Data, Models, and Decisions:

THE FUNDAMENTALS OF MANAGEMENT SCIENCE

DIMITRIS BERTSIMAS

MASSACHUSETTS INSTITUTE OF TECHNOLOGY

ROBERT M. FREUND

MASSACHUSETTS INSTITUTE OF TECHNOLOGY

South-Western College Publishing
Thomson Learning™

Australia • Canada • Denmark • Japan • Mexico • New Zealand • Philippines
Puerto Rico • Singapore • South Africa • Spain • United Kingdom • United States

Data, Models, and Decisions: The Fundamentals of Management Science by Dimitris Bertsimis and Robert Freund

Acquisitions Editor: Charles McCormick
Developmental Editor: Tina Edmondson
Marketing Manager: Joseph A. Sabatino
Production Editor: Anne Chimenti
Manufacturing Coordinator: Sandee Mileweski
Internal Design: Liz Harasymczuk Design
Cover Design: Liz Harasymczuk Design
Cover Image: Craig LaGesse Ramsdell
Production House: D&G Limited, LLC
Printer: R. R. Donnelley & Sons Company

Printed in the United States of America
1 2 3 4 5 03 02 01 00

For more information contact South-Western College Publishing, 5101 Madison Road, Cincinnati, Ohio, 45227 or find us on the Internet at http://www.swcollege.com

For permission to use material from this text or product, contact us by
- **telephone: 1-800-730-2214**
- **fax: 1-800-730-2215**
- **web: http://www.thomsonrights.com**

Library of Congress Cataloging-in-Publication Data

Bertsimas, Dimitris
    Data, models, and decisions : the fundamentals of management science / by Dimitris Bertsimas and Robert M. Freund.
        p. cm.
    Includes bibliographical references and index.
    ISBN 0-538-85906-7 (hbk.)
        1. Management science. 2. Decision making. I. Freund, Robert Michael. II. Title.

T56 .B43 2000
658.5--dc21   99-049421

This book is printed on acid-free paper.

Preface

MANY MANAGERIAL DECISIONS—REGARDLESS OF THEIR FUNCTIONAL ORIENTATION—
are increasingly being based on analysis using quantitative models from the discipline
of management science. Management science tools, techniques, and concepts (decision
trees, probability and statistics, simulation, regression, linear optimization, and nonlinear and discrete optimization) have dramatically changed the way business operates in
finance, service operations, manufacturing, marketing, and consulting. When used
wisely, management science models and tools have enormous power to enhance the
competitiveness of almost any company or enterprise.

This book is designed to introduce management students—from a wide variety
of backgrounds—to the fundamental techniques of using data and management science tools and models to think structurally about decision problems, make more informed management decisions, and ultimately enhance decision-making skills.

EDUCATIONAL PHILOSOPHY

We believe that the use of management science tools and models represents the future of best-practices for tomorrow's successful companies. It is therefore imperative
that tomorrow's business leaders be well-versed in the underlying concepts and
modeling tools of management science, broadly defined. George Dantzig, a founding
father of modern management science, wrote, "The final test of any theory is its capacity to solve the problems which originated it."[1] It is our objective in this book to
contribute to preparing today's management students to become tomorrow's business leaders, and thereby demonstrate that the tools and models of management science pass Dantzig's test.

This book is designed with the following three principles in mind:

- **Rigor.** In order to become tomorrow's business leaders, today's managers need to
  know the fundamental quantitative concepts, tools, and modeling methods. The
  focus here is on *fundamental concepts*. While management students should not be
  expected to remember specific formulas, spreadsheet commands, or technical

---

[1] *Linear Programming and Extensions* by George B. Dantzig, Princeton University Press, Princeton, New
Jersey, 1963.

details after they graduate, it is important for them to retain fundamental concepts necessary for managing in an increasingly technically-oriented business environment. Simply teaching students to plug numbers into black-box models is not relevant to a student's education. This book emphasizes how, what, and why certain tools and models are useful, and what their ramifications would be when used in practice. In recognition of the wide variety of backgrounds of readers of this book, however, we have indicated with a star (*) some sections that contain more advanced material, and their reading can be omitted without loss of continuity.

- **Relevance.** All of the material presented in the book is immediately applied to realistic and representative business scenarios. Because students recognize a spreadsheet as a standard business environment, the spreadsheet is the basic template for almost every model that is presented in the book. Furthermore, the book features over thirty business cases that are drawn from our own consulting experience or the experience of our students and cover a wide spectrum of industries, management functions, and modeling tools.

- **Readability.** We have deliberately written the book in a style that is engaging, informative, informal, conversational in tone, and imbued with a touch of humor from time to time. Many students and colleagues have praised the book's engaging writing style. Most of the chapters and cases have been pre-tested in classrooms at MIT Sloan, Harvard Business School, Wharton, Columbia University, University of British Columbia, Ohio State University, Northwestern University, and McGill University, plus several universities overseas.

DISTINGUISHING CHARACTERISTICS OF THIS BOOK

Unified Treatment of Quantitative Methods. The book combines topics from two traditionally distinct quantitative subjects: probability/statistics, and optimization models, into one unified treatment of quantitative methods and models for management and business. The book stresses those fundamental concepts that we believe are most important for the practical analysis of management decisions. Consequently, it focuses on modeling and evaluating uncertainty explicitly, understanding the dynamic nature of decision-making, using historical data and limited information effectively, simulating complex systems, and allocating scarce resources optimally.

Concise Writing. Despite its wide coverage, the book is designed to be more concise than most existing textbooks. That is, the relevant points are made in the book once or twice, with appropriate examples, and then reinforced in the exercises and in the case modules. There is no excess repetition of material.

Appropriate Use of Spreadsheets. Because students recognize a spreadsheet as a standard business environment, the spreadsheet is the basic template for almost every model presented in the book. In addition, for simulation modeling, linear regression, and linear, nonlinear and discrete optimization, we present command instructions on how to construct and run these models in a spreadsheet environment. However, the book presumes that students already have a basic familiarity with spreadsheets, and so the book is not a spreadsheet user's manual. Unlike many existing textbooks, the use of spreadsheets in our book is designed not to interfere with the development of key concepts. For example, in Chapters 7–9, which cover optimization models, we introduce and develop the concept of an optimization model by defining decision variables and by explicitly constructing the relevant constraints and objective function. Only then do we translate the problem into a spreadsheet for solution by appropriate software. In context, spreadsheets are a vehicle for working with models, but are not a substitute for thinking through the construction of models and analyzing modeling-related issues.

Case Material for Tomorrow's Managers. The book features over thirty business cases that are rich in context, realistic, and are often designed with the protagonist being a relatively young MBA graduate facing a difficult management decision. They cover a wide spectrum of industries, functional areas of management, and modeling tools.

A Capstone Chapter on Integration in the Art of Decision Modeling. Chapter 10, which is the last chapter in the book, illustrates the integrated use of decision modeling in three sectors: the airline industry, the investment management industry, and the manufacturing sector. This chapter contains much material to motivate students about the power of using management science tools and models in their careers.

AUXILIARY MATERIAL

The book is accompanied by a Student Resource CD-ROM that contains:

1. Spreadsheet data and partially- and/or fully-constructed spreadsheet models for many of the cases in the book.

2. Crystal Ball® simulation software, which is a Microsoft Excel® add-on, for use in the construction and use of the simulation case models in Chapter 5.

3. Answers to half of the exercises in each chapter.

For instructors, there is an Instructor's Resource CD-ROM that contains the Solutions Manual, Microsoft PowerPoint® Presentation Slides, Test Bank, and Thomson Learning Testing Tools™ Testing Software. The Solutions Manual provides answers to all the exercises and cases in the book. PowerPoint Slides detail the concepts presented in each chapter and are designed to enhance lecture presentations. A comprehensive test bank comes in two formats: Microsoft Word® document files, and Testing Tools, which allows easy selection and arrangement of only the chosen questions.

In addition to the auxiliary material listed above, resources for both students and instructors are available on the text web site: bertsimas.swcollege.com.

A TOUR OF THE BOOK

Chapter 1: Decision Analysis. This chapter starts right out by introducing decision trees and the decision tree methodology. This material is developed from an intuitive point of view without any formal theory of probability. Students immediately see the value of an easy-to-grasp model that helps them to structure a decision problem, and they also see the need for a theory of probability to model uncertainty, which is developed in the next chapter.

Chapter 2: Fundamentals of Discrete Probability. This chapter covers the laws of probability, including conditional probability. We cover the arithmetic of conditional probability by using probability tables instead of a "Bayes' Theorem" formula in order to keep the concepts as intuitive as possible. We then cover discrete random variables and probability distributions, including the binomial distribution. As preparation for finance, we cover linear functions of a random variable, covariance and correlation of two random variables, and sums of random variables.

Chapter 3: Continuous Probability Distributions and their Applications. This chapter introduces continuous random variables, the probability density function, and the cumulative distribution function. We cover the continuous uniform distribution and the Normal distribution in detail, showing how the Normal distribution arises in models of many management problems. We then cover sums of Normally distributed random variables and the Central Limit Theorem. The Central Limit Theorem points the way to statistical inference, which is covered in the next chapter.

Chapter 4: Statistical Sampling. This chapter covers the basics of statistical sampling: collecting random samples, statistics of a random sample, confidence intervals for the mean of a distribution and for the sample proportion, experimental design, and confidence intervals for the mean of the difference of two random variables.

Chapter 5: Simulation Modeling: Concepts and Practice. In this chapter, we return to constructing and using models, in this case simulation models based on random number generators. We develop the key ideas of simulation with a prototypical management decision problem involving the combination of different random variables. We show how simulation models are constructed, used, and analyzed in a management context.

Chapter 6: Regression Models: Concepts and Practice. This chapter introduces linear regression as a method of prediction. We cover all of the basics of multiple linear regression. Particular care is taken to ensure that students learn how to evaluate and validate a regression model. We also discuss warnings and issues that arise in using linear regression, and we cover extended regression modeling techniques such as nonlinear transformations and dummy variables. We present instructional material on constructing, solving, and interpreting regression models using spreadsheet software.

Chapter 7: Linear Optimization. In this chapter, we develop the basic concepts for constructing, solving, and interpreting the solution of a linear optimization model. We present instructional material on using linear optimization in a spreadsheet. In addition to standard topics, we also focus on shadow prices and the importance of sensitivity analysis of a linear optimization model as an adjunct to informed decision-making. As an optional topic, we show how to model uncertainty in linear optimization using two-stage linear optimization under uncertainty.

Chapter 8: Nonlinear Optimization. This chapter focuses on the extension of the linear optimization model to nonlinear optimization, stressing the key similarities and differences between linear and nonlinear optimization models. We present instructional material on solving a nonlinear optimization model in a spreadsheet. We also focus on portfolio optimization as an important application of nonlinear optimization modeling in management.

Chapter 9: Discrete Optimization. In this chapter, we show how discrete optimization arises in the modeling of many management problems. We focus on binary optimization, integer optimization, and mixed-integer optimization models. We present instructional material on solving a discrete optimization model in a spreadsheet. We also illustrate how discrete optimization problems are solved, to give students a feel for the potential pros and cons of constructing large scale models.

Chapter 10: Integration in the Art of Decision Modeling. This is the "capstone" chapter of the book, which illustrates how management science models and tools are used in an integrative way in today's successful enterprises. This is accomplished by focusing on three sectors: the airline industry, the investment management industry, and the manufacturing sector. This chapter contains much material to motivate students about the power of using management science tools and models in their careers.

USING THE BOOK IN COURSE DESIGN

This book can be used to teach several different types of courses to management students. For a one-semester course in all of management science, we recommend using all of Chapters 1–10 in order. For a half-semester course focusing only on the most basic material, we recommend Chapters 1–3, 6, and 7. Alternatively, Chapters 1–6 can be used in their entirety as part of a course on the fundamentals of probability and statistical modeling, including regression. Yet a fourth alternative is to use Chapters 1 and 7–10 for a half-semester course on optimization modeling for managers.

ACKNOWLEDGMENTS

Foremost, we thank Viên Nguyen for her expository contributions to this book and for her feedback and constructive suggestions on many aspects of this book.

We also thank the following colleagues and former students who have participated in the development of cases, exercises, and other material in this book: Hernan Alperin, Andrew Boyd, Matthew Bruck, Roberto Caccia, Alain Charewicz, David Dubbin, Henk van Duynhoven, Marina Epelman, Ludo Van Der Heyden, Randall Hiller, Sam Israelit, Chuck Joyce, Tom Kelly, Barry Kostiner, David Merrett, Adam Mersereau, Ilya Mirmin, Yuji Morimoto, Vivek Pandit, Brian Rall, Mark Retik, Brian Shannahan, Yumiko Shinoda, Richard Staats, Michael Stollenwerk, Tom Svrcek, Kendra Taylor, Teresa Valdivieso, and Ed Wike.

Many of our colleagues have influenced the development of this book through discussions about management science and educational/pedagogical goals. We thank Arnold Barnett, Gordon Kaufman, John Little, Thomas Magnanti, James Orlin, Nitin Patel, Georgia Perakis, Hoff Stauffer, and Larry Wein.

We also thank all of our former students at MIT's Sloan School of Management, and especially our former teaching assistants, whose feedback in the class *15.060: Data, Models and Decisions* has shaped our educational philosophy towards the teaching of quantitative methods and has significantly influenced our approach to writing this book.

We would also like to express our appreciation to the production and editorial team at Southwestern College Publishing, and especially to Tina Edmondson and Charles McCormick, for all of their efforts.

Finally, and perhaps most importantly, we are grateful to our families and our friends, but especially to our wives, Georgia and Sandy, for their love and support in the course of this extensive project.

Dimitris Bertsimas
Robert M. Freund
Cambridge, December 1999

About the Authors

Dimitris Bertsimas is the Boeing Professor of Management Science and Operations Research at the MIT Sloan School of Management, where he has been teaching quantitative methods to management students for over twelve years. He has won numerous scholarly awards for his research in combinatorial optimization, stochastic processes, and applied modeling, including the SIAM Optimization Prize and the Erlang Prize in probabilistic methods. He serves on the editorial boards of several journals. Professor Bertsimas is also the co-author, together with John Tsitsiklis, of the textbook *Introduction to Linear Optimization*, published by Athena Scientific in 1997.

Robert M. Freund is the Theresa Seley Professor of Management Science and Operations Research at the MIT Sloan School of Management. He has also been responsible for the design, development, and delivery of the quantitative methods curriculum at the Harvard Business School. He has been teaching quantitative methods to management students for over sixteen years. He has won a variety of teaching awards, including being named the Teacher of the Year for the Sloan School three times. His research is in the areas of linear and nonlinear optimization, and in applied modeling. Professor Freund is also a co-editor of the journal *Mathematical Programming*.

DEDICATION

To my parents Aspa and John Bertsimas, and to Georgia.
DB

To the memory of my mother Esta, to my father Richard Freund, and to Sandy.
RMF

Brief Table of Contents

Table of Contents

Decision Analysis

CONTENTS

PERHAPS THE MOST FUNDAMENTAL AND IMPORTANT TASK THAT A MANAGER FACES is to make decisions in an uncertain environment. For example, a manufacturing manager must decide how much capital to invest in new plant capacity, when future demand for products is uncertain. A marketing manager must decide among a variety of different marketing strategies for a new product, when consumer response to these different marketing strategies is uncertain. An investment manager must decide whether or not to invest in a new venture, or whether or not to merge with another firm in another country, in the face of an uncertain economic and political environment.

In this chapter, we introduce a very important method for structuring and analyzing managerial decision problems in the face of uncertainty, in a systematic and rational manner. The method goes by the name **decision analysis.** The analytical model that is used in decision analysis is called a **decision tree.**

1.1   A DECISION TREE MODEL AND ITS ANALYSIS

Decision analysis is a logical and systematic way to address a wide variety of problems involving decision-making in an uncertain environment. We introduce the method of **decision analysis** and the analytical model of constructing and solving a **decision tree** with the following prototypical decision problem.

BILL SAMPRAS' SUMMER JOB DECISION

Bill Sampras is in the third week of his first semester at the Sloan School of Management at the Massachusetts Institute of Technology (MIT). In addition to spending time preparing for classes, Bill has begun to think seriously about summer employment for the next summer, and in particular about a decision he must make in the next several weeks.

On Bill's flight to Boston at the end of August, he sat next to and struck up an interesting conversation with Vanessa Parker, the Vice President for the Equity Desk of a major investment banking firm. At the end of the flight, Vanessa told Bill directly that she would like to discuss the possibility of hiring Bill for next summer, and that he should contact her directly in mid-November, when her firm starts their planning for summer hiring. Bill felt that she was sufficiently impressed with his experience (he worked in the Finance Department of a Fortune 500 company for four years on short-term investing of excess cash from revenue operations) as well as with his overall demeanor.

When Bill left the company in August to begin studying for his MBA, his boss, John Mason, had taken him aside and also promised him a summer job for the following summer. The summer salary would be $12,000 for twelve weeks back at the company. However, John also told him that the summer job offer would only be good until the end of October. Therefore, Bill must decide whether or not to accept John's summer job offer before he knows any details about Vanessa's potential job offer, as Vanessa had explained that her firm is unwilling to discuss summer job opportunities in detail until mid-November. If Bill were to turn down John's offer, Bill could either accept Vanessa's potential job offer (if it indeed were to materialize), or he could search for a different summer job by participating in the corporate summer recruiting program that the Sloan School of Management offers in January and February.

Bill's Decision Criterion

Let us suppose, for the sake of simplicity, that Bill feels that all summer job opportunities (working for John, working for Vanessa's firm, or obtaining a summer job through corporate recruiting at school) would offer Bill similar learning, networking, and resumé-building experiences. Therefore, we assume that Bill's only criterion on which to differentiate between summer jobs is the summer salary, and that Bill obviously prefers a higher salary to a lower salary.

Constructing a Decision Tree for Bill Sampras' Summer Job Decision Problem

A **decision tree** is a systematic way of organizing and representing the various decisions and uncertainties that a decision-maker faces. Here we construct such a decision tree for Bill Sampras' summer job decision.

Notice that there are, in fact, two decisions that Bill needs to make regarding the summer job problem. First, he must decide whether or not to accept John's summer job offer. Second, if he were to reject John's offer, and Vanessa's firm were to offer him a job in mid-November, he must then decide whether to accept Vanessa's offer or to instead participate in the school's corporate summer recruiting program in January and February.

These decisions are represented chronologically and in a systematic fashion in a drawing called a **decision tree.** Bill's first decision concerns whether to accept or reject John's offer. A decision is represented with a small box that is called a **decision node,** and each possible choice is represented as a line called a **branch** that emanates from the decision node. Therefore, Bill's first decision is represented as shown in Figure 1.1. It is customary to write a brief description of the decision choice on the top of each branch emanating from the decision node. Also, for future reference, we have given the node a label (in this case, the letter "A").

If Bill were to accept John's job offer, then there are no other decisions or uncertainties Bill would need to consider. However, if he were to reject John's job offer, then Bill would face the uncertainty of whether or not Vanessa's firm would subsequently offer Bill a summer job. In a decision tree, an uncertain event is represented with a small circle called an **event node,** and each possible outcome of the event is represented as a line (or branch) that emanates from the event node. Such an event node with its outcome branches is shown in Figure 1.2, and is given the label "B." Again, it is customary to write a brief description of the possible outcomes of the event above each outcome branch.

Unlike a decision node, where the decision-maker gets to select which branch to opt for, at an event node the decision-maker has no such choice. Rather, one can think that at an event node, "nature" or "fate" decides which outcome will take place.

The outcome branches that emanate from an event node must represent a **mutually exclusive** and **collectively exhaustive** set of possible events. By mutually exclusive, we mean that no two outcomes could ever transpire at the same time. By collectively exhaustive, we mean that the set of possible outcomes represents the entire range of possible outcomes. In other words, there is no probability that another non-represented outcome might occur. In our example, at this event node there are two, and only two, distinct outcomes that could occur: one outcome is that Vanessa's firm will offer Bill a summer job, and the other outcome is that Vanessa's firm will not offer Bill a summer job.

If Vanessa's firm were to make Bill a job offer, then Bill would subsequently have to decide to accept or to reject the firm's job offer. In this case, and if Bill were to accept the firm's job offer, then his summer job problem would be resolved. If Bill were to instead reject their offer, then Bill would then have to search for summer employment through the school's corporate summer recruiting program. The decision tree shown in Figure 1.3 represents these further possible eventualities, where the additional decision

FIGURE 1.1
Representation of a
decision node.

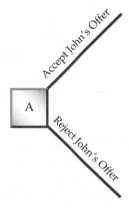

FIGURE 1.2
Representation of an event node.

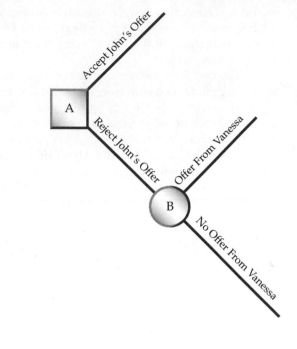

FIGURE 1.3
Further representation of the decision tree.

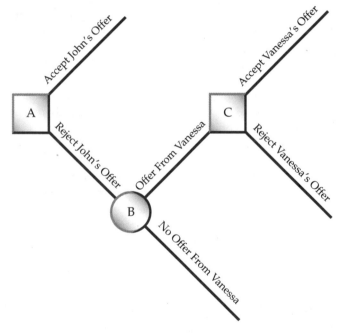

node C represents the decision that Bill would face if he were to receive a summer job offer from Vanessa's firm.

Assigning Probabilities

Another aspect of constructing a decision tree is the assignment or determination of the probability, i.e., the likelihood, that each of the various uncertain outcomes will transpire.

Let us suppose that Bill has visited the career services center at Sloan and has gathered some summary data on summer salaries received by the previous class of

MBA students. Based on salaries paid to Sloan students who worked in the Sales and Trading Departments at Vanessa's firm the previous summer, Bill has estimated that Vanessa's firm would make offers of $14,000 for twelve weeks' work to summer MBA students this coming summer.

Let us also suppose that we have gathered some data on the salary range for all summer jobs that went to Sloan students last year, and that this data is conveniently summarized in Table 1.1. The table shows five different summer salaries (based on weekly salary) and the associated percentages of students who received this salary. (The school did not have salary information for 5% of the students. In order to be conservative, we assign these students a summer salary of $0.)

Suppose further that our own intuition has suggested that Table 1.1 is a good approximation of the likelihood that Bill would receive the indicated salaries if he were to participate in the school's corporate summer recruiting. That is, we estimate that there is roughly a 5% likelihood that Bill would be able to procure a summer job with a salary of $21,600, and that there is roughly a 25% likelihood that Bill would be able

TABLE 1.1
Distribution of summer salaries.

Weekly Salary	Total Summer Pay (based on 12 weeks)	Percentage of Students Who Received This Salary
$1,800	$21,600	5%
$1,400	$16,800	25%
$1,000	$12,000	40%
$500	$6,000	25%
$0	$0	5%

FIGURE 1.4
Further representation of the decision tree.

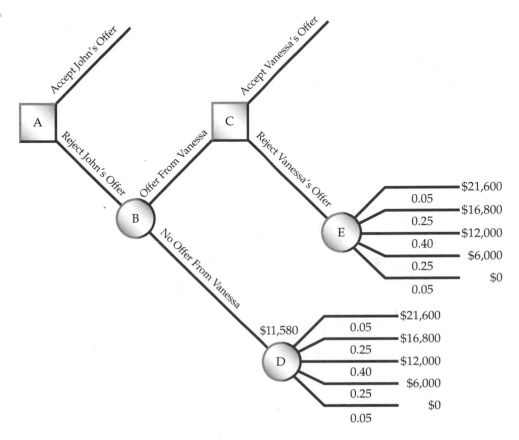

to procure a summer job with a salary of $16,800, etc. The now-expanded decision tree for the problem is shown in Figure 1.4, which includes event nodes D and E for the eventuality that Bill would participate in corporate summer recruiting if he were not to receive a job offer from Vanessa's firm, or if he were to reject an offer from Vanessa's firm. It is customary to write the probabilities of the various outcomes underneath their respective outcome branches, as is done in the figure.

Finally, let us estimate the likelihood that Vanessa's firm will offer Bill a job. Without much thought, we might assign this outcome a probability of 0.50, that is, there is a 50% likelihood that Vanessa's firm would offer Bill a summer job. On further reflection, we know that Vanessa was very impressed with Bill, and she sounded certain that she wanted to hire him. However, very many of Bill's classmates are also very talented (like him), and Bill has heard that competition for investment banking jobs is in fact very intense. Based on these musings, let us assign the probability that Bill would receive a summer job offer from Vanessa's firm to be 0.60. Therefore, the likelihood that Bill would not receive a job offer from Vanessa's firm would then be 0.40. These two numbers are shown in the decision tree in Figure 1.5.

Valuing the Final Branches

The next step in the decision analysis modeling methodology is to assign numerical values to the outcomes associated with the "final" branches of the decision tree, based on the decision criterion that has been adopted. As discussed earlier, Bill's decision criterion is his salary. Therefore, we assign the salary implication of each final branch and write this down to the right of the final branch, as shown in Figure 1.6.

FIGURE 1.5
Further representation of the decision tree.

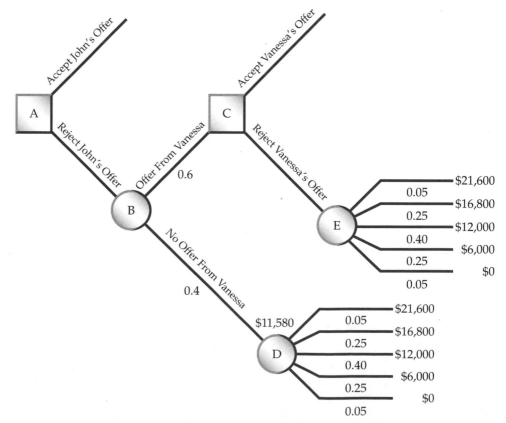

FIGURE 1.6

The completed decision tree.

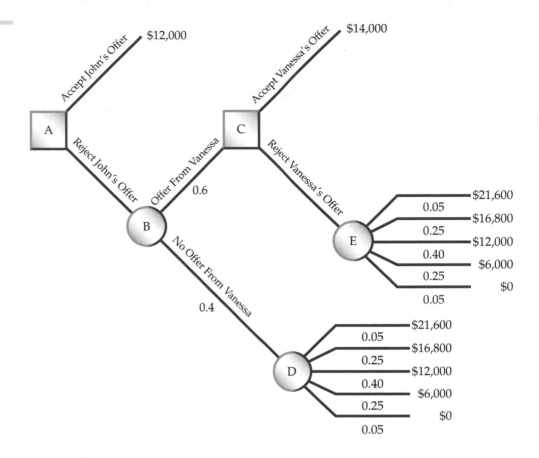

Fundamental Aspects of Decision Trees

Let us pause and look again at the decision tree as shown in Figure 1.6. Notice that time in the decision tree flows from left to right, and the placement of the decision nodes and the event nodes is logically consistent with the way events will play out in reality. Any event or decision that must logically precede certain other events and decisions is appropriately placed in the tree to reflect this logical dependence.

The tree has two decision nodes, namely node A and node C. Node A represents the decision Bill must make soon: whether to accept or reject John's offer. Node C represents the decision Bill might have to make in late November: whether to accept or reject Vanessa's offer. The branches emanating from each decision node represent all of the possible decisions under consideration at that point in time under the appropriate circumstances.

There are three event nodes in the tree, namely nodes B, D, and E. Node B represents the uncertain event of whether or not Bill will receive a job offer from Vanessa's firm. Node D (and also Node E) represents the uncertain events governing the school's corporate summer recruiting salaries. The branches emanating from each event node represent a set of mutually exclusive and collectively exhaustive outcomes from the event node. Furthermore, the sum of the probabilities of each outcome branch emanating from a given event node must sum to one. (This is because the set of possible outcomes is collectively exhaustive.)

These important characteristics of a decision tree are summarized as follows:

Key Characteristics of a Decision Tree

1. Time in a decision tree flows from left to right, and the placement of the decision nodes and the event nodes is logically consistent with the way events will play out in reality. Any event or decision that must logically precede certain other events and decisions is appropriately placed in the tree to reflect this logical dependence.

2. The branches emanating from each decision node represent all of the possible decisions under consideration at that point in time under the appropriate circumstances.

3. The branches emanating from each event node represent a set of mutually exclusive and collectively exhaustive outcomes of the event node.

4. The sum of the probabilities of each outcome branch emanating from a given event node must sum to one.

5. Each and every "final" branch of the decision tree has a numerical value associated with it. This numerical value usually represents some measure of monetary value, such as salary, revenue, cost, etc.

(By the way, in the case of Bill's summer job decision, all of the numerical values associated with the final branches in the decision tree are dollar figures of salaries, which are inherently objective measures to work with. However, Bill might also wish to consider subjective measures in making his decision. We have conveniently assumed for simplicity that the intangible benefits of his summer job options, such as opportunities to learn, networking, resumé-building, etc., would be the same at either his former employer, Vanessa's firm, or in any job offer he might receive through the school's corporate summer recruiting. In reality, these subjective measures would not be the same for all of Bill's possible options. Of course, another important subjective factor, which Bill might also consider, is the value of the time he would have to spend in corporate summer recruiting. Although we will analyze the decision tree ignoring all of these subjective measures, the value of Bill's time should at least be considered when reviewing the conclusions afterward.)

Solution of Bill's Problem by Folding Back the Decision Tree

If Bill's choice were simply between accepting a job offer of $12,000 or accepting a different job offer of $14,000, then his decision would be easy: he would take the higher salary offer. However, in the presence of uncertainty, it is not necessarily obvious how Bill might proceed.

Suppose, for example, that Bill were to reject John's offer, and that in mid-November he were to receive an offer of $14,000 from Vanessa's firm. He would then be at node C of the decision tree. How would he go about deciding between obtaining a summer salary of $14,000 with certainty, and the distribution of possible salaries he might obtain (with varying degrees of uncertainty) from participating in the school's corporate summer recruiting? The criterion that most decision-makers feel is most appropriate to use in this setting is to convert the distribution of possible salaries to a single numerical value using the **expected monetary value** (EMV) of the possible outcomes:

> The **expected monetary value** or **EMV** of an uncertain event is the weighted average of all possible numerical outcomes, with the probabilities of each of the possible outcomes used as the weights.

Therefore, for example, the EMV of participating in corporate summer recruiting is computed as follows:

$$EMV =$$
$$0.05 \times \$21,600 + 0.25 \times \$16,800 + 0.40 \times \$12,000 + 0.25 \times \$6,000 + 0.05 \times \$0$$
$$= \$11,580.$$

The EMV of a certain event is defined to be the monetary value of the event. For example, suppose that Bill were to receive a job offer from Vanessa's firm, and that he were to accept the job offer. Then the EMV of this choice would simply be \$14,000.

Notice that the EMV of the choice to participate in corporate recruiting is \$11,580, which is less than \$14,000 (the EMV of accepting the offer from Vanessa's firm), and so under the EMV criterion, Bill would prefer the job offer from Vanessa's firm to the option of participating in corporate summer recruiting.

The EMV is one way to convert a group of possible outcomes with monetary values and probabilities to a single number that weighs each possible outcome by its probability. The EMV represents an "averaging" approach to uncertainty. It is quite intuitive, and is quite appropriate for a wide variety of decision problems under uncertainty. (However, there are cases where it is not necessarily the best method for converting a group of possible outcomes to a single number. In Section 1.5, we discuss several aspects of the EMV criterion further.)

Using the EMV criterion, we can now "solve" the decision tree. We do so by evaluating every event node using the EMV of the event node, and evaluating every decision node by choosing that decision which has the best EMV. This is accomplished by starting at the final branches of the tree, and then working "backwards" to the starting node of the decision tree. For this reason, the process of solving the decision tree is called **folding back the decision tree.** It is also occasionally referred to as **backwards induction.** This process is illustrated in the following discussion.

Starting from any one of the "final" nodes of the decision tree, we proceed backwards. As we have already seen, the EMV of node E is \$11,580. It is customary to write the EMV of an event node above the node, as is shown in Figure 1.7. Similarly, the EMV of node D is also \$11,580, which we write above node D. This is also displayed in Figure 1.7.

We next examine decision node C, which corresponds to the event that Bill receives a job offer from Vanessa's firm. At this decision node, there are two choices. The first choice is for Bill to accept the offer from Vanessa's firm, which has an EMV of \$14,000. The second choice is to reject the offer, and instead to participate in corporate summer recruiting, which has an EMV of \$11,580. As the EMV of \$11,580 is less than the EMV of \$14,000, it is better to choose the branch corresponding to accepting Vanessa's offer. Pictorially, we show this by crossing off the inferior choice by drawing two lines through the branch, and by writing the monetary value of the best choice above the decision node. This is shown in Figure 1.7 as well.

We continue by evaluating event node B, which is the event node corresponding to the event where Vanessa's firm either will or will not offer Bill a summer job. The methodology we use is the same as evaluating the salary distributions from participating in corporate summer recruiting. We compute the EMV of the node by computing the

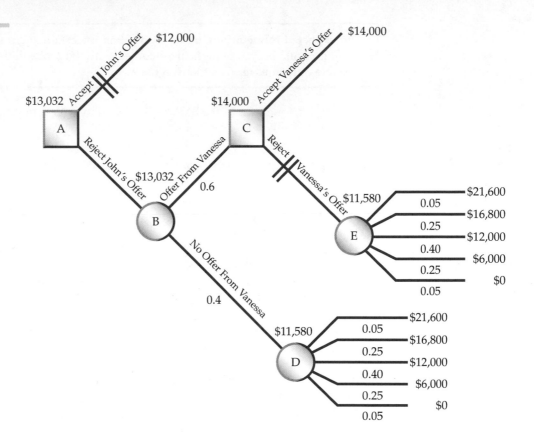

weighted average of the EMVs of each of the outcomes, weighted by the probabilities corresponding to each of the outcomes. In this case, this means multiplying the probability of an offer (0.60) by the $14,000 value of decision node C, then multiplying the probability of not receiving an offer from Vanessa's firm (0.40) times the EMV of node D, which is $11,580, and then adding the two quantities. The calculations are:

$$\text{EMV} = 0.60 \times \$14,000 + 0.40 \times \$11,580 = \$13,032.$$

This number is then placed above the node, as shown in Figure 1.7.

The last step in solving the decision tree is to evaluate the remaining node, which is the first node of the tree. This is a decision node, and its evaluation is accomplished by comparing the better of the two EMV values of the branches that emanate from it. The upper branch, which corresponds to accepting John's offer, has an EMV of $12,000. The lower branch, which corresponds to rejecting John's offer and proceeding onward, has an EMV of $13,032. As this latter value is the highest, we cross off the branch corresponding to accepting John's offer, and place the EMV value of $13,032 above the initial node. The completed solution of the decision tree is shown in Figure 1.7.

Let us now look again at the solved decision tree and examine the "optimal decision strategy" under uncertainty. According to the solved tree, Bill should not accept John's job offer, i.e., he should reject John's job offer. This is shown at the first decision node. Then, if Bill receives a job offer from Vanessa's firm, he should accept this offer. This is shown at the second decision node. Of course, if he does not receive a job offer from Vanessa's firm, he would then participate in the school's corporate summer recruiting program. The EMV of John's optimal decision strategy is $13,032.

Summarizing, Bill's optimal decision strategy can be stated as follows:

Bill's Optimal Decision Strategy:

- Bill should reject John's offer in October.

- If Vanessa's firm offers him a job, he should accept it. If Vanessa's firm does not offer him a summer job, he should participate in the school's corporate summer recruiting.

- The EMV of this strategy is $13,032.

Note that the output from constructing and solving the decision tree is a very concrete plan of action, which states what decisions should be made under each possible uncertain outcome that might prevail.

The procedure for solving a decision tree can be formally stated as follows:

Procedure for Solving a Decision Tree

1. Start with the final branches of the decision tree, and evaluate each event node and each decision node, as follows:

   - For an event node, compute the EMV of the node by computing the weighted average of the EMV of each branch weighted by its probability. Write this EMV number above the event node.

   - For a decision node, compute the EMV of the node by choosing that branch emanating from the node with the best EMV value. Write this EMV number above the decision node, and cross off those branches emanating from the node with inferior EMV values by drawing a double line through them.

2. The decision tree is solved when all nodes have been evaluated.

3. The EMV of the optimal decision strategy is the EMV computed for the starting branch of the tree.

As we mentioned already, the process of solving the decision tree in this manner is called **folding back the decision tree.** It is also sometimes referred to as **backwards induction.**

Sensitivity Analysis of the Optimal Decision

If this were an actual business decision, it would be naive to adopt the optimal decision strategy derived above, without a critical evaluation of the impact of the key data assumptions that were made in the development of the decision tree model. For example, consider the following data-related issues that we might want to address:

- **Issue 1: The probability that Vanessa's firm would offer Bill a summer job.** We have subjectively assumed that the probability that Vanessa's firm would offer Bill a summer job to be 0.60. It would be wise to test how changes in this probability might affect the optimal decision strategy.

- **Issue 2: The cost of Bill's time and effort in participating in the school's corporate summer recruiting.** We have implicitly assumed that the cost of Bill's time and effort in participating in the school's corporate summer recruiting would be zero. It would be wise to test how high the implicit cost of participating in corporate summer recruiting would have to be before the optimal decision strategy would change.

- **Issue 3: The distribution of summer salaries that Bill could expect to receive.** We have assumed that the distribution of summer salaries that Bill could expect to receive is given by the numbers in Table 1.1. It would be wise to test how changes in this distribution of salaries might affect the optimal decision strategy.

The process of testing and evaluating how the solution to a decision tree behaves in the presence of changes in the data is referred to as **sensitivity analysis.** The process of performing sensitivity analysis is as much an art as it is a science. It usually involves choosing several key data values and then testing how the solution of the decision tree model changes as each of these data values are modified, one at a time. Such a process is very important for understanding what data are driving the optimal decision strategy and how the decision tree model behaves under changes in key data values. The exercise of performing sensitivity analysis is important in order to gain confidence in the validity of the model and is necessary before one bases one's decisions on the output from a decision tree model. We illustrate next the art of sensitivity analysis by performing the three data changes suggested previously.

Note that in order to evaluate how the optimal decision strategy behaves as a function of changes in the data assumptions, we will have to solve and re-solve the decision tree model many times, each time with slightly different values of certain data. Obviously, one way to do this would be to re-draw the tree each time and perform all of the necessary arithmetic computations by hand each time. This approach is obviously very tedious and repetitive, and in fact we can do this much more conveniently with the help of a computer spreadsheet. We can represent the decision tree problem and its solution very conveniently on a spreadsheet, illustrated in Figure 1.8 and explained in the following discussion.

FIGURE 1.8

Spreadsheet representation of Bill Sampras' summer job problem.

Spreadsheet Representation of Bill Sampras' Decision Problem			
Data			
Value of John's offer	$12,000		
Value of Vanessa's offer	$14,000		
Probability of offer from Vanessa's firm	0.60		
Cost of participating in Recruiting	$0		
	Distribution of Salaries from Recruiting		
	Weekly Salary	**Total Summer Pay**	**Percentage of Students**
		(based on 12 weeks)	**who Received this Salary**
	$1,800	$21,600	5%
	$1,400	$16,800	25%
	$1,000	$12,000	40%
	$500	$6,000	25%
	$0	$0	5%
	EMV of Nodes		
	Nodes	**EMV**	
	A	$13,032	
	B	$13,032	
	C	$14,000	
	D	$11,580	
	E	$11,580	

In the spreadsheet representation of Figure 1.8, the data for the decision tree is given in the upper part of the spreadsheet, and the "solution" of the spreadsheet is computed in the lower part in the "EMV of Nodes" table. The computation of the EMV of each node is performed automatically as a function of the data. For example, we know that node E of the spreadsheet has its EMV computed as follows:

$$\text{EMV of node E} =$$
$$0.05 \times \$21,600 + 0.25 \times \$16,800 + 0.40 \times \$12,000 + 0.25 \times \$6,000 + 0.05 \times \$0$$
$$= \$11,580.$$

The EMV of node D is computed in an identical manner. As presented earlier, the EMV of node C is the maximum of the EMV of node E and the value of an offer from Vanessa's firm, and is computed as

$$\text{EMV of node C} = \text{MAX}\{\text{EMV of node E}, \$14,000\}.$$

Similarly, the EMV of nodes B and A are given by

$$\text{EMV of node B} = (0.60) \times (\text{EMV of node C}) + (1 - 0.60) \times (\text{EMV of node D})$$

and

$$\text{EMV of node A} = \text{MAX}\{\text{EMV of node B}, \$12,000\}.$$

All of these formulas can be conveniently represented in a spreadsheet, and such a spreadsheet is shown in Figure 1.8. Note that the EMV numbers for all of the nodes in the spreadsheet correspond exactly to those computed "by hand" in the solution of the decision tree shown in Figure 1.7.

We now show how the spreadsheet representation of the decision tree can be used to study how the optimal decision strategy changes relative to the three key data issues discussed above at the start of this subsection. To begin, consider the first issue, which concerns the sensitivity of the optimal decision strategy to the value of the probability that Vanessa's firm will offer Bill a summer job. Denote this probability by p, i.e.,

$$p = \text{probability that Vanessa's firm will offer Bill a summer job.}$$

If we test a variety of values of p in the spreadsheet representation of the decision tree, we will find that the optimal decision strategy (which is to reject John's job offer, and to accept a job offer from Vanessa's firm if it is offered) remains the same for all values of p greater than or equal to $p = 0.174$. Figure 1.9 shows the output of the spreadsheet when $p = 0.18$, for example, and notice that the EMV of node B is $12,016, which is just barely above the threshold value of $12,000. For values of p at or below $p = 0.17$, the EMV of node B becomes less than $12,000, which results in a new optimal decision strategy of accepting John's job offer. We can conclude the following:

- As long as the probability of Vanessa's firm offering Bill a job is 0.18 or larger, then the optimal decision strategy will still be to reject John's offer and to accept a summer job with Vanessa's firm if they offer it to him.

This is reassuring, as it is reasonable for Bill to be very confident that the probability of Vanessa's firm offering him a summer job is surely greater than 0.18.

We next use the spreadsheet representation of the decision tree to study the second data assumption issue, which concerns the sensitivity of the optimal decision strategy to the implicit cost to Bill (in terms of his time) of participating in the school's corporate summer recruiting program. Denote this cost by c, i.e.,

$$c = \text{implicit cost to Bill of participating in}$$
$$\text{the school's corporate summer recruiting program.}$$

FIGURE 1.9
Output of the
spreadsheet of Bill
Sampras' summer
job problem when
the probability that
Vanessa's firm will
make Bill an offer is
0.18.

	Spreadsheet Representation of Bill Sampras' Decision Problem		
Data			
Value of John's offer	$12,000		
Value of Vanessa's offer	$14,000		
Probability of offer from Vanessa's firm	0.18		
Cost of participating in Recruiting	$0		
	Distribution of Salaries from Recruiting		
	Weekly Salary	**Total Summer Pay**	**Percentage of Students**
		(based on 12 weeks)	**who Received this Salary**
	$1,800	$21,600	5%
	$1,400	$16,800	25%
	$1,000	$12,000	40%
	$500	$6,000	25%
	$0	$0	5%
	EMV of Nodes		
	Nodes	**EMV**	
	A	$12,016	
	B	$12,016	
	C	$14,000	
	D	$11,580	
	E	$11,580	

If we test a variety of values of c in the spreadsheet representation of the decision tree, we will notice that the current optimal decision strategy (which is to reject John's job offer, and to accept a job offer from Vanessa's firm if it is offered) remains the same for all values of c less than $c = \$2{,}578$. Figure 1.10 shows the output of the spreadsheet when $c = \$2{,}578$. For values of c above $c = \$2{,}578$, the EMV of node B becomes less than $12,000, which results in a new optimal decision strategy of accepting John's job offer. We can conclude the following:

- As long as the implicit cost to Bill of participating in summer recruiting is less than $2,578, then the optimal decision strategy will still be to reject John's offer and to accept a summer job with Vanessa's firm if they offer it to him.

This is also reassuring, as it is reasonable to estimate that the implicit cost to Bill of participating in the school's corporate summer recruiting program is much less than $2,578.

We next use the spreadsheet representation of the decision tree to study the third data issue, which concerns the sensitivity of the optimal decision strategy to the distribution of possible summer job salaries from participating in corporate recruiting. Recall that Table 1.1 contains the data for the salaries Bill might possibly realize by participating in corporate summer recruiting. Let us explore the consequences of changing all of the possible salary offers of Table 1.1 by an amount S. That is, we will explore modifying Bill's possible summer salaries by an amount S. If we test a variety of values of S in the spreadsheet representation of the model, we will notice that the current optimal decision strategy remains optimal for all values of S less than $S = \$2{,}419$. Figure 1.11 shows the output of the spreadsheet when $S = \$2{,}419$. For values of S above $S = \$2{,}420$, the EMV of node E will become greater than or equal to $14,000, and consequently Bill's optimal decision strategy will change: he would reject an offer from Vanessa's firm if it materialized, and instead would participate in the school's corporate summer recruiting program. We can conclude:

FIGURE 1.10

Output of the spreadsheet of Bill Sampras' summer job problem if the cost of Bill's time spent participating in corporate summer recruiting is $2,578.

Spreadsheet Representation of Bill Sampras' Decision Problem		
Data		
Value of John's offer	$12,000	
Value of Vanessa's offer	$14,000	
Probability of offer from Vanessa's firm	0.60	
Cost of participating in Recruiting	$2,578	
Distribution of Salaries from Recruiting		
Weekly Salary	**Total Summer Pay (based on 12 weeks)**	**Percentage of Students who Received this Salary**
$1,800	$21,600	5%
$1,400	$16,800	25%
$1,000	$12,000	40%
$500	$6,000	25%
$0	$0	5%
EMV of Nodes		
Nodes	**EMV**	
A	$12,001	
B	$12,001	
C	$14,000	
D	$9,002	
E	$9,002	

FIGURE 1.11

Output of the spreadsheet of Bill Sampras' summer job problem if summer salaries from recruiting were $2,419 higher.

Spreadsheet Representation of Bill Sampras' Decision Problem		
Data		
Value of John's offer	$12,000	
Value of Vanessa's offer	$14,000	
Probability of offer from Vanessa's firm	0.60	
Cost of participating in Recruiting	$0	
Distribution of Salaries from Recruiting		
Weekly Salary	**Total Summer Pay (based on 12 weeks)**	**Percentage of Students who Received this Salary**
$1,800	$24,019	5%
$1,400	$19,219	25%
$1,000	$14,419	40%
$500	$8,419	25%
$0	$2,419	5%
EMV of Nodes		
Nodes	**EMV**	
A	$14,000	
B	$14,000	
C	$14,000	
D	$13,999	
E	$13,999	

- In order for Bill's optimal decision strategy to change, all of the possible summer corporate recruiting salaries of Table 1.1 would have to increase by more than $2,419.

This is also reassuring, as it is reasonable to anticipate that summer salaries from corporate summer recruiting in general would not be $2,419 higher this coming summer than they were last summer.

We can summarize our findings as follows:

- For all three of the data issues that we have explored (the probability p of Vanessa's firm offering Bill a summer job, the implicit cost c of participating in corporate summer recruiting, and an increase S in all possible salary values from corporate summer recruiting), we have found that the optimal decision strategy does not change unless these quantities take on unreasonable values. Therefore, it is safe to proceed with confidence in recommending to Bill Sampras that he adopt the optimal decision strategy found in the solution to the decision tree model. Namely, he should reject John's job offer, and he should accept a job offer from Vanessa's firm if such an offer is made.

In some applications of decision analysis, the decision-maker might discover that the optimal decision strategy is very sensitive to a key data value. If this happens, it is then obviously important to spend some effort to determine the most reasonable value of that data. For instance, in the decision tree we have constructed, suppose that in fact the optimal decision was very sensitive to the probability p that Vanessa's firm would offer Bill a summer job. We might then want to gather data on how many offers Vanessa's firm made to Sloan students in previous years, and in particular we might want to look at how students with Bill's general profile fared when they applied for jobs with Vanessa's firm. This information could then be used to develop a more exact estimate of the probability p that Bill would receive a job offer from Vanessa's firm.

Note that in this sensitivity analysis exercise, we have only changed one data value at a time. In some problem instances, the decision-maker might want to test how the model behaves under simultaneous changes in more than one data value. This is a bit more difficult to analyze, of course.

1.2 SUMMARY OF THE GENERAL METHOD OF DECISION ANALYSIS

The example of Bill Sampras' summer job decision problem illustrates the format of the general method of **decision analysis** to systematically analyze a decision problem. The format of this general method is as follows:

Principal Steps of Decision Analysis

1. Structure the decision problem. List all of the decisions that have to be made. List all of the uncertain events in the problem and all of their possible outcomes.

2. Construct the basic decision tree by placing the decision nodes and the event nodes in their chronological and logically consistent order.

3. Determine the probability of each of the possible outcomes of each of the uncertain events. Write these probabilities on the decision tree.

4. Determine the numerical values of each of the final branches of the decision tree. Write these numerical values on the decision tree.

5. Solve the decision tree using the folding-back procedure:

(a) Start with the final branches of the decision tree, and evaluate each event node and each decision node, as follows:

- For an event node, compute the EMV of the node by computing the weighted average of the EMV of each branch weighted by its probability. Write this EMV number above the event node.

- For a decision node, compute the EMV of the node by choosing that branch emanating from the node with the best EMV value. Write this EMV number above the decision node and cross off those branches emanating from the node with inferior EMV values by drawing a double line through them.

(b) The decision tree is solved when all nodes have been evaluated.

(c) The EMV of the optimal decision strategy is the EMV computed for the starting branch of the tree.

6. Perform sensitivity analysis on all key data values. For each data value for which the decision-maker lacks confidence, test how the optimal decision strategy will change relative to a change in the data value, one data value at a time.

As mentioned earlier, the solution of the decision tree and the sensitivity analysis procedure typically involve a number of mechanical arithmetic calculations. Unless the decision tree is small, it might be wise to construct a spreadsheet version of the decision tree in order to perform these calculations automatically and quickly. (And of course, a spreadsheet version of the model will also eliminate the likelihood of making arithmetical errors!)

1.3 ANOTHER DECISION TREE MODEL AND ITS ANALYSIS

In this section, we continue to illustrate the methodology of decision analysis by considering a strategic development decision problem encountered by a new company called Bio-Imaging, Incorporated.

BIO-IMAGING DEVELOPMENT STRATEGIES

In 1998, the company Bio-Imaging, Incorporated was formed by James Bates, Scott Tillman, and Michael Ford, in order to develop, produce, and market a new and potentially extremely beneficial tool in medical diagnosis. Scott Tillman and James Bates were each recent graduates from Massachusetts Institute of Technology (MIT), and Michael Ford was a professor of neurology at Massachusetts General Hospital (MGH). As part of his graduate studies at MIT, Scott had developed a new technique and a software package to process MRI (magnetic resonance imaging) scans of brains of patients using a personal computer. The software, using state of the art computer graphics, would construct a three-dimensional picture of a patient's brain and could be used to find the exact location of a brain lesion or a brain tumor, estimate its volume and shape, and even locate the centers in the brain that would be affected by the tumor. Scott's work was an extension of earlier two-dimensional image processing work developed by James, which had been used extensively in Michael Ford's medical group at MGH for analyzing the effects of lesions on patients' speech difficulties. Over the last few years, this software program had been used to make relatively accurate measurements and diagnoses of brain lesions and tumors.

Although not yet fully tested, Scott's more advanced three-dimensional software program promised to be much more accurate than other methods in diagnosing lesions. While a variety of other scientists around the world had developed their own MRI imaging software, Scott's new three-dimensional program was very different and far superior to any other existing software for MRI image processing.

At James' recommendation, the three gentlemen formed Bio-Imaging, Incorporated with the goal of developing and producing a commercial software package that hospitals and doctors could use. Shortly thereafter, they were approached by the Medtech Corporation, a large medical imaging and software company. Medtech offered them $150,000 to buy the software package in its then-current form, together with the rights to develop and market the software world-wide. The other two partners authorized James (who was the "businessman" of the partnership) to decide whether or not to accept the Medtech offer. If they rejected the offer, their plan was to continue their own development of the software package in the next six months. This would entail an investment of approximately $200,000, which James felt could be financed through the partners' personal savings.

If Bio-Imaging were successful in their effort to make the three-dimensional prototype program fully operational, they would face two alternative development strategies. One alternative would be to apply after six months time for a $300,000 Small Business Innovative Research (SBIR) grant from the National Institute of Health (NIH). The SBIR money would then be used to further develop and market their product. The other alternative would be to seek further capital for the project from a venture capital firm. In fact, Michael had had several discussions with the venture capital firm Nugrowth Development. Nugrowth Development had proposed that if Bio-Imaging were successful in producing a three-dimensional prototype program, Nugrowth would then offer $1,000,000 to Bio-Imaging to finance and market the software package in exchange for 80% of future profits after the three-dimensional prototype program became fully operational. (Because NIH regulations do not allow a company to receive an NIH grant and also receive money from a venture capital firm, Bio-Imaging would not be able to receive funding from both sources.)

James knew that there was substantial uncertainty concerning the likelihood of receiving the SBIR grant. He also knew that there was substantial uncertainty about how successful Bio-Imaging might be in marketing their product. He felt, however, that if they were to accept the Nugrowth Development offer, the profitability of the product would probably then be higher than if they were to market the product themselves.

If Bio-Imaging was not successful in making the three-dimensional prototype program fully operational, James felt that they could still apply for an SBIR grant with the two-dimensional software program. He realized that in this case, they would be less likely to be awarded the SBIR grant. Furthermore, clinical tests would be needed to fine-tune the two-dimensional program prior to applying for the grant. James estimated that the cost of these additional tests would be around $100,000.

The decision problem faced by Bio-Imaging was whether to accept the offer from Medtech or to continue the research and development of the three-dimensional software package. If they were successful in producing a three-dimensional prototype, they would have to decide either to apply for the SBIR grant or to accept the offer from Nugrowth. If they were not successful in producing a three-dimensional prototype, they would have to decide either to further invest in the two-dimensional product and apply for an SBIR grant, or to abandon the project altogether. In the midst of all of this, James also wondered whether the cost of the Nugrowth offer (80% of future profits) might be too high relative to the benefits ($1,000,000 in much-needed capital). Clearly James needed to think hard about the decisions Bio-Imaging was facing.

Data Estimates of Revenues and Probabilities

Given the intense competition in the market for medical imaging technology, James knew that there was substantial uncertainty surrounding the potential revenues of Bio-Imaging over the next three years. James tried to estimate these revenues under a variety of possible scenarios. Table 1.2 shows James' data estimates of revenues under three scenarios ("high profit," "medium profit," and "low profit") in the event that the three-dimensional prototype were to become operational and if they were to receive the SBIR grant. Under the "high profit" scenario the program would presumably be very successful in the marketplace, yielding total revenues of $3,000,000. In the "medium profit" scenario, James estimated the revenues to be $500,000, while in the "low profit" scenario, he estimated that there would be no revenues. James assigned his estimated probabilities of these three scenarios to be 20%, 40%, and 40% for the "high profit," "medium profit," and "low profit" scenarios, respectively.

Table 1.3 shows James' data estimates of revenues of Bio-Imaging in the event that the three-dimensional prototype were to become operational and if they were to accept the financing offer from Nugrowth Development. Given the higher resources that would be available to them ($1,000,000 of capital), James estimated that under the "high profit" scenario the program would yield total revenues of $10,000,000. In the "medium profit" scenario, James estimated the revenues to be $3,000,000; while in the "low profit" scenario, he estimated that there would be no revenues. As before, James assigned his estimated probabilities of the three scenarios to be 20%, 40%, and 40% for the "high profit," "medium profit," and "low profit" scenarios, respectively.

Table 1.4 shows James' data estimates of revenues of Bio-Imaging in the event that the three-dimensional prototype were not successful and if they were to receive

TABLE 1.2

Estimated revenues of Bio-Imaging, if the three-dimensional prototype were operational and if Bio-Imaging were awarded the SBIR grant.

Scenario	Probability	Total Revenues
High Profit	20%	$3,000,000
Medium Profit	40%	$500,000
Low Profit	40%	$0

TABLE 1.3

Estimated revenues of Bio-Imaging, if the three-dimensional prototype were operational, under financing from Nugrowth Development.

Scenario	Probability	Total Revenues
High Profit	20%	$10,000,000
Medium Profit	40%	$3,000,000
Low Profit	40%	$0

Scenario	Probability	Total Revenues
High Profit	25%	$1,500,000
Low Profit	75%	$0

the SBIR grant for the two-dimensional software program. In this case James considered only two scenarios: "high profit" and "low profit." Note that the revenue estimates are quite low. Under the "high profit" scenario the program would yield total revenues of $1,500,000. In the "low profit" scenario, James estimated that there would be no revenues. James assigned his estimated probabilities of the scenarios to be 25% and 75% for the "high profit" and the "low profit" scenarios, respectively.

James also gave serious thought and analysis to various other uncertainties facing Bio-Imaging. After consulting with Scott, he assigned a 60% likelihood that they would be successful in producing an operational version of the three-dimensional software program. Moreover, after consulting with Michael Ford, James also estimated that the likelihood of winning the SBIR grant after successful completion of the three-dimensional software program to be 70%. However, they estimated that the likelihood of winning the SBIR grant with only the two-dimensional software program would be only 20%.

Construction of the Decision Tree

Let us now construct a decision tree for analyzing the decisions faced by Bio-Imaging. The first decision that must be made is whether Bio-Imaging should accept the offer from Medtech or instead continue with the research and development of the three-dimensional software program. This decision is represented by a decision node with two branches emanating from it, as shown in Figure 1.12. (The label "A" is placed on the decision node so that we can conveniently refer to it later.)

If Bio-Imaging were to accept the offer from Medtech, there would be nothing left to decide. If instead they were to continue with the research and development of the three-dimensional software program, they would find out after six months whether or not they would succeed in making it operational. This event is represented by an event node labeled "B" in Figure 1.13.

If Bio-Imaging were successful in developing the program, they would then face the decision whether to apply for an SBIR grant or to instead accept the offer from Nugrowth Development. This decision is represented as node C in Figure 1.14. If they were to apply for an SBIR grant, they would then either win the grant or not. This event is represented as node E in Figure 1.14. If they were to win the grant, they would then complete the development of the three-dimensional software product and market the product accordingly. The revenues that they would then receive would be in accordance with James' estimates given in Table 1.2. The event node G in Figure 1.14 represents James' estimate of the uncertainty regarding these revenues.

If, however, Bio-Imaging were to lose the grant, the offer from Nugrowth would then not be available either, due to the inherent delays in the grant decision process at NIH. In this case, Bio-Imaging would not have the resources to continue, and would have to abandon the project altogether. This possibility is represented in the lower branch emanating from node E in Figure 1.14.

On the other hand, if Bio-Imaging were to accept the offer from Nugrowth Development, they would then face the revenue possibilities in accordance with James' estimates given in Table 1.3. The event node H in Figure 1.14 represents James' estimate of the uncertainty regarding these revenues.

FIGURE 1.12
Representation of
the first decision
faced by Bio-
Imaging.

FIGURE 1.13
Further construction
of the Bio-Imaging
decision tree.

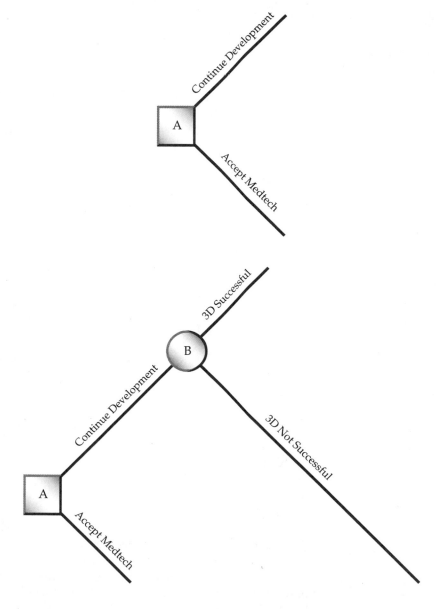

If Bio-Imaging were not successful in making the three-dimensional product operational, there would then be only two alternative choices of action: Abandon the project, or do more work to enhance the two-dimensional software product and then apply for an SBIR grant with the two-dimensional product. These two alternatives are represented at decision node D in Figure 1.15. If Bio-Imaging were to apply for the SBIR grant in this case, they would either win the grant or not. This event is represented as event node F in Figure 1.15. If they were to apply for the SBIR grant and were to win it, they would then complete the development of the two-dimensional software product and market it accordingly. The revenues they would then receive would be in accordance with James' estimates given in Table 1.4. The event node I in Figure 1.15 represents James' estimate of the uncertainty regarding these revenues. Finally, if they were to lose the SBIR grant for the two-dimensional product, they would have to abandon the project, as represented by the lower branch emanating from node F of Figure 1.15.

FIGURE 1.14
Further construction
of the Bio-Imaging
decision tree.

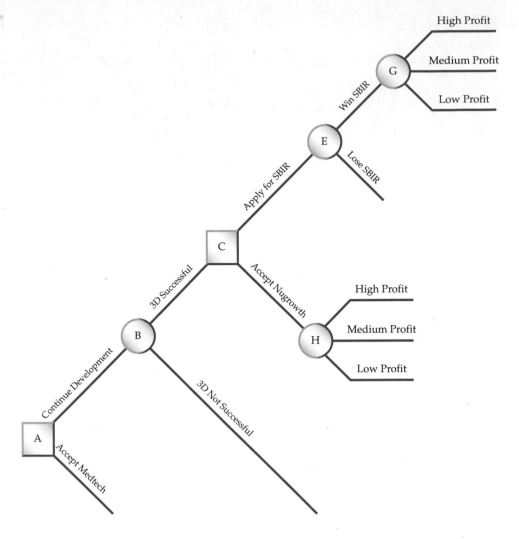

At this point, we have represented a description of the decision problem faced by Bio-Imaging in the decision tree of Figure 1.15. Notice that Figure 1.15 represents all of the decisions and all of the relevant uncertainties in the problem, and portrays the logical unfolding of decisions and uncertain events that Bio-Imaging is facing.

Assigning Probabilities in the Decision Tree

The next task in the decision analysis process is to assign probabilities to all of the uncertain events. For the problem at hand, this task is quite straightforward. For event node B, we place the probability that Bio-Imaging will succeed in producing an operational version of the three-dimensional software under the upper branch emanating from the node. This probability was estimated by James to be 0.60, and so we place this probability under the branch as shown in Figure 1.16. The probability that Bio-Imaging would not be successful in producing a three-dimensional prototype software program is therefore 0.40, and so we place this probability under the lower branch emanating from node B.

For event node E, we place the probability that Bio-Imaging would win the SBIR grant (if they were to succeed at producing an operational version of the three-dimensional software), which James had estimated to be 0.70, under the upper branch emanating from node E. We place the probability of 0.30, which is the proba-

FIGURE 1.15
Representation of
the Bio-Imaging
decision tree.

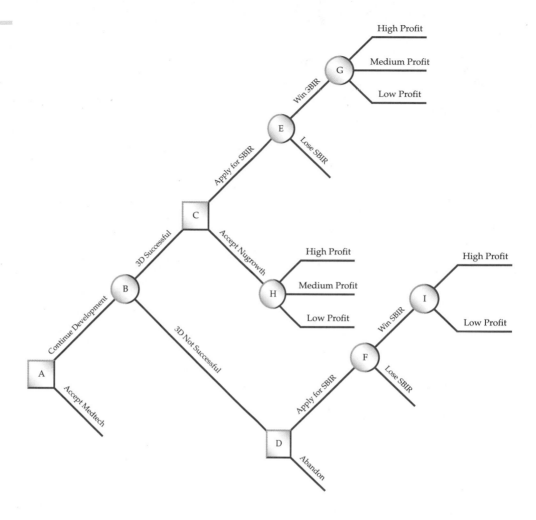

bility that Bio-Imaging would not win the SBIR grant under this scenario, under the lower branch emanating from node E.

For event node F, we have a similar situation. We place the probability that Bio-Imaging would win the SBIR grant (if they were not to succeed at producing an operational version of the three-dimensional software), which James had estimated to be 0.20, under the upper branch emanating from node F. We place the probability of 0.80, which is the probability that Bio-Imaging would not win the SBIR grant under this scenario, under the lower branch emanating from node F.

Finally, we assign the various probabilities of high, medium, and/or low profit scenarios to the various branches emanating from nodes G, H, and I, according to James' estimates of these scenarios as given in Table 1.2, Table 1.3, and Table 1.4.

Valuing the Final Branches

The remaining step in constructing the decision tree is to assign numerical values to the final branches of the tree. For the Bio-Imaging decision problem, this means computing the net profit corresponding to each final branch of the tree. For the branch corresponding to accepting the offer from Medtech, the computation is trivial: Bio-Imaging would receive $150,000 in net profit if they were to accept the offer from Medtech. This is shown in the lower branch emanating from node A, in Figure 1.17. For all other final branches of the tree, the computation is not quite so easy.

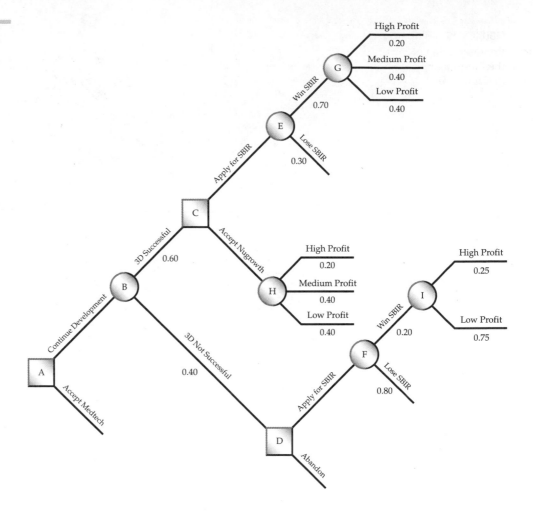

Let us consider first the branches emanating from node G. The net profit is the to-tal revenues minus the relevant costs. For these branches, the total revenues are given in Table 1.2. The relevant costs are the costs of research and development of the operational three-dimensional software (which was estimated by James to be $200,000). The SBIR grant money would be used to cover all final development and marketing costs, and so would not figure into the net profit computation. Therefore, by way of example, the net profit under the "high profit" scenario branch emanating from node G is computed as:

$$\$2,800,000 = \$3,000,000 - \$200,000.$$

The other two net profit computations for the branches emanating from node G are computed in a similar manner. These numbers are then placed next to their respec-tive branches, as shown in Figure 1.17.

Next consider the lower branch emanating from node E, which corresponds to succeeding at making an operational version of the three-dimensional software, ap-plying for the SBIR grant, and losing the competition for the grant. In this case, the revenues would be zero, as Bio-Imaging would abandon the project, but the costs would still be the $200,000 in development costs for the operational version of the three-dimensional software. Therefore the net profit would be −$200,000, as shown in Figure 1.17.

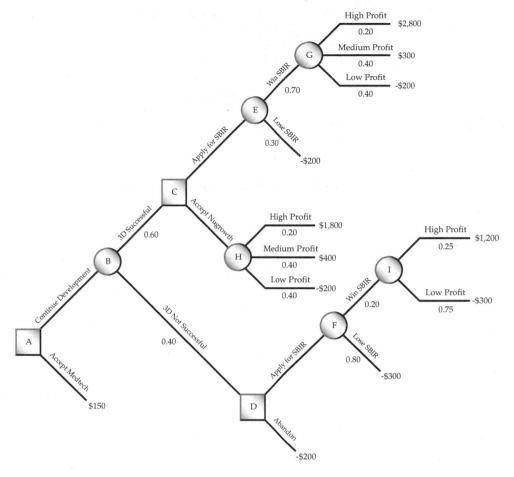

Next consider the three final branches emanating from node H. At node H, Bio-Imaging would have decided to accept the offer from Nugrowth Development, and so Bio-Imaging would only receive 20% of the total revenues. Under the "high profit" scenario, for example, the total revenues would be $10,000,000 (see Table 1.3). Therefore, the net profits to Bio-Imaging would be:

$$\$1,800,000 = 0.20 \times \$10,000,000 - \$200,000.$$

The other two net profit computations for the branches emanating from node H are computed in a similar manner. These numbers are then placed next to their respective branches, as shown in Figure 1.17.

Next consider the two final branches emanating from node I. At node I, Bio-Imaging would have been unsuccessful at producing an operational version of the three-dimensional product (at a cost of $200,000), but would have decided to go ahead and further refine the two-dimensional product (at a cost of $100,000). Under the "high profit" scenario, for example, the total revenues would be $1,500,000, see Table 1.4. Therefore, the net profits to Bio-Imaging would be:

$$\$1,200,000 = \$1,500,000 - \$200,000 - \$100,000.$$

The other net profit computation for the "low profit" scenario branch emanating from node I is computed in a similar manner. These numbers are then placed next to their respective branches, as shown in Figure 1.17.

Finally, we compute the net profits for the lower branches of nodes D and F. Using the logic herein, the net profit for the lower branch of node D is −$200,000 and the net profit for the lower branch of node F is −$300,000. These numbers are shown in Figure 1.17.

At this point, the description of the decision tree is complete. The next step is to solve the decision tree.

Solving for the Optimal Decision Strategy

We now proceed to solve for the optimal decision strategy by folding back the tree. Recall that this entails computing the EMV (expected monetary value) of all event nodes, and computing the EMV of all decision nodes by choosing that decision with the best EMV at the node. Let us start with node H of the tree. At this node, one of the three scenarios ("high profit," "medium profit" and "low profit") would transpire. We compute the EMV of this node by weighting the three outcomes emanating from the node by their corresponding probabilities. Therefore the EMV of node H is computed as:

$$0.20 \ (\$1,800,000) \ + \ 0.40 \ (\$400,000) \ + \ 0.40 \ (-\$200,000) \ = \ \$440,000.$$

We then write the EMV number $440,000 above node H, as shown in Figure 1.18.

FIGURE 1.18

Solution of the Bio-Imaging decision tree (all dollar values are in $1,000).

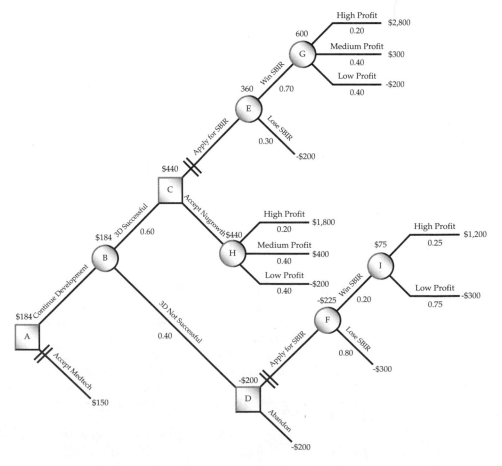

Similarly we compute the EMV of node G as follows:

$$0.20\ (\$2,800,000) + 0.40\ (\$300,000) + 0.40\ (-\$200,000) = \$600,000,$$

and so we write the EMV number $600,000 above node G, as shown in Figure 1.18.

The EMV of node E is then computed as:

$$0.70\ (\$600,000) + 0.30\ (-\$200,000) = \$360,000,$$

and so we write the EMV number $360,000 above node E, as shown in Figure 1.18.

Node C corresponds to deciding whether to apply for an SBIR grant, or to accept the offer from Nugrowth Development. The EMV of the SBIR option (node E) is $360,000, while the EMV of the Nugrowth offer is $440,000. The option with the highest EMV is to accept the offer from the Nugrowth Development. Therefore, we assign the EMV of node C to be the higher of the two EMV values, i.e., $440,000, and we cross off the branch corresponding to applying for the SBIR grant, as shown in Figure 1.18.

The EMV of node I is computed as:

$$0.25\ (\$1,200,000) + 0.75\ (-\$300,000) = \$75,000,$$

and so we write the EMV number $75,000 above node I, as shown in Figure 1.18.

The EMV of node F is

$$0.2\ (\$75,000) + 0.8\ (-\$300,000) = -\$225,000,$$

and so we write the EMV number $-\$225,000$ above node F, as shown in Figure 1.18.

At node D, the choice with the highest EMV is to abandon the project, since this alternative has a higher EMV ($-\$200,000$) compared to that of applying for an SBIR grant with the two-dimensional program ($-\$225,000$). Therefore, we assign the EMV of node D to be the higher of the two EMV values, i.e., $-\$200,000$, and we cross off the branch corresponding to applying for the SBIR grant, as shown in Figure 1.18.

The EMV of node B is computed as

$$0.6\ (\$440,000) + 0.4\ (-\$200,000) = \$184,000,$$

which we write above node B in Figure 1.18.

Finally, at node A, the option with the highest EMV is to continue the development of the software. Therefore, we assign the EMV of node A to be the higher of the two EMV values of the branches emanating from the node, i.e., $184,000, and we cross off the branch corresponding to accepting the offer from Medtech, as shown in Figure 1.18.

We have now solved the decision tree, and can summarize the optimal decision strategy for Bio-Imaging as follows:

Bio-Imaging Optimal Decision Strategy:

- Bio-Imaging should continue the development of the three-dimensional software program and should reject the offer from Medtech.

- If the development effort succeeds, Bio-Imaging should accept the offer from Nugrowth Development.

- If the development effort fails, Bio-Imaging should abandon the project altogether.

- The EMV of this optimal decision strategy is $184,000.

Sensitivity Analysis

Given the subjective nature of many of the data values used in the Bio-Imaging decision tree, it would be unwise to adopt the optimal decision strategy derived herein without a thorough examination of the effects of key data assumptions and key data values on the optimal decision strategy. Recall that sensitivity analysis is the process of testing and evaluating how the solution to a decision tree behaves in the presence of changes in the data. The data estimates that James had developed in support of the construction of the decision tree were developed carefully, of course. Nevertheless, many of the data values, particularly the values of many of the probabilities, are inherently difficult or even impossible to specify with precision, and so should be subjected to sensitivity analysis. Here we briefly show how this might be done.

One of the probability numbers used in the decision tree model is the probability of winning an SBIR grant with the three-dimensional prototype software. Let us denote this probability by q. James' original estimate of the value of q was $q = 0.70$. Because the "true" value of q is also impossible to know, it would be wise to test how sensitive the optimal decision strategy is to changes in the value of q. If we were to construct a spreadsheet model of the decision tree, we would find that the optimal decision strategy remains unaltered for all values of q less than $q = 0.80$. Above $q = 0.80$, the optimal decision strategy changes by having Bio-Imaging reject the offer from Nugrowth in favor of applying for the SBIR grant with the three-dimensional prototype. If James were quite confident that the true value of q were less than 0.80, he would then be further encouraged to adopt the optimal decision strategy from the decision tree solution. If he were not so confident, he would then be wise to investigate ways to improve his estimate of the value of q.

Another probability number used in the decision tree model is the probability that Bio-Imaging would successfully develop the three-dimensional prototype. Let us denote this probability by p. James' original estimate of the value of p was $p = 0.60$. Because the "true" value of p is also impossible to know, it would be wise to test how sensitive the optimal decision strategy is to changes in the value of p. This can also be done by constructing a spreadsheet version of the decision tree, and then testing a variety of different values of p and observing how the optimal decision strategy changes relative to the value of p. Exercise 1.3 treats this and other sensitivity analysis questions that arise in the Bio-Imaging decision tree.

Decision Analysis Suggests Some Different Alternatives

Note from Figure 1.18 that the EMV of the optimal decision strategy, which is $184,000, is not that much higher than the EMV of accepting the offer from Medtech, which is $150,000. Furthermore, the optimal decision strategy, as outlined above, entails substantially more risk. To see this, observe that under the optimal decision strategy, it is possible that Bio-Imaging would realize net profits of $1,800,000, but they might also realize a loss of −$200,000. If they were instead to accept the offer from Medtech, they would realize a guaranteed net profit of $150,000. Because the two EMV values of the two different strategies are so close, it might be a good idea to explore negotiating with Medtech to see if they would raise their offer above $150,000.

In order to prepare for such negotiations, it would be wise to study the product development decision from the perspective of Medtech. With all of the data that has been developed for the decision tree analysis, it is relatively easy to conduct this analysis. Let us presume that Medtech would invest $1,000,000 in the project (which is the same amount that Nugrowth would have invested). And to be consistent, let us assume that the possible total revenues that Medtech might realize would be the same as those that were estimated for the case of Bio-Imaging accepting financing from Nugrowth, and with the same probabilities (as specified in Table 1.3). If we further assume, to be safe, that Medtech would face the same probability of successful development of the three-dimensional software program, then Medtech's net profits from this project can be represented as in Figure 1.19. In the figure, for example, the net profit of the "high profit" outcome is computed as:

$$\$8,850,000 = \$10,000,000 - \$1,000,000 - \$150,000,$$

where the $10,000,000 would be the total revenue, the $1,000,000 would be their investment cost, and the $150,000 would be their offer to Bio-Imaging to receive the rights to develop the product.

The EMV of the node labeled "T" of the tree in Figure 1.19 is computed as:

$$0.20\ (\$8,850,000) + 0.40\ (\$1,850,000) + 0.40\ (-\$1,150,000) = \$2,050,000,$$

and the EMV of the node labeled "S" of the tree in Figure 1.19 is computed as:

$$0.60\ (\$2,050,000) + 0.40\ (-\$1,150,000) = \$770,000.$$

Therefore, it appears that Medtech might still realize a very large EMV after paying Bio-Imaging $150,000 for the rights to develop the software. This suggests that Bio-Imaging might be able to negotiate a much higher offer from Medtech for the rights to develop their three-dimensional imaging software.

One other strategy that Bio-Imaging might look into is to perform the clinical trials to fine-tune the two-dimensional software and apply for an SBIR grant with the two-dimensional software, without attempting to develop the three-dimensional software at all. Bio-Imaging would incur the cost of the clinical trials, which James had estimated to be $100,000, but would save the $200,000 in costs of further development of the three-dimensional software. In order to ascertain whether or not this

FIGURE 1.19

Decision tree faced by Medtech.

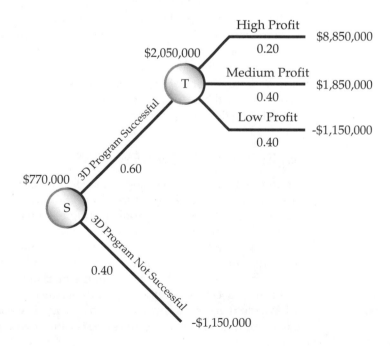

FIGURE 1.20
Evaluation of
another
development
strategy.

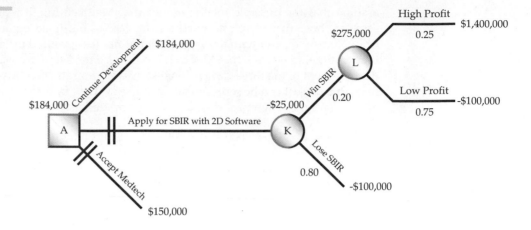

might be a worthwhile strategy, we can draw the decision tree corresponding to this strategy, as shown in Figure 1.20.

The decision tree in Figure 1.20 uses all of the data estimates developed by James for his analysis. As shown in Figure 1.20, the EMV of this alternative strategy is −$25,000, and so it is not wise to pursue this strategy.

As the previous two analyses indicate, decision trees and the decision analysis framework can be of great value not only in computing optimal decision strategies, but in suggesting and evaluating alternative strategies.

1.4   THE NEED FOR A SYSTEMATIC THEORY OF PROBABILITY

In the decision tree for Bill Sampras' summer job choice, as well as the decision tree for Bio-Imaging's development strategy, the probability numbers presented in the problem were exactly in the form needed in order to construct and solve the decision tree. This was very convenient. However, in many management contexts, the probability numbers that one needs to solve the problem must be derived and computed using a formal theory of probability, and such a theory will be developed in Chapter 2. To illustrate the need for such a theory of probability, consider the following relatively simple decision problem.

DEVELOPMENT OF A NEW CONSUMER PRODUCT

Caroline Janes is the marketing manager for a consumer products company that is considering whether to produce a new automatic dishwashing detergent called "Suds-Away." To keep this problem simple, let us assume that the market for Suds-Away will either be weak or it will be strong. If the market is strong, the company will make $18 million on Suds-Away, but if the market is weak, the company will lose $8 million. Based on a combination of experience and intuition, Caroline has estimated that there is a 30% chance that the market for Suds-Away will be strong.

Prior to deciding whether or not to produce Suds-Away, Caroline can conduct a nationwide market survey test of Suds-Away. The cost of the market survey would be $2.4 million. Such market survey tests cannot predict the market for new products with certainty, that is, these survey tests sometimes misread the market for new products. Past results with such surveys indicate that if the market is weak, there is a 10% chance that the test will be positive. Also, if the market is strong, there is a 20% chance that the test will be negative.

Caroline can decide either to not produce Suds-Away, to conduct the market survey test prior to deciding whether or not to produce, or to go ahead with production without conducting such a market survey test.

Figure 1.21 shows the layout for the decision tree for Caroline Janes' decision problem. The immediate decision that Caroline faces is among three different actions: (i) Do not produce Suds-Away; (ii) produce Suds-Away without conducting the market survey test; or (iii) conduct the market survey test prior to deciding whether or not to produce Suds-Away. These three actions are shown as the decision branches emanating from decision node A of the decision tree in Figure 1.21. If Caroline decides to not produce Suds-Away, then her company will realize no revenues, as is shown in the upper branch emanating from node A. If Caroline decides to produce Suds-Away, then the company will either make $18 million (if the market is strong) or lose $8 million (if the market is weak). These possibilities and their respective probabilities are shown in the decision tree at event node B.

Suppose that Caroline decides to conduct the nationwide market survey test, which is the bottom branch emanating from node A. The next event that will transpire will be the outcome of the test. The outcome will be either a "positive" or a "negative" market indication for the success of Suds-Away. These two possibilities are shown at event node C of Figure 1.21.

FIGURE 1.21

Caroline Janes' decision tree for the Suds-Away decision problem.

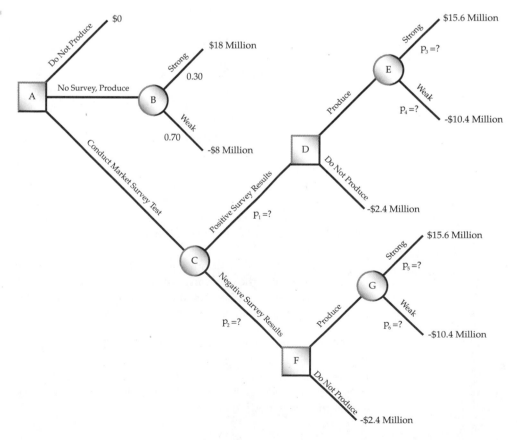

After she receives the information on the outcome of the market survey, Caroline will next have to decide whether or not to produce Suds-Away. Such a decision is shown at decision node D and at decision node E of Figure 1.21. At first glance, it might seem obvious that Caroline should produce Suds-Away if the test results are positive and that she should not produce Suds-Away if the test results are negative. However, the decision to produce Suds-Away at this point depends very much on the accuracy of the market survey test as well as the potential revenue implications of the state of the market for Suds-Away, and so it is prudent to leave this decision in the tree.

Notice that Caroline's decision as to whether or not to produce Suds-Away after receiving the results of the market survey test is drawn in two different places in the decision tree in Figure 1.21. This is because Caroline will face this decision under two different prior sequences of events. She will face this decision if the market survey test outcome is positive; and, of course, she will face the same decision even if the market survey test outcome is negative.

Suppose that the market survey test outcome is positive and that Caroline decides to produce Suds-Away. (This is the upper branch emanating from decision node D in Figure 1.21.) Even though the market survey test is positive in this case, there is still the possibility that the test will misread the market and that the market for Suds-Away might be weak rather than strong. For this reason, we must place an event node, labeled E in Figure 1.21, after Caroline's decision to produce Suds-Away.

Similarly, suppose that the market survey test outcome is negative, and that Caroline decides to produce Suds-Away anyway. This is the upper branch emanating from decision node F in Figure 1.21. Even though the market survey test is negative, there is still the possibility that the test will misread the market and that the market for Suds-Away might be strong rather than weak. Therefore, we must also place an event node, labeled G in Figure 1.21, after Caroline's decision to produce Suds-Away in this case.

The revenue numbers of the final branches in the lower portion of the decision tree in Figure 1.21 are easy to derive. Consider, for example, the case where Caroline has decided to conduct the market survey (at a cost of $2.4 million), and that the outcome of the test is positive. At decision node D, if Caroline decides to produce Suds-Away, then the company will realize a net contribution to earnings of $15.6 million if the market is strong. This is because if the market is strong, the company will earn $18 million directly, but will have expended $2.4 million on the cost of the market survey test, for a net contribution of $15.6 million ($15.6 = 18 - 2.4$). This is shown at the end of the upper branch emanating from event node E.

Similarly, if Caroline decides to produce Suds-Away, then the company will realize a net loss in earnings of $10.4 million if the market is weak. This is because if the market is weak, the company will lose $8 million directly, and will have also expended $2.4 million on the cost of the market survey test, for a total loss of $10.4 million ($10.4 = 8 + 2.4$).

Of course, if Caroline decides not to produce Suds-Away after conducting the market survey test, then the company will lose $2.4 million, which is the cost of the test. This is shown in the bottom branch emanating from decision node D. Similar logic is used to derive all of the other revenue numbers of the final branches of the decision tree.

In order to solve Caroline's decision problem, we have to insert the relevant probability numbers into the decision tree of Figure 1.21. First consider event node B. We know from the statement of the problem that there is a 30% chance that the market for Suds-Away will be strong, and so the probability of the upper branch emanating from node B is $p = 0.30$. Likewise, the probability of the lower branch emanating from node B is $p = 0.70$.

When we consider the probability numbers for the other branches of the decision tree of Figure 1.21, we run into a bit of difficulty. For example, consider event node C of the decision tree. The two event branches emanating from this node represent the possible events that the market survey test result will be positive (the upper branch) or negative (the lower branch). Let p_1 denote the probability that the market survey test result will be positive. Although we are not given the value of p_1 in the statement of Caroline's decision problem, we need to derive p_1 in order to solve the decision tree. As it turns out, there is a way to derive the value of p_1 based on a more systematic approach to probability theory that is based on the **laws of probability** and the use of **probability tables.** This material will be developed in Section 2.2 and Section 2.3 of Chapter 2.

There are a total of six probability numbers, labeled p_1, p_2, p_3, p_4, p_5, and p_6 in Caroline's decision tree in Figure 1.21, that need to be computed and placed in the decision tree before we can solve the decision tree. All of these probability numbers can be derived and computed using the theory of probability, which will be developed in Chapter 2. In fact, we will revisit Caroline Janes' decision tree in Section 2.3 of Chapter 2, where we will use the laws of probability and probability tables to derive these six probability numbers and then solve Caroline Janes' decision tree.

1.5 | FURTHER ISSUES AND CONCLUDING REMARKS ON DECISION ANALYSIS

In this chapter, we have introduced the methodology of decision analysis as a systematic way to analyze a managerial problem under uncertainty. We conclude this chapter with remarks concerning two aspects of the decision analysis methodology: the EMV criterion and considerations of risk, and the issue of non-quantifiable outcomes. Last of all, we discuss some of the many benefits of decision analysis.

The EMV Criterion and the Consideration of Risk

In all of our previous analyses we used the expected monetary value (EMV) criterion to compare various uncertain alternative decisions. The EMV criterion represents an "averaging" approach to compare uncertain alternatives: The EMV is calculated by considering the probabilistic average of all of the possible outcomes. This is a reasonable approach when the range of outcomes is within the realm of normal considerations of risk. However, when the outcomes might represent substantial risk to the decision-maker, the EMV criterion is not so appropriate. This is illustrated below.

Consider a situation where you face a choice between two alternatives as follows. If you choose the first alternative, you will receive $3 million with certainty. If you choose the second alternative, you will receive $10 million with probability 0.50, or you will receive $0 with probability 0.50. The EMV of the first alternative is $3 million, and the EMV of the second alternative is $5 million. Although the EMV of the second alternative is greater (by $2 million) than the EMV of the first alternative, most people (including the authors) would choose the first alternative. This is because the first alternative has less risk: It will assure you of $3 million. The second alternative is more risky; in fact, there is a 50% chance that you will receive nothing at all if you choose the second alternative. Therefore, for this type of problem, the EMV criterion is not appropriate.

On the other hand, suppose that the above decision problem were faced by a very wealthy individual or a large firm. A wealthy individual or a large firm has the financial resources to take the gamble of the second alternative, and might therefore choose among the alternatives using the EMV criterion.

(As it turns out, there is a method that allows one to formally incorporate risk into decision tree models. The method is called **expected utility theory.** However, the method of expected utility theory is not widely used in practice, and so we do not present it.)

In summary, the EMV criterion is a reasonable criterion for a large number of decision problems, especially those in which the relative outcomes are small compared to the resources of the decision-maker.

Non-quantifiable Consequences

When making any decision, a manager needs to consider consequences that are not easily quantifiable. For example, in the case of Bill Sampras' summer job decision, there are many non-quantifiable consequences of the various choices, such as learning and resumé-building opportunities, the physical attractiveness of the job site, and the "quality" of the job (this may include the level of responsibility, exposure to upper management, etc.).

As it turns out, there are sophisticated analytic tools for incorporating many non-quantifiable aspects of decisions into the decision analysis methodology. However, these methods are also not widely used, and so are not presented.

The Many Benefits of Using Decision Analysis

In addition to determining the optimal decision strategy, decision analysis offers many other benefits. These include the following:

- **Clarity of the decision problem.** By constructing the decision tree, the decision-maker is able to see clearly the structure of the sequence of decisions and uncertain events, and to see the interplay between the decisions and the uncertain events.

- **Insight into the decision process.** By solving the decision tree, the decision-maker is able to see what determines the optimal decision strategy.

- **Importance of key data.** By performing sensitivity analysis on key data values, the decision-maker is able to see which data is more important in determining the optimal decision strategy. This is particularly helpful in suggesting where to invest more time and energy in further data gathering.

- **Other benefits.** Quite often, the entire decision analysis process suggests new ways to think about the decision problem that the decision-maker would not otherwise have thought about.

Many management decision problems are complex and involve a large number of decisions and uncertainties that unfold over time. Decision analysis helps to break a problem into smaller, more manageable pieces. Decision analysis is a tool that can be used to enhance and improve a manager's judgment. In the hands of a good manager, the decision analysis process usually leads to more informed, insightful, and therefore better decision-making overall.

CASE MODULES

KENDALL CRAB AND LOBSTER, INC.

It was shortly before noon. Jeff Daniels, director of Overnight Delivery Operations at Kendall Crab and Lobster, Inc. (KCL) in Kendall Square, Cambridge, Mass., anxiously watched the Weather Channel on his office television. A fall storm was rapidly moving along the Atlantic coast toward Boston. If the storm front continued to move north at its current speed, the storm would hit Boston at around 5 P.M. However, many such storms change direction and move out to sea before they reach Boston, leaving Boston with only minor precipitation. The weather forecaster predicted a 50% chance that the storm would hit Boston (at around 5 P.M.), and a 50% chance that the storm would move out to sea and miss Boston and the rest of the northern Atlantic states. Jeff Daniels was not the only employee in Kendall Square watching the Weather Channel so attentively. Because there was a chance that Boston's Logan International Airport might have to shut down operations if the storm hit, many business travelers were nervously awaiting further weather information as well. Historically, when storms of this magnitude hit Boston, one in five are accompanied by severely strong winds that force Logan to close down its operations almost immediately.

Kendall Crab and Lobster, Inc.

Kendall Crab and Lobster, Inc. (KCL) was founded in Cambridge, Massachusetts, in 1962, as a crab and lobster wholesale and delivery company for the Boston area. By 1985, KCL had largely eliminated its crab business and had expanded its operations to include on-demand overnight delivery of lobsters to restaurants, caterers, and consumers in the Northeastern United States, with customers from Washington, D.C. to Presque Isle, Maine. By 1998, KCL's annual sales had reached $22 million. KCL attributed its success to great customer service, focused direct-mail marketing and advertising of its product, and the enormous popularity of lobster as a menu item for special occasions. KCL knew that customer service was critical for the success of any business in the food service sector of the economy, and maintaining an excellent reputation for customer service has always been a very high priority.

Jeff Daniels had worked for KCL part-time while a student at the Sloan School of Management at MIT, and had joined KCL's staff full-time after graduation. He rose quickly through the organization to his current position as director of Overnight Delivery Operations, which has been the company's most profitable department. He knew that the senior management were keeping an eye on him, and he had his mind set on becoming a senior vice-president in the next year.

Lobster

Lobster is a very popular menu item. This popularity stems from its exquisitely rich taste as well as its striking appearance, which decorates any dining table beautifully. People typically dine on lobster to celebrate a special occasion, and the experience of eating lobster is fun and exciting. Furthermore, lobster is extremely simple to cook: One simply places the live lobster in a pot of boiling water for 15 minutes, and it is ready to eat!

However, lobster is so perishable that it must be cooked live. After death, an uncooked lobster's meat rapidly deteriorates. For this reason, lobsters must always be transported live, and this adds significantly to their cost. A lobster is prepared for transport by packing the lobster in a corrugated box with an insulating foam insert, and covering the lobster with frozen non-toxic gel packs inside the insulating foam. A lobster can live in this special box for 36 to 48 hours. It is always necessary to transport lobster by overnight air or truck delivery to ensure that it is delivered live to its recipient.

Overnight Delivery Operations

Customers can order lobsters for next-day delivery any time prior to 5 P.M. on the day before delivery. A typical day's orders amount to approximately 3,000 lobsters that need to be delivered to customers. The staff of the KCL Overnight Delivery Operations spend most of their workday processing orders in their ordering and accounting computer systems and packing the lobsters for shipment. At 5:30 P.M., trucks from United Express Overnight Delivery (a prominent overnight package delivery company) pick up the packed lobsters and truck them to their Logan Airport facility. A United Express plane normally takes off from Logan Airport with the lobsters (and other packages from other Boston clientele) at 6:30 P.M. and flies the packages to United Express' central processing and sorting facility near Washington, D.C. At this facility, all packages (including the lobsters) are sorted and classified by their final destinations, and transported by air and then local trucks during the night, typically arriving at their destination by 10:30 A.M. the next day. The price that KCL charges its customers for delivered lobsters depends on the lobster's size, but typically this price is $30 per lobster, which includes all transportation costs. When KCL ships a lobster via United Express, its unit contribution to earnings is close to $10 per lobster.

If, for any reason due to weather, KCL is not able to deliver a customer's lobster order, it is KCL's policy to notify the customer by telephone (or FAX), to refund the purchase price of the lobster, and to give the customer a $20 discount coupon per lobster, which can be used towards the purchase of lobster from KCL at any time in the next twelve months. When this happens, customers are typically disappointed that they will not receive their lobster order, but they usually understand the relationship between delivery and weather conditions, and they appreciate the discount coupon. Marketing data has shown that approximately 70% of customers who receive such coupons eventually redeem them.

Changes in Operations Due to Weather Activity

Serious coastal storms that have the potential to close down Logan International Airport hit Boston about ten times per year. However, these storms virtually never threaten inland transportation operations on the ground or in the air. For this reason, KCL has often in the past relied on the services of Massachusetts Air Freight (MAF), which operates out of Worcester, Massachusetts (approximately 50 miles west and inland from Boston) for assistance in the transport of lobsters when adverse weather closes down Logan International Airport. If contacted before 5:30 P.M., MAF will pick up the packaged lobsters from KCL in Kendall Square, deliver them by truck to their airport in Worcester, Mass., and then fly them to United Express Overnight Delivery's sorting facility in Washington, D.C., whereupon United Express will take over the further routing and eventual delivery of the lobsters to customers. The costs associated with using MAF to transport lobsters to United Express' sorting facility in Washington, D.C. are typically quite high. According to Jeff's spreadsheet records, the additional transportation cost of using MAF was $13 per lobster in roughly 67% of the times that MAF was used, and was $19 per lobster in the remaining 33% of the times that MAF was used.

The other option that KCL would have if the storm were to force Logan Airport to close would be to simply cancel all orders for delivery to customers for the next day. This option involves notifying customers by telephone and informing them that they will be receiving a coupon in the mail for each lobster ordered. Also, if the lobsters have already been packed for transport, they would have to be unpacked and returned to their holding tanks for processing the following day. If the lobsters were not already packed, the incremental cost of canceling the orders is approximately $1.00 per lobster. If the lobsters were already packed, the cost is instead $1.25 per lobster, since most of the packaging materials are reusable.

With the storm approaching, Jeff faced one other immediate option: He could use a truck delivery company to deliver the lobsters. If Jeff were to make arrangements with Eastern Parcel Delivery (EPD), a regional truck package delivery company, by noon, they would hold trucks for KCL, and pick up the lobsters at 5:30 P.M. for delivery to all customers by late the next morning. EPD was very reliable as a trucking package delivery service, but there were two problems with using EPD. First, KCL would need to commit to using trucks by noon, well before they would know additional information about the storm. Second, truck delivery via EPD was more costly than delivery via air from United Express. EPD's delivery fees typically depended on the total distance that their trucks have to travel. However, because KCL would still be accepting orders from new customers until 5 P.M., the costs of using EPD could not be known at noon with any certainty. Depending on the distance the trucks had to travel, the cost of truck delivery could range from $2 to $4 higher than normal air delivery per lobster. A quick scan of the data in his spreadsheet on previous instances when KCL arranged transportation from EPD showed that in 50% of the times EPD was used, the average additional transportation cost was around $4 per lobster (above the normal cost of delivery by air). In another 25% of the cases, the average additional transportation cost was around $3 per lobster. In the remaining 25% of the cases, the average additional transportation cost was only $2 per lobster.

Many Options to Choose From

If Jeff were to choose to transport the lobsters by truck using EPD, he would have to make the arrangements almost immediately. If he chose not to use EPD, he could wait and see if the storm hit Boston and if the storm forced Logan to close down. If the storm were to hit Boston, it would do so at around 5 P.M. and Logan Airport would either close immediately or not at all, depending on the severity of accompanying winds. If the storm were not to hit Boston and/or the storm were not strong enough to force Logan to close, Jeff would presumably know this by 5:30 P.M., and he could then go ahead with KCL's regular plan of having United Express Overnight Delivery pick up the lobsters for air transport out of Logan Airport. If the storm were to hit Boston and close down Logan Airport, Jeff would also know this by 5:30 P.M., and he would then face the decision of whether to cancel the customers' deliveries altogether, or to transport the lobsters via MAF to Worcester and on to United Express' sorting facility in Washington, D.C., where the lobsters would then be incorporated into United Express' delivery operations.

Regardless of which options Jeff chose, he knew that on Friday he would have to explain his decision to senior management at their weekly operations review meeting. As he sat down to do a decision tree analysis, he also thought it would be an excellent idea to standardize the decision tree methodology so that it could be used semi-automatically in the future. Standardizing the methodology made good sense as a means of keeping KCL's operations consistently efficient. As a side benefit, Jeff hoped that this would also impress the senior managers at the meeting.

Assignment:

(a) Structure the delivery operations decision problem as a decision tree.

(b) Solve for Jeff Daniels' optimal decision strategy.

BUYING A HOUSE

Debbie and George Calvert are thinking of making an offer to purchase a house in Shaker Heights, Ohio. Both George and Debbie saw the house this morning and fell in love with it. The asking price for the house is $400,000, and it has been on the market for only one day. Their broker told them that there were more than 20 potential buyers who saw the house that day. She also added that another broker told her that an offer on the house was going to be presented by that broker this afternoon. Their broker has advised them that if they decide to make an offer on the house, they should offer very close to the asking price of $400,000. She also added that if there are competing offers on the house that are close in value, then it is common practice for the seller to ask the potential buyers to submit their final offers the following day.

Trying to be objective about this decision, Debbie has decided to construct a decision tree to help her with this decision. She has assumed that the "fair market value" of the house under consideration is $400,000. She has assigned an "emotional value" of $10,000 if she and George are successful in purchasing the house. That is, whereas the fair market value of the house is $400,000, the house is worth $410,000 to Debbie and George. Thus, if they were to be successful in purchasing the house for $390,000, the value of this outcome would be $20,000. Of course, if they were not successful in purchasing the house, the value of this outcome would be simply $0. Debbie has also assigned a probability of 0.30 that they will be the only bidders on the house.

Debbie has decided to consider making one of only three offers: $390,000, $400,000, or $405,000. She estimates that if they are the only bidders, the probability that an offer of $390,000 is accepted is 0.40, the probability that an offer of $400,000 is accepted is 0.60, and the probability that an offer of $405,000 is accepted is 0.90.

If, however, there are other bidders, Debbie assumes that the seller will ask them to submit a final offer the following day. In such a scenario, she will then have to rethink what to do: She can withdraw her offer, submit the same offer, or increase her offer by $5,000. She feels that in the event of multiple bids, the probability that an offer of $390,000 is accepted is 0.20, the probability that an offer of $395,000 is accepted is 0.30, the probability that an offer of $400,000 is accepted is 0.50, the probability that an offer of $405,000 is accepted is 0.70, and the probability that an offer of $410,000 is accepted is 0.80.

Assignment:

(a) Structure Debbie and George's problem as a decision tree.

(b) Solve for Debbie and George's optimal decision strategy.

THE ACQUISITION OF DSOFT

Polar, Inc. and ILEN are the two largest companies that produce and sell database software. They each have been negotiating to buy DSOFT, the third largest company in the database software market. Polar currently has 50% of the world market for database software, ILEN has 35%, DSOFT has 10%, and there are several other smaller companies that share the remaining 5% of the market for database software. Financial and market analysts at Polar have estimated the value of DSOFT to be $300 million in net worth.

Throughout the preliminary negotiations, DSOFT has made it clear that they will not accept a purchase offer below $300 million. Jacob Pratt, the CEO of Polar, figures that acquiring DSOFT will make Polar the dominant player in the industry as Polar would then have 60% of the market. In addition, Jacob knows that DSOFT has been developing a new product that has tremendous earnings potential. Jacob has estimated that the new product would increase the net worth of DSOFT by an additional $300 million with probability 0.50, by an additional $150 million with probability 0.30, or have no impact on net worth with probability 0.20.

To simplify matters, Jacob has decided to consider three possible strategies regarding the possible purchase of DSOFT: (i) Make a "high" offer of $400 million; (ii) make a "low" offer of $320 million; or (iii) make no offer at all. If he pursues this third strategy (making no offer), Jacob is certain that ILEN will buy DSOFT. If Polar makes an offer to DSOFT (either a "high" or a "low" offer), Jacob figures that ILEN will increase the offer further. He is uncertain about what ILEN will offer in this case, but he has made the following intelligent estimates of possible outcomes: ILEN would increase Polar's offer by 10% with probability 0.30, by 20% with probability 0.40, or by 30% with probability 0.30. If ILEN were to make such an offer, Jacob would then need to decide whether he would make a final offer to DSOFT. His thinking is that after ILEN makes a counter-offer, Polar would either withdraw from the bidding, match the counter-offer, or make a final offer at 10% above ILEN's counter-offer. If Polar's offer and ILEN's offer are identical, Jacob estimates that the probability that DSOFT will accept Polar's final offer is 0.40 ; however, if Polar counters with an offer which is 10% higher than ILEN's offer, Jacob estimates that DSOFT will accept Polar's final offer with probability 0.60.

Assignment:

(a) Structure Polar's acquisition offer problem as a decision tree.

(b) Solve for the optimal decision strategy for Polar.

NATIONAL REALTY INVESTMENT CORPORATION

National Realty Investment Corporation is a firm that is principally engaged in the purchase, development, management, and sale of real estate properties, particularly residential properties. It is currently evaluating whether or not to purchase the old Bronx Community Hospital, located in the East Bronx of New York City in a neighborhood undergoing rapid growth and rejuvenation. The Bronx Community Hospital operated unprofitably until 1991 when it closed and filed for bankruptcy. National Realty is considering purchasing the building, converting it to apartment units, and operating it as an apartment complex.

The hospital and its property are currently being offered for sale. National has performed an extensive evaluation of the site and neighborhood, and has projected the value of the property to be $2 million. After considering its size and location, National thinks that this is an attractive price and is considering offering to purchase the property at this price. Carlos Melendez is in charge of the hospital project for National. Carlos has thought that this property could be converted into 96 "low-income" apartments. The location seems ideal for such a conversion, and with the help of state agencies that would cooperate with (and subsidize) this type of development, the remodeling could be quite a profitable investment.

The New York Housing and Development Agency (NYHDA) has been administering the Low-Income Housing plan (LIH) for many years, in an effort to accommodate families in need of affordable housing. Because of the high demand for housing in New York City, rents have been increasing at rates higher than 10% per year in many neighborhoods, leaving large numbers of families without affordable housing. For this reason, the NYHDA started the LIH plan, which provides financial incentives for real-estate developers to become involved in the rehabilitation of properties for low-income families. Under normal circumstances such projects might not be appealing to developers, since other investments might yield a higher return (with similar risk). With LIH financial incentives, which represent large subsidies to the developer from the NYHDA, these projects become attractive enough to warrant investment. The NYHDA takes many things into consideration before approving any project under the LIH plan, and all applications are carefully reviewed by different area specialists. The LIH plan subsidies represent long term investments of large amounts of money. Therefore, the NYHDA takes great pains to ensure that all projects are fully completed and that they serve their original purpose of providing housing for low-income families.

Carlos Melendez needs to decide whether National should offer to purchase the hospital or not; however, the decision process is more complex than this, since there are many factors that are uncertain. One of the key issues is whether the 96-unit renovation plan would be granted approval by the NYHDA. In some instances when a developer applies for NYHDA subsidies under the LIH plan, the NYHDA evaluation process can take as long as five months. Unfortunately, National Realty has to make some decisions quite soon.

According to Carlos, some of the uncertainty concerning the approval of a potential application for the hospital property could be resolved if he could postpone his decision for at least one month, until after the coming November elections, when New York City voters will elect a new mayor. One of the candidates is fully supportive of the LIH plan, and she has been encouraging more low-income housing for quite some time. The other candidate has not been supportive of the low-income housing concept or the LIH plan of subsidizing private development. Obviously, the chances of approval of an application for the hospital property to qualify for LIH plan subsidies would increase or decrease according to the outcome of the elections. Carlos thought that if he were to wait until after November to make a decision on the property, he would have a better idea of whether his LIH plan application was going to be approved. Unfortunately, there is always the risk that the property would be purchased by some other buyer if National waited until after the elections. Carlos therefore needs to decide whether to make an offer now or to wait until after the elections and risk that the property would already be sold.

If and when National were to offer to purchase the hospital, they must also offer a non-refundable deposit of 10% of the purchase offer (in this case, $200,000). Once National has made an offer to purchase the hospital, National can then apply for the LIH plan subsidies. After 60 days from the date that the offer and deposit are drawn up, National must either complete the offer to buy the property, in which case the remaining 90% of the value of the property is paid, or withdraw the offer, forfeiting their 10% deposit.

There is no guarantee, unfortunately, that National's LIH subsidy application would be processed and decided upon within the 60-day period National has before making a final decision. (In the past, the NYHDA approval process has taken anywhere from one month to five months.) If the NYHDA were to decide on National's application within the 60-day time period, then this would make National's evaluation process easier. However, there is a distinct possibility that if National were to offer to purchase the hospital (to develop it for low-income housing), they would not hear from NYHDA regarding the status of their application before the 60-day limit that the hospital trustees have. National would have to decide either to withdraw their offer (and lose their 10% deposit) or to purchase the property without knowing whether their application for LIH plan subsidies is going to be accepted.

Initially, Carlos Melendez thought that the hospital renovation project would be profitable only if it received the LIH plan subsidies from the NYHDA. Renovation as well as maintenance costs on the property were projected to be quite high, and consequently higher rents would ordinarily have to be charged to tenants to cover these costs. However, because of the location of the property in the East Bronx, Carlos did not think this would be possible. At the same time, because of all of the new development and construction that has been going on in the neighborhood, Carlos thought that medium-income families might find the renovated apartments attractive and be willing to pay the higher rents. This might make the renovation project cost-effective even if it were not approved for LIH development (and subsidies).

Analyzing the Problem

Carlos Melendez sat at his desk trying to conceptualize his problem. What were the key decisions? What were the key uncertainties? What was the timing of decisions? What was the timing of the resolution of uncertainty? What data would he need in order to make an intelligent, defensible decision? After some hard thinking, he drew up the following list of uncertainties for the hospital renovation project.

- The chance that the 96-unit LIH plan would be approved.

- The chance that the LIH application decision would be delayed beyond 60 days after submission.

- The chance that the mayoral candidate who is favorable to low-income housing would be elected.

- The chance that the hospital property would still be available for purchase if National waited until after the November election.

- The chance that the LIH plan would be approved, given that the outcome of the mayoral election was favorable.

Valuing Uncertainty

Carlos reviewed some past history of LIH applications and estimated the probability that the application decision would be delayed beyond 60 days to be 0.30. Carlos then mused that the probability that the outcome of the mayoral election is favorable is 0.60. Given that the outcome of the mayoral elections were favorable, Carlos estimated that the probability of the LIH plan to be approved is 0.70; if the outcome were unfavorable, the probability of approval is 0.20. Finally, Carlos estimated the probability that the property would still be available for purchase after the election (if National took no action) to be 0.80.

The Value of the Two Development Alternatives

Carlos next went to work on the financial analysis of the development project. Armed with financial numbers, cost estimates, and a business calculator, Carlos estimated that the value of the development project under the LIH plan would be $428,817. This value includes the purchase cost of the property, the cost of renovations, annual maintenance costs, annual rental incomes, and applicable tax shelters. (The details of the computation of this number are presented in the appendix for students who are curious to see how these sorts of computations are developed. However, the details of the computations are not needed in order to do the assignment below.)

If LIH plan approval were not granted for the project, National would lose some of the attractive subsidies and tax shelters offered by NYHDA. On the other hand, there would be no restriction on the percentage of low-income tenants that could occupy the building (nevertheless, not too many high- or medium-income families would be attracted to the neighborhood). Carlos estimated that the value of the development project in the absence of LIH approval would be $42,360. Once again, the details of the computation of this number are presented in the appendix for the interested reader.

Assignment:

(a) Construct a spreadsheet model of the decision problem, and solve for the optimal decision strategy.

(b) Carlos assumed that the probability of LIH approval given a favorable election outcome was $p = 0.7$. Perform sensitivity analysis on this probability, letting p vary in the range between 0.6 and 0.8. In what way, if at all, does the optimal decision strategy change?

(c) (Optional Challenge!) According to the appendix, Carlos assumed a discount rate of $\beta = 7\%$. Perform sensitivity analysis on the discount rate, letting β vary in the range between 6% and 9%. In what way, if at all, does the optimal decision strategy change?

(d) What is your overall recommendation?

Appendix: Computation of the Value of the Development Project

In this appendix we illustrate how the value of the development project is computed. In order to evaluate the project, Carlos must properly account for income from the project, which comes from rents on the units, and costs, including renovation costs, maintenance costs, and taxes.

Estimating Rental Income for the Hospital Renovation Project

If a real estate development project is approved under the LIH plan, a specified percentage of the building must be occupied by low-income families. Tenants have been classified into three main groups according to their level of income. The first are class A tenants, which have an annual income of over $20,000 but less than $30,000. The second class are called class B tenants, who have an annual income between $15,000 and $20,000. Class C tenants are those with an income of $15,000 or less.

According to the specific housing conditions, the NYHDA requires that 20% of all tenants in a building supported by the LIH plan should belong to class A, 30% to class B, and 50% to class C. Once the LIH plan approval is granted, the only requirement that has to be satisfied is to maintain this distribution of tenants in the buildings. This distribution is important in determining what the investment return of the project will be, since this implies different levels of rents according to the class of tenant. On average, the actual amount of monthly rent charged to the tenants plus the subsidy paid by the agency (which accounts for an additional 20% of what the tenant pays) is: $685 for a class A tenant, $484 for a class B tenant, and $418 for a class C tenant.

If the LIH plan approval is not granted for the project, there is obviously no restriction on the percentage of low-income tenants that could occupy the building. However, there would also not be too many medium- or high-income families that would be attracted to the neighborhood. Carlos has estimated that the average monthly rent in this case would be $520 per rental unit.

Costs of Renovation

Carlos has been working with some of the building planners at National and has developed a good feel for renovation costs. He has estimated that the cost of the renovation would be about $1,152,000, which works out to $12,000 per apartment. However, this cost would be lower if the project was approved for LIH subsidies. If their project was approved, National would receive architectural and other technical expertise for free, as well as subsidies for material and labor costs, except for windows and window and door frames, which have to be purchased at market value. Carlos has figured that the total cost would be about 20% lower if the LIH plan was approved.

Annual Maintenance Costs

Maintenance costs for apartment buildings can be divided into two categories, general costs and unit costs. General maintenance costs include costs associated with operating the entire building, such as the supervisors' salaries, the cost of operating the elevators, etc. Carlos estimated this cost to be $56,000 per year for the project.

Unit maintenance costs are the costs of maintaining the individual apartments, such as utility costs (gas, water, electricity) as well as routine repairs in the apartments. Without LIH approval, this cost would be close to $75,000 per year. With LIH approval, subsidies of utility costs would reduce this cost to $60,000 per year.

Taxes

Most of the real estate investments of this dimension are taxed at the annual rate of 45%. However, if granted LIH approval, National would be entitled to a tax rebate of 5%, reducing their effective tax rate to 40%.

Time Horizon

In order to estimate the cash flows of the hospital project, Carlos used a 30-year planning horizon.

Valuing Cash Flows over Time

Suppose that there is an investment opportunity that will pay you $10,000 next year and $17,000 the year after, once you make an initial investment this year of $20,000. Then the total cash flow from the investment would be

$$\$7,000 = -20,000 + 10,000 + 17,000.$$

However, this cash flow analysis assumes that $1 received today is no different than $1 received next year. This is obviously not true. Almost all people prefer $1 today to $1 next year, if for no other reason than the fact that they could put the $1 in a savings account and earn interest on it. Therefore cash flows in the future are valued less than cash flows in the present. Financial calculations take this into account by discounting cash flows in the future, using a *discount rate*. For example, at a discount rate of $\beta = 0.07 = 7\%$ per year, the value of the above investment would be

$$\$4,194 = -20,000 + \frac{1}{(1.07)}10,000 + \frac{1}{(1.07)^2}17,000.$$

Notice that instead of weighting all future cash flows the same, we have discounted each year's cash flow by the factor $0.9346 = 1/1.07$. The number 1.07 is computed as

$1 + \beta$ where β is the discount rate, and so $1 + \beta = 1 + 0.07 = 1.07$. Cash flows that occur t years into the future are discounted using the factor $\dfrac{1}{(1 + \beta)^t}$. More generally,

---

The value of a cash flow that pays K_0 now, K_1 in one year, K_2 in two years, $\ldots$, K_t in year t is:

$$\text{Value} = K_0 + \frac{K_1}{1 + \beta} + \frac{K_2}{(1 + \beta)^2} + \cdots + \frac{K_t}{(1 + \beta)^t}$$

where β is the discount rate used in the cash flow analysis.

This way of computing cash flows over time is called **NPV** or **Net Present Value** analysis, and also goes by the name **discounted cash flow** analysis.

In computing the cash flows over time, Carlos used a discount rate of 7%, which is a fairly standard rate to use for this sort of computation. He computed the value of the cash flows of the hospital project under the LIH plan as follows:

The average monthly rent from each of the 96 units is

$$\$491.20 = 0.20 \cdot 685 + 0.30 \cdot 484 + 0.50 \cdot 418,$$

which accounts for the breakdown of rents by income class.

The total income each year (after taxes) is

$$\$269{,}917 = (1.0 - 0.40)(12 \cdot 96 \cdot 491.2 - 56{,}000 - 60{,}000),$$

which accounts for rental income as well as annual maintenance costs, and a tax rate of 40%.

Using a the discount rate of $\beta = 0.07$ on a cash flow of \$269,917 every year for the next 30 years, Carlos computed:

$$\$3{,}349{,}417 = \sum_{t=1}^{30} \left(\frac{1}{1.07} \right)^t \cdot 269{,}917.$$

The overall value of the project after taxes is therefore:

$$\$427{,}817 = -2{,}000{,}000 - (1.0 - 0.20) \cdot 1{,}152{,}000 + 3{,}349{,}417.$$

This last computation accounts for the purchase cost of the property (\$2,000,000) and the cost of renovation (\$1,152,000), less 20% due to LIH subsidies.

Without LIH approval, using a similar analysis, the value of the project would be

$$\$42{,}360 = -2{,}000{,}000 - 1{,}152{,}000$$
$$+ \sum_{t=1}^{30} (1 - 0.45) \cdot \left(\frac{1}{1.07} \right)^t \cdot (12 \cdot 96 \cdot 520 - 56{,}000 - 75{,}000).$$

1.7   EXERCISES

EXERCISE 1.1 Mary is organizing a special outdoors show which will take place on August 15. The earnings from the show will depend heavily on the weather. If it rains on August 15, the show will lose \$20,000; if it is sunny on August 15, the show will earn $15,000. Historically, the likelihood of it raining on any given day in mid-August is 27%. Suppose that today is July 31. Mary has the option of canceling the show by the end of the day on July 31, but if she does so, she will then lose her $1,000 deposit on the facilities.

(a) What is Mary's optimal decision strategy?

(b) Suppose that Mary can also cancel the show on August 14, but if she waits until then to do so, she must pay a fee of $10,000. The advantage of waiting until August 14 is that she can listen to the weather forecast for the next day on the local news station. According to station records, the weather was forecast to be sunny 90% of the days in mid-August in previous years. Also, when the weather was forecast to be sunny, it turned out to be sunny 80% of the time. When the weather was forecast to be rainy, it turned out to be rainy 90% of the time. What is Mary's optimal decision strategy in this case?

EXERCISE 1.2 The Newtowne Art Gallery has a valuable painting that it wishes to sell at auction. There will be three bidders for the painting. The first bidder will bid on Monday, the second will bid on Tuesday, and the third will bid on Wednesday. Each bid must be accepted or rejected that same day. If all three bids are rejected, the painting will be sold for a standing offer of $900,000. Newtowne's chief auctioneer's estimates for the bid probabilities are contained in Table 1.5. For example, the auctioneer has estimated that the likelihood the second bidder will bid $2,000,000 is $p = 0.90$.

(a) Formulate the problem of deciding which bid to accept as a decision tree.

(b) Solve for the optimal decision strategy.

EXERCISE 1.3 Set up a spreadsheet to analyze the following issues arising in the Bio-Imaging development strategies example:

(a) How does the optimal decision strategy change relative to the probability of successful development of the three-dimensional computer program? Recall that in James' decision tree model, he estimated the probability of the successful development of the three-dimensional computer program to be $p = 0.60$. To answer this question, let p denote the probability of successful development of the three-dimensional computer program. Then let p vary between $p = 0.0$ and $p = 1.0$ in your spreadsheet, and observe how the optimal decision strategy changes. What do you notice?

(b) Suppose that James' estimates of the total revenues to Bio-Imaging under the "high profit" scenarios are too low. Suppose that Bio-Imaging's total revenues would be $15,000,000 instead of $3,000,000 under the "high profit" scenario if three-dimensional software is successful and they win the SBIR grant, and that their total revenue under the "high profit" scenario would be $50,000,000 rather than $10,000,000 if they were to accept the financing offer from Nugrowth. How would their optimal decision strategy change?

TABLE 1.5

Estimates of the probabilities of bids by the three bidders.

Amount of Bid	Bidder 1 (Monday)	Bidder 2 (Tuesday)	Bidder 3 (Wednesday)
$1,000,000	0.0	0.0	0.7
$2,000,000	0.5	0.9	0.0
$3,000,000	0.5	0.0	0.0
$4,000,000	0.0	0.1	0.3

(c) How does the optimal decision strategy change relative to a change in the probability of the "high-profit" scenario? What additional assumptions do you need to make in order to answer this question?

EXERCISE 1.4 Anders and Michael were classmates in college. In their spare time while undergraduates, they developed a software product that regulates traffic on internet sites. Their product uses very imaginative and original ideas, and they have applied for a patent. They estimate that there is an 80% chance their patent will be approved by the US Patent Office.

Anders and Michael have also formed a start-up company called ITNET, and they have started to market their software product. Last month, they presented some of their ideas tof Singular, Inc., the dominant player in this growing market, after Singular had signed a confidentiality agreement with ITNET that ITNET's lawyer had prepared.

Yesterday, Singular announced a new software product that seemed suspiciously similar to the one that Anders and Michael have developed. Anders' first reaction was to plan to sue Singular immediately. However, Michael felt that they should wait until they have received notification of their patent, which is still pending before the U.S. Patent Office. Michael reasoned that their case would be much stronger if they had a patent for their product.

Suppose that Anders and Michael have a 90% chance of winning a lawsuit against Singular if their patent application is approved, and that they still have a 60% chance of winning such a lawsuit even while their patent application is pending (because Singular had signed the confidentiality agreement). However, if their patent application is not approved, suppose that the chance of winning the lawsuit would drop to 40%.

Anders feels that if they sue Singular immediately, there is a 70% chance that Singular would settle out of court for $400,000, and a 30% chance that Singular would not settle out of court. If they win the lawsuit, their settlement would be $1 million. However, they estimate that the legal costs of going to court would be $100,000.

(a) Structure ITNET's problem of whether or not to sue Singular as a decision tree.

(b) Solve for the optimal decision strategy.

EXERCISE 1.5 Javier Peña has always been interested in financing artistic projects. He has recently been offered two financing opportunities in the fashion industry: financing a new line of avant-garde youth fashions designed by Jorge Vera, and financing a line of business attire designed by Paolo Ricci. Javier has had a lot of past experience with these two designers, and has observed that 20% of Vera's fashion lines are "hits" and 80% of them are "misses." Furthermore, Ricci's fashion lines are "hits" 30% of the time, and are "misses" 70% of the time.

Javier's net liquid assets amount to $750,000. As a result, he can afford to finance at most one of the two fashion lines. However, he does have the option of pre-testing at most one of the fashion lines at the upcoming design show in San Francisco, before deciding which, if any, fashion line he would like to finance for the entire U.S. market for the fall fashion season. The costs and revenue associated with the two fashion lines are given in Table 1.6.

Javier has observed, based on previous years, that of the avant-garde fashion lines that were hits nationwide, 80% were hits in the San Francisco pre-test; of the avant-garde fashion lines that were misses nationwide, 40% were hits in the San

TABLE 1.6

Costs and revenue
for the two fashion
lines. Net costs are
given for pre-testing
the lines in San
Francisco.

Fashion Line:	Jorge Vera (avant-garde)	Paolo Ricci (business attire)
Net cost of San Francisco pre-test	$200,000	$75,000
Additional cost of U.S. production of line after a San Francisco pre-test	$500,000	$275,000
Cost of U.S. production if not pre-tested in San Francisco	$600,000	$325,000
Revenue if fashion line is a "hit"	$4,000,000	$1,000,000
Revenue if fashion line is a "miss"	$300,000	$100,000

TABLE 1.7

James McGill's
remaining lifetime in
years.

Tumor	Remove Tumor	Leave Tumor
Benign	5	8
Malignant	5	1

Francisco pre-test. Of the business attire fashion lines that were hits nationwide, 90% were hits in the San Francisco pre-test; of the business attire fashion lines that were misses nationwide, 60% were hits in the San Francisco pre-test. While Javier may find pre-test results useful, he knows the accuracy of this kind of test is not high enough to compel him in all cases to act in accordance with the pre-test results. In any event, Javier is willing to act on the basis of expected monetary values.

(a) Develop a decision tree to assist Javier in deciding what to do.

(b) What probabilities need to be computed in order to solve the decision tree?

(c) After reading Chapter 2, compute the necessary probabilities, and solve for Javier's optimal decision strategy.

EXERCISE 1.6 James McGill, age 68, was recently diagnosed with a particular type of brain tumor, and was referred to Dr. Mitchell Zylber, chief of surgery at the university hospital, for further evaluation. This type of tumor is benign in 50% of cases and is malignant in the other 50% of cases. James McGill's remaining lifetime will depend on the type of tumor (benign or malignant) and on the decision whether or not to remove the tumor. Table 1.7 shows estimates of James McGill's remaining lifetime according to the most up-to-date information known about this type of tumor.

Dr. Zylber could perform exploratory surgery prior to the decision whether or not to remove the tumor, in order to better assess the status of the tumor. Exploratory surgery is known to indicate a benign tumor 75% of the time, if the tumor is indeed benign. The surgery is known to indicate a malignant tumor 65% of the time, if the tumor is indeed malignant. Exploratory surgery itself is dangerous: there is a 5% chance that patients with profiles like James McGill's will not survive such surgery due to complications from anesthesia, etc.

If no exploratory surgery isf performed, James McGill must decide whether or not to have the tumor removed. And if exploratory surgery is performed, James must decide whether or not to have the tumor removed based on the results of the exploratory surgery.

(a) Draw the decision tree for this problem.

(b) What probabilities need to be computed in order to solve the decision tree?

(c) After reading Chapter 2, compute the necessary probabilities, and solve for the decision strategy that maximizes James McGill's expected lifetime.

(d) James McGill's children are expected to have children of their own within the next two or three years. Suppose James McGill wants to maximize the probability that he will live to see his grandchildren. How should this affect his decision strategy?

(e) What ethical questions does this medical problem pose?

Fundamentals of Discrete Probability

CONTENT

IN THE PREVIOUS CHAPTER, WE INTRODUCED THE METHOD OF DECISION ANALYSIS and decision trees for solving managerial decision problems under uncertainty. Recall that a key component of decision analysis involves the use of estimates of the likelihood of an uncertain event in terms of its probability. In this chapter, we introduce the fundamental tools to model an uncertain event and calculate its probability.

We define the concepts of an outcome, an event, and the probability of an event. We also introduce the laws of probability and use these laws to compute probabilities of different types of uncertain events in a variety of management contexts. We then show how to use probability tables to facilitate the calculation of probabilities.

We next introduce the very important concept of a random variable and the probability distribution of a random variable. We also introduce the concepts of the mean, variance, and standard deviation, as summary measures of the probability distribution of a random variable. We then introduce the concept of a joint probability distribution of a collection of random variables, as well as the summary measures of covariance and correlation, which measure the interdependence between two random variables. We include a wide variety of examples drawn from the fields of marketing, finance, manufacturing, and service operations, in which the tools of this chapter are used to provide important information for managing in an uncertain environment.

2.1   OUTCOMES, PROBABILITIES AND EVENTS

Consider the experiment of flipping a coin. The flipped coin will wind up facing either "heads" or "tails," but it is not known in advance which of the two sides will face up. That is, the outcome of the experiment is uncertain. We say that in this experiment, there are two possible outcomes: "heads" and "tails." More generally, the **outcomes** of an experiment are the events that might possibly happen. The outcomes are the ways in which uncertainty will be resolved.

As another example, consider the experiment of picking a card at random from an ordinary deck of 52 cards. There are 52 possible outcomes for the face value of the card. One possible outcome is "ten of diamonds."

For our purposes, the outcomes of an experiment must be specified in such a way that they are **mutually exclusive** and **collectively exhaustive.** By **mutually exclusive** we mean that no two outcomes can occur together. In the case of flipping a coin, the coin cannot be both "heads" and "tails." In the case of picking a card from a deck, the card cannot be both "ten of diamonds" and "queen of spades."

By **collectively exhaustive,** we mean that at least one of the outcomes must occur when the experiment is performed, i.e., when the uncertainty is resolved. A flipped coin must come up either "heads" or "tails." In the case of picking a card from a deck, the picked card must be one of the 52 outcomes "ace of clubs," "two of clubs," "three of clubs," . . . , "king of spades." Since the outcomes are mutually exclusive and collectively exhaustive, exactly one of them occurs at the conclusion of the experiment, that is, when the uncertainty is resolved.

The **probability** of an outcome is the likelihood that the outcome will occur when the uncertainty is resolved. In the case of flipping a coin, the probability of "heads" is 0.50. A physical interpretation of this is that if we flip a coin a very large number of times, say 1,000,000 times, then the number of heads will be extremely close to 500,000. On average, the outcome "heads" will occur 50% of the time. Put another way, the number 0.50 is the fraction of the times when the outcome of the experiment is "heads." In this way, we interpret the notion of a probability of an outcome as its relative frequency. Similarly, in the case of picking a card from a deck, the probability of "ten of diamonds" is 1/52, that is, there is a 1 in 52 chance that the card picked will be the ten of diamonds.

An **event** is a collection of outcomes. For example, in the case of picking a card from a deck, a possible event is "the card picked is a spade." Other events might be "the card picked is a seven," "the card picked is an odd numbered card," "the card picked is a jack, queen, or king," etc. We usually name an event symbolically with a

TABLE 2.1

Events and probabilities from picking a card at random from an ordinary deck of cards.

Event	Symbol	Probability
"The card picked is a spade"	E	13/52
"The card picked is a seven"	F	4/52
"The card picked is an odd numbered card"	G	20/52
"The card picked is a jack, queen, or king"	H	12/52

capital letter, such as A or B. Table 2.1 lists four events related to picking a card from a deck. The second column of Table 2.1 assigns a symbolic name to each of these four possible events. For example, the event "the card picked is a spade" is referred to symbolically as event E.

We will say that two events A and B are mutually exclusive if they contain different outcomes. The events "the card picked is a spade" and "the card picked is a diamond" are mutually exclusive (because a card cannot be both a spade and a diamond). The events "the card picked is a spade" and "the card picked is a seven" are not mutually exclusive.

The probability of an event is the sum of the probabilities of the outcomes comprising the event. For example, the probabilities of the events E, F, G, and H of Table 2.1 are depicted in the third column of the Table.

For a given event A, the symbol $P(A)$ denotes the probability of event A. For example, we write $P(H) = 12/52$ for the event H in Table 2.1.

We conclude this first section with a brief discussion of the philosophy of randomness and probability. When faced with the concept of probability, it is natural to want to know the root cause of the uncertainty being modeled. Sometimes we use probability to model situations where we simply lack information. At other times, we use probability to model a naturally random process, such as flipping a coin. For example, suppose that the weather person announces that the probability of rain tomorrow is 0.30. What does she mean? Does she mean that the genuinely random fluctuations of the atmospheric molecules will, with probability of 0.30, "congeal" into a rainstorm sometime tomorrow? Or does she mean that in 30% of the situations where similar weather patterns have been observed, rain has occurred on the following day? More likely, it is the latter. The problem of what is genuine randomness in a physical or economic process, as opposed to simply lack of information, is a rather deep philosophical question. All of us have an intuitive notion of what randomness means. Our goal here is not to probe this question to its depth. Rather, we simply want to develop methods that will lead to consistent and systematic ways to measure randomness by calculating probabilities of uncertain events based on sound intuition.

2.2   THE LAWS OF PROBABILITY

In this section, we develop a set of four fundamental **laws of probability** that will enable us to work effectively with probabilities of various uncertain events.

> **The First Law of Probability:** *The probability of any event is a number between zero and one. A larger probability corresponds to the intuitive notion of greater likelihood. An event whose associated probability is 1.0 is virtually certain to occur; an event whose associated probability is 0.0 is virtually certain not to occur.*

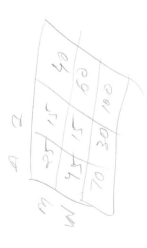

> **The Second Law of Probability:** *If A and B are mutually exclusive events, then*
> $$P(A \text{ or } B) = P(A) + P(B).$$

Returning to the example of picking a card at random from a deck, if A denotes the event "ten of diamonds" and B denotes the event "jack of any suit," then A and B are mutually exclusive events and

$$P(A \text{ or } B) = P(A) + P(B) = 1/52 + 4/52 = 5/52.$$

Note that because outcomes are mutually exclusive and collectively exhaustive, the sum of the probabilities of all the outcomes must equal one.

Suppose that we know that event B has occurred, that is, we know that one of the outcomes in B has been realized, but we do not know which one. The symbol $A|B$ denotes the event A **given** that the event B has occurred. The probability $P(A|B)$ is called the **conditional probability** of A given B. The conditional probability $P(A|B)$ denotes the probability of event A occurring conditional on knowing that event B has occurred.

> **The Third Law of Probability:** *If A and B are two events, then*
> $$P(A|B) = \frac{P(A \text{ and } B)}{P(B)}.$$
>
> *Equivalently,*
> $$P(A \text{ and } B) = P(A|B) \times P(B).$$

The following example illustrates the third law of probability.

Example 2.1 — Conditional Probability Calculation in a Deck of Cards

Let A denote the event "the card picked is the queen of any suit" and let B denote the event "the card picked is a face card." The event $A|B$ then is the event of obtaining a queen given that we have picked a face card. Let us calculate $P(A|B)$ in two different ways. In the first way, we will calculate this probability by applying the third law of probability. In the second way, we will compute this probability by counting.

In the first way, we apply the third law of probability. By the third probability law we have:

$$P(A|B) = \frac{P(A \text{ and } B)}{P(B)} = \frac{4/52}{12/52} = 1/3.$$

In the second way, we note that the event $A|B$ is the event of obtaining a queen given that we have picked a face card. Since a face card is always either a jack, a queen, or a king, the probability that we have picked a queen given that we have picked a face card is simply $1/3$. Note that this agrees perfectly (as it should) with the conclusion of the calculation using the third law of probability, and so verifies the validity of the third law of probability.

Example 2.2 — Picking a Student at Random in a Class

Consider a class of 100 students, 40 of whom are men and 60 of whom are women. Suppose that 70 of the students are Americans and 30 are international students. Of the 70 American students, 25 are men and 45 are women; and of the 30 international students, 15 are men and 15 are women. Table 2.2 summarizes this information.

TABLE 2.2

Distribution of students in a class.

	American	International	Total
Men	25	15	40
Women	45	15	60
Total	70	30	100

TABLE 2.3

Percentage of students in the class.

	American	International	Total
Men	0.25	0.15	0.40
Women	0.45	0.15	0.60
Total	0.70	0.30	1.00

Now suppose that we perform the experiment of choosing a student at random from the class. The probability that a student chosen at random will be an American is therefore the fraction of the students in the class who are American, which is 0.70 = 70/100. Table 2.3 portrays all such probabilities derived this way, i.e., Table 2.3 presents the fraction of students in each of the possible categories. For example, the entry 0.25 in the table represents the fraction of American men in the class. We interpret this number to mean the probability that the student selected is an American man.

Let A, I, M, and W denote the events that the randomly chosen student is American, International, a Man, and a Woman, respectively. (Note that "A" is for American, "I" is for International, etc.) We would like to calculate the probability of various events. From Table 2.3, $P(A) = 0.70$, $P(I) = 0.30$, $P(M) = 0.40$ and $P(W) = 0.60$. Let us next calculate the probability $P(A|M)$. In words, $P(A|M)$ denotes the probability that the student chosen is American, given that the student is a man. By the third law of probability,

$$P(A|M) = \frac{P(A \text{ and } M)}{P(M)}.$$

Since $P(M) = 0.40$ and $P(A \text{ and } M) = 0.25$, we obtain that

$$P(A|M) = \frac{0.25}{0.40} = 0.625.$$

(An alternative and entirely equivalent way to calculate this probability is to reason as follows: there are 40 men, of whom 25 are Americans. Therefore, given that the student is a man, the probability that he is American is 25/40 = 0.625.)

Two events A and B are **independent** if knowing that B has occurred does not influence the probability of A occurring. In contrast, two events A and B are **dependent** if knowing that B has occurred influences the probability of A occurring. For example, let A denote the event that the Standard & Poor 500 index (S&P500) will increase tomorrow and let B denote the event that interest rates will decrease tomorrow. Then, A and B are dependent events. This is because if interest rates decrease, then it is more likely that the S&P500 will increase. In the language of probability, if event B takes place, this then changes the probability that event A will take place.

As another example, let us consider picking a card at random from a deck. Let A denote the event "the card picked is a five" and let B denote the event "the card picked is a club." Then events A and B are independent, because knowing that the card picked is a club (event B) does not influence the probability that the card picked is a five (event A).

> **The Fourth Law of Probability:** *If A and B are independent events, then*
> $$P(A|B) = P(A).$$

The fourth law of probability states that if A and B are independent events, then the conditional probability of event A given event B is the same as the probability of event A. That is, event B has no bearing on the probability of event A.

Let us verify the fourth law of probability in the preceding example, where A is the event "the card picked is a five" and B is the event "the card picked is a club." As remarked previously, events A and B are independent. Note that $P(A) = 4/52$, since there are four "fives" in a deck of 52 cards. Also $P(B) = 13/52$, since there are thirteen clubs in a deck of 52 cards. The event "A and B" is the event "the card picked is the five of clubs." Then $P(A \text{ and } B) = 1/52$, since only one card in the deck is the five of clubs. Now notice that

$$P(A|B) = \frac{P(A \text{ and } B)}{P(B)} = \frac{1/52}{13/52} = 1/13 = 4/52 = P(A)$$

verifies the fourth law of probability.

Now suppose that events A and B are independent. Recall that the third law of probability states that

$$P(A \text{ and } B) = P(A|B) \times P(B).$$

Also, the fourth law of probability states that

$$P(A|B) = P(A).$$

Combining these two equations yields the following equation:

$$P(A \text{ and } B) = P(A) \times P(B),$$

which we formally record as the following implication:

> **Implication of the Fourth Law of Probability:** *If A and B are independent events, then*
> $$P(A \text{ and } B) = P(A) \times P(B).$$

2.3   WORKING WITH PROBABILITIES AND PROBABILITY TABLES

In Example 2.2 of the previous section, we used Table 2.3 to make the computation of probabilities easier and more transparent. Table 2.3 is an example of a **probability table.** In this section, we present several examples of probability tables and their use in computing probabilities of quantities of interest.

Example 2.3 — Using Probability Tables to Compute Probabilities in a Decision Tree

Recall the relatively simple decision analysis problem that was outlined in Section 1.4 of Chapter 1:

DEVELOPMENT OF A NEW CONSUMER PRODUCT

Caroline Janes is the marketing manager for a consumer products company that is considering whether to produce a new automatic dishwashing detergent called "Suds-Away." To keep this problem simple, let us assume that the market for Suds-Away will either be weak or it will be strong. If the market is strong, the company will make $18 million on Suds-Away; but if the market is weak, the company will lose $8 million. Based on a combination of experience and intuition, Caroline has estimated that there is 30% chance that the market for Suds-Away will be strong.

Prior to deciding whether or not to produce Suds-Away, Caroline can conduct a nationwide market survey test of Suds-Away. The cost of the market survey would be $2.4 million. Such market survey tests cannot predict the market for new products with certainty, that is, these survey tests sometimes misread the market for new products. Past results with such surveys indicate that if the market is weak, there is a 10% chance that the test will be positive. Also, if the market is strong, there is a 20% chance that the test will be negative.

Caroline can decide either to not produce Suds-Away, to conduct the market survey test prior to deciding whether or not to produce, or to go ahead with production without conducting such a market survey test.

In Section 1.4 of Chapter 1, we constructed the decision tree for Caroline Janes' decision problem, which is repeated here in Figure 2.1. As is shown in Figure 2.1, there are six probability numbers in Caroline's decision tree, labeled $p_1, p_2, p_3, p_4, p_5,$ and p_6, that need to be computed and placed in the decision tree before we can solve the tree. We now show how all of these probability numbers can be derived and computed using the laws of probability in conjunction with probability tables.

Let S denote the event that the market for Suds-Away is strong and let W denote the event that the market for Suds-Away is weak. Let Q denote the event that the market survey test results are positive and let N denote the event that the market survey test results are negative. Then in the language of probability, we are given the following information about this problem:

$$P(S) = 0.30, \ P(Q|W) = 0.10, \text{ and } P(N|S) = 0.20.$$

Our first goal will be to fill in the probability table shown in Table 2.4. Notice in Table 2.4 that we have filled in the bottom row of the table. This is because we are given in the data for the problem that

$$P(S) = 0.30,$$

and so

$$P(W) = 1.0 - P(S) = 1.0 - 0.30 = 0.70.$$

Now notice that from the third law of probability, we can compute

$$P(Q \text{ and } W) = P(Q|W) \times P(W) = 0.10 \times 0.70 = 0.07.$$

This allows us to fill in first row of the second column of the Table 2.4, which is shown in the completed version of the table in Table 2.5.

Because $P(N|S) = 0.20$, it follows that

$$P(Q|S) = 0.80.$$

Similarly, because $P(Q|W) = 0.10$, it also follows that

$$P(N|W) = 0.90.$$

From the third law of probability, we then have

$$P(N \text{ and } W) = P(N|W) \times P(W) = 0.90 \times 0.70 = 0.63,$$
$$P(Q \text{ and } S) = P(Q|S) \times P(S) = 0.80 \times 0.30 = 0.24,$$
$$P(N \text{ and } S) = P(N|S) \times P(S) = 0.20 \times 0.30 = 0.06.$$

FIGURE 2.1

Caroline Janes'
incomplete decision
tree for the Suds-
Away decision
problem.

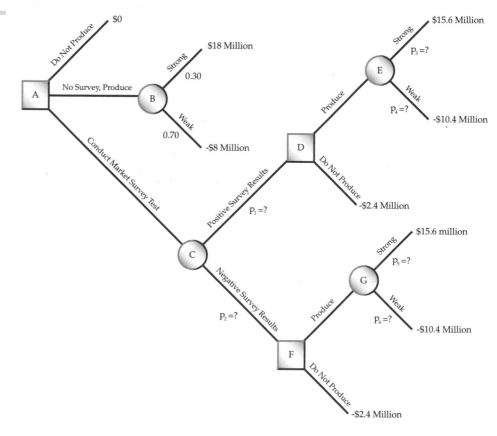

TABLE 2.4

Incomplete
probability table for
Caroline Janes'
decision problem.

	Market is Strong	Market is Weak	Total
Market Test is Positive			
Market Test is Negative			
Total	0.30	0.70	1.00

TABLE 2.5

Complete
probability table for
Caroline Janes'
decision problem.

	Market is Strong	Market is Weak	Total
Market Test is Positive	0.24	0.07	0.31
Market Test is Negative	0.06	0.63	0.69
Total	0.30	0.70	1.00

We can then use these probabilities to create Table 2.5, which contains all possible combinations of events and their corresponding probabilities, as calculated herein. Note that the last column of Table 2.5 is the sum of the other columns. Therefore, Table 2.5 tells us in particular that:

$$P(Q) = 0.31 \text{ and } P(N) = 0.69.$$

Now let us compute the required probability numbers needed for the decision tree in Figure 2.1. We need to compute the six probability numbers $p_1, p_2, p_3, p_4, p_5,$ and p_6. We begin with p_1. Note that p_1 is simply the probability that the outcome of the market survey is positive, which in our new notation is $P(Q)$. From Table 2.5, we have that $p_1 = P(Q) = 0.31$. It then follows easily, using identical reasoning, that $p_2 = P(N) = 0.69$.

We next turn our attention to the computation of p_3. First notice that p_3 is the probability that the market is strong, given that the survey results are positive. That is, p_3 is the conditional probability that the market is strong, conditioned on the event that the survey results are positive. In our notation, we have

$$p_3 = P(S|Q).$$

From the third law of probability, we have

$$p_3 = P(S|Q) = \frac{P(S \text{ and } Q)}{P(Q)}.$$

Then with the aid of Table 2.5, we can compute

$$p_3 = P(S|Q) = \frac{P(S \text{ and } Q)}{P(Q)} = \frac{0.24}{0.31} = 0.774.$$

In a similar manner, we can compute the remaining three probability quantities, as follows:

$$p_4 = P(W|Q) = \frac{P(W \text{ and } Q)}{P(Q)} = \frac{0.07}{0.31} = 0.226,$$

$$p_5 = P(S|N) = \frac{P(S \text{ and } N)}{P(N)} = \frac{0.06}{0.69} = 0.087,$$

$$p_6 = P(W|N) = \frac{P(W \text{ and } N)}{P(N)} = \frac{0.63}{0.69} = 0.913.$$

We then can place these probability numbers in the decision tree, as shown in the completed decision tree in Figure 2.2. Finally, using the folding-back procedure for solving the decision tree, we can obtain the solution to this decision tree problem, which is also shown in Figure 2.2.

Example 2.4 — Quality Control in Manufacturing

A manufacturing process produces microprocessors using an entirely new technology. Historical results suggest that 70% of the final product is damaged and therefore not usable. In the past, the manufacturer has used an extremely expensive (but extremely reliable) diagnostic procedure to test if a microprocessor is damaged. In order to cut costs, management is considering using a very inexpensive test that is not as reliable. Preliminary data suggest that if a microprocessor is damaged, then the

FIGURE 2.2
Caroline Janes'
completed decision
tree for the Suds-
Away decision
problem.

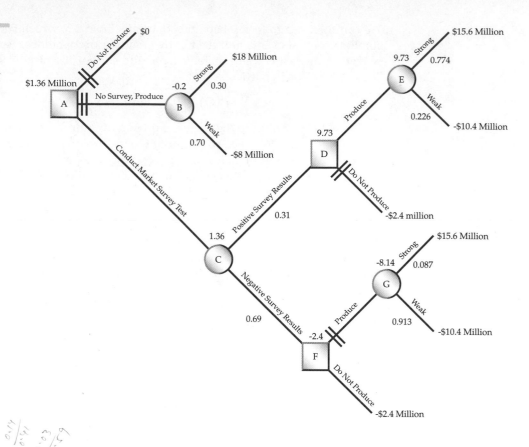

probability that the new test would be negative (i.e., the test declares that the micro-processor is damaged), is 0.80. If the microprocessor is working properly, the proba-bility that the test is negative is 0.10.

Clearly there are two types of errors that can occur with the new test. The first type of error is that a damaged microprocessor might test positive, and so be shipped to a customer. The second type of error is that a perfectly good microprocessor might test negative and so be unnecessarily discarded. Management would therefore like to know the probabilities that each of these two errors might occur.

To answer these questions, we will construct a probability model. Let D denote the event that a microprocessor is damaged and let W denote the event that a micro-processor is working properly (that is, not damaged). Let Q denote the event that a microprocessor tests positive and let N denote the event that the microprocessor tests negative. We are interested in computing the quantity

$$P(D|Q)$$

which is the probability that a microprocessor is damaged given that it tests positive. We are also interested in computing the quantity

$$P(W|N)$$

which is the probability that a microprocessor is working properly given that it tests negative.

We will first fill in the probability table shown in Table 2.6. From the data in the problem, we know the following information:

$$P(D) = 0.70, \ P(N|D) = 0.80, \text{ and } P(N|W) = 0.10.$$

Events D and W are mutually exclusive. Therefore, from the second law of probability,

$$P(W) = 0.30.$$

Therefore we can fill in the bottom row of the probability table, as is shown in the completed probability table in Table 2.7.

Reasoning in a similar way, we conclude also that

$$P(Q|D) = 0.20 \text{ and } P(Q|W) = 0.90.$$

From the third law of probability, we can therefore compute

$$P(N \text{ and } D) = P(N|D) \times P(D) = 0.80 \times 0.70 = 0.56,$$
$$P(N \text{ and } W) = P(N|W) \times P(W) = 0.10 \times 0.30 = 0.03,$$
$$P(Q \text{ and } D) = P(Q|D) \times P(D) = 0.20 \times 0.70 = 0.14,$$
$$P(Q \text{ and } W) = P(Q|W) \times P(W) = 0.90 \times 0.30 = 0.27.$$

We can then use these probabilities to fill in Table 2.7, which contains all possible combinations of events and their corresponding probabilities, as calculated herein. Notice that the last column of Table 2.7 is the sum of the other columns. Therefore, the probability that the test is positive is computed as

$$P(Q) = P(Q \text{ and } D) + P(Q \text{ and } W) = 0.14 + 0.27 = 0.41,$$

and the probability that the test is negative is

$$P(N) = P(N \text{ and } D) + P(N \text{ and } W) = 0.56 + 0.03 = 0.59.$$

We can now use the third law of probability in conjunction with Table 2.7 to calculate the quantities of interest, namely $P(D|Q)$ and $P(W|N)$. From the third law of probability and Table 2.7, we obtain:

$$P(D|Q) = \frac{P(Q \text{ and } D)}{P(Q)} = \frac{0.14}{0.41} = 0.341,$$

$$P(W|N) = \frac{P(N \text{ and } W)}{P(N)} = \frac{0.03}{0.59} = 0.051.$$

TABLE 2.6

Incomplete probability table for the quality control example.

	D	W	Total
Q			
N			
Total			

TABLE 2.7

Completed probability table for the quality control example.

	D	W	Total
Q	0.14	0.27	0.41
N	0.56	0.03	0.59
Total	0.70	0.30	1.00

Based on these two computations, we can conclude that the test would be relatively reliable when it is negative, i.e., only 5% of microprocessors that test negative would be working properly and would be unnecessarily discarded. However, 34% of microprocessors that pass the test (and therefore are shipped to customers) would be damaged. This is a rather significant number in today's quality-oriented business environment. Based on these calculations, we might recommend to management that they not employ this test.

Example 2.5—The Probability of Success of a New Consumer Service

Suppose that a new consumer service will be successful either if the demand for the service is high or if the competition does not react quickly. Suppose that the probability of high demand is 0.60, whereby the probability of low demand is 0.40. Suppose also that the probability that the competition will react quickly is 0.70, and so the probability that the competition will not react quickly is 0.30. Furthermore, suppose that the probability that the competition does react quickly, given that the demand is high, is 0.90. We would like to compute the probability that the new consumer service will be successful.

In order to compute the probability that the new consumer service will be successful, we construct a probability model with events and outcomes as follows. Let H denote the event that the demand for the new consumer service is high and let L denote the event that the demand the new consumer service is low. Let Q denote the event that the competition will react quickly and let R denote the event that the competition will not react quickly. Last of all, let S denote the event that the new consumer service is successful. From the statement of the problem it follows that the event S is the event "H or R." Therefore,

$$P(S) = P(H \text{ or } R).$$

We would like to compute $P(S)$.

We will proceed by constructing a probability table based on all known information. From the data in the problem we know that

$$P(H) = 0.60, \quad P(L) = 0.40, \quad P(Q) = 0.70,$$
$$P(R) = 0.30, \quad \text{and} \quad P(Q|H) = 0.90.$$

Therefore from the third law of probability, it follows that

$$P(Q \text{ and } H) = P(Q|H) \times P(H) = 0.90 \times 0.60 = 0.54.$$

We can place these numbers in a table, as shown in Table 2.8, in which we write the probabilities we have calculated so far. Note that Table 2.8 is not yet complete.

We can then fill in all of the missing probabilities of Table 2.8 as follows. The sum of the probabilities in column Q in Table 2.8 must be 0.70. Since we have already found that $P(Q \text{ and } H) = 0.54$, we obtain:

$$P(Q \text{ and } L) = 0.70 - 0.54 = 0.16.$$

TABLE 2.8

Partial construction of the probability table for the success of a new consumer service.

	Q	R	Total
H	0.54		0.60
L			0.40
Total	0.70	0.30	1.00

	Q	R	*Total*
H	0.54	0.06	0.60
L	0.16	0.24	0.40
Total	0.70	0.30	1.00

This value is then placed in the appropriate cell of the probability table, as shown in Table 2.9, which is the completed version of Table 2.8.

Proceeding in this manner, the sum of the probabilities in row L in Table 2.8 must be 0.40. Since we have already found that $P(Q \text{ and } L) = 0.16$, we obtain:

$$P(R \text{ and } L) = 0.40 - 0.16 = 0.24.$$

Finally, the sum of the probabilities in column R in Table 2.8 must be 0.30. Since we have already found that $P(R \text{ and } L) = 0.24$, we obtain:

$$P(R \text{ and } H) = 0.30 - 0.24 = 0.06.$$

The complete table of probabilities is shown in Table 2.9.

We now can easily calculate the probability of success of the new consumer service: $P(S) = P(R \text{ or } H)$. The events "$R$ and H," "R and L," and "Q and H" are mutually exclusive. Therefore we can apply the second law of probability to obtain:

$$P(S) = P(R \text{ or } H) = P(R \text{ and } H) + P(R \text{ and } L) + P(Q \text{ and } H)$$
$$= 0.06 + 0.24 + 0.54 = 0.84.$$

Example 2.6 — DNA Evidence in a Murder Trial

Jacob Sorenson is a juror in a well-publicized murder trial. Suppose that from the evidence he has heard in the first few days of the trial, he is not very certain whether the defendant is innocent or guilty of the crime. If pressed by a confidant, he would estimate the probability that the defendant committed the crime to be p, where $p = 0.50$ or maybe $p = 0.60$ at most.

Yesterday, a DNA expert testified that the blood found at the crime scene matched the blood of the defendant. The expert testified that she used a new DNA test that is 99% reliable. Asked by one of the defendant's lawyers what she meant by 99% reliable, the DNA expert stated that if the two blood types belong to the same person, then the test declares a match 99 out of 100 times. Moreover, if the two blood types do not belong to the same person, then the test declares a mismatch also 99 out of 100 times. Based on this information, what would be Jacob's revised probability that the defendant is guilty?

We will analyze this problem by constructing a probability model and an associated probability table. Let G denote the event that the defendant is guilty and let I denote the event that the defendant is innocent. Let M denote the event that the blood type found at the crime scene matches the blood type of the defendant and let N denote the event that the blood type found at the crime scene does not match the blood type of the defendant. Let D denote the event that the DNA test is positive, i.e., that the test indicates a match. Let E the event that the DNA test is negative, i.e., that the DNA test indicates a mismatch.

Let us assume that the events G and M are the same. This means that if the defendant is guilty, then the two blood types match; and that if the two blood types match, then the defendant is guilty. Let p denote Jacob's prior belief (before he heard the testimony from the DNA expert) that the defendant is guilty. That is,

$$P(G) = P(M) = p,$$

where p is a number between 0.0 and 1.0. We will interpret this number as the probability that the defendant is guilty.

Our goal is to calculate the probability that the defendant is guilty given the testimony of the DNA expert. The DNA expert testified that the DNA match was positive. Therefore, our goal is to calculate the probability $P(G|D)$ or, equivalently, $P(M|D)$. We will do so by first filling in the probability table shown in Table 2.10, which at the moment only contains the information that $P(M) = p$.

From the second law of probability, we know that

$$P(N) = 1 - P(M) = 1 - p.$$

We also know that the DNA test is 99% reliable. This means that

$$P(D|M) = 0.99 \text{ and } P(E|N) = 0.99.$$

From the second law of probability, then, we can deduce that:

$$P(E|M) = 0.01 \text{ and } P(D|N) = 0.01.$$

From the third law of probability, then,

$$P(D \text{ and } M) = P(D|M) \times P(M) = 0.99p,$$

and

$$P(D \text{ and } N) = P(D|N) \times P(N) = 0.01(1 - p).$$

Table 2.11 summarizes all of the information given or just derived.

We next complete Table 2.11 by calculating all of the missing probabilities as follows. The sum of the probabilities in row M in Table 2.11 must be p. Since we have already found that $P(D \text{ and } M) = 0.99p$, we obtain:

$$P(E \text{ and } M) = 0.01p.$$

Similarly, the sum of the probabilities in row N in Table 2.11 must be $1 - p$. Therefore,

$$P(E \text{ and } N) = 0.99(1 - p).$$

Finally, to complete the table, we add the probabilities $P(D \text{ and } M) + P(D \text{ and } N)$ to find

$$P(D) = P(D \text{ and } M) + P(D \text{ and } N) = 0.99p + 0.01(1 - p) = 0.01 + 0.98p,$$

and similarly,

$$P(E) = P(E \text{ and } M) + P(E \text{ and } N) = 0.01p + 0.99(1 - p) = 0.99 - 0.98p.$$

The preceding information is summarized in Table 2.12.

TABLE 2.10

Incomplete probability table for the DNA evidence problem.

	D	E	Total
M			p
N			
Total			1.00

TABLE 2.11

Partial construction of the probability table for the DNA evidence problem.

	D	E	Total
M	$0.99p$		p
N	$0.01(1 - p)$		$1 - p$
Total			1.00

TABLE 2.12

Complete probability table for the DNA evidence problem.

	D	E	Total
M	$0.99p$	$0.01p$	p
N	$0.01(1-p)$	$0.99(1-p)$	$1-p$
Total	$0.01 + 0.98p$	$0.99-0.98p$	1.00

We now can derive an expression for the probability that the defendant is guilty, given that the DNA test is positive. From the third law of probability and the information in Table 2.12, we have

$$P(G|D) = P(M|D) = \frac{P(D \text{ and } M)}{P(D)} = \frac{0.99p}{0.01 + 0.98p}.$$

Notice that this formula expresses the probability that the defendant is guilty given a positive DNA test, as a function of p, which is the initial level of Jacob's certainty regarding the guilt of the defendant.

Suppose that $p = 0.50$, i.e., that Jacob initially thinks that the defendant is equally likely to be guilty as he is to be innocent. Then his assessment of the probability that the defendant is guilty given a positive DNA test is

$$P(G|D) = P(M|D) = \frac{0.99 \times 0.50}{0.01 + 0.98 \times 0.50} = 0.99.$$

In order to observe the sensitivity of the answer as p changes, let us suppose that $p = 0.10$, i.e., Jacob believes initially that the defendant is most likely innocent. However, his assessment of guilt after the hearing of the positive DNA test would be:

$$P(G|D) = \frac{0.99 \times 0.10}{0.01 + 0.98 \times 0.10} = 0.92.$$

This last number is important; it indicates the power of the very reliable DNA test. Given that the DNA test is positive, Jacob's assessment of the probability of guilt rises from 10% to 92%.

Example 2.7 – Reliability in a Flexible Manufacturing System

Consider a flexible manufacturing system with two machines, denoted by M_1 and M_2. The system is operational if both machines M_1 and M_2 are operational. If either one of machines M_1 or M_2 fails on a given day, the system is no longer operational for that day. The probability that machine M_1 fails on a given day is $p = 0.10$, and the probability that machine M_2 fails on a given day is also $p = 0.10$.

The operations manager of the system is considering the purchase of a new flexible machine M_3 that could do the work of either machine M_1 or M_2 if one of them were to fail. If either one of machines M_1 or M_2 fails, machine M_3 can be substituted for the failed machine. The probability that machine M_3 fails on a given day is also $p = 0.10$. Let us calculate the probability that the system is operational on a given day, with and without the purchase of machine M_3.

Let W_i denote the event that machine M_i is operational (W for "working"), for $i = 1, 2, 3$, and let F_i be the event that machine M_i is not operational (F for "failing"), for $i = 1, 2, 3$. Let S be the event that the system is operational. We are given that $P(F_i) = p = 0.10$ and therefore $P(W_i) = 1 - p = 0.90$ for $i = 1, 2, 3$.

We first calculate $P(S)$ when only machines M_1 and M_2 are available. In this case, in order for the manufacturing system to be operational, both machines M_1 and M_2 must be operational. Therefore,

$$P(S) = P(W_1 \text{ and } W_2).$$

Since the two machines fail independently, the events W_1 and W_2 are independent. Applying the implication of the fourth law of probability, we obtain

$$P(S) = P(W_1 \text{ and } W_2) = P(W_1) \times P(W_2)$$
$$= (1 - p)(1 - p) = 0.90 \times 0.90 = 0.81.$$

That is, without the purchase of the flexible machine M_3, the probability that the system is operational on a given day is 0.81.

We next calculate $P(S)$ for the case when the third machine has been purchased. From the problem description, the system is operational if either one of the following three events transpires:

- both machines M_1 and M_2 are operational, or

- machine M_1 fails, but both machines M_2 and M_3 are operational, or

- machine M_2 fails, but both machines M_1 and M_3 are operational.

Therefore,

$$P(S) = P((W_1 \text{ and } W_2) \text{ or } (F_1 \text{ and } W_2 \text{ and } W_3) \text{ or } (W_1 \text{ and } F_2 \text{ and } W_3)).$$

Notice that the preceding events are mutually exclusive. By the second law of probability, we obtain

$$P(S) = P(W_1 \text{ and } W_2) + P(F_1 \text{ and } W_2 \text{ and } W_3) + P(W_1 \text{ and } F_2 \text{ and } W_3).$$

Since the events W_1 and W_2 are independent, we obtain from the implication of the fourth law of probability that

$$P(W_1 \text{ and } W_2) = P(W_1) \times P(W_2) = (1 - p)(1 - p).$$

Similarly, the events F_1, W_2 and W_3 are independent. Therefore, from the implication of the fourth law of probability,

$$P(F_1 \text{ and } W_2 \text{ and } W_3) = P(F_1) \times P(W_2) \times P(W_3) = p(1 - p)(1 - p),$$

Similarly,

$$P(W_1 \text{ and } F_2 \text{ and } W_3) = P(W_1) \times P(F_2) \times P(W_3) = (1 - p)p(1 - p).$$

Combining all these relations, we obtain

$$P(S) = (1 - p)(1 - p) + 2p(1 - p)(1 - p).$$

For $p = 0.10$, the probability that the system is operational is

$$P(S) = (1 - 0.10)(1 - 0.10) + 2 \times 0.10 \times (1 - 0.10)(1 - 0.10) = 0.972.$$

Notice that the purchase of the flexible machine M_3 would increase the probability that the system is operational on a given day from 0.81 to 0.972.

Let us summarize how we have analyzed the probability problems in the examples in this section. In all of the examples, we have used a common general approach to perform the calculations of probabilities of various uncertain events. This approach is as follows:

General Approach for Performing Probability Calculations

1. Define the various events that characterize the uncertainties in the problem. These definitions need to be clear and unambiguous.

2. Formalize how these events interact, i.e., how they depend on each other, using the language of probability, such as conditional probability ("$A|B$"), conjunctions ("A and B"), disjunctions ("A or B"), etc.

3. When appropriate, organize all the information regarding the probabilities of the various events in a table.

4. Using the laws of probability, calculate the probability of the events that characterize the uncertainties in question. (This last task might take a certain amount of arithmetical ingenuity.)

Despite their simplicity, the laws of probability are very powerful and can be used very effectively in a wide variety of problems involving the evaluation of uncertainty. The general approach outlined herein usually improves one's insight and understanding of the interdependencies of the various uncertainties in question.

2.4 | RANDOM VARIABLES

In the previous sections we introduced a probability model, or experiment, as a list of outcomes for an uncertain quantity with a given probability for each outcome. When the outcomes in a probability model are numbers, we will refer to this uncertain quantity as a **random variable.** A random variable can generally be classified into one of two categories: either it is a **discrete** random variable, or it is a **continuous** random variable. A discrete random variable can only assume values that are distinct and separate. A continuous random variable, by contrast, can take on any value within some interval of numbers.

As an example, suppose that General Avionics is a manufacturer of commercial jet aircraft. Let X denote the number of orders that General Avionics will receive next year for its new 636 aircraft. The value of X is uncertain. Therefore X is a random variable. The possible values for X might be the discrete list of numbers: 42, 43, 44, 45, 46, 47, 48. The variable X is an example of a discrete random variable. Other examples of discrete random variables include: the number of customers who dine at a given restaurant on a given day, the number of contracts a consulting company has in a given year, and the winning number in the weekly Massachusetts state lottery.

In contrast, let Y denote the number of inches of rainfall that Boston will receive next month. Then the value of Y is uncertain, and so Y is a random variable. However, Y can take on any value within the range of, say, zero to fifteen inches. The value of Y is not limited to whole numbers in inches, centimeters, or any other measure. For example, the value of Y could be 3.0 inches, 2.783 inches, 4.92736 inches, etc. Therefore, Y is a continuous random variable. The lifetime of a startup biotechnology firm is another example of a continuous random variable. Continuous random variables are natural models for uncertain times or distances, because these quantities vary continuously, with no gaps.

In this chapter, we focus our attention on discrete random variables. In the next chapter, we will study continuous random variables.

2.5 DISCRETE PROBABILITY DISTRIBUTIONS

A probability model for a discrete random variable consists of a list of each of the possible numerical values that the random variable can take, along with the probability that the random variable will take on that particular value. This list of values (or outcomes) and associated probabilities is called the **probability distribution** of the random variable.

As an example, suppose that General Avionics is a manufacturer of large commercial jet aircraft and let X denote the number of orders for the General Avionics 636 aircraft for next year. Suppose that Ms. Alice Jones has estimated that the number of orders for the General Avionics 636 next year can be described according to Table 2.13. The first column in Table 2.13 lists the possible values that X can take. The second column in Table 2.13 describes the probability that the random variable X assumes these values: for example, the probability that X will have the value 42 is 0.05. We write this mathematically as:

$$P(X = 42) = 0.05.$$

Similarly, we also have

$$P(X = 43) = 0.10,$$
$$\vdots$$
$$P(X = 48) = 0.10.$$

Table 2.13 describes the probability distribution of the random variable X. Notice that the probabilities in the second column of the table sum to one. Because order numbers below 42 and above 48 do not appear in the table, the probability that the number of orders is either below 42 or is above 48 must be zero.

A graphical way to represent the information of Table 2.13 is shown in Figure 2.3. In the figure, we have displayed the values of the random variables on the horizontal axis and their probabilities on the vertical axis.

We will use the following notation when working with a probability distribution. We will say that the random variable X equals x_1 with probability p_1, x_2 with probability p_2, . . . , and x_n with probability p_n. All the p_i's are between zero and one, and they sum to one. For example, consider the probability distribution of the orders for General Avionics 636 aircraft given in Table 2.13. Then we would have $x_1 = 42$ and $p_1 = 0.05$, $x_2 = 43$ and $p_2 = 0.10$, and so forth.

In the previous example, we modeled the random variable X by exhibiting the probability $P(X = x_i)$ for $x_i = 42, 43, \ldots, 48$. More generally, consider a discrete random variable X that assumes values $x_1, \ldots, x_n$ with probabilities $p_1, \ldots, p_n$.

The quantity $P(X = x_i)$ is denoted by $f(x_i)$ for all i and is called the **probability distribution function** or probability distribution of the random variable X.

TABLE 2.13

Probability distribution of the number of orders of General Avionics 636 aircraft next year.

Orders for General Avionics 636 Aircraft	Probability
x_i	p_i
42	0.05
43	0.10
44	0.15
45	0.20
46	0.25
47	0.15
48	0.10

FIGURE 2.3
Graph of the probability distribution of the number of orders for General Avionics 636 aircraft next year

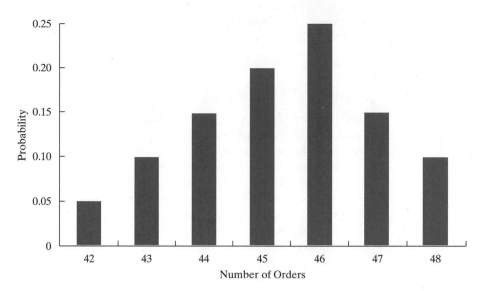

Note that the probability distribution function $f(x_i)$ is simply a rule that specifies the probability that the random variable X will take on a particular value x_i. The probabilities $p_i = f(x_i)$ should always be nonnegative and must satisfy

$$p_1 + p_2 + \cdots + p_n = 1.$$

2.6   THE BINOMIAL DISTRIBUTION

There is one type of probability distribution that arises in so many management domains, ranging from manufacturing quality control to opinion polling for marketing analysis, that it is given a special name: the **binomial distribution.** To understand how a binomial distribution arises, consider a probability experiment consisting of a sequence of n independent trials. Each trial has exactly two possible outcomes: either the outcome is a "success," or the outcome is a "failure." The probability of "success" is the same value p for each and every one of the n trials, and the probability of "failure" then is always $1 - p$ for each and every one of the n trials. Let the random variable X denote the number of "success" outcomes among the n trials. Then the possible values that X might take are the numbers $0, 1, 2, 3, \ldots, n$, with a specific probability of each of these numbers being the realized value of X. Because the value of X is uncertain, then X is a discrete random variable. We will say that X is a **binomial random variable** drawn from a **sample size** n and with **probability of success** p. Note that a binomial random variable X is characterized by two parameters: the sample size n and the probability of success p. We will also say that X **obeys** a binomial distribution with sample size n and probability of success p.

Let us consider two simple examples where the binomial distribution arises.

Example 2.8—Quality in a Production Process

Suppose that completed units produced by a production process are of good quality with probability 0.92 and are of poor quality (and are consequently scrapped) with probability 0.08. Suppose the production process produces 140 units per shift. Let X denote the number of good quality units produced in a given shift. Then X obeys a binomial distribution with sample size $n = 140$ and probability of success $p = 0.92$. Note that X can take on any of the possible values $0, 1, 2, 3, \ldots, 140$, each with a different probability.

Example 2.9 — Flipping a Coin n Times

Another example of a random variable that obeys a binomial distribution is the number of "heads" in n flips of a coin. Let H be the number of "heads" in 10 flips of a coin. Then H will obey a binomial distribution with $n = 10$ and $p = 0.5$.

We now describe the probability distribution of a random variable that obeys a binomial distribution. Let X denote a random variable that obeys a binomial distribution with sample size n and probability of success p. Clearly, X takes on one of the whole number values between 0 and n. Let us first study the probability that X takes the value n, which is the probability that all of the trials are successes. Since each of the n trials is independent, the probability that all n trials are successes is equal to

$$p^n.$$

Therefore the probability that X is equal to n is given by the formula:

$$p^n.$$

We write this as

$$P(X = n) = p^n,$$

which is read "the probability that X equals n is equal to p^n." Arguing in a similar manner, the probability that $X = 0$ is the probability that all n trials are failures, which is given by the formula

$$P(X = 0) = (1 - p)^n.$$

In order to describe the formula for the value $P(X = x)$ for $x = 1, 2, 3, \ldots, n - 1$, we first need some more notation. The symbol $5!$ is called "five factorial" and denotes the number $1 \cdot 2 \cdot 3 \cdot 4 \cdot 5 = 120$. The symbol $k!$ denotes the multiplicative sequence $1 \cdot 2 \cdot 3 \cdot \ldots \cdot (k - 1) \cdot (k)$, and $0!$ is defined to be equal to 1. Then, as it turns out, the general formula for $P(X = x)$ is given as follows:

If X is a random variable that obeys a binomial distribution with sample size n and probability of success p, then

$$P(X = x) = \frac{n!}{(x!)\,(n - x)!}\, p^x(1 - p)^{n-x} \quad \text{for} \quad x = 0, 1, \ldots, n.$$

Note that this formula provides a complete characterization of the probability distribution of X. In order to compute $P(X = x)$ for $x = 0, 1, 2, 3, \ldots, n$, one simply substitutes the appropriate value of x, p, and n into the preceding formula.

Before presenting the intuition behind this formula, we pause to illustrate its use.

Example 2.10 — Computers in the Office

Suppose that there are eight desktop computers in a small retail office, and the probability of any one computer being used during the lunch hour is 0.70. Let X denote the number of computers in use during the lunch hour. Then X obeys a binomial dis-

TABLE 2.14

The binomial distribution with sample size $n = 8$ and probability of success $p = 0.70$.

x	Formula	Probability
0	$\frac{8!}{(0!)\,(8!)}(0.7)^0(0.3)^8$	0.00007
1	$\frac{8!}{(1!)\,(7!)}(0.7)^1(0.3)^7$	0.00122
2	$\frac{8!}{(2!)\,(6!)}(0.7)^2(0.3)^6$	0.01000
3	$\frac{8!}{(3!)\,(5!)}(0.7)^3(0.3)^5$	0.04668
4	$\frac{8!}{(4!)\,(4!)}(0.7)^4(0.3)^4$	0.13614
5	$\frac{8!}{(5!)\,(3!)}(0.7)^5(0.3)^3$	0.25412
6	$\frac{8!}{(6!)\,(2!)}(0.7)^6(0.3)^2$	0.29648
7	$\frac{8!}{(7!)\,(1!)}(0.7)^7(0.3)^1$	0.19765
8	$\frac{8!}{(8!)\,(0!)}(0.7)^8(0.3)^0$	0.05765

tribution with sample size $n = 8$ and probability of success $p = 0.70$. Note that X can take on any of the possible values 0, 1, 2, 3, ... , 8. Table 2.14 shows the probability distribution for X based on the preceding formula.

For example,

$$P(X = 5) = \frac{8!}{(5!)\,(8 - 5)!}\,0.7^5(0.3)^{8-5} = 0.25412,$$

and

$$P(X = 8) = \frac{8!}{(8!)\,(8 - 8)!}\,0.7^8(0.3)^{8-8} = 0.05765.$$

Although we will not present a mathematical derivation of the formula for the binomial distribution, we now give some intuition as to why it correctly describes the probability distribution of X. First, note that because we have defined 0! to be equal to 1, then the formula agrees with the preceding logic for $P(X = n)$ and $P(X = 0)$. Now let us consider $P(X = x)$ for any other value of x, i.e., $x = 1, 2, 3, \ldots, n - 1$. In order for the number of successes to be exactly x, there must also be exactly $n - x$ failures. One way for this to happen is for the first x trials to be successes and for the remaining $n - x$ trials to be failures. The probability of this happening is precisely:

$$p^x(1 - p)^{n-x}.$$

Another way for this to happen is for the first $n - x$ trials to be failures, and then for the last x trials to be successes. There are many other ways that exactly x of the n trials will be successes. As it turns out, the number of different ways that there can be exactly x successes among the n trials is given by the formula:

$$\frac{n!}{(x!)\,(n - x)!}.$$

This then leads to the formula for $P(X = x)$:

$$P(X = x) = \frac{n!}{(x!)\,(n - x)!}\,p^x(1 - p)^{n-x} \text{ for } x = 0, 1, \ldots, n.$$

To illustrate the use of the binomial distribution, let us consider a slightly different version of the production process example shown earlier.

Example 2.11 — Quality Control in a Production Process

Suppose that completed units produced by a production process are of good quality with probability 0.83 and are of poor quality (and are consequently scrapped) with probability 0.17. Suppose the production process produces 5 units per shift.

Let us first compute the probability that there are exactly 2 units in a shift that are of poor quality. Let X denote the number of units that are of poor quality. Then X obeys a binomial distribution with parameters $n = 5$ and $p = 0.17$. By the formula for the binomial distribution, we obtain

$$P(X = 2) = \frac{5!}{(2!)(5-2)!}(0.17)^2(1 - 0.17)^{5-2} = 0.165.$$

Now, let us compute the probability that there is at least 1 unit in a shift that is of poor quality. We are interested in computing $P(X \geq 1)$. Notice that

$$P(X \geq 1) = 1 - P(X = 0).$$

Therefore, we first compute

$$P(X = 0) = \frac{5!}{(0!)(5-0)!}(0.17)^0(1 - 0.17)^{5-0} = (1 - 0.17)^5 = 0.394.$$

Next, we substitute this value into the preceding expression and obtain:

$$P(X \geq 1) = 1 - P(X = 0) = 1.0 - 0.394 = 0.606.$$

Example 2.12 — Staffing at the Service Centers at Netway Computers

Frank Duffield is the regional manager of Netway Computers in Seattle, Washington. Over the years, Netway has sold 50 NX-4000 mainframe computers that are currently operating in the Seattle area and that need servicing from time to time. If a particular NX-4000 computer has a problem, the customer calls the Seattle service facility and an engineer is then dispatched to the customer's location for same-day service. If a customer calls in for service and all of the engineers at the service center are already out servicing other customer locations for the day, then the customer will not be serviced. Frank would like to decide how many engineers to staff at the service facility, in order that all customer requests for service can be fulfilled, with a sufficiently high probability.

Using past history as a guide, Frank has estimated that the likelihood of any customer requiring service on any given day is 0.02. (This means that out of 250 working days in a year, a customer will typically require service on 5 days out of the 250 days.) Obviously, the more engineers that are available to visit customers, the smaller will be the likelihood of a customer not receiving service. Frank would like to staff the service facility with just enough engineers to meet Netway's quality assurance target that there is at most a 5% probability that a customer will not receive service on any given day.

Let us solve this problem for Frank. We know that the probability that a customer requires service on any given day is

$$p = 0.02.$$

Let X be the random variable of the number of customers that require service on a given day. Then X is a random variable, and X obeys a binomial distribution with parameters $n = 50$ and $p = 0.02.$

Let us first examine the case when the service facility has one engineer. On a particular day, if there are at least two customers that call for service, then at least one customer will not receive service. The probability of this event is

$$P(X \geq 2).$$

Let us calculate this probability. First notice that

$$P(X \geq 2) = 1 - P(X = 0) - P(X = 1).$$

We then use the formula for the binomial distribution to compute:

$$P(X = 0) = \frac{50!}{0!(50 - 0)!}\, p^0(1 - p)^{(50-0)} = (1 - p)^{50} = 0.364,$$

and

$$P(X = 1) = \frac{50!}{1!(50 - 1)!}\, p^1(1 - p)^{(50-1)} = 50 \times p \times (1 - p)^{49} = 0.371.$$

Therefore,

$$P(X \geq 2) = 1 - P(X = 0) - P(X = 1) = 1 - 0.364 - 0.371 = 0.265.$$

Therefore, with one engineer in the service facility, the probability that at least one customer will not receive service on a given day is 0.265.

We next examine the case when the service facility has two engineers. On a particular day, if there are at least three customers that call for service, then at least one customer will not receive service. The probability of this event is

$$P(X \geq 3).$$

As before, observe that

$$P(X \geq 3) = 1 - P(X = 0) - P(X = 1) - P(X = 2).$$

We have already computed the values of $P(X = 0)$ and $P(X = 1)$, namely

$$P(X = 0) = 0.364$$

and

$$P(X = 1) = 0.371.$$

We need also to compute $P(X = 2)$, which by the formula for the binomial distribution, is:

$$P(X = 2) = \frac{50!}{2!(50 - 2)!}\, p^2(1 - p)^{(50-2)} = \frac{50 \cdot 49}{2}(0.02)^2(1 - 0.02)^{48} = 0.185.$$

Therefore,

$$P(X \geq 3) = 1 - P(X = 0) - P(X = 1) - P(X = 2)$$
$$= 1 - 0.364 - 0.371 - 0.185 = 0.080.$$

Therefore, with two engineers in the service facility, the probability that at least one customer will not receive service on a given day is 0.080, i.e., 8%. This probability is not yet lower than 5%, which is the quality assurance target.

We continue, by examining the case when the service facility has three engineers. On a particular day, if there are at least four calls for service, then at least one customer will not receive service. The probability of this event is

$$P(X \geq 4) = 1 - P(X = 0) - P(X = 1) - P(X = 2) - P(X = 3).$$

We have already computed the values of $P(X = 0)$, $P(X = 1)$, and $P(X = 2)$, namely

$$P(X = 0) = 0.364,$$
$$P(X = 1) = 0.371,$$

and

$$P(X = 2) = 0.185.$$

We need also to compute $P(X = 3)$, which by the formula for the binomial distribution is

$$P(X = 3) = \frac{50!}{3!(50-3)!} \, p^3(1-p)^{(50-3)} = \frac{50 \cdot 49 \cdot 48}{6} \, p^3(1-p)^{47} = 0.060.$$

Therefore,

$$P(X \geq 4) = 1 - P(X = 0) - P(X = 1) - P(X = 2) - P(X = 3)$$
$$= 1 - 0.364 - 0.371 - 0.185 - 0.060 = 0.020.$$

Therefore, with three engineers in the service facility, the probability that at least one customer will not receive service on a given day is 0.020, i.e., 2%. Therefore, by staffing the service facility with three engineers, Frank will meet the quality assurance target.

2.7   SUMMARY MEASURES OF PROBABILITY DISTRIBUTIONS

We have seen that the probability distribution of a discrete random variable X gives a complete description of the behavior of the random variable X. The information content of the probability distribution is given by a list of the possible values $x_1, x_2, \ldots, x_n$ that the random variable X can take, together with the probabilities $p_1, p_2, \ldots, p_n$ that X will take on each of these possible values. However, it can be overwhelming at times to make intuitive sense of the behavior of X by trying to absorb the information value of the various numbers $x_1, x_2, \ldots, x_n$ and $p_1, p_2, \ldots, p_n$. For this reason, we now present some summary measures that convey much intuitive information about the behavior of the random variable X with just a few relatively straightforward numbers.

The most common summary measure of a probability distribution of a random variable X is the **mean** of the probability distribution. This measure is so common that it also is called by some other names, including the **average**, the **expected value**, and the **expectation** of the random variable X. The mean of the random variable X is computed by multiplying each of the possible values $x_1, \ldots, x_n$ by its corresponding probability $p_1, \ldots, p_n$ and summing up the result:

> If the discrete random variable X assumes values $x_1, \ldots, x_n$ with probability $p_1, \ldots, p_n$, then the **mean** or **expected value** of X is
>
> $$\mu_X = E(X) = \sum_{i=1}^{n} P(X = x_i) \times (x_i) = \sum_{i=1}^{n} p_i x_i.$$

If X is a random variable, we will denote its mean by $E(X)$, although the Greek letter μ_X (pronounced "mu") is often used as well.

Recall that we have already seen the notion of expected value in our discussion of the expected monetary value (EMV) in the context of decision trees in Chapter 1.

Example 2.13 — Rolling a Die

Suppose we roll a die. Let X be the number that the die shows on its uppermost face. Then X is a random variable that obeys the simple distribution shown in Table 2.15.

The expected value of the random variable X is computed as:

$$E(X) = \frac{1}{6} \cdot (1) + \frac{1}{6} \cdot (2) + \frac{1}{6} \cdot (3) + \frac{1}{6} \cdot (4) + \frac{1}{6} \cdot (5) + \frac{1}{6} \cdot (6) = 3.5.$$

As this example makes clear, the expectation is not necessarily a value that is taken by the random variable. Nevertheless, if we were to roll the die many times, the average value of the random variable X would be very close to 3.5.

Example 2.14 — Orders for General Avionics 636 Aircraft

Let X be the number of order of General Avionics 636 aircraft next year, whose probability distribution is given in Table 2.13. Then the expected value of X is computed as:

$$E(X) = 0.05 \cdot (42) + 0.10 \cdot (43) + 0.15 \cdot (44) + 0.20 \cdot (45)$$
$$+ 0.25 \cdot (46) + 0.15 \cdot (47) + 0.10 \cdot (48) = 45.35.$$

Example 2.15 — Sales Performance in Two Regions

Let X denote the sales of a product in the eastern sales division of a company for the next year and let Y denote the sales of the product in the western sales division of the company for the next year. Suppose that Ellis Sterling has estimated that the sales in the eastern division can be described according to the probability distribution function in Table 2.16, and that the sales in the western division can be described according to the probability distribution function in Table 2.17.

Then the expected value of X is computed as

$$E(X) = 0.05 \cdot (3.0) + 0.20 \cdot (4.0) + 0.35 \cdot (5.0) + 0.30 \cdot (6.0) + 0.10 \cdot (7.0)$$
$$= \$5.2 \text{ million,}$$

TABLE 2.15

Probability distribution of the face of die.

Face of Die	Probability
1	1/6
2	1/6
3	1/6
4	1/6
5	1/6
6	1/6

TABLE 2.16

Probability distribution of sales in the eastern division.

Sales ($ million)	Probability
3.0	0.05
4.0	0.20
5.0	0.35
6.0	0.30
7.0	0.10

TABLE 2.17

Probability
distribution of sales
in the western
division.

Sales ($ million)	Probability
3.0	0.15
4.0	0.20
5.0	0.25
6.0	0.15
7.0	0.15
8.0	0.10

and the expected value of Y is computed as:

$$E(Y) = 0.15 \cdot (3.0) + 0.20 \cdot (4.0) + 0.25 \cdot (5.0) + 0.15 \cdot (6.0)$$
$$+ \ 0.15 \cdot (7.0) + 0.10 \cdot (8.0) = \$5.25 \text{ million.}$$

This shows that the expected sales next year from the eastern division and the western are almost identical, namely $E(X) = \$5.2$ million and $E(Y) = \$5.25$ million.

To gain more intuition regarding the distributions X and Y, we can plot the probability distribution functions of eastern sales and western sales from Table 2.16 and Table 2.17. These plots are shown in Figure 2.4 and Figure 2.5. As Figure 2.4 and Figure 2.5 show, the distributions of sales for the eastern division and western division are quite different, even though the two distributions have almost the same means. Notice from the figures that sales in the eastern division are more likely to be closer to the mean of $5.2 million than they are in the western division.

As illustrated in Example 2.15, one problem with the mean is that although it tells us twhat will happen "on average" or "in the long run," it does not reveal how much the individual outcomes vary around the mean. To make this point even more obvious, notice that a mean of 30 could arise because a random variable X is equally likely to be 29 and 31, or because X is equally likely to be 0 and 60.

We would therefore like to have an estimate of the average *deviation* or *volatility* of a random variable around its mean. One can imagine various indicators of the average deviation of a random variable from its mean. However, there is one such measure in particular that has emerged pre-eminently, which is called the **variance** of the random variable X. The symbol VAR(X) denotes the variance of a random variable X. The shorthand σ_X^2 (pronounced "sigma squared") is also be used to denote the variance. The variance is defined as follows:

If the discrete random variable X assumes values $x_1, \ldots, x_n$ with probability $p_1, \ldots, p_n$ and has mean μ_X, then **the variance** of X is

$$\sigma_X^2 = \text{VAR}(X) = \sum_{i=1}^{n} p_i(x_i - \mu_X)^2.$$

Note that the variance measures the average *squared* difference between the possible values x_i and the mean μ_X, weighted by the probabilities p_i.

(Perhaps a more intuitive measure of such deviation would be:

$$\sum_{i=1}^{n} p_i |x_i - \mu_X|,$$

where $| \cdot |$ denotes the absolute value. This quantity measures the average absolute value of the difference from the mean, and so it is a bit more intuitive than the vari-

FIGURE 2.4

Probability distribution function of eastern division sales.

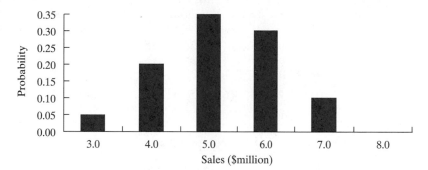

FIGURE 2.5

Probability distribution function of western division sales.

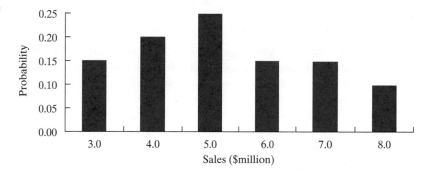

ance. It turns out, however, that the variance has some remarkable properties that make it by far the better measure of average deviation from the mean.)

Example 2.16 — Rolling a Die, continued

The variance of the roll of a die is computed as:

$$\sigma_X^2 = \frac{1}{6} \cdot (1 - 3.5)^2 + \frac{1}{6} \cdot (2 - 3.5)^2 + \frac{1}{6} \cdot (3 - 3.5)^2 +$$

$$\frac{1}{6} \cdot (4 - 3.5)^2 + \frac{1}{6} \cdot (5 - 3.5)^2 + \frac{1}{6} \cdot (6 - 3.5)^2 = 2.92.$$

Example 2.17 — Orders for General Avionics 636 Aircraft, continued

Consider the distribution of orders for General Avionics 636 aircraft given in Table 2.13, and whose mean is $\mu_X = 45.35$, as computed in Example 2.14. The variance of the number of orders for General Avionics 636 aircraft is computed as:

$$\sigma_X^2 = 0.05 \cdot (42 - 45.35)^2 + 0.10 \cdot (43 - 45.35)^2 + 0.15 \cdot (44 - 45.35)^2$$

$$+ 0.20 \cdot (45 - 45.35)^2 + 0.25 \cdot (46 - 45.35)^2 + 0.15 \cdot (47 - 45.35)^2$$

$$+ 0.10 \cdot (48 - 45.35)^2$$

$$= 2.627.$$

Example 2.18 — Sales Performance in Two Regions, continued

Consider the probability distribution of sales for next year for the eastern and the western division of a company from Example 2.15, as shown in Table 2.16 and Table 2.17. Let X denote the sales of the product in the eastern sales division of the company for the next year, and let Y denote the sales of the product in the western sales division of the company for the next year. Then as was computed in Example 2.15, $\mu_X = \$5.2$ million and $\mu_Y = \$5.25$ million. The variance of X is computed as:

$$\sigma_X^2 = 0.05 \cdot (3.0 - 5.2)^2 + 0.20 \cdot (4.0 - 5.2)^2 + 0.35 \cdot (5.0 - 5.2)^2$$
$$+ 0.30 \cdot (6.0 - 5.2)^2 + 0.10 \cdot (7.0 - 5.2)^2$$
$$= 1.06,$$

and the variance of Y is computed as:

$$\sigma_Y^2 = 0.15 \cdot (3.0 - 5.25)^2 + 0.20 \cdot (4.0 - 5.25)^2 + 0.25 \cdot (5.0 - 5.25)^2$$
$$+ 0.15 \cdot (6.0 - 5.25)^2 + 0.15 \cdot (7.0 - 5.25)^2 + 0.10 \cdot (8.0 - 5.25)^2$$
$$= 2.3875.$$

Notice that the variance of western division sales (which is σ_Y^2) is greater than the variance of eastern division sales (which is σ_X^2). This agrees with our intuition based on Figure 2.4 and Figure 2.5 that the distribution of western division sales has more "spread" about the mean than does eastern division sales.

One difficulty with the variance is that it is not measured in the same units as the random variable itself. If X (and thus μ_X) is expressed in dollars, then σ_X^2 is expressed in "dollars squared," which is not very intuitive. To make the measure of deviation of X more compatible with the measure of its mean, statisticians have taken to recording the square root of the variance, which is called the **standard deviation** of the random variable X. The standard deviation is usually denoted by the symbol σ_X, which is pronounced "sigma."

If the discrete random variable X assumes values $x_1, \ldots, x_n$ with probability $p_1, \ldots, p_n$ and has mean μ_X, then **the standard deviation** of X is

$$\sigma_X = \sqrt{\text{VAR}(X)} = \sqrt{\sum_{i=1}^{n} p_i(x_i - \mu_X)^2}.$$

Thet standard deviation is measured in the same units as the mean, and suggests the typical distance between individual outcomes of an experiment and the long-term average of outcomes. If μ_X is a measure of the middle of the distribution, σ_X is a comparable measure of the distribution's *spread around the middle*.

As an example, the standard deviation of the random variable X when rolling a fair die is $\sigma_X = \sqrt{2.92} = 1.7$, while the standard deviation of the number of orders of General Avionics 636 aircraft is $\sigma_X = \sqrt{2.627} = 1.62$. In the example of sales performance, the standard deviation of eastern division sales is $\sigma_X = \sqrt{1.060} = \$1.030$ million, and the standard deviation of western division sales is $\sigma_Y = \sqrt{2.3875} = \$1.5452$ million.

It has become traditional to report the mean and variance (or standard deviation) of a discrete random variable at the same time that one presents its full distribution. While the full probability distribution is needed for a thorough understanding of the behavior of a random variable, the two summary measures of the mean μ_X and the standard deviation σ_X present a very good initial sense of how a random variable behaves.

Example 2.19—The Mean and Standard Deviation of the Binomial Distribution

If X is a random variable that obeys a binomial distribution, then there are convenient formulas for the mean, variance, and standard deviation of X, as follows:

If X is a random variable that obeys a binomial distribution with sample size n and probability of success p, then the mean, variance, and standard deviation of X are:

$$\mu_X = np, \quad \sigma_X^2 = np(1 - p) \quad \text{and} \quad \sigma_X = \sqrt{np(1 - p)}.$$

Although we will not derive these formulas here, we can see the plausibility of these formulas as follows. If X obeys a binomial distribution with sample size n and probability of success p, then the "expected" number of successes in n trials should be np, which is the mean μ_X. The intuition regarding the formula for the standard deviation σ_X (or the variance σ_X^2) is a bit harder to come by. However, we can see how the formula for the standard deviation makes a certain amount of sense, as follows. Notice that if p is either close to 1 or close to 0, then the standard deviation will be lower. This makes sense, because if the probability of success is either very high or very low, then there will not be much deviation from the mean, on average. In fact, the value of p that leads to the highest standard deviation is $p = 0.5$, which will result in the most volatility in the value of the random variable X. Also, notice that the standard deviation is higher when n is higher.

Example 2.20—Staffing at the Service Centers at Netway Computers, continued

Recall Example 2.12, where the number of customers who require service on a given day, denoted by the random variable X, obeys a binomial distribution with parameters $n = 50$ and $p = 0.02$. Then

$$\mu_X = np = 50 \times 0.02 = 1.0,$$
$$\sigma_X^2 = np(1 - p) = 50 \times 0.02 \times (1 - 0.02) = 0.98,$$

and

$$\sigma_X = \sqrt{np(1 - p)} = \sqrt{50 \times 0.02 \times (1 - 0.02)} = 0.99.$$

Note that $\mu_X = 1.0$. This means that on average, there will be one customer requiring service per day.

Example 2.21—Probability Distributions and Decision Trees

In this example we investigate how probability distributions arise naturally in the context of decision trees. Consider again Bill Sampras' summer job search that we discussed in Chapter 1. In Chapter 1 we computed the optimal decision strategy for Bill: Bill should reject John's offer and he should apply for a summer job at Vanessa's firm. If Vanessa's firm were to make Bill an offer, he should accept the offer. If not, he should participate in corporate summer recruiting. Under this decision strategy, Bill's summer salary is uncertain, and therefore Bill's summer salary is a random

TABLE 2.18

Probability distribution of summer salaries from participating in corporate summer recruiting.

Summer Salary	Probability
$21,600	0.05
$16,800	0.25
$12,000	0.40
$6,000	0.25
$0	0.05

TABLE 2.19

Probability distribution of Bill Sampras' summer salary under his optimal decision strategy.

Summer Salary	Probability
$21,600	0.02
$16,800	0.10
$14,000	0.60
$12,000	0.16
$6,000	0.10
$0	0.02

variable. Let us denote this random variable by X. We now derive the probability distribution of X and then compute its mean μ_X and standard deviation σ_X.

We first consider what are the possible values the random variable X can take. If Bill were to receive an offer from Vanessa's firm, then $X = \$14,000$. The probability that he would receive an offer from Vanessa's firm is 0.60. Therefore,

$$P(X = 14{,}000) = 0.60.$$

If he twere not to receive an offer from Vanessa's firm, an event that occurs with probability 0.40, then he would participate in corporate summer recruiting. The possible summer salaries that Bill could obtain if he were to participate in corporate summer recruiting are the five salaries shown in Table 1.1, and replicated here in Table 2.18. Therefore,

$$P(X = 21{,}600) = 0.05 \cdot 0.40 = 0.02,$$
$$P(X = 16{,}800) = 0.25 \cdot 0.40 = 0.10,$$
$$P(X = 12{,}000) = 0.40 \cdot 0.40 = 0.16,$$
$$P(X = 6{,}000) = 0.25 \cdot 0.40 = 0.10,$$
$$P(X = 0) = 0.05 \cdot 0.40 = 0.02.$$

Table 2.19 summarizes the distribution of X.

Let us now compute the mean and standard deviation of this distribution. The expected value of X is

$$\mu_X = 0.02 \cdot 21{,}600 + 0.10 \cdot 16{,}800 + 0.60 \cdot 14{,}000$$
$$+ 0.16 \cdot 12{,}000 + 0.10 \cdot 6{,}000 + 0.02 \cdot 0$$
$$= \$13{,}032.$$

Notice that the expected value of Bill's summer salary is equal to the EMV of his decision tree, as one would expect.

We calculate the variance of X as follows:

$$\sigma_X^2 = 0.02 \cdot (21{,}600 - 13{,}032)^2 + 0.10 \cdot (16{,}800 - 13{,}032)^2$$
$$+ 0.60 \cdot (14{,}000 - 13{,}032)^2 + 0.16 \cdot (12{,}000 - 13{,}032)^2$$
$$+ 0.10 \cdot (6{,}000 - 13{,}032)^2 + 0.02 \cdot (0 - 13{,}032)^2$$
$$= 11{,}962{,}176.$$

The standard deviation of X is $\sigma_X = \sqrt{11{,}962{,}176} = \$3{,}458.60$.

Note that different decision strategies will yield different probability distributions for Bill's summer salary. For example, the strategy "accept John's offer" would lead to a summer salary of $12,000 with certainty. (Therefore, the variance of the Bill's summer salary under this strategy would be zero!)

Let us next compute the probability that the optimal decision strategy is at least as good as the strategy "accept John's offer." In order to answer this question, we need to calculate the probability $P(X \geq 12{,}000)$. From Table 2.19, we have

$$P(X \geq 12{,}000) = P(X = 21{,}600) + P(X = 16{,}800)$$
$$+ P(X = 14{,}000) + P(X = 12{,}000) = 0.88.$$

2.8 | LINEAR FUNCTIONS OF A RANDOM VARIABLE

Suppose that the daily demand for croissants at a bakery shop obeys the probability distribution given in Table 2.20.

If we let X denote the daily demand for croissants, then X is a random variable and we can compute its mean, variance, and standard deviation, as follows:

$$E(X) = \mu_X = \sum_{i=1}^{7} p_i x_i = 71.15,$$

$$\mathrm{VAR}(X) = \sigma_X^2 = \sum_{i=1}^{7} p_i (x_i - \mu_X)^2 = 29.5275,$$

and

$$\sigma_X = \sqrt{29.5275} = 5.434.$$

Suppose that it costs $135 per day to run the croissant operation at the bakery, and that the unit cost of producing a croissant is $0.75 per croissant. Then the daily cost of croissant operations is given by the formula

$$0.75X + 135.$$

Notice that the daily cost of croissant operations is uncertain, and so is itself a random variable. If we let Y denote this random variable, then we have:

$$Y = 0.75X + 135.$$

TABLE 2.20

Probability distribution of the daily demand for croissants.

Daily Demand for Croissants	Probability
x_i	p_i
60	0.05
64	0.15
68	0.20
72	0.25
75	0.15
77	0.10
80	0.10

In fact, we can compute the probability distribution of Y by suitably modifying Table 2.20 above, to produce Table 2.21 below.

Note, for example, that the number 180 in the first row of Table 2.21 is computed as $180 = 0.75 \times 60 + 135$, with the other numbers in the table computed similarly. Based on this table, which describes the probability distribution of Y, we can compute the mean, variance, and standard deviation of Y as follows:

$$E(Y) = \mu_Y = \sum_{i=1}^{7} p_i y_i = 188.3625,$$

$$\text{VAR}(Y) = \sigma_Y^2 = \sum_{i=1}^{7} p_i (y_i - \mu_Y)^2 = 16.6092,$$

and

$$\sigma_Y = \sqrt{16.6092} = 4.075.$$

Notice that Y is a *linear function* of the random variable X, that is,

$$Y = aX + b$$

for some constant numbers a and b. (In this case, $a = 0.75$ and $b = 135.0$). As it turns out, when Y is a linear function of a random variable X, there are simple formulas for the mean, variance, and standard deviation of Y, as a function of the mean, variance, and standard deviation of X. These formulas are given as follows.

If $Y = aX + b$, then

$$\mu_Y = a\mu_X + b,$$
$$\sigma_Y^2 = a^2\sigma_X^2,$$
$$\sigma_Y = |a|\sigma_X.$$

These formulas make intuitive sense as follows. If $Y = aX + b$, then the distribution of X is being scaled by the amount a and then translated by the amount b. It therefore makes sense that the mean of Y would be scaled by the amount a and then translated by the amount b. However, we would anticipate that the standard deviation of Y would be unchanged by any translation and only affected by the absolute value of the scaling amount a.

We could use these formulas to compute the mean, variance, and standard deviation of Y for the example of the daily costs of croissant operations. Doing so, we obtain

$$\mu_Y = a\mu_X + b = 0.75 \times 71.15 + 135 = 188.3625,$$
$$\sigma_Y^2 = a^2\sigma_X^2 = (0.75)^2 \times 29.5275 = 16.6092,$$

TABLE 2.21	
Probability distribution of the daily cost of the croissant operation.	

Daily Cost of Croissants Operation (in dollars)	Probability
y_i	p_i
$180.00	0.05
$183.00	0.15
$186.00	0.20
$189.00	0.25
$191.25	0.15
$192.75	0.10
$195.00	0.10

and

$$\sigma_Y = |a|\sigma_X = |0.75| \times 5.434 = 4.075,$$

which agrees (as it should) with the earlier and more cumbersome computation of these numbers at the start of this section.

It is very easy to derive the preceding formulas for the mean, variance, and standard deviation of a linear function of a random variable, which we do now. Because $Y = aX + b$, the mean of Y is simply

$$E(Y) = \mu_Y = \sum_{i=1}^{n}(ax_i + b) \cdot P(X = x_i) = a\sum_{i=1}^{n}x_iP(X = x_i) + b\sum_{i=1}^{n}P(X = x_i),$$

and since

$$\sum_{i=1}^{n}x_iP(X = x_i) = E(X) = \mu_X$$

and

$$\sum_{i=1}^{n}P(X = x_i) = 1,$$

the preceding expression works out to be:

$$E(Y) = \mu_Y = aE(X) + b = a\mu_X + b.$$

The formula for the variance of Y is derived by noting that

$$\sigma_Y^2 = \sum_{i=1}^{n}p_i(ax_i + b - [a\mu_X + b])^2$$

$$= \sum_{i=1}^{n}p_i(a[x_i - \mu_X])^2 = a^2\sum_{i=1}^{n}p_i(x_i - \mu_X)^2 = a^2\sigma_X^2.$$

Therefore, the standard deviation of Y is given by

$$\sigma_Y = \sqrt{\sigma_Y^2} = \sqrt{a^2\sigma_X^2} = |a|\sigma_X,$$

where $|a|$ denotes the absolute value of a (for example $|4| = 4$, $|-4| = 4$).

Example 2.22 — Compensation of a Business Executive

Karen Donahue, a middle manager at a finance firm, is anxiously awaiting the announcement of next year's salaries. She has an extra reason to be impatient for the news this year, because she has received a somewhat unusual offer from a competing firm. The competing firm has offered Karen a 20% increase above her new salary, plus a signing bonus of $12,000. Karen has estimated that her salary next year at her current employer will obey the probability distribution shown in Table 2.22.

Let X denote the random variable that represents Karen's salary next year at her current job. Then the mean of X is

$$\mu_X = E(X) = (0.15)95,000 + (0.20)100,000 + (0.25)103,000$$
$$+ (0.20)107,000 + (0.20)109,000$$
$$= \$103,200.$$

The variance of X is

TABLE 2.22

Probability distribution of Karen's salary next year at her current employer.

Salary	Probability
x_i	p_i
$95,000	0.15
$100,000	0.20
$103,000	0.25
$107,000	0.20
$109,000	0.20

$$\text{VAR}(X) = (0.15)(95{,}000 - 103{,}200)^2 + (0.20)(100{,}000 - 103{,}200)^2$$
$$+ (0.25)(103{,}000 - 103{,}200)^2 + (0.20)(107{,}000 - 103{,}200)^2$$
$$+ (0.20)(109{,}000 - 103{,}200)^2$$
$$= 21{,}760{,}000.$$

The standard deviation of X is therefore

$$\sigma_X = \sqrt{21{,}760{,}000} = \$4{,}665.$$

If Karen accepts the offer from the competitor firm, her compensation would be

$$Y = 1.20 \cdot X + 12{,}000.$$

Notice that Y is linear function of the random variable X, that is,

$$Y = aX + b$$

where $a = 1.20$ and $b = 12{,}000$. Therefore, the mean of Y is

$$E(Y) = a \cdot E(X) + b = 1.20 \cdot E(X) + 12{,}000$$
$$= 1.20 \cdot (103{,}200) + 12{,}000 = \$135{,}840.$$

The variance of Y is

$$\sigma_Y^2 = a^2 \cdot \sigma_X^2 = (1.20)^2 \cdot \sigma_X^2 = \$31{,}334{,}400,$$

and the standard deviation of Y is

$$\sigma_Y = |a| \cdot \sigma_X = 1.20 \cdot \sigma_X = \$5{,}597.71.$$

2.9   COVARIANCE AND CORRELATION

It is often said that the unemployment rate and the crime rate are "highly correlated." Another popular dictum is that rates of returns of stock in companies in the same industry are "positively correlated." Yet another credo often heard is that the rate of return in the stock market and the rate of return in the bond market are "negatively correlated." In this section, we introduce a formal and intuitively appealing notion of interdependence and correlation between two random variables, that will help to quantify and lend further intuition to the notions of interdependence and correlation among random variables.

Let us first consider the following example. Suppose that X is the number of sunglasses sold per day at a local pharmacy, and Y is the number of umbrellas sold per day at the pharmacy. From past sales data, suppose that we know that sales of sunglasses and umbrellas on a given day obeys the probability distribution for the pair (X, Y) given in Table 2.23. For example, according to the first row of Table 2.23, on any given day there is probability of 0.10 that the pharmacy will sell 35 sunglasses and 41

TABLE 2.23

Daily sales of sunglasses and umbrellas.

Probability	Number of Sunglasses Sold	Number of Umbrellas Sold
p_i	x_i	y_i
0.10	35	41
0.15	78	10
0.05	81	0
0.10	30	13
0.20	16	42
0.05	29	22
0.10	35	1
0.10	14	26
0.10	52	11
0.05	46	23

FIGURE 2.6

Scatter-plot of daily sales of sunglasses and umbrellas.

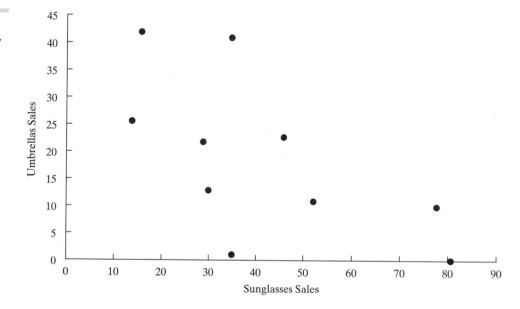

umbrellas. According to the second row of Table 2.23, on any given day there is probability of 0.15 that the pharmacy will sell 78 sunglasses and 10 umbrellas, etc.

In order to develop a feeling for the relationship between X and Y, we might begin with a scatter-plot of the second and third columns of Table 2.23, which is shown in Figure 2.6.

The scatter-plot suggests that smaller sales of sunglasses sold is often, but not always, accompanied by larger sales of umbrellas. Likewise, larger sales of sunglasses sold is often (but not always) accompanied by smaller sales of umbrellas. This makes intuitive sense, since sales of these items tend to be weather-related: When it is sunny, consumers will tend to buy sunglasses; and when it is rainy, consumers will tend to buy umbrellas. Of course, as Figure 2.6 shows, smaller sales of sunglasses is not *always* accompanied by larger sales of umbrellas. One can think of the uncertainty in the sales of umbrellas and sunglasses as arising from two sources. One source would be the idiosyncratic risk of consumers, who might or might not visit the pharmacy on a given day, and who might or might not be in the mood to make purchases. The other source of uncertainty would be the weather, which will influence whether consumers will tend to buy sunglasses or umbrellas.

Because smaller sales of sunglasses is often accompanied by larger sales of umbrellas, we might therefore be tempted to say that the number of sunglasses sold per

FIGURE 2.7

Scatter-plot of daily
sales of sunglasses
and umbrellas
together with their
means.

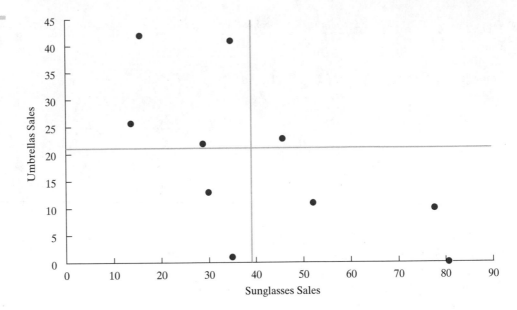

day and the number of umbrellas sold per day are "negatively correlated." We need
to be more careful, however, because not all dots in the scatter-plot are "equal." As
shown in Table 2.23, some of the dots ought to be weighted with a higher probability than others, so our statement about correlation should take into account these
probabilities. We would like to say, for example, "Sunglasses sales that are greater
than the average number of sunglasses sold per day are on average accompanied by
umbrella sales that are smaller than the average number of umbrellas sold per day."

To verify this statement, we compute the mean number of sunglasses and umbrellas sold each day. These means are easily computed as

$$\mu_X = 39.30 \quad \text{and} \quad \mu_Y = 21.35.$$

Figure 2.7 shows the scatter-plot with lines placed in the plot for these two
means. The figure does lend further justification to the assertion that "sunglasses
sales greater than the average number of sunglasses sold per day are typically accompanied by umbrella sales that are smaller than the average number of umbrellas
sold per day."

Armed with this notion, let us now define the **covariance** of two random variables X and Y. The covariance of two random variables X and Y having means μ_X
and μ_Y, respectively, is defined as follows:

Let X and Y be two random variables with respective means μ_X and μ_Y. We define the **covariance** of X and Y by

$$\text{COV}(X, Y) = \sum_{i=1}^{n} p_i (x_i - \mu_X)(y_i - \mu_Y).$$

The covariance of X and Y measures the extent to which the two random variables
vary together. If $\text{COV}(X, Y)$ is positive, then the two random variables vary in the
same direction. That is, higher values of X are apt to occur with higher values of Y,

and low values of X are apt to occur with low values of Y. An example of two random variables with positive covariance would be the number of inches of rainfall in April and the number of umbrellas sold in April. If the covariance is negative, then higher values of X are apt to occur with lower values of Y. Such is the case with the example of sunglasses and umbrellas discussed herein.

Returning to this example, let us now compute $COV(X, Y)$. As we noted before, $\mu_X = 39.30$ and $\mu_Y = 21.35$. Then the covariance of X and Y is

$$COV(X, Y) = 0.10(35 - 39.30)(41 - 21.35) + 0.15(78 - 39.30)(10 - 21.35)$$
$$+ \cdots + 0.05(46 - 39.30)(23 - 21.35)$$
$$= -223.26.$$

Notice that when x_i is larger than μ_X, y_i tends to be smaller than μ_Y, and the product $(x_i - \mu_X)(y_i - \mu_Y)$ tends to be negative. Moreover, the amount of deviation from the means is weighted by the respective probabilities to arrive at a final statement regarding covariance.

It is sometimes difficult to interpret the exact meaning of the number $COV(X, Y)$, because $COV(X, Y)$ is measured in units of X multiplied by Y. (In the previous example, the unit is sunglasses times umbrellas!) To overcome this difficulty, we introduce a standardized measure of interdependence between two random variables called the **correlation** of X and Y:

The **correlation** of X and Y, which is denoted by $CORR(X, Y)$ is defined as:

$$CORR(X, Y) = \frac{COV(X, Y)}{\sigma_X \sigma_Y}.$$

Note first that $CORR(X, Y)$ is a unit-free quantity. This is because the units of the numerator of the formula for $CORR(X, Y)$ is in units of X times the units of Y, and so is the denominator. In fact, it turns out that $CORR(X, Y)$ is always between -1.0 and 1.0.

If the value of $CORR(X, Y)$ is close to 1.0, then this means that X and Y tend to vary in the same direction; analogously, if the value of $CORR(X, Y)$ is close to -1.0, then this means that X and Y tend to vary in the opposite direction. If the correlation is very close to either 1.0 or -1.0, we say that the two random variables are "highly correlated."

In the extreme case where the correlation equals -1.0 or 1.0, we say that X and Y are perfectly correlated, which implies that one random variable is simply a linear function of the other. Also, if the correlation is 0.0, we say that there is no correlation between X and Y. In practice, however, it is very rare to encounter random variables that have either no correlation or perfect correlation, due to measurement errors or other external factors.

Let us now compute $CORR(X, Y)$ for the example of the sunglasses and umbrellas. To do so, we first compute the standard deviations of X and Y, which are easily computed as:

$$\sigma_X = \sqrt{\sum_{i=1}^{10} p_i(x_i - \mu_X)^2} = 22.81.$$

$$\sigma_Y = \sqrt{\sum_{i=1}^{10} p_i(y_i - \mu_Y)^2} = 15.08.$$

Then CORR(X, Y) is computed as:

$$CORR(X, Y) = \frac{COV(X, Y)}{\sigma_X \sigma_Y} = \frac{-223.26}{(22.81)(15.08)} = -0.649.$$

2.10   JOINT PROBABILITY DISTRIBUTIONS AND INDEPENDENCE

We now take a closer look at the example of sales of sunglasses and umbrellas of the previous section. The starting point of the description of the behavior of sales of sunglasses and sales of umbrellas was Table 2.23, which represents the joint probabilities of the daily sales of sunglasses, denoted by the random variable X, and the daily sales of umbrellas, denoted by the random variable Y. The covariance and correlation measures developed in the previous section summarize the extent to which the two random variables X and Y vary together. However, more detailed information is contained in Table 2.23, which lists the probabilities p_i for every pair (x_i, y_i).

More generally, consider two random variables (X, Y) that assume values (x_1, y_1), $(x_2, y_2), \ldots, (x_n, y_n)$ with probabilities $p_1, \ldots, p_n$. Analogous to the case of a single random variable, we have the following definition of the **joint probability distribution** of two random variables:

> The quantity $p_i = P(X = x_i$ and $Y = y_i)$ is denoted by $f(x_i, y_i)$ for all i and is called **the joint probability distribution function** of the pair of random variables (X, Y).

Consider the height, denoted by the random variable H, the weight, denoted by the random variable W, and the GMAT score, denoted by the random variable S, of a randomly chosen business school student. If we were to examine the probability distribution of H, W, and S, we would undoubtedly find that H and W are **dependent,** since individuals that are taller tend also to weigh more. However, we would also undoubtedly find that H and S are **independent,** since the height of a student and the student's ability to do well on a standardized test have nothing to do with one another. We now define this intuitive notion of independence more carefully.

> Two random variables X and Y are **independent** if
> $$P(X = x, Y = y) = P(X = x) \cdot P(Y = y).$$

Notice the connection between this definition and the implication of the fourth law of probability presented at the end of Section 2.2. If we interpret "$X = x$" as the event A and "$Y = y$" as the event B, then the independence of X and Y is equivalent to the statement that

$$P(A \text{ and } B) = P(A) \cdot P(B).$$

This latter statement is exactly the implication of the fourth law of probability stated at the end of Section 2.2.

An immediate and important consequence of the definition of independence is the following formula for independent random variables X and Y:

Let X and Y be two independent random variables. Then
$$E(X \cdot Y) = E(X) \cdot E(Y).$$

This formula can then be used to demonstrate the following relation between independence and correlation:

Let X and Y be two independent random variables. Then
$$COV(X, Y) = 0 \text{ and therefore } CORR(X, Y) = 0.$$

Example 2.23 – A Simple Model of the Stock Market

Consider the following very simple model of the stock market: We suppose that money invested in the stock market in a given month will increase by 5.0% in that month with probability 0.60 and will decrease by 5.5% in that month with probability 0.40. We also assume that the performances of the stock market in different months are independent. If Sam Atkinson invests $100,000 on January 1, what is his expected wealth on February 1? What is his expected wealth on March 1?

In order to answer these two questions, let X denote the stock market return for the month of January and let Y denote the stock market return for the month of February. Let F denote Sam's wealth on February 1 and let M denote Sam's wealth on March 1. Clearly

$$\mu_X = E(X) = 0.6 \cdot (1 + 0.05) + 0.4 \cdot (1 - 0.055) = 1.008.$$

Then the random variable F, which is Sam's wealth February 1, has the formula:

$$F = 100,000X.$$

Therefore,

$$\mu_F = 100,000 \cdot \mu_X = \$100,800.$$

Since the probability distributions of X and Y are the same, it must also be true that

$$\mu_Y = 1.008.$$

Then the random variable M, which is Sam's wealth on March 1, has the formula

$$M = 100,000 \cdot X \cdot Y.$$

Since it is assumed in this problem that the stock market's performance in different months are independent, then X and Y are independent random variables. Therefore,

$$\mu_M = E(100,000 \cdot X \cdot Y) = 100,000 \cdot E(X) \cdot E(Y)$$
$$= 100,000(1.008)(1.008) = \$101,606.4.$$

2.11   SUMS OF TWO RANDOM VARIABLES

In this section, we develop the arithmetic of working with sums of random variables. To see why this might be important, suppose that the random variable X denotes the market return of a particular manufacturing firm for the next year, and that the random variable Y denotes the market return of a particular service company for the next year. If we invest \$5,000 in the manufacturing firm and \$8,000 in the service company, then the random variable Z representing for the total value of our investment would have the formula

$$Z = 5{,}000 \cdot X + 8{,}000 \cdot Y,$$

and so Z is the weighted sum of the random variables X and Y. In fact, the arithmetic we will develop in this section will be used to demonstrate one of the most important (and useful) conclusions of modern financial theory, namely that a mutual fund significantly decreases investment risk.

We start by examining the weighted sum of two random variables. Let X and Y be two random variables, and let $Z = aX + bY$, where a and b are given numbers. Then Z is an unknown quantity, and so is itself a random variable. The formula for the mean of Z is given as follows:

Let X and Y be two random variables, and let $Z = aX + bY$, where a and b are given numbers. Then

$$E(Z) = E(aX + bY) = aE(X) + bE(Y).$$

In words, this formula states that the expectation of the weighted sum of several random variables is the weighted sum of the expectations of the random variables. This formula is true, whether or not the random variables X and Y are independent.

Our next task is to examine the variance of the random variable $Z = aX + bY$. We have

---

Let X and Y be two random variables, and let $Z = aX + bY$, where a and b are given numbers. Then

$$VAR(Z) = VAR(aX + bY) = a^2 VAR(X) + b^2 VAR(Y) \\ + 2 \cdot a \cdot b \cdot \sigma_X \cdot \sigma_Y CORR(X, Y),$$

or, equivalently,

$$VAR(Z) = VAR(aX + bY) = a^2 VAR(X) + b^2 VAR(Y) \\ + 2 \cdot a \cdot b \cdot COV(X, Y).$$

Note that the two formulas given previously are equivalent because

$$CORR(X, Y) = \frac{COV(X, Y)}{\sigma_X \sigma_Y},$$

and so

$$COV(X, Y) = CORR(X, Y)\sigma_X \sigma_Y.$$

When X and Y are positively correlated, the formula for VAR(Z) indicates that the variance of their sum will be greater than the sum of their individual variances. Similarly, if X and Y are negatively correlated, then the variance of their sum will be less than the sum of their individual variances.

As we have already seen, if the random variables X and Y are independent, then COV(X, Y) = 0 and CORR(X, Y) = 0. Therefore, an important consequence of the preceding formula is:

Let X and Y be two **independent** random variables, and let $Z = aX + bY$, where a and b are given numbers. Then

$$\mathrm{VAR}(Z) = \mathrm{VAR}(aX + bY) = a^2\mathrm{VAR}(X) + b^2\mathrm{VAR}(Y).$$

For the interested reader, we now present a derivation of the preceding formulas. During this derivation, the covariance of the two random variables X and Y arises naturally. Here is the derivation:

$$\mathrm{VAR}(Z) = \mathrm{VAR}(aX + bY) = \sum_{i=1}^{n} p_i[ax_i + by_i - (a\mu_X + b\mu_Y)]^2$$

$$= \sum_{i=1}^{n} p_i[(ax_i - a\mu_X + by_i - b\mu_Y)^2].$$

By expanding the square, we obtain

$$\mathrm{VAR}(Z) = \mathrm{VAR}(aX + bY)$$

$$= \sum_{i=1}^{n} p_i[(ax_i - a\mu_X)^2 + (by_i - b\mu_Y)^2 + 2ab(x_i - \mu_X)(y_i - \mu_Y)]$$

$$= a^2 \sum_{i=1}^{n} p_i(x_i - \mu_X)^2 + b^2 \sum_{i=1}^{n} p_i(y_i - \mu_Y)^2 + 2ab \sum_{i=1}^{n} p_i(x_i - \mu_X)(y_i - \mu_Y)$$

$$= a^2\,\mathrm{VAR}(X) + b^2\,\mathrm{VAR}(Y) + 2 \cdot a \cdot b \cdot \mathrm{COV}(X, Y).$$

The following example illustrates the use of the formulas developed in this section and explains the principle on which a mutual fund operates.

Example 2.24 – Mutual Funds Decrease Investment Risk

Consider the two companies Cinematics, Inc. and RTV, Inc. Cinematics owns and operates a large chain of cinema theaters across the country, and RTV is a producer of television sets. The annual rate of return from investing in Cinematics is uncertain, and therefore is a random variable. We suppose that the expected annual return from investing in Cinematics is 10% per year. Similarly, the annual rate of return from investing in RTV is uncertain, and therefore is a random variable. We suppose that the expected annual return from investing in RTV is also 10% per year.

We further suppose that the standard deviation of the return from investing in Cinematics is 8% per year, and that the standard deviation of the return from investing in RTV is 4% per year. Let us also suppose that the correlation between the rate of return from investing in Cinematics and the rate of return from investing in RTV is -0.75. (This negative correlation might be due to the fact that consumers who watch a lot of television do not go to the cinema very often.)

Let us convert the preceding information into statements about random variables. Let the random variable X denote the annual return from investing in Cinematics and let the random variable Y denote the annual return from investing in RTV. Then we have

$$\mu_X = 1.10 \text{ and } \mu_Y = 1.10,$$

and

$$\sigma_X = 0.08 \text{ and } \sigma_Y = 0.04,$$

whereby

$$\sigma_X^2 = 0.0064 \text{ and } \sigma_Y^2 = 0.0016.$$

Furthermore,

$$CORR(X, Y) = -0.75.$$

Therefore, since

$$CORR(X, Y) = \frac{COV(X, Y)}{\sigma_X \sigma_Y},$$

the covariance of X and Y is:

$$COV(X, Y) = CORR(X, Y)\,\sigma_X\sigma_Y = (-0.75)(0.08)(0.04) = -0.0024.$$

Suppose that we invest a fraction a of our money in Cinematics and the remaining fraction $1 - a$ in RTV. Let Z denote the annual return of our investment. Then

$$Z = aX + (1 - a)Y.$$

Notice that Z is a weighted sum of two random variables. Therefore, we can apply the formulas of this section to determine the mean and variance of Z. We first compute the mean of Z:

$$\mu_Z = E(Z) = aE(X) + (1 - a)E(Y) = a(1.10) + (1 - a)(1.10) = 1.10.$$

That is, the expected return from investing a fraction of our money in Cinematics and the remaining fraction in RTV is precisely 10%. This is true regardless of the value of the fraction a, because both companies have the same expected return of 10%. Thus, regardless of the fraction a, we will have an expected return of 10% on our investment.

Investors are usually interested in maximizing their expected return and minimizing their risk, where risk is measured in terms of the standard deviation of their return. That is, investors seek to maximize their expected value of their return and to minimize the standard deviation of their return. Let us now compute the variance and then the standard deviation of the return of the investment, which is Z. From the formula for the variance of the weighted sum of two random variables, we have:

$$\begin{aligned}
\sigma_Z^2 = VAR(Z) &= VAR(a\,X + (1 - a)\,Y) \\
&= a^2 VAR(X) + (1 - a)^2 VAR(Y) + 2a(1 - a)\sigma_X\sigma_Y CORR(X, Y) \\
&= 0.0064\,a^2 + 0.0016\,(1 - a)^2 + 2a(1 - a)(0.08)(0.04)(-0.75).
\end{aligned}$$

Therefore, the standard deviation of the return of the portfolio is:

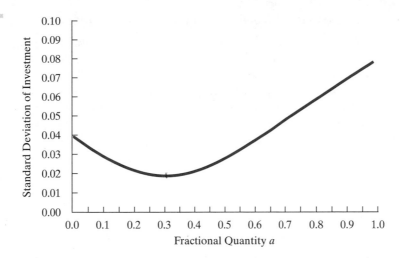

FIGURE 2.8
The standard deviation of the investment as a function of the fraction a.

$$\sigma_Z = \sqrt{0.0064\, a^2 + 0.0016\,(1-a)^2 + 2a(1-a)(0.08)(0.04)(-0.75)}.$$

In Figure 2.8, we plot this formula, which is the standard deviation of the return of the investment, as a function of the fractional quantity a, as a varies between 0.0 to 1.0. Examining the figure, we see that for $a = 0.30$, the standard deviation of the investment is:

$$\sigma_Z = \sqrt{\text{VAR}(Z)} = 0.019.$$

Notice what we have achieved. If we had invested entirely in Cinematics, we would have an expected return of 10% with a standard deviation of 8%. If we had instead invested entirely in RTV, we would have an expected return of 10% with a standard deviation of 4%. However, if we invest 30% of our money in Cinematics and 70% of our money in RTV, we would also have an expected return of 10%, but with a standard deviation of only 1.9%. That is, by diversifying our holdings, we have achieved the same expected return, but with a lower standard deviation, and hence risk, than if we had invested entirely in one or the other of the two companies.

This finding is remarkable, and forms the basis of how a mutual fund is constructed. By taking appropriate combinations of various stocks that are correlated, an investor can form a portfolio of stocks that has much lower risk than any of the individual stocks that are represented in the fund. We will revisit this phenomenon in Chapter 8, in our discussion of nonlinear optimization models.

2.12 SOME ADVANCED METHODS IN PROBABILITY*

(This section contains somewhat more advanced material, and can be omitted without loss of continuity.)

This section contains two advanced topics in probability. The first topic concerns two formulas for manipulating conditional probabilities that are useful when there are a large number of uncertain events. The second topic consists of an alternate formula for the variance of a random variable, which is used to perform some more advanced analysis of investing in the stock market.

Two Formulas Involving Conditional Probabilities

The methodology of constructing a probability table that was illustrated in Section 2.3 can be very effective in performing probability calculations when the number of uncertain events is small. However, when the number of uncertain events is large, it is usually more efficient to work with formulas rather than tables. Herein we present methods for calculating probabilities when there are a large number of uncertain events. We proceed first abstractly and then present an application.

Given two uncertain events A and B, the third law of probability is written

$$P(A|B) = \frac{P(A \text{ and } B)}{P(B)}.$$

This implies that

$$P(A \text{ and } B) = P(A|B) \times P(B).$$

The event $B|A$ means that B occurs given that A has occurred. Also from the third law of probability, it is true that

$$P(B|A) = \frac{P(B \text{ and } A)}{P(A)}.$$

Therefore, if we substitute the formula $P(A \text{ and } B) = P(A|B) \times P(B)$ into the preceding expression, we obtain the following very important formula, which is called **Bayes' Theorem.**

Bayes' Theorem:

$$P(B|A) = \frac{P(A|B)P(B)}{P(A)}.$$

The usefulness of Bayes' Theorem stems from the fact that it allows the revision of the probability of uncertain events in light of new information.

Given an event A and n mutually exclusive and collectively exhaustive events B_1, $B_2, \ldots, B_n$, then the events "A and B_1," "A and B_2," $\ldots$, "A and B_n" are also mutually exclusive. Therefore, from the second law of probability,

$$P(A) = P(A \text{ and } B_1) + P(A \text{ and } B_2) + \cdots + P(A \text{ and } B_n).$$

Furthermore, by the third law of probability,

$$P(A \text{ and } B_1) = P(A|B_1) \times P(B_1),$$
$$P(A \text{ and } B_2) = P(A|B_2) \times P(B_2),$$
$$\vdots$$
$$P(A \text{ and } B_n) = P(A|B_n) \times P(B_n).$$

Combining these last equations we obtain the following formula, which is known as the **Law of Total Probability.**

Law of Total Probability:

$$P(A) = P(A|B_1) \times P(B_1) + P(A|B_2) \times P(B_2) + \cdots + P(A|B_n) \times P(B_n).$$

Example 2.25 — A Birthday Problem

Suppose there are N people in a room. What is the probability that no two of the people in the room share the same birthday?

In order to address this question, we make the following two assumptions. First, we assume that there is no prior relationship among the birthdays of the people in the room (there are no twins present, for example). Second, we assume that the probability of any person being born on any particular day is 1 in 365 (we neglect leap years). In order to test your intuition, think a bit about this problem before reading further. In particular, if there are $N = 60$ people in the room, how likely do you think it is that there are no two people in the room who share the same birthday?

Let us now solve this problem using the laws of probability. Suppose we ask each of the people his or her birthday, in turn. Let A_i be the event that the ith person states a date that has not been stated by any of the previous $i - 1$ people. Let B be the event that all N people have different birthdays. Then

$$P(B) = P(A_1 \text{ and } A_2 \text{ and } \cdots A_N).$$

By the third law of probability, notice that

$$P(A_1 \text{ and } A_2 \text{ and } \cdots A_N) =$$
$$P(A_N | A_1 \text{ and } A_2 \text{ and } \cdots A_{N-1}) \times P(A_1 \text{ and } A_2 \text{ and } \cdots A_{N-1}).$$

Similarly,

$$P(A_1 \text{ and } A_2 \text{ and } \cdots A_{N-1}) =$$
$$P(A_{N-1} | A_1 \text{ and } A_2 \text{ and } \cdots A_{N-2}) \times P(A_1 \text{ and } A_2 \text{ and } \ldots A_{N-2}).$$

Continuing in this way we obtain that

$$P(B) =$$
$$P(A_1) \times P(A_2 | A_1) \times P(A_3 | A_1 \text{ and } A_2) \times \ldots \times P(A_N | A_1 \text{ and } A_2 \cdots A_{N-1}).$$

Clearly, $P(A_1) = 1$, since the first person asked cannot repeat a new date. The second person will announce a new date unless the second person was born the same day as the first person. Therefore

$$P(A_2 | A_1) = 1 - 1/365 = 364/365.$$

To calculate $P(A_3 | A_1 \text{ and } A_2)$, note that if both A_1 and A_2 have occurred, there are two days the third person must avoid in order to prevent repetition. Therefore,

$$P(A_3 | A_1 \text{ and } A_2) = 363/365.$$

Applying this logic more generally, we obtain that

$$P(A_i | A_1 \text{ and } A_2 \text{ and } \cdots A_{i-1}) = \frac{365 - (i - 1)}{365} = \frac{366 - i}{365}.$$

Therefore, we can express $P(B)$ as follows

$$P(B) = \frac{(365)(364)(363)}{(365)(365)(365)} \cdots \frac{(366 - N)}{(365)}.$$

Let us evaluate this expression at particular values of N. For $N = 25$, the probability that there are no shared birthdays among 25 people in a room is computed as

$$P(B) = \frac{(365)(364)(363)}{(365)(365)(365)} \cdots \frac{(341)}{(365)} = 0.43.$$

For $N = 60$, the probability drops to approximately

$$P(B) = \frac{(365)\,(364)\,(363)}{(365)\,(365)\,(365)} \cdots \frac{(306)}{(365)} = 0.006.$$

Finally for $N = 100$ people, the probability that all 100 people in a room will have a different birthday drops to approximately

$$P(B) = \frac{(365)\,(364)\,(363)}{(365)\,(365)\,(365)} \cdots \frac{(266)}{(365)} = 0.0000003.$$

At first glance these results are somewhat surprising. For instance, when $N = 60$ there are six times as many dates as individuals, leaving plenty of room for the people to spread out their birthdays among all possible dates. However, the calculation suggests that it is almost inevitable that there will be a match.

An Alternate Formula for the Variance

Herein we derive an alternate formula for the variance of a random variable, and we use this formula to perform some more advanced analysis of investing in the stock market.

Let X be a random variable. By definition, the variance of X is:

$$\sigma_X^2 = \sum_{i=1}^{n} p_i (x_i - \mu_X)^2.$$

If we expand the square, we obtain

$$\sigma_X^2 = \sum_{i=1}^{n} p_i [(x_i)^2 - 2x_i\mu_X + \mu_X^2].$$

Therefore,

$$\sigma_X^2 = \sum_{i=1}^{n} p_i [(x_i)^2] - \sum_{i=1}^{n} p_i [2x_i\mu_X] + \sum_{i=1}^{n} p_i [\mu_X^2].$$

Because μ_X is not a random variable (it is a number), we obtain

$$\sigma_X^2 = \sum_{i=1}^{n} p_i [(x_i)^2] - 2\mu_X \sum_{i=1}^{n} p_i x_i + \sum_{i=1}^{n} p_i \mu_X^2$$
$$= E[X^2] - 2\mu_X^2 + \mu_X^2 = E[X^2] - \mu_X^2.$$

We summarize this finding as:

$$\sigma_X^2 = E[X^2] - \mu_X^2.$$

The following example is an extension of Example 2.23, but is a more advanced application of discrete random variables.

Example 2.26 — The Effect of Information on Investing in the Stock Market

Recall the very simple model of the stock market posed in Example 2.23: We suppose that money invested in the stock market in a given month will increase by 5.0% in that month with probability 0.60 and will decrease by 5.5% in that month with probability 0.40. We also assume that the performance of the stock market in different months are independent. Suppose Sam Atkinson has $1.00 to invest in the stock market. We would like to answer the following questions:

Questions:

(a) If Sam invests $1.00 on January 1, what is the expected value of his return one year later? What is the standard deviation of his return?

(b) If Sam invests $1.00 on January 1, what is the expected value of his return fifty years later?

(c) Suppose that Sam has perfect information about stock market performance. Therefore, he only invests in the stock market in those months in which the market increases. If he invests $1.00 on January 1, what is the expected value of his return fifty years later?

Answers to the Questions:

(a) Let $X_1, \ldots, X_{12}$ denote the discrete random variables representing the return from investing $1.00 in the twelve months of January through December. These random variables are independent. Each X_i is equal to 1.05 (a 5% increase) with probability 0.60 and is equal to 0.945 (a 5.5% decrease) with probability 0.40. Let Z be the return of $1.00 invested in the stock market over the twelve-month period. Then

$$Z = X_1 \cdot X_2 \cdots X_{12},$$

because stock market returns are multiplicative.

Let us first calculate the expected value of X_1. Simple computation yields:

$$E(X_1) = 0.60 \cdot (1.05) + 0.40 \cdot (0.945) = 1.008,$$

that is, the expected return per month is 0.8%. Because each of the X_i's have the same distribution, each X_i also has the same mean. Furthermore, because returns of different months are independent, then

$$E(Z) = E(X_1 \cdot X_2 \cdots X_{12}) = E(X_1) \cdot E(X_2) \cdots E(X_{12}) = 1.008^{12} = 1.1003,$$

that is, Sam's expected return over the year is 10.03%.

In order to compute the variance of Sam's return over the year, we apply the formula derived previously:

$$VAR(Z) = E[Z^2] - (E[Z])^2.$$

Now notice that

$$E(Z^2) = E[(X_1)^2 \cdots (X_{12})^2].$$

Because the stock market returns from different months are independent, we have

$$E(Z^2) = E[(X_1)^2] \cdots E[(X_{12})^2].$$

Let us then calculate

$$E[(X_1)^2] = \ldots = E[(X_{12})^2] = 0.60 \cdot (1.05)^2 + 0.40 \cdot (0.945)^2 = 1.01871.$$

Therefore,

$$E[Z^2] = 1.01871^{12} = 1.249.$$

The variance of Sam's return over the year is then

$$VAR[Z] = E[Z^2] - (E[Z])^2 = 1.249 - (1.10)^2 = 0.038.$$

Therefore, the standard deviation of Sam's return over the year is

$$\sigma_Z = \sqrt{0.038} = 0.195,$$

i.e., 19.5%.

(b) Let $Z_1, \ldots, Z_{50}$ denote the annual return from investing \$1.00 in the stock market for each of the fifty years. Let Y be the return of \$1.00 invested in the stock market over the entire fifty years. Then

$$E[Y] = E[Z_1 \cdots Z_{50}] = E[Z_1] \cdots E[Z_{50}],$$

because returns of different years are independent. From question (a),

$$E[Z_1] = \ldots = E[Z_{50}] = 1.1003.$$

Therefore,

$$E[Y] = 1.1003^{50} = \$119.21.$$

(c) We next assume that Sam will invest only in those months in which the stock market increases. Otherwise, Sam does not invest his money at all. Let $I_1, \ldots, I_{12}$ be the discrete random variables representing Sam's return from investing \$1.00 in January, $\ldots$, December under the strategy that Sam invests only in those months that in which the stock market increases. Each of the I_i's is then 1.05 with probability 0.60 and 1.00 (he does not invest if the stock market decreases) with probability 0.40. Therefore

$$E[I_1] = \ldots = E[I_{12}] = 0.60 \cdot (1.05) + 0.40 \cdot (1.00) = 1.03.$$

That is, Sam's strategy has an expected return of 3% per month. Then, following the methodology used above, the expected return per year is

$$E[Z] = E[I_1 \ldots I_{12}] = E[I_1] \ldots E[I_{12}] = 1.03^{12} = 1.426,$$

which is a 42.6% return per year. The expected return from investing in this manner over fifty years is therefore

$$E[Y] = 1.426^{50} = \$50.39 \text{ million.}$$

This very simple model dramatically demonstrates the tremendous effect of information on the returns from investing in the stock market.

2.13 | SUMMARY

In this chapter, we have introduced the basic tools that are used to model uncertainty. We defined the concepts of an outcome, an event, and the probability of an event. We also introduced the laws of probability and used these laws to calculate probabilities of uncertain events in a variety of contexts. We used probability tables to facilitate the calculation of probabilities.

We then introduced the notion of a discrete random variable and its probability distribution. We examined one particular distribution, the binomial distribution, in great detail. We also introduced the concepts of mean, variance, and standard deviation, as summary measures of the behavior of a random variable. Last of all, we introduced the concept of a probability distribution of a collection of random variables, as well as the notions of covariance and correlation that summarize the interdependence between two random variables.

Managers often need to work with probabilities of uncertain events within the context of a more general decision problem. The tools and methods of this chapter, in conjunction with those of the previous chapter on decision analysis, provide a powerful methodology for managers to make optimal decisions under uncertainty.

2.14   CASE MODULES

ARIZONA INSTRUMENTATION, INC. AND THE ECONOMIC DEVELOPMENT BOARD OF SINGAPORE

In 1989, Arizona Instrumentation, Inc. (AII) was experiencing depressed sales and earnings due to setbacks in its semiconductor business. New wafer fabs, which are plants that manufacture semiconductors, were very expensive to build, but were necessary in order to remain competitive in the semiconductor market. DRAMs (Dynamic Random Access Memory chips) was one of AII's major semiconductor products, and a new DRAM wafer fab would cost $350 million to build.

Faced with a shortage of capital for such an investment, AII invited the Singapore Economic Development Board (EDB) to invest in a new DRAM wafer fab to be located in Singapore, with technology supplied by AII. Such an arrangement would hopefully yield benefits to both parties: AII would have a new wafer fab for producing DRAMs, and Singapore would advance its interests in moving towards higher-technology manufacturing in its growing economy. EDB would contribute $350 million in capital (as a shareholder) plus other inducements such as subsidized loans and manpower training grants. If the wafer fab project were successful, EDB estimated that the project would generate returns to Singapore of $950 million, so that the net present value would be $950 − $350 = $600 million. If it were not successful, however, all of the investment of $350 million in the project would be lost.

There were several uncertainties surrounding this investment. Competition in the global semiconductor market was fierce. A number of giant Japanese electronics companies, such as Hitachi and Toshiba, had large amounts of excess cash and could flood the market with competitively-priced DRAMs. Earlier, in fact, Intel and Motorola had exited the DRAM market precisely because of the intense competition from these Japanese companies.

AII was one of only two American companies that was manufacturing DRAMs (the other was D-Cron Technology based in Helena, Montana). In addition to struggling to produce DRAMs in the marketplace, AII was also aggressively using the legal system to attack its competitors by initiating lawsuits for patent right infringement. One unintended consequence of its legal activities was that AII was developing a bad reputation as a company more interested in attacking its competitors than in producing a competitive product.

Although DRAM prices were depressed during most of 1989, forecasts showed strong future demand from new software products under development that would need large amounts of memory (such as operating systems for the next generation of personal computers). There were other consumer electronics products that were also projected to contribute to higher future demand for DRAM chips.

In addition to forming a strategic partnership with one another, EDB and AII were also considering forming a larger alliance with two other semiconductor firms. Under this larger alliance, referred to as AESS ("A" for Arizona Instrumentation, "E" for EDB, and "SS" for the other two semiconductor firms), EDB would contribute $100 million in capital and other inducements. If the project were successful, EDB estimated that the project would generate returns to Singapore of $500 million, so that the net present value would be $500 − $100 = $400 million. If it were not successful, however, all of the investment of $100 million in the project would be lost.

Mr. Boon Chye Tan, a project manager at EDB, was asked to evaluate the proposed alliance of EDB with AII, as well as the alternative plan of the AESS alliance, and to make a recommendation to the senior management of EDB.

Mr. Tan estimated that there were four main areas of uncertainty that would contribute to the success or failure of the wafer fab:

- whether or not the large Japanese semiconductor manufacturers would succeed in flooding the DRAM market with competitively-priced DRAMs;

- whether or not the future demand for DRAMs would be high;

- whether or not the reputation of AII would adversely affect the project;

- whether or not EDB and AII, or AESS would be able to secure the necessary financing for the project.

Mr. Tan felt that all of these events were approximately independent of one another. He then estimated the probabilities of the various events under both alliances. Table 2.24 presents his estimates of these probabilities.

Mr. Tan estimated that if all four events were to turn out favorable, there was a 90% chance that the project would succeed. If any three of the four events were to turn out favorable and only one was unfavorable, then there was a 50% chance that the project would succeed. Finally, if two or more of the events were to turn out unfavorable, then there was virtually no possibility that the project would succeed.

Assignment:

Given these estimated probabilities, what recommendation would you make to the senior management of EDB?

SAN CARLOS MUD SLIDES

Extensive logging has exposed a hillside in San Carlos to the possibility of a mudslide. Reforestation is underway, but it will be a year before the new vegetation will be mature enough to remove the danger. If a slide occurs in the interim, human injuries will

TABLE 2.24

Mr. Tan's probability estimates under the two possible alliances.

Event	Alliance	Probability
Japanese Manufacturers Are Unable to Flood Market	EDB & AII	0.70
Future Demand for DRAMs is High	EDB & AII	0.60
Reputation of AII Does Not Adversely Affect Project	EDB & AII	0.50
Alliance is Able to Secure Necessary Financing	EDB & AII	0.90
Japanese Manufacturers Are Unable to Flood Market	AESS	0.70
Future Demand for DRAMs is High	AESS	0.70
Reputation of AII Does Not Adversely Affect Project	AESS	0.30
Alliance is Able to Secure Necessary Financing	AESS	0.95

be avoided because mud moves slowly. The damage from such a slide would be limited to the road that passes beneath the hill. Construction of a retaining wall on the uphill side of the road has been suggested as a possible step to prevent this damage.

The Mayor of San Carlos is puzzled by the uncertainty concerning the issue. He has consulted with an expert who states that there is only one chance in 100 that a slide will occur within the next year. The expert adds that roughly 5% of all such slides break through retaining walls like the one proposed. The retaining wall would cost $40,000 to build. The road would cost about $1,000,000 to repair if damaged by a mudslide.

The expert points out that she can better assess the likelihood of a slide occurring in the next year if she conducts a geological test of the igneous rock layer below the hillside. Like any test, this one is imperfect. A positive test outcome would indicate a higher chance of a slide than a negative test outcome. The test has been conducted at sites at which slides eventually occurred and at sites at which slides did not subsequently occur. The information from these previous tests can be summarized as follows. Positive test outcomes had been reported on 90% of the sites at which slides subsequently occurred. Negative test results had been reported at 85% of the sites at which slides did not subsequently occur.

Assignment:

As an aide to the mayor of San Carlos, what action would you recommend be taken?

GRAPHIC CORPORATION

Dana Meseroll, President of Graphic Corporation, has signed a $1,050,000 contract to deliver and install a sophisticated detection system called G-LAN to a major shipbuilding corporation. Graphic has built a variety of versions of the G-LAN system before. Although the quality of the G-LAN system is quite good, site-specific installation problems still persist. The likelihood that the G-LAN system will perform up to specifications depends very much on engineering characteristics at the installation site.

Using normal production techniques, Graphic can produce and install the G-LAN for $600,000. However, if they took every possible precaution, they could build and install a G-LAN that would be just about perfect, at a cost of $720,000.

If Graphic installed the G-LAN built the normal way, there is an 8% chance that it would not perform up to specifications. It would then have to be shipped back to Graphic's plant, rebuilt for an additional cost of $150,000, and then sent back and reinstalled at the shipbuilder's site. The shipping and reinstallation costs would be an additional $210,000. If the G-LAN is rebuilt, it will be done so as to guarantee that it will work free of defects.

Dana Meseroll has asked George Waitt, division head for test and evaluation, to look into the possibility of pre-testing the circuits in the G-LAN before it is sent out to the shipbuilder. According to George, such a test costs about $20,000. The output of the test is a rating of "Positive," "Neutral," or "Negative." If the G-LAN is all right (i.e., it will perform up to specifications), then the chance that it would test Positive is 70%, and the chance that it would test Neutral is 20%. (This implies that the chance that it would test Negative is 10% in this case.) If the G-LAN is not all right (i.e., it will not perform up to specifications), then the chance that it would test Negative is 75%, and the chance that it would test Neutral is 10%. (This implies that the chance that it would test Positive is 15% in this case.)

Dana Meseroll thought things over. She felt very uneasy about the possibility of installing the G-LAN, having it not perform up to specifications, and suffering the embarrassment of having to rebuild it, reship it, and reinstall it. She guessed that this embarrassment could cost the company around $100,000 in lost goodwill, reputation, and/or effects on future earnings.

Assignment:

If you were Dana Meseroll, what decision strategy would you recommend?

2.15   EXERCISES

EXERCISE 2.1 A four-sided die is engraved with the numbers 1 through 4 on its four different sides. Suppose that when rolled, each side (and hence each number) has an equal probability of being the bottom face when it lands. We roll two such dice. Let X be the sum of the numbers on the bottom faces of the two dice.

(a) What is the probability that X is at least five?

(b) How does your answer to (a) change if you are told that the bottom face of *the first die* has the number "3" on it?

(c) How does your answer to (a) change if you are told that the bottom face of *one of the dice* has the number "3" on it?

EXERCISE 2.2 We toss a coin three times. Let the outcome of this experiment be the sequence of heads (H) and tails (T) resulting from the three tosses.

(a) Enumerate all of the possible outcomes of this experiment.

(b) What is the probability of the outcome "HHT"?

(c) What is the probability of the event "The first two tosses resulted in heads"?

(d) What is the probability of the event "There were two heads in a row among the three tosses"?

EXERCISE 2.3 Suppose that there are 100 MBA students in the first-year class. Of these students, 20 of them have two years of work experience, 30 have three years of work experience, 15 have four years of work experience, and 35 have five or more years of work experience. Suppose that a first-year MBA student is selected at random.

(a) What is the probability that this student has at least four years of work experience?

(b) Suppose that you are told that this student has at least three years of work experience. What is the conditional probability that this student has at least four years of work experience?

EXERCISE 2.4 An oil company is drilling for oil at three promising sites. According to geological tests, the probabilities of finding oil at these three sites are 0.70, 0.85, and 0.80, respectively. The presence of oil at any one of the sites is presumed to be independent of the presence of oil at any of the other sites.

(a) What is the probability of finding oil at all three of the sites?

(b) What is the probability of not finding oil at any of the three sites?

EXERCISE 2.5 In Oblako County, any day can be either sunny or cloudy. If a day is sunny, the following day will be sunny with probability 0.60. If a day is cloudy, the following day will be cloudy with probability 0.70. Suppose it is cloudy on Monday.

(a) What is the probability that it will be sunny on Wednesday?

(b) What is the probability that it will be sunny on both Tuesday and Wednesday?

EXERCISE 2.6 An athletic footwear company is attempting to estimate the sales that will result from a television advertisement campaign of its new athletic shoe. The contribution to earnings from each pair of shoes sold is $40. Suppose that the probability that a television viewer will watch the advertisement (as opposed to turn his/her attention elsewhere) is 0.40. Furthermore, suppose that 1% of viewers who watch the advertisement on a local television channel will buy a pair of shoes. The company can buy television advertising time in one of the time slots according to Table 2.25.

(a) Suppose that the company decides to buy one minute of advertising time. Which time slot would yield the highest expected contribution to earnings net of costs? What is the total expected contribution to earnings resulting from the advertisement?

(b) Suppose the company decides to buy two one-minute advertisements in different time slots. Which two different time slots should the company purchase to maximize the expected contribution to earnings? What is the total expected contribution to earnings resulting from these two advertisements?

EXERCISE 2.7 It is a relatively rare event that a new television show becomes a long-term success. A new television show that is introduced during the regular season has a 10% chance of becoming a long-term success. A new television show that is introduced as a mid-season replacement has only a 5% chance of becoming a long-term success. Approximately 60% of all new television shows are introduced during the regular season. What is the probability that a randomly selected new television show will become a long-term success?

EXERCISE 2.8 On a television game show, there are three boxes. Inside one of the boxes there is a check for $10,000. If you pick the box that contains the check, you keep the money. Suppose you pick one of the boxes at random. The host of the game opens one of the other boxes and reveals that it is empty. The host then offers you the chance to change your pick. Should you change your pick? If so, why? If not, why not?

Carefully construct a probability model of this problem. Please state clearly all assumptions you make in your model. Then answer the questions.

EXERCISE 2.9 There are 550,000 people in the US infected with HIV. Of these people, 275,000 are drug users, and the rest are not drug users. The total population of the US is 250 million. There are 10 million drug users in the US.

TABLE 2.25

Television advertising costs and viewers.

Time Slot	Cost of Advertisement ($/minute)	Estimated number of Viewers
Morning	$120,000	1,000,000
Afternoon	$200,000	1,300,000
Prime Time	$400,000	3,200,000
Late Evening	$150,000	800,000

The standard blood test for HIV infection is not always accurate. The probability that someone who is infected with HIV will test positive for HIV is 0.99. The probability that someone who is not infected with HIV will test negative for HIV is also 0.99. Answer the following questions, clearly stating any assumptions that you need to make.

(a) Suppose that a randomly chosen person takes the standard blood test for HIV, and the outcome of the test is positive. What is the probability that this person is infected with HIV? Is your answer surprising?

(b) Suppose that a randomly chosen *drug user* takes the standard blood test for HIV, and the outcome of the test is positive. What is the probability that this person is infected with HIV?

EXERCISE 2.10 A hardware store has received two shipments of halogen lamps. The first shipment contains 100 lamps, 4% of which are defective. The second shipment contains 50 lamps, 6% of which are defective. Suppose that Emanuel picks a lamp (at random) off of the shelf and purchases it, and he later discovers that the lamp he purchased is defective. Is the defective lamp more likely to come from the first shipment or from the second shipment?

EXERCISE 2.11 It is estimated that one third of the population in a given county is infected with the tuberculosis (TB) bacteria. The human body is usually able to successfully fight the TB bacteria and so prevent the onset of the TB disease. Consequently, a person infected with the TB bacteria has only a 10% chance developing the TB disease over his/her lifetime.

(a) Suppose that we choose a person at random from all of the people in the county. What is the probability that this person has the TB disease?

(b) Suppose that among those people who have died in the county in the last year, we perform an autopsy on one of the bodies chosen at random, and we find that this person did not have the TB disease. What is the probability that this person had been infected with the TB bacteria?

EXERCISE 2.12 An investment consultant believes that the probability distribution of the return on investment (in percent per year) on a certain international portfolio is as given in Table 2.26.

(a) Verify that the numbers in Table 2.26 correspond to a proper probability distribution.

(b) According to this consultant, what is the probability that the portfolio's return on investment will be at least 12%?

(c) According to this consultant, what is the expected return on investment of the portfolio?

TABLE 2.26

Probability distribution of the return on investment of the international portfolio.

Return on Investment (% per year)	Probability
x_i	p_i
9	0.07
10	0.15
11	0.23
12	0.25
13	0.15
14	0.12
15	0.03

(d) According to this consultant, what are the variance and the standard deviation of the return on investment of the portfolio?

EXERCISE 2.13 The probability distribution of the number of sales per week of a particular type of microwave oven is shown in Table 2.27.

(a) What is the probability that between 1 and 3 of the microwave ovens will be sold per week?

(b) Compute the mean, the variance, and the standard deviation of the number of weekly sales of the microwave ovens.

EXERCISE 2.14 A construction job is comprised of two tasks, which we will call "task A" and "task B." The two tasks are initiated simultaneously and their completion times are uncertain. The entire construction job is completed as soon as both tasks are completed. The possible outcomes for the completion times of task A and task B, and the associated probabilities, are given in Table 2.28.

(a) What is the probability distribution of the duration of task A? of task B? of the job as a whole?

(b) What is the mean and the standard deviation of the duration of task A? of task B? of the job as a whole?

(c) Suppose that task A costs $800 for every week that it is in progress, and that task B costs $1,000 per week for every week that it is in progress, and that there is an additional charge of $400 for every week that the job as a whole is still in progress. Compute the probability distribution, the mean, and the standard deviation of the cost of this construction job.

EXERCISE 2.15 An industrial training company that offers week-long courses to corporations has three instructors on its permanent staff. The company receives requests for its courses from its many corporate clients. The course fee charged by the training company is $20,000 per course. The company also has a pool of qualified instructors in the local area (predominantly retired business school faculty) that it can draw upon whenever demand for their courses exceeds their supply of permanent

TABLE 2.27

Probability distribution of weekly sales of a microwave oven.

Number of Sales x_i	Probability p_i
0	0.05
1	0.07
2	0.22
3	0.29
4	0.25
5	0.12

TABLE 2.28

Probabilities of time to completion of tasks A and B.

Time to Complete Task A (in weeks)	Time to Complete Task B (in weeks)	Probability
1	1	0.07
1	2	0.27
1	3	0.06
2	1	0.13
2	2	0.31
2	3	0.16

TABLE 2.29

Probability distribution of weekly demand for courses.

Number of Courses x_i	Probability p_i
0	0.05
1	0.15
2	0.25
3	0.25
4	0.15
5	0.10
6	0.05

TABLE 2.30

Probability distribution of monthly construction of sailboats.

Number of Sailboats	Probability
2	0.15
3	0.20
4	0.30
5	0.25
6	0.05
7	0.05

instructors. Under a standardized arrangement, an instructor in the pool receives 55% of the course fee whenever he/she teaches a course. The weekly demand for courses obeys the probability distribution given in Table 2.29.

The company will obviously utilize its own instructors to teach courses whenever possible. Pool instructors will be scheduled to teach only if the demand for courses exceeds the number of permanent staff.

(a) Verify that the data in Table 2.29 corresponds to a probability distribution.

(b) What is the probability that all of the permanent staff are idle in a particular week?

(c) What is the probability that all of the permanent staff is busy in a particular week?

(d) One of the permanent staff is a star teacher. The company schedules her to teach on every possible occasion to maximize the chances of repeat customers. What is the probability that she will be busy in a given week?

(e) What is the mean and standard deviation of the weekly revenue after deducting payments to pool instructors?

(f) Adding more instructors to the staff involves an incremental cost of $2,500 per instructor per week. How many instructors, if any, should the company add to its permanent staff in order to maximize expected profit?

EXERCISE 2.16 The number of wooden sailboats constructed per month in a small shipyard is a random variable that obeys the probability distribution given in Table 2.30.

Suppose that the sailboat builders have fixed monthly costs of $30,000 and an additional construction cost of $4,800 per boat.

(a) Compute the mean and standard deviation of the number of boats constructed each month.

(b) What is the mean and standard deviation of the monthly cost of the sailboat construction operation?

(c) How do your answers in part (b) change if the fixed monthly cost increases from $30,000 to $53,000? Try to compute your answer using the results of the calculation in part (b) only.

(d) How do your answers in part (b) change if the construction cost per boat increases from $4,800 to $7,000, but the fixed monthly cost stays at $30,000? Try to compute your answer using the results of the calculations of parts (a) and (b) only.

EXERCISE 2.17 In a particular town there are two automobile rental agencies that offer different prices for a weekend out-of-state automobile rental. An automobile rental at Express Car Rentals (ECR) costs $195 and includes free unlimited mileage. An automobile rental at Discount Rentals Agency (DRA) costs $130 plus a mileage charge; the first 300 miles are free and each additional mile costs $0.20 per mile. A market survey indicates that the miles driven by rent-a-car customers for weekend rentals obeys the probability distribution shown in Table 2.31.

(a) Last weekend, Ann rented a car from ECR and Bill rented a car from DRA. They were charged the same amount for their rentals. How many miles did Bill drive?

(b) What is the probability that a randomly selected rent-a-car customer will find a better price at ECR?

(c) Carol handles reservations at DRA. A customer calls and says that he would like to rent a car for the weekend. He also says that according to his estimate of the distance he is going to travel, it will be less expensive for him to rent a car from DRA. What is the expected cost that Carol will charge this customer?

EXERCISE 2.18 Last winter, temperatures recorded in Bismarck, North Dakota ranged from $-36°F$ to $+72°F$. Assume that the standard deviation of the distribution of daily winter temperatures is approximately 18°F. What is the corresponding standard deviation in degrees Celsius? (Note: If A is the temperature in Fahrenheit and B is the same temperature expressed in Celsius, then $B = (5/9) \times (A - 32)$.)

EXERCISE 2.19 A package delivery company experiences high variability in daily customer demand, which in turn results in high variability in the daily workload at the central sorting facility. The company relies on its sorting facility employees working overtime to provide on-time delivery when the workload demand is very high. A sorting facility employee receives a salary of $12/hour for a 40 hour week, and the employee receives $18/hour for every hour worked overtime, that is, for every hour worked over 40 hours in a given week. The number of overtime hours that an employee works in any given week is a random variable, with a mean of 15 hours and a standard deviation of 4 hours. What are the mean, the standard deviation, and the variance of an employee's *total* weekly salary?

EXERCISE 2.20 A manufacturing company of children's clothing has three production plants located in Andover, Bedford, and Concord. The number of items produced per day (in 1,000s) in Andover has a mean of 91 and a standard deviation of 3.2; the mean

TABLE 2.31

Probability distribution of miles driven for weekend automobile rentals.

Miles Driven	Probability
200	0.07
300	0.19
400	0.23
500	0.14
600	0.07
700	0.13
800	0.09
900	0.08

daily production rate in Bedford is 67 with a standard deviation of 2.2; and the mean daily production rate in Concord is 69 with a standard deviation of 5.7. Let X be the total number of items produced per day by the company at all three sites (in 1,000s).

(a) What is the mean of X?

(b) Suppose that production levels in Andover, Bedford, and Concord are independent. What is the variance of X? What is the standard deviation of X?

EXERCISE 2.21 The joint probability distribution of the size of a company's sales force and its yearly sales revenue is as shown in Table 2.32.

(a) Compute the mean, variance, and the standard deviation of the size of the sales force.

(b) Compute the mean, variance, and the standard deviation of yearly sales revenue.

(c) Compute the covariance and correlation of the size of the sales force and yearly sales revenue.

EXERCISE 2.22 A large retail company has stores at two locations in a city: a large department store and a discount outlet store. Weekly sales of umbrellas at the department store have a mean of 147.8 and a standard deviation of 51.0. Weekly sales of umbrellas at the discount outlet store have a mean of 63.2 and a standard deviation of 37.0. Sales of umbrellas in the two stores have a correlation of 0.7.

Umbrellas cost $17 each at the department store and $9 each at the outlet store. Compute the mean, variance, and standard deviation of the total (combined) umbrella sales revenue from the two stores.

EXERCISE 2.23 Let X and Y be the daily sales of Super-Laser printers at the Burtonville and the Arbortown outlets of a consumer electronics department store chain. Suppose that

$$E(X) = 25.0 \text{ and } E(Y) = 33.1,$$
$$SD(X) = 7.0 \text{ and } SD(Y) = 6.2,$$

and $COV(X, Y) = -17.7$. What is $CORR(X, Y)$?

EXERCISE 2.24 In this exercise, we examine the effect of combining investments with positively correlated risks, negatively correlated risks, and uncorrelated risks. A firm is considering a portfolio of assets. The portfolio is comprised of two assets, which we will call "A" and "B." Let X denote the annual rate of return from asset A in the following year, and let Y denote the annual rate of return from asset B in the following year. Suppose that

$$E(X) = 0.15 \text{ and } E(Y) = 0.20,$$
$$SD(X) = 0.05 \text{ and } SD(Y) = 0.06,$$

and $CORR(X, Y) = 0.30$.

TABLE 2.32

Joint probability distribution of sales force and yearly sales revenues.

Probability (p_i)	Number of Sales People (x_i)	Yearly Sales Revenues ($100,000) (y_i)
0.10	15	1.53
0.20	20	1.06
0.25	25	2.61
0.25	30	3.85
0.20	35	4.03

(a) What is the expected return of investing 50% of the portfolio in asset A and 50% of the portfolio in asset B? What is the standard deviation of this return?

(b) Replace $CORR(X, Y) = 0.30$ by $CORR(X, Y) = 0.60$ and answer the questions in part (a). Do the same for $CORR(X, Y) = -0.60, -0.30$, and 0.0.

(c) (Spreadsheet Exercise). Use a spreadsheet to perform the following analysis. Suppose that the fraction of the portfolio that is invested in asset B is f, and so the fraction of the portfolio that is invested in asset A is $(1 - f)$. Letting f vary from $f = 0.0$ to $f = 1.0$ in increments of 5% (that is, $f = 0.0, 0.05, 0.10, 0.15, \ldots$), compute the mean and the standard deviation of the annual rate of return of the portfolio (using the original data for the problem). Notice that the expected return of the portfolio varies (linearly) from 0.15 to 0.20, and the standard deviation of the return varies (non-linearly) from 0.05 to 0.06. Construct a chart plotting the standard deviation as a function of the expected return.

(d) (Spreadsheet Exercise). Perform the same analysis as in part (c) with $CORR(X, Y) = 0.30$ replaced by $CORR(X, Y) = 0.60, 0.0, -0.30$, and -0.60.

EXERCISE 2.25 Suppose a fraction 5% of the microchips produced by a leading microchip manufacturer are defective. Historically, given that a microchip is defective, the inspector (wrongly) accepts the chip 10% of the time, thinking it has no defect. If a microchip is not defective, he always correctly accepts it. Suppose that the inspector inspects 10 microchips.

(a) What is the probability that all 10 microchips in the sample are not defective?

(b) What is the probability that the inspector accepts a particular microchip?

(c) What is the probability that the inspector accepts 9 (out of 10) microchips?

(d) Given that the inspector accepts a microchip, what is the probability that it has no defect?

(e) Given that the inspector accepts all 10 microchips, what it the probability that they all have no defects?

EXERCISE 2.26 According to the "January theory," if the stock market is up in January, it will be up for the whole year (and *vice versa*). Suppose that there is no truth whatever in this theory, and that the likelihood of the stock market moving up or down in any given year is completely independent of the direction of movement in January. Suppose furthermore that the probability of the stock market being up in January is 0.60, and that the probability that the stock market is up for the year is 0.90.

(a) What is the probability that the stock market movement in January will agree with the stock market movement for the entire year?

(b) Over a twenty year time period, what is the probability that the January movement and the annual movement of the stock market will agree for all twenty years?

(c) What is the probability of agreement between the January and annual movements in the stock market in at least 15 of the 20 years?

(d) What is the probability of agreement between the January and annual movements in the stock market in at least 17 of the 20 years?

(e) (Thought exercise.) Given your answers to the previous parts, how might you test whether the January theory is true or false?

EXERCISE 2.27 In this exercise we examine the effects of overbooking in the airline industry. Ontario Gateway Airlines' first class cabins have 10 seats in each plane. Ontario's overbooking policy is to sell up to 11 first class tickets, since cancellations and no-shows are always possible (and indeed are quite likely). For a given flight on Ontario Gateway, there were 11 first class tickets sold. Suppose that each of the 11 persons who purchased tickets has a 20% chance of not showing up for the flight, and that the events that different persons show up for the flight are independent.

(a) What is the probability that at most 5 of the 11 persons who purchased first class tickets show up for the flight?

(b) What is the probability that exactly 10 of the persons who purchased first class tickets show up for the flight?

(c) Suppose that there are 10 seats in first class available and that the cost of each first class ticket is $1,200. (This $1,200 contributes entirely to profit since the variable cost associated with a passenger on a flight is close to zero.) Suppose further that any overbooked seat costs the airline $3,000, which is the cost of the free ticket issued the passenger plus some potential cost in damaged customer relations. (First class passengers do not expect to be bumped!) Thus, for example, if 10 of the first class passengers show up for the flight, the airline's profit is $12,000. If 11 first class passengers show up, the profit is $9,000. What is the expected profit from first class passengers for this flight?

(d) Suppose that only 10 first class tickets were sold. What would be the expected profit from first class passengers for this flight?

(e) (Thought Exercise) People often travel in groups of two or more. Does this affect the independence assumption about passenger behavior? Why or why not?

EXERCISE 2.28 A large shipment of computer chips is known to contain 15% defective chips. Suppose you select 500 chips at random.

(a) What is the expected number of defective chips in your sample?

(b) What is the standard deviation of the number of defective chips in your sample?

EXERCISE 2.29 According to VRT consultants, the probability that your federal tax return will be audited next year is about 0.06 if your income is at least $300,000 and you have not been audited in the previous three years; this probability increases to 0.12 if your income is at least $300,000, and you have been audited in the previous three years.

(a) Suppose that nine taxpayers with incomes of at least $300,000 are randomly selected, and that none of them have been audited in the past three years. What is the probability that exactly one of them will be audited next year? What is the probability that more than one of them will be audited next year?

(b) Suppose that six taxpayers with incomes of at least $300,000 are randomly selected, and that each of them has been audited in the past three years. What is the probability that exactly one of them will be audited next year? What is the probability that more than one of them will be audited next year?

(c) If five taxpayers with incomes of at least $300,000 are randomly selected and exactly two of them have been audited in the past three years, what is the probability that none of these taxpayers will be audited by the IRS next year?

EXERCISE 2.30 In a given area, the probability that a person is exposed to an advertisement of Simco Paper Company is 0.30. Suppose that six people are randomly chosen from among the population in the area.

(a) What is the probability that at least four of these people were exposed to the advertisement?

(b) What is the probability that at most two of these people were exposed to the advertisement?

EXERCISE 2.31 A particular system in a space vehicle must work properly in order for the space vehicle to re-enter the Earth's atmosphere. One particular component of the system operates successfully only 85% of the time. To increase the reliability of the system, four identical versions of the components will be installed in such a way that the system will operate successfully if at least one component is working successfully. Assume that the four components operate independently. What is the probability that the system will fail?

EXERCISE 2.32 It is estimated that 80% of all customers at Speedy Pizza prefer thin crust pizza to thick crust pizza. The remaining 20% prefer thick crust pizza to thin crust pizza. Of the many orders received by Speedy Pizza on a Friday night, six separate orders fail to mention the type of crust desired. Unable to contact the six customers and hoping to minimize disappointments, the manager of Speedy Pizza has decided to send all of the six customers thin crust pizzas.

(a) Let X be the number of customers (among the six) who prefer the thin crust pizza. What assumptions must be satisfied in order for X to obey a binomial distribution?

(b) Write down the probability distribution of X.

(c) What is the probability that exactly three of the six customers will prefer thick crust pizza, and so be unsatisfied?

(d) What is the expected number of customers who will prefer thin crust pizza? What is the standard deviation of the number of customers who will prefer thin crust pizza?

EXERCISE 2.33 The FNO Market Index Fund is a mutual fund that trades on the stock exchange, and whose stock price varies from day to day. In any given month, the probability that its stock price will increase is 0.65. On average, on months that its stock price increases, the expected increase in its stock price is 5%. On months that its stock price decreases, the expected decrease in the stock price is 4%.

(a) What is the probability that the FNO Market Index Fund will increase in exactly seven of the next twelve months?

(b) What is the expected change in the FNO Market Index Fund for next year? For the purposes of this question, you may assume that the increase in the stock price is exactly 5% in months when the stock price increases, and the decrease in the stock price is exactly 4% in months when the stock price decreases.

EXERCISE 2.34 A customer at ShoreBank is called a "frequent ATM user" if he/she uses an ATM (Automated Teller Machine) for a majority of his/her transactions. According to bank records of transactions, 40% of all ShoreBank customers are frequent ATM users. Anna and Bill are part of a team of market research specialists at ShoreBank that are investigating ways to improve customer services at the bank.

The team has decided to form a customer focus group by choosing ten ShoreBank customers at random.

(a) Anna is of the opinion that frequent ATM users have the most to contribute to the focus group. She hopes that at least four members of the focus group will be frequent ATM users. What is the probability of this event happening?

(b) Bill, on the other hand, thinks that the input from those customers who are not frequent ATM users is even more important for the focus group. He hopes that the focus group will include at least four customers who are not frequent ATM users. What is the probability of this event happening?

(c) What is the probability that the focus group will satisfy both Anna's and Bill's wishes?

EXERCISE 2.35 There are five tennis clubs in Cambridge. Each club can only accept a limited number of members, due to space and capacity limitations. Jim would like to join one of these tennis clubs. He assumes that membership decisions are made independently by each club, and he estimates that his chances of being accepted for membership by any particular club is 65%.

(a) If Jim applies for membership at all five clubs, what are his chances of being accepted for membership by exactly three clubs?

(b) What are his chances of being accepted for membership by at least three clubs?

(c) Three of the five clubs are located within walking distance of Jim's apartment. What are his chances of being accepted for membership by at least one of these three clubs?

EXERCISE 2.36 The owner of a charter fishing boat has found that 12% of his passengers become seasick during a half-day fishing trip. He has only two beds below deck to accommodate those who become ill. About to embark on a typical half-day trip, he has 6 passengers on board. What is the probability that there will be enough room below deck to accommodate those who become ill?

EXERCISE 2.37 A company has installed five intrusion-detection devices in an office building. The devices are very sensitive and, on any given night, each one has a 10% chance of mistakenly sounding an alarm when no intruder is present. If two or more of the devices are activated on the same night, the intrusion system automatically sends a signal to the local police. If no intruder is present on a given night, what is the probability that the system will make the mistake of calling the police?

EXERCISE 2.38 Ninety percent of residential gas customers in Illinois use gas for residential heating. Sixteen residential gas customers are randomly selected to participate in a panel discussion for a state energy fair. A gas industry executive is hopeful that at least twelve of the panel members, i.e., 75%, will come from homes in which gas is used for residential heating. If you were the executive's assistant, what degree of assurance could you give the executive that her 75% goal might be reached or exceeded?

Continuous Probability Distributions and Their Applications

CONTENTS

IN THIS CHAPTER, WE INTRODUCE AND DEVELOP METHODS FOR WORKING WITH **continuous** random variables. We develop the notions of the **probability density function** and the **cumulative distribution function** of a random variable as ways to describe and work effectively with a continuous random variable. We then present the **Normal distribution**, which is used to model the vast majority of continuous random variables that arise in practice. We also present the **Central Limit Theorem**, which is the most far-reaching result in all of probability and which explains why the Normal distribution is so pervasive in practice. The Central Limit Theorem also lays the foundation for statistical sampling, which is the subject of Chapter 4.

3.1 | CONTINUOUS RANDOM VARIABLES

In the previous chapter, we introduced the notion of a random variable, which is a numerical outcome of a probability model. We then discussed the distinction between a discrete random variable (which can only take on numerical values that are distinct and separate) as opposed to a continuous random variable (which can take on any numerical value within some interval, with no gaps between adjacent values). In this chapter, we concentrate entirely on the fundamentals of continuous random variables, their distributions, and their properties. We start with a simple example.

As an example of a **continuous** random variable, let X denote the width of a steel plate, measured in millimeters (mm), that is produced in a production process at Lancaster Steel, Inc. As a consequence of random errors due to minor temperature changes, mechanical tolerances, etc., the value of X is uncertain, and so X is a random variable. Suppose that X can take on any value within the range from 52.2 mm to 65.8 mm. The value of X is not limited to whole numbers in millimeters (or in centimeters, inches, feet, or any other measure). Therefore, X is a continuous random variable.

Other examples of continuous random variables include the time it takes to unload railroad cars at a depot, the height of a randomly chosen person, the amount of rainfall in Boston next April, and the temperature at noon tomorrow in Washington, D.C. Continuous random variables are natural models for uncertain times, distances, and measurements, because these quantities vary continuously with no gaps in the possible values that they can take.

Let us return to the example of the random variable X denoting the width of a steel plate produced at Lancaster Steel, Inc. Because there are an infinite number of values that X might take, the probability assigned to any one particular value is essentially zero. But this does not mean that we cannot speak probabilistically about a continuous random variable. It might make little sense to ask what is the probability that the value of X is exactly 59.2364 mm, but it *is* sensible to ask what is the probability that the value of X will be between 58.1 mm and 60.4 mm. In general, for continuous random variables, a probabilistic question is well-posed if it refers to a range of values on an *interval*, rather than to one single specific value.

A natural question is how do we describe the distribution of a continuous random variable? In the discrete case, we were able to give a complete description of the distribution of the random variable by listing all of the possible values x_i of the discrete random variable and their corresponding probabilities p_i. For a continuous random variable, we describe its probability distribution in two different ways: one way is called the **probability density function**, or **pdf** for short. The other description is called the **cumulative distribution function**, or **cdf** for short. We start our discussion with the pdf, as it is a bit more intuitive.

3.2   THE PROBABILITY DENSITY FUNCTION

The first way that we describe the distribution of a continuous random variable is in terms of its **probability density function**, or **pdf**, which is usually denoted by $f(t)$.

> The probability density function (pdf) of a random variable X has the following two characteristics:
>
> **(a)** The area lying under the pdf curve is equal to one, and
>
> **(b)** The probability that X lies between any two given values a and b is equal to the area under the curve between a and b.

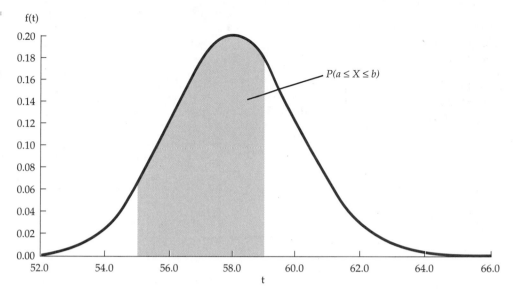

The probability density function $f(t)$ of a random variable X. The area shown is $P(55.0 \leq X \leq 59.0)$.

An example of a probability density function is displayed in Figure 3.1. The probability density function can be thought of as a smoothed histogram of the random variable X. The pdf curve captures our intuition as to where the more likely and the less likely values of X will lie.

Returning again to the example of the random variable X denoting the width of a steel plate produced at Lancaster Steel, Inc., suppose that the probability density function for the random variable X is the function shown in Figure 3.1. Then notice that X is more likely to take on values near 58.0 mm, and is less likely to take on values greater than 62.0 mm or less than 54.0 mm. In fact, the figure indicates that X is less and less likely to take on values farther away from 58.0 mm (in either direction). Notice that the probability density function gives us a visually intuitive portrait of the distribution of the random variable X.

The probability density function portrayed in Figure 3.1 is not uniform in nature; some values of X are indeed more likely than others. In particular, values near 58.0 mm are more likely than values near 63.0 mm.

THE UNIFORM DISTRIBUTION

If the random variable X is equally likely to take on any value in the range from a to b (where $b > a$) then we say that X obeys a **uniform distribution** over the range from a to b. From its definition, the probability density function $f(t)$ for X must have the same height over the entire range from a to b. Therefore the probability density function for X must be shaped as pictured in Figure 3.2. Notice in the figure that the pdf of a uniformly distributed random variable is flat in the range from a to b.

Again looking at Figure 3.2, notice that the pdf $f(t)$ has a height of h for all values between a and b. Because the area lying under the curve of the probability density function $f(t)$ must equal to one, then from Figure 3.2, we see that this area is $h \cdot (b - a)$. Since this area must be equal to one, it follows that

$$h = \frac{1}{b - a}.$$

FIGURE 3.2
The probability
density function $f(t)$
of a uniformly
distributed random
variable X.

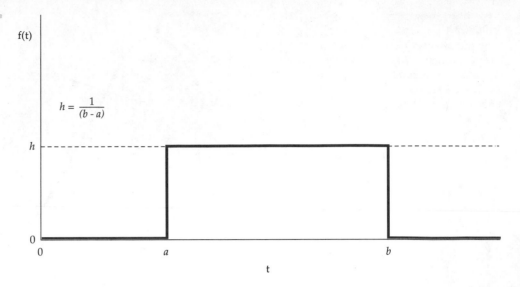

Therefore, if X obeys a uniform distribution over the range from a to b, its probability density function is given by

$$f(t) = \begin{cases} \dfrac{1}{b-a} & \text{if } a \leq t \leq b, \\ 0 & \text{otherwise.} \end{cases}$$

If X obeys a uniform distribution over the range from a to b, we write this in shorthand as

$$X \sim U[a, b],$$

which is read as "X is uniformly distributed over the range from a to b" or "X obeys a uniform distribution over the range from a to b."

We summarize the preceding presentation as follows:

The random variable X obeys a uniform distribution over the range from a to b if X is equally likely to take on any value in the range from a to b. We write this as $X \sim U[a, b]$. The probability density function of $f(t)$ of X is given by:

$$f(t) = \begin{cases} \dfrac{1}{b-a} & \text{if } a \leq t \leq b, \\ 0 & \text{otherwise.} \end{cases}$$

Example 3.1 — Lifetime of an Automobile Exhaust System

Suppose that Michigan Motors, Inc. has determined that the lifetime of the exhaust system of its automobiles obeys a uniform distribution in the range between 2.5 years and 7.0 years. Let L be the random variable that denotes the lifetime of the exhaust system of any one of the automobiles manufactured by Michigan Motors. Then L obeys a uniform distribution in the range from $a = 2.5$ years to $b = 7.0$ years. Note that $b - a = 7.0 - 2.5 = 4.5$. Therefore the probability density function $f(t)$ of L is given by

FIGURE 3.3
The probability density function $f(t)$ of the lifetime of the exhaust system.

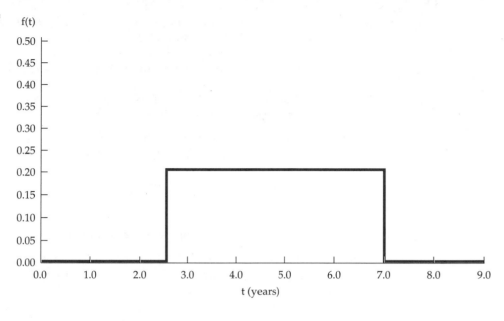

$$f(t) = \begin{cases} \dfrac{1}{4.5} & \text{if } 2.5 \le t \le 7.0, \\ 0 & \text{otherwise.} \end{cases}$$

Figure 3.3 shows the probability density function of L.

3.3   THE CUMULATIVE DISTRIBUTION FUNCTION

We have just seen that the probability density function (pdf) of a continuous random variable conveys an intuitive picture of the distribution of a continuous random variable. In most applications involving continuous random variables, we need to compute the probability that the random variable X takes on a value in a pre-specified range. That is, for some numbers a and b, we need to compute the probability that X lies somewhere between a and b. We write this probability as

$$P(a \le X \le b),$$

which is read as "the probability that X takes on a value no smaller than a and no larger than b." Unfortunately, if we want to actually compute $P(a \le X \le b)$, we would have to compute the area under the curve of the pdf in the range from a to b as in Figure 3.1, which is very inconvenient to do. To bypass this difficulty, we instead work with the **cumulative distribution function** of the random variable, abbreviated **cdf**, which is defined as follows:

For a given number t, the **cumulative distribution function (cdf)** $F(t)$ of a continuous random variable X is defined by
$$F(t) = P(X \le t).$$

In words, $F(t)$ is the probability that X does not exceed t. In general, if we have a description of the cumulative distribution function $F(t)$, we can answer all relevant questions about the behavior of the random variable X. Notice that for any random variable X, the cdf $F(t)$ must have the following two properties:

(a) $F(t) \geq 0.0$ and $F(t) \leq 1.0$. This is because the value of $F(t)$ is a probability and so must be between 0.0 and 1.0.

(b) $F(t)$ is an increasing function of t. This is because as t gets larger, there is of course a greater likelihood that X will take on a value less than or equal to t.

An example of a cdf is shown in Figure 3.4.

Example 3.2 — Width of a Steel Plate, continued

Let us return again to the example of the random variable X denoting the width of a steel plate produced at Lancaster Steel, Inc. Suppose that the cumulative distribution function of X is as shown in Figure 3.4. According to Figure 3.4, for example,

$$F(56.0) = P(X \leq 56.0 \text{ mm}) = 0.17.$$

This means that 17% of all steel plates produced in the production process will have a width of 56.0 mm or less. Clearly

$$P(X > 56.0) = 1 - P(X \leq 56.0) = 1.0 - 0.17 = 0.83,$$

and so 83% of all steel plates produced in the production process will have a width greater than 56.0 mm.

Suppose that we would like to know the probability that X will take on a value in the range from 56.0 mm to 59.0 mm. We write this as

$$P(56.0 \leq X \leq 59.0).$$

FIGURE 3.4

The cumulative distribution function $F(t)$ of X, the width of a steel plate.

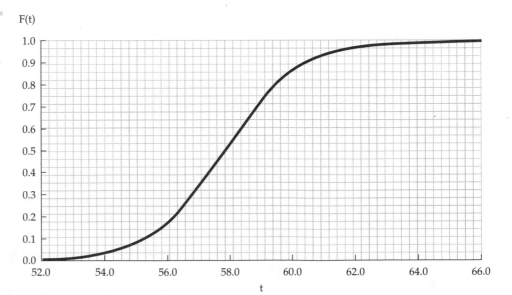

Now notice that

$$P(56.0 \leq X \leq 59.0) = P(X \leq 59.0) - P(X \leq 56.0)$$
$$= F(59.0) - F(56.0)$$
$$= 0.70 - 0.17 = 0.53.$$

This means that 53% of all steel plates produced by Lancaster Steel will have a width that is at least 56.0 mm and is at most 59.0 mm.

As we have just seen, the knowledge of the cumulative distribution function $F(t)$ of a random variable X enables us to answer many questions about the random variable. Suppose that we wish to compute

$$P(X > t)$$

for some value of t. Then

$$P(X > t) = 1 - P(X \leq t) = 1 - F(t).$$

Suppose that we wish to compute

$$P(c \leq x \leq d)$$

for two given numbers c and d, where $d > c$. Then

$$P(X \leq d) = P(X < c) + P(c \leq X \leq d)$$

or, equivalently,

$$P(c \leq X \leq d) = F(d) - F(c).$$

Hence a simple subtraction involving $F(t)$ at two different values of t yields the answer.

Notice that since the probability that X takes on any particular value is zero, we have

$$P(X \leq t) = P(X < t),$$

and so we can interchange "$\leq$" and "$<$" freely in any probability expressions involving continuous random variables. We summarize this discussion as follows:

Suppose that X is a continuous random variable whose cdf is given by $F(t)$. Then

- $P(X \leq t) = F(t)$

- $P(X > t) = 1 - F(t)$,

- $P(c \leq X \leq d) = F(d) - F(c)$, and

- we can interchange "$\leq$" and "$<$" in any probability expressions involving X.

The Cumulative Distribution Function of the Uniform Distribution

Suppose that X is a random variable that obeys the uniform distribution in the range from a to b. Let us calculate the cumulative distribution function $F(t)$ for X. If t is below a, then $F(t)$, the probability that X does not exceed t, must be zero. After all, X must be at least a, so it necessarily falls above any number lower than a. By similar reasoning, $F(t) = 1.0$ when $t > b$, because X can never achieve a value greater than b. Let us next calculate $F(t)$ for t in the range between a and b. From the second property of a probability density function, the probability that X lies between any two given values is equal to the area under the pdf curve between these two values. From Figure 3.2, the area under the pdf curve of the uniform distribution between a and t is $h \cdot (t - a)$ where $h = \dfrac{1}{b - a}$, and so we conclude that for t in the range between a and b that

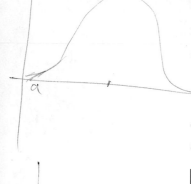

$$F(t) = \frac{t - a}{b - a}.$$

The complete description of the cdf of the uniform distribution is summarized below and is illustrated in Figure 3.5.

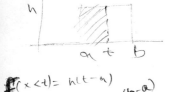
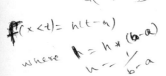

Suppose that X obeys a uniform distribution in the range from a to b. Then the cumulative distribution function $F(t)$ of X is given by

$$F(t) = \begin{cases} 0.0 & \text{if } t < a, \\ \dfrac{t - a}{b - a} & \text{if } a \le t \le b \\ 1.0 & \text{if } t > b. \end{cases}$$

The next example illustrates an application of the uniform distribution.

FIGURE 3.5

The cumulative distribution function $F(t)$ of a uniformly distributed random variable X.

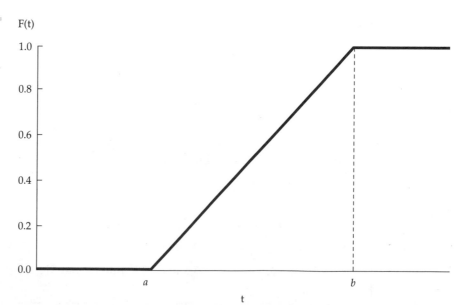

Example 3.3 — Lifetime of an Automobile Exhaust System, continued

Recall Example 3.1, which concerns the distribution of the lifetime of the exhaust system of the automobiles produced by Michigan Motors, Inc. Suppose that Michigan Motors has determined that the lifetime of the exhaust system of any one of its automobiles obeys a uniform distribution in the range from $a = 2.5$ years to $b = 7.0$ years. Suppose that Michigan Motors has a five-year warranty on all parts, and that they will replace any defective part within five years of purchase. What is the probability that any one of their automobiles will need to have its exhaust system replaced within the warranty period?

To answer this question, we first rephrase the question in terms of probability. Let L be the random variable that denotes the lifetime of the exhaust system of one of the automobiles produced by Michigan Motors. We would like to compute the probability that L is less than or equal to 5.0, namely:

$$P(L \leq 5.0).$$

Now notice that $P(L \leq 5.0) = F(5.0)$ where $F(t)$ is the cumulative distribution function of L. From the formula above,

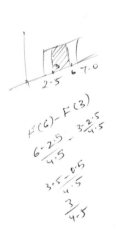

$$F(5.0) = P(L \leq 5.0) = \frac{5.0 - 2.5}{7.0 - 2.5} = \frac{2.5}{4.5} = 0.556.$$

This means that there is a 55.6% likelihood that any one of the automobiles produced by Michigan Motors will need to have its exhaust system replaced within the warranty period.

Continuing the example, suppose that we would like to know the probability that the lifetime of the exhaust system of any one of the automobiles will be between 3 and 6 years. That is, we would like to compute

$$P(3.0 \leq L \leq 6.0).$$

From the properties of the cdf, we have that

$$P(3.0 \leq L \leq 6.0) = F(6.0) - F(3.0).$$

And from the formula for the cdf of the uniform distribution, we have that

$$P(3.0 \leq L \leq 6.0) = F(6.0) - F(3.0) = \frac{6.0 - 2.5}{7.0 - 2.5} - \frac{3.0 - 2.5}{7.0 - 2.5} = 0.667.$$

Therefore there is a 66.7% likelihood that the exhaust system of any of their automobiles will have a lifetime between 3 and 6 years.

Summary Measures for Continuous Random Variables

Recall from Chapter 2 that for a discrete random variable X, we defined the mean $\mu = E(X)$, the variance $\text{VAR}(X) = \sigma^2$, and the standard deviation $\text{SD}(X) = \sigma$ of X, in terms of relatively straightforward formulas involving the possible values x_i of the discrete random variable and their corresponding probabilities p_i. As it turns out, when X is a continuous random variable, it is also possible to define the mean $E(X) = \mu$, the variance $\text{VAR}(X) = \sigma^2$, and the standard deviation $\text{SD}(X) = \sigma$ of X.

However, the formulas for these summary measures involve tools from calculus.[1] Nevertheless when X is a continuous random variable, we will still talk about and refer to the mean, the variance, and the standard deviation of X, just as we did for discrete random variables. Furthermore these summary measures have the exact same interpretations as in the case of a discrete random variable, namely $E(X) = \mu$ is a measure of central tendency, $\mathrm{VAR}(X) = \sigma^2$ is the expected squared deviation from the mean, and $\mathrm{SD}(X) = \sigma$ is the square root of the variance.

3.4   THE NORMAL DISTRIBUTION

By far the most important continuous distribution model in all of probability and statistics is the **Normal** (or Gaussian) distribution. In fact, the name "Normal" derives from the fact that this distribution arises so frequently and in so many different applications that it is simply the "normal" model of probability, and it has played an important role in probability from the 16th century to the present. The probability density function $f(t)$ of a Normal distribution is the well-known bell-shaped curve pictured in Figure 3.6.

A random variable X that obeys a Normal distribution is completely characterized by two parameters, its mean μ and its standard deviation σ. Thus if X obeys a

FIGURE 3.6

The probability density function $f(t)$ of a Normally distributed random variable.

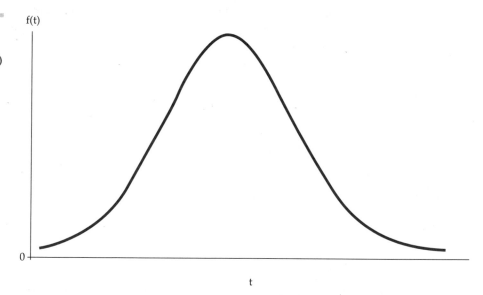

---

[1] If $f(t)$ is the pdf of a continuous random variable X that takes values between a and b, the total area under the curve is

$$\int_a^b f(t)dt = 1,$$

then the mean μ, and the variance σ^2 are given by

$$\mu = \int_a^b t \cdot f(t)dt,$$

$$\sigma^2 = \int_a^b (t - \mu)^2 \cdot f(t)dt.$$

Normal distribution, then $E(X) = \mu$, $SD(X) = \sigma$, and $VAR(X) = \sigma^2$. If X obeys a Normal distribution with mean μ and standard deviation σ, we write this as

$$X \sim N(\mu, \sigma),$$

which is read as "X is Normally distributed with mean μ and standard deviation σ" or "X is a random variable that obeys the Normal distribution with mean μ and standard deviation σ."

The mathematical formula for the probability density function of the Normal distribution is somewhat complex.[2] However, it is fortunate that we will *not* need the formula for the pdf in order to work effectively with the Normal distribution in applications.

The Normal probability density function has a number of very important characteristics. The high point of the bell shape occurs at the mean μ of the distribution. Therefore its bell-shape tells us that X is more likely to take values closer to its mean μ than far from its mean. The bell-shaped curve is also symmetric about the mean, which means that for any number t one has $f(\mu + t) = f(\mu - t)$. Therefore, the Normal random variable X is equally likely to take on values about t units above its mean as it is to take on values about t units below its mean.

In order to develop further intuition regarding the Normal distribution, in Figure 3.7 we plot the probability density functions of three Normally distributed random variables X, Y, and W that have the same standard deviation $\sigma = 1.0$, but the mean of X is less than the mean of Y, which is in turn less than the mean of W. We see from Figure 3.7 that for different values of the mean, the bell-shaped curve of the probability density function of the Normal distribution has the exact same shape, but is simply shifted to the left or to the right.

FIGURE 3.7

The probability density functions of three Normally distributed random variables, X, Y, and W, with different means but with the same standard deviation.

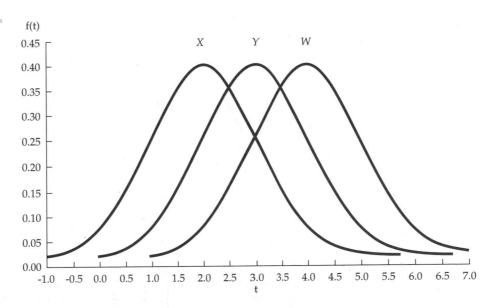

---

[2]If X obeys a Normal distribution with mean μ and standard deviation σ, then the pdf of X is given by

$$f(t) = \frac{1}{\sqrt{2\pi}\sigma} e^{\left(-\frac{(t-\mu)^2}{2\sigma^2}\right)}.$$

Note that this formula involves three of the most important constants in mathematics, namely $\pi = 3.14159\ldots$, $e = 2.718\ldots$, and $\sqrt{2} = 1.4142\ldots$.

FIGURE 3.8

The probability density functions of three Normally distributed random variables, *R*, *S*, and *T*, with different standard deviations but with the same mean.

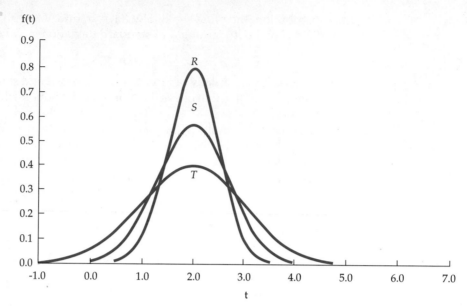

FIGURE 3.9

The distribution of the monthly rates of return of Valley Textile Company approximately obeys a Normal distribution.

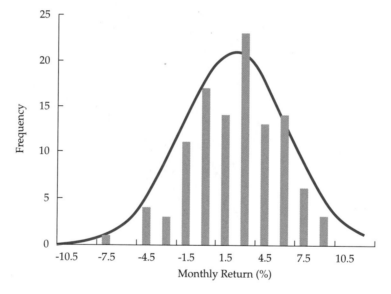

In Figure 3.8, we plot the probability density functions of three Normally distributed random variables, *R*, *S*, and *T*, that have the same mean $\mu = 2.0$, but the standard deviation of *R* is less than the standard deviation of *S*, which is less than the standard deviation of *T*. Notice that for larger values of the standard deviation, the bell shape of the probability density function gets flatter and more spread out. This is as expected, since the standard deviation measures the extent of the spread around the mean.

Many uncertain phenomena in everyday life obey or approximately obey a Normal distribution. Examples include distributions of returns on stocks and the distributions of returns on mutual funds, the distribution of sales of products, the distribution of standardized test scores such as the GMAT, the distribution of a per-

TABLE 3.1

Monthly rate of
return of Valley
Textile Company
from January, 1988
through February,
1997.

Month	Rate of Return(%)	Month	Rate of Return(%)	Month	Rate of Return(%)	Month	Rate of Return(%)
Jan-88	3.58	May-90	−4.77	Sep-92	5.26	Jan-95	1.74
Feb-88	2.41	Jun-90	6.43	Oct-92	0.86	Feb-95	3.99
Mar-88	2.47	Jul-90	−4.07	Nov-92	2.30	Mar-95	2.74
Apr-88	1.99	Aug-90	1.30	Dec-92	−2.10	Apr-95	4.56
May-88	−1.40	Sep-90	0.24	Jan-93	−2.38	May-95	−0.07
Jun-88	7.50	Oct-90	−1.46	Feb-93	1.51	Jun-95	−1.39
Jul-88	4.60	Nov-90	1.85	Mar-93	1.54	Jul-95	5.69
Aug-88	4.18	Dec-90	2.77	Apr-93	2.02	Aug-95	3.82
Sep-88	−2.13	Jan-91	5.72	May-93	3.35	Sep-95	2.89
Oct-88	4.84	Feb-91	5.94	Jun-93	−0.72	Oct-95	−2.64
Nov-88	5.00	Mar-91	−1.11	Jul-93	−0.44	Nov-95	−1.06
Dec-88	3.53	Apr-91	2.76	Aug-93	−1.56	Dec-95	3.10
Jan-89	3.22	May-91	2.28	Sep-93	3.69	Jan-96	1.46
Feb-89	5.32	Jun-91	−2.19	Oct-93	2.28	Feb-96	0.72
Mar-89	−2.18	Jul-91	3.33	Nov-93	−3.48	Mar-96	7.24
Apr-89	−1.47	Aug-91	−0.46	Dec-93	3.68	Apr-96	−1.65
May-89	−5.69	Sep-91	0.65	Jan-94	−1.78	May-96	2.66
Jun-89	6.65	Oct-91	4.80	Feb-94	3.66	Jun-96	7.87
Jul-89	8.76	Nov-91	0.46	Mar-94	1.12	Jul-96	7.00
Aug-89	−0.24	Dec-91	2.03	Apr-94	0.03	Aug-96	5.93
Sep-89	3.00	Jan-92	−0.07	May-94	2.99	Sep-96	0.89
Oct-89	−1.19	Feb-92	5.11	Jun-94	4.64	Oct-96	6.52
Nov-89	−1.12	Mar-92	−7.68	Jul-94	−2.69	Nov-96	0.76
Dec-89	−1.63	Apr-92	4.16	Aug-94	−0.75	Dec-96	−1.43
Jan-90	2.16	May-92	1.89	Sep-94	−4.83	Jan-97	0.43
Feb-90	1.73	Jun-92	2.12	Oct-94	0.23	Feb-97	0.56
Mar-90	6.40	Jul-92	−3.51	Nov-94	5.06		
Apr-90	−5.59	Aug-92	2.07	Dec-94	−0.90		

son's height or weight in the general population, etc. Later in this chapter, we will see why so many different quantities "must" approximately obey a Normal distribution as a consequence of a broad dictum known as the Central Limit Theorem.

Example 3.4 – The Distribution of Monthly Rates of Return of the Valley Textile Company

The monthly returns of the Valley Textile Company in the period from January, 1988 through February, 1997 is shown in Table 3.1. If we plot a histogram of these numbers in increments of 1.5%, we obtain the bar chart shown in Figure 3.9. Overlayed on the bar chart is the plot of a Normal probability density function. Notice that the Normal pdf curve is in close agreement with the data. This is but one illustration that many uncertain quantities approximately obey a Normal distribution.

Example 3.5 – The Distribution of Revenues among Sales Districts at Simco Foods, Inc.

Table 3.2 shows the net revenue last year of the 185 sales districts at Simco Foods, Inc. If we plot a histogram of these number in increments of $4 million, we obtain the bar chart shown in Figure 3.10. Overlayed on the bar chart is the plot of a Normal probability density function. Notice that the Normal pdf curve is in close agreement with the data.

TABLE 3.2

Net revenues of 185 sales districts of Simco Foods, Inc.

District	Net Revenues ($ Million)	District	Net Revenues ($ Million)	District	Net Revenues ($ Million)	District	Net Revenues ($ Million)
1	−6.83	48	15.77	95	16.98	142	3.55
2	13.64	49	15.94	96	10.04	143	9.48
3	16.72	50	−3.65	97	12.30	144	11.42
4	14.23	51	27.37	98	3.82	145	8.01
5	16.65	52	11.03	99	17.30	146	13.83
6	12.37	53	14.38	100	8.43	147	−9.82
7	12.87	54	15.12	101	14.14	148	12.89
8	7.80	55	4.96	102	13.65	149	5.10
9	6.41	56	16.39	103	10.10	150	19.32
10	8.06	57	15.48	104	8.02	151	31.18
11	26.56	58	7.58	105	22.68	152	6.77
12	−3.23	59	19.16	106	−4.40	153	12.52
13	10.10	60	7.24	107	18.53	154	6.15
14	16.17	61	8.57	108	10.78	155	14.66
15	14.08	62	8.97	109	7.63	156	16.69
16	10.31	63	14.79	110	19.59	157	9.25
17	9.10	64	23.36	111	18.08	158	6.20
18	9.82	65	7.44	112	−6.82	159	11.57
19	13.00	66	3.38	113	15.86	160	23.27
20	13.06	67	−0.94	114	26.88	161	−0.59
21	14.60	68	19.28	115	16.55	162	26.31
22	6.24	69	−5.17	116	13.44	163	16.47
23	4.82	70	3.06	117	9.35	164	16.84
24	11.31	71	10.79	118	14.02	165	7.18
25	4.03	72	6.15	119	16.67	166	11.63
26	9.92	73	1.67	120	0.58	167	12.64
27	6.62	74	6.98	121	9.12	168	12.53
28	22.29	75	3.70	122	−0.04	169	9.23
29	−3.71	76	12.15	123	13.17	170	19.39
30	6.50	77	9.54	124	5.35	171	17.93
31	−4.18	78	14.34	125	14.28	172	14.88
32	8.21	79	6.58	126	26.83	173	1.14
33	12.13	80	3.85	127	31.85	174	2.22
34	−5.90	81	−1.95	128	1.49	175	11.84
35	10.32	82	9.04	129	17.44	176	12.09
36	13.97	83	8.22	130	12.16	177	−3.03
37	4.45	84	13.71	131	26.42	178	10.90
38	3.46	85	25.99	132	−4.62	179	6.71
39	19.53	86	6.64	133	22.73	180	15.31
40	20.97	87	11.47	134	14.43	181	15.01
41	15.51	88	2.30	135	20.97	182	−0.95
42	14.20	89	17.72	136	8.28	183	1.07
43	11.41	90	4.81	137	17.29	184	5.10
44	11.13	91	7.28	138	10.19	185	13.61
45	17.49	92	12.98	139	16.74		
46	10.72	93	21.36	140	7.98		
47	15.87	94	15.70	141	9.80		

Example 3.6—The Distribution of Daily Lunch-time Revenue at a Fast-Food Restaurant

Table 3.3 shows the relative frequency of lunch-time revenue at a fast-food restaurant for 210 weekdays in 1997, in various bands of $200 increments, and Figure 3.11 displays a bar chart of the relative frequency of the lunch-time revenue, taken from the

FIGURE 3.10

The distribution of net revenue of the sales districts of Simco Foods approximately obeys a Normal distribution.

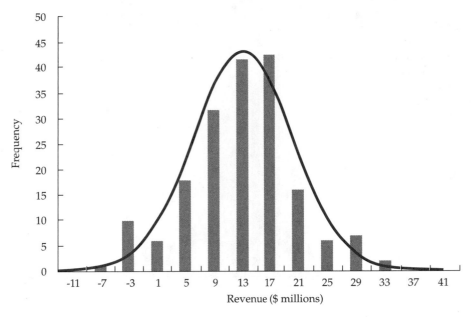

FIGURE 3.11

The distribution of daily lunch-time revenue at a fast-food restaurant approximately obeys a Normal distribution.

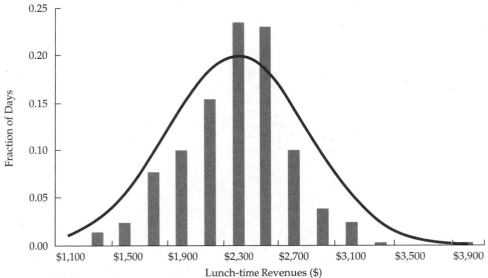

TABLE 3.3

Relative frequency of lunch-time revenues at a fast-food restaurant for 210 days in 1997.

Range of Revenue	Number of Days	Fraction of Days
$1,000 to $1,200	0	0.000
$1,200 to $1,400	3	0.014
$1,400 to $1,600	5	0.024
$1,600 to $1,800	16	0.076
$1,800 to $2,000	21	0.100
$2,000 to $2,200	32	0.152
$2,200 to $2,400	49	0.233
$2,400 to $2,600	48	0.229
$2,600 to $2,800	21	0.100
$2,800 to $3,000	8	0.038
$3,000 to $3,200	5	0.024
$3,200 to $3,400	1	0.005
$3,400 to $3,600	0	0.000
$3,600 to $3,800	0	0.000
$3,800 to $4,000	1	0.005

The distribution of income of full-time year-round female workers does not obey a Normal distribution.

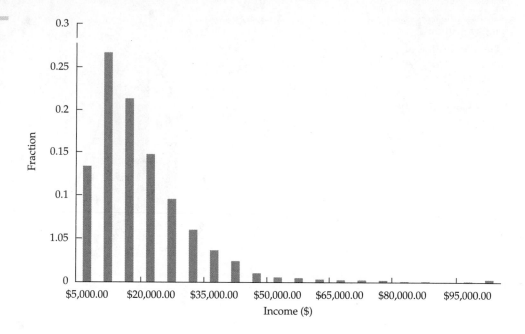

TABLE 3.4
Income of full-time year-round female workers based on the U.S. Census, 1990.

Range of Incomes	Fraction of Full-time Female Workers
$0 to $5,000	0.132
$5,000 to $10,000	0.264
$10,000 to $15,000	0.211
$15,000 to $20,000	0.145
$20,000 to $25,000	0.094
$25,000 to $30,000	0.058
$30,000 to $35,000	0.035
$35,000 to $40,000	0.023
$40,000 to $45,000	0.009
$45,000 to $50,000	0.004
$50,000 to $55,000	0.003
$55,000 to $60,000	0.002
$60,000 to $65,000	0.002
$65,000 to $70,000	0.001
$70,000 to $75,000	0.002
$75,000 to $80,000	0.000
$80,000 to $85,000	0.000
$85,000 to $90,000	0.000
$90,000 to $95,000	0.001
$95,000 and higher	0.014

final column of Table 3.3. Overlayed on the bar chart is the plot of a Normal probability density function. Notice that the Normal pdf curve is in close agreement with the data.

Example 3.7 — Income of Full-Time Female Workers

Table 3.4 and Figure 3.12 show the data and a plot of the histogram of the income of full-time female workers based on the U.S. Census of 1990. Notice that a Normal probability density function is *not* consistent with the data as portrayed in the figure.

While the Normal distribution arises in very many arenas, there are also occasions where it does not arise. As the figure shows, it would be inappropriate to model the distribution of income of full-time female workers as a random variable obeying a Normal distribution.

3.5 COMPUTING PROBABILITIES FOR THE NORMAL DISTRIBUTION

In this section, we show how to compute probabilities for a random variable X that obeys a Normal distribution with mean μ and standard deviation σ. We will show how to compute any probability such as

$$P(a \leq X \leq b)$$

for given numbers a and b. As a means toward this goal, we first show how to compute such probabilities when our random variable obeys a specific instance of the Normal distribution called the **standard Normal** distribution, defined as follows.

> A random variable Z obeys a **standard Normal** distribution if Z is Normally distributed with mean $\mu = 0.0$ and standard deviation $\sigma = 1.0$. In this case, we write
>
> $$Z \sim N(0, 1).$$

We usually reserve the symbol Z for a random variable that obeys a standard Normal distribution.

Suppose that the random variable Z obeys a standard Normal distribution. We would like to have a formula for the cumulative distribution function (cdf) $F(z)$ of Z, where

$$F(z) = P(Z \leq z) \quad \text{for any value of } z.$$

It turns out that no such explicit formula for $F(z)$ exists. Recall that for any particular value of z, the value of $F(z)$ is the area under the probability density function to the left of z in the bell-shaped curve for a standard Normal density function, as shown in Figure 3.13. Scientists have computed the area under the pdf curve of the standard Normal distribution to a high degree of accuracy for a wide variety of values of z and have compiled their computations into a **standard Normal table**. A standard Normal table is a listing of the values $F(z) = P(Z \leq z)$ for all z, and such a table appears in the Appendix of this book in Table A.1.

Let us see just how to use a standard Normal table. Suppose that Z obeys a standard Normal distribution, and that we would like to compute $F(z)$ where $z = 1.63$, for example. That is, we want to compute:

$$F(1.63) = P(Z \leq 1.63).$$

Examining Table A.1, we look up the first two digits "1.6" of the number "1.63" in the first column of the table and then look up the third digit "3" of the number "1.63" in the column heading. We then read the number "0.9484" in the body of the table. This means that

$$F(1.63) = P(Z \leq 1.63) = 0.9484.$$

FIGURE 3.13

The standard Normal table shows values of the cdf of a standard Normal random variable. It corresponds to the area under the pdf curve to the left of z.

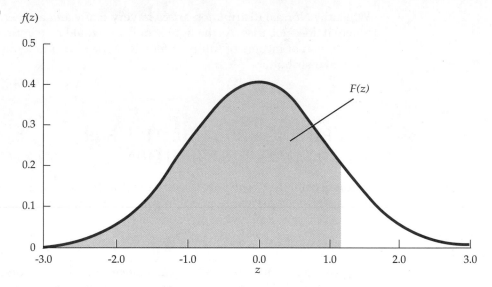

Similarly, we can use the table to determine:

$$P(Z \le 1.00) = 0.8413,$$
$$P(Z \le 0.00) = 0.5,$$
$$P(Z \le -1.55) = 0.0606,$$

for example.

We can also use Table A.1 to answer another important type of question related to the standard Normal distribution called the "reverse" probability question. Suppose that we want to know the value of z for which

$$F(z) = P(Z \le z) = 0.67.$$

If we look up the number "0.67" in the body of the standard Normal table, we find that "0.6700" appears in the body of the table corresponding to a value of z of $z = 0.44$, that is,

$$F(0.44) = P(Z \le 0.44) = 0.67.$$

Suppose instead that we want to know that value of z for which

$$F(z) = P(Z \le z) = 0.80.$$

If we look up the number "0.80" in the body of the standard Normal table, we find that "0.8000" does not appear, but the number that is the closest is "0.7995," which corresponds to a value of z of $z = 0.84$. Therefore, to a reasonable level of accuracy, we can state

$$F(0.84) = P(Z \le 0.84) = 0.80.$$

Similarly, we can use the table in "reverse" to determine:

$$P(Z \le 0.25) = 0.60$$
$$P(Z \le 0.52) = 0.70$$
$$P(Z \le -1.28) = 0.10.$$

Although it would appear that the standard Normal table is only useful in the special case when the random variable obeys a Normal distribution with mean $\mu = 0.0$ and standard deviation $\sigma = 1.0$, it turns out that this table can be used to perform probability computations for any random variable that obeys a Normal distribution with any mean μ and any standard deviation σ. This is because there is a very special relationship between the standard Normal distribution and a general Normal distribution with mean μ and standard deviation σ, summarized as follows:

If X is a random variable that obeys a Normal distribution with mean μ and standard deviation σ, then the random variable Z defined by

$$Z = \frac{X - \mu}{\sigma}$$

obeys a standard Normal distribution, and in particular

$$\mu_Z = 0.0$$

and

$$\sigma_Z = 1.0.$$

(To see why this must be true, observe first that

$$E(Z) = E\left(\frac{X - \mu}{\sigma}\right) = \frac{1}{\sigma} E(X - \mu) = \frac{1}{\sigma}(E(X) - \mu) = 0.0$$

and

$$\text{VAR}(Z) = \text{VAR}\left(\frac{X - \mu}{\sigma}\right) = \text{VAR}\left(\frac{X}{\sigma} - \frac{\mu}{\sigma}\right) = \text{VAR}\left(\frac{X}{\sigma}\right) = \frac{1}{\sigma^2}\text{VAR}(X) = 1.0.$$

Therefore $\sigma_Z = \sqrt{1.0} = 1.0$, and so Z has a mean of zero and a standard deviation of 1.0. What is also surprising is that Z is itself Normally distributed, i.e., $Z = (X - \mu)/\sigma$ obeys a Normal distribution. We will not derive this last statement, as its derivation is beyond the scope of this book.)

Let us now make use of this important fact. Suppose that X obeys a Normal distribution with mean μ and standard deviation σ, and that we would like to calculate $P(a \le X \le b)$ for some numbers a and b. Then

$$
\begin{aligned}
P(a \le X \le b) &= P\left(\frac{a - \mu}{\sigma} \le \frac{X - \mu}{\sigma} \le \frac{b - \mu}{\sigma}\right) \\
&= P\left(\frac{a - \mu}{\sigma} \le Z \le \frac{b - \mu}{\sigma}\right) \\
&= P\left(Z \le \frac{b - \mu}{\sigma}\right) - P\left(Z \le \frac{a - \mu}{\sigma}\right)
\end{aligned}
$$

where Z is a standard Normal random variable. We summarize this as:

If X obeys a Normal distribution with mean μ and standard deviation σ, then

$$P(a \le X \le b) = P\left(Z \le \frac{b - \mu}{\sigma}\right) - P\left(Z \le \frac{a - \mu}{\sigma}\right)$$

where Z is a standard Normal random variable.

Let us see how to use this fact. Suppose that X obeys a Normal distribution with mean $\mu = 3.2$ and standard deviation $\sigma = 1.3$, for example. Suppose that we wish to compute

$$P(2.7 \leq X \leq 4.1).$$

We substitute the following numbers into the formula:

$$a = 2.7, \quad b = 4.1, \quad \mu = 3.2, \quad \sigma = 1.3$$

and obtain

$$P(2.7 \leq X \leq 4.1) = P\left(Z \leq \frac{4.1 - 3.2}{1.3}\right) - P\left(Z \leq \frac{2.7 - 3.2}{1.3}\right)$$
$$= P(Z \leq 0.69) - P(Z \leq -0.38).$$

Since Z is a standard Normal random variable, then from Table A.1 we have:

$$P(Z \leq 0.69) = 0.7549$$

and

$$P(Z \leq -0.38) = 0.3520.$$

Therefore

$$P(2.7 \leq X \leq 4.1) = P(Z \leq 0.69) - P(Z \leq -0.38) = 0.7549 - 0.3520 = 0.4029.$$

Example 3.8 – The Time to Process an Insurance Policy

At Emerson Insurance, the process of issuing an insurance policy consists of two steps, *underwriting* the policy (which is the process of evaluation and classification of the policy) and *rating* the policy (which is the calculation of premiums). Let X denote the time to underwrite a policy and let Y denote the time to rate a policy. Suppose that X obeys a Normal distribution with mean $\mu_X = 150$ minutes and $\sigma_X = 30$ minutes. Suppose that Y obeys a Normal distribution with $\mu_Y = 75$ minutes and $\sigma_Y = 25$ minutes. Consider the following questions:

(a) What is the probability that it takes 120 minutes or less to underwrite a policy?

(b) What is the probability that it takes more than 25 minutes to rate a policy?

(c) What is the 95th percentile of the underwriting time? In other words, find x such that $P(X \leq x) = 0.95$.

Let us now answer these three questions.
Consider the first question. We want to find the probability

$$P(X \leq 120).$$

However

$$P(X \leq 120) = P\left(\frac{X - \mu_X}{\sigma_X} \leq \frac{120 - \mu_X}{\sigma_X}\right).$$

Let

$$Z = \frac{X - \mu_X}{\sigma_X}.$$

Then Z is a standard Normal random variable, and we can use the Normal table to find the answer:

$$P(X \leq 120) = P\left(\frac{X - \mu_X}{\sigma_X} \leq \frac{120 - \mu_X}{\sigma_X}\right)$$

$$= P\left(Z \leq \frac{120 - 150}{30}\right) = P(Z \leq -1.00) = 0.1587.$$

Now consider the second question. We want to find the probability

$$P(Y > 25).$$

However

$$P(Y > 25) = P\left(\frac{Y - \mu_Y}{\sigma_Y} > \frac{25 - \mu_Y}{\sigma_Y}\right).$$

Now let

$$Z = \frac{Y - \mu_Y}{\sigma_Y}.$$

Then Z is a standard Normal random variable, and we can use the Normal table to find the answer:

$$P(Y > 25) = P\left(\frac{Y - \mu_Y}{\sigma_Y} > \frac{25 - \mu_Y}{\sigma_Y}\right)$$

$$= P\left(Z > \frac{25 - 75}{25}\right) = P(Z > -2.00)$$

$$= 1.0 - P(Z \leq -2.00)$$

$$= 1.0 - 0.0228 = 0.9772.$$

Last of all, consider the third question. We seek the value of x for which

$$P(X \leq x) = 0.95.$$

We write:

$$0.95 = P(X \leq x) = P\left(\frac{X - \mu_X}{\sigma_X} \leq \frac{x - \mu_X}{\sigma_X}\right).$$

If we let

$$Z = \frac{X - \mu_X}{\sigma_X},$$

then Z is a standard Normal random variable. Substituting this into the above equation yields:

$$0.95 = P(X \leq x) = P\left(Z \leq \frac{x - \mu_X}{\sigma_X}\right).$$

However from Table A.1, we see that

$$P(Z \leq 1.65) = 0.95.$$

Comparing this expression with that above, we must therefore equate

$$\frac{x - \mu_X}{\sigma_X} = 1.65.$$

Solving this for x yields

$$x = 1.65 \cdot \sigma_X + \mu_X = 1.65 \cdot 30 + 150 = 199.5 \text{ minutes.}$$

That is,

$$P(X \leq 199.5) - 0.95.$$

In order to obtain a more intuitive understanding of how variability affects the behavior of a Normally distributed random variable, we can use the standard Normal table to derive the following:

If X obeys a Normal distribution with mean μ and standard deviation σ, then

$$P(\mu - \sigma \leq X \leq \mu + \sigma) = 0.6826$$
$$P(\mu - 2\sigma \leq X \leq \mu + 2\sigma) = 0.9544$$
$$P(\mu - 3\sigma \leq X \leq \mu + 3\sigma) = 0.9974.$$

According to the above statement, the likelihood that X is within one standard deviation from its mean is 68%. Moreover, the likelihood that X is within two standard deviations from its mean is 0.9544. Finally, the likelihood that X is within three standard deviations from its mean is 0.9974. Another useful summary that is easily derived from the standard Normal table is:

If X obeys a Normal distribution with mean μ and standard deviation σ, then

$$P(\mu - 1.65\sigma \leq X \leq \mu + 1.65\sigma) = 0.90$$
$$P(\mu - 1.96\sigma \leq X \leq \mu + 1.96\sigma) = 0.95$$
$$P(\mu - 2.81\sigma \leq X \leq \mu + 2.81\sigma) = 0.995.$$

According to this statement, there is a 90% likelihood that X is within 1.65 standard deviations from its mean. Moreover, there is a 95% likelihood that X is within 1.96 standard deviations from its mean, and there is a 99.5% likelihood that X is within 2.81 standard deviations from its mean.

3.6   SUMS OF NORMALLY DISTRIBUTED RANDOM VARIABLES

Suppose that X and Y are random variables that each obey a Normal distribution with means μ_X and μ_Y and standard deviations σ_X and σ_Y, respectively. Suppose also that X and Y do not have any peculiar dependence[3]. Suppose that a, b, and c are three given numbers and let us define

---

[3]More formally, suppose that the joint distribution of X and Y is a multivariate Normal distribution. The reason we make this assumption is that if X and Y have peculiar dependencies, then the results of this section are not true.

$$U = aX + bY + c.$$

Then the value of U is uncertain, and therefore U is a random variable. The following important result summarizes what is known about the probability distribution of U:

Suppose that X and Y are random variables that obey Normal distributions with means μ_X and μ_Y and standard deviations σ_X and σ_Y, respectively. Suppose that a, b and c are three given numbers, and define the random variable

$$U = aX + bY + c.$$

Then U obeys a Normal distribution. The mean, variance, and standard deviation of U are given by the following formulas:

$$\mu_U = a\mu_X + b\mu_Y + c,$$
$$\sigma_U^2 = a^2\sigma_X^2 + b^2\sigma_Y^2 + 2ab\sigma_X\sigma_Y\,\mathrm{CORR}(X, Y),$$
$$\sigma_U = \sqrt{a^2\sigma_X^2 + b^2\sigma_Y^2 + 2ab\sigma_X\sigma_Y\,\mathrm{CORR}(X, Y)}.$$

The formulas above for the mean and standard deviation of U are the same as those derived in Chapter 2. But the important fact in the above statement is that the random variable U is itself a Normally distributed random variable whenever X and Y are Normally distributed. That is, the weighted sum of random variables that obey a Normal distribution is another random variable that also obeys a Normal distribution.

Example 3.9 – The Time to Process an Insurance Policy, continued

In Example 3.8, we derived several probabilities related to the underwriting and rating of insurance policies at Emerson Insurance. Let us suppose that the time to underwrite a policy and the time to rate a policy are positively correlated (as one would expect) and that $\mathrm{CORR}(X, Y) = 0.37$, where recall that X and Y are the random variables denoting the time to underwrite and rate an insurance policy, respectively. We now continue the example by asking the following questions:

(a) What is the probability that it takes less than 180 minutes to issue a policy (that is, both to underwrite and rate the policy)?

(b) What is the 95th percentile of the time to issue a policy? In other words, find u such that $P(X + Y \leq u) = 0.95$.

(c) What is the probability that an underwriter will complete three policies (both underwriting and rating) within one 8-hour day?

In order to answer these three questions, let U be the random variable that represents the total time to issue a policy. Clearly, $U = X + Y$. Because U is the sum of Normally distributed random variables, U is itself Normally distributed. The mean of U is computed as

$$\mu_U = \mu_X + \mu_Y = 150.0 + 75.0 = 225.0$$

and variance of U is computed as

$$\sigma_U^2 = \sigma_X^2 + \sigma_Y^2 + 2\sigma_X\sigma_Y\mathrm{CORR}(X, Y) = 30^2 + 25^2 + 2 \cdot 30 \cdot 25 \cdot 0.37 = 2{,}080.0.$$

Therefore, the standard deviation of U is $\sigma_U = \sqrt{2{,}080.0} = 45.61$ minutes.

To answer the first question, we need to compute

$$P(U \leq 180).$$

This is computed as follows:

$$P(U \leq 180) = P\left(\frac{U - \mu_U}{\sigma_U} \leq \frac{180 - \mu_U}{\sigma_U}\right) = P\left(\frac{U - \mu_U}{\sigma_U} \leq -0.99\right).$$

However, the quantity

$$Z = \frac{U - \mu_U}{\sigma_U}$$

obeys a standard Normal distribution, and so from Table A.1, we have

$$P(Z \leq 0.99) = 0.1611$$

and so

$$P(U \leq 180) = 0.1611.$$

Let us now consider the second question. We need to find that value of u for which

$$0.95 = P(U \leq u).$$

We write:

$$0.95 = P(U \leq u) = P\left(\frac{U - \mu_U}{\sigma_U} \leq \frac{u - \mu_U}{\sigma_U}\right).$$

The random variable

$$Z = \frac{U - \mu_U}{\sigma_U}$$

obeys a standard Normal distribution, and the 95th percentile of a standard Normal distribution is 1.65, i.e.,

$$P(Z \leq 1.65) = 0.95.$$

Therefore

$$\frac{u - \mu_U}{\sigma_U} = 1.65$$

and solving for u yields

$$u = 1.65 \times \sigma_U + \mu_U = 300.25 \text{ minutes.}$$

Last of all, let us answer the third question. Let U_1, U_2, and U_3 denote the time it takes to process the first, second, and third policies. From the above analysis, we know that $E(U_i) = 225.0$ and $SD(U_i) = 45.61$ for $i = 1, 2, 3$. Also, notice that U_1, U_2, and U_3 are independent. Let $V = U_1 + U_2 + U_3$. Then V is the total time it takes to complete all three policies. The random variable V is the sum of Normally distributed random variables and so is itself Normally distributed. The mean, variance, and the standard deviation of V are computed as follows:

$$\mu_V = \mu_{U_1} + \mu_{U_2} + \mu_{U_3} = 225.0 + 225.0 + 225.0 = 675.0 \text{ minutes,}$$
$$\sigma_V^2 = \sigma_{U_1}^2 + \sigma_{U_2}^2 + \sigma_{U_3}^2 = 2{,}080 + 2{,}080 + 2{,}080 = 6{,}240,$$

and so

$$\sigma_V = \sqrt{6,240} = 78.99 \text{ minutes.}$$

Because each working day consists of $480 = 8 \times 60$ minutes, we are interested in computing

$$P(V \le 480).$$

Note that

$$P(V \le 480) = P\left(\frac{V - \mu_V}{\sigma_V} \le \frac{480 - \mu_V}{\sigma_V}\right)$$

$$= P\left(\frac{V - \mu_V}{\sigma_V} \le \frac{480 - 675}{78.99}\right)$$

$$= P\left(\frac{V - \mu_V}{\sigma_V} \le -2.47\right).$$

Because

$$Z = \frac{V - \mu_V}{\sigma_V}$$

is a standard Normal random variable, from a standard Normal table we compute

$$P(Z \le -2.47) = 0.0068.$$

Therefore

$$P(V \le 480) = 0.0068.$$

3.7 | THE CENTRAL LIMIT THEOREM

In this section, we present the Central Limit Theorem, which is the most powerful and far-reaching statement in all of probability theory. To set the stage for the theorem, we first make the following definition: Two random variables are **identically distributed** if they obey the same probability distribution.

Suppose that $X_1, \ldots, X_n$ are independent and identically distributed random variables. (The short-hand for this statement is that $X_1, \ldots, X_n$ are **i.i.d.**) Then each of the random variables $X_1, X_2, \ldots, X_n$ has the same mean μ and the same standard deviation σ. Let

$$S_n = \sum_{i=1}^{n} X_i$$

denote the sum of these random variables. We now present the Central Limit Theorem.

The Central Limit Theorem (for the sum). If n is moderately large (say, n is larger than 30), then S_n is approximately Normally distributed with mean $n\mu$ and standard deviation $\sigma\sqrt{n}$.

This is indeed a remarkable result: It states that the sum of a number of independent identically distributed random variables is distributed in a Normal fashion no matter what the distribution of the random variables themselves is. For example, the random variables $X_1, \ldots, X_n$ could each obey a uniform distribution, they could each obey a binomial distribution, or they could each obey some other discrete distribution. The distribution of the sum of the random variables will be approximately Normally distributed, regardless of the distribution of the $X_1, \ldots, X_n$ so long as n is reasonably large. Put another way, the distribution of the sum no longer reflects the distribution of its terms!

Let the numerical average, or "mean," of $X_1, \ldots, X_n$ be denoted by $\overline{X}$. That is,

$$\overline{X} = \frac{\sum\limits_{i=1}^{n} X_i}{n}.$$

We will often use a different, but equivalent, version of the Central Limit Theorem, which concerns itself with the distribution of the mean $\overline{X}$.

> **The Central Limit Theorem (for the mean).** If n is moderately large (say, n is larger than 30), then $\overline{X}$ is approximately Normally distributed with mean μ and standard deviation $\sigma/\sqrt{n}$.

This version of the Central Limit Theorem is the same as the first version, except that we have divided by n, with subsequent changes in the conclusions of the theorem.

Example 3.10 — An Illustration of the Central Limit Theorem

Recall in Example 3.6 that the distribution of lunch-time revenues at the fast-food restaurant approximately obeys a Normal distribution. Let us see why this "must" be true as a consequence of the Central Limit Theorem. Suppose that n different customers visit the restaurant during the lunch hour on a given day and let $X_1, \ldots, X_n$ denote the revenues from each of these customers, respectively. Then it is reasonable to assume that $X_1, \ldots, X_n$ are independent and identically distributed random variables. Furthermore, total lunch-time revenues at the restaurant is given by

$$S_n = \sum_{i=1}^{n} X_i.$$

From the Central Limit Theorem, S_n must be approximately Normally distributed.

Example 3.11 — Another Illustration of the Central Limit Theorem

Suppose we roll a die n times. Let $X_1, X_2, \ldots, X_n$ be the number that the die shows on its uppermost face on the first, second, $\ldots$, nth roll. Let $S_n = X_1 + \ldots + X_n$. In Figure 3.14, we plot the distribution function of the sum S_n for $n = 1, 2,$ and 3. When $n = 1$, the distribution of S_1 is just the distribution of the face value of one roll of a die, which is just

$$P(S_1 = i) = 1/6 \quad \text{for} \quad i = 1, 2, \ldots, 6.$$

This distribution is a discrete version of the uniform distribution, as shown in Figure 3.14. When $n = 2$, the distribution of S_2 is less uniform and looks somewhat like a bell shape, as shown in Figure 3.14. When $n = 3$, the distribution of S_3 is remarkably close to the bell-shaped curve of the Normal distribution.

FIGURE 3.14

The distribution of the sum of n rolls of a die is approximately Normally distributed, even for very small values of n.

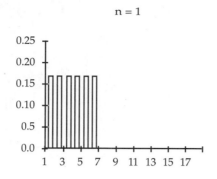

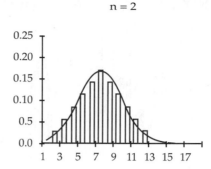

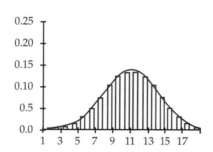

Example 3.12 — Approximation of the Binomial Distribution by the Normal Distribution

Suppose we toss a coin that has probability p of coming up heads and probability $1 - p$ of coming up tails. Suppose we toss the coin n times. Let us define the random variable X_i by the rule: $X_i = 1$ if the coin comes up heads at toss i and $X_i = 0$ if the coin comes up tails at toss i, for $i = 1, 2, \ldots, n$. Then $X_i = 1$ with probability p and $X_i = 0$ with probability $1 - p$. Let $S_n = X_1 + \ldots + X_n$. Then S_n is the number of heads in n tosses. We have seen in Chapter 2 that S_n obeys a binomial distribution with parameters n and p. From the properties of the binomial distribution presented in Chapter 2, we have the following formulas for the mean and the standard deviation of S_n:

$$E(S_n) = np$$

and

$$\mathrm{SD}(S_n) = \sqrt{np(1 - p)}.$$

Applying the Central Limit Theorem, we find that for large values of n, S_n will be approximately Normally distributed. In other words, the Normal distribution is a good approximation of the binomial distribution, when n is large. A good rule of thumb is to use the Normal distribution as an approximation of the binomial distribution if both $np \geq 5$ and $n(1 - p) \geq 5$.

In Figure 3.15, we plot the binomial distribution for $p = 0.8$ and for four different values of n, namely for $n = 10, 15, 20, 25$. Notice that even for these relatively low values of n, the shape of the binomial distribution resembles the Normal distribution's bell-shaped curve quite closely.

We have just argued that the Normal distribution is a good approximation of the binomial distribution when n is moderately large. Suppose that X obeys a binomial

Binomial distribution.

FIGURE 3.15
The binomial distribution is closely approximated by a Normal distribution with the same mean and standard deviation.

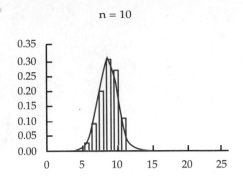

n = 10

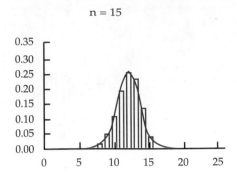

n = 15

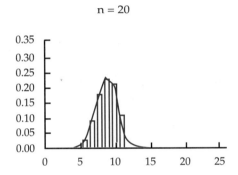

n = 20

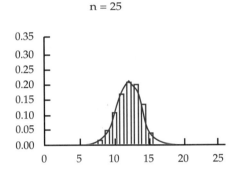

n = 25

distribution with parameters n and p. Then $\mu_X = np$ and $\sigma_X = \sqrt{np(1-p)}$. Now suppose that Y is a Normally distributed random variable with $\mu_U = np$ and $\sigma_Y = \sqrt{np(1-p)}$. Then because X and Y have the same mean and standard deviation, the distributions of X and Y will be approximately the same, since X is approximately Normally distributed and Y is exactly Normally distributed. Therefore, if we wish to compute $P(a \leq X \leq b)$ for some particular values of a and b, we can approximate this probability by instead computing $P(a \leq Y \leq b)$. We summarize this in the following statement:

> Suppose that X obeys a binomial distribution with parameters n and p. If n is moderately large ($np \geq 5$ and $n(1-p) \geq 5$), then X is approximately Normally distributed. If we wish to compute $P(a \leq X \leq b)$ for particular values of a and b, a good approximation is:
>
> $$P(a \leq X \leq b) \approx P(a \leq Y \leq b),$$
>
> where Y is a Normally distributed random variable with mean $\mu_Y = np$ and standard deviation $\sigma_Y = \sqrt{np(1-p)}$.

Example 3.13 — Random Testing of a Production Process

Suppose that a manufacturing process for semiconductors has a defect rate of one defect for every thousand components. What is the likelihood that there will be at least 10 defective semiconductors in a batch of 6,000 semiconductors?

To answer this question, let X denote the number of defective semiconductors among the batch of 6,000 semiconductors. Then X obeys a binomial distribution with parameters $p = 0.001$ and $n = 6{,}000$. We need to compute $P(X \geq 10)$. First note that

$$\mu_X = np = 6{,}000 \cdot 0.001 = 6.0$$

and

$$\sigma_X = \sqrt{np(1 - p)} = \sqrt{6{,}000 \cdot 0.001 \cdot (1 - 0.001)} = 2.448.$$

Because $np = 6{,}000 \cdot 0.001 = 6 \geq 5$ and $n(1 - p) = 6{,}000 \cdot (1 - 0.001) = 5{,}994 \geq 5$, then we can approximate X with a Normally distributed random variable Y with mean $\mu_Y = 6.0$ and $\sigma_Y = 2.448$. Therefore,

$$P(X \geq 10) \approx P(Y \geq 10) = P\left(\frac{Y - 6.0}{2.448} \geq \frac{10.0 - 6.0}{2.448}\right)$$
$$= P\,(Z \geq 1.63).$$

Using a standard Normal table, this last quantity is 0.0516. That is,

$$P(X \geq 10) \approx 0.0516.$$

3.8 SUMMARY

In this chapter, we have developed the important constructs of continuous random variables. We introduced the probability density function and the cumulative distribution function as ways to describe a continuous random variable and to perform probability computations for a continuous random variable. We introduced the Normal distribution, which can arise in at least three ways: (i) as a natural model for many physical processes, (ii) as a sum of several Normally distributed random variables, or (iii) as an approximation of a sum (or average) of many independent and identically distributed random variables.

We then presented the Central Limit Theorem, which is the most far-reaching statement in all of probability. The Central Limit Theorem states that the sum of n independent and identically distributed random variables X_i is closely approximated by a Normal distribution irrespective of the distribution of the random variables X_i. Moreover, n does not have to be very large for this approximation to hold. Last of all, we showed how the Normal distribution can be used to approximate the binomial distribution.

3.9 EXERCISES

EXERCISE 3.1 The personnel of a police patrol station are responsible for handling all traffic incidents that occur on a 30-mile highway. The station is located at the entrance to the highway, diagrammed in Figure 3.16. When a traffic incident occurs, the patrol has to travel from the station to the site of the traffic incident to respond. Assume that a traffic incident is equally likely to occur at any point on the highway (whereby the distance the patrol has to travel is uniformly distributed between 0 and 30 miles).

FIGURE 3.16
Diagram of the
highway and police
station.

Police Station Location

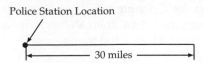

30 miles

(a) What is the probability that the police patrol has to travel more than 10 miles to the site of an incident?

(b) Suppose the patrol station has relocated to the midpoint of the highway. Under the assumption that a traffic incident is equally likely to occur at any point on the highway, what is the new answer to (a)?

EXERCISE 3.2 The men's 100 meter sprint at the 1996 Olympic Games in Atlanta was a hotly contested event between Donovan Bailey of Canada, Frankie Fredericks of Namibia, and Ato Boldon of Trinidad. Assume that the probability distribution of the time to run the race is the same for all three runners, and that this time obeys a (continuous) uniform distribution between 9.75 seconds and 9.95 seconds.

(a) What is the probability that Donovan Bailey's time will beat the previous record of 9.86 seconds?

(b) What is the probability that the winning time will beat the previous record of 9.86 seconds?

(c) In answering part (b) with the data you were given, you had to assume that the running times for the three athletes were independent of each other. Give one reason why this may not be valid.

EXERCISE 3.3 The weekly sales of a brand-name kitchen cleanser at a supermarket is believed to be Normally distributed with a mean 2,550 bottles and a standard deviation 415 bottles. The store manager places an order at the beginning of each week for the cleanser. She would like to carry enough bottles of the cleanser so that the probability of stocking out (i.e., not having enough bottles of cleanser) is only 2.5%. How many bottles should she order each week?

EXERCISE 3.4 KLEERCO supplies under-hood emission-control air pumps to the automotive industry. The pump is vacuum-powered and works while the engine is operating, cleaning the exhaust by pumping extra oxygen into the exhaust system. If a pump fails before the vehicle in which it is installed has travelled 50,000 miles, Federal emission regulations require that it be replaced at no cost to the vehicle owner. The company's current air pump lasts an average of 61,000 miles, with a standard deviation of 9,000 miles. The number of miles a pump operates before becoming ineffective has been found to obey a Normal distribution.

(a) For the current pump design, what percentage of the company's pumps will have to be replaced at no charge to the vehicle owner?

(b) What percentage of the company's pumps will fail at exactly 50,000 miles?

(c) What percentage of the company's pumps will fail at mileage between 42,000 and 57,000?

(d) For what number of miles does the probability become 80% that a randomly selected pump will no longer be effective?

EXERCISE 3.5 Helen has an early class tomorrow morning. She knows that she needs to get to bed by 10:00 P.M. in order to be sufficiently rested to concentrate and participate in class. However, before she goes to bed, she must start and then complete a homework assignment which is due tomorrow morning. According to her experience, the time it takes her to complete a homework assignment for this class is Normally distributed with mean $\mu = 3.5$ hours and standard deviation $\sigma = 1.2$ hours. Helen looks at her watch and sees that it is now 6:00 P.M. What is the probability that she will be able to get to bed in time to be sufficiently rested for the next day's class?

EXERCISE 3.6 Winter lasts from December 21 through March 21. The average winter temperature in Boston is Normally distributed with mean $\mu = 32.5\,°F$ and standard deviation $\sigma = 1.59\,°F$. In New York City, the average winter temperature is Normally distributed with mean $\mu = 35.4\,°F$ and standard deviation $\sigma = 2.05\,°F$.

(a) What is the probability that the average winter temperature in Boston this coming winter will be above freezing ($32\,°F$)?

(b) Assume that average winter temperatures in Boston and New York are independent. What is the probability that the average temperature in Boston in the coming winter will be higher than in New York?

(c) Do you think the independence assumption above is reasonable?

EXERCISE 3.7 In a large shipment of tomatoes, the weight of each tomato is Normally distributed with mean $\mu = 4.2$ ounces and standard deviation $\sigma = 1.0$ ounce. Tomatoes from this shipment are sold in packages of three.

(a) Assuming the weight of each tomato is independent of the weights of other tomatoes, compute the mean and the standard deviation of the weight of a package.

(b) Compute the probability that a package weighs between 11.0 and 13.0 ounces.

EXERCISE 3.8 MIT's pension plan has two funds, the fixed income fund and the variable income fund. Let X denote the annual return of the fixed income fund. Let Y denote the annual return of the variable income fund. We assume that X obeys a Normal distribution with mean 7% and standard deviation 2%, and that Y obeys a Normal distribution with mean 13% and standard deviation 8%. We also assume that $CORR(X, Y) = -0.4$. A particular professor has invested 30% of his pension money in the fixed income fund and 70% of his pension money in the variable income fund.

(a) What is the expected annual return of the Professor's pension money?

(b) What is the standard deviation of the annual return of the Professor's pension money?

(c) What is the distribution of the annual return of the Professor's pension money?

(d) What is the probability that the annual return of the Professor's pension money is between 10% and 15%?

EXERCISE 3.9 Let X denote the percentage increase in the Dow Jones Index in the coming year and let Y denote the percentage increase in the S&P 500 Index in the coming year. Suppose that X and Y obey a joint Normal distribution, and that the mean of X is 11% and its standard deviation is 13%, and the mean of Y is 10% and its standard deviation is 12%. Suppose that $CORR(X, Y) = 0.43$.

(a) What is the probability that the Dow Jones Index will increase by more than 11% in the coming year?

(b) What is the probability that the Dow Jones Index will decrease by more than 11% in the coming year?

(c) What is the probability that the S&P 500 Index will increase in the coming year by an amount less than 15%?

(d) Suppose that a person places 30% of a portfolio in the Dow Jones Index and the remaining 70% of the portfolio in the S&P 500 Index. What is the expected return of the combined portfolio? What is the standard deviation of this return?

(e) What is the distribution of $X - Y$? What is the probability that X is greater than Y?

EXERCISE 3.10 According to a recent census, 52.2% of Boston residents are female. Suppose a group of 100 Bostonians is selected at random.

(a) What is the mean and the standard deviation of the number of female members of the group?

(b) Use the Normal approximation to find the probability that less then one half of the members of the group are female.

(c) Use the Normal approximation to find the probability that the number of female members of the group is between 45 and 55.

EXERCISE 3.11 Historical data indicate that the starting salary for a new MBA graduate in a leading management consulting firm can be modeled using a Normal distribution with mean $90,000 and standard deviation $20,000. Suppose that second-year salaries increase by exactly 20%. Suppose also that the bonus each year can be modeled using a Normal distribution with mean $25,000 and standard deviation $5,000. Suppose that the bonus is independent of the initial salary (and is also independent of the annual salary increase).

(a) What is the expected annual compensation (salary plus bonus) for a new hire?

(b) What is the standard deviation of the annual compensation for a new hire?

(c) What is the expected annual compensation of an employee after completing one year at the firm, i.e., just after his/her salary increase is announced?

(d) What is the standard deviation of an employee's annual compensation after completing one year at the firm, i.e., just after his/her salary increase is announced?

(e) What is the probability that an employee's annual compensation after completing one year in the firm, i.e., just after the salary increase is announced, will exceed $140,000?

EXERCISE 3.12 A portfolio manager believes that tomorrow's foreign exchange rate of German marks per U.S. dollar will be Normally distributed with mean 2.03 and standard deviation 0.08. Using the manager's numbers, answer the following questions:

(a) What is the probability that tomorrow's rate will be above 2.08?

(b) What is the probability that tomorrow's rate will be below 1.85?

(c) What is the probability that tomorrow's rate will be between 2.00 and 2.20?

EXERCISE 3.13 You are presented with two portfolios, each of which consists of various amounts invested in the common stock of three companies, whose annual returns are mutually independent, and Normally distributed with respective means and standard deviations as shown in Table 3.5. The compositions of the two portfolios are given in Table 3.6. Which portfolio has a greater probability of not losing money?

TABLE 3.5

Mean and standard deviation of annual rate of return for three companies.

Company	Expected Annual Rate of Return	Standard Deviation of Rate of Return
Avco, Inc.	8.0%	0.5%
Boscom, Inc.	11.0%	6.0%
Caltrans, Inc.	17.0%	20.0%

TABLE 3.6

Composition of the two portfolios.

Portfolio	Percentage in Avco, Inc.	Percentage in Boscom, Inc.	Percentage in Caltrans, Inc.
Explorer Fund	70%	15%	15%
Integrity Fund	34%	33%	33%

EXERCISE 3.14 Wenjun Chen and Tim Schwartz have analyzed the sport of five-pin bowling, which is the leading participant sport in Canada. After studying scores from an Ontario league, they concluded that the logarithm of any given player's score (the "logscore") obeys a Normal distribution and is independent of the logscore of any of the other players. While the mean of the distribution varies from one player to another player, their evidence suggested that the standard deviation, σ, for any player was the same and was equal to 0.205.

(a) If player A has a mean logscore that exceeds player B's mean logscore by 0.15, what is the probability that A will have a higher score than, and thereby defeat, B in a single game?

(b) What is the probability that A will beat B in 3 or more games in a series of 5 games?

EXERCISE 3.15 A software company sells a shrink-wrapped product at a price of $500 per package under a 30-day return policy. This policy permits a customer to return the product within 30 days of purchase for a refund of the full purchase price if the customer is not satisfied for any reason.

(a) In January of the current year, the firm's retail sales division sold 2,500 packages. Historically, 10% of the products sold by the division are returned for a full refund. What is the mean and standard deviation of the number of packages that will be returned from January's sales?

(b) What is the mean and standard deviation of revenue from January sales, after allowing for returns?

(c) What is the probability that January revenue (after allowing for returns) will exceed the division's target of $1.3 million?

EXERCISE 3.16 A key concern in using Normal approximations for sums and averages of n independent identically distributed random variables $X_1, \ldots, X_n$ is how large n has to be for the approximation to be good. Though it is commonplace to assume that $n \geq 30$ is adequate, the quality of the approximation depends on the shape of the distribution of the X_i's. This exercise illustrates why it is difficult to give a definitive answer to the question: "How large is large enough?"

The binomial distribution with parameters n, the number of trials, and p, the probability of a success, can be approximated by the Normal distribution with $\mu = np$ and $\sigma = \sqrt{np(1 - p)}$. A reliable rule of thumb for the approximation to be good is that both np and $n(1 - p)$ should be at least 5.

(a) What is the minimum value of n for which the Normal approximation is good when $p = 0.5$? Show how your answer changes with p by using values $p = 0.1, p = 0.01$ and $p = 0.001$.

(b) If $p = 0.01$ and $n = 20$, compare the Normal approximation for the probability of the binomial random variable being less than or equal to 0 with its true value.

EXERCISE 3.17 André is a fearless circus performer who gets shot from a special cannon during the grand finale of the show. After being shot from the cannon, André is supposed to land on a safety net at the other side of the arena. The distance he travels varies, but is Normally distributed with a mean of 150 feet and a standard deviation of 10 feet. The landing net is 30 feet long.

(a) To maximize André's probability of landing on the net, how far away from the cannon should he position the nearest edge of the net?

(b) Given the net position in part (a), what is the probability that André will land on the safety net and so be able to return for tomorrow night's show?

EXERCISE 3.18 In 1996, after an extensive investigation by the Consumer Product Safety Commission, an automotive manufacturer agreed to recall 43,000 cars of one of its models. The commission suggested that about 30% of the cars exhibited a potentially dangerous problem in their electrical wiring. However, the manufacturer found only five cars having a problem in the electrical wiring in a random sample of 2,000 cars and claimed the recalls were not justified.

(a) What assumptions must be made in order to characterize the number of cars having an electrical wiring problem found in a random sample of 2,000 as a binomial random variable? Do these assumptions appear to be satisfied?

(b) Assume that the conditions of part (a) hold. Determine the approximate probability of finding five or fewer cars having an electrical wiring problem in a random sample of 2,000 if, in fact, 30% of all cars have an electrical wiring problem.

(c) Assume that the manufacturer's sample data have been reported accurately. Is it likely that 30% of the cars have a problem in their electrical wiring?

EXERCISE 3.19 *Investor's Market Times* is a magazine that rates stocks and mutual funds and publishes predictions of stock performance. Suppose that *Investor's Market Times* has predicted that stock A will have an expected annual return of 10% with a standard deviation of 4%, and stock B will have an expected annual return of 20% with a standard deviation of 10%. *Investor's Market Times* has also estimated that the correlation between the return of these stocks is -0.20.

(a) What fraction of your portfolio should you invest in each of stocks A and B so that the expected annual return is 13%?

(b) What is the standard deviation of the return of the portfolio that has an expected annual return of 13% (part (a))?

(c) The magazine recommends 50 small international stocks as great buying opportunities in the next year. They claim that each of these 50 stocks has an expected annual return of 20% and a standard deviation of 20%. They also claim that these returns are independent. For diversification reasons, they recommend that investors invest 2% of their money in each stock and hold the portfolio for a year. What is the expected return and standard deviation of the annual return of this portfolio?

(d) What is the probability that the portfolio of 50 stocks will have an annual return between 18% and 24%?

EXERCISE 3.20 The paint department in an automobile factory applies two processes when painting cars: (i) painting and (ii) polishing. The painting process is defective 20% of the time, while the polishing process is defective 10% of the time. Each car first goes through the painting and then through the polishing process. Each car is inspected after it has completed the two processes. If either the painting or the polishing is defective, the car is returned to a special station for re-work, where the two processes are applied once again. Rework at the special station is 100% reliable (although it is also very expensive).

(a) What is the probability that a car is returned to the special station for rework?

(b) In a batch of 1,000 cars, what is the expected number of cars that will be returned for rework?

(c) In a batch of 1,000 cars, what is the probability that the number of returned cars is less than or equal to 200?

(d) Let X be the number of cars in a group of 1,000 cars that have painting defects. Let Y be the number of cars in a group of 1,000 cars that have polishing defects. What is the distribution of X? What is the distribution of Y?

(e) What is the probability that the total number of defects, $X + Y$, is less than or equal to 300?

Statistical Sampling

CONTENTS

THE USE OF A SAMPLE OF DATA TO ESTIMATE PROPERTIES OF A POPULATION IS A KEY component of many management decisions. For example, marketing managers often need to estimate the potential sales of a product as part of the broad spectrum of product development decisions. In order to do so, they typically estimate the distribution of sales based on a small sample of actual sales data in a test market. As another example, operations managers often need to estimate the proportion of defective parts in a production process and then use this information to make recommendations about alterations in the production process. Again, such managers typically estimate the proportion of defects based on a small sample of parts chosen for intensive inspection. In these two cases, as well as many others, a manager needs to estimate key parameters of a population based on a sample drawn from this population; and of course, the manager needs also to assess the reliability of his/her estimates.

In this chapter, we introduce methods to construct estimates of the essential components of a probability distribution, such as the shape of a probability distribution function $f(x)$, the mean μ, and the standard deviation σ, based on information from a sample of n observations drawn from the distribution. We also present methods for constructing an estimate of the proportion p of a population, based on information from a sample of n observations drawn from the population.

A core issue in computing estimates of distribution parameters has to do with the reliability of the estimates. The basic analytical construct that is used to understand the relative reliability of an estimate based on sample data is the **confidence interval** of the estimate. We develop and apply the methodology for constructing confidence intervals of sample estimates to a wide variety of managerial paradigms that arise in sampling.

4.1   RANDOM SAMPLES

We introduce the issues we will address in this chapter by way of the following example.

Example 4.1 – NEXNet Corporation

NEXNet Corporation is a relatively small but aggressive company in the telecommunications market in the mid-Atlantic region of the United States. They are now considering a move to the Boston area, and they are targeting relatively higher income communities. NEXNet has been using a growth and development strategy based on marketing in communities with high telephone use. Based on past experience, they have found that they are able to operate profitably in communities with the following characteristics in current telephone usage:

- The mean monthly household telephone bill is at least $75.00.

- The percentage of households whose monthly telephone bills are under $45.00 is no more than 15%.

- The percentage of households whose monthly telephone bills is between $60.00 and $100.00 is at least 30%.

As part of her analysis of potential communities to target for marketing and sales, Lisa Strom would like to estimate the distribution of monthly household telephone bills for the month of October in the communities of Weston, Wayland, and Sudbury, based on data from a telephone survey of households in these communities. (As an enticement to participate in the survey, NEXNet offers discount coupons on certain products to survey participants.) Lisa has arranged for such a survey to be conducted for 70 randomly chosen households in these three towns. The results of the survey are shown in Table 4.1.

Based on the survey results shown in Table 4.1, Lisa would like to answer the following questions:

(a) What is an estimate of the shape of the distribution of October household telephone bills?

(b) What is an estimate of the percentage of households whose October telephone bill is below $45.00?

(c) What is an estimate of the percentage of households whose October telephone bill is between $60.00 and $100.00?

TABLE 4.1

Sample of 70 monthly telephone bills for the month of October.

Respondent Number	October Phone Bill	Respondent Number	October Phone Bill	Respondent Number	October Phone Bill
1	$95.67	25	$79.32	49	$90.02
2	82.69	26	89.12	50	61.06
3	75.27	27	63.12	51	51.00
4	145.20	28	145.62	52	97.71
5	155.20	29	37.53	53	95.44
6	80.53	30	97.06	54	31.89
7	80.81	31	86.33	55	82.35
8	60.93	32	69.83	56	60.20
9	86.67	33	77.26	57	92.28
10	56.31	34	64.99	58	120.89
11	151.27	35	57.78	59	35.09
12	96.93	36	61.82	60	69.53
13	65.60	37	74.07	61	49.85
14	53.43	38	141.17	62	42.33
15	63.03	39	48.57	63	50.09
16	139.45	40	76.77	64	62.69
17	58.51	41	78.78	65	58.69
18	81.22	42	62.20	66	127.82
19	98.14	43	80.78	67	62.47
20	79.75	44	84.51	68	79.25
21	72.74	45	93.38	69	76.53
22	75.99	46	139.23	70	74.13
23	80.35	47	48.06		
24	49.42	48	44.51		

(d) What is an estimate of the mean of the distribution of October household telephone bills?

(e) What is an estimate of the standard deviation of the distribution of October household telephone bills?

In order to answer these as well as other questions about the distribution of monthly household telephone bills in the three towns, we introduce the notion of a **random sample** and examine its properties. We start with some definitions of the terms we will use.

A **population** (or "universe") is the set of all units of interest. A **sample** is a subset of the units of a population. A **random sample** is a sample collected in such a way that every unit in the population is equally likely to be selected.

For the NEXNet example, the **population** is the collection of all of the October telephone bills of the households in the three towns of Weston, Wayland, and Sudbury. The **sample** is the collection of the 70 October telephone bills from the 70 households that were chosen and interviewed. This sample is a **random sample** if the manner of choosing the households was done in such a way that all households in the site area were equally likely to be chosen.

Throughout the chapter, we will presume that the popuation is large enough that when collecting a random sample from the population, there is virtually no chance of selecting the same unit more than once. For the NEXNet example, this means that the likelihood of selecting the same household more than once when collecting the random sample is essentially zero.

We now briefly discuss the issue of how to obtain a random sample. For the NEXNet example, let us suppose that each household in the three towns of Weston, Wayland, and Sudbury has one listed telephone number. Then one way to choose a household "at random" would be to use the telephone book and pick a page at random, then pick a name on the page at random and then telephone the household chosen and interview them. One would then repeat this process 70 times to obtain a random sample of 70 households and their associated October telephone bills.

Of course, it might seem that another way to obtain a random sample might be to go to one of the local gourmet food markets that services these three towns and survey the first 70 people who exit the food market. However, this might bias the sample in favor of those residents who shop at that type of market, whose household incomes might be higher (on average) than that of the general population of the site area and hence whose telephone bills might be higher. Therefore, choosing the sample in this manner might not produce a truly random sample. The sample would be **biased** in favor of higher telephone bills. The issue of how to obtain samples that are truly random, and so exhibit no bias, often involves a variety of factors including using good sense, good judgement, and insight.

4.2   STATISTICS OF A RANDOM SAMPLE

Let us return to the problem of estimating the distribution of monthly telephone bills in the site area in Example 4.1. Suppose that we were to choose a household in the site area at random, interview them, and record their October telephone bill as some number X. Then X is an uncertain quantity, and so X is a random variable. Therefore, X will obey a probability distribution with some mean μ and standard deviation σ, and the probability density function (pdf) of the random variable X will be some function $f(x)$ and the cumulative distribution function (cdf) of X will be some function $F(x)$.

Continuing this line of reasoning, suppose that we are about to choose n households at random in the site area in order to interview them regarding their October telephone bill. (In this case, $n = 70$.) Let $X_1, X_2, \ldots, X_n$ denote the October telephone bill of households $1, 2, \ldots, n$. Then each $X_i, i = 1, 2, \ldots, n$ is a random variable. And each X_i will be drawn from the same probability distribution that has mean μ, standard deviation σ, pdf $f(x)$, and cdf $F(x)$. In fact, the random variables $X_i, i = 1, 2, \ldots, n$ will be independent and identically distributed.

Now let us move to a point in time **after** we have chosen the random sample of n October telephone bill values. Let $x_1, \ldots, x_n$ be the observed values **after** we have collected them. That is, $x_1, \ldots, x_n$ are the observed October household telephone bills for the first, second, . . . ,nth household in the sample. From Table 4.1, $x_1 = \$95.67$, $x_2 = \$82.69, \ldots, x_{70} = \$74.13$. Notice that if we were to ask a different group of randomly selected households, we would of course obtain a different collection of observed values. A very important observation is that **before** collecting the n observations, each observation is a random variable X_i for $i = 1, 2, \ldots, n$ that is distributed according to the unknown probability density function $f(x)$ and cumulative distribution function $F(x)$, and whose mean is μ and whose standard deviation is σ. After we have gathered the data from the random sample, the n observed values are 70 numbers that are realizations of the random variables. We denote the random variables by capital letters $X_1, \ldots, X_n$ and their realizations by $x_1, x_2, \ldots, x_n$.

To gain intuition about the shape of the distribution of X, it is useful to create a **frequency table** and a **histogram** of the sample values $x_1, x_2, \ldots, x_{70}$ of Table 4.1. A

TABLE 4.2

Frequency table of the 70 October telephone bills.

Interval Limit From	Interval Limit To	Number in Sample	Fraction of the Sample
$30.00	$40.00	3	0.04
$40.00	$50.00	6	0.09
$50.00	$60.00	7	0.10
$60.00	$70.00	13	0.19
$70.00	$80.00	12	0.17
$80.00	$90.00	11	0.16
$90.00	$100.00	9	0.13
$100.00	$110.00	0	0.00
$110.00	$120.00	0	0.00
$120.00	$130.00	2	0.03
$130.00	$140.00	2	0.03
$140.00	$150.00	3	0.04
$150.00	$160.00	2	0.03

frequency table of the 70 observed October telephone bills is presented in Table 4.2. The frequency table is constructed by first dividing the range of sample observation values into a series of intervals, shown in the first two columns of Table 4.2. The third column of Table 4.2 shows the number of sample observations in each interval, and this number is converted to a fraction of the total number of observations in the fourth column of Table 4.2. Each entry in the third column of Table 4.2 is computed by simply counting the number of occurrences of the sample values $x_1, x_2, \ldots, x_{70}$ that lie in each of the intervals of the table. For example, there are 3 occurrences of the 70 sample telephone bill values that fall in the interval from $30.00 to $40.00, namely respondent number 29 ($37.53), respondent number 54 ($31.89), and respondent number 59 ($35.09). Therefore, the fraction of the sample that is in the interval from $30.00 to $40.00 is 0.04 = 3/70, which is shown in the fourth column of Table 4.2.

A graph of the frequency values from a frequency table is called a histogram of the sample observations. Such a histogram is shown in Figure 4.1. This graph gives a nice pictorial view of the distribution of the values of the sample. Because the values of the sample obey the underlying (unknown) distribution of the random variable X, this graph is also an approximation of the shape of the probability density function of X. (If X were instead a discrete random variable, the graph would be an approximation of the probability distribution function of X.) We see from the graph in Figure 4.1 that the more probable values of X are mostly clustered in the range from $65.00 to $95.00. Notice that the shape is somewhat like a Normal distribution in the range up through $105.00, but that the shape also contains a significant number of telephone bills above $115.00. We might hypothesize at this point that the pattern of telephone bills is approximately Normally distributed, except for some very high users. Perhaps these high users have friends and/or relatives in other countries that they speak with often by telephone, or perhaps these high users are tele-commuters who work from a home office. Notice that the pictorial information from the histogram in Figure 4.1 gives us valuable information that we might put to good use in developing a marketing or sales strategy for these communities.

We are now in a position to answer Lisa Strom's first question, based on the histogram of the frequency table:

- An estimate of the shape of the distribution of October telephone bills in the site area is that it is shaped like a Normal distribution, with a peak near $65.00, except for a small but significant group in the range between $125.00 and $155.00.

More generally, suppose that we are interested in estimating the shape of the probability density function $f(x)$ of the random variable X. We proceed as follows:

FIGURE 4.1

Histogram of the 70 October telephone bills.

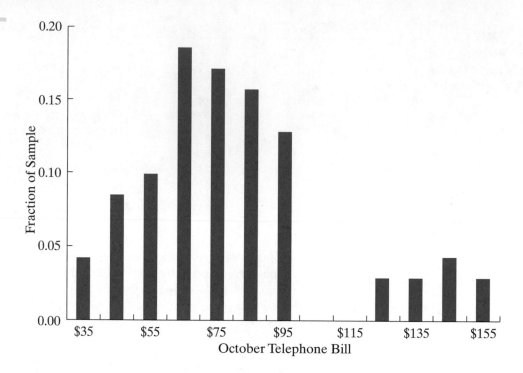

In order to estimate the shape of the probability density function $f(x)$ of X, one can create a **frequency table** of the sample values $x_1, x_2, x_3, \ldots, x_n$. This is done by first dividing up the range of values of $x_1, x_2, x_3, \ldots, x_n$ into a set of intervals. Then for each of the intervals, compute the fraction of the sample whose values fall in between the endpoints of the interval. Then the set of fractions, one for each interval over the entire range of values, is called the frequency table. This table can then be plotted as a bar graph, which is called a **histogram**. This histogram is an estimate of the shape of the probability density function $f(x)$.

The preceding method for estimating the probability density function $f(x)$ of a random variable X based on sample data is not the only method that is used in practice. Especially when the sample size n is small or when intuition suggests that the shape of the distribution might be highly unusual, more sophisticated methods that try to "smooth" the shape of the curve of the estimated probability density function $f(x)$ are used instead of the straightforward counting method presented here.

Now let us look at the next two questions posed by Lisa Strom in Example 4.1. Rephrased in the language of probability, these questions are: "What is an estimate of $P(X \le \$45.00)$?" and "What is an estimate of $P(\$60.00 \le X \le \$100.00)$?", where X is the October telephone bill of a randomly chosen household (and so is a random variable). More generally, suppose we are interested in estimating the probability that X will take on a value in some range, say between a and b, for some given numbers a and b. To be more concrete, suppose that $a = \$75.00$ and $b = \$90.00$. That is, we would like to estimate:

$$P(\$75.00 \le X \le \$90.00).$$

How might we estimate this probability? Suppose, for the sake of argument, that it happened to be true that $P(\$75.00 \leq X \leq \$90.00) = 0.33$. Then we would expect roughly 33% of the values of the sample values $x_1, x_2, \ldots, x_{70}$ in Table 4.1 to be in the range between $75.00 and $90.00. If, instead, it happened to be true that $P(\$75.00 \leq X \leq \$90.00) = 0.38$, then we would expect roughly 38% of the values of the sample values $x_1, x_2, \ldots, x_{70}$ in Table 4.1 to be in the range between $75.00 and $90.00. Conversely, the percentage of values of $x_1, x_2, \ldots, x_{70}$ in Table 4.1 that are in the range between $75.00 and $90.00 is an estimate of the true probability p for which $p = P(\$75.00 \leq X \leq \$90.00)$. If we count the observed fraction $\bar{p}$ of the data values $x_1, x_2, \ldots, x_{70}$ in Table 4.1 that have a value of at least $75.00 and at most $90.00, then this fraction $\bar{p}$ is

$$\bar{p} = 0.29 = \frac{20}{70},$$

since 20 of the 70 observed values in Table 4.1 are in the range between $75.00 and $90.00. Therefore, $\bar{p} = 0.29$ is our estimate of $p = P(\$75.00 \leq X \leq \$90.00)$.

We summarize this method as follows:

Suppose that we are given two numbers a and b and that we wish to estimate the probability $p = P(a \leq X \leq b)$. Let $\bar{p}$ denote that fraction of the sample data $x_1, x_2, x_3, \ldots, x_n$ whose observed values are greater than or equal to a and are less than or equal to b. Then $\bar{p}$ is an estimate of the true probability $p = P(a \leq X \leq b)$.

Now let us answer Lisa Strom's second question: "What is an estimate of $P(X \leq \$45.00)$?" To answer this question, we simply count the number of values of $x_1, x_2, \ldots, x_{70}$ in Table 4.1 that are less than or equal to $45.00. This number is 5. Therefore, our estimate of $p = P(X \leq \$45.00)$ is:

$$\bar{p} = \frac{5}{70} = 0.07.$$

The answer to Lisa Strom's second question is therefore:

- An estimate of the percentage of households whose October telephone bill is below $45.00 is 7%.

Similarly, let us answer Lisa Strom's third question: "What is an estimate of $P(\$60.00 \leq X \leq \$100.00)$?" To answer this question, we simply count the number of values of $x_1, x_2, \ldots, x_{70}$ in Table 4.1 that are greater than or equal to $60.00 and are also less than or equal to $100.00. This number is 45. Therefore, our estimate of $p = P(\$60.00 \leq X \leq \$100.00)$ is

$$\bar{p} = \frac{45}{70} = 0.64.$$

The answer to Lisa Strom's second question is therefore:

- An estimate of the percentage of households whose October telephone bill is between $60.00 and $100.00 is 64%.

After we have collected the n observations $x_1, \ldots, x_n$, we can estimate the mean μ and standard deviation σ of the distribution of October telephone bills in the site area by computing the **observed sample mean**, the **observed sample variance**, and the **observed sample standard deviation**, which are defined as follows:

The **observed sample mean,** denoted by $\bar{x}$, is defined as:

$$\bar{x} = \frac{x_1 + \cdots + x_n}{n}.$$

The **observed sample variance,** denoted by s^2, is defined as:

$$s^2 = \frac{\sum_{i=1}^{n}(x_i - \bar{x})^2}{n-1}.$$

The **observed sample standard deviation,** denoted by s, is defined as:

$$s = \sqrt{\frac{\sum_{i=1}^{n}(x_i - \bar{x})^2}{n-1}}.$$

The observed sample mean is just the sum of all observed values divided by the number of observations, n. It is a natural and intuitive estimate of μ, because we would expect the observed sample mean to have a value that is close to the value of the mean μ.

Notice that the observed sample variance is the sum of the squared deviations from the observed sample mean, divided by $n-1$. A more intuitive definition of the observed sample variance would be:

$$\frac{\sum_{i=1}^{n}(x_i - \bar{x})^2}{n},$$

which is the sum of the squared deviations from the observed sample mean divided by n. The reason why we divide by $n-1$, instead of n, is not very intuitive; and of course when n is large, the choice of n or $n-1$ has only a negligible effect on computations.

Let us calculate these quantities for the problem faced by NEXNet in Example 4.1. For this example, $n = 70$, and so:

$$\bar{x} = \frac{x_1 + \cdots + x_n}{n} = \frac{95.67 + 82.69 + \cdots + 74.13}{70} = \$79.40,$$

$$s^2 = \frac{\sum_{i=1}^{n}(x_i - \bar{x})^2}{n-1}$$

$$= \frac{(95.67 - 79.40)^2 + (82.69 - 79.40)^2 + \cdots + (74.13 - 79.40)^2}{69}$$

$$= 829.08,$$

and

$$s = \sqrt{829.08} = \$28.79.$$

We estimate the mean of the distribution with the observed sample mean $\bar{x}$, and we estimate the standard deviation of the distribution with the observed sample standard deviation s. Therefore, we now have answers to the last two questions posed by Lisa Strom in Example 4.1:

- An estimate of the mean of the distribution of October household telephone bills is $\bar{x} = \$79.40$.

- An estimate of the standard deviation of the distribution of October household telephone bills is $s = \$28.79$.

More generally, of course, we have:

We estimate the true mean μ of the random variable X by using the observed sample mean $\bar{x}$.

We estimate the true standard deviation σ of the random variable X by using the observed sample standard deviation s.

Example 4.2 — NEXNet Corporation, continued

Recall that NEXNet Corporation has been using a growth and development strategy targeted on communities with the following telephone usage characteristics:

- The mean monthly household telephone bill is at least $75.00.

- The percentage of households whose monthly telephone bills are under $45.00 is no more than 15%.

- The percentage of households whose monthly telephone bills is between $60.00 and $100.00 is at least 30%.

Based on a survey of 70 households in the site area of Weston, Wayland, and Sudbury, Lisa Strom has arrived at the following estimates:

(a) An estimate of the shape of the distribution of October telephone bills in the site area is that it is shaped like a Normal distribution, with a peak near $65.00, except for a small but significant group in the range between $125.00 and $155.00.

(b) An estimate of the percentage of households whose October telephone bill is below $45.00 is 7%.

(c) An estimate of the percentage of households whose October telephone bill is between $60.00 and $100.00 is 64%.

(d) An estimate of the mean of the distribution of October household telephone bills is $\bar{x} = \$79.40$.

(e) An estimate of the standard deviation of the distribution of October household telephone bills is $s = \$28.79$.

Based on Lisa Strom's preceding estimates, it appears that the site area has the necessary telephone usage characteristics to merit targeting this area for marketing. In addition, Lisa Strom might also recommend further analysis of the high-use telephone market (those households with monthly telephone bills above $115.00) to develop a special marketing campaign, for example.

The observed sample mean is not the only measure of central tendency in a sample of n observations. The following definition embraces an alternate way to measure the notion of central tendency in a sample of n observations:

The **median** of a sample of n observations is the observation below which lie half the data (that is, the 50th percentile).

TABLE 4. 3

Sample of previous job experience of nine MBA students.

Student	Previous Job Experience (years)
John	3
Alice	5
Manuel	5
Sarah	4
Lee	3
Vivek	2
Tom	5
Elaine	4
Vien	9

We illustrate this definition in the following example:

Example 4.3 – Number of Years of Job Experience of MBA Students

Table 4.3 shows the number of years of previous job experience for nine randomly selected MBA students.

The observed sample mean of this sample is

$$\bar{x} = \frac{3 + 5 + 5 + 4 + 3 + 2 + 5 + 4 + 9}{9} = 4.44 \text{ years.}$$

The median of the sample is 4 years, since 50% of the 9 observations lie on or below the value of 4 years.

The observed sample variance is

$$s^2 = \frac{(3 - 4.44)^2 + (5 - 4.44)^2 + \cdots + (9 - 4.44)^2}{9 - 1} = 4.03.$$

The observed sample standard deviation is

$$s = \sqrt{4.03} = 2.007 \text{ years.}$$

In general, the observed sample mean accounts equally for the numerical value of each observation, but might be distorted by extreme values. The median is not affected by the magnitude of extreme values, but conveys information about position only, not about magnitude.

The definitions of the observed sample mean, observed sample variance, and observed sample standard deviation pertain to the observed values $x_1, x_2, \ldots, x_n$ of the random sample, that is, **after the sample has been collected**. Let us instead look at the problem **before** the random sample is collected. Recall that before the sample is collected, the random variables $X_1, X_2, \ldots, X_n$ denote the uncertain values that will be obtained from the random sample. We have the following definitions:

The **sample mean**, denoted by $\overline{X}$, is defined as:

$$\overline{X} = \frac{X_1 + \cdots + X_n}{n}.$$

The **sample variance**, denoted by S^2, is defined as:

$$S^2 = \frac{\sum_{i=1}^{n} (X_i - \overline{X})^2}{n - 1}.$$

The **sample standard deviation**, denoted by S, is defined as:

$$S = \sqrt{\frac{\sum_{i=1}^{n}(X_i - \overline{X})^2}{n-1}}.$$

Notice that the sample mean $\overline{X}$ and the sample standard deviation S are random variables, since they depend on the random variables $X_1, \ldots, X_n$, which are uncertain before the sample is collected. Notice that we distinguish between the **sample mean** $\overline{X}$, which is a random variable and the **observed sample mean** $\overline{x}$, which is a number. Similarly, the **sample standard deviation** S is a random variable and the **observed sample standard deviation** s is a number.

Because the sample mean $\overline{X}$ is a random variable, it will have a mean and a standard deviation. Let us calculate the mean and the standard deviation of the sample mean $\overline{X}$. Since the expected value of each X_i is $E(X_i) = \mu$, then

$$E(\overline{X}) = E\left(\frac{X_1 + \cdots + X_n}{n}\right) = \frac{1}{n}(E(X_1) + \cdots + E(X_n)) = \frac{1}{n}(\mu + \cdots + \mu) = \mu.$$

This states that the expected value of the sample mean is the true mean of the population, which is reassuring. We say that the sample mean is an **unbiased** estimator of the true mean because of this fact.

Now let us compute the standard deviation of the random variable $\overline{X}$. We start by computing the variance of $\overline{X}$:

$$\text{VAR}(\overline{X}) = \text{VAR}\left(\frac{X_1 + \cdots + X_n}{n}\right) = \frac{1}{n^2}(\text{VAR}(X_1) + \cdots + \text{VAR}(X_n)),$$

because the random variables X_i are independent. Therefore,

$$\text{VAR}(\overline{X}) = \frac{1}{n^2}(\sigma^2 + \cdots + \sigma^2) = \frac{\sigma^2}{n}.$$

Therefore, the standard deviation of the sample mean $\overline{X}$ is

$$\sigma_{\overline{X}} = \sqrt{\frac{\sigma^2}{n}} = \frac{\sigma}{\sqrt{n}}.$$

We summarize these findings as follows:

The expected value of the sample mean $\overline{X}$ is
$$E(\overline{X}) = \mu.$$
The standard deviation of the sample mean $\overline{X}$ is
$$\sigma_{\overline{X}} = \frac{\sigma}{\sqrt{n}}.$$

Notice that when n is large the standard deviation of the sample mean tends to zero.

It is also possible to derive the following fact:

$$E(S^2) = \sigma^2.$$

(We omit the calculation as it is technical and not very intuitive.) This means that the sample variance is an **unbiased** estimator of the true variance σ^2 of the population. This observation explains why we divided by $n - 1$, and not by n, in the computation of the sample variance and the sample standard deviation. That is, by dividing by $n - 1$, the sample variance turns out to be an unbiased estimator of the true variance σ^2 of the population.

At this point, it is natural to ask: "How good an estimate of the mean μ is the observed sample mean $\bar{x}$?" That is, how reliable is this estimate? In order to address this question, we need to understand the shape of the distribution of the sample mean $\bar{X}$. We have already seen that $E(\bar{X}) = \mu$ and $\sigma_{\bar{X}} = \sigma/\sqrt{n}$. Now recall the Central Limit Theorem (for the mean) of Chapter 3:

Central Limit Theorem for the Sample Mean. For n large (say, $n \geq 30$), the sample mean $\bar{X}$ is approximately Normally distributed with mean μ and standard deviation $\dfrac{\sigma}{\sqrt{n}}$.

We illustrate this result with the following example.

Example 4.4 — Berkshire Power Company

Berksire Power Company (BPC) is an electric utility company that provides electric power in Berkshire County in western Massachusetts. BPC has recently implemented a variety of incentive programs to encourage households to conserve energy in winter months. Sarah Woodhouse is in charge of measuring the effectiveness of these new incentive programs. Sarah would like to estimate the mean μ and standard deviation σ of the distribution of household electricity consumption for the upcoming month of January in Berkshire County. Sarah chose 100 households in the county at random, and she arranged to send meter-readers to all of these households on January 1 and again on January 31 to record the meter levels of the 100 households. (The electricity consumption of a household for the month of January is the difference between the meter levels on January 1 and January 31.) Table 4.4 shows the observed electricity consumption of the 100 randomly chosen households for the month of January.

From the sample observations in Table 4.4, we can compute the observed sample mean, the observed sample variance, and the observed sample standard deviation for January electricity usage as follows:

$$\bar{x} = \frac{x_1 + \cdots + x_n}{n} = \frac{2{,}424 + 4{,}242 + \cdots + 2{,}165}{100} = 3{,}011 \text{ KWH,}$$

$$
\begin{aligned}
s^2 &= \frac{\sum_{i=1}^{n}(x_i - \bar{x})^2}{n - 1} \\
&= \frac{(2{,}424 - 3{,}011)^2 + (4{,}242 - 3{,}011)^2 + \cdots + (2{,}165 - 3{,}011)^2}{99} \\
&= 540{,}483.7,
\end{aligned}
$$

and

TABLE 4.4

Sample of January electricity usage in 100 households (in KWH).

Household Number	Usage (KWH)	Household Number	Usage (KWH)	Household Number	Usage (KWH)	Household Number	Usage (KWH)
1	2,424	26	2,803	51	3,487	76	3,896
2	4,242	27	3,933	52	3,797	77	1,964
3	1,803	28	1,901	53	4,052	78	2,133
4	2,286	29	3,071	54	3,638	79	2,774
5	2,475	30	3,837	55	4,170	80	2,225
6	3,234	31	1,806	56	2,088	81	2,865
7	1,901	32	2,153	57	2,360	82	3,630
8	3,141	33	2,801	58	2,170	83	3,021
9	4,303	34	3,192	59	4,002	84	2,096
10	3,622	35	2,137	60	4,399	85	3,481
11	2,907	36	3,494	61	2,197	86	3,711
12	3,677	37	2,950	62	3,731	87	3,525
13	2,153	38	3,282	63	3,796	88	2,225
14	2,892	39	2,748	64	3,076	89	3,332
15	1,878	40	4,007	65	1,807	90	2,841
16	3,014	41	3,797	66	4,395	91	2,911
17	3,284	42	2,980	67	3,370	92	4,090
18	2,695	43	2,390	68	3,363	93	3,313
19	2,870	44	3,274	69	4,119	94	2,776
20	3,621	45	3,785	70	3,217	95	2,314
21	2,947	46	2,497	71	2,510	96	3,798
22	2,009	47	3,018	72	3,570	97	2,772
23	2,320	48	2,051	73	2,126	98	3,644
24	1,885	49	4,398	74	3,207	99	2,461
25	3,557	50	3,053	75	1,958	100	2,165

$$s = \sqrt{540,483.7} = 735.18 \text{ KWH.}$$

Suppose that instead of choosing a sample size of $n = 100$, Sarah had chosen a sample size of $n = 10$ households for her random sample of electricity consumption in the month of January. She would have obtained ten different observed consumption numbers $x_1, \ldots, x_{10}$ whose observed sample mean might have been, for example, 3,056 KWH. If she were to have chosen ten other random households instead, she might have obtained a different observed sample mean, of say, 2,867 KWH. Suppose we repeat this experiment a number of different times, and each time we choose ten households at random and then collect the electricity consumption numbers and compute the observed sample mean each time. We would, of course, obtain a different value of the observed sample mean each time. Furthermore, a histogram of all of the different observed sample means would look like Figure 4.2, and the shape of the probability density function of $\overline{X}$ would approximately be the shape of the histogram in Figure 4.2.

Now suppose that instead of choosing a sample size of $n = 10$ households, that we choose a larger sample size of $n = 100$ households and repeat the previous experiment. We would obtain 100 different observed consumption numbers $x_1, \ldots, x_{100}$, whose observed sample mean might have been, for example, 2,964 KWH. If we were to have chosen 100 other random households instead, we might have obtained a different observed sample mean, of say, 3,027 KWH. Suppose we repeat this experiment a number of different times, and each time we choose 100 households at random and then collect the electricity consumption numbers and compute the observed sample mean each time. We would, of course, obtain a different value of the observed sample mean each time. Furthermore, a plot of the histogram of all of the different observed sample means would look like Figure 4.3, and the shape of the probability density function of $\overline{X}$ would approximately be the shape

FIGURE 4.2
Histogram of the
observed sample
mean for a sample
size of $n = 10$.

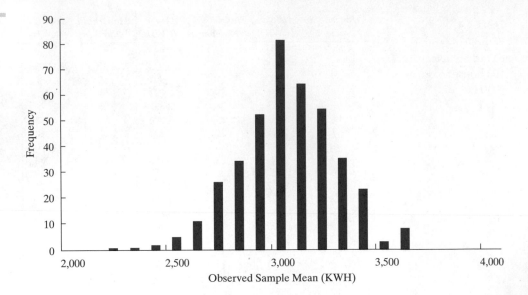

FIGURE 4.2
Histogram of the
observed sample
mean for a sample
size of $n = 10$.

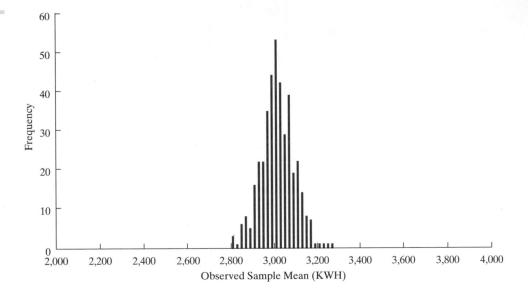

FIGURE 4.3
Histogram of the
observed sample
mean for sample
size of $n = 100$.

of the histogram in Figure 4.3. Notice that Figure 4.3 is approximately bell-shaped. Also notice that the spread of the histogram of Figure 4.3 is much less than the corresponding spread in the histogram of Figure 4.3. This illustrates the fact from the Central Limit Theorem that the standard deviation of the distribution of the sample mean $\overline{X}$ is lower when the sample size n is larger. The sample size of Figure 4.2 is $n = 10$ and the sample size of Figure 4.3 is $n = 100$. Therefore, we would expect the spread in Figure 4.3 to be less by a factor of $3.162 = \sqrt{10}$ according to the Central Limit Theorem.

Reconsidering Example 4.1, if we used $n = 7{,}000$ as the size of the sample of households as opposed to $n = 70$, intuition suggests that the observed sample mean $\overline{x}$ and the observed sample standard deviation s would be very reliable estimates of the mean μ and the standard deviation σ of the underlying distribution of the random variable X. On the other hand, if we used $n = 7$ as the size of the sample of households, intuition suggests that the observed sample mean $\overline{x}$ and the observed sample standard deviation s would not necessarily be very reliable estimates of the mean μ and the standard deviation σ of the underlying distribution of the random variable X. In the next section, we will translate this loose intuition of "reliability" into an exact measure by developing the very important concept of a confidence interval.

4.3 CONFIDENCE INTERVALS FOR THE MEAN, FOR LARGE SAMPLE SIZE

In the previous section, we introduced the basic methodology for estimating the mean μ and the standard deviation σ of a probability distribution of a random variable X based on a random sample of n observations. Intuition suggests that the observed sample mean $\bar{x}$ will be a more reliable estimate of the mean μ when the sample size n is larger. In this section, we quantify this intuitive notion of reliability of an estimate by developing the concept of a confidence interval for an estimate of the mean μ of a random variable.

The sample mean $\overline{X}$ is an estimate of the mean μ of the distribution of the random variable X; however, a particular observed value $\bar{x}$ of the sample mean will typically not be equal to the mean μ.

Consider the following problem: Compute a quantity b such that, with probability $p = 0.95$, the observed value of the sample mean $\overline{X}$ will lie within b units of the mean μ. That is, we would like to compute a quantity b such that

$$p = P(\mu - b \le \overline{X} \le \mu + b) = 0.95.$$

It is useful to reflect on what the random variable is in this statement. The population mean μ is **not known**, but it is **not random**. It is the sample mean $\overline{X}$ that is the random variable. The previous statement says that the probability that $\overline{X}$ will fall within b units of the mean μ is $p = 0.95$.

Let us now compute the value of b for which the preceding expression is true. In order to do so, we do a bit of further rearrangement of the expression. By subtracting the mean μ from all of the expressions inside the probability, we obtain:

$$P(-b \le \overline{X} - \mu \le b) = 0.95.$$

Next let us divide all of the terms inside the probability expression by the quantity $\sigma/\sqrt{n}$, to obtain:

$$P\left(-\frac{b}{\sigma/\sqrt{n}} \le \frac{\overline{X} - \mu}{\sigma/\sqrt{n}} \le \frac{b}{\sigma/\sqrt{n}}\right) = 0.95.$$

Recall that $E(\overline{X}) = \mu$ and $\sigma_{\overline{X}} = \sigma/\sqrt{n}$. Furthermore, from the Central Limit Theorem (for the sample mean), $\overline{X}$ is approximately Normally distributed when n is large. Therefore, the random variable

$$Z = \frac{\overline{X} - \mu}{\sigma/\sqrt{n}}$$

will obey a standard Normal distribution when n is large (say, $n \ge 30$). Substituting Z in the middle expression, we obtain

$$P\left(-\frac{b}{\sigma/\sqrt{n}} \le Z \le \frac{b}{\sigma/\sqrt{n}}\right) = 0.95.$$

However, since Z is a standard Normal random variable, we know that

$$P(-1.96 \le Z \le 1.96) = 0.95.$$

Therefore it must be true that

$$\frac{b}{\sigma/\sqrt{n}} = 1.96$$

and so

$$b = \frac{1.96\sigma}{\sqrt{n}}.$$

Substituting this expression back in the original probability equation, we obtain:

$$P\left(\mu - \frac{1.96\sigma}{\sqrt{n}} \le \overline{X} \le \mu + \frac{1.96\sigma}{\sqrt{n}}\right) = 0.95.$$

Rearranging this expression, we find that

$$P\left(\overline{X} - \frac{1.96\sigma}{\sqrt{n}} \le \mu \le \overline{X} + \frac{1.96\sigma}{\sqrt{n}}\right) = 0.95.$$

Now suppose that we have collected our n samples and have computed the observed sample mean $\bar{x}$ and the observed sample standard deviation s. We will use s as an approximation of the true standard deviation σ. We construct an interval estimate of the mean μ by replacing $\overline{X}$ by $\bar{x}$ and σ by s in the preceding expression. This yields the following interval:

$$\left[\bar{x} - \frac{1.96s}{\sqrt{n}}, \bar{x} + \frac{1.96s}{\sqrt{n}}\right].$$

This interval is called a **95% confidence interval** for the mean of the distribution of X. We formally record this as:

If n is sufficiently large, say $n \ge 30$, then a 95% **confidence interval for the mean** μ is the interval:

$$\left[\bar{x} - \frac{1.96s}{\sqrt{n}}, \bar{x} + \frac{1.96s}{\sqrt{n}}\right].$$

Note that if we were to repeat our sampling experiment over and over again, each time we would compute a different observed sample mean $\bar{x}$ and a different observed sample standard deviation s and therefore, a different confidence interval. However, 95% of the resulting confidence intervals would, on average, contain the actual mean μ. We summarize this interpretation as follows:

Interpretation of a confidence interval. Since both the sample mean $\overline{X}$ and the sample standard deviation S are random variables, each time we take random samples, we find different values for the observed sample mean $\bar{x}$ and the observed sample standard deviation s. This results in a different confidence interval each time we sample. A 95% confidence interval means that 95% of the resulting intervals will contain the actual mean μ.

Example 4.5 — Berkshire Power Company, continued

Recall Example 4.4, where Sarah has collected $n = 100$ random sample observations of household electricity consumption for the month of January. In that example, we computed the observed sample mean $\bar{x} = 3{,}011$ KWH and the observed sample standard deviation $s = 735.18$ KWH. Let us construct a 95% confidence interval for the mean μ of the distribution of January household electricity consumption. Substituting in the formula, we obtain:

$$\left[\bar{x} - \frac{1.96s}{\sqrt{n}}, \bar{x} + \frac{1.96s}{\sqrt{n}} \right] = \left[3{,}011 - \frac{1.96 \times 735.18}{\sqrt{100}}, 3{,}011 + \frac{1.96 \times 735.18}{\sqrt{100}} \right]$$
$$= [2{,}866.9, 3{,}155.1].$$

That is, we are 95% confident that the mean μ of January household electricity consumption lies in the interval between 2,866.9 KWH and 3,155.1 KWH.

Let us pause to observe that the 95% confidence interval for the mean μ has some appealing intuitive features. First, notice that the center of the interval is the observed sample mean $\bar{x}$ (which is our estimate of the mean μ). Second, as the sample size n increases, the width of the confidence interval decreases (due to the $\sqrt{n}$ factor in the denominator). This is natural, because we expect that we will be more confident in our estimate if the sample size n is larger. Third, as the observed sample standard deviation decreases, the confidence interval becomes tighter. This also makes good sense, since one would expect that it is easier to make estimates about the mean of a random variable if the random variable has less spread to begin with, that is, if the random variable has a smaller standard deviation.

Example 4.6 — Newspaper Waste

In the printing of a newspaper, frequent mistakes in the printing process often require that many tons of newsprint must be thrown away. A large newspaper company is concerned that its printing operations waste too much newsprint. To judge the severity of their problem and to help decide if management action is warranted, the company has collected data on the weight of daily newsprint waste for each of the last 50 days of operations. The observed sample mean of these observations is 273.1 tons (per day) and the observed sample standard deviation is 64.2 tons (per day).

Let us compute a 95% confidence interval for the mean μ of the distribution of wasted newsprint. The observed sample mean is $\bar{x} = 273.1$ tons, and the observed sample standard deviation is $s = 64.2$ tons. From the expression for a 95% confidence interval for the mean, we obtain:

$$\left[\bar{x} - \frac{1.96s}{\sqrt{n}}, \bar{x} + \frac{1.96s}{\sqrt{n}} \right] = \left[273.1 - \frac{1.96 \times 64.2}{\sqrt{50}}, 273.1 + \frac{1.96 \times 64.2}{\sqrt{50}} \right]$$
$$= [255.3, \ 290.8].$$

That is, we are 95% confident that the mean of the distribution of daily newsprint waste lies between 255.3 tons per day and 290.8 tons per day.

It is natural at this point to wonder where the number "1.96" comes from in the formula for the 95% confidence interval for the mean. Going back into the derivation on the previous pages, we see that the number "1.96" arises because $P(-1.96 \leq Z \leq 1.96) = 0.95$, where Z is a standard Normal random variable. Suppose that we wanted the probability that our interval contains the mean to be some number other than 0.95. More generally, suppose that β is our desired level of confidence, that is, we want to compute a β% confidence interval, where, for example,

$\beta = 90$ or perhaps $\beta = 99$. Using the logic of this section, we can establish the following general method for computing a β% confidence interval for the mean μ for any value of β:

Suppose that $\bar{x}$ is the observed sample mean and s is the observed sample standard deviation. If n is sufficiently large, say $n \geq 30$, then a β% **confidence interval for the mean** μ is the interval:

$$\left[\bar{x} - \frac{c \times s}{\sqrt{n}}, \bar{x} + \frac{c \times s}{\sqrt{n}}\right],$$

where the number c is that number for which

$$P(-c \leq Z \leq c) = \beta/100.$$

For $\beta = 90\%, c = 1.645.$

For $\beta = 95\%, c = 1.960.$

For $\beta = 98\%, c = 2.326.$

For $\beta = 99\%, c = 2.576.$

Example 4.7 — Newspaper Waste, continued

In Example 4.6, we computed a 95% confidence interval for the mean of the daily newspaper waste. Let us instead compute a 99% confidence interval for the mean of the daily newspaper waste. The observed sample mean is $\bar{x} = 273.1$ tons and the observed sample standard deviation is $s = 64.2$ tons. From the expression for a 99% confidence interval for the mean shown above, we obtain:

$$\left[\bar{x} - \frac{2.576s}{\sqrt{n}}, \bar{x} + \frac{2.576s}{\sqrt{n}}\right] = \left[273.1 - \frac{2.576 \times 64.2}{\sqrt{50}}, 273.1 + \frac{2.576 \times 64.2}{\sqrt{50}}\right]$$
$$= [249.71, \ 296.49].$$

That is, we are 99% confident that the mean of the distribution of daily newsprint waste lies between 249.71 tons per day and 296.49 tons per day.

Tradeoffs in confidence intervals

Ideally, we would like to have a confidence interval whose width is small, but whose confidence level is high (that is, β is large). Let us look at the formula for a β% confidence interval more closely to see how this might or might not be possible. For a fixed confidence level β, if we increase the sample size n, then the confidence interval will have a smaller width, due to the $\sqrt{n}$ in the denominator. Clearly, the larger the sample size n, the more accurate will be our estimate, and so the smaller will be the width of the confidence interval for the mean.

However, for a fixed sample size n, if we want to make a statement with a higher level of confidence (higher β), we must use a wider interval. Conversely, for a fixed sample size n, statements about narrower intervals must be made with a lower confidence (lower β).

For a fixed sample size n and a fixed confidence level β, we can obtain a narrower interval with populations that have less spread, that is, whose standard deviation σ or whose sample standard deviation s are smaller. That is, it is easier to make more confident estimates of the mean μ when the spread or variation is smaller.

All of the results of this section presume that the sample size n is "large," that n is at least 30. However, there are many situations in estimation where the sample size n is small. In Section 4.5, we will develop confidence intervals for small sample sizes. Before doing so, however, we first must make a slight digression to describe a particular continuous probability distribution called the *t*-distribution.

THE *t*-DISTRIBUTION

The *t*-distribution is a special probability distribution that arises when computing confidence intervals with small sample sizes (typically when the sample size n is less than 30). The shape of the *t*-distribution depends on a parameter k associated with the distribution that is called the "degrees of freedom" of the distribution. The probability density function of the *t*-distribution with k degrees of freedom is shown in Figure 4.4 for a variety of values of k. Also included in Figure 4.4 is the probability density function of a standard Normal distribution. Notice that the *t*-distribution is roughly bell-shaped. Also, the *t*-distribution is symmetric around zero, which is its mean. However, in contrast with the standard Normal distribution, the standard deviation σ of the *t*-distribution with k degrees of freedom is $\sigma = \sqrt{\dfrac{k}{k-2}}$, which is larger than one. This is because the *t*-distribution has more area in the tails of the distribution, as Figure 4.4 shows. However, for k sufficiently large, $\sigma = \sqrt{\dfrac{k}{k-2}}$ is approximately equal to one. Furthermore, as the value of the degrees of freedom k becomes larger, the shape of the probability density function of the *t*-distribution becomes closer to the shape of the standard Normal distribution.

It is helpful to think of the *t*-distribution as a slightly "flattened" version of the standard Normal distribution, where the extent of the flattening depends on the value of the degrees of freedom k. For the purposes of statistical computation, when the degrees of freedom k is 30 or more, then the *t*-distribution and the standard Normal distribution are virtually identical.

FIGURE 4.4

The probability density function $f(x)$ of the *t*-distribution and the standard Normal distribution. Notice that the *t*-distribution has more area in the tails than the standard Normal distribution.

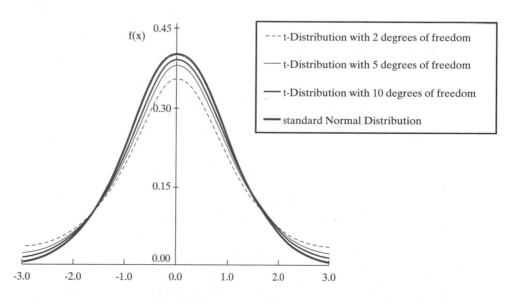

- - -	t-Distribution with 2 degrees of freedom
——	t-Distribution with 5 degrees of freedom
——	t-Distribution with 10 degrees of freedom
——	standard Normal Distribution

Let T be a random variable that obeys the t-distribution with k degrees of freedom. In a typical statistical application of the t-distribution, one is interested in knowing the value of the number c for which the following expression is true:

$$P(-c \leq T \leq c) = 0.95.$$

More generally speaking, for a given confidence level $\beta\%$ (such as $\beta = 90, \beta = 95$, or $\beta = 99$), one is interested in knowing the value of the number c for which the following expression is true:

$$P(-c \leq T \leq c) = \beta/100.$$

Table A.2 of the Appendix shows the value of c which makes the above expression true. Referring to Table A.2, suppose that T is a random variable that obeys a t-distribution with $k = 15$ degrees of freedom. Then from the table, we find that

$$P(-2.131 \leq T \leq 2.131) = 0.95.$$

As another example, suppose that T is a random variable that obeys a t-distribution with $k = 8$ degrees of freedom. Then from the table, we find that

$$P(-3.355 \leq T \leq 3.355) = 0.99.$$

Note that Table A.2 has only values for k less than 30 degrees of freedom. When the degrees of freedom k is 30 or higher, we instead use a standard Normal distribution, since the t-distribution is virtually identical to the standard Normal distribution when the degrees of freedom k is 30 or more.

4.5   CONFIDENCE INTERVALS FOR THE MEAN, FOR SMALL SAMPLE SIZE

In many management decisions, it is often important to make inferences with only a small sample size. For example, federal legislation requires pharmaceutical companies to perform extensive tests on new drugs before they can be marketed. After successfully testing a new drug on animals, a pharmaceutical company is permitted to perform tests on humans on a very small number of patients (often ten or fewer) who have been randomly selected from the population of all patients. It is therefore important to be able to make estimates about the effects of a new drug using a small sample.

The method of constructing confidence intervals that we used in Section 4.3 assumed that we had available a large sample of observations, say $n \geq 30$ observations. The derivation of the confidence interval for large samples was based on the fact that the random variable

$$Z = \frac{\overline{X} - \mu}{\sigma/\sqrt{n}}$$

obeys a standard Normal distribution if n is sufficiently large, say $n \geq 30$. Instead, we will consider the random variable T defined by

$$T = \frac{\overline{X} - \mu}{S/\sqrt{n}}.$$

When the sample observations $X_i, i = 1, \ldots, n$ each obey a Normal distribution, then the random variable T obeys a t-distribution with $k = (n - 1)$ degrees of freedom. If the underlying distribution of the sample observations X_i are almost Normally distributed, then T approximately obeys a t-distribution with $k = (n - 1)$ degrees of freedom. This approximation will be better to the extent that the distribution of the sample observations X_i is closer to being a Normal distribution. Therefore if the underlying distribution is "well-behaved," that is, not heavily skewed, then the approximation of T by a t-distribution works well.

We now present the method for constructing a $\beta\%$ confidence interval for the mean μ for a small sample size:

Suppose that the distribution of the sample observations is "well-behaved" in the sense that it is not too different in shape from a Normal distribution. Let $\bar{x}$ be the observed sample mean and s be the observed sample standard deviation. Then a $\beta\%$ **confidence interval for the mean** μ is computed as follows:

First, use a t-distribution table to find the number c for which

$$P(-c \le T \le c) = \beta/100,$$

where T obeys a t-distribution with $k = (n - 1)$ degrees of freedom.
Then the $\beta\%$ confidence interval is:

$$\left[\bar{x} - \frac{c \times s}{\sqrt{n}}, \bar{x} + \frac{c \times s}{\sqrt{n}} \right].$$

Before demonstrating why this method is valid, let us first illustrate how the method is used in an example.

Example 4.8 – A Printer Manufacturer

Suppose that a printer manufacturer is concerned with estimating the mean μ of the distribution of the lifetime of a printhead. It is assumed that the lifetime of a printhead approximately obeys a Normal distribution. The manufacturer has tested 15 randomly selected printheads. The observed sample mean of the 15 samples is $\bar{x} = 1.23$ million characters, and the observed sample standard deviation is $s = 0.27$ million characters. Let us compute a 99% confidence interval for the mean μ of the distribution of the lifetime of a printhead. Then we are interested in computing a $\beta\%$ confidence interval for the mean, where $\beta = 99$. Using the preceding method, we first must find c for which

$$P(-c \le T \le c) = \beta/100$$

where T obeys a t-distribution with $k = (n - 1)$ degrees of freedom. Since the sample size is $n = 15$, the value of k is $k = 15 - 1 = 14$. From Table A.2, the value of c is $c = 2.977$. Applying the preceding method, the 99% confidence interval for the mean μ of the lifetime of a printhead is

$$\left[\bar{x} - \frac{2.977s}{\sqrt{15}}, \bar{x} + \frac{2.977s}{\sqrt{15}} \right] = \left[1.23 - \frac{2.977 \times 0.27}{\sqrt{15}}, 1.23 + \frac{2.977 \times 0.27}{\sqrt{15}} \right]$$

$$= [1.022, \ 1.437]$$

million characters. That is, we are 99% confident that the mean μ of the distribution of the lifetime of a printhead lies between 1.022 million characters and 1.437 million characters.

Notice the similarity between the method for computing a β% confidence interval for the mean for a small sample size and for a large sample size. The only difference between the two methods is in the computation of the number c. When the sample size n is large, then a Normal distribution is the appropriate distribution for computing the value of c. When the sample size n is small, then a t-distribution is the appropriate distribution for computing the value of c.

Derivation of the Confidence Interval for Small Sample Size

In the remainder of this section, we illustrate how the method for computing the confidence interval for the mean μ for a small sample size is derived. *This discussion is more mathematical and can be skipped without a loss in continuity or general understanding.*

Suppose that we are interested in computing a $\beta = 95\%$ confidence interval for the mean μ for a sample size of $n = 20$ observations. That is, we would like to find a quantity b such that the observed value of the sample mean $\overline{X}$ will lie within b units of the mean μ. Equivalently, we would like to compute a quantity b such that

$$P(\mu - b \leq \overline{X} \leq \mu + b) = 0.95.$$

This statement says that the probability that $\overline{X}$ will fall within b units of the mean μ is $p = 0.95$.

By subtracting the mean μ from all of the expressions inside the probability we obtain

$$P(-b \leq \overline{X} - \mu \leq b) = 0.95.$$

Next we divide all of the terms inside the probability expression by the quantity $S/\sqrt{n}$ to obtain

$$P\left(-\frac{b}{S/\sqrt{n}} \leq \frac{\overline{X} - \mu}{S/\sqrt{n}} \leq \frac{b}{S/\sqrt{n}}\right) = 0.95.$$

If we define the random variable T by

$$T = \frac{\overline{X} - \mu}{S/\sqrt{n}},$$

then one can demonstrate based on mathematical analysis that T will obey a t-distribution with $k = (n - 1)$ degrees of freedom provided that the distribution of the sample observations X_i, $i = 1, \ldots, n$, is well-behaved (not too skewed). We record this fact formally as follows:

Consider the random variable T defined as:

$$T = \frac{\overline{X} - \mu}{S/\sqrt{n}}.$$

Then T will obey a t-distribution with $k = (n - 1)$ degrees of freedom provided that the distribution of the sample observations X_i, $i = 1, \ldots, n$, is well-behaved (not too skewed).

We next substitute the value of T in the probability expression derived previously:

$$P\left(-\frac{b}{S/\sqrt{n}} \leq \frac{\overline{X} - \mu}{S/\sqrt{n}} \leq \frac{b}{S/\sqrt{n}}\right) = 0.95.$$

Substituting T in the middle expression, we obtain:

$$P\left(-\frac{b}{S/\sqrt{n}} \leq T \leq \frac{b}{S/\sqrt{n}}\right) = 0.95.$$

However, since T obeys a t-distribution with $k = (n - 1) = 20 - 1 = 19$ degrees of freedom, we find from Table A.2 that

$$P(-2.093 \leq T \leq 2.093) = 0.95.$$

Therefore it must be true that

$$\frac{b}{S/\sqrt{n}} = 2.093$$

and so

$$b = \frac{2.093S}{\sqrt{n}}.$$

Note that b is a random variable because b depends on the sample standard deviation S.
Substituting this expression back in the original probability equation, we obtain

$$P\left(\mu - \frac{2.093S}{\sqrt{n}} \leq \overline{X} \leq \mu + \frac{2.093S}{\sqrt{n}}\right) = 0.95.$$

Rearranging this expression, we find that

$$0.95 = P\left(\overline{X} - \frac{2.093S}{\sqrt{n}} \leq \mu \leq \overline{X} + \frac{2.093S}{\sqrt{n}}\right).$$

It follows from the above expression that with probability 0.95, the interval

$$\left[\overline{X} - \frac{2.093S}{\sqrt{n}}, \ \overline{X} + \frac{2.093S}{\sqrt{n}}\right]$$

will contain the mean μ of the distribution of random variable X. This interval is therefore the 95% confidence interval for the mean of the distribution of X.

If we replicate this derivation for a general $\beta\%$ confidence level and for a general sample size n, we then obtain the general method for computing a confidence interval for the mean, which was presented earlier in this section.

4.6   ESTIMATION AND CONFIDENCE INTERVALS FOR THE POPULATION PROPORTION

In many management domains, one is interested in estimating the **proportion** of a population that has a certain characteristic. For example, a product manager might want to estimate the proportion of commuters who have cellular telephones in their automobiles. A marketing manager might want to estimate the proportion of teenagers who prefer a certain clothing style. A political campaign manager might want to estimate the proportion of registered voters who intend to vote for her candidate.

In each of these cases, one is concerned with estimating the proportion of a population that has a certain characteristic. In this section, we develop a method for estimating such a proportion, and we also develop a method for computing a confidence interval for the proportion. We motivate the development with the following example:

Example 4.9 — A Cable Television Company

Suppose that a cable television company would like to estimate the proportion p of households in Boston who own two or more television sets. The company has polled 200 households in Boston and has found that 124 of the 200 households own two or more television sets.

What is a good estimate of the proportion of Boston households who own two or more television sets? Obviously, a natural estimate of the proportion of Boston households who own two or more television sets is $124/200 = 0.62$.

More generally, suppose we are interested in estimating the proportion p of a targeted population that has a particular characteristic, based on a random sample of n observations from the population. Each element of the sample either does or does not possess the particular characteristic. Suppose that we have collected the n sample observations, and let x denote the number of the sample elements that possess the particular characteristic.

The **observed sample proportion** $\bar{p}$ is defined to be:

$$\bar{p} = \frac{x}{n}$$

and is an estimate of the proportion p of the targeted population that has the particular characteristic.

Example 4.10 — Teenage Cigarette Smoking

Suppose that the National Institute of Health (NIH) would like to estimate the proportion of teenagers that smoke cigarettes. Suppose that NIH has randomly sampled 1,000 teenagers, and that 253 of the teenagers stated that they smoke cigarettes. We therefore estimate the proportion of teenagers who smoke cigarettes to be the observed sample proportion $\bar{p} = 253/1,000 = 0.253$.

In addition to the proportion of teenagers who smoke cigarettes, we would like to compute a confidence interval for the estimate of the proportion of teenagers who smoke cigarettes.

More generally, we now develop the method for computing a confidence interval for the population proportion. In order to do so, we first study the sampling procedure **before** we have conducted the sample. Let p denote the proportion of the population that possesses the particular characteristic that we are studying. (Remember, we do not know what the actual value of p is; we are attempting to estimate the value of p.) Suppose that we have decided to collect observations from a random sample of n individuals. Let X be the number of individuals in the sample of n individuals that will possess the particular characteristic. Then X will obey a binomial distribution with n trials and probability of success p, and therefore

$$E(X) = np$$

and

$$\sigma_X = \sqrt{np(1-p)}.$$

We define the **sample proportion** as:

The **sample proportion** $\overline{P}$ is

$$\overline{P} = \frac{X}{n}.$$

Note that the sample proportion $\overline{P}$ is a random variable because X is a random variable. In fact, $\overline{P}$ is a linear function of the random variable X, and so from the formulas for the mean and standard deviation of a linear function of a random variable, we have

$$E(\overline{P}) = \frac{E(X)}{n} = \frac{np}{n} = p$$

and

$$\sigma_{\overline{P}} = \frac{\sigma_X}{n} = \frac{\sqrt{np(1-p)}}{n} = \sqrt{\frac{p(1-p)}{n}}.$$

These observations are used in conjunction with the Central Limit Theorem to derive a method for computing a confidence interval for the population proportion. We now present this method. The derivation of the method is deferred to the end of this section.

Suppose that $\overline{p}$ is the observed sample proportion. If n and $\overline{p}$ satisfy:

$$n\overline{p} \geq 5 \quad \text{and} \quad n(1 - \overline{p}) \geq 5,$$

then a $\beta\%$ **confidence interval for the population proportion** p is the interval:

$$\left[\overline{p} - c\sqrt{\frac{\overline{p}(1-\overline{p})}{n}}, \overline{p} + c\sqrt{\frac{\overline{p}(1-\overline{p})}{n}} \right],$$

where the number c is that number for which

$$P(-c \leq Z \leq c) = \beta/100.$$
$$\text{For } \beta = 90\%, c = 1.645.$$
$$\text{For } \beta = 95\%, c = 1.960.$$
$$\text{For } \beta = 98\%, c = 2.326.$$
$$\text{For } \beta = 99\%, c = 2.576.$$

We first illustrate the use of the method by computing the 95% confidence interval for the proportion in Example 4.9. Recall in Example 4.9 that the cable television company would like to estimate the proportion p of households in Boston who own two or more television sets. The company has polled 200 households in Boston and has found that 124 of the 200 households own two or more television sets. For this example, $n = 200$, $\bar{p} = 124/200 = 0.62$, and $\beta = 95$. Note that $n\bar{p}$ is greater than 5 and that $n(1 - \bar{p})$ is also greater than 5. Therefore, we can use the above method. We compute the value of c to be $c = 1.96$ because $\beta = 95$, and so the 95% confidence interval is

$$\left[0.62 - 1.96\sqrt{\frac{0.62(1 - 0.62)}{200}}, 0.62 + 1.96\sqrt{\frac{0.62(1 - 0.62)}{200}} \right] = [0.553, 0.687].$$

That is, we are 95% confident that the proportion of households in Boston who own two or more television sets is between 0.553 and 0.687.

We next illustrate this method by computing the 99% confidence interval for the proportion in Example 4.10. Recall in Example 4.10 that the NIH would like to estimate the proportion p of teenagers who smoke cigarettes. NIH has polled 1,000 teenagers and has found that 253 of the 1,000 teenagers smoke cigarettes. For this example, $n = 1,000$, $\bar{p} = 253/1,000 = 0.253$, and $\beta = 99$. Again, note that $n\bar{p}$ is greater than 5 and that $n(1 - \bar{p})$ is also greater than 5. Therefore, we can use the preceding method. We compute the value of c to be $c = 2.576$ because $\beta = 99$, and so the 99% confidence interval is

$$\left[0.253 - 2.576\sqrt{\frac{0.253(1 - 0.253)}{1,000}}, 0.253 + 2.576\sqrt{\frac{0.253(1 - 0.253)}{1,000}} \right]$$
$$= [0.218, 0.288].$$

That is, we are 99% confident that the proportion of teenagers who smoke cigarettes is between 0.218 and 0.288.

Example 4.11 — Age of First-year MBA students at Harvard Business School

Suppose we have randomly sampled 36 first-year MBA students at the Harvard Business School and have found that 30 of the 36 randomly sampled students are over 25 years old. Let us construct a 90% confidence interval for the proportion of first-year Harvard Business School students who are over 25 years old. For this example, $n = 36$, and $\bar{p} = 30/36 = 0.8333$, and $\beta = 90$. Once again, note that $n\bar{p}$ is greater than 5 and that $n(1 - \bar{p})$ is also greater than 5. Therefore, we can use the preceding method. We compute the value of c to be $c = 1.645$ because $\beta = 90$, and so the 90% confidence interval is

$$\left[0.8333 - 1.645\sqrt{\frac{0.8333(1 - 0.8333)}{36}}, 0.8333 + 1.645\sqrt{\frac{0.8333(1 - 0.8333)}{36}} \right]$$
$$= [0.731, 0.936].$$

That is, we are 90% confident that the proportion of first-year Harvard Business School students who are over 25 years old is between 0.731 and 0.936.

Derivation of the Confidence Interval for the Proportion

In the remainder of this section, we illustrate how the method for computing the confidence interval for the proportion is derived. *This discussion is more mathematical, and can be skipped without a loss in continuity or general understanding.*

Note that the sample proportion $\bar{P} = X/n$ is a random variable because X is a random variable. (Furthermore, we know that X obeys a binomial distribution with n trials and probability of success p.) In fact, $\bar{P}$ is a linear function of the Binomial random variable X, and we saw earlier in this section the formulas for the mean and the standard deviation of $\overline{P}$:

$$E(\overline{P}) = p \quad \text{and} \quad \sigma_{\overline{P}} = \sqrt{\frac{p(1-p)}{n}}.$$

As it turns out, using either the Central Limit Theorem or the fact that the binomial distribution can be approximated by the Normal distribution, we have the following observation:

The random variable Z defined by

$$Z = \frac{\overline{P} - p}{\sqrt{\overline{P}(1-\overline{P})/n}}$$

approximately obeys a standard Normal distribution. This approximation is very good whenever n and p satisfy

$$np \geq 5 \quad \text{and} \quad n(1-p) \geq 5.$$

Now suppose that we are interested in computing a $\beta = 95\%$ confidence interval for the proportion p for a sample size of $n = 100$ observations. That is, we would like to find a quantity b such that the observed value of the sample proportion $\overline{P} = X/n$ will lie within b units of the proportion p. Equivalently, we would like to compute a number b such that

$$P(p - b \leq \overline{P} \leq p + b) = 0.95.$$

This statement says that the probability that the sample proportion $\overline{P}$ will fall within b units of the proportion p is 0.95.

By subtracting the proportion p from all of the expressions inside the probability, we obtain

$$P(-b \leq \overline{P} - p \leq b) = 0.95.$$

Next we divide all of the terms inside the probability expression by the quantity $\sqrt{\overline{P}(1-\overline{P})/n}$ to obtain

$$P\left(-\frac{b}{\sqrt{\overline{P}(1-\overline{P})/n}} \leq \frac{\overline{P} - p}{\sqrt{\overline{P}(1-\overline{P})/n}} \leq \frac{b}{\sqrt{\overline{P}(1-\overline{P})/n}}\right) = 0.95.$$

If we define the random variable Z by

$$Z = \frac{\overline{P} - p}{\sqrt{\overline{P}(1-\overline{P})/n}},$$

then as we previously stated, Z will approximately obey a standard Normal distribution provided that np is greater than or equal to 5 and $n(1-p)$ is greater than or equal to 5. We next substitute the value of Z in the probability expression derived previously:

$$P\left(-\frac{b}{\sqrt{\overline{P}(1-\overline{P})/n}} \leq Z \leq \frac{b}{\sqrt{\overline{P}(1-\overline{P})/n}}\right) = 0.95.$$

However, since Z obeys a standard Normal distribution, we obtain

$$P(-1.96 \leq Z \leq 1.96) = 0.95.$$

Therefore, it must be true that

$$\frac{b}{\sqrt{\overline{P}(1-\overline{P})/n}} = 1.96,$$

and so

$$b = 1.96\sqrt{\frac{\overline{P}(1-\overline{P})}{n}}.$$

Note that b is a random variable because b is a function of the sample proportion $\overline{P}$.

Substituting this expression back in the original probability equation, we obtain

$$P\left(p - 1.96\sqrt{\frac{\overline{P}(1-\overline{P})}{n}} \leq \overline{P} \leq p + 1.96\sqrt{\frac{\overline{P}(1-\overline{P})}{n}}\right) = 0.95.$$

Rearranging this expression, we find that

$$0.95 = P\left(\overline{P} - 1.96\sqrt{\frac{\overline{P}(1-\overline{P})}{n}} \leq p \leq \overline{P} + 1.96\sqrt{\frac{\overline{P}(1-\overline{P})}{n}}\right).$$

It follows from the above expression that with probability 0.95 the interval

$$\left[\overline{P} - 1.96\sqrt{\frac{\overline{P}(1-\overline{P})}{n}}, \overline{P} + 1.96\sqrt{\frac{\overline{P}(1-\overline{P})}{n}}\right]$$

will contain the proportion p. This interval is therefore the 95% confidence interval for the proportion p.

If we replicate this derivation for a general $\beta\%$ confidence level and for a general sample size n, then we obtain the general method for computing a confidence interval for the proportion that was presented earlier in this section.

Note that the methodology of this section applies only when both $n\overline{p}$ and $n(1-\overline{p})$ are greater than or equal to 5. When $n\overline{p} < 5$ or $n(1-\overline{p}) < 5$, then the approximations involving the binomial distribution and the Normal distribution do not work very well. It turns out that there are methods for computing confidence intervals in these cases nevertheless, but they are quite sophisticated and are beyond the agenda of this book.

4.7   EXPERIMENTAL DESIGN

We have seen in the previous sections how the sample size n affects the computation of a confidence interval. We have also seen that as the sample size n is increased, the confidence interval becomes more narrow. Quite often in the use of sampling, a manager needs to estimate how large a sample n he or she needs to gather in order to satisfy a pre-specified tolerance in the width of the confidence interval. This problem is often referred to as **experimental design**.

Experimental Design for Estimating the Mean μ

We have seen that the $\beta\%$ confidence interval for the mean μ of the distribution of a random variable is:

$$\left[\bar{x} - \frac{c \times s}{\sqrt{n}}, \bar{x} + \frac{c \times s}{\sqrt{n}} \right],$$

where the number c is that number for which

$$P(-c \leq Z \leq c) = \beta/100,$$

and Z obeys a standard Normal distribution. (As a reminder, for $\beta = 95\%$, then $c = 1.96$.) Notice that the confidence interval is $[\bar{x} - L, \bar{x} + L]$, where

$$L = \frac{c \times s}{\sqrt{n}}.$$

One can think of L as the "tolerance level" of the experiment. That is, our estimate $\bar{x}$ is within plus or minus L of the value of μ with probability $\beta/100$. Suppose that we have a pre-specified tolerance level L that we must attain, and that we would like to compute the sample size n for which we can attain the pre-specified tolerance level L. If we solve for n in the above expression, we obtain:

$$n = \frac{c^2 s^2}{L^2}.$$

In practice, if the value of n computed in this expression is less than 30, then we set $n = 30$ to ensure that the previous derivation is statistically valid.

One difficulty in using this formula directly for computing the required sample size n is that we do not know the value of the sample standard deviation s in advance. However, one can typically obtain a rough estimate of the sample standard deviation s by conducting a small pilot sample first. We summarize this as follows:

Suppose that we want to construct a $\beta\%$ confidence interval for the mean μ with a tolerance level of L, that is, the confidence interval will be of the form $[\bar{x} - L, \bar{x} + L]$. Suppose that s is a rough estimate of the observed sample standard deviation of the distribution. Then the required sample size n is

$$n = \frac{c^2 s^2}{L^2},$$

where the number c is that number for which

$$P(-c \leq Z \leq c) = \beta/100,$$

and Z obeys a standard Normal distribution.

For $\beta = 90\%$, $c = 1.645$.
For $\beta = 95\%$, $c = 1.960$.
For $\beta = 98\%$, $c = 2.326$.
For $\beta = 99\%$, $c = 2.576$.

Furthermore, n should be at least 30 to ensure that the above expressions are statistically valid.

Notice that certain aspects of the above formula are intuitive. If we want to have a narrow confidence interval (small L), then we will need a large sample size n. Notice that the higher the confidence level β, the higher is the value of c. (For example, for $\beta = 95\%$, $c = 1.96$. For $\beta = 99\%$, $c = 2.576$.) Therefore, if we desire a high degree of confidence (higher β), then the sample size n needs to be larger. A final remark is that the value of n should be rounded up so that n is a whole number.

Example 4.12 – Market Research

Suppose that a marketing research firm wants to conduct a survey to estimate the mean μ of the distribution of the amount spent on entertainment by each adult who visits a certain popular resort. The firm would like to estimate the mean of this distribution to within $120.00 with 95% confidence. From data regarding past operations at the resort, it is has been estimated that the standard deviation of entertainment expenditures is no more than $400.00. How large does the firm's sample size need to be?

To answer this question, we will apply the formula above with $L = 120.00$ and $s = 400.00$. Also, since $\beta = 95\%$, then $c = 1.96$. We therefore compute:

$$n = \frac{c^2 s^2}{L^2} = \frac{(1.96)^2 (400)^2}{120^2} = 42.68.$$

We then round this number up to 43. That is, the market research firm needs to conduct a random sample of 43 adults who have visited the resort.

Experimental Design for Estimating the Proportion p

Recall that the $\beta\%$ confidence interval for the proportion p is

$$[\bar{p} - L , \bar{p} + L],$$

where

$$L = c\sqrt{\frac{\bar{p}(1 - \bar{p})}{n}},$$

and c is that number for which the standard Normal random variable Z satisfies

$$P(-c \leq Z \leq c) = \beta/100.$$

Here we assume that n is large, namely $n\bar{p} \geq 5$ and $n(1 - \bar{p}) \geq 5$.

Suppose that we have a pre-specified tolerance level L that we must attain, and that we would like to compute the sample size n for which we can attain the pre-specified tolerance level L. If we solve for n in the above expression, we obtain

$$n = \frac{c^2 \bar{p}(1 - \bar{p})}{L^2}.$$

The problem with using this formula directly for computing the required sample size n is that we do not know the value of the observed sample proportion $\bar{p}$ in advance, and so we do not know the value of the expression $\bar{p}(1 - \bar{p})$ in the formula in advance. However, mathematical manipulation can be used to demonstrate that the expression $\bar{p}(1 - \bar{p})$ always satisfies

$$\bar{p}(1 - \bar{p}) \leq \frac{1}{4},$$

because $\bar{p}$ is always between 0.0 and 1.0. Thus, if we use the value of 1/4 instead of $\bar{p}(1 - \bar{p})$ in the expression for n above, we obtain the "conservative" estimate

$$n = \frac{c^2}{4L^2}$$

for the sample size. We record this formally as follows:

Suppose that we want a β% confidence interval for the proportion with a tolerance level of L, that is, the confidence interval will be of the form $[\bar{p} - L, \bar{p} + L]$. Then an estimate of the required sample size is:

$$n = \frac{c^2}{4L^2},$$

where the number c is that number for which

$$P(-c \le Z \le c) = \beta/100,$$

and Z obeys a standard Normal distribution.

For $\beta = 90\%$, $c = 1.645$.
For $\beta = 95\%$, $c = 1.960$.
For $\beta = 98\%$, $c = 2.326$.
For $\beta = 99\%$, $c = 2.576$.

Example 4.13 — Conducting a Public Opinion Poll

Suppose that a major American television network is interested in estimating the proportion p of American adults who are in favor of a particular national issue such as handgun control. The television network would like to compute a 95% confidence interval whose tolerance level is plus or minus 3%. How many adults would the television network need to poll?

In order to answer this question, we use the formula above. In this case, we have $L = 0.03$ and $\beta = 95$, and so we find that $c = 1.96$. Therefore we compute

$$n = \frac{c^2}{4L^2} = \frac{(1.96)^2}{4 \times (0.03)^2} = 1,067.11.$$

We then round this number up to $n = 1,068$. That is, we must poll 1,068 adults in order to obtain the desired tolerance level of 3%.

This is a rather remarkable fact. No matter how small or large is the proportion we want to estimate, if we randomly sample 1,068 adults, then in 19 cases out of 20 (that is, 95%), the results based on such a sample will differ by no more than three percentage points in either direction from what would have been obtained by polling all American adults.

Example 4.14 — Conducting Another Public Opinion Poll

Suppose that a major American newspaper company is interested in estimating the proportion p of American adults who intend to join a private militia. The newspaper would like to compute a 98% confidence interval whose tolerance level is plus or minus 4%. How many adults would the newspaper company need to poll?

In order to answer this question, we use the formula

$$n = \frac{c^2}{4L^2}.$$

In this case, we have $L = 0.04$ and $\beta = 98$, and so we find that $c = 2.326$. Therefore we compute

$$n = \frac{c^2}{4L^2} = \frac{(2.326)^2}{4 \times (0.04)^2} = 845.36.$$

We then round this number up to $n = 846$. That is, we must poll 846 adults in order to obtain the desired tolerance level of 4%.

4.8 COMPARING ESTIMATES OF THE MEAN OF TWO DISTRIBUTIONS

In many management decisions, it is important to estimate the difference between the means of two populations. For example, a marketing manager might be interested in the difference between the sales in two successive months in order to assess the effectiveness of a marketing campaign that took place in the second month. In this section, we develop methods to estimate the difference between the means of two populations.

Example 4.15 – A Product-Promotion Decision

Suppose that a national department store chain is considering whether or not to promote its products via a direct-mail promotion campaign. Because the promotion campaign will be expensive, the company would like to test the effectiveness of the campaign beforehand. They have chosen two randomly selected groups of consumers, where each group consists of 600 consumers. They plan to mail the promotional material to all of the consumers in the first group, but not to any of the consumers in the second group. They then plan to monitor the spending of each consumer in each group in their stores during the coming month in order to estimate the effectiveness of the promotional campaign.

We now construct a general model that will later be applied to this example. Suppose that two independent populations 1 and 2 have population means μ_1 and μ_2 and standard deviations σ_1 and σ_2. Our objective is to estimate the difference between the means of the two populations, that is, $\mu_1 - \mu_2$.

Suppose that we plan to randomly sample from both populations, obtaining n_1 observations $X_1, \ldots, X_{n_1}$ from the first population and n_2 observations $Y_1, \ldots, Y_{n_2}$ from the second population. The two sample means are

$$\overline{X}_1 = \frac{X_1 + \cdots + X_{n_1}}{n_1} \quad \text{and} \quad \overline{X}_2 = \frac{Y_1 + \cdots + Y_{n_2}}{n_2}.$$

From the properties of linear functions of random variables, we have

$$E[\overline{X}_1 - \overline{X}_2] = E[\overline{X}_1] - E[\overline{X}_2] = \mu_1 - \mu_2,$$

and

$$\mathrm{VAR}(\overline{X}_1 - \overline{X}_2) = \mathrm{VAR}(\overline{X}_1) + \mathrm{VAR}(\overline{X}_2),$$

because the two sets of random samples are independent. Furthermore, since

$$\mathrm{VAR}(\overline{X}_1) = \frac{\sigma_1^2}{n_1} \quad \text{and} \quad \mathrm{VAR}(\overline{X}_2) = \frac{\sigma_2^2}{n_2},$$

we have

$$\mathrm{VAR}(\overline{X}_1 - \overline{X}_2) = \frac{\sigma_1^2}{n_1} + \frac{\sigma_2^2}{n_2}.$$

Therefore, the standard deviation of $\overline{X}_1 - \overline{X}_2$ is simply

$$\sqrt{\frac{\sigma_1^2}{n_1} + \frac{\sigma_2^2}{n_2}}.$$

If the observed sample means are $\bar{x}_1$ and $\bar{x}_2$ and the observed sample standard deviations are s_1 and s_2, then the estimate for $\mu_1 - \mu_2$ is $\bar{x}_1 - \bar{x}_2$. We record this as:

> The difference between the observed sample means $\bar{x}_1 - \bar{x}_2$ is an estimate of the difference between the sample means $\mu_1 - \mu_2$.

In order to construct a confidence interval for the difference between the means, we can apply a version of the Central Limit Theorem to assert that the random variable Z defined as

$$Z = \frac{\overline{X}_1 - \overline{X}_2 - (\mu_1 - \mu_2)}{\sqrt{\dfrac{\sigma_1^2}{n_1} + \dfrac{\sigma_2^2}{n_2}}}$$

approximately obeys a standard Normal distribution, as long as n_1 and n_2 are each large (both n_1 and n_2 are 30 or more). By following the same kind of logic that was used in Section 4.3, we can construct a $\beta\%$ confidence interval for $\mu_1 - \mu_2$ as follows:

> Suppose that both n_1 and n_2 are large ($n_1 \geq 30$ and $n_2 \geq 30$). A $\beta\%$ confidence interval for the difference $\mu_1 - \mu_2$ of the two population means is
>
> $$\left[\bar{x}_1 - \bar{x}_2 - c\sqrt{\frac{s_1^2}{n_1} + \frac{s_2^2}{n_2}}, \ \bar{x}_1 - \bar{x}_2 + c\sqrt{\frac{s_1^2}{n_1} + \frac{s_2^2}{n_2}} \right],$$
>
> where the number c is that number for which
>
> $$P(-c \leq Z \leq c) = \beta/100,$$
>
> and Z obeys a standard Normal distribution.
>
> For $\beta = 90\%$, $c = 1.645$.
> For $\beta = 95\%$, $c = 1.960$.
> For $\beta = 98\%$, $c = 2.326$.
> For $\beta = 99\%$, $c = 2.576$.

We remark that if one or more of the sample sizes n_1 and n_2 is small, this method cannot be applied, and in fact there is no known method for satisfactorily constructing such confidence intervals in this case.

Example 4.16 — A Product-Promotion Decision, Revisited

Here we reconsider Example 4.15. Let us denote the group of randomly selected consumers who received the promotional material in the mail as "sample 1," and let us denote the group of randomly selected consumers who did not receive the promotional material in the mail as "sample 2." Suppose that due to problems in their computer systems, the company has only been able to obtain consumer sales data for 500 consumers in group 1 and for 400 consumers in group 2. Suppose that the observed sample mean of consumer sales (per consumer per month) in group 1 is $387.00, and the observed sample mean of consumer sales (per consumer per month) in group 2 is $365.00. The observed sample standard deviation of consumer sales is $223.00 in group 1 and is $274.00 in group 2.

Let us first compute an estimate of the difference in the means $\mu_1 - \mu_2$ of the distribution of sales between the first group and and second group. For this example, $\bar{x}_1 = \$387.00$ and $\bar{x}_2 = \$365.00$. Therefore, the estimate of the difference of the means $\mu_1 - \mu_2$ is $\bar{x}_1 - \bar{x}_2 = \$387.00 - \$365.00 = \$22.00$.

Next let us compute the 98% confidence interval for the difference between the means $\mu_1 - \mu_2$ of the distribution of sales between the first group and second group. In order to do so, we will apply the formula above. We have $s_1 = \$223.00$ and $s_2 = \$274.00$, and $n_1 = 500$ and $n_2 = 400$. Therefore, we compute

$$\sqrt{\frac{s_1^2}{n_1} + \frac{s_2^2}{n_2}} = \sqrt{\frac{223^2}{500} + \frac{274^2}{400}} = \$16.95.$$

Because $\beta = 98\%$, we find that $c = 2.326$. Finally, since both sample sizes are larger than 30, then the $\beta = 98\%$ confidence interval is

$$\left[\bar{x}_1 - \bar{x}_2 - c\sqrt{\frac{s_1^2}{n_1} + \frac{s_2^2}{n_2}}, \bar{x}_1 - \bar{x}_2 + c\sqrt{\frac{s_1^2}{n_1} + \frac{s_2^2}{n_2}} \right] = [-\$17.43, \$61.43].$$

That is, we are 98% confident that the difference in the means of the distributions of consumer spending at the department stores with and without the promotional campaign is between $-\$17.43$ (per consumer per month) and $\$61.43$ (per consumer per month). Because this confidence interval contains zero, we are *not* 98% confident that the promotional campaign will result in any increase in consumer spending.

4.9 | COMPARING ESTIMATES OF THE POPULATION PROPORTION OF TWO POPULATIONS

It is often the case that a manager needs to estimate the difference between the proportions of two independent populations. For example, a marketing manager might need to estimate the difference between the proportion of men who buy a new product and the proportion of women who buy the new product. In this section, we develop the tools to estimate the difference between the proportions of two independent populations.

We start by considering a general model as follows. Suppose that two independent populations 1 and 2 have population proportions p_1 and p_2 of a certain characteristic of interest. Our objective is to estimate $p_1 - p_2$, the difference between the proportions of the two populations. Suppose that we sample from both populations, obtaining n_1 observations from the first population and n_2 observations from the second population. Let X_1 denote the number of observations in the first population that will have the characteristic of interest and let X_2 denote the number of observations in the second population that will have this characteristic. The sample proportions of the two populations are $\overline{P}_1 = X_1/n_1$ and $\overline{P}_2 = X_2/n_2$. From the results of Section 4.6 for the mean and standard deviation of the sample proportion, as well as the rules for linear combinations of random variables, we have

$$E[\overline{P}_1 - \overline{P}_2] = E[\overline{P}_1] - E[\overline{P}_2] = p_1 - p_2$$

and

$$\text{VAR}(\overline{P}_1 - \overline{P}_2) = \text{VAR}(\overline{P}_1) + \text{VAR}(\overline{P}_2) = \frac{p_1(1 - p_1)}{n_1} + \frac{p_2(1 - p_2)}{n_2},$$

because the two sets of random samples are independent. Therefore, the standard deviation of $\overline{P}_1 - \overline{P}_2$ is simply

$$\sqrt{\frac{p_1(1 - p_1)}{n_1} + \frac{p_2(1 - p_2)}{n_2}}.$$

If the observed sample proportions are $\bar{p}_1$ and $\bar{p}_2$, then the estimate for $p_1 - p_2$ is $\bar{p}_1 - \bar{p}_2$. We record this as:

> The difference between the observed sample proportions $\bar{p}_1 - \bar{p}_2$ is an estimate of the difference between the proportions $p_1 - p_2$.

In order to construct a confidence interval for the difference between the proportions of the two populations, we can apply a version of the Central Limit Theorem to assert that the random variable Z defined as

$$Z = \frac{\overline{P}_1 - \overline{P}_2 - (p_1 - p_2)}{\sqrt{\dfrac{\overline{P}_1(1 - \overline{P}_1)}{n_1} + \dfrac{\overline{P}_2(1 - \overline{P}_2)}{n_2}}}$$

approximately obeys a standard Normal distribution as long as $n_1\bar{p}_1$, $n_2\bar{p}_2$, $n_1(1 - \bar{p}_1)$ and $n_2(1 - \bar{p}_2)$ are all greater than or equal to 5. By following the same kind of logic that was used in Section 4.6, we can construct a $\beta\%$ confidence interval for $p_1 - p_2$ as follows:

> Suppose that both n_1 and n_2 are each large ($n_1\bar{p}_1 \geq 5$, $n_1(1 - \bar{p}_1) \geq 5$, $n_2\bar{p}_2 \geq 5$, and $n_2(1 - \bar{p}_2) \geq 5$). Then the $\beta\%$ confidence interval for the difference $p_1 - p_2$ of the two population proportions is
>
> $$\left[\bar{p}_1 - \bar{p}_2 - c\sqrt{\frac{\bar{p}_1(1 - \bar{p}_1)}{n_1} + \frac{\bar{p}_2(1 - \bar{p}_2)}{n_2}},\right.$$
> $$\left.\bar{p}_1 - \bar{p}_2 + c\sqrt{\frac{\bar{p}_1(1 - \bar{p}_1)}{n_1} + \frac{\bar{p}_2(1 - \bar{p}_2)}{n_2}}\right]$$
>
> where the number c is that number for which
>
> $$P(-c \leq Z \leq c) = \beta/100,$$

and Z obeys a standard Normal distribution.

$$\text{For } \beta = 90\%, c = 1.645.$$
$$\text{For } \beta = 95\%, c = 1.960.$$
$$\text{For } \beta = 98\%, c = 2.326.$$
$$\text{For } \beta = 99\%, c = 2.576.$$

Example 4.17 — A Cholesterol Study

In a ten year study sponsored by the National Heart, Lung, and Blood Institute, 3,806 middle-aged men with high cholesterol levels but no known heart problems were randomly divided into two equal groups. Members of the first group received a new drug designed to lower cholesterol levels, while the second group received daily dosages of a placebo. Besides lowering cholesterol levels, the drug appeared to be effective in reducing the incidence of heart attacks. During the ten years, 155 of those in the first group had a heart attack, compared to 187 in the placebo group.

Let p_1 denote the proportion of middle-aged men with high cholesterol who will suffer a heart attack within ten years if they receive the new drug. Let p_2 denote the proportion of middle-aged men with high cholesterol who will suffer a heart attack within ten years if they do not receive the new drug. Let us compute the estimate of the difference between the two proportions $p_1 - p_2$. The estimate of $p_1 - p_2$ is $\bar{p}_1 - \bar{p}_2 = 155/1{,}903 - 187/1{,}903 = -0.0168$.

Now let us compute the 90% confidence interval of the difference between the proportions $p_1 - p_2$ using the preceding formula. Here we have $n_1 = 1{,}903$ and $n_2 = 1{,}903$, and $\bar{p}_1 = 155/1{,}903 = 0.08145$ and $\bar{p}_2 = 187/1{,}903 = 0.09827$. For $\beta = 90\%$, we find that $c = 1.645$. Therefore a 90% confidence interval is

$$\left[\bar{p}_1 - \bar{p}_2 - c\sqrt{\frac{\bar{p}_1(1-\bar{p}_1)}{n_1} + \frac{\bar{p}_2(1-\bar{p}_2)}{n_2}}, \bar{p}_1 - \bar{p}_2 + c\sqrt{\frac{\bar{p}_1(1-\bar{p}_1)}{n_1} + \frac{\bar{p}_2(1-\bar{p}_2)}{n_2}} \right]$$
$$= [-0.032, \ -0.0016].$$

That is, we are 90% confident that the difference between the two population proportions $p_1 - p_2$ lies in the range between -0.032 and -0.0016. Note that this entire range is less than zero. Therefore, we are 90% confident that the new drug is effective in reducing the incidence of heart attacks in middle-age men with high cholesterol.

4.10   SUMMARY AND EXTENSIONS

In this chapter, we introduced methods to estimate the shape of the probability distribution of a random variable and to estimate probabilities associated with a random variable, based on constructing a frequency table and a histogram of a random sample of observed values. We also introduced methods to estimate the mean μ and the standard deviation σ of a probability distribution and of the proportion p of a population, based on a random sample of observed values. We defined the notions of the observed sample mean, the observed sample standard deviation, and the observed population proportion as estimates of the mean μ, the standard deviation σ, and population proportion p. We further presented methods for computing confidence intervals for μ, p, and for the difference between two population means and for the difference between two population proportions. These are the most often used confidence intervals in a managerial setting. However, there are certain management settings where one is interested in computing confidence intervals for the standard deviation (to measure risk, for example), for the difference between two standard deviations (to estimate which of two decisions might have greater risk, for example), as well as for a variety of other estimates of interest. The tools needed to compute these other types of confidence intervals go well beyond the intended interest of most management students, and so are not developed or used in this book.

4.11 CASE MODULES

CONSUMER CONVENIENCE, INC.

Five months ago, Kim LePage was promoted to director of telemarketing operations at Consumer Convenience, Inc. (CCI), which is a retail catalog company that offers consumer products by mail-order and by telephone ordering. CCI's corporate target is to achieve $45,000 per day in sales revenues from telemarketing operations. Both Kim LePage and her manager have been concerned about the variability in the sales revenues from the telemarketing operations, and so Kim has decided to study the daily sales revenue data from the last five months of operations in order to get a better understanding of the sales revenues variability. Kim has obtained the daily sales revenue in a spreadsheet that is shown in Table 4.5. The daily cost of the telemarketing operations is $40,000 per day. A quick look at Table 4.5 indicates that there were at least a few days in which revenues were less than costs, which was not good.

Kim would like to report to her manager as much information regarding sales revenues as possible.

Assignment:

The spreadsheet CCI.XLS contains the data shown in Table 4.5. Using this spreadsheet, answer the following questions:

(a) What is the shape of the distribution daily sales revenue from telemarketing operations?

(b) What is an estimate of the expected daily sales revenue from telemarketing operations? How confident should Kim be about this estimate? Is there a need for more data?

(c) What is an estimate of the standard deviation of the daily sales revenue from telemarketing operations?

(d) On any given day, what is an estimate of the probability that daily sales revenue from telemarketing operations will be at least $45,000? How confident should Kim be about this estimate? Is there a need for more data?

(e) On any given day, what is an estimate of the probability that daily sales revenue from telemarketing operations will be less than $40,000? How confident should Kim be about this estimate? Is there a need for more data?

TABLE 4.5

Sample of 150 daily sales revenues of telemarketing operations (in dollars).

Date	Sales Revenues	Date	Sales Revenues	Date	Sales Revenues
1-Feb	$49,887.78	23-Mar	$45,716.91	12-May	$40,185.18
2-Feb	61,440.47	24-Mar	47,283.17	13-May	56,076.65
3-Feb	40,644.97	25-Mar	47,807.66	14-May	58,921.80
4-Feb	42,811.79	26-Mar	39,437.27	15-May	37,948.46
5-Feb	48,145.60	27-Mar	45,959.62	16-May	39,364.31
6-Feb	39,025.98	28-Mar	54,508.11	17-May	35,964.13
7-Feb	56,855.29	29-Mar	50,166.20	18-May	54,230.25
8-Feb	52,069.28	30-Mar	40,722.15	19-May	64,697.71
9-Feb	41,353.28	31-Mar	63,593.24	20-May	49,907.70
10-Feb	61,110.75	1-Apr	39,728.90	21-May	50,072.89
11-Feb	52,067.93	2-Apr	36,947.77	22-May	54,801.06
12-Feb	46,255.42	3-Apr	58,810.62	23-May	58,914.52
13-Feb	47,437.37	4-Apr	41,929.42	24-May	44,374.26
14-Feb	35,913.85	5-Apr	62,517.95	25-May	50,320.26
15-Feb	51,006.90	6-Apr	58,958.33	26-May	34,754.95
16-Feb	51,916.32	7-Apr	44,150.94	27-May	40,410.26
17-Feb	48,316.69	8-Apr	49,477.70	28-May	40,785.87
18-Feb	58,179.03	9-Apr	54,623.36	29-May	47,082.23
19-Feb	45,195.08	10-Apr	53,765.15	30-May	50,655.90
20-Feb	45,274.06	11-Apr	41,398.38	31-May	37,727.27
21-Feb	30,000.00	12-Apr	49,264.65	1-Jun	50,349.69
22-Feb	40,440.08	13-Apr	49,260.73	2-Jun	59,997.03
23-Feb	51,244.84	14-Apr	30,000.00	3-Jun	56,171.33
24-Feb	46,848.92	15-Apr	40,309.05	4-Jun	43,917.70
25-Feb	45,216.40	16-Apr	63,235.51	5-Jun	35,945.86
26-Feb	38,582.15	17-Apr	52,851.02	6-Jun	46,329.04
27-Feb	47,553.81	18-Apr	56,128.86	7-Jun	49,694.23
28-Feb	59,089.63	19-Apr	50,697.70	8-Jun	52,447.06
1-Mar	40,823.95	20-Apr	45,157.53	9-Jun	65,820.83
2-Mar	37,171.39	21-Apr	50,481.36	10-Jun	54,239.87
3-Mar	59,416.87	22-Apr	57,739.92	11-Jun	40,501.48
4-Mar	30,000.00	23-Apr	39,567.94	12-Jun	58,087.21
5-Mar	50,762.22	24-Apr	44,534.88	13-Jun	54,378.58
6-Mar	40,157.58	25-Apr	54,427.55	14-Jun	49,950.13
7-Mar	49,934.94	26-Apr	57,848.26	15-Jun	49,234.40
8-Mar	54,549.14	27-Apr	51,011.35	16-Jun	50,645.49
9-Mar	58,655.00	28-Apr	40,058.62	17-Jun	30,000.00
10-Mar	48,683.40	29-Apr	30,000.00	18-Jun	52,796.12
11-Mar	56,727.74	30-Apr	47,677.31	19-Jun	54,896.83
12-Mar	61,504.60	1-May	56,820.43	20-Jun	60,760.31
13-Mar	71,280.90	2-May	51,865.85	21-Jun	45,644.64
14-Mar	51,839.67	3-May	64,014.88	22-Jun	40,096.17
15-Mar	51,903.67	4-May	51,759.17	23-Jun	54,705.09
16-Mar	58,660.49	5-May	34,818.02	24-Jun	46,739.59
17-Mar	55,272.50	6-May	58,397.65	25-Jun	49,014.71
18-Mar	42,544.51	7-May	58,337.14	26-Jun	44,226.34
19-Mar	45,033.38	8-May	48,187.68	27-Jun	58,289.80
20-Mar	50,753.84	9-May	54,060.26	28-Jun	54,789.39
21-Mar	55,549.87	10-May	41,694.70	29-Jun	64,267.29
22-Mar	45,282.94	11-May	48,808.57	30-Jun	63,038.82

POSIDON, INC.

POSIDON, Inc. is a partnership of private investors that develop and run large retail shopping centers around the country. POSIDON only builds two types of shopping centers: "value-oriented" shopping centers aimed at medium-income consumers, and "luxury-oriented" shopping centers aimed at high-income consumers. POSIDON's criterion for choosing which of the two types of shopping centers to develop depends on the average family income in a 15-mile radius around of the proposed shopping center; their break-point between between medium-income consumers and high-income consumers is a family income of $75,000. POSIDON has recently been considering a particular property that they own in Framingham, Massachusetts. They now must decide which of the two types of shopping centers to develop on the property.

Table 4.6 presents the results of a survey of 200 randomly selected households whose homes lie within 15 miles of the site of the proposed shopping center, and who had agreed to provide POSIDON with information about their family income.

Assignment:

The spreadsheet POSIDON.XLS contains the data shown in Table 4.6. Answer the following questions based on aqn analysis of the data:

(a) What is the shape of the distribution of family income within the site area?

(b) What is an estimate of the mean family income in the site area?

(c) What is an estimate of the standard deviation of family income in the site area?

(d) Construct a 95% confidence interval of the mean family income in the site area.

HOUSING PRICES IN LEXINGTON, MASSACHUSETTS

VALMAX is one of the largest real estate companies in New England. John Porter is the manager of VALMAX's Lexington, Massachusetts office, which is one of their most profitable offices. VALMAX has received complaints from a number of their recent clients in Lexington who believe that they were advised to post asking-prices for their houses that were too low, especially relative to the asking-prices for houses brokered by other realtors. VALMAX has also received complaints from other clients in Lexington who believe that they were advised to accept selling-prices for houses that they purchased that were too high relative to the selling-prices for houses brokered by other realtors. John Porter has decided to perform an analysis of recent real estate transactions in Lexington in order to estimate the truthfulness of these claims.

Asking-prices and selling-prices of houses sold are public information, and John has obtained this data from the Lexington Town Hall. John has collected the asking-prices and selling-prices for the 79 housing sales in Lexington in the last three months, and has divided the sales into the 35 sales brokered by VALMAX and the other 44 sales that were brokered by other realtors. The price data for these two sets of housing sales are shown in Tables 4.7 and 4.8, and are contained in the spreadsheet VALMAX.XLS.

Are the clients' complaints justified?

SCALLOP SAMPLING[1]

In order to guard the future supply of scallops in coastal waters, the United States Fisheries and Wildlife Service (USFWS) requires that, in any given catch of a commercial fishing boat, the average meat per scallop for the entire catch must weigh at least 0.5 ounces. Typically, scallops grow (and hence the weight of their meat increases) as they age. The USFWS has instituted rather severe penalties for catches whose average meat per scallop is less than 0.5 ounces.

The weight of scallops is not Normally distributed, just as one would not expect the age of scallops to be Normally distributed. Since it is impractical to weigh every scallop

[1]This case is motivated by an article in the journal *Interfaces* in 1995 by Arnold Barnett.

TABLE 4.6

Sample of 200 family incomes in the site area.

Number	Income	Number	Income	Number	Income	Number	Income
1	$97,957	51	$72,787	101	$79,673	151	$71,358
2	$63,334	52	$63,123	102	$69,177	152	$74,370
3	$62,565	53	$67,739	103	$70,358	153	$58,881
4	$69,877	54	$62,881	104	$74,733	154	$65,586
5	$63,475	55	$81,190	105	$80,711	155	$56,139
6	$54,352	56	$76,828	106	$84,569	156	$73,197
7	$74,883	57	$62,842	107	$61,222	157	$45,488
8	$57,306	58	$65,520	108	$59,163	158	$65,762
9	$78,451	59	$70,258	109	$80,875	159	$70,243
10	$60,189	60	$62,873	110	$51,535	160	$82,067
11	$44,662	61	$70,216	111	$58,311	161	$66,481
12	$55,978	62	$69,174	112	$56,590	162	$49,899
13	$55,322	63	$82,498	113	$70,312	163	$48,480
14	$48,142	64	$55,792	114	$69,564	164	$66,106
15	$68,978	65	$75,613	115	$67,090	165	$58,437
16	$51,090	66	$62,819	116	$54,009	166	$70,693
17	$73,778	67	$42,440	117	$56,720	167	$71,531
18	$63,659	68	$65,468	118	$61,843	168	$76,217
19	$64,915	69	$71,927	119	$82,663	169	$72,542
20	$81,714	70	$67,520	120	$71,864	170	$62,696
21	$46,164	71	$76,903	121	$54,412	171	$75,288
22	$67,780	72	$60,521	122	$61,503	172	$55,834
23	$68,292	73	$74,947	123	$75,326	173	$58,662
24	$60,102	74	$82,303	124	$78,964	174	$73,923
25	$57,026	75	$65,629	125	$61,432	175	$52,023
26	$63,516	76	$71,283	126	$76,101	176	$72,178
27	$74,880	77	$62,535	127	$79,616	177	$67,025
28	$82,384	78	$51,594	128	$72,171	178	$64,307
29	$57,641	79	$65,011	129	$60,648	179	$65,043
30	$70,496	80	$80,130	130	$62,616	180	$69,408
31	$68,650	81	$70,341	131	$71,230	181	$68,298
32	$87,175	82	$76,609	132	$55,206	182	$72,695
33	$64,237	83	$76,926	133	$64,771	183	$55,466
34	$58,840	84	$69,418	134	$52,021	184	$65,675
35	$73,866	85	$54,750	135	$52,861	185	$48,219
36	$47,967	86	$53,562	136	$59,268	186	$62,057
37	$66,208	87	$70,701	137	$53,354	187	$81,266
38	$67,462	88	$71,293	138	$82,295	188	$78,538
39	$58,975	89	$68,834	139	$73,293	189	$60,465
40	$68,377	90	$68,968	140	$79,542	190	$57,819
41	$62,800	91	$64,123	141	$61,334	191	$58,015
42	$79,146	92	$64,869	142	$49,234	192	$52,814
43	$80,346	93	$71,976	143	$55,310	193	$55,718
44	$66,141	94	$71,870	144	$52,904	194	$59,985
45	$47,975	95	$49,964	145	$52,435	195	$61,596
46	$65,021	96	$64,176	146	$64,014	196	$58,032
47	$74,831	97	$49,191	147	$53,863	197	$67,107
48	$59,909	98	$66,657	148	$76,943	198	$64,402
49	$58,290	99	$76,893	149	$72,353	199	$52,548
50	$52,207	100	$65,606	150	$72,243	200	$73,490

in a catch, the USFWS inspectors base their assessment of the weight of the scallop meat on a sample of scallops. For a given catch, the inspectors first collect 1,000 random scallops from the catch using appropriate randomization techniques. The inspectors then compute the average meat per scallop for the sample. Let $\bar{x}$ and s denote the observed sample mean and the observed sample standard deviation of the meat per scallop for a given sample collected by USFWS inspectors. If $\bar{x} \geq 0.5$ ounces, the USFWS inspectors

TABLE 4.7

Sales of houses in
Lexington
represented by
VALMAX in the last
three months.

House Number	Asking Price ($)	Selling Price ($)	Difference ($)
1	290,000	275,000	15,000
2	315,000	314,000	1,000
3	299,000	310,000	−11,000
4	615,000	610,000	5,000
5	345,000	345,000	0
6	230,000	221,000	9,000
7	420,000	418,000	2,000
8	399,000	382,000	17,000
9	549,000	555,000	−6,000
10	299,000	292,000	7,000
11	430,000	431,000	−1,000
12	330,000	303,000	27,000
13	395,000	381,000	14,000
14	675,000	661,000	14,000
15	460,000	443,000	17,000
16	437,000	449,000	−12,000
17	680,000	668,000	12,000
18	380,000	385,000	−5,000
19	325,000	310,000	15,000
20	435,000	435,000	0
21	304,000	300,000	4,000
22	552,000	560,000	−8,000
23	403,000	389,000	14,000
24	419,000	425,000	−6,000
25	227,000	217,000	10,000
26	340,000	342,000	−2,000
27	619,000	615,000	4,000
28	312,000	308,000	4,000
29	320,000	319,000	1,000
30	299,000	270,000	29,000
31	289,000	280,000	9,000
32	316,000	319,000	−3,000
33	328,000	320,000	8,000
34	610,000	615,000	−5,000
35	350,000	353,000	−3,000

will impose no penalty. If $\bar{x} \leq 0.45$ ounces, then the USFWS will confiscate the entire catch of scallops. If $\bar{x}$ lies between 0.45 ounces and 0.5 ounces, that is, $0.45 \leq \bar{x} \leq 0.50$, the USFWS will confiscate $20 \times (0.5 - \bar{x}) \times 100\%$ of the catch.

Suppose that the USFWS boards a ship whose catch is 10,000,000 scallops and that the USFWS inspector collects a random sample of 1,000 scallops. Suppose further that the mean meat per scallop of the sample is $\bar{x} = 0.48$ ounces, and that the sample standard deviation is $s = 0.3$ ounces.

(a) What is the penalty imposed on this ship stated both as a percentage of the catch and also in terms of the number of scallops confiscated?

(b) Let w denote the average meat per scallop of the 10,000,000 scallops on this ship. How confident are you that w is less than or equal to 0.50 ounces? In other words, how confident are you that the catch is really in violation of the standards set by the USFWS?

(c) Assuming that a given ship's catch has an average weight per scallop of 0.50 ounces and that the standard deviation of this weight is 0.30 ounces, what is the probability that the average weight of a sample of size $n = 1,000$ will be 0.48 ounces or lower?

(d) Is the question in part (c) equivalent to the question in part (b)?

TABLE 4.8

Sales of houses in
Lexington
represented by other
realtors in the last
three months.

House	Asking Price ($)	Selling Price ($)	Difference ($)
1	295,000	280,000	15,000
2	425,000	411,000	14,000
3	299,000	285,000	14,000
4	299,000	299,000	0
5	475,000	471,000	4,000
6	350,000	348,000	2,000
7	429,000	418,000	11,000
8	399,000	401,000	-2,000
9	489,000	476,000	13,000
10	299,000	270,000	29,000
11	539,000	531,000	8,000
12	225,000	214,000	11,000
13	749,000	735,000	14,000
14	689,000	664,000	25,000
15	469,000	476,000	-7,000
16	299,000	270,000	29,000
17	539,000	531,000	8,000
18	199,000	205,000	-6,000
19	349,000	335,000	14,000
20	689,000	687,000	2,000
21	485,000	479,000	6,000
22	299,000	285,000	14,000
23	305,000	275,000	30,000
24	479,000	469,000	10,000
25	699,000	677,000	22,000
26	339,000	325,000	14,000
27	195,000	209,000	-14,000
28	539,000	535,000	4,000
29	279,000	268,000	11,000
30	459,000	469,000	-10,000
31	679,000	659,000	20,000
32	729,000	725,000	4,000
33	215,000	214,000	1,000
34	539,000	525,000	14,000
35	289,000	270,000	19,000
36	479,000	469,000	10,000
37	389,000	390,000	-1,000
38	419,000	410,000	9,000
39	339,000	339,000	0
40	469,000	462,000	7,000
41	299,000	280,000	19,000
42	289,000	280,000	9,000
43	419,000	403,000	16,000
44	289,000	275,000	14,000

(e) The USFWS has been severely criticized over the years for basing their penalty on the observed sample mean of a sample of size 1,000. Scallop ship owners have argued that the penalties are "capricious" and random. The USFWS is considering the following more conservative approach for determining penalties:

- Whenever the USFWS inspectors collect a sample, obtaining a sample mean $\bar{x}$ and a sample standard deviation s, the inspectors will then compute a value b (which depends on $\bar{x}$ and on s) for which inspectors are 95% confident that $w \le b$. (Recall that w is the average meat per scallop for the entire catch. Since the inspectors are using sampling, w is not known.)

- The inspectors will then assess the penalty using the value b rather than $\bar{x}$ using the same penalties as before:

  If $b \geq 0.5$ ounce, there will be no penalty.

  If $b \leq 0.45$ ounce, then the USFWS will confiscate the entire catch of scallops.

  If b lies between 0.45 ounces and 0.5 ounces, that is, $0.45 \leq b \leq 0.50$, the USFWS will confiscate $20 \times (0.5 - b) \times 100\%$ of the catch.

Now suppose that $\bar{x} = 0.48$ ounces and that $s = 0.3$ ounces. What is the value of b, and how many scallops will be confiscated by the USFWS?

(f) Now suppose that the USFWS auctions off the scallops that they confiscate from catches that they found in violation of their regulations using the policy stated in part (e) for determining the amount of scallops to be confiscated. The USFWS earns $1 per 100 scallops, or one penny per scallop, in such auctions. Notice that by using a larger sample size, the USFWS might obtain a tighter confidence interval and hence a larger number of confiscated scallops. However, the cost of collecting and sampling the weight of the scallops is $0.05 per scallop on average. Suppose that on the next ship that arrives, the USFWS inspectors collect a sample of 1,000 scallops and compute its observed sample mean of 0.46 ounces and its observed sample standard deviation of 0.3 ounces. What would be the ship's penalty using the confiscation rules given in part (e)? Suppose further that the inspectors are permitted to take an additional sample of size n to narrow the confidence interval. How large should n be so as to maximize the net expected revenue to the USFWS? Please justify your answer. (HINT: Try different values for n and try to obtain an answer that approximately maximizes net revenues to the USFWS. If you need to make any simplifying assumptions in order to carry out your analysis, please state your assumptions.)

4.12 | EXERCISES

EXERCISE 4.1 According to Census data, household incomes in Boston have a mean of $37,907 and a standard deviation of $15,102. Suppose that a sample of household incomes of 100 Boston households will be selected at random. Let $\overline{X}$ denote the sample mean of this proposed sample.

(a) What is the distribution of $\overline{X}$?

(b) What is the probability that $\overline{X}$ will exceed $35,000?

EXERCISE 4.2 An insurance company would like to estimate the average amount claimed by its policyholders over the past year. A random sample of 300 policyholders was chosen, whose observed sample mean was $739.98 and whose sample standard deviation was $312.70.

(a) Construct a 95% confidence interval for the average amount claimed by policyholders in the last year.

(b) Construct a 99% confidence interval for the average amount claimed by policyholders in the last year.

(c) Determine the required sample size in order to estimate the average amount claimed by policyholders to within $\pm\$30.00$ at the 95% confidence level.

(d) (Challenge) The company's primary concern is to avoid underestimating the average amount claimed by its policyholders. Determine a value b so that the insurance company is 95% confident that the average amount claimed by its policyholders is b or less.

EXERCISE 4.3 According to annual precipitation data kept for the past 75 years, the average precipitation in New York City is 41.76 inches per year and the observed sample standard deviation is 5.74 inches per year.

(a) Construct a 99% confidence interval for the mean of the distribution of yearly precipitation in New York City.

(b) Determine the required sample size in order to estimate the mean of the distribution of yearly precipitation in New York City to within 1.2 inches at the 99% confidence level.

(c) During the same 75-year period, the average precipitation in Tokyo was 34.37 inches per year and the observed sample standard deviation was 4.98 inches per year. Construct a 95% confidence interval for the difference between the mean yearly precipitation in New York and Tokyo.

EXERCISE 4.4 A company manufacturing stereo equipment claims that their personal CD player can be used for approximately 8 hours of continuous play when used with alkaline batteries. To provide this estimate, the company tested 35 CD players with new alkaline batteries and recorded the time at which the batteries in the players "lost power." The average time was 8.3 hours with a sample standard deviation of 1.2 hours.

(a) Construct a 95% confidence interval for the mean time until a new alkaline battery used in the CD player loses power.

(b) Determine the required sample size in order to estimate the mean time until a new alkaline battery used in the CD player loses power to within ± 10 minutes at the 99% confidence level.

EXERCISE 4.5 A sporting equipment company manufactures 15-pound dumbbells. To ensure that the production line is functioning properly, 50 dumbbells were selected at random, and their weights were recorded. The observed sample mean weight of the 50 dumbbells was 16.87 lb. and the observed sample standard deviation was 1.44 lb.

(a) Construct a 90% confidence interval for the mean of the distribution of the weight of the manufactured dumbbells.

(b) Determine the required sample size in order to estimate the mean of the distribution of the weight of the manufactured dumbbells to within ± 0.2 lb., at the 98% confidence level.

EXERCISE 4.7 An investment analyst would like to estimate the average amount invested in a particular mutual fund by institutional investors. A random sample of 15 institutional investors' portfolios has been chosen. The observed sample mean of the amounts invested in the mutual fund by these 15 investors is $11.32 million and the observed sample standard deviation is $4.4 million.

(a) Construct a 90% confidence interval for the mean amount invested by all institutional investors in the mutual fund.

(b) Determine the required sample size in order to estimate the mean amount invested by all institutional investors in this mutual fund to within $500,000, at the 95% confidence level.

EXERCISE 4.7 A long-distance telephone company has offered Alex a new discount plan. According to the plan, Alex would receive a significant discount if he makes long-distance telephone calls for at least 80 minutes per month. Before deciding whether or not to accept the new plan, Alex would naturally like to estimate his monthly long-distance telephone usage. Alex has conveniently held onto his monthly telephone bills for the past 12 months, which he has now decided to use to estimate his monthly long-distance telephone usage. Based on these 12 bills, his observed sample mean of monthly long-distance usage is $\bar{x} = 85.8$ minutes, and the observed sample standard deviation is $s = 19.3$ minutes. Construct a 95% confidence interval for the mean of the distribution of Alex's long-distance telephone usage. What assumptions must you make in order to construct the confidence interval?

EXERCISE 4.8 A supermarket manager is trying to decide how many checkout registers to keep open during the early-morning hours. To aid her analysis, she recorded the number of customers who came to the supermarket during the early-morning hours for the past 10 days. The data collected is presented in Table 4.9.

(a) Construct a 95% confidence interval for the mean number of early-morning customers in the supermarket.

(b) What assumptions must you make in order to compute your confidence interval?

EXERCISE 4.9 A soft-drink company would like to estimate the proportion of consumers who like the taste of their new carbonated beverage. In a random sample of 200 consumers, 54 of the consumers liked the taste of the new beverage.

(a) Construct a 99% confidence interval for the proportion of consumers who like the taste of the new beverage.

(b) Determine the required sample size in order to estimate the proportion of consumers who like the taste of the new beverage to within 1% at the 95% confidence level.

EXERCISE 4.10 During a local election between two candidates, exit polls based on a sample of 400 voters indicated that 54% of the voters supported the incumbent candidate.

(a) Construct a 98% confidence interval for the percentage of votes that the incumbent has received in this election.

(b) How large a sample is required in order to declare the incumbent candidate a winner at the 99% confidence level?

EXERCISE 4.11 The MetroBridge Transit Authority (MBTA) would like to estimate the average time of the morning commute (in minutes) of city residents. The Authority would like to be 95% confident that their estimate does not differ from the

TABLE 4.9

The number of early-morning customers in the last ten days.

Day	Number of early-morning customers
1	167
2	172
3	150
4	178
5	160
6	164
7	167
8	140
9	190
10	150

true population mean by more than 5 minutes. From past experience it is known that the standard deviation of the distribution of commute times is at most 20 minutes. How many commuters does the Authority need to poll?

EXERCISE 4.12 A subscription literary magazine would like to "profile" their subscribers by mailing a questionnaire to a random sample of their subscribers. In particular, they would like to determine an estimate of the average income of their subscribers to the nearest $1,000 with 99% confidence. The standard deviation of the distribution of their subscribers' incomes is believed to be at most $5,000. Determine a conservative estimate of the required sample size.

EXERCISE 4.13 A polling company is trying to estimate the average age of a Boston resident. The company would like to be 95% confident that their estimate will be within three years of the true mean of the population. Based on an earlier census, the standard deviation of distribution of ages the population is presumed to be no more than 23 years. Find the smallest sample size that will satisfy the polling company's requirement.

EXERCISE 4.14 Before deciding whether or not to undertake a large mailing to advertise a reduced price of a certain product, a company would like to estimate the proportion of consumers who would respond positively to an advertisement for the product. The marketing division wants to know the minimum sample size required to estimate the population proportion to within ± 0.15 at the 99% confidence level. Find the minimum required sample size.

EXERCISE 4.15 A public opinion group is trying to estimate the percentage of registered voters in the state who are registered as "Independent." It is desirable to estimate the true percentage to within $\pm 3\%$ at the 99% confidence level. Determine an estimate of the required sample size that is needed.

EXERCISE 4.16 An information technology service at a large university surveyed 200 students from the College of Engineering and 100 students from the College of Arts. Among the survey participants, 91 Engineering students and 73 Arts students owned a laptop computer. Construct a 98% confidence interval for the difference between the proportions of laptop owners among Engineering and Arts students.

EXERCISE 4.17 At two different branches of a department store, pollsters randomly sampled 100 customers at store 1 and 80 customers at store 2, all on the same day. At Store 1, the average amount purchased was $41.25 per customer with a sample standard deviation of $24.25. At Store 2, the average amount purchased was $45.75 with a sample standard deviation of $34.76.

(a) Construct a 95% confidence interval for the mean amount purchased per customer in each of the two stores.

(b) Construct a 95% confidence interval for the difference between the means of purchases per customer of the two stores.

EXERCISE 4.18 Daily Express Airlines is concerned about the occupancy levels and the on-time performance of their flights.

(a) To estimate the occupancy level of their flights, the airline has randomly sampled 20 of its flights. The observed sample mean in the sample is 8.1 unoccupied seats per flight and the observed sample standard deviation is 3.9 unoccupied seats per flight. Construct a 99% confidence interval for the mean number of unoccupied seats per flight.

(b) To estimate the length of delays in flights, the airline has randomly sampled 80 of its flights. The observed sample mean is 15.5 minutes of delay per flight, and the observed sample standard deviation is 6.7 minutes. Construct a 95% confidence interval for the mean delay per flight.

(c) How many flights should the airline sample in order to estimate the mean delay per flight to within 1 minute at the 99% confidence level?

(d) A very important statistic in understanding customer satisfaction in the airline industry is the fraction of flights that arrive on time. In the sample of 80 flights (part (b)), 60 flights arrived on time, while 20 experienced some delay. Construct a 95% confidence interval for the proportion of flights that arrive on time.

(e) How many flights should the airline sample in order to predict the proportion of flights that arrive on time to within 2%, at the 95% confidence level?

EXERCISE 4.19 A book club is planning to conduct a telephone survey to estimate the proportion of members of the club who would be inclined to enroll in a new service specializing in cassette-tape recordings of books. The book club would like to estimate this proportion to within plus or minus 5 percentage points at the 95% confidence level.

(a) What is the size of the sample that would need to be surveyed?

(b) Suppose that the book club has decided to call 500 randomly selected members to perform the telephone survey. Suppose that there is a 10% chance that any randomly selected member will not answer the telephone. Let X be the number of randomly selected members among the 500 who will answer the telephone call. What is the distribution of X?

(c) What is the expected value of X?

(d) What is the standard deviation of X?

(e) What is the approximate probability that X is larger than 400?

EXERCISE 4.20 It is estimated that there are 117 million "TV homes" in the United States. Most media research organizations use only 5,000 TV homes to collect information on television viewership patterns. In the language of media research, a television show "rating" measures the percentage of the nation's 117 million TV homes that have watched a particular television program. Thus, for example, if a program has a rating of 27, this means that 27% of all TV homes watched the program.

(a) A popular television program received a rating of 20 on a particular evening based on a sample of 5,000 TV homes. Construct a 99% confidence interval for the actual percentage of all TV homes that were watching this television program.

(b) Suppose a television network would like to estimate the ratings of a new show. The network executives would like to obtain a 95% confidence interval whose tolerance level is within 2 rating points. Calculate the size of the sample required to obtain such an estimate.

Simulation Modeling: Concepts and Practice

CONTENTS

THIS CHAPTER PRESENTS THE BASIC CONCEPTS AND DEMONSTRATES THE MANAGERIAL use of a **simulation model,** which is a computer representation of a problem that involves random variables. The chief advantage of a simulation model of a problem is that the simulation model can forecast the consequences of various management decisions before such decisions must be made. Simulation models are used in a very wide variety of management settings, including modeling of manufacturing operations, modeling of service operations where queues form (such as in banking, passenger air travel, food services, etc.), modeling of investment alternatives, and analyzing and pricing of sophisticated financial instruments. A simulation model is an extremely useful tool to help a manager make difficult decisions in an environment of uncertainty.

A SIMPLE PROBLEM: OPERATIONS AT CONLEY FISHERIES

The central ideas of a simulation model are best understood when presented in the context of a management problem. To initiate these ideas, consider the following practical problem faced by Conley Fisheries, Inc.

OPERATIONS AT CONLEY FISHERIES, INC.

Clint Conley, president of Conley Fisheries, Inc., operates a fleet of fifty cod fishing boats out of Newburyport, Massachusetts. Clint's father started the company forty years ago but has recently turned the business over to Clint, who has been working for the family business since earning his MBA ten years ago. Every weekday of the year, each boat leaves early in the morning, fishes for most of the day, and completes its catch of codfish (3,500 lbs. of codfish) by mid-afternoon. The boat then has a number of ports where it can sell its daily catch. The price of codfish at some ports is very uncertain and can change quite a bit even on a daily basis. Also, the price of codfish tends to be different at different ports. Furthermore, some ports have only limited demand for codfish, and so if a boat arrives relatively later than other fishing boats at that port, the catch of fish cannot be sold and so must be disposed of in ocean waters.

To keep Conley Fisheries' problem simple enough to analyze with ease, assume that Conley Fisheries only operates one boat, and that the daily operating expenses of the boat are $10,000 per day. Also assume that the boat is always able to catch all of the fish that it can hold, which is 3,500 lb. of codfish.

Assume that the Conley Fisheries' boat can bring its catch to either the port in Gloucester or the port in Rockport, Massachusetts. Gloucester is a major port for codfish with a well-established market. The price of codfish in Gloucester is $3.25/lb., and this price has been stable for quite some time. The price of codfish in Rockport tends to be a bit higher than in Gloucester but has a lot of variability. Clint has estimated that the daily price of codfish in Rockport is Normally distributed with a mean of $\mu = \$3.65/\text{lb.}$ and with a standard deviation of $\sigma = \$0.20/\text{lb.}$

The port in Gloucester has a very large market for codfish, and so Conley Fisheries never has a problem selling their codfish in Gloucester. In contrast, the port in Rockport is much smaller, and sometimes the boat is unable to sell part or all of its daily catch in Rockport. Based on past history, Clint has estimated that the demand for codfish in Rockport that he faces when his boat arrives at the port in Rockport obeys the discrete probability distribution depicted in Table 5.1.

It is assumed that the price of codfish in Rockport and the demand for codfish in Rockport faced by Conley Fisheries are independent of one another. Therefore, there is no correlation between the daily price of codfish and the daily demand in Rockport faced by Conley Fisheries.

At the start of any given day, the decision Clint Conley faces is which port to use for selling his daily catch. The price of codfish that the catch might command in Rockport is only known if and when the boat docks at the port and negotiates with buyers. After the boat docks at one of the two ports, it must sell its catch at that port or not at all, since it takes too much time to pilot the boat out of one port and power it all the way to the other port.

Clint Conley is just as anxious as any other business person to earn a profit. For this reason, he wonders if the smart strategy might be to sell his daily catch in Rockport. After all, the expected price of codfish is higher in Rockport, and although the

TABLE 5.1

Daily demand in
Rockport faced by
Conley Fisheries.

Demand (lbs. of codfish)	Probability
0	0.02
1,000	0.03
2,000	0.05
3,000	0.08
4,000	0.33
5,000	0.29
6,000	0.20

standard deviation of the price is high, and hence there is greater risk with this strategy, he is not averse to taking chances when they make good sense. However, it also might be true that the smart strategy could be to sell the codfish in Gloucester, since in Gloucester there is ample demand for his daily catch, whereas in Rockport there is the possibility that he might not sell all of his catch (and so potentially lose valuable revenue). It is not clear to him which strategy is best.

One can start to analyze this problem by computing the daily earnings if Clint chooses to sell his daily catch of codfish in Gloucester. The earnings from using Gloucester, denoted by G, is simply:

$$G = (\$3.25)(3,500) - \$10,000 = \$1,375,$$

which is the revenue of $3.25 per pound times the number of pounds of codfish (3,500 lbs.) minus the daily operating costs of $10,000.

The computation of daily earnings if Clint chooses Rockport is not so straightforward, because the price and the demand are each uncertain. Therefore the daily earnings from choosing Rockport is an uncertain quantity, i.e., a random variable. In order to make an informed decision as to which port to use, it would be helpful to answer such questions as:

(a) What is the shape of the probability distribution of daily earnings from using Rockport?

(b) On any given day, what is the probability that Conley Fisheries would earn more money from using Rockport instead of Gloucester?

(c) On any given day, what is the probability that Conley Fisheries will lose money if they use Rockport?

(d) What is the expected daily earnings from using Rockport?

(e) What is the standard deviation of the daily earnings from using Rockport?

The answers to these five questions are, in all likelihood, all that is needed for Clint Conley to choose the port strategy that will best serve the interests of Conley Fisheries.

5.2   PRELIMINARY ANALYSIS OF CONLEY FISHERIES

One can begin to analyze the decision problem at Conley Fisheries by looking at the problem in terms of random variables. We first define the following two random variables:

PR = price of codfish at the port in Rockport in \$/lb.

D = demand faced by Conley Fisheries at the port in Rockport in lbs.

According to the statement of the problem, the assumptions about the distributions of these two random variables are as shown in Table 5.2.

In order to analyze the decision problem at Conley Fisheries, we next define one new random variable F to be the daily earnings (in dollars) if the boat docks at the port in Rockport to sell its catch of codfish. Note that F is indeed a random variable. The quantity F is uncertain, and in fact, F is a function of the two quantities PR and D, which are themselves random variables. In fact, it is easy to express F as a function of the random variables PR and D. The formula for F is as follows:

$$F = \begin{cases} PR \times 3{,}500 - 10{,}000, & \text{if } D \geq 3{,}500. \\ PR \times D - 10{,}000, & \text{if } D < 3{,}500, \end{cases}$$

i.e., F is simply the price times the quantity of codfish that can be sold (total sales revenue) minus the cost of daily operations. However, in this case, the quantity of codfish that can be sold is the minimum of the quantity of the catch (3,500 lbs.) and the demand for codfish faced by Conley Fisheries at the dock (D). In fact, the above expression can alternatively be written as:

$$F = PR \times \min(3{,}500, D) - 10{,}000,$$

where the expression $\min(a, b)$ stands for the minimum of the two quantities a and b.

This formula is a concise way of stating the problem in terms of the underlying random variables. With the terminology just introduced the questions at the end of Section 5.1 can be restated as:

(a) What is the shape of the probability density function of F?

(b) What is $P(F > \$1{,}375)$?

(c) What is $P(F < \$0)$?

(d) What is the expected value of F?

(e) What is the standard deviation of F?

Now that these five questions have been restated concisely in terms of probability distributions, one could attempt to answer the five questions using the tools of Chapters 2 and 3. Notice that each of these five questions pertains to the random variable F. Furthermore, from the formula above for F, we see that that F is a relatively simple function of the two random variables PR and D. However, it turns out that when random variables are combined, either by addition, multiplication, or some more complicated operation, the new random variable rarely has a convenient form for which there are convenient formulas. (An exception to this dictum is the case of the sum of jointly Normally distributed random variables.) Almost all other instances where random variables are combined are very complex to analyze; and there are seldom formulas for

TABLE 5.2

Summary of random variables and their distributions.

Random Variable	Distribution
PR	Normal, $\mu = 3.65$, $\sigma = 0.20$
D	Discrete distribution, as given in Table 5.1.

the mean, the standard deviation, for the probability density function, or for the cumulative distribution function of the resulting random variable.

In light of the preceding remarks, there are no formulas or tables that will allow us to answer the five questions posed above about the random variable F. However, as we shall soon see, a computer simulation model can be used to effectively gain all of the information we need about the distribution of the random variable F, and so enable us to make an informed and optimal strategy decision about which port to use to sell the daily catch of codfish.

5.3   A SIMULATION MODEL OF THE CONLEY FISHERIES PROBLEM

Suppose for the moment that Clint Conley is a very wealthy individual, who does not need to earn any money, and who is simply curious to know the answers to the five questions posed above for the pure intellectual pleasure it would give him! With all of his time and money, Clint could afford to perform the following experiment. For each of the next 200 weekdays, Clint could send the boat out to fish for its catch and then bring the boat to the port in Rockport at the end of the day to sell the catch. He could record the daily earnings from this strategy each day and, in so doing, would obtain sample data of 200 observed values of the random variable F. Clint could then use the methodology of Chapter 4 to answer questions about the probability distribution of F based on sample data to obtain approximate answers to the five questions posed earlier.

Of course, Clint Conley is not a very wealthy individual, and he does need to earn money, and so he cannot afford to spend the time and money to collect a data set of 200 values of daily earnings from the Rockport strategy. We now will show how to construct an elementary simulation model on a computer, which can be used to answer the five questions posed by Clint.

The central notion behind most computer models is to somehow re-create the events on the computer which one is interested in studying. For example, in economic modeling, one builds a computer model of the national economy to see how various prices and quantities will move over time. In military modeling, one constructs a "war game" model to study the effectiveness of new weapons or military tactics, without having to go to war to test these weapons and/or tactics. In weather or climate forecasting, one constructs an atmospheric model to see how storms and frontal systems will move over time in order to predict the weather with greater accuracy. Of course, these three examples are obviously very complex models involving sophisticated economic principles, or sophisticated military interactions, or sophisticated concepts about the physics of weather systems.

In the Conley Fisheries problem, one can also build a computer model that will create the events on the computer which one is interested in studying. For this particular problem, the events of interest are the price of codfish and the demand for codfish that Conley Fisheries would face in Rockport over a 200 day period. For the sake of discussion, let us reduce the length of the period from 200 days to 20 days, as this will suffice for pedagogical purposes.

As it turns out, the Conley Fisheries problem is a fairly elementary problem to model. One can start by building the blank table shown in Table 5.3. This table has a list of days (numbered 1 through 20) in the first column, followed by blanks in the remaining columns. Our first task will be to fill in the second column of the table by

TABLE 5.3

Computer worksheet for a simulation of Conley Fisheries.

Day	Demand in Rockport (lbs.)	Quantity of Codfish Sold (lbs.)	Price of Codfish in Rockport ($/lb.)	Daily Earnings in Rockport ($)
1				
2				
3				
4				
5				
6				
7				
8				
9				
10				
11				
12				
13				
14				
15				
16				
17				
18				
19				
20				

modeling the demand for codfish faced by Conley Fisheries. Recall that this demand obeys a discrete probability distribution and is given in Table 5.1. Thus, we would like to fill in all of the entries of the column "Demand in Rockport" with numbers that obey the discrete distribution for demand of Table 5.1. Put a slightly different way, we would like to fill in all of the entries of the column "Demand in Rockport" with numbers *drawn* from the discrete probability distribution of Table 5.1.

Once we have filled in the entries of the demand column, it is then easy to fill in the entries of the next column labeled "Quantity of Codfish Sold." Because the Conley Fisheries boat always has a daily catch of 3,500 lbs. of codfish, the quantity sold will be either 3,500 or the "Demand in Rockport" quantity, whichever of the two is smaller. (For example, if the demand in Rockport is 5,000, then the quantity sold will be 3,500. If the demand is Rockport is 2,000, then the quantity sold will be 2,000.)

The fourth column of the table is labeled "Price of Codfish in Rockport." We would like to fill in this column of the table by modeling the price of codfish in Rockport. Recall that the price of codfish obeys a Normal distribution with mean $\mu = \$3.65$ and standard deviation $\sigma = \$0.20$. Thus, we would like to fill in the all of the entries of the column "Price of Codfish in Rockport" with numbers that obey a Normal distribution with mean $\mu = \$3.65$ and standard deviation $\sigma = \$0.20$. Put a slightly different way, we would like to fill in all of the entries of the fourth column with numbers *drawn* from a Normal distribution with mean $\mu = 3.65$ and standard deviation $\sigma = 0.20$.

The fifth column of Table 5.3 will contain the daily earnings in Rockport for each of the numbered days. This quantity is elementary to compute given the entries in the other columns. It is:

Daily Earnings = (Quantity of Codfish Sold) × (Price of Cod) − $10,000.

That is, the daily earnings for each of the days is simply the price times the quantity, minus the daily operating cost of $10,000. Put in a more convenient light, for each row of the table, the entry in the fifth column is computed by multiplying the corresponding entries in the third and fourth columns and then subtracting $10,000.

Summarizing so far, we would like to fill in the entries of Table 5.3 for each of the 20 rows of days. If we can accomplish this, then the last column of Table 5.3 will contain a sample of computer-generated, i.e., simulated, values of the daily earnings in Rockport. The sample of 20 simulated daily earnings values can then be used to answer the five questions posed about the random variable F, using the methods of statistical sampling that were developed in Chapter 4.

In order to simulate the events of 20 days of selling the codfish in Rockport, we will need to fill in all of the entries of the column "Demand in Rockport" with numbers drawn from the discrete probability distribution of Table 5.1. We will also need to fill in all of the entries of the column "Price of Codfish in Rockport" with numbers drawn from a Normal distribution with mean $\mu = 3.65$ and standard deviation $\sigma = 0.20$. Once we are able to do this, the computation of all of the other numbers in the table is extremely simple.

There are two critical steps in filling in the entries of Table 5.3 that are as yet unclear. The first is to somehow generate a sequence of numbers that are drawn from and hence obey the discrete distribution of Table 5.1. These numbers will be used to fill in the "Demand in Rockport" column of the table. The second step is to somehow generate a sequence of numbers that are drawn from and hence obey a Normal distribution with mean $\mu = 3.65$ and standard deviation $\sigma = 0.20$. These numbers will be used to fill in the "Price of Codfish in Rockport" column of the table. Once we have filled in all of the entries of these two columns, the computations of all other numbers in the table can be accomplished with ease.

Therefore, the critical issue in creating the simulation model is to be able to generate a sequence of numbers that are drawn from a given probability distribution. To understand how to do this, one needs a computer that can generate random numbers. This is discussed in the next section.

5.4 RANDOM NUMBER GENERATORS

A **random number generator** is any means of automatically generating a sequence of different numbers each of which is independent of the other, and each of which obeys the uniform distribution on the interval from 0.0 to 1.0.

Most computer software packages that do any kind of scientific computation have a mathematical function corresponding to a random number generator. In fact, most hand-held scientific calculators also have a random number generator function. Every time the user presses the button for the random number generator on a hand-held scientific calculator, the calculator creates a different number and displays this number on the screen; and each of these numbers is drawn according to a uniform distribution on the interval from 0.0 to 1.0.

The Excel® spreadsheet software also has a random number generator. This random number generator can be used to create a random number between 0.0 and 1.0 in any cell by entering "=RAND()" in the desired cell. Every time the function RAND() is called, the software will return a different number (whose value is always between 0.0 and 1.0); and this number will be drawn from a uniform distribution between 0.0 and 1.0. For example, suppose one were to type "=RAND()" into the first row of column "A" of an Excel® spreadsheet. Then the corresponding spreadsheet might look like that shown in Figure 5.1.

Let X denote the random variable that is the value that will be returned by a call to a random number generator. Then X will obey a uniform distribution on the interval from 0.0 to 1.0. Here are some consequences of this fact:

$$P(X \le 0.5) = 0.5,$$
$$P(X \ge 0.5) = 0.5,$$
$$P(0.2 \le X \le 0.9) = 0.7.$$

In fact, for any two numbers a and b for which $0 \le a \le b \le 1$, then:

$$P(a \le X \le b) = b - a.$$

Stated in plain English, this says that for any interval of numbers between zero and one, the probability that X will lie in this interval is equal to the width of the interval. This is a very important property of the uniform distribution on the interval from 0.0 to 1.0, which we will use shortly to great advantage.

(One might ask, "How does a computer typically generate a random number that obeys a uniform distribution between 0.0 and 1.0?" The answer to this question is rather technical, but usually random numbers are generated by means of examining the digits that are cut off when two very large numbers are multiplied together and placing these digits to the right of the decimal place. The extra digits that the computer cannot store are in some sense random and are used to form the sequence of random numbers.)

(Actually, on an even more technical note, the random number generators that are programmed into computer software are more correctly called "pseudo-random number generators." This is because a computer scientist or other mathematically trained professional could in fact predict the sequence of numbers produced by the software if he/she had a sophisticated knowledge of the way the number generator's software program is designed to operate. This is a minor technical point that is of no consequence when using such number generators, and so it suffices to think of such number generators as actual random number generators.)

FIGURE 5.1

Spreadsheet illustration of a random number generator.

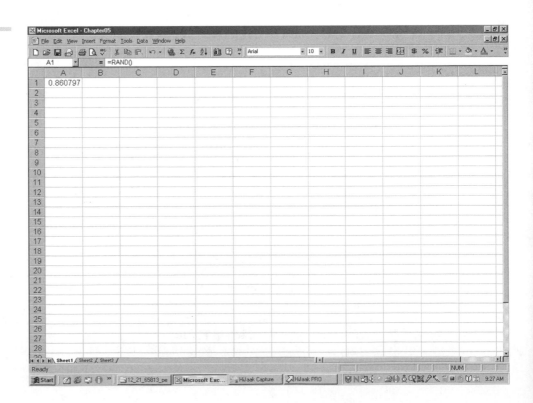

We next address how we can use a random number generator to create numbers that obey a discrete probability distribution.

5.5   CREATING NUMBERS THAT OBEY A DISCRETE PROBABILITY DISTRIBUTION

Returning to the Conley Fisheries problem, recall that our next task is to generate a sequence of demand values for each of the 20 days being simulated. Recall that the demand values must obey the discrete probability distribution of Table 5.1.

According to Table 5.1, the probability that the demand will be 0 lbs. is 0.02. Also, the probability that the demand is 1,000 lbs. is 0.03, etc. Now consider the following rule for creating a sequence of demands that will obey this distribution. First, make a call to a random number generator. The output of this call will be some value x, and recall that x will be an observed value from a uniform distribution on the interval from 0.0 to 1.0. Suppose that we create a demand value of $d = 0$ whenever x lies between 0.0 and 0.02. Then because x has been drawn from a uniform distribution on the interval from 0.0 to 1.0, the likelihood that x will lie between 0.0 and 0.02 will be precisely 0.02; and so the likelihood that d is equal to 0 will be precisely 0.02. This is exactly what we want. We can develop a similar rule in order to decide when to create a demand value of $d = 1,000$ as follows: Create a demand value of $d = 1,000$ whenever x lies between 0.02 and 0.05. Note that because x has been drawn from a uniform distribution on the interval from 0.0 to 1.0, the likelihood that x will lie between 0.02 and 0.05 will be precisely 0.03 (which is the width of the interval, i.e., $0.03 = 0.05 - 0.02$), which is exactly what we want. Similarly, we can develop a rule in order to decide when to create a demand value of $d = 2,000$ as follows: Create a demand value of $d = 2,000$ whenever x lies between 0.05 and 0.10. Note once again that because x has been drawn from a uniform distribution on the interval from 0.0 to 1.0, the likelihood that x will lie between 0.05 and 0.10 will be precisely 0.05 (which is the width of the interval, i.e., $0.05 = 0.10 - 0.05$), which is also exactly what we want. If we continue this process for all of the seven possible demand values of the probability distribution of demand, we can summarize the method in Table 5.4.

Table 5.4 summarizes the interval rule for creating a sequence of demand values that obey the probability distribution of demand. For each of the 20 days under consideration, call the random number generator once in order to obtain a value x that is drawn from a uniform distribution on the interval from 0.0 to 1.0. Next, find which of the seven intervals of Table 5.4 contains the value x. Last of all, use that interval to create the demand value d in the second column of the table.

For example, suppose the random number generator has been used to generate 20 random values, and these values have been entered into the second column

TABLE 5.4

Interval rule for creating daily demand in Rockport faced by Conley Fisheries.

Interval	Demand Value Created (lbs. of codfish)
0.00 − 0.02	0
0.02 − 0.05	1,000
0.05 − 0.10	2,000
0.10 − 0.18	3,000
0.18 − 0.51	4,000
0.51 − 0.80	5,000
0.80 − 1.00	6,000

TABLE 5.5

Worksheet for
generating demand
for codfish in
Rockport.

Day	Random Number	Demand in Rockport (lbs. of codfish)
1	0.3352	4,000
2	0.4015	4,000
3	0.1446	3,000
4	0.4323	4,000
5	0.0358	1,000
6	0.4999	4,000
7	0.8808	6,000
8	0.9013	6,000
9	0.4602	4,000
10	0.3489	4,000
11	0.4212	4,000
12	0.7267	5,000
13	0.9421	6,000
14	0.7059	5,000
15	0.1024	3,000
16	0.2478	4,000
17	0.5940	5,000
18	0.4459	4,000
19	0.0511	2,000
20	0.6618	5,000

of Table 5.5. Consider the first random number in Table 5.5, which is 0.3352. As this number lies between 0.18 and 0.51, we create a demand value on day 1 of 4,000 lbs. using the interval rule of Table 5.4. Next, consider the second random number in Table 5.5, which is 0.4015. As this number lies between 0.18 and 0.51, we also create a demand value on day 2 of 4,000 lbs. using the interval rule of Table 5.4. Next, consider the third random number in Table 5.5, which is 0.1446. As this number lies between 0.10 and 0.18, we create a demand value on day 3 of 3,000 lbs. using the interval rule of Table 5.4. If we continue this process for all of the 20 days portrayed in Table 5.5, we will create the demand values as shown in the third column of Table 5.5.

Notice that if we generate the demand values according to the interval rule of Table 5.4, then the demand values will indeed obey the probability distribution for demand as specified in Table 5.1. To see why this is so, consider any particular value of demand, such as demand equal to 5,000 lbs. A demand of 5,000 lbs. will be generated for a particular day whenever the random number generated for that day lies in the interval between 0.51 and 0.80. Because this interval has a width of 0.29 ($0.80 - 0.51 = 0.29$), and because x was drawn from a uniform distribution between 0.0 and 1.0, the likelihood that any given x will lie in this particular interval is precisely 0.29. This argument holds for all of the other six values of demand, because the width of the assignment intervals of Table 5.4 are exactly the same as the probability values of Table 5.1. In fact, that is why they were constructed this particular way. For example, according to Table 5.1, the probability that demand for codfish will be 4,000 lbs. is 0.33. In Table 5.4, the width of the random number assignment interval is $0.51 - 0.18 = 0.33$. Therefore, the likelihood in the simulation model that the model will create a demand of 4,000 lbs. is 0.33.

Notice how the entries in Table 5.4 are computed. One simply divides up the numbers between 0.0 and 1.0 into non-overlapping intervals whose widths correspond to the probability distribution function of interest. The general method for generating a sequence of numbers that obey a given discrete probability distribution is summarized as follows:

> **General Method for Creating Sample Data drawn from a Discrete Probability Distribution**
>
> 1. Divide up the number line between 0.0 and 1.0 into non-overlapping intervals, one interval for each of the possible values of the discrete distribution, and such that the width of each interval corresponds to the probability for each value.
>
> 2. Use a random number generator to generate a sequence of random numbers that obey the uniform distribution between 0.0 and 1.0.
>
> 3. For each random number generated in the sequence, assign the value corresponding to the interval that the random number lies in.

There is one minor technical point that needs to be mentioned about the endpoints of the assignment intervals of Table 5.4. According to Table 5.4, it is not clear what demand value should be created if the value of the random number x is exactly 0.51 (either $d = 4,000$ or $d = 5,000$), or if x is exactly any of the other endpoint values (0.02, 0.05, 0.10, 0.18, 0.51, or 0.80). Because the number x was drawn from a continuous uniform distribution, the probability that it will have a value of precisely 0.51 is zero, and so this is extremely unlikely to occur. But just in case, we can be more exact in the rule of Table 5.4 to specify that when the number is exactly one of the endpoint values, then choose the smaller of the possible demand values. Thus, for example, if $x = 0.51$, one would choose $d = 4,000$.

The final comment of this section concerns computer software and computer implementation of the method. It should be obvious that it is possible by hand to implement this method for any discrete probability distribution, as has been done, for example, to create the demand values in Table 5.5 for the Conley Fisheries problem. It should also be obvious that it is fairly straightforward to program a spreadsheet to automatically create a sequence of numbers that obey a given discrete probability distribution, using commands such as RAND(), etc. In addition, there are special simulation software programs that will do all of this automatically, where the user only needs to specify the discrete probability distribution, and the software program does all of the other work. This will be discussed further in Section 5.10.

We next address how we can use a random number generator to create numbers that obey a continuous probability distribution.

5.6 CREATING NUMBERS THAT OBEY A CONTINUOUS PROBABILITY DISTRIBUTION

Again returning to the problem of Conley Fisheries, the next task is to create a sequence of daily prices of codfish at the port in Rockport, one price for each of the 20 days under consideration, in such a way that the prices generated are observed values that have been drawn from the probability distribution of the daily price of codfish in Rockport. Recall that the daily price of codfish in Rockport obeys a Normal distribution with mean $\mu = \$3.65/\text{lb.}$ and with a standard deviation $\sigma = \$0.20/\text{lb.}$ Thus the price of codfish obeys a continuous probability distribution, and so unfortunately the method of the previous section, which was developed for discrete random variables, cannot be directly applied. For the case when it is necessary to create numbers that are drawn from a continuous probability distribution, there is a very simple method that is described as follows in generality.

Suppose that Y is any random variable that obeys a continuous probability distribution whose cumulative distribution function (cdf) is $F(y)$, where recall that

$$F(y) = P(Y \leq y),$$

and that it is necessary as part of a simulation model to create a sequence of numbers that obeys this particular continuous probability distribution. There is a graphical procedure for creating such a sequence of numbers, which is quite simple and is stated as follows:

Graphical Method for Creating Sample Data drawn from a Continuous Probability Distribution

1. Use a random number generator to generate a sequence of random numbers that obey the uniform distribution between 0.0 and 1.0.

2. For each random number x generated in the sequence of Step 1, place that number on the vertical axis of the graph of the cumulative distribution function (cdf) $F(y)$. Then find the point y on the horizontal axis whose cdf value $F(y)$ equals x.

We now illustrate this graphical method. Suppose Y is a continuous random variable whose probability density function (pdf) $f(y)$ is given in Figure 5.2, and whose cumulative distribution function (cdf) $F(y)$ is given in Figure 5.3. Suppose that we are interested in creating a sample of ten values drawn from this distribution. First, in Step 1, we generate a sequence of ten random numbers using a random number generator, whose values might look like those in the first column of Table 5.6.

FIGURE 5.2

Probability density function $f(y)$ of the random variable Y.

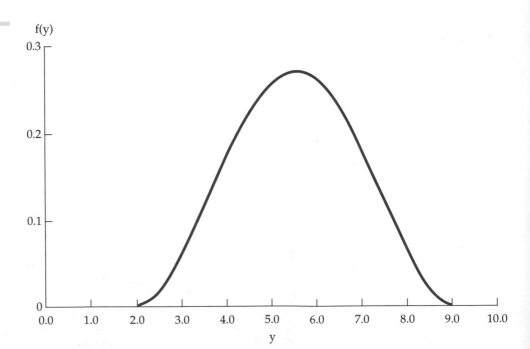

FIGURE 5.3

Cumulative
distribution function
$F(y)$ of the random
variable Y.

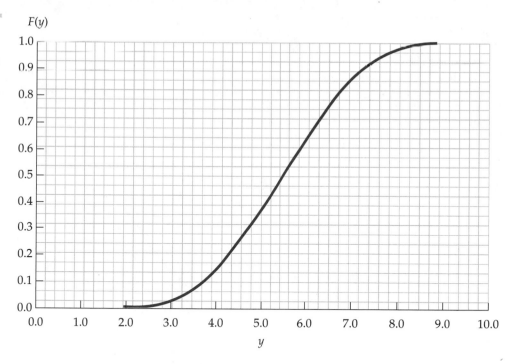

TABLE 5.6

A sequence of ten
random numbers.

Random Number (x)	Value of y
0.8054	
0.6423	
0.8849	
0.6970	
0.2485	
0.0793	
0.7002	
0.1491	
0.4067	
0.1658	

In order to create the sample value for the first random number, which is $x = 0.8054$, we place that value on the vertical axis of the cumulative distribution function $F(y)$ of Figure 5.3 and determine the corresponding y value on the horizontal axis from the graph. This is illustrated in Figure 5.4. For $x = 0.8054$, the corresponding y value is (approximately) $y = 6.75$. Proceeding in this manner for all of the ten different random number values x, one obtains the ten values of y depicted in Table 5.7. These ten values of y then constitute a sample of observed values drawn from the probability distribution of Y.

As just shown, it is quite easy to perform the necessary steps of the graphical method. However, it may not be obvious why this method creates a sequence of values of y that are in fact drawn from the probability distribution of Y. We now give some intuition as to why the method accomplishes this.

Consider the probability density function (pdf) $f(y)$ of Y shown in Figure 5.2 and its associated cumulative distribution function (cdf) $F(y)$ shown in Figure 5.3. Remember that the cdf $F(y)$ is the area under the curve of the pdf $f(y)$. Therefore, the slope of $F(y)$ will be steeper for those values of y where the pdf $f(y)$ is higher, and

FIGURE 5.4

Illustration of the graphical method for creating observed values of a continuous random variable with cumulative distribution function $F(y)$.

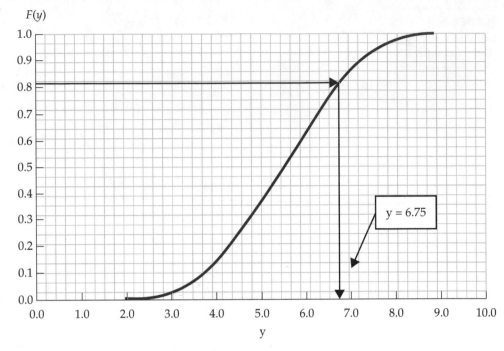

TABLE 5.7

Values of x and y.

Random Number (x)	Value of y
0.8054	6.75
0.6423	6.04
0.8849	7.16
0.6970	6.24
0.2485	4.51
0.0793	3.58
0.7002	6.28
0.1491	4.02
0.4067	5.15
0.1658	4.12

the slope of $F(y)$ will be flatter for those values of y where the pdf $f(y)$ is lower. For example, at $y = 5.5$, $f(y)$ is quite large, and the slope of $F(y)$ is quite steep. Also, for example, at $y = 3.0$, $f(y)$ is quite small, and the slope of $F(y)$ is quite flat.

Now consider the application of the graphical method for creating values of y. Note that by way of the construction, the method will produce a greater concentration of values of y where the slope of the cdf $F(y)$ is steeper. Likewise, the method will produce a lesser concentration of values of y where the slope of the cdf $F(y)$ is flatter. Therefore, using the observation in the paragraph above, the method will produce a greater concentration of values of y where the pdf $f(y)$ is higher and will produce a lesser concentration of values of y where the pdf $f(y)$ is lower. As it turns out, this correspondence is precise, and so indeed the method will produce values of y that are exactly in accord with the underlying probability distribution of Y.

Although the method is best illustrated by considering a graph of the cdf $F(y)$, it is not necessary to have a literal graph of the cumulative distribution function in order to use the method. In fact, another way to state the method without the use of graphs is as follows:

General Method for Creating Sample Data Drawn from a Continuous Probability Distribution

1. Use a random number generator to generate a sequence of random numbers that obey the uniform distribution between 0.0 and 1.0.

2. For each random number x generated in the sequence of Step 1, compute that value of y whose cumulative distribution function value is equal to x. That is, given x, solve the equation:

$$F(y) = P(Y \leq y) = x$$

to obtain the value y. Then assign y as the value created.

This more general form of the method is now illustrated on the Conley Fisheries problem, where the task at hand is to create a sequence of prices for codfish at the port in Rockport, one price for each of the 20 days under consideration, in such a way that the created prices are samples drawn from the probability distribution of the daily price of codfish in Rockport. Recall that the daily price of codfish in Rockport obeys a Normal distribution with mean μ = $3.65/lb. and with a standard deviation σ = $0.20/lb.

The first step is to use a random number generator to generate 20 random numbers. Suppose this has been done, and the 20 random numbers are as shown in the second column of Table 5.8.

The second step is then to compute that value of y for which the equation

$$F(y) = P(Y \leq y) = x$$

TABLE 5.8

Worksheet for generating the price of codfish in Rockport.

Day	Random Number	Price of Codfish in Rockport ($/lb.)
1	0.3236	3.5585
2	0.1355	3.4299
3	0.5192	3.6596
4	0.9726	4.0342
5	0.0565	3.3330
6	0.2070	3.4866
7	0.2481	3.5139
8	0.8017	3.8196
9	0.2644	3.5240
10	0.2851	3.5365
11	0.7192	3.7661
12	0.7246	3.7693
13	0.9921	4.1330
14	0.5227	3.6614
15	0.0553	3.3309
16	0.5915	3.6963
17	0.0893	3.3810
18	0.3136	3.5529
19	0.0701	3.3550
20	0.8309	3.8416

is solved, for each of the 20 different random number values x in Table 5.8, and where $F(y)$ is the cdf for a Normal distribution with mean $\mu = \$3.65/\text{lb}$. and with standard deviation $\sigma = \$0.20/\text{lb}$. Consider the first random number value, which is $x = 0.3236$. Then the corresponding value of y is that value of y which solves:

$$P(Y \leq y) = 0.3236,$$

and where Y obeys a Normal distribution with mean $\mu = 3.65$ and with a standard deviation $\sigma = 0.20$. But then, if we define

$$Z = \frac{Y - \mu}{\sigma},$$

and recall that Z is a standard Normal random variable, then

$$P(Y \leq y) = 0.3236$$

is equivalent to

$$P\left(Z \leq \frac{y - \mu}{\sigma}\right) = 0.3236.$$

Solving this equation via a standard Normal table, one obtains that

$$\frac{y - \mu}{\sigma} = -0.4575,$$

and substituting the values of $\mu = \$3.65/\text{lb}$. and $\sigma = \$0.20/\text{lb}$. in this expression and solving for y yields

$$y = \mu - 0.4575\sigma = 3.65 - 0.4575 \times 0.20 = \$3.5585/\text{lb}.$$

Therefore, with $y = \$3.5585$, it is true that

$$F(y) = P(Y \leq y) = 0.3236,$$

and so we create a price of $\$3.5585/\text{lb}$. in the first row of the third column of Table 5.8. Continuing in precisely this manner for all of the other 19 random number values, we create the remaining entries in the table.

The final comment of this section concerns computer software and computer implementation of the general method. It should be obvious that it is possible by hand to implement either the graphical method or the more general method for any continuous probability distribution, so long as it is possible to work with the cumulative distribution function of the distribution via either a graph or a table. For the Conley Fisheries problem, for example, the method is implemented by using the table for the Normal distribution. When the continuous distribution is of a very special form, such as a Normal distribution or a uniform distribution, it is quite easy to create a spreadsheet that will do all of the necessary computations automatically. When the continuous distribution is other than the Normal or a uniform distribution, there are special simulation software programs that will do all of the computation automatically, where the user only needs to specify the general parameters of the continuous distribution, and the software program does all of the other work. This will be discussed further in Section 5.10

5.7

COMPLETING THE SIMULATION MODEL OF CONLEY FISHERIES

We can now complete the simulation of the Conley Fisheries problem by combining the demand values of Table 5.5 and the price values of Table 5.8 to complete the analysis. This is shown in Table 5.9, which is now discussed in detail. Table 5.9 portrays the results of the simulation efforts on the simulation of the first 20 days of the 200-day period. The second and third columns of Table 5.9 are simply the simulated values of demand in Rockport (column 3) based on the random number in Column 2, as created in Table 5.5 and simply copied over to Table 5.9. The fourth column of Table 5.9 is the quantity of codfish sold, which, as one may recall, is the minimum of the demand (Column 3) and the daily catch of 3,500 lbs. The fifth and sixth columns of Table 5.9 are simply the simulated values of the price of codfish in Rockport (Column 6) based on the random number in Column 5, as created in Table 5.8 and simply copied over to Table 5.9. Last of all, Column 7 of Table 5.9 is the daily earnings in Rockport, which is computed by the formula:

$$\text{Daily Earnings} = (\text{Quantity of Codfish Sold}) (\text{Price of Cod}) - \$10,000.$$

Thus, for example, for day 1, the daily earnings is:

$$\text{Daily Earnings} = (3,500 \text{ lbs.}) (\$3.5585/\text{lb.}) - \$10,000 = \$2,455.$$

The computations are repeated in a similar fashion for all of the 20 days in the table.

The important numbers in Table 5.9 are the daily earnings numbers in the last column of the table. By generating the daily earnings numbers for a large number of days, it should be possible to get a fairly accurate description of the probability distribution of the daily earnings in Rockport, i.e., the probability distribution of the random variable F.

Although the number $n = 20$ has been used to show some of the intermediary detailed work in the simulation of the Conley Fisheries problem, there is no reason why the model cannot be extended to run for $n = 200$ simulated days, and hence simulate

TABLE 5.9

Completed worksheet for the Conley Fisheries problem.

Day Number	Random Number	Demand in Rockport (lbs.)	Quantity of Codfish Sold (lbs.)	Random Number	Price of Codfish in Rockport ($/lb.)	Daily Earnings in Rockport ($)
1	0.3352	4,000	3,500	0.3236	3.5585	$2,455
2	0.4015	4,000	3,500	0.1355	3.4299	$2,005
3	0.1446	3,000	3,000	0.5192	3.6596	$979
4	0.4323	4,000	3,500	0.9726	4.0342	$4,120
5	0.0358	1,000	1,000	0.0565	3.3330	($6,667)
6	0.4999	4,000	3,500	0.2070	3.4866	$2,203
7	0.8808	6,000	3,500	0.2481	3.5139	$2,299
8	0.9013	6,000	3,500	0.8017	3.8196	$3,368
9	0.4602	4,000	3,500	0.2644	3.5240	$2,334
10	0.3489	4,000	3,500	0.2851	3.5365	$2,378
11	0.4212	4,000	3,500	0.7192	3.7661	$3,181
12	0.7267	5,000	3,500	0.7246	3.7693	$3,193
13	0.9421	6,000	3,500	0.9921	4.1330	$4,465
14	0.7059	5,000	3,500	0.5227	3.6614	$2,815
15	0.1024	3,000	3,000	0.0553	3.3309	($7)
16	0.2478	4,000	3,500	0.5915	3.6963	$2,937
17	0.5940	5,000	3,500	0.0893	3.3810	$1,834
18	0.4459	4,000	3,500	0.3136	3.5529	$2,435
19	0.0511	2,000	2,000	0.0701	3.3550	($3,290)
20	0.6618	5,000	3,500	0.8309	3.8416	$3,445

$n = 200$ days of daily earnings. Indeed, Table 5.10 shows 200 different daily earnings numbers generated by using the simulation methodology for 200 different days. Note that the first 20 entries in Table 5.10 are simply the daily earnings in Rockport of the first 20 days of the simulation, i.e., they are the numbers from the final column of Table 5.9.

TABLE 5.10

Simulation output for $n = 200$ simulation trials of the Conley Fisheries model.

Day Number	Daily Earnings in Rockport ($)	Day Number	Daily Earnings in Rockport ($)	Day Number	Daily Earnings in Rockport ($)	Day Number	Daily Earnings in Rockport ($)
1	$2,455	51	$2,870	101	$3,188	151	($3,039)
2	$2,005	52	$2,530	102	$2,907	152	$1,822
3	$979	53	$4,289	103	$4,192	153	$2,217
4	$4,120	54	$1,968	104	$2,792	154	$3,068
5	($6,667)	55	($2,382)	105	$2,727	155	($224)
6	$2,203	56	$3,271	106	$1,930	156	$3,662
7	$2,299	57	$2,457	107	$2,569	157	$3,829
8	$3,368	58	$2,240	108	$2,858	158	$1,628
9	$2,334	59	$2,658	109	$3,783	159	($10,000)
10	$2,378	60	$1,443	110	($2,523)	160	$2,254
11	$3,181	61	($6,491)	111	($2,290)	161	$3,406
12	$3,193	62	$1,954	112	$4,229	162	$441
13	$4,465	63	($6,284)	113	$3,317	163	($3,159)
14	$2,815	64	$2,494	114	($1,769)	164	$3,243
15	($7)	65	$3,649	115	$2,581	165	$1,351
16	$2,937	66	$3,258	116	$2,361	166	$3,649
17	$1,834	67	($2,034)	117	($10,000)	167	$3,156
18	$2,435	68	$2,791	118	$919	168	$2,104
19	($3,290)	69	$2,856	119	$2,493	169	$2,573
20	$3,445	70	$2,026	120	$3,973	170	$2,011
21	$2,076	71	$2,677	121	$3,189	171	$3,706
22	$3,583	72	$3,364	122	($3,654)	172	$2,017
23	$2,169	73	$3,472	123	$2,492	173	($2,860)
24	$3,064	74	$1,873	124	$2,843	174	$2,247
25	($6,284)	75	$2,104	125	($3,020)	175	$2,165
26	$3,602	76	$2,586	126	$2,725	176	$4,134
27	$4,406	77	$2,201	127	$2,194	177	$3,031
28	$2,911	78	$1,825	128	$1,883	178	$2,345
29	$2,389	79	$2,955	129	$3,329	179	$1,416
30	$2,752	80	$1,469	130	$2,372	180	$3,025
31	$2,163	81	$1,843	131	$1,010	181	$156
32	$3,553	82	$3,936	132	$3,161	182	$2,737
33	$3,315	83	$2,572	133	$2,769	183	$3,025
34	$1,936	84	($10,000)	134	$3,184	184	($3,328
35	$3,013	85	$1,601	135	$2,786	185	$2,163
36	$405	86	$4,238	136	$3,233	186	($2,383)
37	$2,443	87	$2,423	137	$2,230	187	$1,641
38	$2,825	88	$1,072	138	$3,338	188	$2,310
39	$1,818	89	$2,651	139	$2,670	189	$2,980
40	($1,808)	90	$1,823	140	($6,362)	190	$3,109
41	$3,104	91	$2,782	141	$2,500	191	$3,246
42	$2,802	92	($5,963)	142	($3,068)	192	$2,567
43	$556	93	$2,904	143	$2,036	193	$3,340
44	$2,554	94	$3,972	144	$4,030	194	$2,244
45	$2,792	95	$2,539	145	$3,826	195	$3,219
46	$3,099	96	$1,530	146	$3,527	196	$2,496
47	$2,465	97	$1,629	147	$3,196	197	$2,011
48	$2,909	98	$2,610	148	$3,573	198	$2,731
49	$2,386	99	$2,821	149	$4,020	199	($6,464)
50	$2,505	100	$2,067	150	$3,012	200	$3,614

| 5.8 | # USING THE SAMPLE DATA FOR ANALYSIS |

Table 5.10 contains a sample of $n = 200$ observed values of the earnings from using Rockport. Fixing some notation, let x_i denote the daily earnings from using Rockport for day number i, for all values of $i = 1, \ldots, 200$. That is, $x_1 = \$2{,}455$, $x_2 = \$2{,}005, \ldots, x_{200} = \$3{,}614$. Then each x_i is the observed value of the random variable F and has been drawn from the (unknown) probability distribution of the random variable F. In fact, the array of values $x_1, x_2, \ldots, x_{200}$ constitutes a fairly large sample of $n = 200$ different observed values of the random variable F. Therefore, we can use this sample of observed values to estimate the answers to the five questions posed in Section 5.1 and Section 5.2, which we rephrase below in the language of statistical sampling:

(a) What is the shape of the probability density function of F ?

(b) What is $P(F > \$1{,}375)$?

(c) What is $P(F < \$0)$?

(d) What is the expected value of F?

(e) What is the standard deviation of F?

We now proceed to answer these five questions.

Question (a):
What is an estimate of the shape the probability density function of F?

Recall from Chapter 4 that in order to gain intuition about the shape of the distribution of F, it is useful to create a frequency table and a histogram of the observed sample values $x_1, x_2, \ldots, x_{200}$ of Table 5.10. Such a frequency table is presented in Table 5.11.

A histogram of the values of Table 5.11 is shown in Figure 5.5. This histogram gives a nice pictorial view of the distribution of the observed values of the sample, and it also is an approximation of the shape of the probability density function (pdf) of F. We see from the histogram in Figure 5.5 that the values of F are mostly clustered in the range $\$0$ through $\$4{,}500$, in a roughly bell shape or Normal shape, but that there are also a significant number of other values scattered below $\$0$, whose values can be as low as $-\$10{,}000$. This histogram indicates that while most observed values of earnings from Rockport are quite high, there is some definite risk of substantial losses from using Rockport.

Question (b):
What is an estimate of $P(F > \$1{,}375)$?

This question can be answered by using the counting method developed in Chapter 4. Recall from Chapter 4 that the fraction of values of $x_1, x_2, \ldots, x_{200}$ in Table 5.10 that are larger than $\$1{,}375$ is an estimate of the probability p for which

$$p = P(F > \$1{,}375).$$

If we count the number of values of $x_1, x_2, \ldots, x_{200}$ in Table 5.10 that are larger than $\$1{,}375$, we obtain that 165 of these 200 values are larger than $\$1{,}375$. Therefore, an estimate of $p = P(F > \$1{,}375)$ is:

$$\frac{165}{200} = 0.83.$$

We therefore estimate that there is an 83% likelihood that the earnings in Rockport on any given day would exceed the earnings from Gloucester. This supports the strategy option of choosing Rockport over Gloucester.

TABLE 5.11

Frequency table of the 200 observed values of earnings in Rockport.

Interval From	Interval To	Number in the Sample
($10,500)	($10,000)	3
($10,000)	($9,500)	0
($9,500)	($9,000)	0
($9,000)	($8,500)	0
($8,500)	($8,000)	0
($8,000)	($7,500)	0
($7,500)	($7,000)	0
($7,000)	($6,500)	1
($6,500)	($6,000)	5
($6,000)	($5,500)	1
($5,500)	($5,000)	0
($5,000)	($4,500)	0
($4,500)	($4,000)	0
($4,000)	($3,500)	1
($3,500)	($3,000)	5
($3,000)	($2,500)	2
($2,500)	($2,000)	4
($2,000)	($1,500)	2
($1,500)	($1,000)	0
($1,000)	($500)	0
($500)	$0	2
$0	$500	3
$500	$1,000	3
$1,000	$1,500	6
$1,500	$2,000	17
$2,000	$2,500	43
$2,500	$3,000	41
$3,000	$3,500	35
$3,500	$4,000	16
$4,000	$4,500	10
$4,500	$5,000	0

FIGURE 5.5

Histogram of earnings from Rockport.

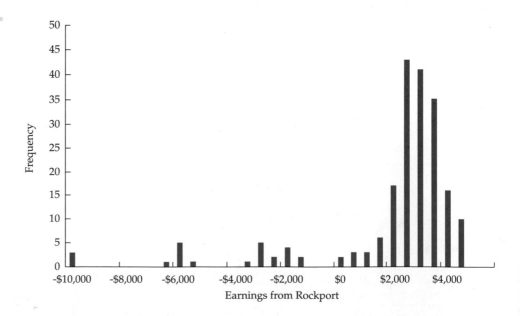

Question (c):

What is an estimate of $P(F < 0)$?

This question can also be answered by using the counting method of Chapter 4. Recall from Chapter 4 that the fraction of values of $x_1, x_2, \ldots, x_{200}$ in Table 5.10 that are less than \$0 is an estimate of the probability p for which $p = P(F < \$0)$. If we count the number of values of $x_1, x_2, \ldots, x_{200}$ in Table 5.10 that are less than \$0, we obtain that 26 of these 200 values are less than \$0. Therefore, an estimate of $p = P(F < \$0)$ is:

$$\frac{26}{200} = 0.13.$$

We therefore estimate that there is a 13% likelihood that Conley Fisheries would lose money on any given day, if they chose to sell their catch in Rockport. This shows that the risk of choosing Rockport is not too large, but it is not insubstantial either.

Question (d):

What is an estimate of the expected value of F?

We know that the observed sample mean $\bar{x}$ of this sample of 200 observed values is a good estimate of the actual expected value μ of the underlying distribution of F, especially when the sample size is large (and here, the sample size is $n = 200$, which is quite large). Therefore, the observed sample mean of the 200 values $x_1, x_2, \ldots, x_{200}$ in Table 5.10 should be a very good estimate of the expected value μ of the random variable F. It is straightforward to obtain the sample mean $\bar{x}$ for the sample given in Table 5.10. Its value is

$$\bar{x} = \frac{2{,}445 + 2{,}005 + \ldots + 3{,}614}{200} = \$1{,}768.38.$$

Therefore our estimate of the mean of the random variable F is \$1,768.38. Notice that this value is larger than \$1,375, which is the earnings that Conley Fisheries can obtain (with certainty) by selling its fish in Gloucester. Thus, an estimate of the expected increase in revenues from selling in Rockport is

$$\$393.38/\text{day} = \$1{,}768.38/\text{day} - \$1{,}375.00/\text{day}.$$

Question (e):

What is an estimate of the standard deviation of F?

Recall from the statistical sampling methodology of Chapter 4 that the observed sample standard deviation s is a good estimate of the actual standard deviation σ of the random variable F, especially when the sample size is large. It is straightforward to obtain the observed sample standard deviation for the sample given in Table 5.10, as follows:

$$s^2 = \frac{\sum_{i=1}^{n}(x_i - \bar{x})^2}{n-1}$$

$$= \frac{(2{,}455 - 1{,}768.38)^2 + (2{,}005 - 1{,}768.38)^2 + \ldots + (3{,}614 - 1{,}768.38)^2}{200 - 1}$$

$$= 7{,}142{,}715.87.$$

Therefore

$$s = \sqrt{7,142,715.87} = \$2,672.59,$$

and our estimate of the standard deviation of F is $s = \$2,672.59$. This standard deviation is rather large, which confirms Clint Conley's intuition that there is substantial risk involved in using Rockport as the port at which to sell his daily catch.

An additional question that one might want to answer is: What is a 95% confidence interval for the mean of the distribution of daily earnings from selling the catch of codfish in Rockport? The answer to this question is provided by the formula in Chapter 4 for a 95% confidence interval for the mean of a distribution when n is large. This formula is:

$$[\bar{x} - 1.96s/\sqrt{n}, \bar{x} + 1.96s/\sqrt{n}].$$

Substituting the values of $\bar{x} = \$1,768.38$, $s = \$2,672.59$, and $n = 200$, we compute the 95% confidence interval for the true mean of the distribution of daily earnings to be

$$[\$1,397.98, \$2,138.78].$$

Notice that this interval does not contain the value $1,375. Therefore, at the 95% confidence level, we can conclude that the expected daily earnings from selling the catch of codfish in Rockport is higher than from selling the catch of codfish in Gloucester.

Finally, suppose Clint Conley were to construct and use the simulation model that has been developed herein. With the answers to the questions posed earlier, he would be in a good position to make an informed decision. Here is a list of the key data garnered from the analysis of the simulation model:

- We estimate that the shape of the distribution of daily earnings from Rockport will be as shown in Figure 5.5. On most days the earnings will be between $0 and $4,500 per day. However, on some days this number could be as low as $-\$10,000$.

- We estimate that the probability is 0.83 that the daily earnings in Rockport would be greater than in Gloucester on any given day.

- We estimate that the probability is 0.13 that the daily earnings in Rockport will be negative on any given day.

- We estimate that the expected daily earnings from Rockport is $1,768.38. This is higher than the earnings in Gloucester would be, by $393.38/day.

- We estimate that the standard deviation of the daily earnings in Rockport is $2,672.59.

- The 95% confidence interval for the actual expected daily earnings from using Rockport excludes $1,375. Therefore, we are 95% confident that the expected daily earnings from Rockport is higher than from Gloucester.

Based on this information, Clint Conley would probably optimally choose to sell his catch in Rockport, in spite of the risk. Note that the risk is not trivial, as there is always the possibility that he could lose money on any given day (with probability 0.13), and in fact he could have cash-flow problems if he were extremely unlucky. But unless he is extremely averse to taking risks (in which case he might not want to be in the fishing industry to begin with), he would probably further the long-term interests of Conley Fisheries by choosing to sell his fish in Rockport.

5.9 SUMMARY OF SIMULATION MODELING, AND GUIDELINES ON THE USE OF SIMULATION

A simulation model attempts to measure aspects of uncertainty that simple formulas cannot. As we saw in the Conley Fisheries problem, even this simple problem has no convenient analysis via formulas related to probability and random variables. Of course, when formulas and tables can be used instead of a simulation model, then the manager's task is that much easier. But all too often, there are situations that must be analyzed where a simulation model is the only appropriate methodological tool.

The successful application of a simulation model depends on the ability to create sample values of random variables that obey a variety of discrete and continuous probability distributions. This is the key to constructing and using a simulation model. Through the use of a random number generator, it is possible to create sample data values that obey any discrete distribution or any continuous distribution by applying the general methods outlined in Section 5.5 (for discrete random variables) and Section 5.6 (for continuous random variables).

Unlike decision trees and certain other modeling tools, a simulation has no internal optimal decision-making capability. Note that the simulation model constructed for analyzing the Conley Fisheries problem only produced data as the output, and the model itself did not choose the best port strategy. Suppose that Conley Fisheries faced the decision of choosing among five different ports. A simulation model would be able to analyze the implications of using each port, but unlike a decision tree model, the simulation model would not choose the optimal port strategy. In order to use a simulation model, the manager must enumerate all possible strategy options and then direct the simulation model to analyze each and every option.

The results that one can obtain from using a simulation model are not precise due to the inherent randomness in a simulation. The typical conclusions that one can draw from a simulation model are estimates of the shapes of distributions of particular quantities of interest, estimates of probabilities of events of interest, and means and standard deviations of the probability distributions of interest. One can also construct confidence intervals and other inferences of statistical sampling.

The question of the number of trials or runs to perform in a simulation model is mathematically complex. Fortunately, with today's computing power, this is not a paramount issue for most problems, because it is possible to run even very large and complex simulation models for many hundreds or thousands of trials, and so obtain a very large set of sample data values to work with.

Finally, one should recognize that gaining managerial confidence in a simulation model will depend on at least three factors:

- a good understanding of the underlying management problem,

- one's ability to use the concepts of probability and statistics correctly, and

- one's ability to communicate these concepts effectively.

5.10 COMPUTER SOFTWARE FOR SIMULATION MODELING

The Conley Fisheries example illustrates how easy it is to construct a simulation model using standard spreadsheet software. The "input" to the Conley Fisheries example consisted of the following information:

- the description of probability distribution of the random variable D, the daily demand in Rockport. This distribution was shown in Table 5.1.

- the description of the probability distribution of the random variable PR, the daily price of codfish in Rockport. This is a Normal distribution with mean $\mu = \$3.65$ and standard deviation $\sigma = \$0.20$.

- the formula for the earnings from selling the catch in Rockport, namely

$$F = PR \times \min(3{,}500, D) - 10{,}000.$$

Based on these inputs, we constructed a simulation model predicated on the ability to generate random variables that obey certain distributions, namely a discrete distribution (for daily demand in Rockport) and the Normal distribution (for daily prices in Rockport). The output of the model was the sample of observed values of earnings in Rockport shown in Table 5.10. Based on the information in Table 5.10, we constructed a histogram of the sample observations (shown in Figure 5.5), and we performed a variety of other computations, such as counting the number of observations in a given range, the computation of the sample mean and the sample standard deviation, etc.

Because simulation modeling is such a useful tool, there are a variety of simulation modeling software products that facilitate the construction of a simulation model. A typical simulation software package is usually designed to be used as an add-on to the Excel® spreadsheet software and has pull-down menus that allows the user to choose from a variety of probability distributions for the generation of random variables (such as the uniform distribution, the Normal distribution, the binomial distribution, a discrete distribution, etc.) The software is designed to automatically generate random numbers that obey these distributions. Furthermore, the typical simulation software package will automatically perform the routine tasks involved in analyzing the output of a simulation model, such as creating histograms, estimating probabilities, and estimating means and standard deviations. All of this capability is designed to free the manager to focus on managerial analysis of the simulation model, as opposed to generating random numbers and creating chart output. An example of such a software package that is used in some of the cases in Section 5.12 is called CrystalBall® and is described at the end of the Ontario Gateway case.

There are also a large number of "specialty simulation" software packages that are designed for specific uses in specific applications domains. For example, there are some simulation modeling software packages designed to model manufacturing operations, and that offer special graphics and other features unique to a manufacturing environment. There are other simulation modeling software packages designed for other special application domains, such as service applications, military applications, and financial modeling.

5.11   TYPICAL USES OF SIMULATION MODELS

Perhaps the most frequent use of simulation models is in the analysis of a company's production operations. Many companies use simulation to model the events that occur in their factory production processes, where the times that various jobs take is uncertain and where there are complex interactions in the scheduling of tasks. These models are used to evaluate new operations strategies, to test the implications of using new processes, and to evaluate various investment possibilities that are intended to improve production and operational efficiency.

Another frequent use of simulation models is in the analysis of operations where there are likely to be queues (that is, waiting lines). For example, the best managed fast-food chains use simulation models to analyze the effects of different staffing strategies on how long customers will wait for service, and on the implications of offering new products, etc. Banks use simulation models to assess how many tellers or how many ATMs (automated teller machines) to plan for at a given location. Airlines use simulation modeling to analyze throughput of passengers at ticket counters, at gates, and in baggage handling. With the increasing use of toll-free numbers for serving customers in a variety of businesses (from catalog shopping to toll-free software support for software products), many telecommunications companies now offer simulation modeling as part of their basic service to all of their "800" business customers to help them assign staffing levels for their toll-free services.

Another use of simulation modeling is in capital budgeting and the strategic analysis of investment alternatives. Simulation models are used to analyze the implications of various assumptions concerning the distribution of costs of an investment, possible market penetration scenarios, and the distribution of cash-flows, both in any given year as well as over the life of the investment.

As mentioned earlier, simulation models are used quite abundantly in the analysis of military procurement and in the analysis of military strategy. Here in particular, simulation modeling is used to great advantage, as the alternative of testing new hardware or tactics in the field is not particularly attractive.

Simulation is also used in financial engineering to assign prices and analyze other quantities of interest for complex financial instruments, such as derivative securities, options, and futures contracts.

This is only a small list of the ways that simulation models are currently used by managers. With the rapid advances in both computer hardware and the ease of use of today's simulation modeling software, there is enormous potential for simulation models to add even more value to the educated and creative manager who knows how to wisely use the tools of simulation.

5.12 CASE MODULES

THE GENTLE LENTIL RESTAURANT

An Excellent Job Offer

Sanjay Thomas, a second-year MBA student at the M.I.T. Sloan School of Management, is in a very enviable position: He has just received an excellent job offer with a top-flight management consulting firm. Furthermore, the firm was so impressed with Sanjay's performance during the previous summer that they would like Sanjay to start up the firm's practice in its new Bombay office. The synergy of Sanjay's previous consulting experiences (both prior to Sloan and during the previous summer), his Sloan MBA education, and his fluency in Hindi offer an extremely high likelihood that Sanjay would be very successful, if he were to accept the firm's offer and develop the Bombay office's practice in India and southern Asia.

Sanjay is a rather contemplative individual who tries to see the bigger picture of events and decisions in life. He is very excited about the job offer for a number of good reasons. He likes the intellectual and business stimulation of management consulting, and the great variety of assignments and business situations that consultants have the opportunity to deal with. Also, the salary offer is excellent ($80,000 for the first year). However, he is also apprehensive. The lifestyle of management consultants is taxing. There is constant travel, and much of the travel is rather routine. Furthermore, in Sanjay's summer consulting experience he often had to cancel his personal plans at the last minute in order to accommodate spurts of unexpected work in the evenings and on weekends. While Sanjay is very energetic and motivated, and he enjoys hard work, he is also committed to maintaining a healthy personal life as well. Career development is but one piece of his many aspirations.

A Different Career Path?

The job offer has catalyzed Sanjay to think more seriously about one particular career alternative he has pondered over the last two years, namely to open his own upscale restaurant serving gourmet Indian cuisine. Sanjay is attracted to this plan for a number of reasons. For one, he has always wanted to start his own business. Second, he has always had a passion and talent for gourmet Indian cuisine. Third, he enjoys being a good host, and in fact hospitality has always been an integral part of his lifestyle.

In terms of lifestyle issues, Sanjay knows several restaurant owners who also work extremely long hours; his Aunt Sona owns a restaurant in Bethesda, Maryland, and she is always working. But as hard as his aunt works, Sanjay feels that these hours constitute a very different lifestyle from that of a management consultant. There would be very little if any travel involved and so he would be able to participate more in his community. And although the restaurant business might demand extreme effort from time to time, Sanjay figures that such situations would not arise as often as in a consulting career. The most important difference for Sanjay is that he would be working for himself, and that the business would be more fun than consulting (although he also has enjoyed consulting quite a bit as well). Sanjay believes that his high energy, management skills, and interest in gourmet Indian cuisine would form the essential ingredients needed to open and successfully operate his own restaurant, which he has temporarily named the Gentle Lentil Restaurant.

The non-financial advantages of consulting (variety of work, intellectual challenge) seem to be evenly matched against the non-financial advantages of opening the Gentle Lentil Restaurant (less travel, business ownership). The financial implications of the two alternatives might be very different, however. In addition to his desire to earn a good salary, Sanjay also would like to pay off his educational debt obligations, which are rather substantial. (Like many other students attending top business schools, Sanjay financed a big portion of his education through student loans.) In order to maintain a reasonable lifestyle while paying off his loans after graduation, Sanjay has figured that he would need to earn approximately $5,000 per month before taxes.

Making an Informed Decision

As part of one of his course projects last semester on entepreneurship, Sanjay actually conducted a profitability analysis of a sample of gourmet Indian restaurants in major East Coast cities, starting with his aunt's restaurant. After adjusting the data to reflect the cost-of-living standard in Boston, Sanjay used the information to define benchmark costs and revenues for the Gentle Lentil Restaurant concept. These data are based on siting the restaurant, with a seating capacity of 50 patrons, in the Harvard Square area, borrowing money to construct the interior structure, and leasing all capital equipment for the restaurant.

Sanjay estimated the monthly non-labor fixed costs of operating the Gentle Lentil Restaurant to be $3,995 per month, see the cost analysis in Appendix 1 at the end of the case. He also estimated the variable costs of food to be $11/meal served. Among the many uncertainties in the restaurant business, there were three uncertain variables that tended to dominate the profitability equation: the number of meals sold (per month), the revenue per meal, and the (fixed) labor costs of the restaurant. From his conversations with many restaurant owners, Sanjay was able to estimate actual distributions for these three crucial uncertain variables, as follows.

- **Number of meals sold.** Sanjay estimated that for a restaurant like the Gentle Lentil suitably sited in the environs of Harvard Square with a seating capacity of 50 persons, the number of meals sold per month would obey a Normal distribution with a mean of $\mu = 3,000$ meals and a standard deviation of $\sigma = 1,000$ meals.

- **Revenue per Meal.** Since The Gentle Lentil Restaurant would provide a gourmet dining experience, Sanjay would plan to offer prix fixe (fixed price) meals and would set the price of the meals according to his own estimate of what the local economy and what the market for gourmet dining would support. His own personal estimate, based on discussions with friends and gourmet food aficionados, is shown in Table 5.12. In this range of meal prices, we will assume, for modeling purposes, that the monthly demand will not be affected by the meal price.

- **Labor Costs.** Sanjay estimated that the labor costs for the Gentle Lentil Restaurant would be somewhere between $5,040 per month and $6,860 per month. (For the details of how he arrived at these two numbers, see Appendix 2 at the end of the case.) Without any other information, Sanjay assumed that actual labor costs would obey a continuous uniform distribution in this range.

An Unusual Partnership Opportunity

It was obvious to Sanjay that there would be substantially more risk involved in the Gentle Lentil Restaurant than in accepting the consulting position. When he mentioned this to his aunt in a phone conversation, she offered him the following financial "partnership" opportunity to increase his incentive to undertake the Gentle Lentil venture. Under the financial partnership, his aunt would guarantee Sanjay a monthly salary of at least $3,500. That is, if earnings in a given month fell below $3,500, she would cover the difference. In exchange for this, his aunt would receive 90% of all monthly earnings in excess of $9,000. If earnings were between $3,500 and

TABLE 5.12

Likelihood of prix fixe meal price.

Scenario	Prix Fixe Meal Price	Probability
Very healthy market	$20.00	25%
Healthy market	$18.50	35%
Not so healthy market	$16.50	30%
Unhealthy market	$15.00	10%

$9,000, all such moneys would go to Sanjay. It seemed to Sanjay that the effect of this partnership was to reduce the likelihood that his monthly salary would be very low, but it would also reduce the likelihood that his monthly salary would be very high.

Assignment:

(a) Without considering the partnership opportunity, what would be Sanjay's expected monthly salary at Gentle Lentil? How does this compare to his monthly salary at the consulting firm?

(b) Without considering the partnership opportunity, try to compute the standard deviation of Sanjay's monthly salary at Gentle Lentil. What problems do you encounter?

(c) If you were Sanjay, what quantitative questions about the potential salary at Gentle Lentil (with and without the partnership opportunity) would you want to answer before deciding whether to launch the Gentle Lentil Restaurant or to accept the consulting position?

Appendix 1

Monthly Non-Labor Fixed Costs for the Gentle Lentil Restaurant

Table 5.13 shows Sanjay Thomas' estimate of the monthly non-labor fixed costs for the Gentle Lentil Restaurant.

Notes:

1. Sanjay assumed that Gentle Lentil would lease all restaurant equipment, and that all other capital expenditures would be financed through loans.

2. Description of fixed cost categories is as follows:

   • Rent: cost of restaurant space

   • Leased Equipment: kitchen equipment, furniture, cash register, computer

   • Utilities: gas, electricity, water

   • Insurance: general liability, fire

   • Loan repayment: repayment on 5-year bank loan at market rate

   • Advertising/Promotion: general marketing activities (advertisements, matchbooks, etc.)

   • Miscellaneous: menus, furniture repair, etc.

TABLE 5.13

Monthly non-labor fixed costs for the Gentle Lentil Restaurant.

Category	Monthly Cost ($)
Rent	$3,000
Leased Equipment	$275
Utilities	$265
Insurance	$155
Loan Repayment	$125
Advertising/Promotion	$100
Miscellaneous	$75
Total Non-Labor Fixed Costs	$3,995

Appendix 2

Labor Costs for the Gentle Lentil Restaurant

Sanjay estimated the minimum and maximum monthly labor costs as shown in Table 5.14.

TO HEDGE OR NOT TO HEDGE?

Digitron, Inc. is a large computer hardware company based in Philadelphia, Pennsylvania. Digitron manufactures a variety of computer products ranging from color printers and scanners to modems and computer screens. In 1997, Digitron had net earnings of $367 million based on revenues of $2.1 billion. The breakdown of revenues by geographical region is shown in Table 5.15.

Because 50% of Digitron's revenues are from countries outside the U.S., a significant portion of the company's cash-flows are denominated in foreign currencies. Digitron relies on sustained cash-flows generated from domestic and foreign sources to support its long-term commitment to U.S. dollar-based research and development. If the dollar were to strengthen against foreign currencies, Digitron's revenues (and hence its earnings) would be adversely affected, and the company's ability to fund research and other strategic initiatives would be adversely affected as well.

At the end of 1997, there was widespread internal concern among managers at Digitron about a potential strengthening of the dollar in 1998 against the German mark (DM) and the British pound (BP), and its implications for Digitron's cash-flows. Jonathan Calbert, CEO of Digitron, decided to explore the use of currency put options in order to decrease the company's exposure to the risk of currency fluctuations. He asked Bill Joyce, vice president of finance at Digitron, to look into the problem of currency exchange rate fluctuations and to make a recommendation whether Digitron should hedge its revenues from Germany and Great Britain using put options.

Currency Put Options

In 1997, Digitron had revenues of 645 million German marks, which works out to $420 million, using the exchange rate of 0.6513 US$/DM ($420 million = 645 million × 0.6513). If the dollar were to strengthen against the German mark, then the

TABLE 5.14

Monthly labor costs for the Gentle Lentil Restaurant.

Position	Wage ($/hour)	Minimum Staff	Maximum Staff
Chef	$16.00	1	1
Wait Staff	$3.00	2	4
Kitchen Staff	$7.00	2	3
Total Labor Cost		$5,040	$6,860

Note: Employee hours worked is based on a seven hour day, five days per week, four weeks per month.

TABLE 5.15

1997 revenues at Digitron from various regions of the world.

Region	Revenues ($ million)	Percent of all Revenues (%)
United States	1,050	50
Germany	420	20
Great Britain	336	16
Rest of Europe	84	4
Asia	210	10

exchange rate would decrease from 0.6513 US$/DM to some lesser value, and consequently the value of Digitron's German revenues would be diminished. For example, if the exchange were to decrease to 0.6072 US$/DM, then the value of 645 million German marks would only be $392 million ($392 million = 645 million $\times$ 0.6072), which is $28 million less than if the exchange rate were to remain at 0.6513 US$/DM.

Digitron can address the risk of a future strengthening of the dollar against the German mark by purchasing German mark put options. A put option on the DM (German mark) rate is an option to sell German marks at a guaranteed dollar price. We now explain how a put option works.

A put option on the DM rate is defined by the expiration date, the strike price (k), and the cost (c). Such a put option on the DM rate gives the holder of the option the right (but not the obligation) to sell German marks at the strike price k at the expiration date of the option. The expiration date is a fixed future date, such as one year from now. Let DM_1 be the random variable that is the DM rate at the expiration date of the option. Note that DM_1 is indeed a random variable, because the DM rate at the future expiration date is an uncertain quantity. Clearly, if the strike price k is greater than the DM rate at the expiration date (DM_1), then the holder will exercise the option, and he/she will then have a payoff of $k - DM_1$. Otherwise, the holder will not exercise the option, and his/her payoff will be zero. The cost c of the put option is simply the amount of money that the put option costs to obtain. Therefore the net payoff of a German mark put option with strike price k and cost c is

$$\text{Net Payoff} = \begin{cases} k - DM_1 - c & \text{if } DM_1 \leq k, \\ -c, & \text{if } DM_1 > k. \end{cases}$$

This expression can also be written as:

$$\text{Net Payoff} = \max(k - DM_1, 0) - c.$$

Here we see that the put option net payoff is itself a random variable, because it is a function of the random variable DM_1, which is the future DM rate at the expiration date. We also see in this formula that the put option net payoff is also a function of the strike price k and the cost c.

Let us see how the formula for the net payoff works out. Suppose that the current DM rate is 0.6513 US$/DM, and that an investor buys a put option today on the DM rate with an expiration date of one year from now, a strike price k = $0.62 US$/DM, and cost c = $0.0137. If the German mark were to depreciate in one year to DM_1 = 0.60, then this option would have the following net payoff:

$$\text{Net Payoff} = \max(k - DM_1, 0) - c = \max(0.62 - 0.60, 0) - 0.0137 = \$0.0063.$$

If, instead, the German mark were to depreciate in one year to DM_1 = 0.50 US$/DM, then this put option would have a net payoff of

$$\text{Net Payoff} = \max(k - DM_1, 0) - c = \max(0.62 - 0.50, 0) - 0.0137 = \$0.1063.$$

If, however, the German mark were to depreciate in one year to DM_1 = 0.64 US$/DM, then this option would have a net payoff of

$$\text{Net Payoff} = \max(k - DM_1, 0) - c = \max(0.62 - 0.64, 0) - 0.0137 = -\$0.0137,$$

that is, a loss of $0.0137.

TABLE 5.16

The DM rate, in US$/DM, from 1989 through 1997.

Year	Average DM rate (US$/DM)	Change from previous year (%)
1989	0.4914	—
1990	0.4562	−7.16
1991	0.5368	17.66
1992	0.5789	7.84
1993	0.5326	−7.99
1994	0.5542	4.05
1995	0.6285	13.40
1996	0.6394	1.73
1997	0.6513	1.86

A Model for the German Mark Rate

Foreign exchange rates are susceptible to potentially large fluctuations. For example, Table 5.16 shows the average DM rate (against the dollar) over the nine year period from 1989 through 1997. The last column of Table 5.16 is the percentage change in the DM rate from the previous year, and is computed by the simple formula:

$$\text{Change from previous year} = 100 \times \left(\frac{\text{DM Rate in year } (t+1)}{\text{DM Rate in year } t} - 1 \right).$$

Based on the eight numbers in the last column of Table 5.16, we can compute the sample mean of the percentage change in the DM rate as well as the sample standard deviation of the percentage change in the DM rate. Direct computation yields that the sample mean of the percentage change in DM rate was 3.92% over the period from 1989 to 1997, and the sample standard deviation of the percentage change in the DM rate was 9.01%. Let R_{DM} be the random variable that is the future annual percentage change in the DM rate. As it turns out, the future change in the DM rate is more accurately modeled if we assume that the future change in the DM rate has a mean of zero, as opposed to estimating this mean based on historical data. However, the estimate of the standard deviation of R_{DM} based on historical data is usually quite accurate. Therefore, we will model the future change in the DM rate as the random variable R_{DM} obeying a Normal distribution with mean $\mu = 0.0\%$ and standard deviation $\sigma = 9.0\%$. The current DM rate is 0.6513 US$/DM. The DM rate next year, denoted by DM_1, is then given by the formula:

$$DM_1 = 0.6513 \times \left(1 + \frac{R_{DM}}{100} \right).$$

Note then in particular that DM_1, which is the DM exchange rate next year, is a random variable, since it is a function of the random variable R_{DM}.

A Model for the British Pound Rate

Let R_{BP} denote the future annual percentage change in the BP exchange rate. We can estimate the distribution of R_{BP} using historical data analogous to that shown in Table 5.16 and using the same type of analysis as for the German mark. Doing so, we will assume that R_{BP} obeys a Normal distribution with mean $\mu = 0.0\%$ and standard deviation $\sigma = 11.0\%$. The current BP rate is 1.234 US$/BP. The BP rate next year, denoted by BP_1, is then given by the formula:

$$BP_1 = 1.234 \times \left(1 + \frac{R_{BP}}{100} \right).$$

Note, just as for the German mark, that BP_1, which is the BP exchange rate next year, is a random variable, since it is a function of the random variable R_{BP}.

Moreover, one can also use historical data to estimate the correlation between R_{BP} and R_{DM}, which we estimate to be 0.675. That is, we will assume that

$$\text{CORR}(R_{BP}, R_{DM}) = 0.675 .$$

Revenue under Hedging

For simplicity, let us first assume that Digitron is only interested in hedging the foreign exchange risk due to future fluctuations in the exchange rate for the German mark.

The marketing department at Digitron has forecast that the 1998 revenues of Digitron in Germany will remain at the same level as in 1997 (in German marks), which was 645 million German marks. If Digitron does not hedge against its foreign exchange rate risk, then Digitron's revenue in $million at the end of next year from Germany will be

$$\text{Unhedged Revenue} = 645 \times DM_1 = 645 \times 0.6513 \times \left(1 + \frac{R_{DM}}{100}\right),$$

where R_{DM}, which is the future percentage change in the DM exchange rate, obeys a Normal distribution with mean $\mu = 0.0\%$ and standard deviation $\sigma = 9.0\%$.

If, however, Digitron buys a number n_{DM} (in million) of put options with strike price k_{DM} and cost c_{DM}, then the revenue in $million at the end of next year will be

$$\text{Hedged Revenue} = \text{Unhedged Revenue} +$$
$$\text{Number of Options} \times (\text{Net Payoff of the put option}).$$

This then leads to the following formula:

$$\text{Hedged Revenue} = 645 \times DM_1$$
$$+ n_{DM} \times [\max(k_{DM} - DM_1, 0) - c_{DM}]$$
$$= 645 \times 0.6513 \times \left(1 + \frac{R_{DM}}{100}\right)$$
$$+ n_{DM} \times \left[\max\left(k_{DM} - 0.6513\left(1 + \frac{R_{DM}}{100}\right), 0\right) - c_{DM}\right].$$

For example, suppose Digitron buys $n_{DM} = 500$ million put options on the DM rate with an expiration date of one year from now, a strike price of $k_{DM} = \$0.62$ US\$/DM, and at a cost of $c_{DM} = \$0.0137$. The current DM rate is 0.6513 US\$/DM. If the change in the DM rate over the next year turns out to be -23.23%, then the observed value of the random variable R_{DM} would be $r_{DM} = -23.23$. If Digitron did not hedge their revenues by buying any put options, then Digitron's total revenue in 1998 would be

$$\text{Unhedged Revenue} = 645 \times 0.6513 \times \left(1 + \frac{-23.23}{100}\right) = \$322.502 \text{ million.}$$

If Digitron had purchased $n_{DM} = 500$ million put options on the DM rate, then their total revenue in 1998 would be

$$\text{Hedged Revenue} = \text{Unhedged Revenue}$$
$$+ 500 \times \left[\max\left(0.62 - 0.6513 \times \left(1 + \frac{-23.23}{100}\right), 0\right) - 0.0137\right]$$
$$= \$322.502 + \$53.148$$
$$= \$375.650 \text{ million.}$$

Notice that even though the DM rate would have dropped by 23.23% in this case, the total revenue dropped by only 10.6%, that is, from $420 million to $375.650 million. This is what makes put options so attractive.

If, however, the change in the DM rate over the next year turns out to be 10.84%, then the observed value of the random variable R_{DM} would be $r_{DM} = 10.84$. If Digitron did not hedge their revenues by buying any put options, then Digitron's total revenue in 1998 would be

$$\text{Unhedged Revenue} = 645 \times 0.6513 \times \left(1 + \frac{10.84}{100}\right) = \$465.626 \text{ million.}$$

On the other hand, if Digitron had purchased $n_{DM} = 500$ million put options on the DM rate, then their total revenue in 1998 would be

$$\text{Hedged Revenue} = \text{Unhedged Revenue}$$
$$+ 500 \times \left[\max\left(0.62 - 0.6513 \times \left(1 + \frac{10.84}{100}\right), 0\right) - 0.0137\right]$$
$$= \$465.626 - \$6.85$$
$$= \$458.776 \text{ million.}$$

In this instance, while the DM exchange went up by 10.84%, Digitron's revenues only went up by 9.23%, that is, from $420 million to $458.776 million.

The Hedging Problem

Bill Joyce felt that the main source of foreign exchange risk in 1998 would be from fluctuations in the German mark and the British pound, because revenue from Germany and Great Britain represents the major portion of the company's revenue from foreign markets (a total of $756 million out of $1.05 billion from all foreign markets). Although Digitron's marketing department has predicted that 1998 revenues in Germany and Great Britain will remain at their 1997 levels (in German marks and British pounds, respectively), the revenues in dollars could fluctuate due to uncertainty in foreign exchange markets. Jonathan Calbert and Bill Joyce wanted to ensure, as much as possible, that possible dollar losses due to foreign exchange rates be limited to a maximum of $50 million.

Based on conversations with his CEO, Bill Joyce decided to focus on minimizing the likelihood that next year's revenue from Germany and Great Britain would be less than $706 million, that is, $50 million less than the current revenue of $756 million. Bill Joyce instructed his staff to obtain quotes on put options on the German mark and the British pound with one-year expiration dates. The results of his staff's inquiries are shown in Tables 5.17 and 5.18. Tables 5.17 and 5.18 show the strike prices and costs of nine different put options on the DM and BP rates respectively.

TABLE 5.17

Strike price and cost of nine different put options on the DM exchange rate, with a one-year expiration date.

Strike Price for DM (in $)	Cost (in $)
0.66	0.085855
0.65	0.032191
0.64	0.020795
0.63	0.017001
0.62	0.013711
0.61	0.010851
0.60	0.008388
0.59	0.006291
0.55	0.001401

TABLE 5.18

Strike price and cost of nine different put options on the BP exchange rate with a one-year expiration date.

Strike Price for BP (in $)	Cost (in $)
1.30	0.137213
1.25	0.082645
1.20	0.045060
1.15	0.028348
1.10	0.016146
1.05	0.007860
1.00	0.003277
0.95	0.001134
0.90	0.000245

Assignment:

(a) Construct a simulation model to help Bill Joyce select a hedging strategy using put options to minimize the risk of exchange rate fluctuations on the German mark and British pound.

(b) Suppose that Digitron buys 500 million put options on the DM rate and 500 million put options on the BP rate. For each combination of the various put options described in Table 5.17 and Table 5.18, run the simulation model and estimate the likelihood that next year's revenue from Germany and Great Britain would be at least $706 million. Which combination of put options maximizes this likelihood? What is your estimate of the mean and standard deviation of revenues next year using this combination? Do you think that Digitron should purchase these put options?

(c) By changing the number of put options that Digitron could buy on the DM exchange rate (n_{DM}), and the number of put options that Digitron could buy on the BP exchange rate (n_{BP}), it might be possible to further increase the likelihood that next year's revenue from Germany and Great Britain would be at least $706 million. Re-run the simulation model using the combination of put options from part (b) but with $n_{DM} = 100, 300$ and 500 million, and with $n_{BP} = 100, 300$ and 500 million. Do any of these combinations increase the likelihood that next year's revenue from Germany and Great Britain would be at least $706 million?

ONTARIO GATEWAY

Mary Litton, Chief Operating Officer of Ontario Gateway, re-read the memo she had just dictated and sighed. She did not envy her Operations staff the task she had just assigned to them. Making sense of all the available data and quotes to choose the best aircraft insurance policy for the Ontario Gateway fleet of aircraft would not be an easy job. Furthermore, if the wrong policy was chosen, the company would have to live with the consequences until the policy expired in five years time. She hoped her staff would be able to make good sense of all the data in her memo and would turn the data into a sound (and defensible) insurance policy recommendation in time for the Board of Directors' meeting on December 11. At that time, she would have to put forward the recommended insurance policy to the rest of the Board, and be prepared to justify her choice with supporting data and analysis.

Background

Ontario Gateway Corporation was the brainchild of Ontario Airlines CEO, Robert McDermott. Mr. McDermott, a French-Canadian, had built Ontario Airlines from a small cargo-carrying enterprise serving Canada into a respectable but marginal passenger carrier serving North American air transportation hubs. In the Spring of 1995, while attending a European Union Aviation Convention in Paris, France, he approached the Chairman of Air Prix Corporation (a French passenger carrier serving selective parts of Europe) about a possible merger. After several months of consultation, a memorandum of understanding was reached that led to the merger of both firms and the creation of a new world class airline, Ontario Gateway.

The Global Airline Industry

The airline industry in North America had become extremely competitive since deregulation over a decade ago. Furthermore, competition in the European airline industry had been heating up as well, mostly as a result of market initiatives within the European Union. State-owned airlines were being considered for privatization, while the market itself was being deregulated under "open skies" initiatives that allowed all European Union (EU) based airlines to fly without restriction within the EU. The EU retained restrictions on non-EU airline firms, as did the United States and Canada. Thus, EU based firms had a competitive advantage over non-EU firms within Europe, while North American firms likewise essentially competed only among themselves.

Ontario Airlines

Ontario Airlines drew little notice within North America until it began upgrading its fleet of largely older leased DC-8 and DC-9 aircraft in 1994. The first of 47 Boeing 757 aircraft was delivered in the fall of that year, and the firm held an option to buy 28 more aircraft at the same price and financing terms over the next three years. This allowed Ontario Airlines to modernize virtually overnight, giving the firm a homogenous fleet of the most advanced passenger aircraft in the world.

Mr. McDermott was determined to make his firm the most efficient airline in North America. The firm aggressively priced its way into the major North American hubs, and created a highly-trained pool of pilots and service personnel dedicated only to the operation of the 757 fleet. Ontario Airlines tended to routinely fill their flights, helping the firm to cover costs on even the most aggressively priced routes.

Air Prix

Formed in 1992 to coincide with the opening of markets in the European Community, Air Prix was a "Southwest Airlines style" upstart airline in France. Although its major competitor was state-owned Air France, it managed to eke out positive earnings on routes between Paris, Lille, Lyons, and Marseilles by efficiently operating only in these profitable routes. Preparing for aggressive operations throughout Europe in the coming years, Air Prix negotiated in 1993 with both Airbus and Boeing to obtain preferable arrangements to acquire new aircraft. A deal was finally reached for the EU to finance the purchase of 39 Airbus A340 aircraft. By Spring of 1995, Air Prix was flying its fleet of A340s within France and parts of Europe but was having difficulty competing with British Airways and other firms. Even though Air Prix enjoyed generous financing subsidies, it had trouble filling up the large A340s on a consistent basis.

The Merger Strategy

Air Prix and Ontario Airlines were very similar. Both firms were relatively small and had recently purchased new aircraft, and both firms were serving their respective continental markets. A merger would create a truly world class airline with the legal right to serve both the North American and EU markets. Furthermore, it could then exercise the option to buy more of the Boeing 757s and use them on the European routes, while shifting the A340s (which have more seat capacity and can fly longer distances) into trans-Atlantic service. The objective was to exploit operational economies of scale on a global basis.

Managing Risk

Partially because of the peculiarities of the financing terms for its fleets of aircraft, the newly formed Ontario Gateway Corporation was highly leveraged, requiring much of its cash flow to service its substantial debt obligations. The situation was further complicated by pre-existing loan agreements that restricted the firm's freedom to issue any further debt for a minimum of five years. If, for any reason, the firm were to face a cash flow problem, creditors could easily bring the firm into bankruptcy for failing to meet current debt obligations. Mr. McDermott felt that his firm faced several major risks over and above the normal business risks in the air transportation industry. These risks were exchange rate risk, political risk, and accident risk.

Exchange rate risk was analyzed in detail during the merger negotiations. Both firms intended to avoid the exchange-rate-driven bankruptcy that brought down Sir Freddie Laker's Laker Airlines a decade earlier. Even after thorough analysis, it was found that Ontario Gateway's costs and revenues were fairly balanced in ECU (European Currency Unit) and US dollar terms. McDermott had directed the Treasurer to implement a fairly standard currency hedging strategy in the currency options markets to ensure that exchange rate risk was minimized.

Political risk essentially entailed the exposure to potential government interference in both the North American and EU market operations. The firm's lawyers believed that they had firm legal grounds to ward off protectionist regulatory attacks in either market. Nonetheless, Mr. McDermott took every opportunity to promote his airline in France and Europe as a Franco-French Canadian venture that supported Airbus and the concept of EU economic integration. Furthermore, he made sure that press coverage in the United States regularly reminded the public of the firm's close relationship with Boeing, and its furtherance of open skies under the NAFTA framework.

Accident risk was traditionally handled in both firms by insurance contracts that would separately cover legal liability for loss-of-life and the replacement cost of the aircraft. The firm was covered for loss-of-life liability claims by a standard policy that was competitively priced. Aircraft loss coverage was another matter. The Airbus A340s were covered under a policy issued to Air Prix by Lloyds of London. The Boeing 757s were covered by an initial purchase insurance policy issued through the U.S. Export-Import Bank by the Reinsurance Corporation of Northern California (RCNC). The loan agreement with the U.S. Export-Import Bank required that all of the aircraft must be insured at replacement cost. The expensive Lloyds of London policy on the A340s was scheduled to terminate on March 1, 1997 and would not be renewed.

Thus on December 1, 1996, Mr. McDermott directed his Chief Operating Officer, Mary Litton, to obtain alternative insurance policy bids (see Enclosure 1) and make a recommendation regarding aircraft loss insurance coverage after March 1, 1997. Although Mr. McDermott was reasonably happy with the RCNC policy, he wanted to investigate the cost effectiveness of alternative insurance plans before he decided what to do after March 1, 1997. His specific guidance was as follows:

> I want to keep the 757s completely covered to keep the Export-Import Bank happy; furthermore, I want the A340s insured on a cost-effective basis—no more Lloyds of London over-priced policies! But don't forget—we have got

to maintain cash flow at its current level. This means we must be thoroughly covered for any loss of aircraft; if we lose a plane, we will need the cash to replace it quickly—otherwise we will be driven straight into bankruptcy court.

Mary returned to her office to contemplate her boss's guidance. She reached into the file containing the recently obtained aircraft insurance proposals from the RCNC, the Canadian Trust Company (CTC), and Hawthorne Insurance Corporation (HIC). Although the mechanics of the policies were very easy to understand, it was not easy to translate the numbers into a workable sense of the risk coverage that each proposal offered. She was determined to create an accurate picture of the costs and benefits of each of the policies in order to make an informed recommendation to the CEO.

Enclosure 1: Insurance Proposal Breakdown for Ontario Gateway

General Information:

Government statistics and industry publications indicate that the probability of aircraft loss is relatively straightforward to estimate, as follows. Aircraft are at the greatest risk of crash during take-offs and landings (and not during flight in mid-air), and so the likelihood of a crash of an aircraft is proportional to the number take-offs and landings of the aircraft. This likelihood is usually expressed as the accident rate per given number of flights of the aircraft. The OECD-based airline industry experiences a very low and virtually constant accident rate per flight. Current data shows an industry-wide accident rate of about one accident per five million flights. Incidental aircraft damages (minor takeoff/landing damage, bird strikes, etc.) tend to be firm specific.

Ontario's fleet characteristics are outlined in Table 5.19. A baseline assumption of about 342 flying days per plane per year is an appropriate operational benchmark. The Executive Vice President for Maintenance and Services estimates an annual cost of incidental aircraft damages varying between $1 million to $5 million per year.

Insurance Plans:

I. RCNC offers two plans:

    A. RCNC1: This plan covers complete accident replacement cost of the aircraft fleet for an annual fee of 0.45% of fleet value and carries a 10% deductible on all aircraft losses. However, there is a rebate clause, wherein RCNC will rebate to Ontario Gateway 20% of any cumulative profits (premiums minus claims) at the end of the five year term of the plan.

    B. RCNC2: This plan calls for an annual fixed premium of 0.10% of the insured value of the fleet, plus an annual variable premium paid at the end of the year consisting of the lesser of:

        (i) 90% of all losses during the year, and

        (ii) 1.00% of the insured value of the fleet.

II. CTC: CTC has offered the following insurance plan. Ontario Gateway would pay $13 million annually. CTC would then cover 90% of losses up to $80 million of annual aircraft losses. Losses in excess of $80 million would not be covered.

III. HIC: HIC developed this policy specifically for Ontario Gateway. For a premium of 0.165% of fleet value, this policy will pay for all fleet losses above $24 million. This plan also has a rebate clause: HIC would rebate 3.5% of any cumulative profits to be paid at the end of the five year term of the plan.

Enclosure 2: Memo To Operations Staff from Mary Litton

TO: Operations Staff

FROM: Mary Litton

DATE: December 4, 1996

SUBJECT: Insurance Proposal Analysis

This firm must choose an insurance policy to cover our fleet from aircraft crash losses for the five-year period beginning March 1, 1997. We have four viable policies to choose from at this time. You are to conduct a thorough analysis of the cost and benefits of each proposal, and recommend one of the policies to me by December 11, 1996.

As you know, this firm is currently trying to grow global operations under a highly leveraged capital structure. We need to maintain high revenue levels in order to continue meeting existing debt obligations. Hence, we cannot afford to take chances with respect to unanticipated negative cash flow. The insurance policy we choose must protect us from unanticipated losses of aircraft, especially during the next year. Specifically, we must be insured so we do not incur a liability for more than $41 million in aircraft crash losses and insurance costs combined in the next year (March 1, 1997 to February 28, 1998). As this is the absolute maximum loss we can incur, it would be wise to leave ourselves a margin of safety of about 10% which means we should aim to minimize the chance of losses exceeding $37 million. Contingent on this, our other major goal is to obtain this insurance coverage at lowest cost over the entire five-year period.

I look forward to your report.

Mary Litton
Chief Operating Officer

TABLE 5.19

Ontario Gateway Aircraft Fleet.

Aircraft	Number	Replacement Cost[1] ($ million)	Flights per Day
Boeing 757			
Model 200	47	$56.4[2]	6.0
Airbus A340[3]			
Model 200	15	$78.9[4]	2.25
Model 300	24	$88.5[5]	2.0
Total	86	$5,958	

[1]Ontario Gateway chooses to insure airplanes at the cost of a new airplane with the same options.
[2]Source: UAL and AMR 1995 Annual Reports: Case writer estimates.
[3]Airbus A340 models differ by model based on flying range, number of seats, fuel capacity, and type of engine.
[4]Source: Aviation Week & Space Technology, January 8, 1996: Case writer estimates.
[5]Source: Aviation Week & Space Technology, January 8, 1996: Case writer estimates.

Assignment:

A simulation model of the Ontario Gateway insurance decision is provided in the spreadsheet OGSIM.XLS. This model is designed to run with the Crystal Ball® simulation software spreadsheet add-in that can be conveniently embedded in Microsoft Excel®.

(a) Run the simulation model OGSIM.XLS built for this insurance decision. Make sure you understand how the model works as you might want to modify the model to do your analysis.

(b) To add clarity to the analysis, modify the model so that you can analyze the cost savings between the plans that are viable.

(c) Check the sensitivity of your analysis to the presumed probability of a crash. Because Ontario Gateway operates a newer fleet of aircraft with only two different types of aircraft, it may be reasonable to suppose that they are slightly safer than the industry as whole. Change the probability of a crash to make Ontario Gateway 25% safer than the industry average, and see what effect this has on the output and the consequent insurance decision.

(d) Based on your simulation results and analysis/judgment, prepare a concise but detailed decision recommendation with supporting analysis and justification. Your recommend should account for the nature of the uncertainty and risk involved in the decisions under consideration.

GETTING STARTED WITH CRYSTAL BALL® FOR THE ONTARIO GATEWAY CASE

Here we show how to get started using the Crystal Ball® simulation software spreadsheet add-in.

Launching Crystal Ball®

After loading Crystal Ball® onto your computer, you can run Crystal Ball® by clicking the Start button, and then select Programs, and you will see the menu selection for Crystal Ball®. When you click on Crystal Ball®, it will load Excel® automatically. **(Note: Although Crystal Ball® is an Excel® add-in, you should always start Crystal Ball® first.)** After Excel® loads, you will see a window that warns you that this software has macros which could have viruses. Do not be alarmed by this. You should select the "Enable Macros" option to continue. You will next see the Crystal Ball® logo on the screen as it finishes loading. You will notice that there is now a new tool bar and new menus that Crystal Ball® provides. You are now ready to open the Ontario Gateway simulation model spreadsheet provided with the case, which is called OGSIM.XLS.

Guidelines on Understanding and Using Crystal Ball® for the Ontario Gateway Case

Introduction

Crystal Ball® is a powerful simulation tool that is conveniently embedded in the familiar Excel® software. Crystal Ball® allows you to simulate events that are based on random occurrences. For this case, aircraft crashes and incidental aircraft damage for the next five years are the random variables. While we may be able to make reasonable assumptions about the number of crashes and the amount of incidental aircraft damage, it is not possible to know precisely which planes in the fleet will crash in each of the next five years nor what the amount of annual other incidental damage will be. These variables directly affect the relative attractiveness of the different insurance policies. If we could predict the future, the insurance policy decision would be a trivial exercise in arithmetic. Since we cannot predict the future, the insurance policy decision is a more complicated one. This is precisely where simulation plays a valuable role, and where the Crystal Ball® simulation software can be used to great advantage.

Crystal Ball® allows you to:

- Make the assumption that crashes and other aircraft damage obey specific probability distributions.

- Run an n-trial simulation of crashes and other damage for the five-year period.

- Calculate the costs under the insurance policies for each of the n trials.

- Generate a probability distribution for the costs of the policies (and the cost differences) based on the n-trial simulation.

In turn, this should assist you in deciding which is the most attractive insurance policy.

Understanding The Model: Assumption Cells and Forecast Cells

Although the model appears to be a normal Excel® spreadsheet, it is in fact slightly different. There are certain cells that are important to Crystal Ball®. Green-colored cells are so-called **Assumption Cells** and blue-colored cells are **Forecast Cells.**

Assumption Cells take on values from a defined probability distribution. The five incidental aircraft damage Assumption Cells are uniform distributions and the fifteen aircraft loss Assumption Cells are binomial distributions (there might be other equally plausible distributions to use as well). To view the specific distribution, select the Assumption Cell and choose the **Define Assumption...** command under the **"Cell"** menu. Note the parameters for the distribution (min and max values for the uniform distributions; probability and number of trials for the binomial distributions).

Forecast Cells are cells for which a probability distribution is generated based on the simulation. These cells contain formulas that are driven by the values of the Assumption Cells. As the Assumption Cells take on different values, the Forecast Cell values change accordingly. Forecast Cells can be viewed by selecting the cell and choosing the **Define Forecast...** command under the **"Cell"** menu.

Before running the simulation, you should spend some time learning the spreadsheet model in general, and the Assumption Cells and Forecast Cells in particular. Start by clicking through the spreadsheet to understand the policy cost tables. Then go to the color coded Assumption Cells and verify that they are built correctly. This can be done by clicking on the **"Cell"** command, and then selecting the **"Define assumption"** command. The assumption will be illustrated by an appropriate probability distribution. Next, go to the Forecast Cells. Check the formulas in the cells. Then click on the **"Cell"** command, and then on the **"Define forecast"** to verify that the Forecast Cell and the output title match. Note that the Forecast Cells have been built with the "automatic forecast display feature" turned OFF; otherwise, the simulation may "choke" during a complicated run due to lack of memory.

Running The Model

To run the model, click on **"Run,"** and then click on **"Run preferences"** to choose the number of trials (try 5,000 to start). Choose "Run" again and wait until the simulation stops. That's it!

You can stop and continue the simulation at any time using the applicable commands from the **"Run"** menu.

Viewing the Output

Click on **"Run,"** and then on **"Forecast windows."** From there, click on the reports you want to see and open them. Two additional menus, **"Preferences"** and **"View"** also appear on the menu bar. The **"View"** menu selects the type of statistics that are displayed for each Forecast Cell. The **"Preferences"** menu alters the format of the displayed charts. By the way, the reports can be copied and pasted into a Word® document using **"Paste special"** as a **"picture."**

Saving and Re-running

Your simulation run can be saved using the **"Save Run"** command in the **"Run"** menu. To re-run the simulation, say with a different number of trials or with a different probability of a crash, etc., select **"Reset"** from the **"Run"** menu, make any necessary changes, and then choose **"Run"** once again.

Final Word

These directions are enough to teach you the basics of this software and to allow you to get started with Crystal Ball®. You should be able to work effectively with the simulation model in a short period of time. Use the on-line help menu for additional pointers.

CASTERBRIDGE BANK

Susan Newson returned to Casterbridge Bank refreshed and revitalised from a long weekend hiking in the Lake District, ready to begin the annual recruiting drive for analysts at the bank's London office. The scent of late spring flora and the roar of cascading waterfalls were still fresh in her mind as she gazed out over a bustling London morning. Beginning with the first of twenty waiting voice-mail messages (all marked urgent, of course), she recognised the booming voice of the Chairman, Michael Henchard:

> Sharon, I've been getting a lot of flack from division managers about frequent shortages in analysts in London. It strikes me that our analyst hiring targets were too low last year. But in some months there seem to be loads of analysts with no projects to work on. I can't sense whether we over-hired or under-hired last year!
>
> I'm convinced we need to get a handle on our hiring policies for the new analyst recruiting cycle: It's costing us money when we are understaffed and when we are overstaffed. Either come up with one of your MBA equations or get an HR consultant to sort it all out. Kindly book a time on Friday to discuss this with me.

Well, here it was, the proverbial "deep end." This is why Susan had fought so hard to get this prime position in personnel at Casterbridge: the challenge. Putting her MBA networking skills to work, she immediately phoned an ex-classmate, Don Farfrae, who had started up an HR consulting company in London after graduating from business school:

"Well Sue, I think we could do a quick but effective study of your problem and help you to decide the right analyst staffing levels for the coming year. I can put three of my best people on it right away, shouldn't take much more than a few weeks, and cost £20,000 at the most."

"Hmm, since you put it that way, can I give you a call back?"

Surely she could put together a relatively simple model of the bank's analyst staffing problem and come up with an answer for Henchard by Friday. Perhaps then he would start getting her name right!

The Bank

Even as a relatively new London investment bank, Casterbridge had a reputation for excellence in client service. Casterbridge routinely attracted the best clients and prided itself in its excellent professional staff. In its earliest years, the bank's focus had been on expanding rapidly and taking aggressive advantage of the lucrative banking opportunities in the 1980's. With high profitability and high growth, no one paid much attention to developing sound internal management practices and decision-making.

Now that its market position had stabilized, Casterbridge was sorely in need of more efficient internal management. Many of the methods and standards used at the bank were beginning to become a liability as the business matured and growth and profitability rates settled down. For the first time Casterbridge had to consider costs seriously and improve staffing efficiency. Internally the bank was in a state of flux, struggling to get its costs under control, while retaining its much envied reputation and clientele.

The Analyst Position

The best and brightest from top colleges and universities around the world vied for the lucrative and demanding position of analyst at Casterbridge. After graduating with a Bachelors Degree, analysts would join the bank in the summer to work in any number of areas providing analysis, research, and support skills to the MBA professional staff. A new graduate could expect to be involved in anything from preparing privatization "beauty contest" proposals, to aiding mergers and acquisitions, to research and analysis for large clients. In addition, a large part of the bank's business consisted of the more standard debt and equity financing for major clients' business activities. These "projects" could take anywhere between a few days to six months to come to fruition.

Analysts were paid extremely well and were typically expected to work any hours necessary to serve the clients' interests. On an annual salary of around £32,000 ($48,000), analysts could expect to be very busy much of the time. In addition to a direct salary cost of $4,000 per month, an analyst's labour cost to Casterbridge typically also included another $2,000 per month in indirect support costs such as training, health insurance, and other employee benefits. In common with most international investment banks, Casterbridge performed all internal accounting and client charging in US $—a sad indication of the decline of the once great British Pound.

Most analysts found that three years of strain and stress at Casterbridge was about all anyone could stand. Departing analysts usually enrolled in MBA programs at top business schools, joined finance departments of major multinational corporations, or transferred to management consulting.

Work Flow Management Problems

The investment banking industry has always been characterized by uncertainty in the level and timing of banking engagements, which are driven by the needs of its clients. Because the business world is fundamentally unpredictable and subject to large swings in fortune, the future demands of the bank's clients are uncertain.

Clients' demand for analyst services fluctuated quite a bit. In some months, the demand for analyst time on client projects exceeded the number of analysts in the London office. The operations department would handle these shortages by temporarily transferring staff from other Casterbridge offices in Europe (mostly Paris and Frankfurt) and/or by pooling analysts from various departments within the London office. Unfortunately, despite the promise of global staffing optimization, transferred staff tended to be less efficient than those working in their home office, typically by a factor of 60%, due to factors such as language, culture, and training differences.

In other months, however, there were not enough client projects in the London office to keep all of the analysts busy. When this happened, the otherwise idle analysts would be assigned to do internal research work.

In this environment the bank tried to recruit the "right" number of analysts from the main pool of graduating students in June. Offers were made after the April recruiting round with responses due in May. Newly hired analysts were asked to start work on July 1.

The immediate cost of recruiting too many analysts was obviously the salary and indirect support costs that would have to be paid when no profitable work was being done. On the other hand, the cost of recruiting too few analysts was the implicit cost of staffing projects with transferred staff from other offices or departments, who were inherently less efficient.

Demand for analysts was affected by both market and internal factors, resulting in a clear seasonal cycle with peaks in September and March. Over the long hot summer as clients (and senior bankers) basked in the Mediterranean sun, the demand for analysts experienced a prolonged lull known as "the beach effect." Come September the backlog became pressing causing a sudden flurry of activity in order to complete the work. Just as this was accomplished the Christmas season arrived and the Alps filled with snow, drawing the fun-loving bankers and corporate leaders to the slopes and après-ski. The low demand at this time was exacerbated by the reluctance of clients to consider committing to new projects before the new budget year beginning in January. Once flush with a year's worth of funding, clients would be eager to engage the bank to perform work and the flood gates opened once again, with work levels building to a peak in March.

In addition to these month-to-month changes, there was a significant economic effect on the levels of client work in any year. If the global or European economy was particularly buoyant, then workloads would rise significantly as mergers, acquisitions, and privatizations were proposed in the bullish stock markets. The converse was true when economic activity slowed.

The bank charged its customers fixed fees or percentages of the value of deals or issues, based on an internal billing rate of $10,000 per month for an analyst's time. For example, if the M&A division had a one-month project for a client that they anticipated would use three person-months of analysts' time, they would charge the client a fixed fee of $30,000 for the project.

Alternative hiring strategies

Casterbridge's past analyst hiring strategy was straightforward:

Estimate the 'right' number of analysts to hire for July 1, and then hope for the best.

Trying to remember some of the lessons she learned in her HR courses at business school, Susan Newson thought that a more creative hiring strategy might be much more effective. For example, there was an inherent inefficiency in having all of the new analysts start work on July 1. Perhaps if they allowed new recruits to choose to start at the beginning or at the end of the summer (either July 1 or September 1), then any remaining imbalance might be less costly.

However, some of the new recruits who would choose to take the summer off and start in September might happen upon better job opportunities while enjoying their last free summer, and therefore might not show up for work in the autumn. Susan recalled the experience of a classmate in Personnel at a large consulting firm, whose firm had adopted a flexible start-date strategy for its university recruits; about half of the new recruits chose to start work in July. Of the remaining half who chose to delay their start-date to September, between 70% and 100% fulfilled their promise to join the firm.

Susan also thought there might be some merit to engaging in December recruiting in order to capture students who graduate at mid-year. Susan thought that mid-year recruiting, if done correctly, could help to alleviate analyst staffing shortages. In fact, the option to do December recruiting might even allow Casterbridge to hire fewer analysts for July 1 and then make a mid-year correction if need be. Analysts hired in the December round would be asked to start work at the beginning of January.

Data gathering

A brief conversation with Tom Hardy (whom Susan had replaced after he had been promoted to head of personnel for global operations at Casterbridge) clarified the basic facts of the situation. As of April 1, Casterbridge had 63 analysts and was about to enter the usual round of recruiting leading to final offers for July. Of the offers extended, not all would be accepted, despite the reputation of Casterbridge. Tom estimated that the bank was most likely to employ about 70% of the graduates that were extended offers, which was Casterbridge's historical acceptance rate for analyst offers.

Throughout the year the bank experienced some degree of analyst attrition, which varied between 0% and 20% per month. Tom, however, treated retention as being 95% (the rough average rate) in all months as he was considering the year as a whole. According to Tom, the bank had generally tried to match the expected staff levels with the average workload, which seemed quite reasonable. Tom then explained the elegantly simple formula he had used in the past to match expected analyst levels with average workload:

> We want to try to hire the right number of analysts to match the average demand of about 90 in any month. Therefore what I do as a rule of thumb is to use the following equation to find Q, the number of offers to make for July:

> Average demand = (estimate of number of analysts as of July 1 + number of accepted offers) × (average annual retention rate)

> So this year's relationship would be:

$$90 = (63 \times (0.95)^3 + 0.70 Q) \times (0.95)^6$$

(Note: $(0.95)^6$ here is an approximation to $(1 + 0.95 + 0.95^2 + 0.95^3 + \ldots + 0.95^{11})/12$, the average retention rate based on Tom Hardy's assumption of a retention rate of 95% in each month.)

That is to say we should make about, erm... about 98 offers. It's that simple!

With the new pressure on costs, Susan was not so sure that it was "that simple," and so she decided to inquire into the matter further. As it turned out, the bank had kept data on past staffing levels and workload on a reasonably consistent basis in activity reports generated by the HR department. Susan found the file of dog-eared paper. Although the numbers went back five years or so, she thought that it would take only a little manipulation to prepare some useful numbers.

Deciding that a good basic set of historic numbers was the first priority, Susan had her assistant Anthony compile average analyst months worked by month from the five years of data that she had found. Given this pattern, she could now estimate the number of analysts that would be required in the coming year (see Figure 5.6 and Table 5.20). However, a number of complications existed. The average numbers, Anthony noticed, hid quite a wide variation both in month to month levels and between years. A quick look back at some market trends showed that the yearly variation seemed to depend quite heavily on the state of the global economy; during recessions

FIGURE 5.6

Demand fluctuation at Casterbridge bank.

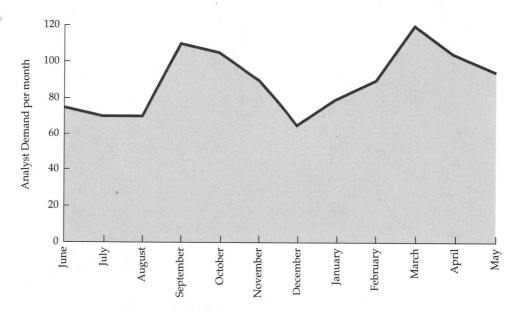

TABLE 5.20

Estimated analyst demand levels at Casterbridge bank.

Month	Analyst Demand
June	75
July	70
August	70
September	110
October	105
November	90
December	65
January	80
February	90
March	120
April	105
May	95
Total	1,075
Average per month	90

work was down, and in periods of expansion it was higher throughout the year. The monthly variability did not seem to have such a simple explanation, and after failing to find any link between it and the average length of engagement, they decided to live with a little uncertainty. Both sources of variability would have to be added to the basic forecast that Susan had developed in order to arrive at realistic demand numbers.

The data began to spin in Susan's head: This much complexity and uncertainty required a break for lunch in the park! Having picked a quiet spot under a huge old beech tree, she contemplated the hiring problem over an avocado and bacon sandwich. With so many related variables, it was clear that the problem would require some sort of structure. Reaching for a napkin, Susan spent a while jotting down what she had discovered that morning about hiring at the bank.

First, she knew that analyst demand was not deterministic, as the historic numbers might suggest if taken at face value. Both the uncertain economic climate over the year and monthly "random" uncertainty had to be considered. These two factors could dramatically change the level of analyst demand from the historic levels.

Obviously the bank had a pretty good idea of the way in which the economy was expected to perform each year, so that the main effect on analyst demand levels would come from unexpected economic growth or decline. Susan guessed that estimates of economic growth would be extremely unlikely to be more than 10% different (either higher or lower) from the actual outcome. Therefore, it seemed reasonable to model the change in the demand for analysts due to unexpected economic conditions as a random variable that obeys a Normal distribution with mean $\mu = 0\%$ and a standard deviation of $\sigma = 5\%$.

In addition to economic growth influences over the whole year, Susan had also noted the variability in analyst demand each month. Demand seemed to fluctuate quite widely from expected levels, again in both directions. A Normal distribution also with a mean $\mu = 0\%$, but with a much larger spread indicated by a standard deviation of around $\sigma = 10\%$ sounded about right. The actual demand in any month would therefore be based on the historic level, but scaled up or down with random economic effects for the year (as a whole) as well as random fluctuation for the month in question.

Turning to the supply side of the equation, Susan knew that the bank had 63 analysts and would retain something upwards of 80% of them at the end of each month, on average around 95% per month over the whole year. Looking more closely at the monthly average retention rates (see Table 5.21), Susan began to try to fit a story that would make sense with the numbers that she had collected. In January (once year end bonuses were received) and in September (after a relaxing summer and as the business schools kicked off a new term) the bank would probably experi-

TABLE 5.21

Observed average analyst retention levels at Casterbridge Bank.

Month	Average Retention Rate
January	90.0%
February	95.0%
March	95.0%
April	95.0%
May	97.5%
June	97.5%
July	97.5%
August	97.5%
September	90.0%
October	95.0%
November	95.0%
December	95.0%
Simple Average	95.0%

ence higher than average rates of attrition. In contrast, during the summer months, retention would be higher as many analysts applied to business schools and began researching other job opportunities. Thus the peculiarities of the banking year seemed to fit the observed behaviour of analysts, reassuring Susan that she had sufficiently detailed information with which to work. A uniform distribution between 80% and 100% appeared to be the most realistic way to model the uncertainty in the retention rate for January and September, 95% to 100% for the summer months and 90% to 100% for the rest of the year.

Now, she thought, if the bank makes offers to graduating students then they know that they only expect to have 70% of them accept. Susan thought that the number of accepted offers should therefore obey a binomial distribution with a probability of success (i.e., accepted offer) of $p = 0.70$ and the number of trials n would be equal to the number of offers extended, thus resulting in the expected result of a 70% acceptance rate.

Next, the number of analysts at Casterbridge in any month would depend on the level in the previous month and the attrition rate of existing staff. However, for recruiting months the level would also be boosted by incoming new recruits at the start of the month. (Susan summarized these ideas on her napkin, shown in Table 5.22.)

Turning the napkin over, Susan mopped up some mayonnaise and started to think about the costs involved in the analyst hiring decision that Henchard was so worried about. It struck her that the real costs of an imbalance of supply and demand would be the costs to the bank of having staff idle or the cost of using less efficient transferred staff during analyst shortages. Both of these costs would impact the all important contribution to earnings.

Susan knew the analyst salary costs and the indirect support costs for staff members. Given this and the rough amount of revenue that an analyst should earn for the bank in a normal month ($10,000), a contribution to earnings figure could be calculated. If an analyst had to be transferred in from elsewhere to fill a staffing shortage, then costs would rise by about 60% and hence reduce the contribution accordingly. It thus appeared to be marginally better for the bank to have too few rather than too many analysts. (See Table 5.23 for Susan's analysis of costs and earnings contributions.)

TABLE 5.22

Susan Newson's napkin formulation of the hiring problem.

Henley's Sandwich Bar

Hiring Problem

Units: Number of Analysts

Model of Demand for Analysts

H_i = Historic average analyst demand in month i
X = percentage unanticipated economic growth per year
$X \sim N(0\%, 5\%)$
Y_i = Random noise in demand in month i compared to expected historic level in month i
$Y_i \sim N(0\%, 10\%)$
D_i = Demand for analysts in month i
$D_i = H_i (1 + X) (1 + Y_i)$

Model of Supply of Analysts

Q_i = Number of offers made by bank to analysts to start in month i
A_i = Number of analysts who accept offer to start in month i
$A_i \sim B(Q_i, 0.7)$
R_i = Percentage retention rate of analysts in month i
$R_i \sim U(80\%, 100\%)$ for September and January
$R_i \sim U(95\%, 100\%)$ for May, June, July and August
$R_i \sim U(90\%, 100\%)$ for February, March, April, October, November and December
P_i = Number of analysts employed at start of month i
$P_{i+1} = (P_i)(R_i) + A_{i+1}$
$P_0 = 63$

TABLE 5.23

Susan Newson's back of the napkin analysis of costs and earnings contributions.

	Henley's Sandwich Bar
Monthly salary and indirect labor support cost	
Monthly Salary	$4,000
Monthly Indirect Cost	$2,000
Monthly Total Cost	$6,000
Monthly Contribution to Earnings of productive analyst	
Revenue per analyst month	$10,000
Monthly Total Cost	$6,000
Contribution per analyst	$4,000
Costs and Contribution of Transferred Workers	
Inefficiencies of Transfers	60%
Monthly Total Cost of Transfer	$9,600 (= $6,000 × 1.60)
Revenue per month	$10,000
Monthly Total Cost	$9,600
Contribution per transferee:	$400

Calculations of Earnings Contributions

Let E_i = contribution to earnings from analysts' work in month i
If demand equals supply of analysts then $E_i = 4,000 D_i = 4,000 P_i$
But if not then earnings contributions are computed one of two ways each month, depending on whether there is a shortage or an excess of analysts in month i:

Excess of analysts in month i

If $P_i > D_i$ then $E_i = 10,000 D_i - 6,000 P_i$

Shortage of analysts in month i

If $D_i > P_i$ then $E_i = (10,000 - 6,000) P_i + (10,000 - 9,600)(D_i - P_i)$

As the first of the English summer sun attempted to break through the rain clouds, and the birds twittered over the dull rumble of distant traffic, Susan inspected her napkin with pride. She now had a much clearer view of the analyst hiring problem and how the different sources of uncertainty might interact. Given the relatively high cost of a mismatch in analyst numbers, Susan was convinced that Tom Hardy's solution was in fact probably costing the bank money.

Susan now understood how to model the events and then recommend a hiring policy for the new recruiting cycle. Despite some simplifying assumptions, particularly regarding the distributions of variables, Susan was confident that her formulation of the problem retained sufficient realism. She rewarded her efforts with a chocolate fudge brownie and returned to the office with renewed energy. Dusting off her laptop, she quickly replicated the structure of the problem in a spreadsheet on her computer.

All in a day's work

It was Monday afternoon. Susan mulled over her spreadsheet and double cappuccino. How many new analysts should the bank make offers to? Did it make sense to offer recruits the option of starting at the beginning of September? Should the bank be more radical and hire twice each year instead of only once? Which strategy was best for the bank? How could she show Henchard the monetary implications of each strategy? Full of hope that all this would become clear in the next few hours, Susan reached for the mouse, knocking her coffee onto the keyboard.

Assignment:

(a) Briefly, what does it mean to hire the "right" number of analysts? What is the objective in trying to decide the "right" number of analysts to hire?

(b) Briefly explain Tom Hardy's hiring strategy. What are the strengths and weaknesses of his approach?

(c) Prepare a two-paragraph explanation of Susan Newson's basic approach to the analyst hiring decision. What are the strengths and weaknesses of her approach?

(d) Consider the "fixed-start" strategy of making offers to new graduates to start on July 1. A simulation model of the fixed-start strategy is provided in the Excel® spreadsheet CASTRBDG.XLS for use with the simulation software Crystal Ball®. This spreadsheet model is designed to forecast the distribution of earnings as a function of the number of offers Q that Casterbridge makes to new graduates to start on July 1. Review this spreadsheet to make sure that you understand all of its components. The number of offers Q is input to the spreadsheet in cell D6, and the contribution to earnings is computed in cell O19. Run the simulation model with a number of different values of Q in the range between $Q = 10$ and $Q = 110$. Which value of Q results in the greatest expected contribution to earnings? What is your optimal hiring strategy? Is your strategy more profitable or less profitable than Tom Hardy's strategy? What is the expected difference in the contribution to earnings between the two?

(e) Now consider a "flexible-start" strategy of making offers to new graduates to start on either July 1 or September 1. Modify the simulation model CASTRBDG.XLS in Crystal Ball®, to help you decide the optimal number of offers that the bank should make given the flexible-start strategy. Make whatever assumptions that you think are reasonable and are supported by your knowledge of the case. Is the flexible-start strategy more profitable or less profitable than the fixed-start strategy? Why? What is the expected difference in earnings contribution between the two?

(f) **(Challenge)** Now consider a more complicated strategy involving December recruiting. In December recruiting, offers are made in December for graduating students to start work on January 1. December recruiting would cost Casterbridge approximately $22,000 in fixed costs of visiting campuses, interviewing, arranging for call-backs, etc. Develop your own December hiring strategy. Test your strategy out by modifying your simulation model in Crystal Ball®. Then decide the optimal number of offers that the bank should make with a fixed-start strategy combined with December recruiting, as well as with a flexible-start strategy combined with December recruiting. Once again, make whatever assumptions that you think are reasonable and are supported by your knowledge of the case. Is December recruiting worth the cost? Why or why not?

NOTE: There are a number of ways to develop a December recruiting strategy. For example, one strategy might simply be: Make $Q1$ offers for July 1, and make $Q2$ offers for January 1, where $Q1$ and $Q2$ are chosen optimally by testing a bunch of different possible values. Another more sophisticated strategy might be: Make $Q1$ offers for July 1. If, on average, there is a shortage of S analysts in June-December, then make $Q2 = f(S)$ more offers in December, where $f(S)$ is some function of the shortage number, for example $f(S) = S/(0.70)$ (The value of 0.70 accounts for the average acceptance rate).

CHAPTER 6

Regression Models: Concepts and Practice

CONTENTS

ONE OF THE MOST IMPORTANT SKILLS OF A GOOD MANAGER IS THE ABILITY TO perceive trends in business data and to make accurate predictions based on such trends. Marketing and production managers often need to forecast sales, earnings, costs, production levels, inventories, purchases, capital requirements, etc., based on data from past performance and/or industry-wide trends. Financial managers often need to forecast price movements of financial instruments, based on past performance as well as the price movements of related instruments. In this chapter, we introduce a powerful modeling tool for prediction based on data called **linear regression.** The goal of a linear regression model is the development of a specific formula that relates the movements of one variable (such as the production cost of a product) to those of a small set of other relevant variables (such as labor hours in production, expenditures for new machinery, and/or investments in worker training).

For example, we might want to understand how the sales of a product can be predicted based on such factors as advertising expenditures, promotions expenditures, and competitors' prices. The variable that we wish to analyze or predict is called the **dependent variable** and is usually denoted by the capital letter Y. In this case, the dependent variable would be the sales of the product. The small set of variables whose values determine the value of the dependent variable Y are called the **independent variables.** These variables are usually denoted by the lower case letters $x_1, \ldots, x_k$. In this case, the independent variables would be advertising expenditures, promotions expenditures, and competitors' prices. We would denote these three independent variables by x_1 for advertising expenditures, x_2 for promotions expenditures, and x_3 for competitors' prices.

As another example, we might want to understand how the rate of return of a company's stock can be predicted based on the earnings of the company and the growth in the economy as a whole. In this case, the dependent variable Y would be the rate of return of the company's stock, and the independent variables would be the earnings of the company (x_1) and the growth in the economy as a whole (x_2).

6.1   PREDICTION BASED ON SIMPLE LINEAR REGRESSION

In this section, we introduce the linear regression model with a prototypical problem that arises in marketing, namely the prediction of sales of a product based on advertising expenditures:

Example 6.1 — Predicting Sales from Advertising Expenditures

Suppose that John Broder is a marketing manager at J&T Products, a large manufacturer of household products. J&T has begun to roll out a new product called "Apple-Glo," which is an environmentally-safe household cleaner. AppleGlo has been introduced into J&T's Northeastern sales regions over the last two years with expensive advertising campaigns, see Table 6.1. Suppose that John is interested in analyzing the effect of advertising on the sales of AppleGlo. In particular, J&T is now considering introducing AppleGlo into two new regions, accompanied by expensive advertising campaigns of $2.0 million in one of the regions and $1.5 million in the other region. John would like to predict what the expected first-year sales of AppleGlo would be in each of these two regions to assess if the advertising campaigns will be cost-effective.

Based on the information given in this table, John would like to answer questions such as:

(a) What is the relationship between first-year advertising and first-year sales? Is there an equation that relates these two quantities?

(b) What is an estimate of expected first-year sales if advertising expenditures are $1.5 million? What is an estimate of expected first-year sales if advertising expenditures are $2.0 million?

(c) How reliable are the estimates of first-year sales? How good is the predictive power of the equation that relates first-year advertising and first-year sales?

Let us now analyze John's problem with the aim of answering the questions posed above. To begin our analysis, we can plot the data of Table 6.1 in a scatter-plot

TABLE 6.1

Advertising expenditures and first-year sales of AppleGlo by region.

Date of Introduction	Region	Advertising Expenditures ($ million) (x_i)	First-Year Sales ($ million) (y_i)
January, 1994	Maine	1.8	104
February, 1994	New Hampshire	1.2	68
March, 1994	Vermont	0.4	39
April, 1994	Massachusetts	0.5	43
May, 1994	Connecticut	2.5	134
June, 1994	Rhode Island	2.5	127
July, 1994	New York	1.5	87
August, 1994	New Jersey	1.2	77
September, 1994	Pennsylvania	1.6	102
October, 1994	Delaware	1.0	65
November, 1994	Maryland	1.5	101
December, 1994	West Virginia	0.7	46
January, 1995	Virginia	1.0	52
February, 1995	Ohio	0.8	33

FIGURE 6.1

Scatter-plot of first year sales and advertising expenditures.

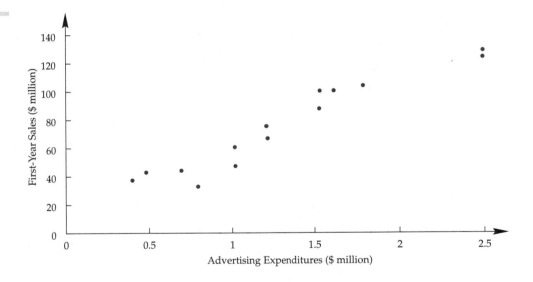

to visually explore any trends or patterns in the data. A scatter-plot of Table 6.1 is presented in Figure 6.1. Figure 6.1 confirms the straightforward intuitive expectation that higher sales are associated with higher advertising, generally speaking. However, as the figure shows, there are exceptions to this rule.

Figure 6.1 suggests that first-year sales of AppleGlo might be roughly described by a linear function of advertising expenditures. That is, all of the data points in Figure 6.1 lie approximately on a straight line. Of course, there is no straight line that passes through all of the points, but it appears that a properly positioned straight line would have most or all of the data points nearby. A linear regression model attempts to find the "best" straight line equation that relates first-year advertising expenditures to first-year sales.

Let Y denote the first-year sales of AppleGlo and let x denote the first-year advertising expenditures for AppleGlo. We would like to predict the value of first-year sales Y as a function of first-year advertising expenditures x. In this case, the dependent variable is Y, which is the first-year sales of AppleGlo; and the independent variable is x, which is the first-year advertising expenditures.

Let us now introduce some more notation that will be used to develop the linear regression model. The **data** for the linear regression model will be the observations of first-year advertising and first-year sales as shown in Table 6.1. Let n denote the number of observations. In this case, $n = 14$ observations. We denote the $n = 14$ values of the independent variable (advertising expenditures) by $x_1, x_2, \ldots, x_n$. We denote the $n = 14$ values of the dependent variable (sales) by $y_1, y_2, \ldots, y_n$. It is helpful to think of the data for the model as the n ordered pairs $(x_1, y_1), (x_2, y_2), \ldots, (x_n, y_n)$. Thus, for example, $(x, y_1) = (1.8, 104), \ldots, (x_{14}, y_{14}) = (0.8, 33)$.

The simplest linear regression model assumes that there is a **linear** relationship between the dependent variable Y and the independent variable x (in this case, between first-year sales and advertising expenditures respectively). Recall that a straight line in a graph is represented as

$$y = \beta_0 + \beta_1 x,$$

where β_0 is the intercept of the line with the vertical axis, and β_1 is the slope of the line. If all of the data observations $(x_1, y_1), (x_2, y_2), \ldots, (x_n, y_n)$ actually lie on a straight line, we would have:

$$y_i = \beta_0 + \beta_1 x_i, \quad \text{for} \quad i = 1, \ldots, n,$$

(where, as is mentioned above, β_0 is the intercept of the line with the vertical axis, and β_1 is the slope of the line). Of course, as the scatter-plot of Figure 6.1 shows, there is no straight line that passes through all of the observations $(x_1, y_1), (x_2, y_2), \ldots, (x_n, y_n)$. Nevertheless, Figure 6.1 does indicate that there is a "roughly" linear relationship (a straight line) that will lie near most or all of the observations. It is therefore helpful to think of the following model:

$$Y_i = \beta_0 + \beta_1 x_i + \text{"noise,"} \quad \text{for} \quad i = 1, \ldots, n,$$

where Y_i is the first-year sales and x_i is the first-year advertising expenditures. Put another way, the model is

$$Y_i = \beta_0 + \beta_1 x_i + \text{"unaccounted difference,"} \quad \text{for} \quad i = 1, \ldots, n.$$

Here, the "unaccounted difference" might include factors due to the idiosyncrasies of consumer behavior, underlying influences of the economy, actions by competitors, etc. Because we either do not have appropriate data to model these factors explicitly, or because we do not know the nature of these differences, we will model these "unaccounted differences" as independent, identically distributed observations from a Normal distribution with mean $\mu = 0$ and some (unknown) standard deviation σ. Later, we will examine how to see if this particular assumption is reasonable. More specifically:

The **simple linear regression model** assumes that

$$Y_i = \beta_0 + \beta_1 x_i + \varepsilon_i, \quad \text{for} \quad i = 1, \ldots, n,$$

where the values of $\varepsilon_1, \varepsilon_2, \ldots, \varepsilon_n$ are observed values of independent Normally distributed random variables with mean $\mu = 0$ and some unknown standard deviation σ.

The quantity β_0 is the "baseline" value of Y; it is the value of the dependent variable Y when the independent variable $x = 0$. The quantity β_1 is the slope of the line; it is the change in the dependent variable Y per unit change in the independent variable x.

Again, it is helpful to think of the $\varepsilon_1, \varepsilon_2, \ldots, \varepsilon_n$ as arising from a catch-all error category that captures the effects of factors that are neglected or are ignored in the model.

Stated a bit differently, the simple linear regression model is as follows.

$$Y = \beta_0 + \beta_1 x + \varepsilon,$$

where ε is a Normally distributed random variable with mean $\mu = 0$ and some standard deviation σ.

Based on this model, note that for a given value x of the independent variable, the expected value of Y is simply $\beta_0 + \beta_1 x$, and the standard deviation of Y is σ. We record these two facts as:

$$E(Y \mid x) = \beta_0 + \beta_1 x$$

and

$$\text{Standard Deviation}(Y \mid x) = \sigma.$$

Note that the expected value of Y depends on the value of the independent variable x, but that the standard deviation of Y does not depend on the value of the independent variable x. For the example of advertising and sales, the above expression states that for a given value of advertising expenditures x, expected sales is a linear function of advertising of the form $\beta_0 + \beta_1 x$, and the standard deviation of sales is some number σ.

We now turn to the task of estimating the value of the intercept β_0 and the value of the slope β_1. Let b_0 and b_1 be estimates of the intercept β_0 and the slope β_1. The values of b_0 and b_1 are called the **regression coefficients.** Intuitively, we would like to choose b_0 and b_1 in a manner such that the resulting line is the "best" fit of the data observations $(x_1, y_1), (x_2, y_2), \ldots, (x_n, y_n)$. If we have trial values of the estimates b_0 and b_1, then the **estimated** or **predicted** values of the dependent variable are:

$$\hat{y}_i = b_0 + b_1 x_i, \quad \text{for} \quad i = 1, \ldots, n.$$

The difference then between the **observed** values of the dependent variables $y_1, y_2, \ldots, y_n$ and the **predicted** values $\hat{y}_1, \hat{y}_2, \ldots, \hat{y}_n$ are called the **residuals** and are:

$$e_i = y_i - \hat{y}_i = y_i - b_0 - b_1 x_i, \quad \text{for} \quad i = 1, \ldots, n.$$

As an example of these definitions, consider the observations of Table 6.1. The fourteenth observation is $(x_{14}, y_{14}) = (0.8, 33)$. Suppose that we have chosen $b_0 = 41.0$ and $b_1 = 29.0$. Then the observed value of y_{14} is $y_{14} = 33$ and the estimated or predicted value is $\hat{y}_{14} = b_0 + b_1 x_{14} = 41.0 + 29.0 \times 0.8 = 64.2$. The residual then is $e_{14} = y_{14} - \hat{y}_{14} = 33 - 64.2 = -31.2$. This is shown visually in Figure 6.2. In Figure 6.2, the residual for each observation is the difference between the height of the observation (the observed value of sales) and the value of the equation (the estimated or predicted value of sales).

Our goal is to select values of b_0 and b_1 in such a way that the residuals are as small as possible. It seems that an intuitive approach would be to choose b_0 and b_1 to ensure that

FIGURE 6.2
The regression line
$y = 41 + 29x$.

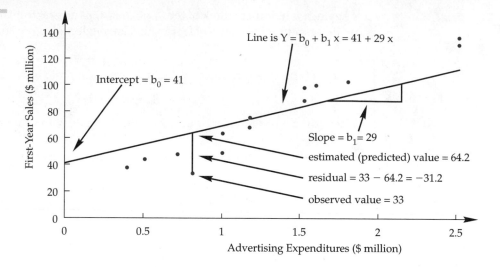

$$\sum_{i=1}^{n} |e_i| = \sum_{i=1}^{n} |y_i - \hat{y}_i| = \sum_{i=1}^{n} |y_i - b_0 - b_1 x_i|$$

is minimized (recall that the expression $|a|$ denotes the absolute value of the number a). Once again, for reasons of tractability, we will instead choose b_0 and b_1 to ensure that

$$\sum_{i=1}^{n} (e_i)^2 = \sum_{i=1}^{n} (y_i - \hat{y}_i)^2 = \sum_{i=1}^{n} (y_i - b_0 - b_1 x_i)^2$$

is minimized. The sum in the equation above is called the **residual sum of squared errors** or simply the **residual sum of squares.** Therefore, we will define the "best" regression line as the one that chooses b_0 and b_1 to minimize the residual sum of squares. We summarize this discussion as follows.

The **data** for the linear regression model consists of the n observations
$$(x_1, y_1), (x_2, y_2), \ldots, (x_n, y_n).$$
The **regression coefficients** are b_0 and b_1.
The **estimate** or **predicted** values of the dependent variable are:
$$\hat{y}_i = b_0 + b_1 x_i, \quad \text{for} \quad i = 1, \ldots, n.$$
The **residuals** are:
$$e_i = y_i - \hat{y}_i = y_i - b_0 - b_1 x_i, \quad \text{for} \quad i = 1, \ldots, n.$$
The **residual sum of squares** is:
$$\sum_{i=1}^{n} (e_i)^2 = \sum_{i=1}^{n} (y_i - \hat{y}_i)^2 = \sum_{i=1}^{n} (y_i - b_0 - b_1 x_i)^2.$$
The **"best"** regression line is the one that chooses b_0 and b_1 to minimize the residual sum of squares.

A computer software package for linear regression will compute the regression coefficients b_0 and b_1 which minimize the residual sum of squares, based on the observation data $(x_1, y_1), (x_2, y_2), \ldots, (x_n, y_n)$. Given the observation data $(x_1, y_1), (x_2, y_2), \ldots, (x_n, y_n)$, the regression coefficients b_0 and b_1 are computed using calculus (see Exercise 6.9) as follows:

First compute the two quantities:

$$\bar{x} = \frac{\sum\limits_{i=1}^{n} x_i}{n}$$

and

$$\bar{y} = \frac{\sum\limits_{i=1}^{n} y_i}{n}.$$

Then compute

$$b_1 = \frac{\sum\limits_{i=1}^{n}(x_i - \bar{x})(y_i - \bar{y})}{\sum\limits_{i=1}^{n}(x_i - \bar{x})^2}$$

and

$$b_0 = \bar{y} - b_1 \bar{x}.$$

For the example of predicting first-year sales based on first-year advertising (Example 6.1), the observation data is given in Table 6.1. If we use such a software package for linear regression with Table 6.1 as the data, the computer will compute the regression coefficients to be

$$b_0 = 13.82 \quad \text{and} \quad b_1 = 48.60.$$

Therefore, for this example, the regression line is given by:

$$y = b_0 + b_1 x = 13.82 + 48.60x.$$

The baseline value of first-year sales is the intercept $b_0 = 13.82$ and the incremental value of sales per unit increase of advertising is the slope $b_1 = 48.60$. That is, an increase in first-year advertising of \$1 million is expected to increase first-year sales by \$48.60 million. A plot of the regression line is shown in Figure 6.3.

Let us use the formulas we outlined earlier to verify the computer's calculation. From Table 6.1 we have $(x_1, y_1) = (1.8, 104), \ldots, (x_{14}, y_{14}) = (0.8, 33)$. We first compute

$$\bar{x} = \frac{\sum\limits_{i=1}^{n} x_i}{n} = \frac{1.8 + 1.2 + \cdots + 0.8}{14} = 1.3$$

and

FIGURE 6.3

The regression line for first-year sales and advertising in Example 6.1.

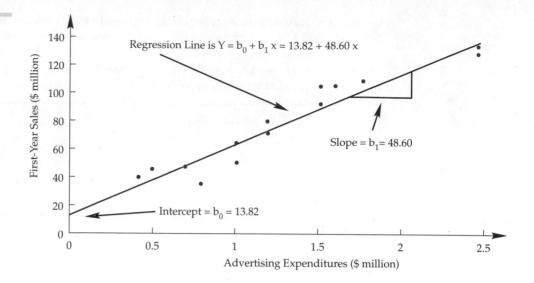

$$\bar{y} = \frac{\sum\limits_{i=1}^{n} y_i}{n} = \frac{104 + 68 + \cdots + 33}{14} = 77.$$

We then compute

$$b_1 = \frac{\sum\limits_{i=1}^{n}(x_i - \bar{x})(y_i - \bar{y})}{\sum\limits_{i=1}^{n}(x_i - \bar{x})^2}$$

$$= \frac{(1.8 - 1.3)(104 - 77) + (1.2 - 1.3)(68 - 77) + \cdots + (0.8 - 1.3)(33 - 77)}{(1.8 - 1.3)^2 + (1.2 - 1.3)^2 + \cdots + (0.8 - 1.3)^2}$$

$$= 48.60$$

and

$$b_0 = \bar{y} - b_1\bar{x} = 77 - 48.60 \times 1.3 = 13.82.$$

As it turns out, these values of b_0 and b_1 can also be computed automatically as part of computer spreadsheet regression software. An example of the regression software spreadsheet output for Example 6.1 is shown in Table 6.2. Notice that the coefficients $b_0 = 13.82$ and $b_1 = 48.60$ appear under the heading "coefficients" in rows 17 and 18 of the spreadsheet. We will explain the use and interpretation of regression software spreadsheet output in Sections 6.3 and 6.4. •

Based on the linear regression model, we can estimate or predict the expected first-year sales of AppleGlo for a given level of first-year advertising. For example, if J&T spends $1.5 million in first-year advertising, the expected first-year sales are predicted to be

$$y = 13.82 + 48.60 \times 1.5 = \$86.72 \text{ million.}$$

If J&T spends $2.0 million in first-year advertising, the expected first-year sales are estimated to be

$$y = 13.82 + 48.60 \times 2.0 = \$111.02 \text{ million.}$$

TABLE 6.2

Microsoft Excel® computer output for the prediction of sales of AppleGlo in Example 6.1.

	A	B	C	D	E	F	G
1	SUMMARY OUTPUT						
2							
3	Regression Statistics						
4	Multiple R	0.964					
5	R Square	0.930					
6	Adjusted R Square	0.924					
7	Standard Error	9.106					
8	Observations	14					
9							
10	ANOVA						
11		dof	SS	MS	F	Significance F	
12	Regression	1	13,130.942	13,130.942	158.354	0.000	
13	Residual	12	995.058	82.921			
14	Total	13	14,126.000				
15							
16		Coefficients	Standard Error	t Stat	P-value	Lower 95%	Upper 95%
17	Intercept	13.82	5.579	2.478	0.029	1.668	25.980
18	Advertising	48.60	3.862	12.584	0.000	40.183	57.011
19							
20							
21							
22	RESIDUAL OUTPUT						
23							
24	Observation	Predicted Sales	Residuals				
25	1	101.299	2.701				
26	2	72.140	-4.140				
27	3	33.263	5.737				
28	4	38.122	4.878				
29	5	135.317	-1.317				
30	6	135.317	-8.317				
31	7	86.719	0.281				
32	8	72.140	4.860				
33	9	91.579	10.421				
34	10	62.421	2.579				
35	11	86.719	14.281				
36	12	47.842	-1.842				
37	13	62.421	-10.421				
38	14	52.701	-19.701				

6.2

PREDICTION BASED ON MULTIPLE LINEAR REGRESSION

In the linear regression model presented in Section 6.1, the value of the dependent variable Y is presumed to be a linear function of the independent variable x. However, in most managerial settings, there are many factors that affect the value of the dependent variable Y. In order to predict the value of sales, for example, we might wish to consider such factors as advertising expenditures, promotional expenditures, the time of year, economic conditions, competitors' actions, etc. The prediction of the dependent variable as a linear function of **multiple** independent variables is called **multiple linear regression.** (The linear regression model of Section 6.1, where there was only one independent variable, is called **simple linear regression.**)

We introduce the multiple linear regression model with a more sophisticated version of the problem of predicting the sales of a product.

Example 6.2 — Predicting Sales of a Product based on Multiple Factors

Suppose that Yen Chin Lee is a marketing manager for Country Kitchen Corporation (CKC), a Northeastern regional processed foods company, and suppose that she is interested in predicting future sales of the company's snack food product "Nature-Bar." Based on good management intuition, Yen Chin has figured that the three most important factors that influence sales of Nature-Bar are advertising expenditures, promotional expenditures, and competitors' sales. Suppose that she has gathered data on CKC's sales, advertising, and promotions of Nature-Bar for the last year, by sales region, in relevant markets where CKC has a significant share of the snack food market. Yen Chin has also gathered data on sales of snack foods by CKC's main competitor for these regions as well, and all of this data is summarized in Table 6.3. Yen Chin would like to predict future sales of Nature-Bar in the regions given in Table 6.3 as a function of advertising, promotions, and competitors' sales.

In Example 6.2, note that there are three separate factors (advertising, promotions, and competitors' sales) that are presumed to have a direct influence on the estimate of sales. This differs from Example 6.1, where there was only one factor (advertising) that was presumed to have a direct influence on the estimate of sales.

(Note also that it is not possible to create a scatter-plot of the data of Table 6.3. This is because there are three separate factors (advertising, promotions, and competitors' sales) that are presumed to have a direct influence on sales, and so there is no convenient way to display the data of Table 6.3 that would visually indicate any patterns or trends.)

We now present the notation that will be used to develop the multiple linear regression model. Let Y denote the dependent variable. In Example 6.2, Y denotes the sales of Nature-Bar. Let k denote the number of independent variables in the model and let $x_1, \ldots, x_k$ denote the independent variables. In Example 6.2, there are $k = 3$ independent variables (advertising, promotions, and competitors' sales). Let x_1 de-

TABLE 6.3

Sales of Nature-Bar, advertising expenditures, promotions expenditures, and competitors' sales, by region, for 1998.

Region	Sales ($ million) (y_i)	Advertising Expenditures ($ million) (x_{1i})	Promotions Expenditures ($ million) (x_{2i})	Competitors' Sales ($ million) (x_{3i})
Selkirk	101.8	1.3	0.2	20.40
Susquehanna	44.4	0.7	0.2	30.50
Kittery	108.3	1.4	0.3	24.60
Acton	85.1	0.5	0.4	19.60
Finger Lakes	77.1	0.5	0.6	25.50
Berkshire	158.7	1.9	0.4	21.70
Central	180.4	1.2	1.0	6.80
Providence	64.2	0.4	0.4	12.60
Nashua	74.6	0.6	0.5	31.30
Dunster	143.4	1.3	0.6	18.60
Endicott	120.6	1.6	0.8	19.90
Five-Towns	69.7	1.0	0.3	25.60
Waldeboro	67.8	0.8	0.2	27.40
Jackson	106.7	0.6	0.5	24.30
Stowe	119.6	1.1	0.3	13.70

note advertising expenditures (in \$ million), let x_2 denote promotional expenditures (in \$ million), and let x_3 denote competitors' sales (in \$ million). Then $x_1, \ldots, x_k$ ($k = 3$) are the independent variables for the multiple linear regression model.

The **data** for the multiple linear regression model will be the observations of the dependent variable (sales) and the observations of the independent variables (advertising, promotions, and competitors' sales), as shown in Table 6.3. Let n denote the number of observations. In this case, $n = 15$ observations. We denote the $n = 15$ observed values of the independent variables (advertising, promotions, and competitors' sales) by (x_{1i}, x_{2i}, x_{3i}) for each $i = 1, \ldots, n$. For example, for $i = 15$, corresponding to Stowe, we have $(x_{1i}, x_{2i}, x_{3i}) = (1.1, 0.3, 13.70)$. We denote the $n = 15$ values of the dependent variable (sales) by $y_1, y_2, \ldots, y_n$. Thus, for example, $y_{15} = 119.6$.

The multiple linear regression model assumes that there is a linear relationship between the dependent variable Y and the independent variables $x_1, \ldots, x_k$ (in this case, between sales and advertising, promotions, and competitors' sales). As in the case of simple linear regression, it is therefore helpful to think of the following model:

$$Y_i = \beta_0 + \beta_1 x_{1i} + \ldots + \beta_k x_{ki} + \text{"unaccounted difference," for } i = 1, \ldots, n.$$

As noted in the case of simple linear regression, the "unaccounted difference" might include factors due to the idiosyncracies of consumer behavior, underlying influences of the economy, etc. Because we either do not have appropriate data to model these factors explicitly, or because we do not know the nature of these differences, we model these "unaccounted differences" as observations from a Normal distribution with mean $\mu = 0$ and some (unknown) standard deviation σ. More specifically:

The **multiple linear regression model** assumes that

$$Y_i = \beta_0 + \beta_1 x_{1i} + \ldots + \beta_k x_{ki} + \varepsilon_i, \text{ for } i = 1, \ldots, n,$$

where the values of $\varepsilon_1, \varepsilon_2, \ldots, \varepsilon_n$ are observed values of independent Normally distributed random variables with mean $\mu = 0$ and some standard deviation σ.

The quantity β_0 is the "baseline" value of Y; it is the value of the dependent variable Y when $x_1 = 0, x_2 = 0, \ldots, x_k = 0$. Each of the quantities $\beta_1, \beta_2, \ldots, \beta_k$ is the change in the dependent variable Y per unit change in each of the independent variables $x_1, x_2, \ldots, x_k$.

Again, it is helpful to think of the $\varepsilon_1, \varepsilon_2, \ldots, \varepsilon_n$ as arising from a catch-all error category that captures the effects of factors that are neglected or are ignored in the model.

Stated a bit differently, the multiple linear regression model is as follows.

$$Y = \beta_0 + \beta_1 x_1 + \beta_2 x_2 + \ldots + \beta_k x_k + \varepsilon,$$

where ε is a Normally distributed random variable with mean $\mu = 0$ and some standard deviation σ.

Based on this model, note that for given values of the independent variables $x_1, x_2, \ldots, x_k$, the expected value of Y is simply $\beta_0 + \beta_1 x_1 + \beta_2 x_2 + \ldots + \beta_k x_k$, and the standard deviation of Y is σ. We record these two facts as:

$$E(Y \mid x_1, x_2, \ldots, x_k) = \beta_0 + \beta_1 x_1 + \beta_2 x_2 + \ldots + \beta_k x_k,$$

and

$$\text{Standard Deviation}(Y \mid x_1, x_2, \ldots, x_k) = \sigma.$$

In words, this expression states that for given values $x_1, x_2, \ldots, x_k$ of the independent variables, the expected value of the dependent variable Y is a linear function of $x_1, x_2, \ldots, x_k$ of the form $\beta_0 + \beta_1 x_1 + \beta_2 x_2 + \ldots + \beta_k x_k$. Furthermore, the standard deviation of the dependent variable Y is σ. Note that the expected value of Y depends on the values of the independent variables $x_1, x_2, \ldots, x_k$, but that the standard deviation of Y does not depend on the value of the independent variables $x_1, x_2, \ldots, x_k$. For Example 6.2, the preceding expression states that for given values of advertising (x_1), promotions (x_2), and competitors' sales (x_3), the expected sales is a linear function of these three quantities of the form $\beta_0 + \beta_1 x_1 + \beta_2 x_2 + \beta_3 x_3$, and that the standard deviation of sales is some number σ.

We now turn to the task of estimating the values of $\beta_0, \beta_1, \ldots, \beta_k$. Let $b_0, b_1, \ldots, b_k$ be estimates of $\beta_0, \beta_1, \ldots, \beta_k$. If we have trial values of the estimates $b_0, b_1, \ldots, b_k$, then the **estimated** or **predicted** values of the dependent variable are:

$$\hat{y}_i = b_0 + b_1 x_{1i} + \ldots + b_k x_{ki}, \quad \text{for } i = 1, \ldots, n.$$

The difference then between the **observed** values of the dependent variables $y_1, y_2, \ldots, y_n$ and the **predicted** values $\hat{y}_1, \hat{y}_2, \ldots, \hat{y}_n$ are called the **residuals** and are:

$$e_i = y_i - \hat{y}_i = y_i - b_0 - b_1 x_{1i} - \ldots - b_k x_{ki}, \quad \text{for } i = 1, \ldots, n.$$

Our goal is to select values of $b_0, b_1, \ldots, b_k$ in such a way that the residuals are as small as possible. Just as in the case of simple linear regression, we will choose $b_0, b_1, \ldots, b_k$ to ensure that

$$\sum_{i=1}^{n} (e_i)^2 = \sum_{i=1}^{n} (y_i - \hat{y}_i)^2 = \sum_{i=1}^{n} (y_i - b_0 - b_1 x_{1i} - \ldots - b_k x_{ki})^2$$

is minimized, that is, so that the **residual sum of squared errors** or more simply the **residual sum of squares** is minimized. We summarize all of this as follows.

The **data** for the multiple linear regression model consists of the observed value of the dependent variable y_i together with the observed values of the k independent variables $(x_{1i}, x_{2i}, \ldots, x_{ki})$ for each of $i = 1, \ldots, n$ observations. The **regression coefficients** are $b_0, b_1, \ldots, b_k$.

The **estimate** or **predicted** values of the dependent variable are:

$$\hat{y}_i = b_0 + b_1 x_{1i} + \ldots + b_k x_{ki} \quad \text{for } i = 1, \ldots, n.$$

The **residuals** are:

$$e_i = y_i - \hat{y}_i = y_i - b_0 - b_1 x_{1i} - \ldots - b_k x_{ki}, \quad \text{for } i = 1, \ldots, n.$$

The **residual sum of squares** is:

$$\sum_{i=1}^{n} (e_i)^2 = \sum_{i=1}^{n} (y_i - \hat{y}_i)^2 = \sum_{i=1}^{n} (y_i - b_0 - b_1 x_{1i} - \ldots - b_k x_{ki})^2.$$

The **"best"** regression line is the one that chooses $b_0, b_1, \ldots, b_k$ to minimize the residual sum of squares.

A computer software package for linear regression will compute the regression coefficients $b_0, b_1, \ldots, b_k$, which minimize the residual sum of squares, based on the data y_i and $(x_{1i}, x_{2i}, \ldots, x_{ki})$ for each of $i = 1, \ldots, n$. (Incidentally, the computation of the regression coefficients $b_0, b_1, \ldots, b_k$ in a multiple linear regression model is **not** done with the use of formulas. Rather, the coefficients $b_0, b_1, \ldots, b_k$ are computed as the solution to a particular system of k equations in k unknowns. The particular equation system that is used in the computation of the regression coefficients arises from a special application of calculus to the problem of minimizing the residual sum of squares.)

For the problem of predicting sales in Example 6.2, the data is given in Table 6.3. If we use a spreadsheet software package for linear regression with Table 6.3 as the data, the spreadsheet will compute the regression coefficients shown in Table 6.4.

Using the coefficients as portrayed in Table 6.4, the regression equation of Example 6.2 is given by:

$$y = b_0 + b_1 x_1 + b_2 x_2 + b_3 x_3 = 65.705 + 48.979 x_1 + 59.654 x_2 - 1.838 x_3.$$

Thus, for example, the incremental value of sales per unit increase of promotions is $b_2 = 59.654$. This number is interpreted as follows: An increase in promotions of \$1 million is expected to increase sales by \$59.654 million.

Based on the regression model, we can estimate or predict the expected sales of Nature-Bar for given levels of advertising, promotions, and competitors' sales. For example, suppose that Yen Chin wishes to predict sales of Nature-Bar in the Nashua sales region for next year. Suppose that she is planning to spend \$0.7 million on advertising and \$0.6 million on promotions in the Nashua region next year, and she estimates that CKC's competitors' sales will remain flat at their current level of \$31.30 million next year. Then, the expected sales in the Nashua region next year are predicted to be

$$Y = 65.705 + 48.979 x_1 + 59.654 x_2 - 1.838 x_3$$
$$= 65.705 + 48.979 \times 0.7 + 59.654 \times 0.6 - 1.838 \times 31.30$$
$$= \$78.253 \text{ million.}$$

As another example, suppose that Yen Chin wishes to estimate sales of Nature-Bar in the Central sales region for next year, and that she is planning to spend \$1.4 million on advertising and \$0.8 million on promotions in the Central region next year. Suppose, in addition, that she has heard that CKC's competitor is planning to cease operations in the Central region next year (their sales were very low in 1998, according to Table 6.3). Then the expected sales of Nature-Bar in the Central region next year are estimated to be

$$Y = 65.705 + 48.979 x_1 + 59.654 x_2 - 1.838 x_3$$
$$= 65.705 + 48.979 \times 1.4 + 59.654 \times 0.8 - 1.838 \times 0$$
$$= \$181.999 \text{ million.}$$

TABLE 6.4

Regression coefficients for prediction of sales of Nature-Bar.

Regression Coefficient	Value
b_0	65.705
b_1	48.979
b_2	59.654
b_3	−1.838

USING SPREADSHEET SOFTWARE FOR LINEAR REGRESSION

It is very easy to perform linear regression using a computer spreadsheet. In this section, we outline the steps involved in using Microsoft Excel® to perform linear regression.

Organizing the Data

The data for the regression model should be organized in a spreadsheet with the dependent and independent variables in columns and with the n different observations of the dependent variable and the independent variables organized by rows. For example, Table 6.5 illustrates a spreadsheet version of the data for Nature-Bar of Example 6.2, which was orginally shown in Table 6.3. It is also recommended that a descriptive label of the dependent variable and the independent variables be placed at the top of the table. For example, in the spreadsheet shown in Table 6.5, the descriptive label "Sales" is used for the dependent variable corresponding to sales, and "Advertising," "Promotions," and "Competitors" are used for the three independent variables corresponding to Advertising Expenditures, Promotions Expenditures, and Competitors' sales. These appear in the first row of the spreadsheet in Table 6.5.

Running the Regression

A convenient way to run a regression model in Microsoft Excel® is as follows:

1. Open Microsoft Excel®. Go to **Tools** in the pull-down menu, and click on **Data Analysis.** (If the option **Data Analysis** is not listed under **Tools,** you will need to load this feature into your configuration of Microsoft Excel®.) Then select **Regression** from among the list of tools. A menu entitled **Regression** should appear.

2. Under **Input**, click the button to the right of **Input Y range** and highlight all of the cells with data for the dependent variable, including the descriptive label at the top. For example, for the spreadsheet shown in Table 6.5, we would highlight the cells B1:B16. A convenient way to do this is to click on the mouse and while holding down the mouse button, highlight the cells for the dependent variable. Press **Enter** to complete this selection.

3. Under **Input**, click the button to the right of **Input X range** and highlight all of the cells with data for the independent variables, including the descriptive labels

TABLE 6.5

Spreadsheet representation of the data for the regression model for predicting sales of Nature-Bar of Example 6.2.

	A	B	C	D	E
1	Region	Sales	Advertising	Promotions	Competitors
2	Selkirk	101.8	1.3	0.2	20.40
3	Susquehanna	44.4	0.7	0.2	30.50
4	Kittery	108.3	1.4	0.3	24.60
5	Acton	85.1	0.5	0.4	19.60
6	Finger Lakes	77.1	0.5	0.6	25.50
7	Berkshire	158.7	1.9	0.4	21.70
8	Central	180.4	1.2	1.0	6.80
9	Providence	64.2	0.4	0.4	12.60
10	Nashua	74.6	0.6	0.5	31.30
11	Dunster	143.4	1.3	0.6	18.60
12	Endicott	120.6	1.6	0.8	19.90
13	Five-Towns	69.7	1.0	0.3	25.60
14	Waldeboro	67.8	0.8	0,2	27.40
15	Jackson	106.7	0.6	0.5	24.30
16	Stowe	119.6	1.1	0.3	13.70

at the top. For example, for the spreadsheet shown in Table 6.5, we would high-light the cells C1:E16. Once again, a convenient way to do this is to click on the mouse and while holding down the mouse button, highlight all of the cells for the independent variables. Press **Enter** to complete this selection.

4. In the boxes below, check off **Labels** and **Confidence Interval**. Make sure that "95%" is the value in the box next to **Confidence Interval**.

5. Under **Output Options**, choose **New Worksheet Ply** and in the box to the right, name the new sheet in which the regression output is to appear. Next, under **Residuals**, select **Residuals** and **Residual Plot**. By selecting **Residuals** and **Residuals Plots**, the software will automatically create certain charts, whose use-fulness will be explained in Section 6.6.

6. The spreadsheet is now ready for the regression to be performed. Simply click on **OK**.

Viewing the Output of the Regression Model

The output of the regression model will be a table generated on a new worksheet and will be displayed automatically. Table 6.6 shows the spreadsheet output for the regression model for the prediction of sales of Nature-Bar of Example 6.2. The out-put table contains a lot of numbers, and explanations of many of these numbers will be covered in Section 6.4. The regression coefficients $b_0, b_1, \ldots, b_k$ appear roughly in the middle of the spreadsheet in the left under the heading "Coeffi-cients." The first coefficient is the value of b_0, which is 65.705, and is called the "In-tercept" in the spreadsheet output. The next three coefficients are the regression coefficients for each of the three independent variables and are $b_1 = 48.079$ (for Ad-vertising Expenditures), $b_2 = 59.654$ (for Promotions Expenditures), and $b_3 = -1.838$ (for Competitors' Sales). Notice that these coefficients are the same as the coefficients in Table 6.4.

As Table 6.6 shows, there are many other numbers in the output table of a re-gression model, in addition to the regression coefficients $b_0, b_1, \ldots, b_k$. The interpre-tation of most of these other numbers is covered in the next section, Section 6.4.

6.4 | INTERPRETATION OF COMPUTER OUTPUT OF A LINEAR REGRESSION MODEL

There are many different computer software packages that perform linear regression. It might seem at first glance that the only output information that is needed from a computer software package is the regression coefficients $b_0, b_1, \ldots, b_k$. However, be-cause linear regression is so easy to perform, it is extremely important to analyze the ex-tent to which the resulting regression model is sensible, useful, and satisfies the underlying assumptions of linearity, normality, etc. before using the regression model in the context of making managerial decisions. The computer output of most software packages for linear regression consists of the regression coefficients $b_0, b_1, \ldots, b_k$, as well as a host of other diagnostic information that is critical in analyzing the sensibility of the underlying regression model. This computer output is fairly standard in terms of the types of output information that the packages compute and then display to a user.

We will illustrate the use of linear regression computer output with the output information contained in the Microsoft Excel® regression software. To be concrete, we

TABLE 6.6

Microsoft Excel® spreadsheet software output for the prediction of sales of Nature-Bar in Example 6.2.

	A	B	C	D	E	F	G
1	SUMMARY OUTPUT						
2							
3	Regression Statistics						
4	Multiple R	0.913					
5	R Square	0.833					
6	Adjusted R Square	0.787					
7	Standard Error	17.600					
8	Observations	15					
9							
10	ANOVA						
11		dof	SS	MS	F	Significance F	
12	Regression	3	16,997.537	5,665.846	18.290	0.000	
13	Residual	11	3,407.473	309.770			
14	Total	14	20,405.009				
15							
16		Coefficients	Standard Error	t Stat	P-value	Lower 95%	Upper 95%
17	Intercept	65.705	27.731	2.369	0.037	4.669	126.740
18	Advertising	48.979	10.658	4.596	0.001	25.521	72.437
19	Promotions	59.654	23.625	2.525	0.028	7.657	111.652
20	Competitors	-1.838	0.814	-2.258	0.045	-3.629	-0.047
21							
22							
23							
24	RESIDUAL OUTPUT						
25							
26	Observation	Predicted Sales	Residuals				
27	1	103.820	-2.020				
28	2	55.873	-11.473				
29	3	106.965	1.335				
30	4	78.038	7.062				
31	5	79.127	-2.027				
32	6	142.749	15.951				
33	7	171.637	8.763				
34	8	86.004	-21.804				
35	9	67.401	7.199				
36	10	130.990	12.410				
37	11	155.225	-34.625				
38	12	85.536	-15.836				
39	13	66.467	1.333				
40	14	80.265	26.435				
41	15	112.302	7.298				

will study the linear regression computer output for the problem of predicting sales of Nature-Bar in Example 6.2. This computer output is shown in Table 6.6. Note that the regression model output in Table 6.6 consists of a large amount of numerical data. We will not discuss the meaning of all of this numerical data. Rather, we will confine our discussion to only the most important output that is needed for a proper evaluation and use of the regession model.

The Regression Coefficients

As mentioned earlier, the regression coefficients $b_0, b_1, \ldots, b_k$ of the linear regression model are displayed in a column in the middle portion of the Excel® computer output under the heading "Coefficients." The first coefficient in that column is the coefficient value of b_0, which is the intercept or base-line. Its value is $b_0 = 65.705$. The values of the coefficients $b_1, \ldots, b_k$ are displayed vertically below the value of b_0, as shown in Table 6.6. These values are $b_1 = 48.979$, $b_2 = 59.654$, and $b_3 = -1.838$.

The Standard Error

Recall that one of the basic assumptions in the linear regression model is that

$$Y_i = \beta_0 + \beta_1 x_{1i} + \ldots + \beta_k x_{ki} + \varepsilon_i, \quad \text{for} \quad i = 1, \ldots, n,$$

where the values of $\varepsilon_1, \varepsilon_2, \ldots, \varepsilon_n$ are the "noise" or "unaccounted differences." It is assumed that $\varepsilon_1, \varepsilon_2, \ldots, \varepsilon_n$ are observed values of independent Normally distributed random variables with mean $\mu = 0$ and some standard deviation σ. The regression output contains a number called the **standard error** of the regression model, which is used as an estimate of σ. The value of the standard error (denoted by s) is displayed in the fourth entry of the first column of the Excel® regression output in Table 6.6. In Table 6.6, the value of s is $s = 17.60$. Therefore, the regression estimate of σ is $s = 17.60$.

The Degrees of Freedom

The **degrees of freedom** of a linear regression model is an important number that is needed in order to construct confidence intervals for the regression coefficients using the t-distribution. The **degrees of freedom** is defined to be:

$$\text{degrees of freedom} = \text{number of observations} \\ - \text{number of independent variables} \\ - 1.$$

In our notation, the number of observations of the regression data is denoted by n and the number of independent variables in the regression model is denoted by k. Therefore, the degrees of freedom (dof) is given by the simple formula:

$$dof = n - k - 1.$$

For the prediction of the sales of Nature-Bar in Example 6.2, the number of observations is $n = 15$ and the number of independent variables is $k = 3$. Therefore, the degrees of freedom is computed as:

$$dof = n - k - 1 = 15 - 3 - 1 = 11.$$

That is, the degrees of freedom is $dof = 11$. In the Excel® computer output, the degrees of freedom dof appears as the second entry in the first column of the middle portion of the output table. It is $dof = 11$.

Standard Errors of the Regression Coefficients, and Confidence Intervals for the Regression Coefficients

Corresponding to each of the regression coefficients $b_0, b_1, \ldots, b_k$ is a number called the **standard error of the regression coefficient.** The standard errors of the regression coefficients are denoted as $s_{b_0}, s_{b_1}, \ldots, s_{b_k}$ and are displayed in the column to the right of the regression coefficients in the Excel® output. For example, in Table 6.6, the standard errors of the regression coefficients are $s_{b_0} = 27.731$, $s_{b_1} = 10.658$, $s_{b_2} = 23.625$, and $s_{b_3} = 0.814$. These numbers will play an important role in the construction of certain confidence intervals related to the regression coefficients $b_0, b_1, \ldots, b_k$, which we now describe.

Recall that the linear regression model assumes that

$$Y_i = \beta_0 + \beta_1 x_{1i} + \ldots + \beta_k x_{ki} + \varepsilon_i, \text{ for } i = 1, \ldots, n,$$

where the values of $\varepsilon_1, \varepsilon_2, \ldots, \varepsilon_n$ are the "noise" or "unaccounted differences." The predicted values of $\beta_0, \beta_1, \ldots, \beta_k$ are the regression coefficients $b_0, b_1, \ldots, b_k$. Because the regression coefficients $b_0, b_1, \ldots, b_k$ are estimates of the actual (but unknown) values of $\beta_0, \beta_1, \ldots, \beta_k$, it is useful to be able to construct confidence intervals for each of the β_m based on the estimate b_m for $m = 0, 1, \ldots, k$. Let us consider a particular value of m, where m is one of the indices $0, 1, \ldots, k$. The estimate of β_m is the regression coefficient b_m. We would like to compute a confidence interval of the form

$$[b_m - b, b_m + b]$$

in such a way that we are, say, 95% confident that the value of β_m lies in this interval. That is, we would like to compute a number b, so that the we are 95% confident that the value of β_m lies in the interval

$$[b_m - b, b_m + b].$$

This is accomplished as follows.

Procedure for Constructing Confidence Intervals for the Regression Coefficients

Let b_m be the regression coefficient for the independent variable x_m and let s_{b_m} be the standard error of the regression coefficient b_m. Then a β% confidence interval for β_m is computed as follows:
First use a t-table to find the number c for which

$$P(-c \leq T \leq c) = \beta/100,$$

where T obeys a t-distribution with $dof = n - k - 1$ degrees of freedom.
Then the β% confidence interval is:

$$[b_m - c \times s_{b_m}, b_m + c \times s_{b_m}]$$

We now illustrate the construction of confidence intervals for the regression coefficients. Suppose that we wish to construct a 90% confidence interval for the value of β_2 in the regression model of sales of Nature-Bar in Example 6.2. According to Table 6.6, the value of the regression coefficient b_2 is $b_2 = 59.654$ and the value of the standard error of the regression coefficient s_{b_2} is $s_{b_2} = 23.625$. Furthermore, the degrees of freedom dof is $dof = n - k - 1 = 15 - 3 - 1 = 11$. Therefore, we seek the value of the number c for which

$$P(-c \leq T \leq c) = \beta/100 = 90/100 = 0.90,$$

where T obeys a t-distribution with $dof = 11$ degrees of freedom. We can use Table A.2 of the Appendix, which presents various values of c for the t-distribution. According to Table A.2, $c = 1.769$ for $dof = 11$ and $\beta = 90$. Therefore, the 90% confidence interval for β_2 is given by

$$[b_2 - c \times s_{b_2}, b_2 + c \times s_{b_2}] = [59.654 - 1.769 \times 23.625, 59.654 + 1.769 \times 23.625]$$
$$= [17.861, 101.447].$$

That is, we are 90% confident that the value of β_2 lies in the range from 17.861 to 101.447.

Note that the standard error of the estimate s_{b_m} plays a role anal[...] the standard deviation of the sample mean in the construction of confide[...] of the mean.

The most commonly used confidence intervals in regression mode[...] $\beta = 95\%$ confidence intervals for $\beta_0, \beta_1, \ldots, \beta_k$. For this reason, the Excel® regressi[...] output conveniently computes and displays the 95% confidence intervals for $\beta_0, \beta_1, \ldots, \beta_k$ in the right side of the third section of the regression output using exactly the same methodology presented previously. For example, if we examine the right-hand corner of the third section of the output of the regression model for sales of Nature-Bar as shown in Table 6.6, we find that the 95% confidence interval for intercept or baseline β_0 is the interval [4.669, 126.740], and that the 95% confidence interval for β_1 is the interval [25.521, 72.437]. Likewise, the 95% confidence interval for β_2 is the interval [7.657, 111.652], and the 95% confidence interval for β_3 is the interval [−3.629, −0.047]. Of course, we also could have computed these 95% confidence intervals by hand using the method just presented.

The *t*-statistics

Recall once again that the linear regression model assumes that

$$Y_i = \beta_0 + \beta_1 x_{1i} + \ldots + \beta_k x_{ki} + \varepsilon_i, \quad \text{for} \quad i = 1, \ldots, n,$$

where the values of $\varepsilon_1, \varepsilon_2, \ldots, \varepsilon_n$ are the "noise" or "unaccounted differences." The estimated values of $\beta_0, \beta_1, \ldots, \beta_k$ are the regression coefficients $b_0, b_1, \ldots, b_k$. Let us consider a particular value of m, where m is one of the indices $1, \ldots, k$. The estimate of β_m is the regression coefficient b_m. Suppose that the regression coefficient b_m is very small, say $b_m = 0.026$ or $b_m = -0.017$, for example. In this case, we might not be sure whether the true value of β_m is different from zero. If it were the case that $\beta_m = 0$, then there is no linear relationship between the dependent variable Y and the independent variable x_m, and so x_m should not be factored into any estimate of the dependent variable Y. We now develop a test that decides whether the true value of β_m is equal to zero or not.

In the previous subsection, we constructed a confidence interval for β_m at the $\beta\%$ confidence level of the form:

$$[b_m - c \times s_{b_m}, b_m + c \times s_{b_m}],$$

where c is found using the *t*-distribution table (Table A.2 of the Appendix). That is, c is that number for which

$$P(-c \leq T \leq c) = \beta/100,$$

where T obeys a *t*-distribution with $dof = n - k - 1$ degrees of freedom. If this confidence interval does not contain zero, then we can assert at the $\beta\%$ level of confidence that β_m is not equal to zero. In order to test whether or not this confidence interval contains zero or not, we compute the quantity

$$\bar{t} = \frac{b_m}{s_{b_m}},$$

which is called the *t*-statistic for the regression coefficient b_m. By rearranging the arithmetic for the computation of the confidence interval

$$[b_m - c \times s_{b_m}, b_m + c \times s_{b_m}],$$

it is straightforward to conclude that this interval will not contain zero so long as the absolute value of the t-statistic, namely $|\bar{t}|$, is larger than the number c. We record this formally as:

Test for the Significance of β_m.

Compute the t-statistic

$$\bar{t} = \frac{b_m}{s_{b_m}}.$$

Let c be that number for which

$$P(-c \le T \le c) = \beta/100,$$

where T obeys a t-distribution with $dof = n - k - 1$ degrees of freedom. If

$$|\bar{t}| > c,$$

then we are confident at the $\beta\%$ confidence level that β_m is different from zero.

We now illustrate the use of the t-statistic to test the significance of the regression coefficients. Suppose that we wish to test the significance of β_2 in the regression model of sales of Nature-Bar in Example 6.2 at the $\beta = 95\%$ level of confidence. According to Table 6.6, the value of the regression coefficient b_2 is $b_2 = 59.654$ and the value of the standard error of the regression coefficient s_{b_2} is $s_{b_2} = 23.625$. Therefore, the t-statistic for this coefficient is

$$\bar{t} = \frac{b_2}{s_{b_2}} = \frac{59.654}{23.625} = 2.525.$$

Using $\beta = 95$ and $dof = n - k - 1 = 15 - 3 - 1 = 11$, the value of c from the t-distribution Table A.2 is $c = 2.201$. Next, note that $|\bar{t}| = \bar{t} = 2.525$, which is larger than $c = 2.201$. Therefore, we are 95% confident that the value of β_2 is different from zero.

As another example, suppose that we wish to test the significance of β_3 in the regression model of sales of Nature-Bar in Example 6.2 at the $\beta = 95\%$ level of confidence. According to Table 6.6, the value of the regression coefficient b_3 is $b_3 = -1.838$ and the value of the standard error of the regression coefficient s_{b_3} is $s_{b_3} = 0.814$. Therefore, the t-statistic for this coefficient is

$$\bar{t} = \frac{b_3}{s_{b_3}} = \frac{-1.838}{0.814} = -2.258.$$

Just as in the previous paragraph, the value of c from the t-distribution Table A.2 is $c = 2.201$. Next, note that $|\bar{t}| = 2.258$, which is larger than $c = 2.201$. Therefore, we are 95% confident that the value of β_3 is different from zero.

If the absolute value of the t-statistic $|\bar{t}|$ is less than c, then we should be skeptical about the assumption that the dependent variable Y depends linearly on the independent variable x_m, and we might want to eliminate the independent variable x_m from the linear regression model.

Because the t-statistics are so important, they are computed automatically in most software packages that perform linear regression. In the Excel® regression software, the t-statistics are computed and displayed in the fourth column of the middle portion of the output table. For the regression model of sales of Nature-Bar in Example 6.2, the t-statistics can be found in Table 6.6. Examining Table 6.6, we find that the t-statistics are as follows: for β_0, $\bar{t} = 2.369$; for β_1, $\bar{t} = 4.596$; for β_2, $\bar{t} = 2.525$; and for β_3, $\bar{t} = -2.258$.

The Coefficient of Determination: R^2

The most important and fundamental question in a linear regression model is whether or not the model does a good job of predicting the value of the dependent variable Y for given values of the independent variables $x_1, x_2, \ldots, x_k$. Put another way, we would like to answer the question, "How good or appropriate is the linear regression model?" The answer to this question often relies heavily on the **coefficient of determination,** which is denoted by R^2 and is most often referred to simply as the "R squared" of the linear regression model. The value of R^2 appears in the Excel® regression computer output table as the second number in the first column of the table. For the regression model of sales of Nature-Bar in Example 6.2, we can read from Table 6.6 that the coefficient of determination is $R^2 = 0.833$. We now explain the meaning and interpretation of the coefficient of determination R^2 in detail.

In order to develop some intuition and to motivate the definition we provide two interpretations of R^2.

First interpretation of R^2

We again consider Example 6.2 in which a linear regression model is used to predict the sales of Nature-Bar based on advertising, promotions, and competitors' sales. The data for Example 6.2 was presented in Table 6.3. The Excel® regression software output for Example 6.2 is shown in Table 6.6, where we see that the value of R^2 is $R^2 = 0.833$.

Now let us return to the examination of Table 6.3. In Table 6.3, there are $n = 15$ observed values of the dependent variable Y, which is the sales of Nature-Bar. These observed values are $y_1 = 101.8$, $y_2 = 44.4$, $\ldots$, $y_{15} = 119.6$. These observed values of the dependent variable Y vary from a low of \$44.4 million to a high of \$180.4 million. The observed values exhibit a lot of variation. The linear regression model attempts to **account** for this variation, as much as is possible, by a linear function of the independent variables $x_1, \ldots, x_k$. The value of R^2 is a measure of the extent to which the regression linear equation of the independent variables $x_1, \ldots, x_k$ successfully accounts for the variation in the dependent variable Y. To make this more precise in a mathematical sense, we proceed as follows.

We first define the **total variation** of the observed values of the dependent variable Y:

$$\text{Total Variation } = \sum_{i=1}^{n} (y_i - \bar{y})^2$$

where

$$\bar{y} = \frac{\sum_{i=1}^{n} y_i}{n}.$$

That is, the total variation of the observed values of the dependent variable y is the sum of the squared differences between the observed values y_i of the dependent variable and their observed sample mean $\bar{y}$.

Next, let us measure the extent to which the regression linear equation does **not** account for the observed values $y_1, y_2, \ldots, y_n$. Using the regression coefficients

$b_0, b_1, \ldots, b_k$, recall that the estimate or the predicted values of the dependent variable are:

$$\hat{y}_i = b_0 + b_1 x_{1i} + \ldots + b_k x_{ki}, \quad \text{for} \quad i = 1, \ldots, n.$$

The **residuals** are:

$$e_i = y_i - \hat{y}_i = y_i - b_0 - b_1 x_{1i} - \ldots - b_k x_{ki}, \quad \text{for} \quad i = 1, \ldots, n,$$

and the **residual sum of squares** is:

$$\sum_{i=1}^{n} (e_i)^2 = \sum_{i=1}^{n} (y_i - \hat{y}_i)^2 = \sum_{i=1}^{n} (y_i - b_0 - b_1 x_{1i} - \ldots - b_k x_{ki})^2.$$

The residual sum of squares measures the variation in the observed values of the dependent variable that are **not** accounted for by the linear regression equation.

We now are ready to define R^2:

$$R^2 = 1 - \frac{\text{residual sum of squares}}{\text{total variation}}.$$

Put another way, we have:

$$R^2 = 1 - \frac{\text{residual sum of squares}}{\text{total variation}}.$$
$$= 1 - \frac{\text{variation not accounted for by the independent variables}}{\text{total variation}}$$
$$= \frac{\text{variation accounted for by the independent variables}}{\text{total variation}}$$

Stated yet another way, we have the following interpretation of the R^2:

> R^2 is the proportion of total variation of the observed values of the dependent variable Y that is **accounted for** by the regression equation of the independent variables $x_1, x_2, \ldots, x_k$.

In this way, we see that the R^2 value is always a number between zero and one. Generally speaking, the higher the value of R^2, the better is the regression model. (However, there are exceptions to this rule, as we will see.)

In order to offer more visual intuition regarding the definition and the interpretation of R^2, let us consider a simple linear regression model with one independent variable x that is used to predict the dependent variable Y. Suppose that a scatter-plot of the data for the regression model together with the regression line is as shown in Figure 6.4. Notice that the observed data points lie almost exactly on the regression line in the figure. In this case, the value of R^2 is $R^2 = 0.99$, because the linear function of the independent variable x almost completely accounts for the observed values of the dependent variable Y. Suppose instead that the data and the regression line are as shown in Figure 6.5. In this case, the points lie fairly near the regression line. For this case, the value of R^2 is $R^2 = 0.70$, because the independent variable x accounts for 70% of the observed variation in the dependent variable Y. Finally, suppose that the data and the regression line are as shown in Figure 6.6. In this case, the value of R^2 is $R^2 = 0.00$, because the independent variable does not account for any of the variation in the observed values of the dependent variable Y.

FIGURE 6.4
Scatter-plot and regression line, where $R^2 = 0.99$.

FIGURE 6.5
Scatter-plot and regression line, where $R^2 = 0.70$.

FIGURE 6.6
Scatter-plot and regression line, where $R^2 = 0.00$.

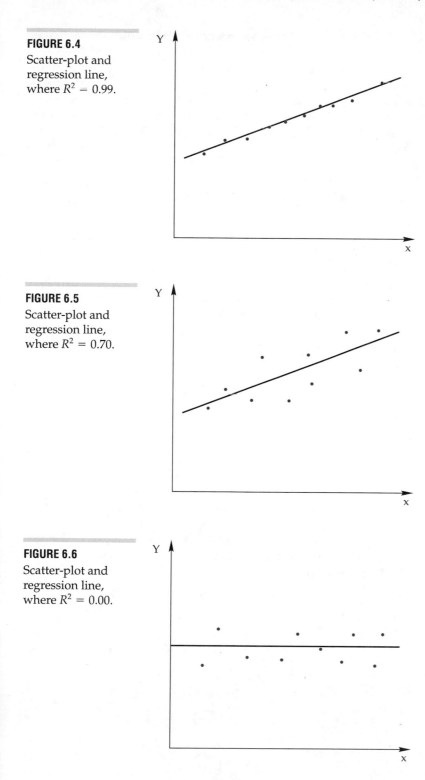

Because R^2 measures the proportion of total variation in the dependent variable Y that has been accounted for by the regression line, we often say that the regression line "accounts for R^2 percent of the variance."

The value of R^2 is frequently used to measure the extent to which the regression model fits the data. However, bear in mind that while a regression model can validate the extent to which the value of one variable can be predicted in terms of the value of another variable, the model cannot, by itself, demonstrate causality between the two variables. For example, consider the fact that in winter months, people use more heating oil, and so sales of heating oil are higher in winter months than in summer months. Also, sales of ski equipment are higher in winter months than in summer months. In fact, if we were to run a linear regression model with sales of ski equipment as the independent variable and sales of heating oil as the dependent variable, the resulting model would be very good, with a high value of R^2. However, we know that sales of ski equipment does not cause people to purchase more home heating oil!

An alternative interpretation of R^2

We now give an alternative interpretation of R^2 that leads to a different kind of insight into its meaning. Given a set of data for linear regression of the form $(x_{1i}, \ldots, x_{ki}$ and $y_i)$ for $i = 1, \ldots, n$, one can imagine at least two linear models based on this data:

Model A: In this model, we suppose that

$$Y = C + \varepsilon_1,$$

where C is a constant and ε_1 obeys a Normal distribution with mean 0 and standard deviation σ_1. This model supposes that the dependent variable Y is actually constant and that the observed variations of the y_i values in the data set are just random "noise" around the true value of C. Pictorially, Model A asserts that the relationship between Y and $x_1, \ldots, x_k$ is a horizontal line, as shown in Figure 6.7.

Model B: $Y = \beta_0 + \beta_1 x_1 + \ldots + \beta_k x_k + \varepsilon$, where the quantities $\beta_0, \beta_1, \ldots, \beta_k$ are constants and ε obeys a Normal distribution with mean 0 and standard deviation σ. Model B is the familiar linear regression model.

The values $b_0, b_1, \ldots, b_k$ of the regression coefficients in a linear regression model are selected so that the residual sum of squares is minimized. The estimate or the predicted values of the dependent variable are:

$$\hat{y}_i = b_0 + b_1 x_{1i} + \ldots + b_k x_{ki} \quad \text{for} \quad i = 1, \ldots, n.$$

FIGURE 6.7

Two alternative models to explain the data.

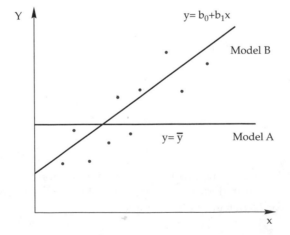

The **residuals** are:

$$e_i = y_i - \hat{y}_i = y_i - b_0 - b_1 x_{1i} - \ldots - b_k x_{ki}, \text{ for } i = 1, \ldots, n,$$

and the **residual sum of squares** under the linear regression model B, denoted by SSR(B), is:

$$\text{SSR}(B) = \sum_{i=1}^{n} (e_i)^2 = \sum_{i=1}^{n} (y_i - \hat{y}_i)^2 = \sum_{i=1}^{n} (y_i - b_0 - b_1 x_{1i} - \ldots - b_k x_{ki})^2.$$

It is easy to show using calculus that the least squares estimate of C in model A is

$$\hat{c} = \bar{y},$$

where $\bar{y}$ is the observed sample mean of $y_1, \ldots, y_n$:

$$\bar{y} = \frac{\sum\limits_{i=1}^{n} y_i}{n}.$$

This formula makes good intuitive sense. If one really believes that the y_i values reflect random scatter about some common value C, it is intuitive to estimate that value by the sample mean of $y_1, \ldots, y_n$. Under Model A, the sum of squared residuals is

$$\text{SSR}(A) = \sum_{i=1}^{n} (y_i - \bar{y})^2.$$

To quantify the improvement of Model B over Model A, we might compare the sum of squared residuals under model A and model B. Then the quantity

$$\frac{\text{SSR}(A) - \text{SSR}(B)}{\text{SSR}(A)} = 1 - \frac{\text{SSR}(B)}{\text{SSR}(A)}$$

is the percentage reduction in the sum of squared residuals when the "best" horizontal line is replaced by the best unrestricted line. The **coefficient of determination** R^2 is defined to be this percentage reduction, namely

$$R^2 = 1 - \frac{\text{SSR}(B)}{\text{SSR}(A)} = 1 - \frac{\sum\limits_{i=1}^{n} (y_i - \hat{y}_i)^2}{\sum\limits_{i=1}^{n} (y_i - \bar{y})^2} .$$

For the regression model of sales of Nature-Bar in Example 6.2, the coefficient of determination is $R^2 = 0.833$. Our interpretation of R^2 is that the sum of squared residuals drops 83% when Y is allowed to depend linearly on $x_1, \ldots, x_k$. From this interpretation of R^2, it follows that R^2 will always be a number between 0.0 and 1.0. If $R^2 = 1.0$, then the regression points lie perfectly along a straight line. If $R^2 = 0.0$, then $SSR(A) = SSR(B)$, and there is no reduction in the sum of residuals if we tilt the horizontal line of Model A.

As mentioned earlier, the value of R^2 is frequently used to measure the extent to which the regression model fits the data. A high R^2 is often interpreted as an indication of an excellent fit. This is not always correct. Consider, for example, the scatter-plot and regression line depicted in Figure 6.8. In this example, the value of R^2 is $R^2 = 0.84$. However, the scatter-plot suggests that the observed values of the dependent variable Y would be better fit by a curve than by a straight line.

FIGURE 6.8
Scatter-plot and
regression line
where $R^2 = 0.84$, but
the data would be
better fit by a curve.

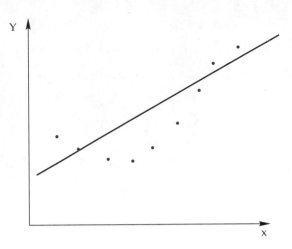

FIGURE 6.9
Scatter-plot and
regression line
where $R^2 = 0.13$, but
a linear model is
appropriate to
describe the fit.

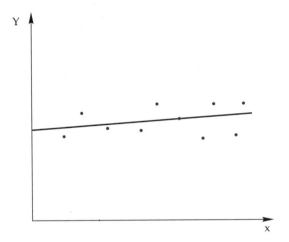

At the same time, a low value of R^2 does not necessarily mean that the regression model lacks credibility. Figure 6.9 shows a regression line with both low values of the sum of squared residuals and very low R^2 ($R^2 = 0.13$). However, intuitively, a linear model fits the data well. The reason is that R^2 is **a relative** and **not an absolute** measure of quality of fit. The improvement in the fit due to a tilted regression line (which is captured in the R^2 value) is very small. In this example, the scatter-plot suggests that the independent variable x seems irrelevant to the observed values of the dependent variable Y, but it does not suggest that a linear regression model is inappropriate.

These last two examples indicate that the value of R^2 can, on occasion, give misleading information about the degree to which the linear regression model is a good fit with the data. However, in general, it is better to have a higher value of R^2 than a lower value of R^2. The determination of what is a "good enough" value of R^2 to accept the linear regression model depends very much on the intended use of the model, as well as on experience and good management sense. For example, in macroeconomic modeling where one attempts to predict, say, growth in GNP as a linear function of other macroeconomic indicators (such as the money supply, the rate of inflation, interest rates, etc.), a value of $R^2 = 0.35$ might be acceptable. In detailed cost modeling where one attempts to predict the cost of producing a complex product as a function of inputs (such as labor hours, management hours, costs of raw materials, etc.), a value of $R^2 = 0.75$ might be unacceptably low. Good judgment in using linear regression and in interpreting the value of R^2 comes with time and experience.

Many users of linear regression tend to become fixated on the value of R^2, but R^2 tells only part of the story in a linear regression model. In Section 6.6, we will develop a number of methods for determining whether a linear regression model is "valid" or not.

Other Regression Output

As Table 6.6 shows, there are many other diagnostic numbers that appear in the computer output of a linear regression model. The interpretation of these other numbers involves statistical concepts that go well beyond the scope of what a manager typically needs to know about linear regression, and so they are not covered in this book.

6.5   SAMPLE CORRELATION AND R^2 IN SIMPLE LINEAR REGRESSION

Recall that the simple linear regression model is:

$$Y = \beta_0 + \beta_1 x + \varepsilon,$$

where ε is a Normally distributed random variable, and the data for the regression are the n ordered pairs (x_1, y_1), (x_2, y_2), . . . , (x_n, y_n) corresponding to the n values of the independent variable $x_1, \ldots, x_n$ and the dependent variable $y_1, \ldots, y_n$. For example, consider the regression model for first-year sales and advertising expenditures of AppleGlo, whose data (x_1, y_1), (x_2, y_2), . . . , (x_n, y_n) were given in Table 6.1. A scatter plot of this data together with the regression line were shown in Figure 6.3. Notice from Figure 6.3 that first-year sales tend to be relatively high when advertising expenditures are relatively high, which suggests that first-year sales are "positively correlated" with advertising expenditures. From the discussion in Section 6.4 on the coefficient of determination R^2, it would seem that the R^2 of this regression ought to correspond to the "correlation" between the variable x (advertising expenditures) and the variable y (first-year sales). In this section we give precise meaning to this intuition.

We start by using several ideas of statistical sampling, as presented in Chapter 4. We can consider the data for our regression model, namely the n ordered pairs (x_1, y_1), (x_2, y_2), . . . , (x_n, y_n), to be sample data. Then, we define the sample means $\bar{x}$ and $\bar{y}$ to be:

$$\bar{x} = \frac{\sum_{i=1}^{n} x_i}{n} \quad \text{and} \quad \bar{y} = \frac{\sum_{i=1}^{n} y_i}{n}.$$

Similarly, we define the sample standard deviations s_x and s_y to be:

$$s_x = \sqrt{\frac{\sum_{i=1}^{n} (x_i - \bar{x})^2}{n - 1}} \quad \text{and} \quad s_y = \sqrt{\frac{\sum_{i=1}^{n} (y_i - \bar{y})^2}{n - 1}}.$$

Then, analogous to the definition of the correlation of two random variables presented in Section 2.9 of Chapter 2, we define the **sample covariance** $\text{cov}(x, y)$ to be:

$$\text{cov}(x, y) = \frac{\sum\limits_{i=1}^{n}(x_i - \bar{x})(y_i - \bar{y})}{n - 1}.$$

We also define the **sample correlation** to be:

$$\text{corr}(x, y) = \frac{\text{cov}(x, y)}{s_x s_y}.$$

Notice the similarity between these formulas and the corresponding formulas for the covariance and correlation of two random variables given in Section 2.9 of Chapter 2.

Let us compute these various quantities for the regression data of first-year sales and advertising expenditures of AppleGlo of Table 6.1. We first compute:

$$\bar{x} = \frac{\sum\limits_{i=1}^{n} x_i}{n} = \frac{1.8 + 1.2 + \ldots + 0.8}{14} = 1.30$$

and

$$\bar{y} = \frac{\sum\limits_{i=1}^{n} y_i}{n} = \frac{104 + 68 + \ldots + 33}{14} = 77.0.$$

We next compute:

$$s_x = \sqrt{\frac{\sum\limits_{i=1}^{n}(x_i - \bar{x})^2}{n - 1}}$$

$$= \sqrt{\frac{(1.8 - 1.30)^2 + (1.2 - 1.30)^2 + \ldots + (0.8 - 1.30)^2}{13}}$$

$$= 0.654$$

and

$$s_y = \sqrt{\frac{\sum\limits_{i=1}^{n}(y_i - \bar{y})^2}{n - 1}}$$

$$= \sqrt{\frac{(104 - 77.0)^2 + (68 - 77.0)^2 + \ldots + (33 - 77.0)^2}{13}}$$

$$= 32.964.$$

Then

$$\text{cov}(x, y) = \frac{\sum_{i=1}^{n} (x_i - \bar{x})(y_i - \bar{y})}{n - 1}$$

$$= \frac{(1.8 - 1.30)(104 - 77.0) + \ldots + (0.8 - 1.30)(33 - 77.0)}{13}$$

$$= 20.785.$$

Therefore

$$\text{corr}(x, y) = \frac{\text{cov}(x, y)}{s_x s_y} = \frac{20.785}{0.654 \times 32.964} = 0.964.$$

Examining Table 6.2, we see that the R^2 for the regression of first-year sales of AppleGlo with advertising expenditures is

$$R^2 = 0.93 = 0.964^2 = (\text{corr}(x, y))^2,$$

and so we see in this example that R^2 is the square of the sample correlation $\text{corr}(x, y)$. This is not a coincidence, and in fact we have the following relationship between the sample correlation and R^2 in simple linear regression:

R^2 is the square of the sample correlation coefficient between the independent variable y and the dependent variable x, that is,

$$R^2 = (\text{corr}(x, y))^2.$$

In other words, the R^2 of a simple linear regression is high only when there is high degree of correlation between the dependent and independent variables. As it turns out, there is another important relationship involving the simple linear regression model and the sample correlation:

The estimate of the slope b_1 in the simple linear regression model $y = b_0 + b_1 x$ can be written as

$$b_1 = \text{corr}(x, y) \times \left(\frac{s_y}{s_x}\right),$$

where s_x and s_y are the sample standard deviations of x and y.

For example, in the regression model for first-year sales of AppleGlo and advertising expenditures, we see from Table 6.2 that $b_1 = 48.60$. Now notice that we also have

$$\text{corr}(x, y) \times \left(\frac{s_y}{s_x}\right) = 0.964 \times \left(\frac{32.964}{0.654}\right) = 48.60 = b_1,$$

which validates the above formula.

6.6 | VALIDATING THE REGRESSION MODEL

In this section, we discuss ways to validate a linear regression model by testing the extent to which the basic assumptions of linear regression are satisfied or not. We will consider four such tests of the assumptions of linear regression:

- Linearity,
- Normality of the $\varepsilon_1, \varepsilon_2, \ldots, \varepsilon_n,$
- Heteroscedasticity, and
- Autocorrelation.

Linearity

Recall that the linear regression model assumes that

$$Y_i = \beta_0 + \beta_1 x_{1i} + \ldots + \beta_k x_{ki} + \varepsilon_i, \quad \text{for} \quad i = 1, \ldots, n,$$

where the values of $\varepsilon_1, \varepsilon_2, \ldots, \varepsilon_n$ are the "noise" or "unaccounted differences." The estimated values of $\beta_0, \beta_1, \ldots, \beta_k$ are the regression coefficients $b_0, b_1, \ldots, b_k$.

The key assumption of **linearity** is that the dependent variable Y depends linearly on the values of the independent variables $x_1, x_2, \ldots, x_k$. When $k = 1$, that is, when there is only one independent variable, one can construct a scatter-plot of the observation data to check visually whether or not there is a linear relationship between the dependent variable Y and the independent variable x.

When the number of independent variables k is large, a scatter-plot cannot be constructed to perform a check of the assumption of linearity. In this case, one has to rely on common sense and good judgment as to whether a linear relationship between the dependent variable and the independent variables is an appropriate assumption to make. One can perform the regression and check the value of R^2. A very high value of R^2 will usually indicate that the linearity assumption is appropriate. But, as discussed in Section 6.4, there are exceptions to this general rule.

Normality of $\varepsilon_1, \varepsilon_2, \ldots, \varepsilon_n$

The linear regression model assumes that

$$Y_i = \beta_0 + \beta_1 x_{1i} + \ldots + \beta_k x_{ki} + \varepsilon_i, \quad \text{for} \quad i = 1, \ldots, n,$$

where the values of $\varepsilon_1, \varepsilon_2, \ldots, \varepsilon_n$ are assumed to obey a Normal distribution with mean $\mu = 0$ and some standard deviation σ. One way to test the assumption of Normality of the $\varepsilon_1, \varepsilon_2, \ldots, \varepsilon_n$ is to plot a histogram of the regression residuals

$$e_i = y_i - \hat{y}_i = y_i - b_0 - b_1 x_{1i} - \ldots - b_k x_{ki}, \quad \text{for} \quad i = 1, \ldots, n.$$

If the histogram appears to have a bell-shape as in the Normal distribution, then the Normality assumption is probably satisfied.

For example, consider the regression model used to predict sales of Nature-Bar in Example 6.2. The Microsoft Excel® spreadsheet output of this regression was presented in Table 6.6. The regression residuals are automatically computed as part of the Microsoft Excel® in the lower left corner of the spreadsheet output of the regression. In the Nature-Bar example, the residuals for each of the 15 observations appear in cells C26:C41 of the spreadsheet output in Table 6.6. Thus for example, the residual for the first observation is -2.02, which is seen to be:

$$e_1 = y_1 - \hat{y}_1 = y_1 - b_0 - b_1 \times (1.3) - b_2 \times (0.2) - b_3 \times (20.40)$$
$$= 101.8 - 65.705 - 48.979 \times (1.3) - 59.654 \times (0.2) - (-1.838) \times (20.40)$$
$$= -2.02.$$

A plot of the histogram of these residuals is shown in Figure 6.10. This histogram appears to be fairly bell-shaped, and so the Normality assumption does not appear to be violated.

(There are sophisticated statistical tests that can be used to check mathematically whether or not the residuals are approximately Normally distributed. These tests are beyond the scope of this book. For our purposes, it will suffice to perform a visual check of the histogram of the residuals.)

Heteroscedasticity

Recall that the linear regression model assumes that

$$Y_i = \beta_0 + \beta_1 x_{1i} + \ldots + \beta_k x_{ki} + \varepsilon_i, \quad \text{for} \quad i = 1, \ldots, n,$$

where the values of $\varepsilon_1, \varepsilon_2, \ldots, \varepsilon_n$ are the "noise" or "unaccounted differences," and where $\varepsilon_1, \varepsilon_2, \ldots, \varepsilon_n$ are assumed to be observed values of independent Normally distributed random variables with mean $\mu = 0$ and some standard deviation σ. One of the key aspects of this assumption is that the different values $\varepsilon_1, \varepsilon_2, \ldots, \varepsilon_n$ are drawn from distributions with the **same** standard deviation σ. This property is called **homoscedasticity**. Consider the regression line portrayed in Figure 6.11. In Figure 6.11, the regression residuals (which are the vertical distances from the points to the regression line) appear to have the same standard deviation. Now consider the regression line portrayed in Figure 6.12. In this regression line, the regression residuals appear to be getting larger with larger values of the independent variable x. This is referred to as **heteroscedasticity** and is a violation of the assumption that the $\varepsilon_1, \varepsilon_2, \ldots, \varepsilon_n$ are drawn from distributions with the **same** standard deviation σ.

One can test for heteroscedasticity by plotting the regression residuals with the observations of each of the independent variables and visually checking that the regression residuals have no pattern as a function of the value of each of the independent variables. For example, Figures 6.13, 6.14, and 6.15 are scatter-plots of the regression residuals for the regression model of the prediction sales of Nature-Bar in

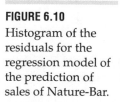

FIGURE 6.10

Histogram of the residuals for the regression model of the prediction of sales of Nature-Bar.

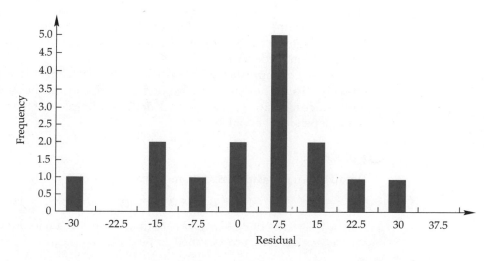

FIGURE 6.11

A regression line
where the residuals
are not influenced
by the value of
independent
variable x.

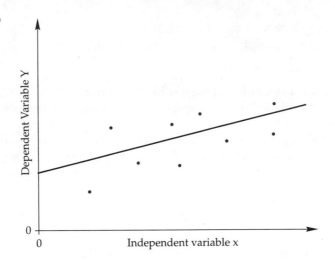

FIGURE 6.12

A regression line
where the residuals
are influenced
by the value of
independent
variable x.

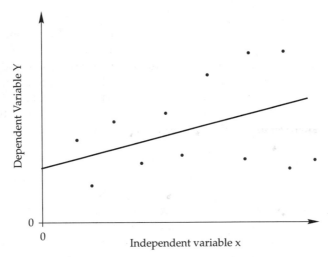

Example 6.2 for each of the three independent variables of the regression model (namely, advertising (x_1), promotions (x_2), and competitors' sales (x_3). In Figure 6.13 and Figure 6.15, there does not appear to be any pattern of change in the residuals as a function of the advertising (Figure 6.13) or of competitors' sales (Figure 6.15). In Figure 6.14, there appears to be some sort of pattern, but it is probably not enough to cause too much concern.

There are sophisticated statistical tests that can be used to check for heteroscedasticity. These tests are beyond the scope of this book. For our purposes, it will suffice to perform a visual check of the scatter-plots of the residuals with each of the independent variables.

Autocorrelation

Recall that the linear regression model assumes that

$$Y_i = \beta_0 + \beta_1 x_{1i} + \ldots + \beta_k x_{ki} + \varepsilon_i, \text{ for } i = 1, \ldots, n,$$

where the values of $\varepsilon_1, \varepsilon_2, \ldots, \varepsilon_n$ are the "noise" or "unaccounted differences," and where $\varepsilon_1, \varepsilon_2, \ldots, \varepsilon_n$ are assumed to be observed values of independent Normally

FIGURE 6.13
Scatter-plot of
regression residuals
with advertising (x_1)
for the regression
model of the
prediction of sales of
Nature-Bar.

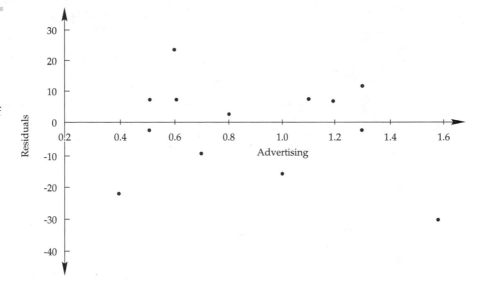

FIGURE 6.13
Scatter-plot of
regression residuals
with advertising (x_1)
for the regression
model of the
prediction of sales of
Nature-Bar.

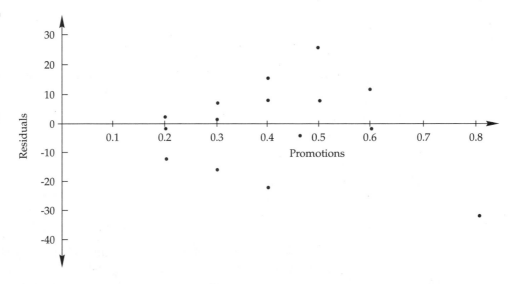

FIGURE 6.14
Scatter-plot of
regression residuals
with promotions (x_2)
for the regression
model of the
prediction of sales of
Nature-Bar.

distributed random variables with mean $\mu = 0$ and some standard deviation σ. The phenomenon of **autocorrelation** can occur if the assumption of the independence of $\varepsilon_1, \varepsilon_2, \ldots, \varepsilon_n$ is violated.

Suppose that we have a regression model for some data that is specified with a time component. (For example, we might have data on sales of our product for each of the last fourteen months.) Suppose that a plot of the residuals of the regression model in time order of the observations is as shown in Figure 6.16. Notice in Figure 6.16 that the residuals exhibit a pattern over the time order of the observations. That is, the values of the regression residuals are not independent. This is probably evidence that the values of $\varepsilon_1, \varepsilon_2, \ldots, \varepsilon_n$ are not independent. The phenomenon whereby the $\varepsilon_1, \varepsilon_2, \ldots, \varepsilon_n$ are not independent is referred to as **autocorrelation.**

Let us re-examine the regression model of the prediction of first-year sales of AppleGlo of Example 6.1. Recall from Table 6.1 that there is a time order for the introduction of AppleGlo in each sales region, and so it is therefore wise to test for

FIGURE 6.15

Scatter-plot of regression residuals with competitors' sales (x_3) for the regression model of the prediction of sales of Nature-Bar.

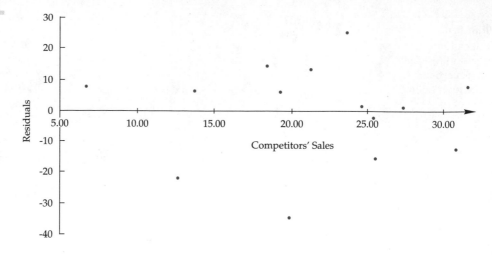

FIGURE 6.16

Scatter-plot of regression residuals in observation order, showing evidence of autocorrelation.

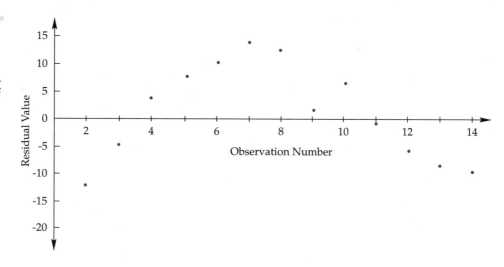

autocorrelation in this regression model. Figure 6.17 shows a plot of the regression residuals (in time order) for the regression model of the prediction of first-year sales of AppleGlo. Figure 6.17 indicates that there is no apparent pattern among the residuals over time, and so there is no evidence of autocorrelation in this regression model.

There are sophisticated statistical tests that can be used to check for autocorrelation. These tests are beyond the scope of this book. For our purposes, it will suffice to perform a visual check of the scatter-plots of the residuals in time order to check for any evidence of a pattern. If there is such a pattern, then there is evidence of autocorrelation. Typically, if there is evidence of autocorrelation, it can be eliminated by incorporating time as one of the independent variables.

Checking for Autocorrelation using Microsoft Excel®

As was discussed previously, we can check for the presence of autocorrelation in a regression model by plotting the regression residuals over time with the goal of finding a pattern in the plot. It is very easy to create such a plot in the Microsoft Excel® spreadsheet software, as follows:

FIGURE 6.17

Scatter-plot of regression residuals (in time order) for the regression model of the first-year sales of AppleGlo of Example 6.1, which shows no evidence of autocorrelation.

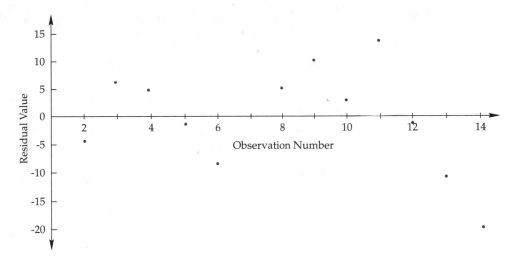

1. Locate the "Residuals" column in the "RESIDUAL OUTPUT" table in your regression output spreadsheet. The "RESIDUAL OUTPUT" table is the bottom-most table in the regression output spreadsheet and the "Residuals" column is the right-most column in this table. For example, as is shown in Table 6.2, the "Residuals" column in the regression output for the regression model of the first-year sales of AppleGlo is located in cells C24:C38 of the regression output spreadsheet.

2. Go to the toolbar and click on the **Chart Wizard** toolbar button. Select **Line Chart** from among Chart type options and then select the sub-type in the second row on the left-hand side, which shows two lines with data marks. Click on **Next >**.

3. Place the cursor in the "Data Range" area and select the cells in the "Residuals" column of the regression output spreadsheet, including the label "Residuals." For example, for the regression output for the regression model of first-year sales of AppleGlo shown in Table 6.2, we would select cells C24:C38 of the regression output spreadsheet. Make sure that the **Series in Columns** button is selected. Click on **Next >**.

4. Click on **Finish**.

6.7 | WARNINGS AND ISSUES IN LINEAR REGRESSION MODELING

In this section, we discuss some further issues that can arise during the linear regression modeling process.

Overspecification by the Addition of Too Many Independent Variables

In the process of developing a regression model, it is tempting to add as many independent variables as possible. The reasoning behind this is that one never knows what might increase the R^2 of the model, and the dictum that "more is better than less" is a tempting strategy.

As it turns out, it is true that the addition of more and more independent variables cannot decrease the R^2 of the model and, in most cases, will at least marginally increase the R^2 of the model. However, this is a dangerous strategy to employ for a number of reasons. First of all, the better regression models are those that make good intuitive sense, and so one should only add additional independent variables if it is sensible to do so. Second, as we have seen in this chapter, a regression model is itself a sophisticated mathematical tool, and such tools are best managed and used when they are kept as simple as possible. For this reason, the better regression models are those that use as few independent variables as possible, and so they are as simple as possible. There is also a third reason not to add too many independent variables to a regression model that has to do with the phenomenon of "multicollinearity," which will be covered shortly.

Extrapolating beyond the Range of the Data

Recall that in Example 6.2 that the regression equation for predicting sales of Nature-Bar is:

$$y = b_0 + b_1 x_1 + b_2 x_2 + b_3 x_3 = 65.705 + 48.979 x_1 + 59.654 x_2 - 1.838 x_3,$$

where x_1 is advertising expenditures (in \$ million), x_2 is promotional expenditures (in \$ million), and x_3 is competitors' sales (in \$ million). This regression equation was developed based on the data for Example 6.2 in Table 6.3. The regression equation indicates, for example, that the incremental sales of Nature-Bar for a \$1 million increase in advertising expenditures is \$48.979 million. Notice from Table 6.3 that all of the advertising expenditures for the regions in the table are between \$0.4 million and \$1.9 million. The regression model is valid in this range of the data. However, it would be unwise to use the model to predict sales if CKC were thinking of a gigantic advertising campaign of, say, \$10 million in a particular region, because the regression model is not based on any data in that range.

In general, it is wise to only use the regression equation to predict values of the dependent variable in the range of the independent variables that were used in the data that created the model in the first place. Outside of this range, the predictive power of the model might not be as good.

Multicollinearity

Table 6.7 shows the undergraduate grade point average (GPA), GMAT score, and graduate school GPA for 25 MBA students. Suppose we would like to predict graduate school GPA based on undergraduate GPA and GMAT scores for prospective students. Table 6.8 shows the key components of the output of a linear regression used to predict graduate school GPA, using the data in Table 6.7. Reading off the the regression coefficients from Table 6.8, we see that the regression equation is:

Graduate School GPA = 0.09540 + 1.12870 × (College GPA) − 0.00088 × (GMAT).

At first glance, this regression equation seems to not make good sense, since we would expect that the regression coefficient for the GMAT score variable should be a positive number, whereas it is −0.00088. However, according to the output information in Table 6.8, the R^2 for this regression model turns out to be $R^2 = 0.960$, which is extremely high, and so indicates that the overall regression model is an extremely good fit with the data.

To better understand and assess this regression model, let us perform a significance test on the regression coefficient for the GMAT score. We first compute the t-statistic for the regression coefficient for the GMAT score variable, which is

TABLE 6.7

Undergraduate GPA, GMAT, and graduate school GPA for 25 MBA students.

	A	B	C	D
1	Student Number	Undergraduate GPA	GMAT	Graduate School GPA
2	1	3.9	640	4.0
3	2	3.9	644	4.0
4	3	3.1	557	3.1
5	4	3.2	550	3.1
6	5	3.0	547	3.0
7	6	3.5	589	3.5
8	7	3.0	533	3.1
9	8	3.5	600	3.5
10	9	3.2	630	3.1
11	10	3.2	548	3.2
12	11	3.2	600	3.8
13	12	3.7	633	4.1
14	13	3.9	546	2.9
15	14	3.0	602	3.7
16	15	3.7	614	3.8
17	16	3.8	644	3.9
18	17	3.9	634	3.6
19	18	3.7	572	3.1
20	19	3.0	570	3.3
21	20	3.2	656	4.0
22	21	3.9	574	3.1
23	22	3.1	636	3.7
24	23	3.7	635	3.7
25	24	4.0	654	3.9
26	25	3.8	633	3.8

TABLE 6.8

Key ingredients of the regression output for the prediction of graduate school GPA based on undergraduate GPA and GMAT scores.

R Square	0.960	
Standard Error	0.080	
Observations	25	

	Coefficients	Standard Error
Intercept	0.09540	0.28451
Undergraduate GPA	1.12870	0.10233
GMAT	−0.00088	0.00092

$$\bar{t} = \frac{b_2}{s_{b_2}} = \frac{-0.00088}{0.00092} = -0.95.$$

Next, we compute the c value for the significance test with $dof = 25 - 2 - 1 = 22$ at the 95% confidence level. According to the t-table shown in Table A.2 of the Appendix, $c = 2.074$. Then noting that $|\bar{t}| = |-0.95| < 2.074 = c$, the coefficient -0.00088 fails the significance test, and so we cannot be confident (at the 95% level) that the coefficient on the GMAT score variable is not zero. This is a bit reassuring, since it is completely against intuition that this coefficient would be negative. However, intuition is still unsatisfied because common sense indicates that we should expect the GMAT score to be a positive predictor of graduate school GPA.

To resolve this paradox, first notice that one problem with this regression model is that the two independent variables (undergraduate GPA and GMAT score) are highly correlated. Using the formulas for the sample correlation given in Section 6.5, we can compute the sample correlation for the 25 undergraduate GPA and GMAT scores shown in Table 6.7, and we find that the sample correlation of these 25 under-graduate GPA and GMAT scores is 0.895. This indicates that the 25 undergraduate GPA and GMAT scores shown in Table 6.7 are very highly correlated. The regression model, in a sense, gets confused as to what extent each of these independent variables is actually contributing to the predicted graduate school GPA. And in minimizing the residual sum of squares, the model has found that it can actually reduce the residual sum of squares by making the regression coefficient for GMAT scores slightly negative.

Let us see what happens if we eliminate the GMAT score independent variable from the model. Table 6.9 shows the key components of the output of a linear regression used to predict graduate school GPA using the undergraduate GPA score as the one and only independent variable. Reading off the the regression coefficients from Table 6.9, we see that the regression equation is:

$$\text{Graduate School GPA} = -0.1287 + 1.0413 \times (\text{Undergraduate GPA}).$$

According to the regression output in Table 6.9, the R^2 of this regression model is $R^2 = 0.958$, which is ever-so-slightly smaller than the previous value of $R^2 = 0.960$, and is still extremely high. Let us perform a significance test on the regression coefficient for the GMAT score. We first compute the t-statistic for the regression coefficient for the Undergraduate GPA score variable, which is

$$\bar{t} = \frac{b_1}{s_{b_1}} = \frac{1.0413}{0.0455} = 22.89.$$

Next, we compute the c value for the significance test with $dof = 25 - 1 - 1 = 23$ at the 95% confidence level. According to the t-table shown in Table A.2 of the Appendix, $c = 2.069$. Then noting that $|\bar{t}| = |22.89| > 2.069 = c$, the coefficient 1.0413 passes the significance test, indicating a valid regression model overall.

The phenomenon whereby two independent variables are highly correlated is called **multicollinearity.** One should suspect the presence of multicollinearity in a given regression model when the model has a high R^2, but when one or more of the t-statistics is lower than the value of c for the significance test. When this happens, it is wise to check for multicollinearity between some pair of independent variables. This can be done by first using intuition to sense whether any pair of the independent variables might be highly correlated. Second, the sample correlation of any suspected pairs of independent random variables can be computed using the formulas developed in Section 6.5. If any of the sample correlation values are highly positive (say, greater than 0.70) or highly negative (say, smaller than -0.70), then there is probably evidence of multicollinearity. The multicollinearity problem can usually be eliminated by removing one of the independent variables in question from the set of independent variables.

TABLE 6.9

Key ingredients of the regression output for the prediction of graduate school GPA based only on undergraduate GPA.

	R Square	0.958	
	Standard Error	0.080	
	Observations	25	
		Coefficients	*Standard Error*
Intercept		−0.1287	0.1604
Undergraduate GPA		1.0413	0.0455

TABLE 6.10

Microsoft Excel®
output of the sample
correlation values
for the data for
Nature-Bar shown in
Table 6.5.

	A	B	C	D
1		Advertising	Promotions	Competitors
2	Advertising	1		
3	Promotions	0.1613	1	
4	Competitors	-0.2131	-0.4939	1

Checking for Multicollinearity using Microsoft Excel®

As mentioned above, the presence of multicollinearity can be detected by computing the sample correlations among pairs of independent variables. The computation of these sample correlation values can be done conveniently in Microsoft Excel® as follows:

1. Go to **Tools** in the pull-down menu and click on **Data Analysis.** Then select **Correlation** from among the list of tools.

2. Under **Input range**, click the button to the right of **Input range** and highlight all cells corresponding to the independent variables and their data values, including the descriptive labels in the row above where the data is presented. For example, for the sample data for Nature-Bar shown in Table 6.5, the relevant range of cells is cells C1:E16.

3. In the boxes below, check off **Labels in First Row** and make sure that the button for **Columns** is selected.

4. Under **Output Options**, choose **New Worksheet Ply**.

5. Click on **OK**.

6. The sample correlations will appear in a table on the new worksheet in the lower left portion of the table. For example, for the sample data for Nature-Bar shown in Table 6.5, the sample correlation table is as shown in Table 6.10. According to this table, the sample correlation of the data for Advertising and Competitors is −0.2131, for example.

6.8 REGRESSION MODELING TECHNIQUES

In this section, we discuss three advanced regression modeling techniques, namely the use of nonlinear relationships, the use of so-called "dummy variables," and the process of stepwise multiple regression.

Nonlinear Relationships

Table 6.11 shows weekly sales data for the first week of March of last year for 26 convenience stores owned and operated by a large chain of convenience stores. The second column of the table shows the weekly sales of each store, and the third column of the table shows the population within one mile of the store, estimated using publicly available census data. The fourth column converts the weekly sales data into a number representing sales per population unit, which we will call the "sales density" of the store. For example, for the first store, the weekly sales were $36,080. With a

TABLE 6.11

Sales data for 26 convenience stores.

Store Number	Weekly Sales ($)	Population within one mile of store	Sales Density (Sales/ Population) ($/person)	Median Income in Vicinity of Store ($)
1	36,080	8,000	4.51	27,000
2	20,700	10,000	2.07	21,000
3	51,030	9,000	5.67	33,000
4	34,260	6,000	5.71	42,000
5	22,520	4,000	5.63	36,000
6	32,060	7,000	4.58	29,000
7	28,700	5,000	5.74	35,000
8	47,080	11,000	4.28	26,000
9	16,660	7,000	2.38	21,000
10	11,280	8,000	1.41	19,000
11	53,280	9,000	5.92	38,000
12	17,950	5,000	3.59	24,000
13	38,000	8,000	4.75	29,000
14	53,460	9,000	5.94	37,000
15	53,730	9,000	5.97	41,000
16	6,300	6,000	1.05	18,000
17	11,560	4,000	2.89	23,000
18	42,280	7,000	6.04	40,000
19	25,200	5,000	5.04	32,000
20	57,700	10,000	5.77	35,000
21	25,800	6,000	4.30	27,000
22	46,640	8,000	5.83	36,000
23	44,640	9,000	4.96	30,000
24	12,000	5,000	2.40	21,000
25	18,160	4,000	4.54	28,000
26	28,860	6,000	4.81	29,000

population of 8,000 people living within one mile of the store, this translates into a sales density of $4.51 = 36,080/8,000$, which is a sales density of $4.51 per person. The fifth column shows the median income of persons living in the vicinity of the convenience store, which has been estimated again using publicly available census data. For the first convenience store, for example, the median income in the vicinity of the store is estimated to be $27,000 per year.

Suppose that we would like to predict the sales density (column 4 of Table 6.11) for new stores, based on the median income in the vicinity of the stores (column 5 of Table 6.11). In order to understand how median income affects sales density, we might start by looking at a scatter-plot of the numbers in the fourth column (sales density) and the fifth column of Table 6.11. Such a scatter-plot is shown in Figure 6.18.

Notice from Figure 6.18 that the data suggests that the sales density of convenience stores is definitely related to the median income, but not in a linear fashion. In fact, it looks like some other type of curve might provide the best fit to the points shown in Figure 6.18. We might therefore suppose that the relationship between sales density and median income is a regression equation of the following form:

$$\text{Sales Density} = \beta_0 + \beta_1 \times (\text{Median Income}) + \beta_2 \times (\text{Median Income})^2.$$

Notice that this regression equation is not a linear function of the independent variable since, in particular, the independent variable is squared. It would seem, therefore, that we cannot use linear regression software to develop the regression equation. However, we can overcome this problem by creating an extra independent variable called "Median Income Squared." Table 6.12 presents the identical

FIGURE 6.18

Scatter-plot of the median income and the sales density of the 26 convenience stores' data from Table 6.11.

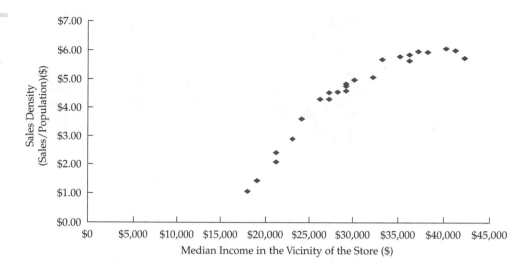

TABLE 6.12

Sales data for 26 convenience stores including the extra column for "median income squared."

Store Number	Weekly Sales ($)	Population within one mile of store	Sales Density (Sales/ Population) ($/person)	Median Income in Vicinity of Store ($)	Median Income Squared ($²)
1	36,080	8,000	4.51	27,000	729,000,000
2	20,700	10,000	2.07	21,000	441,000,000
3	51,030	9,000	5.67	33,000	1,089,000,000
4	34,260	6,000	5.71	42,000	1,764,000,000
5	22,520	4,000	5.63	36,000	1,296,000,000
6	32,060	7,000	4.58	29,000	841,000,000
7	28,700	5,000	5.74	35,000	1,225,000,000
8	47,080	11,000	4.28	26,000	676,000,000
9	16,660	7,000	2.38	21,000	441,000,000
10	11,280	8,000	1.41	19,000	361,000,000
11	53,280	9,000	5.92	38,000	1,444,000,000
12	17,950	5,000	3.59	24,000	576,000,000
13	38,000	8,000	4.75	29,000	841,000,000
14	53,460	9,000	5.94	37,000	1,369,000,000
15	53,730	9,000	5.97	41,000	1,681,000,000
16	6,300	6,000	1.05	18,000	324,000,000
17	11,560	4,000	2.89	23,000	529,000,000
18	42,280	7,000	6.04	40,000	1,600,000,000
19	25,200	5,000	5.04	32,000	1,024,000,000
20	57,700	10,000	5.77	35,000	1,225,000,000
21	25,800	6,000	4.30	27,000	729,000,000
22	46,640	8,000	5.83	36,000	1,296,000,000
23	44,640	9,000	4.96	30,000	900,000,000
24	12,000	5,000	2.40	21,000	441,000,000
25	18,160	4,000	4.54	28,000	784,000,000
26	28,860	6,000	4.81	29,000	841,000,000

data as was shown in Table 6.11, with the addition of a sixth column that contains the squares of the entries in the fifth column. For example, for store number 1, the median income number is $27,000, and so the entry in the sixth column is $27,000 \times 27,000 = 729,000,000$. Using data from this table, our regression equation would be written as:

$$\text{Sales Density} = \beta_0 + \beta_1 \times (\text{Median Income}) + \beta_2 \times (\text{Median Income Squared}).$$

TABLE 6.13

Key ingredients of the regression output for the prediction of sales density based median income.

R Square	0.991	
Standard Error	0.148	
Observations	26	

	Coefficients	Standard Error
Intercept	−10.860	0.550
Median Income	0.000857	0.0000380
Median Income Squared	−0.0000000109	0.00000000063

Now notice that this equation is linear in all of the independent variables, and so we can perform linear regression. Table 6.13 shows the key ingredients of the regression output from this regression. Note in particular in Table 6.13 that $R^2 = 0.99$, and so this nonlinear model is an excellent fit to the convenience store data in Table 6.12.

This example illustrates that while a linear regression might not be appropriate for some data, a nonlinear transformation of the data might work quite well. A variety of nonlinear relationships can be converted to linear relationships in the manner illustrated here, including the use of quadratic terms, logarithmic terms, etc. Furthermore, the conversion process illustrated here can be very effective in creating a regression model that is a good fit with the observed data.

However, there is a drawback in using nonlinear relationships in a regression model. Notice that each time a nonlinear relationship is added to a regression model, the number of independent variables increases by one, and so the model becomes larger, in which case it might be more difficult to gain intuition about the output of the regression model.

The Use of "Dummy Variables"

There are many instances when we would like to use linear regression to predict the effect that a particular phenomenon has on the value of the dependent variable, where the phenomenon in question either takes place or not. For example, we might be interested in predicting annual repair costs of a particular automobile model based on the age of the vehicle and whether or not the vehicle is equipped with an automatic transmission.

Table 6.14 shows the annual repair costs of 19 vehicles of the same automobile model (Column 4 of the table), as well as information on the age of the vehicle (Column 2) and whether or not the vehicle has an automatic transmission (Column 3). In Column 3, note that we use a "1" to denote that the vehicle has an automatic transmission, and we use a "0" to denote that the vehicle does not have an automatic transmission.

We can postulate a regression model equation, based on the data in Table 6.14, of the following form:

$$\text{Repair Cost} = \beta_0 + \beta_1 x_1 + \beta_2 x_2 + \varepsilon,$$

where x_1 is the independent variable for the age of the vehicle, and x_2 has value $x_2 = 1$ or $x_2 = 0$ depending on whether or not the vehicle has an automatic transmission or not. (And, as usual, ε is assumed to be a Normally distributed random variable with mean $\mu = 0$ and standard deviation σ.) The independent variable x_2 is called a **dummy variable**. Regression calculations involving dummy variables are exactly the same as in the usual linear regression model. The only difference is that the corresponding independent variables only take on the values of 0 or 1.

Table 6.15 shows the key ingredients in the regression output from the regression model just developed. According to Table 6.15, the regression equation turns out to be:

$$\text{Repair Cost} = 288.133 + 160.730 \times x_1 + 176.964 \times x_2.$$

TABLE 6.14

Annual repair costs for 19 vehicles at an automobile dealership.

Vehicle	Age of Vehicle (years)	Automatic Transmission (Yes=1, No=0)	Annual Repair Costs ($)
1	3	1	956
2	4	0	839
3	6	0	1,257
4	5	1	1,225
5	4	1	1,288
6	2	1	728
7	4	0	961
8	8	1	1,588
9	7	0	1,524
10	4	0	875
11	3	1	999
12	5	1	1,295
13	3	0	884
14	2	1	789
15	4	0	785
16	3	1	923
17	4	1	1,223
18	9	0	1,770
19	2	1	692

TABLE 6.15

Key ingredients of the regression output for the prediction of automobile repair costs.

R Square	0.913	
Standard Error	97.077	
Observations	19	

	Coefficients	Standard Error
Intercept	288.133	72.332
Age of Vehicle	160.730	12.424
Automatic Transmission	176.964	48.335

Thus, if we want to predict the annual repair cost of a vehicle of this model that is 7 years old and that has an automatic transmission, we would estimate the annual repair cost to be:

$$\$1{,}590.21 = 288.133 + 160.730 \times (7) + 176.964 \times (1).$$

If, on the other hand, this same vehicle did not have an automatic transmission, then we would estimate its annual repair cost to be:

$$\$1{,}413.24 = 288.133 + 160.730 \times (7) + 176.964 \times (0).$$

In particular, we see that we can interpret the regression coefficient on the dummy variable, which is $176.964, as the estimate of the additional annual repair cost due to the vehicle being equipped with an automatic transmission.

Stepwise Multiple Regression

In many settings involving prediction using linear regression, there may be many possible choices of independent variables. For example, in predicting the earnings of a large company, one can choose such independent variables as national economic indicators (GNP growth rate, inflation rate, the prime lending rate, etc.); industry-specific independent variables, such as price-to-earnings ratios in the industry, performance of competitors, etc.; as well as company-specific independent variables such as costs of production, investment in new product research, advertising and marketing expenditures, etc.

However, in order to avoid problems with multicollinearity when developing a multiple linear regression model, it is best to employ as few independent variables as possible. A general rule of thumb is the following:

The number of independent variables k and the number of data observations n should satisfy the relationship:

$$n \geq 5(k + 2).$$

This raises the problem of which subset of all possible independent variables should be chosen to arrive at the "best" regression model for the prediction problem at hand.

Stepwise multiple regression is one procedure commonly used to address this problem. Suppose we are considering a large group of possible independent variables $x_1, \ldots, x_k$, where k is a large number, to predict the value of the independent variable Y. In a stepwise multiple regression, the regression equation is constructed one variable at a time. First, the equation

$$\hat{y} = b_0 + b_i x_i$$

is constructed using the independent variable x_i that is most highly correlated with Y. Then a new variable is brought into the equation to produce

$$\hat{y} = b_0 + b_i x_i + b_j x_j,$$

where x_j is the variable that does the best job of predicting the variation in Y that has not already been predicted by x_i. That is, x_j is the variable that does the best job in eliminating the prediction errors that were present using the first equation. It should be noted that the b_0 and b_i values of the second regression might be somewhat different than the values obtained in the first regression.

This process of adding variables one at a time, in the manner just described, is usually continued until the modeler feels that there are enough variables in the regression equation, or until the R^2 value is sufficiently high for the intended use of the regression model.

6.9 | ILLUSTRATION OF THE REGRESSION MODELING PROCESS

In this section, we present an example of the regression modeling process. Our objective is to illustrate the iterative process of regression analysis during which we run different regression models, analyze regression output, and eventually arrive at a sound regression model that has good predictive capability.

Example 6.3—Compensation at CERNA, Inc.

George Steinbrock is a compensation consultant who advises firms on issues involving salaries and executive compensation for companies. George has recently been hired by CERNA, Inc., an American subsidiary of a large Asia-based insurance company. CERNA has recently lost a disturbingly large number of middle-level managers to its competitors, and management at CERNA wants to determine if compensation is one of the reasons why employees are leaving CERNA. Moreover, in light of a recent lawsuit at another Asia-based insurance company in the United States alleging that Asian managers have received higher compensation than their American counterparts (with comparable qualifications), there has been widespread concern among managers at CERNA that there might be such a bias at CERNA as well.

George collected salary and related data from a sample of 110 middle-level managers at CERNA. This data is presented in the spreadsheet CERNA.xls, and a summary of the first few rows and last few rows of this spreadsheet is shown in Table 6.16. The second column of Table 6.16 shows the salaries of the 110 managers in the sample. The third column contains information on the nationality of the 110 managers in the sample, where a "1" indicates non-Asian and a "0" indicates Asian. The fourth column of Table 6.16 contains the undergraduate grade-point-average (GPA) of these managers, and the fifth column of the table contains information on whether or not the manager has a post-graduate degree (master's degree or higher), where a "1" indicates a post-graduate degree and a "0" indicates only an undergraduate degree. The sixth column of Table 6.16 contains the years of experience that each of the managers has at CERNA. All of the information in Table 6.16 was provided to George (in a confidential format) by the personnel office at CERNA based on CERNA's employee information records.

The data in Table 6.16 was chosen by George for his analysis for several reasons. First of all, the data was available to him, as CERNA keeps such information in its employees' personnel files. Second, George wanted to try to predict salaries at CERNA based on some notion of experience (captured, albeit imperfectly, by the number of years at CERNA) and innate intellectual talent for the job (captured, hopefully, by a combination of undergraduate GPA scores and by a dummy variable for a post-graduate degree). Also, George wanted to test the notion that non-Asian employees might receive lower compensation than their Asian counterparts.

TABLE 6.16

The first few rows and last few rows of the spreadsheet data on salary and related information for 110 employees at CERNA.

Employee Number	Salary ($)	Non-Asian Dummy Variable	Undergraduate GPA	Graduate Degree Dummy Variable	Years of Experience
1	99,026	0	3.36	0	15
2	69,190	1	2.35	1	9
3	95,453	1	3.33	1	10
4	57,695	1	3.37	0	2
5	94,364	1	3.87	1	4
⋮	⋮	⋮	⋮	⋮	⋮
96	86,678	1	3.21	1	8
97	91,450	0	2.56	1	17
98	84,344	1	2.93	1	8
99	70,499	1	2.66	1	8
100	82,779	1	2.79	1	8
101	74,406	1	2.91	0	5
102	64,526	0	2.32	0	10
103	47,487	1	2.31	0	2
104	105,698	0	3.56	1	14
105	55,173	0	2.01	1	4
106	80,765	1	3.12	1	2
107	77,081	0	3.36	0	5
108	60,024	0	2.51	1	3
109	71,606	1	2.89	0	8
110	108,625	1	3.85	1	7

George next prepared to run a linear regression model based on the data in the spreadsheet. The independent variables that he used in his model are as follows:

- **Non-Asian**: a dummy variable that has a value of "1" if the employee's nationality is non-Asian and has a value of "0" if the employee's nationality is Asian.

- **GPA**: the undergraduate GPA of the employee.

- **Graduate Degree**: a dummy variable that has a value of "1" if the employee has a post-graduate degree and has a value of "0" if the employee only has an undergraduate degree.

- **Experience**: the number of years that the employee has worked at CERNA.

Rather than run his regression model using the sample data from all 110 employees in the sample, George decided instead to run the regression on the first 102 employees in the sample, and then to use the results to see if the salary predicted by the model for the remaining 8 employees would be in good agreement with the actual salaries of these 8 employees.

The key ingredients of the output of George's regression model are shown in Table 6.17. Notice first from Table 6.17 that $R^2 = 0.870$, which is quite high. Next, notice that the coefficient on the dummy variable for "non-Asian" is negative, which seems to indicate that an employee's being a non-Asian would contribute negatively to his or her salary.

However, let us perform a significance test on the regression coefficient for the non-Asian dummy variable. We first compute the t-statistic for the regression coefficient for this variable, which is

$$\bar{t} = \frac{b_1}{s_{b_1}} = \frac{-3,624.758}{2,137.292} = -1.696.$$

Next we compute the c value for the significance test with $dof = 102 - 4 - 1 = 97$ at the 95% confidence level. According to the t-table shown in Table A.2 of the Appendix, $c = 1.96$. Then noting that $|\bar{t}| = |-1.696| > 1.96 = c$, the coefficient $-3,624.758$ fails the significance test, and so we cannot be confident (at the 95% level) that the coefficient on the non-Asian dummy variable is not zero.

Because the coefficient $-3,624.758$ fails the significance test, even though the regression R^2 is quite high ($R^2 = 0.870$), we should suspect multicollinearity in the data. In order to test for multicollinearity, we can calculate the sample correlation values for all combinations of the four independent variables. These sample correlation values are shown in Table 6.18.

TABLE 6.17

Key ingredients of the regression output for the prediction of salary at CERNA using four independent variables (non-Asian, GPA, Graduate Degree, and Experience).

R Square	0.870	
Standard Error	5,796.933	
Observations	102	

	Coefficients	Standard Error
Intercept	6,948.178	4,807.554
non-Asian	-3,624.758	2,137.292
GPA	18,591.857	1,122.617
Graduate Degree	10,086.808	1,228.508
Experience	1,805.233	226.033

TABLE 6.18

The sample correlation coefficients among the four independent variables (non-Asian, GPA, Graduate Degree, and Experience).

	non-Asian	GPA	Graduate Degree	Experience
non-Asian	1			
GPA	−0.038	1		
Graduate Degree	0.179	0.104	1	
Experience	−0.842	0.019	−0.153	1

TABLE 6.19

Key ingredients of the regression output for the prediction of salary at CERNA using three independent variables (GPA, Graduate Degree, and Experience).

R Square	0.866	
Standard Error	5,852.163	
Observations	102	

	Coefficients	Standard Error
Intercept	1,649.504	3,688.765
GPA	18,689.862	1,131.810
Graduate Degree	9,883.140	1,234.273
Experience	2,126.167	124.796

Examining the sample correlation values in Table 6.18, we see that the sample correlation between data values for the dummy variables for "non-Asian" and "Experience" is −0.84. This large negative value indicates a high degree of negative correlation between employees' years at CERNA and whether or not they are non-Asian. Upon reflection, this makes good sense, since most CERNA employees with many years of experience are Asian. In fact, ten or fifteen years ago, CERNA hired primarily Asian managers for middle-level management positions.

In order to try to eliminate the multicollinearity problem from the model, let us remove the "non-Asian" dummy variable from the regression model and instead perform the regression using the three independent variables:

- **GPA**: the undergraduate GPA of the employee.

- **Graduate Degree**: a dummy variable that has a value of "1" if the employee has a post-graduate degree and has a value of "0" if the employee only has an undergraduate degree.

- **Experience**: the number of years that the employee has worked at CERNA.

The key ingredients of the regression output for this simpler model are shown in Table 6.19.

Now let us examine the regression output for this second regression in detail. From the regression output in Table 6.19, we see that the R^2 of this second regression has decreased only slightly to $R^2 = 0.866$ from the previous value of $R^2 = 0.870$. So, it appears that this second regression model still is a good fit with the data.

We next perform a sort-of "sanity check" to see if the signs of the regression coefficients make sense. Common-sense indicates that each of the three independent variables should be a positive contributor to the prediction of salary, and indeed we see from Table 6.19 that the signs of the regression coefficients for these three independent variables are indeed all positive.

We next can compute the *t*-statistics for the three independent variables, and the resulting computation shows that the regression coefficients on all three of the independent variables are indeed significant.

We next check for the Normality of the residuals. We do this by computing a histogram of the regression residuals. Such a histogram is shown in Figure 6.19. As Figure 6.19 shows, the residuals appear to be approximately Normally distributed.

We next check for any evidence of heteroscedasticity. To do this we look at the scatter-plot of the regression residuals with the sample data for each of the three independent variables. These scatter-plots are shown in Figure 6.20, Figure 6.21, and Figure 6.22. Examining these three figures, we see no evidence of any unusual patterns among the residuals.

Based on the above analysis and observations, we can conclude that this second regression model is quite satisfactory. One last check on the model would be to see how well the model does at predicting the salaries of curent employees. According to the regression output for the model in Table 6.19, we have the following regression equation:

FIGURE 6.19

A histogram of the regression residuals indicates that the regression residuals approximately obey a Normal distribution.

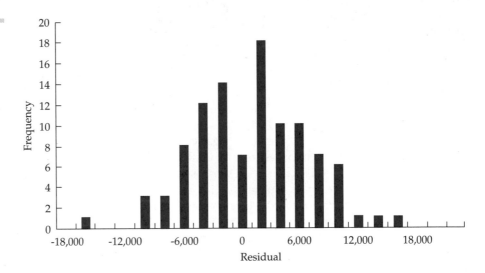

FIGURE 6.20

The residual plot as a function of the GPA independent variable shows no evidence of heteroscedasticity.

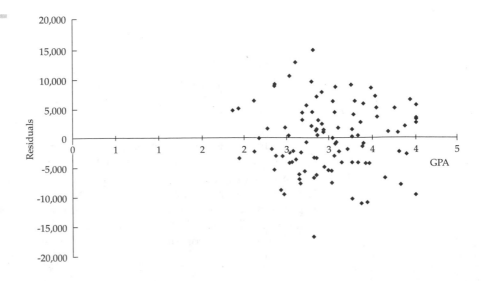

$$\text{Salary} = 1{,}649.504 + 18{,}689.862 \times \text{GPA}$$
$$+ 9{,}883.140 \times \text{Graduate Degree} + 2{,}126.167 \times \text{Experience.}$$

Let us now use this regression equation to predict the salaries of the 8 employees (employee numbers 103-110) that were purposely omitted from the regression model. For example, using this regression equation, we can compute the predicted salary for employee 110, which would be:

$$\$98{,}372 = 1{,}649.504 + 18{,}689.862 \times (3.85)$$
$$+ 9{,}883.140 \times (1) + 2{,}126.167 \times (7).$$

Table 6.20 shows the predicted salary for each of these eight employees along with the other data that George had collected. Note that the predicted values (shown in Column 2 of Table 6.20) are in very close agreement with the actual salaries of these

FIGURE 6.21

The residual plot as a function of the Graduate Degree independent variable shows no evidence of heteroscedasticity.

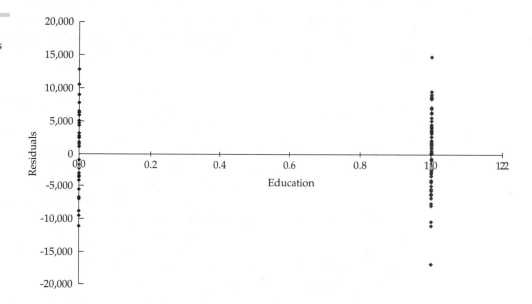

FIGURE 6.22

The residual plot as a function of the Experience independent variable shows no evidence of heteroscedasticity.

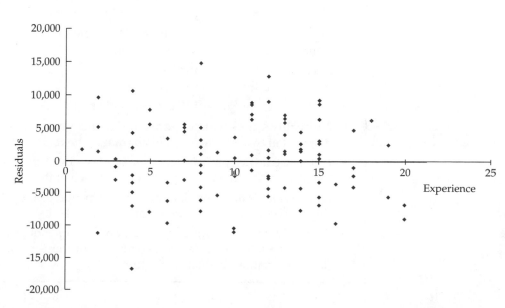

TABLE 6.20

Predicted salary versus actual salary for employees 103-108 at CERNA.

Employee Number	Predicted Salary ($)	Actual Salary ($)	non-Asian Dummy Variable	Undergraduate GPA	Graduate Degree Dummy Variable	Years of Experience
103	49,075	47,487	1	2.31	0	2
104	107,835	105,698	0	3.56	1	14
105	57,604	55,173	0	2.01	1	4
106	74,097	80,765	1	3.12	1	2
107	75,078	77,081	0	3.36	0	5
108	64,823	60,024	0	2.51	1	3
109	72,673	71,606	1	2.89	0	8
110	98,372	108,625	1	3.85	1	7

8 employees, which are shown in Column 3 of the table. In fact, the sample correlation of the data in these two columns turns out to be 0.978, which is very impressive. We can thus conclude that this regression model has excellent predictive capability.

The process we have worked through in this illustration is typical of the iterative process of constructing, evaluating, and updating a linear regression model.

6.10   SUMMARY AND CONCLUSIONS

Regression is one of the most powerful and easy-to-use tools for making accurate predictions in business. As this chapter has tried to make clear, however, there are many subtleties involved in developing, evaluating, and using a linear regression model. The following checklist summarizes the most important issues that should be addressed to evaluate and validate a linear regression model:

Checklist for Evaluating a Linear Regression Model
- **Linearity.** If there is only one independent variable, construct a scatter-plot of the data to visually check for linearity. Otherwise, use common sense to determine whether a linear relationship is sensible.
- **Signs of Regression Coefficients.** Check the signs of the regression coefficients to see if they make intuitive sense.
- **t-statistics.** Use the t-statistics to check if the regression coefficients are significantly different from zero.
- **R^2.** Check if the value of R^2 is reasonably high.
- **Normality.** Check that the regression residuals are approximately Normally distributed by constructing a histogram of the regression residuals.
- **Heteroscedasticity.** Check for heteroscedasticity of the residuals by plotting the residuals with the observed values of each of the independent variables.
- **Autocorrelation.** If the data are time-dependent, plot the residuals over time to check for any apparent patterns.
- **Multicollinearity.** If you suspect that two independent variables are correlated, calculate the correlation coefficient of these variables to see if their data observations exhibit correlation.

We all develop beliefs about the world around us based on personal intuition, social norms, or whim. In the realm of economics, most of us believe that demand for a product increases when the price of the good is decreased. In the social sciences, for example, many believe that there is correlation between executive compensation and the gender and race of executives. In political debate, there are many who believe that less government regulation is best for the health of the economy. Linear regression offers a methodology to examine and empirically test such beliefs. However, as we have stressed in this chapter, we should be careful as to how we construct and then interpret the output of a linear regression model. Good judgment and sound analysis must at all times go hand in hand.

6.11   CASE MODULES

PREDICTING HEATING OIL CONSUMPTION AT OILPLUS

OILPLUS, Inc. provides heating oil to residential customers in Lancaster, Pennsylvania. OILPLUS would like to predict heating oil consumption among its customers in order to plan its own fuel purchases and to budget its revenue flows appropriately.

Table 6.21 shows heating oil consumption of OILPLUS's customer base and average monthly temperature for 55 consecutive months from August, 1989 through February, 1994. The spreadsheet OILPLUS.xls contains all of he data shown in Table 6.21. Figure 6.23 shows a scatter-plot of heating oil consumption and average daily temperature, based on the data in Table 6.21. This scatter-plot shows that there is a relationship between heating oil consumption and average monthly temperature, just as intuition would indicate.

Table 6.22 shows the key ingredients of the output of a linear regression model of heating oil consumption based on average monthly temperature. A scatter-plot of the regression residuals of this regression model is shown in Figure 6.24.

Assignment:

(a) OILPLUS would like to predict the heating oil consumption for next December. According to the temperature data in Table 6.21, the average December monthly temperature over the years 1989-1993 is 35.2 degrees. Use the regression model to predict the heating oil consumption for next December based on this average temperature.

(b) According to the heating oil consumption data in Table 6.21, the average heating oil consumption for the last five Decembers (1989-1993) was 75.92 thousand gallons for the month. It might therefore seem reasonable to use this number as our prediction of next December's heating oil consumption. What advantages does prediction based on the regression model have over this simple averaging method?

(c) Evaluate the regression model by examining the regression model output. Check the R^2, the t-statistics, and the scatter-plot of the regression residuals. What do you notice?

(d) Would you recommend using this regression model to predict heating oil consumption at OILPLUS? Why or why not?

TABLE 6.21
Consumption of heating oil and average monthly temperature for 55 consecutive months.

Month	Heating Oil Consumption (1,000 gallons)	Average Temperature (degrees Fahrenheit)
August, 1989	24.32	72
September, 1989	27.33	69
October, 1989	15.68	53
November, 1989	57.43	40
December, 1989	104.40	31
January, 1990	48.83	40
February, 1990	55.40	34
March, 1990	59.58	50
April, 1990	54.48	52
May, 1990	26.29	60
June, 1990	24.22	74
July, 1990	23.84	74
August, 1990	20.07	71
September, 1990	29.52	70
October, 1990	22.83	61
November, 1990	54.95	53
December, 1990	75.18	37
January, 1991	84.70	32
February, 1991	42.81	36
March, 1991	42.39	45
April, 1991	31.11	59
May, 1991	29.49	73
June, 1991	16.99	72
July, 1991	14.78	74
August, 1991	25.27	77
September, 1991	19.96	67
October, 1991	26.80	55
November, 1991	38.09	45
December, 1991	80.68	37
January, 1992	77.14	31
February, 1992	69.00	38
March, 1992	62.27	35
April, 1992	57.73	53
May, 1992	32.36	57
June, 1992	21.00	67
July, 1992	28.69	72
August, 1992	36.57	75
September, 1992	25.92	61
October, 1992	41.25	51
November, 1992	51.49	48
December, 1992	53.12	36
January, 1993	58.46	30
February, 1993	71.46	32
March, 1993	40.46	34
April, 1993	21.03	56
May, 1993	25.55	65
June, 1993	8.78	70
July, 1993	20.92	82
August, 1993	19.39	70
September, 1993	22.34	63
October, 1993	44.41	57
November, 1993	38.13	43
December, 1993	66.24	35
January, 1994	101.23	23
February, 1994	102.98	33

FIGURE 6.23

Scatter-plot of average monthly temperature and consumption of heating oil for 55 consecutive months.

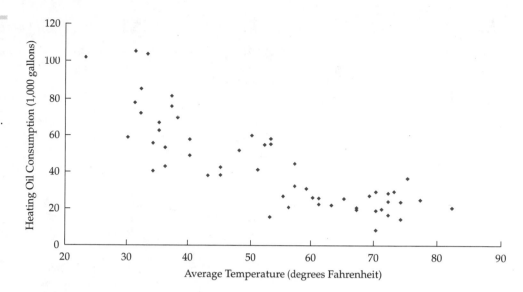

TABLE 6.22

Key ingredients of the regression output for the prediction of heating oil consumption at OILPLUS.

R Square	0.688	
Standard Error	13.519	
Observations	55	
	Coefficients	*Standard Error*
Intercept	109.001	6.351
Temperature	−1.235	0.114

FIGURE 6.24

Scatter-plot of regression residuals for the regression model used to predict heating oil consumption based on average monthly temperature.

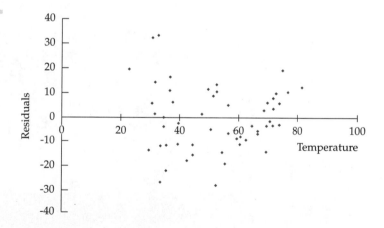

EXECUTIVE COMPENSATION

Highly publicized salaries of corporate chief executive officers (CEOs) in the United States have generated sustained interest in understanding the factors related to CEO compensation in general. Table 6.23 contains data on the annual compensation of the CEO's of 50 large publicly-traded corporations in the United States in the previous year, as well as other information that we would hope could be used to predict CEO compensation. An explanation of the entries in Table 6.23 is as follows:

TABLE 6.23
CEO compensation and related information for 50 corporations.

Company Number	Total Compensation ($ thousand)	Years in current position	Change in Stock Price from previous year (%)	Change in Company's Sales from previous year (%)	MBA dummy variable
1	1,530	7	48	89	1
2	1,117	6	35	19	1
3	602	3	9	24	0
4	1,170	6	37	8	1
5	1,086	6	34	28	0
6	2,536	9	81	−16	1
7	300	2	−17	−17	0
8	670	2	−15	−67	1
9	250	0	−52	49	0
10	2,413	10	109	−27	1
11	2,707	7	44	26	1
12	341	1	28	−7	0
13	734	4	10	−7	0
14	2,368	8	16	−4	0
15	743	4	11	50	1
16	898	7	−21	−20	1
17	498	4	16	−24	0
18	250	2	−10	64	0
19	1,388	4	8	−58	1
20	898	5	28	−73	1
21	408	4	13	31	1
22	1,091	6	34	66	0
23	1,550	7	49	−4	1
24	832	5	26	55	0
25	1,462	7	46	10	1
26	1,456	7	46	−5	1
27	1,984	8	63	28	1
28	1,493	10	12	−36	0
29	2,021	7	48	72	1
30	2,871	8	7	5	1
31	245	0	−58	−16	1
32	3,217	11	102	51	1
33	1,315	7	42	−7	0
34	1,730	9	55	122	1
35	260	0	−54	−41	1
36	250	2	−17	−35	0
37	718	5	23	19	1
38	1,593	8	66	76	1
39	1,905	8	67	−48	1
40	2,283	5	21	64	1
41	2,253	7	46	104	1
42	254	0	−41	99	0
43	1,883	8	60	−12	1
44	1,501	5	10	20	1
45	386	0	−17	−18	0
46	2,181	11	37	27	1
47	1,766	6	40	41	1
48	1,897	8	−24	−41	1
49	1,157	5	21	87	1
50	246	3	1	−34	0

- Column 2 shows the total compensation of the CEO of each company. This number includes direct salary plus bonuses, stock options, and other indirect compensation.

- Column 3 shows the number of years that the executive has been the CEO of the company.

- Column 4 shows the percentage change in the stock price of the company from the previous year.

- Column 5 shows the percentage change in the company's sales from the previous year.

- Column 6 shows information on whether or not the CEO has an MBA. A "1" is used to indicate that the CEO has an MBA, and a "0" is used to indicate that the CEO does not have an MBA.

The spreadsheet CEO-COMPENSATION.xls contains all of the data shown in Table 6.23.

Assignment:

(a) Comment on the extent to which you think that the data shown in Table 6.23 might or might not be an appropriate choice to use to predict the compensation of CEOs.

(b) Construct and run a regression model to predict CEO compensation as a function of the independent variables indicated in Table 6.23.

(c) Evaluate the regression output of your regression model. Is there evidence of multicollinearity?

(d) Try constructing a smaller regression that uses fewer independent variables. You might need to experiment with several different regression models using different combinations of independent variables. Evaluate your best regression model by looking at the regression R^2, the t-statistics, regression residuals, etc. Are you satisfied with your regression model?

(e) Which are the critical factors that are good predictors of CEO compensation? In particular, does having an MBA have an effect on CEO compensation? Why or why not?

THE CONSTRUCTION DEPARTMENT AT CROQ'PAIN

Introduction

PARIS, FRIDAY, JULY 7, 1995—Michel Boutillon was having a bad day. He had just called his wife to tell her that their week-long trip to the Riviera would have to wait a little while longer. His company's president, Jean Gerard, had just asked him to make a presentation to top management the following Monday. Michel, a graduate of the Marseilles Institute of Trade, had been hired two years earlier to be a "transition manager" at Croq'Pain, a chain of quality fast-food restaurants. He was responsible for getting new restaurants ready to open after construction was completed. He also had been asked to develop a better system for the selection of locations for new stores. The new system was to be based on a statistical model. Michel was originally given two months to come up with a proposal but, apparently, Gerard did not have the patience to wait that long. Michel was not surprised because the mid-year revenue figures for all the

Croq'Pain stores had arrived earlier in the week. These figures showed that the performance of eight of the ten stores that opened in the first half of last year were less than satisfactory.

The Company

Jean Gerard founded Croq'Pain in 1981 and opened his first "restaurant rapide" on the "Parvis" de la Defense, the main business center on the outskirts of Paris. This first store was extremely popular among the business clientèle there as well as with the shoppers and visitors to the CNET (a large exhibition hall in the middle of the center). Going after the student clientèle, he opened his second restaurant six months later on the Boulevard St. Michel in the middle of the Latin Quarter, the students' section of town. Other restaurants, located in different parts of the capital, were opened during the next five years. In a 1986 interview with a local business magazine, he said that he saw his stores as the French answer to the American fast food invasion. Indeed, in the early eighties, many fast food chains had set up shop in Paris and other French cities, and most were based on American models. McDonald's and Burger King had already opened in Paris, and a number of French look-alikes had mushroomed as well. His goal, he said, was to offer quality food . . . fast, not fast food. By 1987, Croq'Pain had 15 stores in Paris, Toulouse, and Marseilles.

In 1987, poor financial results at some of the stores prompted Gerard to conduct a large marketing survey among his customers. The results forced him to re-assess the company's marketing strategy. The survey (shown in Table 6.24) revealed that the bulk of the customer base was made up of professionals and baby boomers (now in their late

TABLE 6.24

Summary results of a 1987 marketing survey that was conducted among customers of Croq'Pain between April 1, 1987 and May 15, 1987. The survey was conducted at all Croq'Pain locations.

Sample size	1,150
Male/female Split	
Males	72%
Females	28%
Age distribution	
under 15 yrs old	2%
15-24 yrs old	12%
25-34 yrs old	16%
35-44 yrs old	55%
45-54 yrs old	13%
over 55 yrs old	2%
Family status	
Single	36%
Married	64%
1 child	8%
2 children	25%
3 children and above	9%
Employment	
Not employed	30%
Employed	70%
Current Status/Activity	
Student	17%
Blue collar	8%
White collar	55%
Other	20%
Visits	
Less than 1/month	15%
1-5/month	14%
5-15/month	45%
15-25/month	25%
more than 25 times/month	1%

thirties and early forties). He concentrated new stores in areas that would serve this clientèle and moved away from the student neighborhoods, in effect withdrawing from the competition with other fast food chains. Croq'Pain stores were opened in more cities, but were concentrated in the downtown areas and the business centers. This strategy paid off, and Croq'Pain's expansion continued at a steady pace. In January 1994, the company owned 50 stores throughout France. The expansion continued particularly strongly in the first half of 1994; ten new stores were opened during this period alone.

All store openings were controlled by the Construction Department of Croq'Pain. It was responsible for selecting the location of new stores and coordinating their construction. It was also responsible for supplying and installing all of the equipment necessary to run the restaurant. Management of the store was passed to the store manager "clef en main"—the day of the opening, the store manager was literally given the keys by the transition manager. The store was ready to do business the same day.

The Croq'Pain Concept

The very idea of fast food goes against everything the French culinary culture stands for. Not too long ago, it was common for most workers to take a two-hour lunch and go home to eat what is still regarded as the main meal of the day. But Gerard recognized that more and more workers, especially around Paris, were commuting from towns too far away to get home in the middle of the day. Increasingly, they were eating lunch on or around the job.

Croq'Pain took advantage of this change and offered a range of sandwiches, salads and pies. Among other items, it serves baguette sandwiches. Among the main baguette items, one finds the campagnarde (paté), the tout-jambon (ham with butter), and the complète (eggs, tomatoes, lettuce, and mayo) baguettes. It offers a selection of quiches (mushroom, ham, three-cheese, onion pie among others), salads (niçoise, tuna, or lettuce), yogurts, and cheeses. Drinks include bottled water, soft drinks, red and white wine as well as ten different kinds of beer. Gerard did not aim to offer the lowest prices but rather a good mix of quality food, based on French traditions, and price.

In addition to providing good quality food and convenience, the stores quickly developed a unique look: black-and-white checkered tile floors; red and white counters; "French café" style tables and wood chairs; and black sidewalk tables with red umbrellas.

The Construction Department

The Construction Department, in charge of opening new restaurants, employs 40 people, including architects, lawyers, designers, accountants, and teams of workers involved in different stages of the actual store construction. The process of launching a new restaurant begins approximately one year before the restaurant's scheduled opening date. It includes the following steps:

1. **Choice of location:** The city and location of the new store is selected. At this stage, the company also determines the investment needed to open the store. The investment includes building and land as well as equipment.

2. **Property acquisition:** The building or land is purchased (or possibly leased, in some cases), and all necessary permits and licenses are obtained.

3. **Design:** The architects design the new store, a step that is begun during the property acquisition stage but is finalized at this stage.

4. **Remodeling and/or building:** The actual construction of the store, by hired contractors, takes place.

5. **Logistics:** Prior to the restaurant opening, the transition manager steps in to oversee logistical problems, such as installing the proper equipment, setting up a local supply chain, and hiring staff.

6. **Opening day:** In a morning ceremony, the transition manager passes the key to the store manager (Jean Gerard has never missed a store opening), and the restaurant opens the same day.

After opening day, the store is in the hands of the store manager and the transition manager moves on to his/her next assignment as soon as the store is opened. The store managers have complete control over their store thenceforth. In particular, they frequently adjust the workforce during the year in response to the store's variable workload and financial results. They can also, to a much lesser extent, adjust the store's operating hours.

The location selection step is critical. The decision made at this point, to a large extent, determines the company's future earnings. So far, determining the store's location (as well as its size) has been an imperfect art, and several attempts have been failures. At its current high rate of expansion, the company has a growing need to standardize the location selection process and minimize the risk of failure.

The usual procedure for choosing a location has involved sending a "location expert" to choose several possible options. The expert would then make an estimate of the earnings potential of each location followed by a recommendation to the company's president and the director of construction, Didier Marchand. A location was chosen by this panel based on the expert's estimates and management's opinion.

Developing a Model for the Selection of Store Locations

Soon after he was given responsibility for developing a model to help select new locations for stores, Michel gathered a team that included the location selection experts and asked everyone to devise ideas for the structure of the model. The independent variables of the model were to be those variables that they thought would influence the profitability of a new store. The list established by the team is presented in Table 6.25.

Following the team's recommendations for the model parameters, Michel collected the data for all stores, up to and including the ten stores opened in the first half of 1994. (Data for stores opened afterwards is not complete and thus could not be included.) This data is shown in Table 6.26. Also included are the operating earnings figures for the period July, 1994-June, 1995. He proceeded to run a regression of the earnings figures using all of the parameters of the model (results are shown in Table 6.27).

He was not pleased with this first result and needed to improve on the initial model. To begin with, he did not like the choice of certain parameters. They had little value for predicting financial results because they could not be known in advance. Second, he thought that some of the "homemade" parameters had been recommended because they were used by the experts but, in fact, they were of little use. Overall, he was beginning to have serious doubts about the feasibility of such a model-based approach for selecting store locations.

Once he looked at the results from his regression model, he felt quite uncomfortable with what he saw: some of the regression coefficients did not make sense, and many were not statistically significant. Clearly, this regression model needed improvement.

Second, he thought that a good way of testing the applicability of the regression model was to consider what would have happened last year had the model been used

TABLE 6.25

Parameters for the regression model. The parameter K, i.e., the capital invested in the store, is not included in the model. All French monetary units have been converted to U.S. dollars for the purpose of this case.

Variable	Units	Description
EARN	$1,000	Operating earnings: annual sales minus annual operating costs. Operating costs exclude the fixed costs of property rent and equipment rental (all capital equipment is purchased by headquarters and rented to the stores). Operating costs include variable costs such as salaries, utilities, supplies, inventories and other expenses.
SIZE	m²	Size of store: Total area inside the store.
EMPL		Number of employees employed by the store as of Dec. 31, 1994.
P15		Number of 15-24 year-olds in a 3 km radius around site.
P25		Number of 25-34 year-olds in a 3 km radius around site.
P35		Number of 35-44 year-olds in a 3 km radius around site.
P45		Number of 45-54 year-olds in a 3 km radius around site.
P55		Number of persons above 55 in a 3 km radius around site.
total		Total population in 3 km radius around site.
INC	$1,000	Average income in town or neighborhood around site.
COMP		Number of competitors in a 1 km radius around site. Establishments considered as competitors include fast food restaurants, bars and cafes equipped providing lunch service.
NCOMP		Number of restaurants that do not compete directly with Croq'Pain in 1 km radius around site.
NREST		Number of non-restaurant businesses in 1 km radius around site.
PRICE	$/m²/month	Monthly rent per square meter of the retail properties in the same locale.
CLI		Cost of Living Index. Measures the cost of living in the immediate vicinity to the restaurant site. Aggregate of average cost of living index determined by the commerce department and additional economic measures taken by experts on site.
K	$1,000	Capital invested in the store. This amount is exactly equal to the purchase price of the property (or the lease, in some cases) plus the cost of all equipment and the cost of remodeling the space.)

to evaluate and select the 1994 store locations. In order to do that, of course, he would have to amend the model by using only the data obtained for the first 50 stores. Then he would use this regression model to evaluate the ten stores that were opened in 1994.

Croq'Pain's goal is to have a 16% return on invested capital after taxes. As it turns out (after some laborious computations using a method called discounted cash flow analysis), this is equivalent for our purposes to a ratio of Operating Earnings (EARN) to invested capital (K) of 0.26. Therefore, Croq'Pain defines their "performance ratio" for a store as:

$$\text{Performance Ratio} = \frac{\text{Sales} - \text{Variable Costs}}{\text{Invested Capital}} = \frac{\text{Operating Earnings}}{\text{Invested Capital}}.$$

The target performance ratio is 0.26, i.e., 26%.

Michel wondered which of the ten stores would have been opened had the model been used to predict the performance ratio of these stores.

Third, he needed to consider his recommendations for new stores for 1996. The experts had so far made a list of ten potential locations (see the list in Table 6.28). He wanted to use the model to help him select the potential locations of stores to be opened in 1996.

He also contemplated if his analysis could be parlayed into a different way to think strategically about the way Croq'Pain plans to grow its business.

Finally, after all this, he needed to prepare his presentation to the executives using very definitive arguments. Jean Gerard did not like "maybes." If Michel decided to recommend against using a regression model for selecting locations, he would

STORE	EARN	K	SIZE	EMPL	Total	P15	P25	P35	P45	P55	INC	COMP	NCOMP	NREST	PRICE	CLI
1	28.3	861	129	14	8,580	980	1,280	560	1,000	3,100	27.6	8	1	45	16.10	129
2	−1.5	630	91	12	8,460	1,290	720	1,200	1,490	3,100	28.3	2	2	27	11.40	116
3	68.9	1,074	140	13	19,250	2,940	2,490	3,710	4,030	5,270	30.2	5	4	5	21.70	142
4	202.1	882	184	7	20,920	3,570	4,930	4,420	4,300	2,960	27.6	2	1	7	11.80	138
5	115.8	931	144	14	11,660	1,700	1,140	2,200	2,140	2,630	33.9	1	3	25	16.60	126
6	221.7	1,185	160	11	25,780	4,640	3,150	5,720	5,330	5,920	32.5	3	9	8	22.10	137
7	292.9	907	94	5	19,000	3,600	2,330	4,750	4,970	3,030	33.1	0	11	89	24.30	134
8	134.4	764	100	8	18,500	3,450	2,560	3,630	3,520	4,800	29.7	3	3	14	16.40	132
9	37.4	643	85	14	14,210	1,930	4,280	1,740	2,060	2,960	28.4	4	12	43	12.90	129
10	181.0	666	92	6	17,440	3,520	1,780	4,350	4,020	3,470	28.3	8	1	76	13.00	117
11	246.9	1,245	167	12	22,360	3,970	2,810	4,540	4,770	4,700	38.3	3	10	9	22.80	136
12	178.3	846	199	15	20,360	3,190	3,610	4,380	4,150	3,670	32.1	6	3	11	10.10	121
⋮	⋮	⋮	⋮	⋮	⋮	⋮	⋮	⋮	⋮	⋮	⋮	⋮	⋮	⋮	⋮	⋮
43	94.1	597	76	16	23,180	4,050	2,430	5,060	4,980	5,400	31.0	6	13	19	11.70	134
44	214.2	643	144	14	21,830	3,920	2,810	4,260	4,330	5,970	30.0	1	11	26	7.60	112
45	63.3	761	87	17	22,220	3,230	4,890	3,990	4,050	5,270	25.5	2	3	32	18.70	128
46	237.1	570	73	6	26,700	5,150	2,520	6,280	5,910	6,490	35.2	8	3	14	10.50	134
47	208.8	553	59	11	19,920	3,450	3,990	4,090	4,110	2,760	34.4	7	6	71	11.70	116
48	110.6	861	83	13	26,200	4,070	4,970	5,360	5,190	5,710	29.5	4	10	44	25.00	116
49	165.4	714	125	7	20,550	2,800	3,820	3,370	3,650	5,260	33.8	3	10	12	11.30	122
50	−11.4	575	56	4	14,260	2,150	3,030	2,360	2,240	3,800	29.9	2	5	12	14.10	127
51	216.3	776	146	11	17,440	2,800	2,350	3,180	3,050	5,490	32.1	2	6	26	11.60	124
52	65.7	648	62	11	12,880	2,020	1,780	2,810	3,000	2,010	32.7	7	7	70	18.00	125
53	67.6	690	96	9	14,310	2,320	1,040	2,420	2,770	4,380	30.0	1	6	7	13.60	134
54	127.9	715	86	10	12,990	2,480	2,380	2,530	2,670	1,420	34.4	3	5	17	16.50	122
55	82.9	650	88	8	16,380	1,870	3,290	2,520	2,660	4,390	28.8	3	3	16	12.80	134
56	−2.9	788	72	7	21,360	3,310	3,590	3,730	3,970	5,450	28.7	2	8	10	24.30	129
57	247.7	782	119	7	23,400	3,620	3,820	5,680	4,260	6,060	33.4	2	10	63	13.30	121
58	343.0	1,558	285	8	22,830	4,160	1,230	5,120	5,200	5,670	27.6	2	3	40	18.30	116
59	193.1	936	193	8	13,510	1,950	2,360	2,310	2,320	3,480	28.7	1	9	34	12.50	112
60	277.5	688	92	12	25,490	4,890	1,800	6,070	5,960	5,890	36.0	1	8	31	14.10	127

TABLE 6.26

Data on Croq'Pain stores. (Only stores having been in operation at least one full year are shown). Stores 51-60 have opened in the first half of 1994.

have to defend this decision and offer possible improvements to the existing methodology. If he decided to recommend using the regression model, he also would have to offer strong arguments because the company would be far worse off with a bad model and no experts than it is now, with no model and experts who are sometimes wrong. In addition, he would have to point out possible shortcomings of the model methodology.

Michel felt a little better having spelled out his approach, but he knew that it was going to be a long weekend. He closed the door to his office, unplugged the phone, and went to work.

Assignment:

Using the data for this case, provided in the spreadsheet file entitled CROQPAIN.xls, do the following:

(a) Examine the operating earnings regression model output obtained from the 60 stores, as shown in Table 6.27. Try to improve the model by eliminating certain independent variables or by making any other changes that you think make good sense. You should strive for a model that is simple (i.e., has few independent variables), and that does not violate any of the basic assumptions of multiple regression (e.g., multicollinearity, heteroscedasticity), but nevertheless has good predictive power.

TABLE 6.27

First model run: Operating earnings model based on 60 stores.

	A	B	C	D	E	F	G
1	SUMMARY OUTPUT						
2							
3	Regression Statistics						
4	Multiple R	0.931					
5	R Square	0.867					
6	Adjusted R Square	0.826					
7	Standard Error	38.126					
8	Observations	60					
9							
10	ANOVA						
11		dof	SS	MS	F	Significance F	
12	Regression	14	426,750.607	30,482.186	20.970	0.000	
13	Residual	45	65,411.117	1,453.580			
14	Total	59	492,161.724				
15							
16		Coefficients	Standard Error	t Stat	P-value	Lower 95%	Upper 95%
17	Intercept	-364.267	98.345	-3.704	0.001	-562.345	-166.190
18	SIZE	0.771	0.099	7.803	0.000	0.572	0.970
19	EMPL	-0.866	1.466	-0.591	0.558	-3.818	2.086
20	total	-0.010	0.013	-0.805	0.425	-0.036	0.015
21	P15	0.057	0.028	2.050	0.046	0.001	0.113
22	P25	0.013	0.013	0.978	0.333	-0.014	0.040
23	P35	0.014	0.022	0.658	0.514	-0.030	0.059
24	P45	0.001	0.033	0.032	0.975	-0.065	0.067
25	P55	0.010	0.014	0.727	0.471	-0.018	0.039
26	INC	8.763	1.644	5.331	0.000	5.453	12.074
27	COMP	-2.681	2.320	-1.156	0.254	-7.354	1.992
28	NCOMP	-0.347	1.561	-0.222	0.825	-3.490	2.797
29	NREST	1.451	0.245	5.920	0.000	0.958	1.945
30	PRICE	-3.173	0.966	-3.283	0.002	-5.119	-1.226
31	CLI	0.402	0.700	0.574	0.569	-1.008	1.812

(b) Michel thinks that a good way to validate the model obtained with data from the 60 stores is to see how a similar model, obtained from the 50 stores opened before 1994, would have performed in predicting the performance of the last ten stores opened. Step back one year prior to the opening of the last ten restaurants. Amend the model you have developed using only the data from the first fifty stores. Using Croq'Pain's performance ratio target of 26%, which of the ten stores would you have opened in 1994?

(c) Croq'Pain's strategic planning group has developed a list of ten potential store locations for 1996 shown in Table 6.28. Which of these locations would you select, i.e., which locations meet or exceed the performance ratio? Use the most complete model (60 restaurants) for your analysis.

(d) Prepare a memorandum containing your recommendations as to whether, and how, regression models can be used in the process of location selection. Defend your recommendations with a discussion of the relative strengths and weaknesses of regression models in this setting.

STORE	K	SIZE	EMPL	Total	P15	P25	P35	P45	P55	INC	COMP	NCOMP	NREST	PRICE	CLI
Calais	660	54	—	6,710	600	2,570	430	690	1,440	38	4	5	18	22	131
Montchanin	733	120	—	11,040	1,300	1,400	2,110	1,090	2,680	31	7	6	21	13	115
Aubusson	1,050	135	—	11,910	2,210	1,850	2,330	2,240	2,170	29	1	4	13	22	135
Toulouse	836	245	—	11,350	3,400	3,000	2,570	1,200	1,350	37	5	8	62	13	136
Torcy	784	96	—	3,500	260	700	500	1,200	2,000	30	12	7	38	18	130
Marseilles-1	925	197	—	12,720	1,650	1,960	2,300	1,780	4,390	23	1	9	41	12	136
Marseilles-2	1,090	93	—	16,660	2,570	2,940	2,820	2,720	4,450	25	2	0	5	33	133
Clermont	738	169	—	9,410	780	1,940	880	1,080	3,450	30	4	4	11	9	126
Montpellier	584	149	—	19,020	2,500	2,680	4,600	4,567	3,000	29	4	5	26	13	128
Dijon	681	150	—	12,650	1,650	1,320	1,000	3,400	2,370	35	3	12	54	15	128

TABLE 6.28

Ten new locations considered by the experts. Note that the column for the number of employees is blank. This is because the number of employees is decided and adjusted during a store's operation by each store manager.

SLOAN INVESTORS, PART I

Introduction

In the fall of 1995, Jim Theiser, a second-year MBA student at M.I.T.'s Sloan School of Management, had just returned to campus after completing a summer internship as an equity analyst for a medium-sized investment management firm located in Boston, Massachusetts. During his summer internship, Jim helped the firm select portfolios of stocks. Towards this end, Jim had constructed and used a variety of modeling tools, including multiple linear regression, for use in predicting stock returns. From this experience, Jim was introduced to the entire money management industry in the United States. He also was exposed to a variety of specific ways to statistically "beat" the market. In fact, Jim believed that the models he had constructed represented a *new* way to predict stock returns and to beat the market.

In addition to an interest in investments, Jim also had an entrepreneur's desire to start his own money management company upon graduation. Jim thought that if he could build a company around his new method for predicting stock returns, he could potentially become very wealthy. At first Jim was pessimistic about achieving this goal: In order to raise the many millions of dollars necessary to start a new investment fund, Jim would need a network of contacts. Realistically, he did not have a chance of developing such a network of contacts on his own. After all, who would give millions of dollars to someone who had only worked in the money management industry for a mere three months? Rather than go it alone, Jim decided to approach one of his former professors at MIT about his plan, and hopefully, to persuade the professor to become a partner in his proposed venture. He remembered that this professor had many contacts in the money management industry. The professor was both intrigued and skeptical of Jim's plan. Through persistence, Jim was able to get the professor to join his team as an advisor. If Jim could prove to the professor that his model could make money, then the professor assured him that he could raise the initial capital that Jim needed.

The problem that Jim faced, of course, was finding a way to prove that his prediction method was, in fact, more accurate than other methods. Jim knew that America's stock market is extremely "efficient" and that beating the market is an extremely difficult task. Of course, an investment approach that does not show improvement over the market has very little chance of attracting investors. The professor was not about to put his reputation (not to mention his money) on the line for a predictive model that was in any way questionable. As a result, Jim felt that it was essential that he begin testing and "proving" his model's capabilities as soon as possible. If he could prove that his model works, the professor would back his venture, and Jim would be on his way to starting his money management company.

Overview of the Investment Management Industry

The investment management industry has its roots in Boston, Massachusetts. Beginning in the early part of the 19th century, wealthy individuals in the Boston area began the practice of hiring trustees to manage their investments. In exchange for a small yearly fee (typically on the order of 1% of the value of the assets under management), an investment trustee would manage the individual's assets. The idea, which was novel at the time, was that a professional investment manager could provide a better rate of return on assets than his client could, presuming that the client does not have the time, interest, or skill to manage the money himself. Most trustees in Boston at that time were very conservative in their approach to investing, as they were interested in finding a mix of investments that would guard their clients' wealth over an extended period of time. Beginning around 1930, some of these trustees realized they could market their services to the smaller investor. Firms such as Putnam and Fidelity were born during this period. The enormous mutual fund industry that we see today has sprouted from this rather humble beginning.

Fundamental (Active) Research

Unquestionably, the giant of the mutual fund industry is Fidelity Investments. Fidelity was founded around the year 1930 by Edward Johnson II. Since that time, the company has been handed down to his son, Edward Johnson III, who still runs the company today. Fidelity was founded on the idea that the best way to provide high returns on their clients' assets was to do plenty of high-quality analysis of companies. Analysts at Fidelity fly around the world to visit the companies in their portfolios in order to keep abreast of all of the companies' latest management decisions, as well as to learn more about the overall performance of these companies. Fidelity believes that by doing more work than their competition, they can make better predictions about company returns, and thus make better returns than the market. Given that Fidelity now manages over $500 billion in assets, it is easy to argue that their approach has been quite successful.

Index (Passive) Funds

Besides the actively managed funds, there has been a growing trend in the money management industry toward so-called passive management funds. Proponents of passive management believe that the American stock market is so efficient that *all* of the information about a stock is already reflected in the price of the stock. Accordingly, it is impossible to achieve long-run returns that are better than the market as a whole. One consequence of this tenet, then, is that it is a waste of investors' money to pay to fly analysts around the globe in search of information about companies. Instead, the best approach to money management is to simply mimic a broad market index (such as the S&P 500 index) as efficiently as possible. Such a strategy is, of course, much simpler and easier to implement than an active strategy that calls for amassing, sifting, and analyzing reams of information about the performance of companies under consideration. An index fund manager needs only to make sure that her portfolio is continually updated to match the market index she is trying to follow. This approach is obviously considerably less expensive than hiring a team of analysts. As a result, index funds tend to charge fees on the order of 20 basis points (1 basis point equals 0.01%) as opposed to the typical fees of 100 basis points for an active fund.

Index funds have been around for a long time, but only recently have they gained in popularity. In 1975, John C. Bogle started the Vanguard group of funds in Valley Forge, Pennsylvania. Today Vanguard has over $300 billion under management, and they are still growing quite rapidly. Initially, fundamental active investment companies, like Fidelity, did not consider index funds to be a serious competitor in the investment management industry. However, with the enormous success of companies such as Vanguard, the landscape has changed. In order to compete with Vanguard, Fidelity now manages a considerable number of its own index funds and is planning on launching many more in the near future.

Quantitative (Active) Funds

Whereas an analyst can only keep track of a few stocks in a single industry at any one time, a powerful computer can evaluate thousands of stocks at the same time, and can more easily search and find small anomalies in stock prices. If timed properly, then, an investor can hopefully take advantage of such anomalies (either by buying or selling stocks) and earn an above-market-rate of return. Such is the approach behind quantitative active funds.

The first major advantage of a quantitative fund is that it requires much less manpower than a comparable fundamental fund. The second major advantage is that computers can detect and react to new prices and information quickly. Almost unheard of twenty years ago, there are now numerous companies that use quantitative approaches in the management of assets. One of the largest such companies is State Street Global Advisors, located in Boston. Another relatively new, but interesting, quantitative company is Numeric Investors, co-founded by the son of Vanguard founder John C. Bogle. Numeric Investors uses 100% quantitative techniques in selecting stocks that, they hope, will beat the market index. One major drawback of quantitative funds is that once the fund's model "discovers" a way to beat the market, the predictive power of the model quickly vanishes. The reason for this is that if the model finds a way to beat the market, more and more people will invest in this model. Eventually, this increased investment interest will alter the prices of the securities under investment, thus eliminating the potential for continued profit. As a result, it is essential that quantitative analysts continually re-evaluate their models' predictive power. And of course, the longer that a quantitative model can be kept a secret, the better will be its performance.

Efficient Market Theory

Making above-average returns in the stock market is no simple task. Despite claims to the contrary, most money managers do not beat the market index. In fact, there are a group of theories, known collectively as the Efficient Market Theory, which assert that making above-average returns in the stock market is extremely difficult, if not impossible. Proponents of the Efficient Market Theory divide the theory into the following three classes:

Weak Form

The basic idea behind the Weak Form is that it is impossible to predict future stock returns based on past stock performance. In other words, if IBM's stock has gone up for the last twenty days, there is no more chance that it will continue to increase tomorrow than if it had gone down or simply fluctuated up and down during the last twenty days. If this theory is true, then it is useless to incorporate data on past stock returns into any predictive model of future stock returns.

Semi-Strong Form

In addition to the Weak Form, the Semi-Strong Form also posits that current stock prices incorporate all readily available information. Thus, there is no advantage in analyzing factors such as a firm's P/E ratio (price to earnings ratio), the firm's book value, the firm's cash flows, or anything else, because all of this information is already incorporated into the firm's stock price.

Strong Form

Believers in the Strong Form would probably say that the only way to manage money is to use a passive investment approach. They believe everything in the Semi-Strong Form, with the addition that a firm's current stock price already includes *all* of the information that one could gather by painstaking fundamental analysis of the firm and of the economy. In other words, the fundamental research that is performed by companies such as Fidelity is a waste of time. They are not learning anything that the market does not already know, but they are charging clients 100 basis points for the service.

These theories are, after all . . . just theories. Obviously, if the Strong Form is really true, then the traders on Wall Street probably would not even have their jobs. This is, of course, not the case. But what about mutual funds? As it turns out, there is conflicting evidence concerning the value added to mutual funds from active management. Many people are convinced that active money management adds no value. That is why companies like Vanguard have been so successful. Unfortunately, there is no consensus on how efficient the American stock market really is. Even if you personally believe that the market is completely efficient, you should still ask yourself whether this efficiency *is the result of* a well-functioning mutual fund industry. Perhaps companies like Fidelity are doing such a good job at finding undervalued securities and capitalizing on these findings that to the ordinary investor it appears that the market is incorporating all of this information.

Regardless of whether you believe that the stock market is completely efficient or not, there is no doubt that the market is at least *very* efficient. Accordingly, it should not be surprising that stock data will be very "noisy." Therefore, using statistical models to predict stock returns is one of the most challenging tasks in the money management industry. The next section discusses some of the key issues that stock analysts face when they construct and use statistical models.

Known Pitfalls with Quantitative Statistical Models

In theory, a quantitative model can be an extremely useful tool to help discover stocks with high returns and low risk. However, due to the efficiency of the American stock market, it is very rare that one finds any models with assuredly high predictive power. For example, constructing a linear regression for predicting stock returns with $R^2 = 0.30$ is considered extremely good. Working with this level of noise can be very deceiving. It is very common for people who are not completely thorough in their analysis to fall into a variety of traps. The result is that a particular model might be believed to have great predictive power, when in fact, it does not.

Before a fund manager decides to base investment decisions on a new statistical model, she should test the model on historical data. For example, she might go back and use the stock returns from one year ago through ten years ago as the input to the model, and then use the model to predict the stock returns from last year. If the model accurately predicted last year's stock returns, then that would add to the confidence that the model will work for next year. Eventually, if the model holds up after many such tests of this sort, the model would then be used as the basis of investment decisions with real money. Unfortunately, it is often found that a model that appeared to do a good job of predicting historical returns fails when applied to predicting future returns. This, of course, is not good for business! Why does this happen? Below is a *partial* list of some common traps that analysts fall into when they try to check the validity of a model.

Look-Ahead Bias

Many prediction models use corporate financial numbers as part of the input to the model to predict a company's future stock price. Financial numbers, such as the company's P/E ratio, are often useful in predicting the stock price. Although these financial numbers can be quite useful, it is imperative that someone using them makes sure that the numbers were readily available at the time of the prediction. For example, suppose you are interested in predicting a company's stock price. Now let us say that you compared the December stock price to the company's fourth quarter earnings over a period of years, in order to check for any correlation. That would be a mistake, because fourth quarter earnings are usually not reported until a month or so after the quarter ends. That would mean that the fourth quarter earnings data was not available until January or February of the following year, and so you would be using the future to predict the past. Of course, trying to use your model in the future cannot be successful, because the information that the model needs for its prediction will not yet exist.

Survival Bias

We illustrate the concept of survival bias with a simple example. Suppose that you went back to 1990 and followed the 5,000 largest companies in the United States. Now suppose that you came back again in 1995 and once again looked at the 5,000 largest companies in the United States. Suppose you found out that the value of these companies went up by 60% over this five-year period. At first thought you might think that you could have made a 60% rate of return if you had invested in these companies during this five-year period. Unfortunately, that logic is wrong! The companies in 1995 are not the same set of companies as in 1990. It is likely that many of the companies from the 1990 list would no longer be among the 5,000 largest companies in 1995 (and some might not even exist at all) and would have been replaced in the list by other companies. As a result, your actual return on your 1990 investment would probably be less than 60%. In order to find out what your actual rate of return would have been, you would have to track all the 5,000 companies from the 1990 list, regardless of whether they were still on the list for 1995. This is referred to as Survival Bias, because you have mistakenly only evaluated the companies that have survived (i.e., not been eliminated from the list). Of course, the ones that survive will have been the companies that were more successful.

You could make this same mistake if you were only evaluating the Dow 30 list of companies. Suppose that it is now 1996 and you went back twenty years to 1976 to see how the Dow 30 has performed during the twenty years from 1976 until 1996. The stocks in the Dow 30 change over time, and so if you tracked the returns of the current Dow 30 for the past twenty years, the returns would have been exceptionally good: after all, that is the reason these companies made it into the Dow 30. The problem here is that if you went back to 1976 you could not have known which thirty companies would have made up the Dow 30 in 1996. It would be like asking in 1996 which companies will be in the Dow 30 in the year 2026.

Bid-Ask Bounce

If you want to buy a stock you have to pay the ask price. If you want to sell the stock you will receive the bid price. Typically there is a 1/8 to 1/4 dollar difference between these two price numbers. The difference is the fee that you have to pay the market maker (the person who matches sellers and buyers) to do her job. Most stock databases report one price, either the bid price or the ask price, but quite often the database does not state which price is being reported, and the databases are often not consistent. Therefore, in examining such data, it might appear that a stock increased in value when in fact all that happened was that the reported price changed from the bid price to the ask price, while the actual underlying value of the stock remained unchanged.

Data Snooping

This is probably the most common and most deceptive trap an analyst can fall into. In practice it is not difficult to "prove" anything if you try long enough to find the data you are looking for. To understand this concept, consider a list of randomly generated numbers. What if you tried to use these numbers to predict future stock returns? On average, you would expect these numbers to have no predictive power. However, if you generate enough of these lists, eventually you will randomly generate a list of numbers that will, by chance, have a positive correlation with actual outcomes of stock price data. Therefore, you would be able to "predict" stock prices using purely random numbers. Of course, in order to find these numbers you would have had to generate a large variety of lists that had no correlation at all with the stock prices you are trying to predict. Does that mean that the final list you generated will be any better at predicting actual stock returns outside of your sample than any other randomly generated list? Of course not. Stock analysts do not data snoop intentionally. What happens in practice is that using historical data, analysts often try a variety of approaches to find predictive power. Maybe the first ten attempts will yield no predictive power at all. Eventually they will find some scenario that appears to predict returns that in reality is no better than the first ten attempts.

Jim Theiser's Stock Prediction Model

The basic idea behind Jim Theiser's stock prediction model is to perform linear regression on previous monthly returns of stocks (in this case the Dow 30) using various characteristics of the underlying assets as well as current market valuation statistics as the independent variables. Jim's model is based on twelve factors that he believes are possible good predictors of future stock performance. Of course, different stocks' returns will correlate differently to these factors. This is merely a starting point from which a thorough regression analysis can reduce the list of factors to a smaller subset. The twelve factors can be grouped into four major categories and are presented below:

Valuation (price level)

Probably the most common factor used to predict stock returns are those factors related to current market valuation of a stock. The idea is to find stocks that are valued artificially low by the market, and so the purchase of stocks should yield high returns. In Jim's model he uses the following factors related to valuations:

1. E/P ratio (Earnings to Price ratio): This compares the underlying corporate earnings of a stock to its market price. In theory, higher profits should translate to a higher stock price.

2. Return on Equity (ROE): Another measure of performance is the ratio of the profit to the assets of the company expressed as a percentage. Companies that have a high ROE should have a high stock price.

3. Book Value (per share) to Price (BV/P): Book Value is the value that accountants assign to the underlying assets of a company. In theory, if the stock price falls below the book value, it would be more profitable for the stockholders to liquidate the assets of the company.

4. Cash Flow to Price (CF/P): Since there is a tremendous amount of leeway in reporting accounting profits, many financial analysts believe that cash flows are a better (that is, less biased) measure of a company's profitability. CF/P is meant to be similar to E/P and is another measure of a company's market valuation.

Momentum (Price History)

Simply stated, does the past performance of a stock in any way predict future returns? To test for this possibility, Jim's model incorporates the following factors:

5. Previous 1 Month Return: The particular stock's return from the previous month.

6. Previous 2 Month Return: The cumulative return of the particular stock over the last 2 months.

7. Previous 6 Month Return: The cumulative return of the particular stock over the last 6 months.

8. Previous 12 Month Return: The cumulative return of the particular stock over the last 12 months.

9. Previous 1 Month Return of S&P: This factor is included as a broader test for momentum.

Risk

According to the efficient market theory, risk is the only factor that should have any impact on the expected return of a stock: Investors demand a premium on the rate of return of a company if the investment is risky. That is why stocks are believed to offer a much higher return, on average, than investing in government Treasury Bills. In Jim's model, risk is quantified using the following two factors:

10. The trailing 12-month sample standard deviation of stock returns.

11. The trailing 12-month sample standard deviation of cash flow to price (CF/P).

Liquidity

Many market "observers" believe that the liquidity of an asset is reflected in its price. The idea is that the easier it is to trade a security in for cash, the less vulnerable an investor is to fluctuations in the security's price. In order to understand this better, think of a very non-liquid asset such as a house. If you own a house and the real estate market collapses, it could take you a long period of time to find a buyer. During this period, the value of the house could decline even further. On the other hand, if you own a liquid asset such as a Treasury bill, you can sell it any time you wish in a matter of minutes. It is clearly more desirable to own an asset that can be sold quite easily. Jim's model attempts to account for liquidity with the following factor:

12. The trading volume/market cap (V/MC): It is believed that stocks differ in their liquidity. If you have invested in a small company, it might be difficult to find a buyer of your stock exactly at the moment you want to sell it. In contrast, selling the stock of a large company, such as IBM, should be much easier. It is believed that the relative liquidity of a stock can affect its market price.

Assignment:

You are to take on the role of Jim Theiser's partner. You have been given the task of predicting the Dow 30 stock price returns over the six month period from January, 1996 through June, 1996. You should use linear regression to make predictions of future returns, but you will only have to evaluate two stocks from the Dow 30: IBM and GM. After you have completed your analysis, you are to advise Jim on the quality of the model. Do you believe that the model works and has some predictive power? Why or why not? What are its strengths and weaknesses? Please keep in mind all of the evaluative tools of linear regression, plus the potential pitfalls, when using these tools to predict stock price returns.

The data for the case is contained in the spreadsheet IBMandGM.xls. The spreadsheet contains two worksheets, one for IBM and one for GM. Each worksheet contains monthly data for the twelve factors discussed previously, for the period from January, 1990 through June, 1996. In addition, you are presented with the actual returns from the corresponding stock from January, 1990 through December, 1995, but not for the first six months of 1996. You are to use linear regression to make the best possible predictions for the missing returns from January, 1996 through June, 1996. While constructing your model, you should investigate all of the warnings and issues involved in evaluating and validating a regression model. Remember that stock returns are very noisy and can be extremely difficult to predict. Keep this in mind as you perform your analysis and do not expect to find an "ideal" regression model. Use your best judgment in deciding which variables to keep and which to omit from your model.

What to Hand in

Please hand in your predictions of the stock price returns for GM and IBM from January, 1996 through June, 1996. In addition, for each company, include any relevant charts that you used in your analysis. You should demonstrate that you have investigated all of the issues involved in evaluating a regression model. Please write a brief sentence or two on each issue, explaining its impact on your analysis.

EXERCISES

EXERCISE 6.1 Table 6.29 contains data collected by VARMAX Realty on twenty houses. Column 2 of this table shows the selling price of each house, and Column 3 shows the total area of the house, measured in (feet)^2. The fourth column of Table 6.29 is a rating of the quality of the neighborhood in which the house is located, rated on a scale of 1 through 5 with 1 being the lowest ranking. Similarly, Column

TABLE 6.29

Data for 20 houses for Exercise 6.1.

House Number	Price ($1,000)	Area (feet²)	Neighborhood Quality Rating (1-5)	General Condition Rating (1-5)
1	350	2,100	2	5
2	280	1,560	4	4
3	285	2,420	4	2
4	210	1,201	5	3
5	450	3,020	4	3
6	465	4,200	3	4
7	405	2,100	3	5
8	440	2,356	5	3
9	345	4,005	3	2
10	375	1,980	3	5
11	290	2,220	2	3
12	490	4,500	5	1
13	250	1,450	5	4
14	235	2,300	2	4
15	105	1,354	1	3
16	310	3,560	3	2
17	215	2,580	1	3
18	440	2,300	5	5
19	415	3,890	2	4
20	270	2,100	4	1

5 of Table 6.29 contains a rating of the general condition of the house, also rated as a number between 1 and 5 with 1 being the lowest ranking.

VARMAX would like to use the data in Table 6.29 to develop a linear regression model to predict the price of houses as a function of the area of the house, the neighborhood rating, and the condition rating of the house.

The data in Table 6.29 is provided in the spreadsheet VARMAX.xls.

(a) Construct and run a regression model to predict the price of a house based on the three independent variables for the area, the neighborhood rating, and the condition rating of the house.

(b) Evaluate the regression output of your regression model. Do you recommend using this regression model?

(c) What is the regression equation produced by the linear regression model?

(d) What is the predicted price of a house whose area is 3,000 square feet with a neighborhood ranking of 5 and a general condition ranking of 4?

EXERCISE 6.2 The United States Internal Revenue Service (IRS) is trying to estimate the monthly amount of unpaid taxes that its auditing division in Dallas, Texas is able to uncover. In the past, the IRS has estimated this figure on the basis of the expected number of field-audit labor hours. In recent years, however, field-audit labor hours have become an erratic predictor of the amount of uncovered unpaid taxes.

The Dallas auditing division keeps records of the number of labor hours that are devoted to trying to uncover unpaid taxes, as well as the number of computer hours used to check tax returns to try to uncover unpaid taxes. Table 6.30 contains the labor hours and the computer hours (in units of 100 hours), and unpaid taxes discovered by the audit division (in $ million), for the last ten months. The IRS has decided to test the ability of a linear regression model to predict the amount of uncovered unpaid taxes based on both field-audit labor hours as well as computer hours.

TABLE 6.30

Data on labor hours, computer hours, and uncovered unpaid taxes for Exercise 6.2.

Month	Labor hours (100 hours)	Computer hours (100 hours)	Uncovered unpaid taxes ($ million)
January, 1998	45	16	31
February, 1998	42	14	20
March, 1998	44	15	27
April, 1998	45	13	27
May, 1998	43	13	24
June, 1998	46	14	32
July, 1998	44	16	30
August, 1998	45	16	30
September, 1998	44	15	28
October, 1998	43	15	25

(a) The spreadsheet AUDIT.xls contains the data in Table 6.30. Using this spreadsheet, construct a linear regression model to predict uncovered unpaid taxes.

(b) Perform a significance test of the regression coefficients using the t-statistics in your regression model output. What do you find?

(c) Look at the scatter-plots of the regression residuals with each of the independent variables. Is there evidence of heteroscedasticity?

(d) Would you recommend that the IRS increase the number of computer hours devoted to auditing of tax returns? Would you recommend that the IRS increase the number of field-audit hours? Why or why not?

EXERCISE 6.3 One key component of the mission of the United States Internal Revenue Service (IRS) is to ensure that individuals pay their required taxes. This task is quite difficult, as there are millions of taxpayers and the complexity of the United States tax code is rather mind-boggling. In fact, the IRS only checks a small fraction of all tax returns submitted by taxpayers; they rely on most taxpayers' incentive to submit a truthful tax return either because they are honest or because of the threat of criminal action if they are caught cheating on their taxes. Because auditing a tax return is a very labor-intensive (and hence expensive) undertaking, the IRS needs to develop simple rules that it can use to automatically determine if a given tax return should be fully audited. For example, the IRS might use the following rule:

> If a given taxpayer's gross income is in excess of $200,000, yet his/her taxes paid is under $5,000, then the taxpayer's tax return should be audited.

In order to develop more effective rules, the IRS uses regression models to predict what taxes are typically owed based on the figures in a very small number of entries on their tax return. Table 6.31 shows the figures from 24 tax returns. The spreadsheet IRS-PREDICT.xls contains all of the data shown in Table 6.31.

(a) Construct a linear regression model that can be used to predict the taxes owed based on the independent variables suggested by Table 6.31. Evaluate the validity of your model.

(b) Build a new linear regression model that addresses some of the concerns in part (a).

(c) Is there evidence of heteroscedacity in the model of part (b)? Are the normality assumptions satisfied? What are the 95% confidence intervals on the coefficients of the model?

TABLE 6.31

Tax return data of 24 tax returns, for Exercise 6.3.

Tax Return Number	Taxes Owed ($)	Gross Pre-Tax Income ($)	Schedule-A Deductions ($)	Schedule C Income ($)	Schedule C Deductions Percentage (%)	Home Office Indicator
1	37,056	128,555	17,952	24,720	19	0
2	30,002	105,332	29,696	14,350	45	1
3	16,045	68,557	17,332	25,260	50	1
4	22,345	100,052	18,221	22,213	32	1
5	17,056	78,657	18,737	26,023	64	1
6	35,674	112,575	25,769	22,387	80	1
7	25,678	82,006	15,146	25,510	75	1
8	29,567	111,040	15,073	19,967	54	0
9	22,040	78,860	17,478	22,878	15	0
10	25,639	102,243	20,878	21,893	24	0
11	9,459	46,814	21,769	20,818	11	0
12	46,789	140,918	11,649	16,191	75	0
13	21,050	82,837	26,466	14,452	45	1
14	39,678	133,674	15,380	13,047	56	0
15	36,720	123,498	27,546	26,573	64	1
16	15,932	70,383	21,147	16,731	32	0
17	22,244	88,873	31,658	21,053	25	0
18	25,670	90,101	16,879	17,693	30	1
19	24,568	72,603	23,879	25,947	10	0
20	23,897	91,467	23,020	24,695	5	0
21	29,789	147,042	28,332	20,850	18	1
22	24,378	99,258	25,802	19,419	38	1
23	32,478	123,021	17,297	16,889	70	1
24	11,253	54,782	21,418	9,086	50	0

TABLE 6.32

Dates of earthquakes and related data for Exercise 6.4.

Month of Earthquake	Month Number	Number of months after the most recent earthquake	Number of months after the second-most-recent earthquake
December, 1990	0	—	—
October, 1991	10	10	—
February, 1992	14	4	14
November, 1992	23	9	13
April, 1993	28	5	14
December, 1993	36	8	13
June, 1994	42	6	14
February, 1995	50	8	14
May, 1995	53	3	11
December, 1995	60	7	10
April, 1996	64	4	11
January, 1997	73	9	13
March, 1997	75	2	11
November, 1997	83	8	10

(d) What is your prediction of the taxes owed by a taxpayer with gross pre-tax income of $130,000, deductions claimed in Schedule A $34,500, income on Schedule C of $26,000, having a home office, and Schedule C deductions percentage of 25%?

EXERCISE 6.4 The accurate prediction of the timing of earthquakes is an important undertaking in the interests of public safety. In this exercise, we explore a regression model approach to this problem.

The first column of Table 6.32 shows the month and year of all earthquakes measuring 3.5 or larger on the Richter scale on a small island in the Pacific Ocean between December, 1990 and November, 1997. The dates in first column of the table are converted to a "month number" in the second column of the table starting with December, 1990 being month number 0. Thus, for example, October, 1991 is month number 10, since this month is 10 months after December, 1990. The data in Table 6.32 is reproduced in the spreadsheet EARTHQUAKE.xls.

We might postulate that the time to the next earthquake might be a function of the number of months after the most recent earthquake, as well as the number of months after the second-most-recent earthquake. These numbers are shown in the third and fourth columns of Table 6.32. For example, consider the earthquake that occurred in May, 1995. The most recent earthquake prior to that time was in February, 1995, and so the number of months after the most recent earthquake would be 3 months. Also, the number of months after the second-most-recent earthquake is 11 months, as the second-most-recent earthquake took place in June, 1994.

(a) Construct a regression model to predict the time when earthquakes occur based on the data in Table 6.32.

(b) What is the R^2 of your regression model? Given the very imperfect nature of earthquake prediction, do you consider this value of R^2 to be high or low?

(c) Evaluate the validity of your regression model. Do the regression coefficients pass the significance test? Is there evidence of autocorrelation?

(d) Construct a smaller regression model based on your answers to part (c) and test the validity of this smaller model to ensure that it passes all evaluation tests.

EXERCISE 6.5 A manufacturer of small electric motors uses an automatic milling machine to produce slots in motor shafts. A batch of shafts is run and then checked. All shafts that do not meet required dimensional tolerances are discarded. At the beginning of each new batch, the milling machine needs to be adjusted, because the machine's cutter head wears slightly during batch production.

The manufacturer would like to predict the number of defective shafts per batch as a function of the size of the batch. To this end, the engineering department has gathered the data shown in Table 6.33 on the number of defective shafts per batch. This data is reproduced in the spreadsheet BATCH.xls.

(a) Construct a linear regression model to predict the number of defective shafts per batch as a function of the batch size.

(b) Examine the regression output R^2 and the t-statistics. Is your linear regression model a good fit to the data? Explain your answer.

(c) Look at the residual plot that is produced with the regression output. Do you observe any evidence of heteroscedasticity?

(d) Based on the results of your analysis, construct a new regression model that uses a nonlinear relationship to eliminate any heteroscedasticity. Does your new model eliminate the heteroscedasticity?

EXERCISE 6.6 Jack Meister, the master brewer at Hubbard Brewing Co. (HBC), would like to predict the annual sales of beers that are brewed at HBC. To this end, he has assembled data and run a multiple linear regression model of beer sales based on the following five factors:

- **Hops**: The ounces of hops used in the brewing of a keg of beer.
- **Malt**: The pounds of malt used in the brewing of a keg of beer.

TABLE 6.33

Batch sizes and the number of defective shafts for a sample of 30 batches for Exercise 6.5.

Sample Number	Batch Size	Number of Defective Shafts
1	200	24
2	175	17
3	125	10
4	125	7
5	375	92
6	250	37
7	350	84
8	125	6
9	400	112
10	350	81
11	375	96
12	275	49
13	100	5
14	225	25
15	300	54
16	250	34
17	225	26
18	175	15
19	225	29
20	300	53
21	150	7
22	250	41
23	400	109
24	350	82
25	250	34
26	150	6
27	325	69
28	375	97
29	200	22
30	200	21

TABLE 6.34

Excerpts from the data for 50 beers brewed by HBC for Exercise 6.6.

Beer Number	Annual Sales ($,1000)	Hops (ounces per keg)	Malt (pounds per keg)	Annual Advertising ($)	Bitterness Scale	Initial Investment ($ million)
1	4,800	9.0	8.0	180,000	3	1.4
2	5,100	9.0	8.0	180,000	3	0.6
3	5,100	8.0	8.0	180,000	3	0.7
4	1,900	9.0	7.0	140,000	4	2.4
5	5,300	8.0	8.0	180,000	3	2.3
⋮	⋮	⋮	⋮	⋮	⋮	⋮
46	6,250	8.0	8.0	170,000	2	1.2
47	4,900	5.0	7.0	170,000	3	1.5
48	5,000	5.0	7.0	170,000	2	1.6
49	5,100	8.0	7.0	170,000	3	1.4
50	5,200	8.0	7.0	170,000	1	0.5

- **Annual Advertising**: The annual advertising expenditures for the beer in dollars.

- **Bitterness**: The bitterness rating of the beer. Bitterness is rated on a scale cf 1 to 10 with a 10 being the most bitter.

- **Initial investment**: The initial investment in brewing equipment in $ million.

Jack gathered data on these five factors for 50 different beer brands brewed by HBC. This data is shown in Table 6.34 and is reproduced in the spreadsheet HBC.xls.

TABLE 6.35

Key ingredients of the regression output for the prediction of sales of beer for Exercise 6.6.

R Square	0.8790	
Standard Error	558.9364	
Observations	50	
	Coefficients	**Standard Error**
Intercept	13,707.1386	1,368.4086
Hops	37.3444	42.4970
Malt	1,319.2696	161.0762
Annual Advertising	0.0493	0.0048
Bitterness	−63.1678	83.1086
Initial Investment	53.2305	133.1423

TABLE 6.36

Sample correlations for the independent variables used in the prediction of sales of beer in Exercise 6.6.

	Hops	Malt	Annual Advertising	Bitterness	Initial Investment
Hops	1				
Malt	−0.0508	1			
Annual Advertising	−0.0467	0.2194	1		
Bitterness	0.6744	−0.5468	−0.1554	1	
Initial Investment	−0.0335	0.0173	0.0812	0.0319	1

TABLE 6.37

Data for four proposed new beers, for Exercise 6.6.

Proposed New Beer	Hops (ounces per keg)	Malt (pounds per keg)	Annual Advertising ($)	Bitterness Scale	Initial Investment ($ million)
"Great Ale"	12.0	8.0	150,000	6	1.2
"Fine Brau"	7.0	6.0	155,000	2	1.3
"HBC Porter"	11.0	8.0	180,000	3	2.1
"HBC Stout"	9.0	7.0	150,000	6	1.0

Jack then ran a regression model to predict the annual sales of beers (in $1,000) using the previous five factors as the independent variables. Table 6.35 shows the key ingredients of the regression output from Jack's model. Table 6.36 shows the sample correlations for the data for the five independent variables.

(a) What is the regression equation produced by Jack's regression model?

(b) Compute a 95% confidence interval for each of the regression coefficients in Jack's model. Do you notice anything interesting?

(c) Evaluate the validity of Jack's regression model. In particular, which regression coefficients are significant? How might Jack change the model to arrive at a more valid model?

(d) Construct a new regression model that will still have good predictive power, but whose regression coefficients will be more significant. What is the new regression equation?

(e) Table 6.37 contains data for four proposed new beers being developed for possible production at HBC. What is your prediction of the annual sales of these four new beers based on your new regression model?

(f) HBC's new product development team has created a new beer, temporarily called Final Excalibur, that they believe will be the most bitter beer ever sold. The ingredients consist of 13 ounces of hops and 7 pounds of malt per keg. HBC is thinking of investing $700,000 in initial capital to brew this beer with an annual advertising budget of $150,000. Would you recommend using the regression equation to predict the sales of this new beer? Why or why not?

EXERCISE 6.7 In recent years, many American firms have intensified their efforts to market their products in the Pacific Rim. A consortium of U.S. firms that produce raw materials used in Singapore is interested in predicting the level of exports from the U.S. to Singapore. The consortium would also like to understand the relationship between U.S. exports to Singapore and certain factors affecting the economy of Singapore. The consortium has hired a consultant to help them with this task.

The consultant obtained monthly data on five major economic indicators for 67 months from January, 1989 through July, 1994. These economic indicators are as follows:

- **Exports**: U.S. exports to Singapore in billions of Singapore dollars.

- **Money Supply**: the Singapore money supply indicator in billions of Singapore dollars.

- **Lending Rate**: the minimum Singapore bank lending rate in percentage per year.

- **Price Index**: the Singapore price index.

- **Exchange**: the exchange rate of Singapore dollars per U.S. dollar.

The consultant then constructed three different regression models using three different combinations of the independent variables. The key ingredients of the regression output from these three models are shown in Table 6.38, Table 6.39, and Table 6.40.

(a) What is the number of degrees of freedom associated with the regression output shown in Table 6.38?

TABLE 6.38
Key ingredients of the regression output for the first regression model to predict U.S. exports to Singapore for Exercise 6.7.

| R Square | 0.825 | |
| Observations | 67 | |

	Coefficients	Standard Error
Intercept	−4.015	2.766
Money Supply	0.368	0.064
Lending Rate	0.005	0.049
Price Index	0.037	0.009
Exchange Rate	0.268	1.175

TABLE 6.39
Key ingredients of the regression output for the second regression model to predict U.S. exports to Singapore for Exercise 6.7.

| R Square | 0.825 | |
| Observations | 67 | |

	Coefficients	Standard Error
Intercept	−3.995	2.736
Money Supply	0.364	0.041
Price Index	0.037	0.004
Exchange Rate	0.242	1.135

TABLE 6.40

Key ingredients of the regression output for the third regression model to predict U.S. exports to Singapore for Exercise 6.7.

	Coefficients	Standard Error
R Square	0.825	
Observations	67	
Intercept	−3.423	0.541
Money Supply	0.361	0.039
Price Index	0.037	0.004

TABLE 6.41

The market value and related information for 15 firms for Exercise 6.8.

Firm Number	Market Value of Firm ($ million)	Total Assets ($ million)	Total Sales ($ million)	Number of Employees
1	3,023	8,610	10,328	121,000
2	1,386	2,593	3,712	55,000
3	1,949	2,119	3,099	26,700
4	1,319	1,820	2,553	11,980
5	867	1,407	1,959	21,900
6	254	511	911	4,100
7	191	521	800	7,500
8	1,969	579	795	6,100
9	375	368	578	5,400
10	159	190	527	4,400
11	252	741	524	6,950
12	314	322	466	5,000
13	1,778	398	443	4,890
14	468	199	443	5,700
15	267	250	423	5,100

(b) Compute the 95% confidence interval for each of the four regression coefficients corresponding to the independent variables in Table 6.38. Which variable(s) among the four do you think are important independent variable(s) for predicting U.S. exports to Singapore?

(c) In your opinion, which of the three regression models is best overall? Support your answer with any analysis that you feel is appropriate.

(d) What is your prediction of U.S. exports to Singapore in billions of Singapore dollars if the money supply indicator is 7.3, the lending rate is 12.7%, the Singapore price index is 155.0, and the exchange rate is 2.12 Singapore dollars per U.S. dollar? Use the model that you chose in part (c) to make your prediction.

(e) How would you go about verifying whether autocorrelation exists in the regression model that you chose in part (c)?

EXERCISE 6.8 Juan Martinez is an analyst at SDA, Inc., a leading mutual fund company. Juan has been asked to develop a regression model for use in predicting the market value of a firm. Table 6.41 shows data that Juan has gathered on 15 firms. The second column of the table shows the market value of each of the 15 firms. The third column shows the total assets of the each firm, and the fourth column shows the total sales of each firm, all for the previous year. The fifth column shows the number of employees at each firm. The data from Table 6.41 is also provided in the spreadsheet SDA.xls.

(a) Construct a multiple linear regression model to predict the market value of a firm based on the data that Juan has gathered for the 15 firms.

(b) Examine the regression output of your regression model. Is there evidence of multicollinearity in the model? How would you detect it?

(c) Propose a simpler model by possibly deleting one or more independent variable(s) from your model.

(d) Suppose a firm has assets of $1,800 million, sales of $3,500 million and has 31,000 employees. What is your prediction of the firm's market value using your model from part (c)?

EXERCISE 6.9 The purpose of this exercise is to derive the formulas for the coefficients of a simple linear regression that were introduced in Section 6.1. Please note that this exercise is more mathematical and requires a knowledge of calculus.

(a) Suppose that we have n values $x_1, \ldots, x_n$ of the independent variable x and n values $y_1, \ldots, y_n$ of the dependent variable Y. Use calculus to show that the values of b_0 and b_1 that minimize the residual sum of squares

$$\text{minimize} \quad \sum_{i=1}^{n} (y_i - b_0 - b_1 x_i)^2,$$

are given by the formulas:

$$b_1 = \frac{\sum_{i=1}^{n} (x_i - \bar{x})(y_i - \bar{y})}{\sum_{i=1}^{n} (x_i - \bar{x})^2}$$

and

$$b_0 = \bar{y} - b_1 \bar{x},$$

where

$$\bar{x} = \frac{\sum_{i=1}^{n} x_i}{n} \quad \text{and} \quad \bar{y} = \frac{\sum_{i=1}^{n} y_i}{n}.$$

(b) Show that

$$b_1 = \text{corr}(x, y) \frac{s_y}{s_x},$$

where $\text{corr}(x, y)$ is the sample correlation between x and y, and s_x and s_y are the sample standard deviations of x and y.

(c) Show that R^2 is equal to the square of the sample correlation between x and y. That is, show that

$$R^2 = (\text{corr}(x, y))^2.$$

CHAPTER ⑦

Linear Optimization

CONTENTS

THIS CHAPTER PRESENTS THE FUNDAMENTALS OF A POWERFUL SET OF TOOLS called linear optimization models (also called "linear programming" models) that are very valuable in analyzing a wide variety of management problems. We demonstrate the essential concepts needed to develop and use linear optimization modeling tools, and we show how these tools can help managers obtain the most value from the resources of their firm.

Linear optimization models are used in just about every arena of the global economy, including transportation, telecommunications, production and operations scheduling, as well as in support of strategic decision-making. To quote the late computer scientist Eugene Lawler, "[Linear optimization modeling] is used to allocate resources, plan production, schedule workers, plan investment portfolios and formulate marketing (and military) strategies. The versatility and economic impact of linear optimization models in today's industrial world is truly awesome."

| 7.1 | FORMULATING A MANAGEMENT PROBLEM AS A LINEAR OPTIMIZATION MODEL |

FORMULATING A MANAGEMENT PROBLEM AS A LINEAR OPTIMIZATION MODEL

In this section, we introduce the fundamental ideas of linear optimization through two examples of management problems.

Example 7.1 – The New Bedford Steel

New Bedford Steel (NBS) is a steel producer located in Bedford, Pennsylvania. Coking coal is a necessary raw material in the production of steel, and NBS procures 1.0-1.5 million tons of coking coal per year. It is now time to plan for next year's production, and Stephen Coggins, coal supply manager for NBS, has solicited and received bids from eight potential coal mining companies for next year.

Table 7.1 shows the relevant information on the bids from the eight potential coal suppliers. For example, Ashley Mining Co. has bid to supply NBS with coking coal at a price of $49.50/ton up to their capacity of 300 mtons (300,000 tons) per year (1 "mton" denotes 1,000 tons). The Ashley mine is a union mine, and the mode of delivery of the coal from the mine is by rail. The coal from the Ashley mine has an average volatility of 15% (the volatility of the coal is the percent of volatile (burnable) matter in the coal).

Based on market forecasts and last year's production characteristics, NBS is planning to accept bids for 1,225 mtons (1,225,000 tons) of coking coal for the coming year. This coal must have an average volatility of at least 19%. Also, as a hedge against adverse labor relations, NBS has decided to procure at least 50% of its coking coal from union (United Mine Workers) mines. Finally, Stephen Coggins needs to keep in mind that capacity for bringing in coal by rail is limited to 650 mtons per year, and capacity for bringing in coal by truck is limited to 720 mtons per year.

Stephen Coggins is interested in answering the following three questions:

(a) How much coal should NBS contract for from each supplier in order to minimize the cost of supply of coking coal?

(b) What will be NBS's total cost of supply?

(c) What will be NBS's average cost of supply?

It should be obvious that Stephen Coggins' main objective should be to formulate a supply plan that minimizes the cost of supplying coking coal to NBS. The least expensive coal is the Ashley coal, followed by Bedford, then Consol, etc. However, the less expensive coals also have a lower volatility, which is troubling since the coking coal must have an average volatility of 19%. One strategy that Stephen Coggins could try to employ would be to only contract with mines whose coal has at least 19% volatility. This strategy would eliminate Ashley, Bedford, and Consol from consideration, which is unfortunate since they are the three lowest bidders. Indeed, a smarter strategy is to consider blending the coal, since NBS has blending facilities at its materials handling site. For example, blending equal amounts of coal from Consol and Dunby would produce a blend of coal that has an average volatility of 19%, since Consol's coal has an average volatility level of 18% and Dunby's coal has an average volatility level of 20%.

Formulation of the Coking Coal Supply Problem

At this point, it should be clear that there is no easy way to determine (even from a careful scrutiny of the data) how much Stephen Coggins should contract from each supplier to minimize the cost of the coking coal supply. Let us formulate the problem mathematically. The decisions that Stephen Coggins must make are the quantities of

	Ashley	Bedford	Consol	Dunby	Earlam	Florence	Gaston	Hopt
Price ($/ton)	49.50	50.00	61.00	63.50	66.50	71.00	72.50	80.00
Union/Non-union	Union	Union	Non-union	Union	Non-union	Union	Non-union	Non-union
Truck/Rail	Rail	Truck	Rail	Truck	Truck	Truck	Rail	Rail
Volatility (%)	15	16	18	20	21	22	23	25
Capacity(mtons/year)	300	600	510	655	575	680	450	490

TABLE 7.1

Bids received by NBS from potential coking coal suppliers.

coal to contract from each of the eight suppliers. Formally, let the unknown variable A denote the amount of coal to be contracted from Ashley in mtons (1,000 tons). Similarly, we can define the other seven unknown variables and list all of these as follows:

A = the amount of coal to be contracted from Ashley in mtons,

B = the amount of coal to be contracted from Bedford in mtons,

C = the amount of coal to be contracted from Consol in mtons,

D = the amount of coal to be contracted from Dunby in mtons,

E = the amount of coal to be contracted from Earlam in mtons,

F = the amount of coal to be contracted from Florence in mtons,

G = the amount of coal to be contracted from Gaston in mtons,

H = the amount of coal to be contracted from Hopt in mtons.

With these unknown variables represented as above, the cost of supplying coal to NBS can be represented as:

$$\text{Cost} = 49.50A + 50.00B + 61.00C + 63.50D + 66.50E + 71.00F + 72.50G + 80.00H.$$

The objective, of course, is to determine the values of A, B, C, D, E, F, G, and H that minimize this cost. In so doing, there will be certain restrictions or constraints that must be obeyed. For example, Stephen Coggins must purchase 1,225 mtons of coal. This is represented by the following equation, which we will call the "supply" equation or the supply constraint:

$$\text{Supply:} \quad A + B + C + D + E + F + G + H = 1,225.$$

This equation states simply that the total amount of coking coal to be contracted from all of the suppliers for next year must equal 1,225 mtons, which is the amount of coking coal NBS has determined that they will need for next year. Another constraint that must be satisfied is that at least 50% of the coal must come from union mines. Examining Table 7.1, we see that this constraint is easily represented by the following inequality:

$$A + B + D + F \geq C + E + G + H.$$

Rearranging this expression so that all of the variables appear to the left of the "$\geq$" sign, we obtain the following constraint which we will call the "union" constraint:

$$\text{Union:} \quad A + B - C + D - E + F - G - H \geq 0.$$

Similarly, the capacity restriction on coal deliveries by truck and by rail can each be formulated after examining the "Truck/Rail" row of Table 7.1 and then writing down the constraints as follows:

$$\text{Truck:}\quad B + D + E + F \le 720,$$
$$\text{Rail:}\quad A + C + G + H \le 650.$$

Another important condition that we must bear in mind is that the average volatility of the coal must be at least 19%. We can write this condition as follows:

$$\frac{15A + 16B + 18C + 20D + 21E + 22F + 23G + 25H}{A + B + C + D + E + F + G + H} \ge 19.$$

As it turns out, the form of the above expression is not very convenient, and so we will change this expression to an equivalent expression by first clearing the denominator and obtaining:

$$15A + 16B + 18C + 20D + 21E + 22F + 23G + 25H \ge 19(A + B + C + D + E + F + G + H).$$

By moving all of the terms to the left side of the expression and combining the numbers, we obtain the following constraint, which we will call the "volatility" constraint:

$$\text{Volatility:}\quad -4A - 3B - C + D + 2E + 3F + 4G + 6H \ge 0.$$

Yet another important consideration is the mine capacity of each of the eight mines. We can easily represent these conditions as follows:

$$\text{Acap:}\qquad A \le 300$$
$$\text{Bcap:}\qquad B \le 600$$
$$\text{Ccap:}\qquad C \le 510$$
$$\text{Dcap:}\qquad D \le 655$$
$$\text{Ecap:}\qquad E \le 575$$
$$\text{Fcap:}\qquad F \le 680$$
$$\text{Gcap:}\qquad G \le 450$$
$$\text{Hcap:}\qquad H \le 490.$$

Last but not least, we must ensure that none of the unknowns A, B, C, D, E, F, G, or H are allowed to take on negative quantities. We therefore impose the following conditions, called the nonnegativity conditions:

$$\text{Nonnegativity:}\quad A, B, C, D, E, F, G, H \ge 0.$$

A summary of the formulation of the New Bedford Steel coking coal supply problem appears below. This is just a concise representation of all of the constraints and equations that have been developed above.

Formulation of the New Bedford Coking Coal Supply Problem

minimize $\quad 49.50A + 50.00B + 61.00C + 63.50D + 66.50E$
$\quad\quad\quad\quad + 71.00F + 72.50G + 80.00H$

subject to:

Supply:	$A + B + C + D + E + F + G + H = 1{,}225$
Union:	$A + B - C + D - E + F - G - H \geq 0$
Truck:	$B + D + E + F \leq 720$
Rail:	$A + C + G + H \leq 650$
Volatility:	$-4A - 3B - C + D + 2E + 3F + 4G + 6H \geq 0$
Acap:	$A \leq 300$
Bcap:	$B \leq 600$
Ccap:	$C \leq 510$
Dcap:	$D \leq 655$
Ecap:	$E \leq 575$
Fcap:	$F \leq 680$
Gcap:	$G \leq 450$
Hcap:	$H \leq 490$
Nonnegativity:	$A, B, C, D, E, F, G, H \geq 0.$

As it turns out, it is possible to format this problem into a spreadsheet and to instruct the spreadsheet software to compute the solution to this problem. That is, the computer will compute the values of the variables $A, B, C, D, E, F, G,$ and H that will satisfy all of the constraints and the nonnegativity conditions, and that will yield the minimum value of the cost in the process. If one solves this problem in this way, the supply strategy that minimizes the total cost of supply turns out to be the assignment shown in Table 7.2, with a minimized cost of $73,267.50 (in thousands of dollars), i.e., $73.2675 million. (The method for obtaining this solution will be shown later, in Section 7.4.) A quick check will reveal that all of the constraints of the problem have been satisfied. For example, the rail capacity constraint is:

$$\text{Rail:} \quad A + C + G + H \leq 650.$$

Substituting for the values of $A, B, C, D, E, F, G,$ and H from Table 7.2, we indeed see that

$$A + C + G + H = 55.0 + 0.0 + 450.0 + 0.0 \leq 650.$$

One can also check all of the other constraints of the problem and verify that they are satisfied by this solution as well.

TABLE 7.2

The supply strategy that minimizes the total cost of supplying coking coal to NBS.

Mining Company	Variable	Amount to Purchase (mtons/year)
Ashley	A	55.0 mtons
Bedford	B	600.0 mtons
Consol	C	0.0 mtons
Dunby	D	20.0 mtons
Earlam	E	100.0 mtons
Florence	F	0.0 mtons
Gaston	G	450.0 mtons
Hopt	H	0.0 mtons

We are now in a good position to answer Stephen Coggins' three questions, as follows:

(a) How much coal should NBS contract for from each supplier in order to minimize the cost of supplying coking coal to NBS?

Answer: As indicated previously, the assignment that minimizes the cost of supply of coking coal is shown in Table 7.2.

(b) What will be NBS's total cost of supply of coking coal?

Answer: The total cost of supplying coking coal will be:

$$
\begin{aligned}
\text{Cost} &= 49.50A + 50.00B + 61.00C + 63.50D + 66.50E \\
&\quad + 71.00F + 72.50G + 80.00H \\
&= 49.50(55) + 50.00(600) + 61.00(0) + 63.50(20) + 66.50(100) \\
&\quad + 71.00(0) + 72.50(450) + 80.00(0) \\
&= \$73{,}267.50 \text{ (in thousands of dollars)}.
\end{aligned}
$$

(c) What will be NBS's average cost of supply?

Answer: The average cost of supply will be:

$$\$73{,}267.50/1{,}225 = \$59.81/\text{ton}.$$

Example 7.2 – Gemstone Tool Company

Gemstone Tool Company (GTC) is a privately held firm that competes in the consumer and industrial market for construction tools. In addition to its main manufacturing facility in Seattle, Washington, GTC operates several other manufacturing plants located in the United States, Canada, and Mexico. These plants produce their entire range of products, including power drills and saws, nail guns, and hand-held tools such as hammers, screwdrivers, wrenches, and pliers. For the sake of simplicity, let us suppose that the Winnipeg, Canada plant only produces wrenches and pliers. Wrenches and pliers are made from steel, and the process involves molding the tools on a molding machine and then assembling the tools on an assembly machine. The amount of steel used in the production of wrenches and pliers and the daily availability of steel is shown in the first line of Table 7.3. On the next two lines are the machine utilization rates needed in the production of wrenches and pliers and the capacity of these machines as well. Finally, the last two rows of the table indicate the daily market demand for these tools and their variable (per unit) contribution to earnings.

For example, according to the second column of Table 7.3, each wrench produced by GTC uses 1.5 lbs. of steel, and spends 1.0 hour on the molding machine and 0.3 hour on the assembly machine. The demand for wrenches is 15,000 per day. Every 1,000 wrenches produced (and then sold) contributes $130 to the earnings of GTC. According to the fourth column of Table 7.3, the amount of steel available per day is

		Wrenches	Pliers	Availability
TABLE 7.3	Steel (lbs.)	1.5	1.0	27,000 lbs./day
Data for the	Molding Machine (hours)	1.0	1.0	21,000 hours/day
Gemstone Tool	Assembly Machine (hours)	0.3	0.5	9,000 hours/day
Company.	Demand Limit (tools/day)	15,000	16,000	
	Contribution to Earnings ($/1,000 units)	$130	$100	

27,000 lbs. The amount of molding machine capacity is 21,000 hours per day and the amount of assembly machine capacity is 9,000 hours per day.

GTC would like to plan for the daily production of wrenches and pliers at its Winnipeg plant so as to maximize the contribution to earnings. In particular, GTC would like to answer the following questions:

(a) How many wrenches and pliers should GTC plan to produce per day in order to maximize the contribution to earnings?

(b) What would be the total contribution to earnings from this plan?

(c) Which resources would be most critical in this plan?

For this problem, the main objective is to maximize the contribution to earnings. Because of the complications involving the availability limitations of steel, molding machine capacity, and assembly machine capacity, as well as demand limits for wrenches and pliers, there once again is no obvious way to construct an earnings-maximizing production plan by simply studying the numbers in Table 7.3 and doing basic analysis. We therefore will proceed, just as in the New Bedford Steel problem, to develop a mathematical formulation of the problem.

Formulation of Production Planning Problem

The decisions that GTC must make are the number of wrenches to produce per day and the number of pliers to produce per day. Let us therefore define:

$$W = \text{the number of wrenches produced per day, in 1,000s,}$$

$$P = \text{the number of pliers produced per day, in 1,000s.}$$

We can now represent the contribution to earnings of the production plan as:

$$\text{Contribution} = 130W + 100P.$$

Note that the contribution to earnings is expressed in dollars, since the units for W and P are in thousands (1,000s) of tools, and the units for the contributions from each tool are in dollars per thousand tools.

In this problem, the objective is to determine the values of W and P that maximize the contribution to earnings. In so doing, there will be constraints that must be obeyed, arising from availability restrictions as well as from demand restrictions.

One of the constraints is the daily availability of steel. According to Table 7.3, there are 27,000 lbs. of steel available per day. Also, according to Table 7.3, each wrench uses 1.5 lbs. of steel in its manufacture, and each pliers uses 1.0 lb. of steel in its manufacture. Therefore, if we produce W wrenches per day (in 1,000s) and P pliers per day (in 1,000s), the total amount of steel that will be required per day (in 1,000 lbs.) would be:

$$1.5W + 1.0P.$$

This quantity must not exceed the daily availability of steel, which is 27,000 lbs. The "steel" constraint then is:

$$\text{Steel: } 1.5W + 1.0P \le 27.$$

Another of the constraints is the daily capacity of molding machines. According to Table 7.3, there are 21,000 hours of molding machine capacity per day. Also, according to Table 7.3, each wrench uses 1.0 hour of molding machine time in its manufacture, and each pliers uses 1.0 hour of molding machine time in its manufacture.

Therefore, if we produce W wrenches per day (in 1,000s) and P pliers per day (in 1,000s), the total amount of molding machine hours that will be required per day (in 1,000 hours) would be:

$$1.0W + 1.0P.$$

This quantity must not exceed the daily capacity of molding machine hours, which is 21,000 hours. The "molding" constraint then is:

$$\text{Molding:} \quad 1.0W + 1.0P \leq 21.$$

We need to formulate a similar constraint for the limitation on assembly machine capacity. Proceeding exactly as we just did with the molding constraint, we obtain the following constraint for assembly machine capacity:

$$\text{Assembly:} \quad 0.3W + 0.5P \leq 9.$$

We next turn to the demand restrictions. From Table 7.3, we see that GTC cannot sell more than 15,000 wrenches per day, and they also cannot sell more than 16,000 pliers per day. We can represent these demand limitations as:

$$\text{W-Demand:} \quad W \leq 15,$$
$$\text{P-Demand:} \quad P \leq 16.$$

Finally, we must ensure that neither W nor P is allowed to take on negative quantities. We therefore impose the following nonnegativity conditions:

$$\text{Nonnegativity:} \quad W, P \geq 0.$$

A summary of the formulation for the GTC problem is shown below. This is just a concise representation of all of the constraints and equations that have been developed above.

Formulation of the Gemstone Tool Company Problem

$$
\begin{array}{lr}
\text{maximize} & 130W + 100P \\
\text{subject to:} & \\
\text{Steel:} & 1.5W + 1.0P \leq 27 \\
\text{Molding:} & 1.0W + 1.0P \leq 21 \\
\text{Assembly:} & 0.3W + 0.5P \leq 9 \\
\text{W-demand:} & W \leq 15 \\
\text{P-demand:} & P \leq 16 \\
\text{Nonnegativity:} & W, P \geq 0.
\end{array}
$$

Just as in the case of the New Bedford Steel problem, it is possible to format this problem into a spreadsheet and to instruct the software to compute the solution to this problem. That is, the computer will compute the values of the variables W and P that will satisfy all of the constraints and nonnegativity conditions and that will yield the maximum value of the contribution to earnings in the process. If one solves this problem in this way, the production plan that maximizes the contribution to earnings is given by the following assignment:

$$W = 12.0$$
$$P = 9.0,$$

with a maximized contribution to earnings of \$2,460.00 (in dollars per day). A quick check will reveal that all of the constraints of the problem have been satisfied. For example, the steel availability constraint is:

$$\text{Steel:} \quad 1.5W + 1.0P \leq 27.$$

Substituting in for the values of W and P, we indeed see that

$$1.5W + 1.0P = 1.5(12.0) + 1.0(9.0) \leq 27.$$

One can also check all of the other constraints of the problem and verify that they are satisfied by this solution as well.

We can now answer the three questions posed earlier, as follows:

(a) How many wrenches and pliers should GTC plan to produce per day in order to maximize the contribution to earnings?

Answer: GTC should plan to produce 12,000 wrenches per day and 9,000 pliers per day.

(b) What would be the total contribution to earnings from this plan?

Answer: The total contributions to earnings would be:

$$\begin{aligned} \text{Contribution} &= 130W + 100P \\ &= 130(12.0) + 100(9.0) \\ &= \$2,460 \text{ per day.} \end{aligned}$$

(c) Which resources would be most critical in this plan?

Answer: To answer this question, we must check to see which of the resources (steel, molding machine capacity, and assembly machine capacity) would be used up to their resource limitations. The calculations are straightforward. For example, under the proposed production plan, the daily use of steel would be

$$1.5W + 1.0P = 1.5(12.0) + 1.0(9.0) = 27,$$

which is exactly equal to the daily availability of steel. Therefore, under the proposed plan, GTC would use up its entire daily availability of steel.

Also under the proposed production plan, the daily use of molding machine hours would be

$$1.0W + 1.0P = 1.0(12.0) + 1.0(9.0) = 21,$$

which is exactly equal to the daily molding machine capacity. Therefore, under the proposed plan, GTC would use all of the molding machine capacity.

Let us lastly consider assembly machine hours. Under the proposed production plan, the daily use of assembly machine hours would be

$$0.3W + 0.5P = 0.3(12.0) + 0.5(9.0) = 8.1,$$

which is less than the daily assembly machine capacity of 9 thousand hours. Therefore, under the proposed plan, GTC would not use all of its daily assembly machine capacity.

| 7.2 | KEY CONCEPTS AND DEFINITIONS |

In this section, we use the insights from the previous two examples to define the key concepts in a linear optimization model.

Objective

Both the New Bedford Steel (NBS) problem and the Gemstone Tool Company (GTC) problem are instances of the same type of mathematical model. They both have an **objective** that needs to be optimized. In NBS, the objective is to minimize the procurement cost of the coking coal. In the GTC problem, the objective is to maximize the contribution to earnings from the manufacture of wrenches and pliers.

Decision Variables

Both the NBS problem and the GTC problem have a set of **decision variables** that are the unknowns that the user needs to determine. In the NBS problem, the decision variables are the unknowns A, B, C, D, E, F, G, and H that represent the amount of coal to be contracted from each mine. In the GTC problem, the decision variables are the unknowns W and P that represent the number of wrenches and pliers to be manufactured per day.

Objective Function

Each problem also has an **objective function** that expresses the objective in terms of the decision variables. For the NBS problem, this objective function is given by the cost function:

$$\text{Cost} = 49.50A + 50.00B + 61.00C + 63.50D + 66.50E + 71.00F + 72.50G + 80.00H.$$

For the GTC problem, the objective function is given by the contribution to earnings function:

$$\text{Contribution} = 130W + 100P.$$

Constraints

Another common feature of both problems is that they each have **constraints** that limit or otherwise impose requirements on the relationships between the decision variables. For the NBS problem, the constraints are the mathematical expressions governing the supply requirement, the union/non-union policy, truck and rail capacity, the volatility requirement, and the mine capacities. A list of these constraints is shown below.

Supply: $\qquad A + B + C + D + E + F + G + H = 1{,}225$

Union: $\qquad A + B - C + D - E + F - G - H \geq 0$

Truck: $\qquad\qquad B + D + E + F \leq 720$

Rail: $\qquad\qquad A + C + G + H \leq 650$

Volatility: $\quad -4A - 3B - C + D + 2E + 3F + 4G + 6H \geq 0$

Acap: $\qquad\qquad\qquad\qquad A \leq 300$

Bcap: $\qquad\qquad\qquad\qquad B \leq 600$

Ccap: $\qquad\qquad\qquad\qquad C \leq 510$

Dcap: $\qquad\qquad\qquad\qquad D \leq 655$

Ecap: $\qquad\qquad\qquad\qquad E \leq 575$

Fcap: $\qquad\qquad\qquad\qquad F \leq 680$

Gcap: $\qquad\qquad\qquad\qquad G \leq 450$

Hcap: $\qquad\qquad\qquad\qquad H \leq 490.$

In the GTC problem, the constraints are the daily availability limits on steel, molding machine capacity, and assembly machine capacity, plus the demand limits on wrenches and pliers. A list of these constraints is shown below.

Steel: $\quad 1.5W + 1.0P \leq 27$

Molding: $\quad 1.0W + 1.0P \leq 21$

Assembly: $\quad 0.3W + 0.5P \leq 9$

W-demand: $\qquad\quad W \leq 15$

P-demand: $\qquad\quad P \leq 16.$

Notice that constraints can be equality or inequality constraints. For example, the supply constraint in the NBS problem is an equality constraint. The steel constraint in the GTC problem is an inequality constraint. An inequality constraint can be either a less-than-or-equal-to ("$\leq$") constraint or a greater-than-or-equal-to ("$\geq$") constraint. In the GTC problem, the molding machine capacity constraint is a less-than-or-equal-to ("$\leq$") constraint. In the NBS problem, the union/non-union constraint is a greater-than-or-equal-to ("$\geq$") constraint.

Constraint Function, LHS, RHS

Each of the constraints can be rearranged so that all terms with decision variables are on the left of the constraint relation, and the only part of the constraint that appears on the right is the constant term. For example, the rail capacity constraint in the NBS problem is of the form:

$$\underbrace{A + C + G + H}_{\uparrow} \qquad \underbrace{\leq}_{\uparrow} \qquad \underbrace{650.}_{\uparrow}$$

constraint function   relation   right-hand-side (RHS)

The part of the constraint on the left is called the constraint function ("$A + C + G + H$") and is also referred to as the left-hand-side (LHS), followed by the constraint relation (either "$=$," "$\leq$," or "$\geq$"), followed by the constant, which is referred to as the right-hand-side (RHS).

Nonnegativity Conditions

Finally, notice that each of the two problems has **nonnegativity conditions** on the decision variables. The NBS problem has the nonnegativity conditions:

$$A \geq 0, B \geq 0, C \geq 0, D \geq 0, E \geq 0, F \geq 0, G \geq 0, H \geq 0.$$

The GTC problem has the conditions:

$$W \geq 0, P \geq 0.$$

Feasible Solution

A feasible plan or **feasible solution** is an assignment of decision variables that satisfies all constraints and nonnegativity conditions. For example, in the GTC problem a feasible plan is the following assignment:

$$W = 6, P = 8.$$

It is simple to verify quickly that this assignment satisfies all of the constraints and the nonnegativity conditions for the GTC problem, and so is a feasible solution to the problem. However, this plan only yields a contribution to earnings of

$$\begin{aligned} \text{Contribution} &= 130W + 100P \\ &= 130(6.0) + 100(8.0) \\ &= \$1{,}580 \text{ per day.} \end{aligned}$$

This contribution value is quite substantially less than $2,460 dollars per day, which is the maximal contribution that can be achieved.

Optimal Solution

In both the NBS problem and the GTC problem, the goal is to find a feasible plan that optimizes the objective function, i.e., an assignment of decision variables that satisfies all of the constraints and that optimizes the objective function. An optimal plan or **optimal solution** is a feasible plan that achieves the best value of the objective function over all other feasible plans.

For example, in the NBS problem, as stated earlier, the optimal solution is:

$$A = 55, B = 600, C = 0, D = 20, E = 100, F = 0, G = 450, H = 0.$$

For this optimal solution the supply cost is $73,267.50 (in thousands of dollars).

Linear Optimization Model

Finally, we call the model of a management problem a **linear optimization model** if all of the constraint functions are linear functions, and if the objective function is a linear function, where a linear function is any function which is the sum of variables times constants. For example, a linear function is a function of the form:

$$3.0X + 7.2Y - 5.0Z + 12.5W + 34.4.$$

This expression is a linear function because it is the sum of variables times constants, plus a constant term. The following expressions are not linear functions:

$$AB + 7C + 8D + 3.2 \quad \text{(because the function } AB \text{ is nonlinear)}$$
$$A^2 + 4B - 2C + 5D \quad \text{(because the variable } A \text{ is squared)}$$
$$4A + 5\sin(B) \text{ ° (because the sine function is not a linear function)}.$$

To summarize, we have:

> A **linear optimization model** is a problem of optimizing an **objective function** expressed as a linear function of the **decision variables,** subject to **constraints** that are also linear functions of the decision variables and subject to **nonnegativity conditions** on the decision variables. A **feasible solution** is any assignment of values of the decision variables that satisfies all of the constraints and the nonnegativity conditions. The goal in a linear optimization model is to find an **optimal solution,** which is a feasible solution that optimizes the value of the objective function.

7.3 | SOLUTION OF A LINEAR OPTIMIZATION MODEL

This section covers solution methods for finding an optimal solution to a linear optimization model, i.e., solving a linear optimization model. We first consider a graphical solution method. Although the graphical solution method is not ordinarily used in practice, it offers very important insight into the behavior of linear optimization models in general and the behavior of the optimal solution in particular. Later in this section, we discuss how the insights from the graphical solution method have been utilized to develop the software that is now used to solve linear optimization models by computer.

Recall the Gemstone Tool Company production planning problem that was presented in Example 7.2. The data for this problem has been presented in Table 7.3. The formulation of the problem as a linear optimization model was described in Section 7.1 and is re-stated here for convenience:

maximize	$130W + 100P$	
subject to:		
Steel:	$1.5W + 1.0P \le 27$	
Molding:	$1.0W + 1.0P \le 21$	
Assembly:	$0.3W + 0.5P \le 9$	
W-demand:	$W \le 15$	
P-demand:	$P \le 16$	
Nonnegativity:	$W, P \ge 0.$	

We will solve the GTC linear optimization model by using the following five-step procedure:

Step 1: Plot the Nonnegativity Conditions.

Step 2: Plot each of the Constraints.

Step 3: Plot the Feasible Region.

Step 4: Determine the Objective Function Isoquants.

Step 5: Determine the Optimal Solution.

Each step is described below.

Step 1: Plot the Nonnegativity Conditions

The nonnegativity conditions are:

$$\text{Nonnegativity:} \quad W \geq 0, P \geq 0.$$

Notice that the locus of points that satisfy the nonnegativity conditions is just the first quadrant of the graphical plane. This is shown in Figure 7.1. In the figure, the plane is divided into four regions called "quadrants." The first region corresponds to those values of W and P that satisfy:

$$W \geq 0, P \geq 0.$$

The second region corresponds to those values of W and P that satisfy:

$$W \leq 0, P \geq 0.$$

The third region corresponds to those values of W and P that satisfy:

$$W \leq 0, P \leq 0.$$

The fourth region corresponds to those values of W and P that satisfy:

$$W \geq 0, P \leq 0.$$

Since we are only interested in those values of W and P that are nonnegative, we will restrict our attention to Region 1 in Figure 7.1.

FIGURE 7.1
The four regions of
the plane.

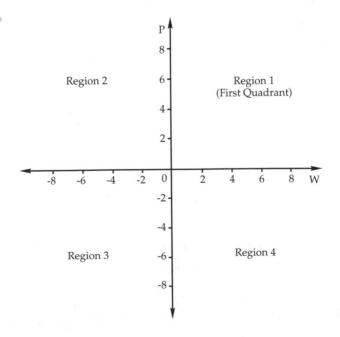

Step 2: Plot Each Constraint

Consider the steel constraint:

$$\text{Steel:} \quad 1.5W + 1.0P \le 27.$$

We can plot this constraint by first plotting the equation

$$1.5W + 1.0P = 27$$

in the plane with horizontal axis W and vertical axis P. Recall that the plot of an equation in two unknowns is a line in the plane. There are several equivalent ways to determine this line. One way to determine the line is to compute the point where the line intersects the W-axis and then compute the point where the line intersects the P-axis and then finally draw the line connecting the two points. For example, we can compute the point where the line intersects the W-axis by setting $P = 0$ and then solving for W, obtaining $W = 18$. Thus the point on the W-axis is given by $(W, P) = (18, 0)$. We can compute the point where the line intersects the P-axis by setting $W = 0$ and then solving for P, obtaining $P = 27$. Thus the point on the P-axis is given by $(W, P) = (0, 27)$. When we connect these two points with a straight line, we obtain the line shown in Figure 7.2.

The line in Figure 7.2 is the locus of all points that satisfy the equation

$$1.5W + 1.0P = 27.$$

However, we are interested in determining those points that satisfy the steel constraint inequality:

$$\text{Steel:} \quad 1.5W + 1.0P \le 27.$$

It is easy to see that all of the points on one of the sides of the line in Figure 7.2 will satisfy

$$1.5W + 1.0P \le 27,$$

and all of the points on the other side of the line in Figure 7.2 will satisfy

FIGURE 7.2
The plot of the steel equation line.

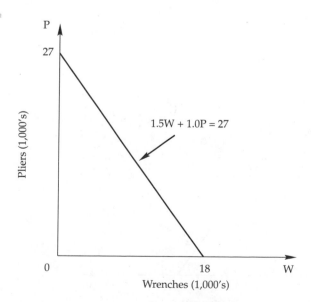

$$1.5W + 1.0P \geq 27.$$

One can figure out which side satisfies the inequality in the correct way by choosing a point on one of the sides and testing. For example, we can choose the point

$$(W, P) = (10,10),$$

which lies to the lower southwest of the steel equation line. When we test whether

$$(W, P) = (10,10)$$

satisfies

$$1.5W + 1.0P \leq 27,$$

or

$$1.5W + 1.0P \geq 27,$$

we see that $1.5(10) + 1.0(10) \leq 27$, and so the southwest region (Region 1 in Figure 7.3) is the locus of points satisfying

$$1.5W + 1.0P \leq 27,$$

and the northeast region (Region 2 in Figure 7.3) is the locus of points satisfying

$$1.5W + 1.0P \geq 27.$$

Typically, the easiest test point to use is the origin, which in this case is $(W, P) = (0,0)$. It is readily seen that $(W, P) = (0, 0)$ satisfies

$$1.5W + 1.0P = 1.5(0) + 1.0(0) \leq 27,$$

and so we see again that the southwest region (Region 1) is the locus of points that satisfy the steel constraint. The last step in plotting the constraint is to indicate on the graph which side of the line is the locus of points that satisfy the constraint. We can do this by indicating the region with an arrow that points into the correct region, as is shown in Figure 7.3.

FIGURE 7.3
The plot of the steel constraint.

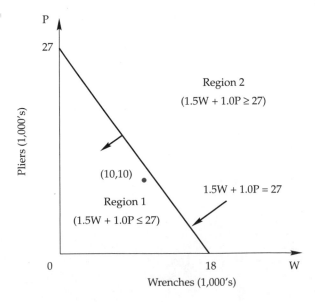

FIGURE 7.4
The plot of all of the constraints.

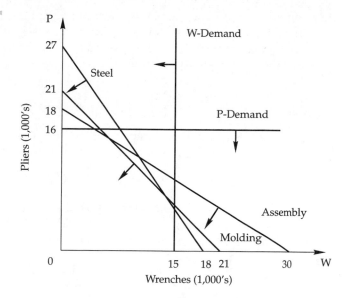

FIGURE 7.5
Plot of the feasible region.

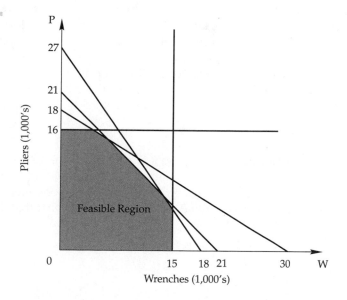

If we follow the above procedure and plot all of the constraints in the problem, namely the steel, molding, assembly, W-demand, and P-demand constraints, we obtain the graph shown in Figure 7.4.

Step 3: Plot the Feasible Region

The next step is to determine the locus of all points (W, P) that are feasible for the linear optimization model. The locus of these points is called the **feasible region** for the linear optimization model. The feasible region therefore corresponds to all points (W, P) that satisfy the nonnegativity conditions as well as all of the constraints in the problem. Using Figure 7.4 as a reference, it is easy to check that the shaded region in Figure 7.5 is the locus of all of the feasible points. Note that this shaded region is in the first quadrant of the plane, and that it lies on the correct side of each of the constraint lines as shown in Figure 7.4. Also, note that any point not in the shaded region is on the wrong side of at least one of the constraint equations, or lies in the wrong quadrant. Therefore, the shaded region corresponds precisely to the feasible region of the linear optimization model, i.e., it is the locus of all points that satisfy all of the constraints and the nonnegativity conditions.

Step 4: Determine the Objective Function Isoquants

The objective in the Gemstone Tool Company linear optimization model is to maximize the contribution to earnings, as expressed in the objective function:

$$\text{Contribution} = 130W + 100P.$$

Suppose we would like to determine the locus of all points (W, P) whose contribution is equal to some given value, say \$1,300. The locus of all points (W, P) whose contribution is equal to \$1,300 corresponds to those points (W, P) which satisfy the equation:

$$130W + 100P = 1,300.$$

The locus of all such points is therefore a line in the plane and is shown in Figure 7.6. The line in Figure 7.6 is an example of an **isoquant of the objective function,** which is defined as the locus of points whose objective function value is equal to a given constant number (in this case, 1,300).

Now suppose that we would like to determine the locus of all points (W, P) whose contribution is equal to \$1,500. The locus of all points (W, P) whose contribution is equal to \$1,500 corresponds to those points (W, P) which satisfy the equation:

$$130W + 100P = 1,500.$$

This line is also an isoquant and is shown in Figure 7.7. Notice that the slope of these two isoquants is the same. In fact, an important observation is that the slope of *all* isoquants is the same. Although the slopes of all isoquants are the same, the intercept with the W-axis and the P-axis is different. The fact that the slope of all of the

FIGURE 7.6
Plot of an objective function isoquant.

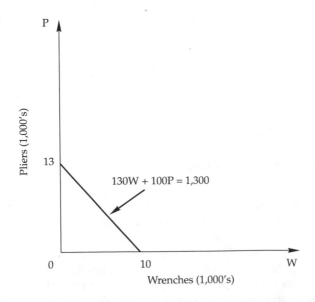

FIGURE 7.7
Plot of two objective function isoquants.

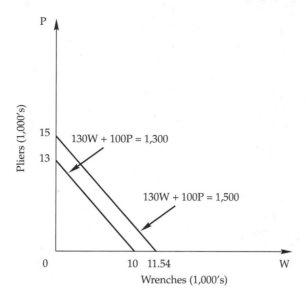

FIGURE 7.8
Isoquants and the feasible region.

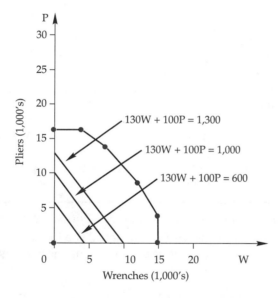

isoquants is the same will be very useful in determining the optimal solution of a linear optimization model, as we will see next.

Step 5: Determine the Optimal Solution

We now show how to find the optimal solution of a linear optimization model. The idea is to compute which point in the feasible region has the best objective function value. We can determine this point by superimposing several of the objective function isoquants onto the feasible region, as is shown in Figure 7.8. We then observe that the isoquants corresponding to larger objective function values are those that are more northeastern in the figure. We therefore can visually determine which point in the shaded region has the best objective function value by visually pushing an isoquant of the objective function further to the northeast until the isoquant just touches

FIGURE 7.9
The optimal
isoquant and the
feasible region.

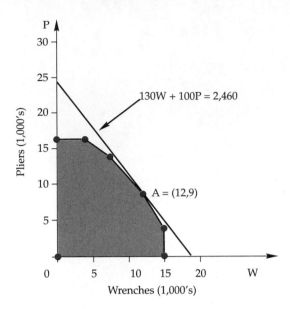

the feasible region. This is shown in Figure 7.9. The point where this isoquant just touches the feasible region is the point labeled "*A*" in Figure 7.9. This point has co-ordinates $(W, P) = (12, 9)$. Therefore, $W = 12$ and $P = 9$ is the optimal solution to the Gemstone Tool Company linear optimization model. The optimal objective function value is given by

$$\text{Contribution} = 130W + 100P = 130(12) + 100(9) = \$2{,}460.$$

Let us review the five step procedure just presented:

The Graphical Method for Solving a Linear Optimization Model

Step 1: Plot the Nonnegativity Conditions. The first step is to plot the non-negativity conditions. This is done by identifying the nonnegativity conditions with the first quadrant of the plane.

Step 2: Plot each of the Constraints. The second step is to plot each of the con-straints. For each constraint, we first plot the constraint equation line. Next, we determine which of the two regions determined by the constraint equation line corresponds to the correct inequality defined in the constraint. We indicate the correct region by drawing arrows that point into the correct region.

Step 3: Plot the Feasible Region. The third step is to determine the feasible re-gion. This is done by checking which area in the plane lies on the correct side of all of the constraints and satisfies the nonnegativity conditions. This area should then be shaded in.

Step 4: Determine the Objective Function Isoquants. The fourth step is to plot several of the objective function isoquants that intercept the feasible region. These isoquants will indicate which direction in the feasible region corre-sponds to improving objective function values. All of the isoquants will have the same slope.

> **Step 5: Determine the Optimal Solution.** The fifth and last step is to visually move an isoquant of the objective function in the direction of improving objective function values, until the isoquant just touches the feasible region. The point where the isoquant just touches the feasible region corresponds to the optimal solution of the linear optimization model.

Observations on the Graphical Method for Solving a Linear Optimization Model

We now summarize several observations gleaned from the graphical method for solving a linear optimization model.

The Optimal Solution solves a System of Equations

Notice from Figure 7.9 that the optimal solution of the GTC problem occurs where the steel and the molding constraint lines meet. Therefore, the optimal solution occurs where the steel constraint is satisfied at equality and where the molding machine constraint is satisfied at equality. It then follows that the optimal solution $(W, P) = (12, 9)$ is also the solution to the two equations corresponding to the equation lines for the steel and the molding constraints:

$$1.5W + 1.0P = 27$$
$$1.0W + 1.0P = 21.$$

It is easy to check that the solution to this system of two equations in two unknowns is $(W, P) = (12, 9)$, that is,

$$1.5(12) + 1.0(9) = 27$$
$$1.0(12) + 1.0(9) = 21.$$

The above arguments regarding the optimal solution are quite general. The optimal solution of a linear optimization model will be the solution to a system of equations corresponding to some of the constraints. In the GTC problem, this system of equations arises from the steel and the molding constraint equations.

Feasible Region

The set of feasible plans is called the feasible set or feasible region. The feasible region is always shaped like a polygon, i.e., its border consists of line segments of different slopes. Figure 7.10 illustrates a variety of ways that a feasible region can be shaped.

Binding and Non-binding Constraints

A constraint is said to be **binding** or **active** if it is satisfied at equality at the optimal solution. A constraint is said to be **non-binding** or **inactive** if it is satisfied with strict inequality at the optimal solution.

Let us examine which of the constraints for the Gemstone Tool Company problem are binding constraints and which constraints are non-binding constraints. The solution of the GTC problem is $(W, P) = (12, 9)$. Let us substitute this solution into each constraint of the GTC linear optimization model to see which constraints are satisfied at equality (and so are binding constraints) and which constraints are satisfied at strict inequality (and so are non-binding constraints). For the steel constraint, we have:

$$1.5W + 1.0P = 1.5(12) + 1.0(9) = 27,$$

FIGURE 7.10
Shapes of some
feasible regions.

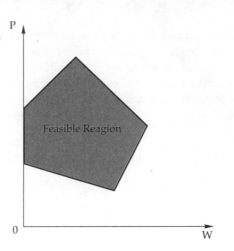

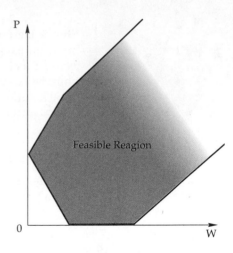

and so the steel constraint is satisfied at equality and therefore the steel constraint is a binding constraint. Similarly, for the molding machine constraint, we have:

$$1.0W + 1.0P = 1.0(12) + 1.0(9) = 21,$$

and so the molding machine constraint is satisfied at equality and therefore the molding machine constraint is a binding constraint. For the assembly machine constraint, we have:

$$0.3W + 0.5P = 0.3(12) + 0.5(9) = 8.1 < 9,$$

and so we see that the assembly machine constraint is a non-binding constraint. For the W-demand constraint, we have:

$$W = 12 < 15,$$

and so we see that the W-demand constraint is a non-binding constraint. Similarly, for the P-demand constraint, we have:

$$P = 9 < 16,$$

and so we see that the P-demand constraint is a non-binding constraint. To summarize for the GTC problem, the binding constraints are the steel and molding machine constraints, and the non-binding constraints are the assembly machine constraint, the W-demand constraint, and the P-demand constraint.

We could also verify which constraints are binding and which constraints are not binding by examining the geometry of the optimal solution of the problem. Examining Figure 7.9, we see that the optimal solution of the GTC problem occurs at the point labeled "A"(corresponding to $(W, P) = (12, 9)$). Now notice from Figure 7.9 that the point A touches the steel constraint equation line and it also touches the molding machine constraint equation line. This means that the solution $(W, P) = (12, 9)$ satisfies the steel and the molding machine constraints at equality, and so the steel and the molding machine constraints are binding constraints. Furthermore, because the point "A" does not touch any of the other constraint lines in Figure 7.9, then the solution $(W, P) = (12, 9)$ satisfies all of the other constraints of the problem with strict inequality. Therefore the non-binding constraints consist of all of the other constraints, namely the assembly, W-demand, and P-demand constraints.

Geometrically, a binding constraint is one that passes through the optimal solution. Geometrically, an non-binding constraint is one that does not pass through the optimal solution. By definition, then, every equality ("=") constraint is a binding constraint.

Multiple Optimal Solutions

Notice that there might be more than one optimal solution to a linear optimization model, i.e., there might be **multiple optima.** This is illustrated in Figure 7.11.

Unbounded Linear Optimization Model

A linear optimization model is **unbounded** if there exist feasible plans with arbitrarily large (for a maximization problem) or arbitrarily small (for a minimization problem) objective values. When this happens in practice, the formulation has in all likelihood been mis-specified. An example of an unbounded linear optimization model is illustrated in Figure 7.12.

Infeasible Linear Optimization Model

A linear optimization model is **infeasible** if there is no plan that satisfies all of the constraints. This means that it is not possible to satisfy all of the constraints of the problem. This is illustrated in Figure 7.13. When this happens in practice, it usually means that the problem has been overly constrained and that some constraint or constraints in the original problem needs to be either removed or otherwise made less restrictive.

Limitations of the Graphical Method

The graphical method is only useful in practice when the linear optimization problem that needs to be solved has only two decision variables. Most applications of linear optimization involve many more than two decision variables and are solved by computer software using a method called the simplex algorithm, which will be discussed shortly.

However, despite its limitations, the graphical method is very useful for studying the behavior of a linear optimization model and for gaining intuition about the behavior of linear optimization in general. For example, through the development of

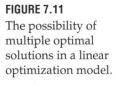

FIGURE 7.11

The possibility of multiple optimal solutions in a linear optimization model.

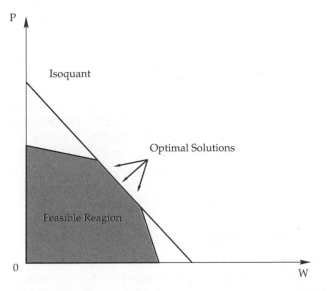

FIGURE 7.12
The possibility of an
unbounded linear
optimization model.

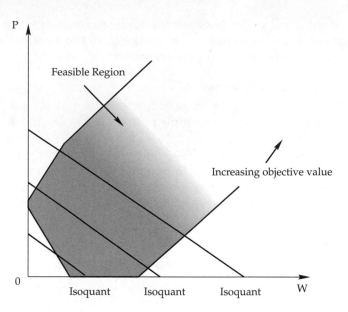

FIGURE 7.13
The possibility of an
infeasible linear
optimization model.

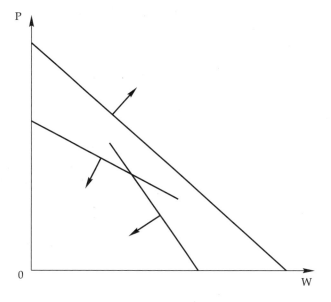

the graphical method, we see that the set of feasible solutions can be viewed as a polygon-shaped region in the plane, and that the optimal solution is (in general) one of the corner points of the feasible region that corresponds to the solution of a system of equations. We also see how it may be possible to have multiple optimal solutions of a linear optimization model. Finally, the graphical method indicates the possibility that a linear optimization model could be unbounded, and it is also possible that a linear optimization model could be infeasible.

The Simplex Algorithm for Solving a Linear Optimization Model

The method that is used to solve most linear optimization models is called the simplex algorithm. The simplex algorithm is based on ideas that we can easily visualize based on the graphical solution method, as we will now describe.

Recall from the graphical method that the feasible region is shaped like a polygon, and that the optimal solution will correspond to one of the corners of the polygon. Next notice that a corner of the polygon is actually the solution of a system of two equations in two unknowns.

In a linear optimization model with two variables, the simplex algorithm would proceed by first solving one of the different systems of two equations in two unknowns corresponding to one of the corners of the feasible region polygon. The simplex algorithm would then test to see if that solution is an optimal solution. If not, the algorithm proceeds by performing what is called a "pivot" in order to find a better corner point solution. It would then proceed to solve another system of two equations in two unknowns, corresponding to another corner of the feasible region polygon, etc. The simplex algorithm continues in this manner until it finds an optimal solution of the linear optimization model.

When the linear optimization model has more than two variables, say m variables where $m > 2$, the simplex algorithm does the analogous steps as indicated above. The simplex algorithm proceeds by first solving a certain system of m equations in m unknowns to arrive at a possible solution. The simplex algorithm then tests to see if that solution is an optimal solution. If not, the algorithm proceeds to find a better system of m equations in m unknowns to solve. It then proceeds to solve this other system of m equations in m unknowns, to find another possible solution, etc. The simplex algorithm continues in this manner until it finds an optimal solution of the linear optimization model.

Thus, we see that the simplex algorithm solves a series of systems of m equations in m unknowns. The number of times it must do this typically is related to the number n of constraints in the model. Therefore, the more decision variables there are (m), and the more constraints there are (n), the more computer time will be needed to solve the linear optimization model.

The simplex algorithm is conceptually simple and easy to learn. However, it is the philosophy of this text to present only those tools which will be of use to managers, and the simplex algorithm is not in this category.

7.4 CREATING AND SOLVING A LINEAR OPTIMIZATION MODEL IN A SPREADSHEET

Microsoft Excel® has an Add-In function that is called "Solver" that uses the simplex algorithm to solve a linear optimization model in a spreadsheet that has been suitably described. In this section, we show how to construct a linear optimization model in a spreadsheet and how to use the "Solver" function to solve the model.

To see if your copy of Microsoft Excel® has the "Solver" function activated, pull down the **Tools** header on the top of your spreadsheet screen and look to see if there is a command called **Solver** . . . . If **Solver** . . . is not listed, either refer to your Microsoft Excel® documentation on "Add-Ins" or ask a system support person for help.

Creating a Linear Optimization Model in the Spreadsheet

The first step in solving a linear optimization model in a spreadsheet is to convert the mental or paper formulation of the problem into a spreadsheet file suitable for solution by the appropriate software program. In our case, this means typing the formulation into the appropriate format in Microsoft Excel®.

There are many different ways to organize a spreadsheet for constructing a linear optimization model. However, we recommend a basic format that will help you to keep your model organized, logical, transparent, and easy to work with. This is done by organizing the spreadsheet into four sections: **Data, Decision Variables, Objective Function,** and **Constraints.** Each of the four sections can be as large or as small as is necessary to build the model, and you can format the cells in any manner that appeals to you.

- The **Data Section** provides the numbers that are used in the optimization model. Raw data can be used in calculations to generate other data, which can be used in other calculations. An example of this is a table of product revenues and costs that can be used to calculate the product contributions to earnings. Wherever possible, try to arrange your data in conveniently organized tables. This will make it easier to use when building other sections of the model.

- The **Decision Variables Section** identifies the cells that will represent, as the name implies, the different decision variables in the model. These cells will be entered to the Solver as the unknowns to be solved for, and they will be filled with the optimal variable values when a solution to the model is found. It is often useful to place descriptive labels above and/or beside the decision variable cells so that you know which cell corresponds to which variable. You might also place a border around each individual decision variable cell to highlight it so that you can quickly identify it when building other sections of the model.

- The **Objective Function Section** contains the cells that are necessary to compute the objective function value. Though several cells can be used to perform intermediate calculations, the final objective function calculation must be contained in a single cell referred to as the objective function cell. The objective function will be a function of the data in the Data Section and the (still unknown) values of the decision variables.

- The **Constraints Section** defines the cells that calculate the left-hand-side (LHS) and right-hand-side (RHS) of the different constraints in the model. Any combination of constants and decision variable cells can be entered into the constraint cells. However, all elements of the LHS of a specific constraint must be contained in one cell and all of those for the RHS of that constraint must be contained in another single cell. It is good practice to align the constraint LHS in one column and the constraint RHS in the next column over. Also, you must remember to enter the nonnegativity conditions of the variables as constraints in the model. Once you have built your model, you are ready to tell the Solver how to optimize it.

Optimizing a Linear Optimization Model in the Spreadsheet

Pull down the **Tools** header and select **Solver . . . .** Once you select Solver you should see the **Solver Parameters** window, which is illustrated in Figure 7.14. This is the main window of Solver; it is used to identify the different elements of the model so that Microsoft Excel® knows what they are. In the upper left corner of the window you will see the label **Set Target Cell:** and a box with a highlighted cell reference in it. This box is where you must enter the cell reference of the objective function cell. You can either type it or click in the appropriate cell on the spreadsheet. If you cannot see the cell, drag the **Solver Parameters** window out of the way and then click on the objective function cell. Next click in either the **Max** or **Min** radio button on the next line in the **Solver Parameters** window to tell Solver whether to maximize or minimize the value of the objective function cell.

To specify the decision variables, which are called the **By Changing Cells:** in a Solver model, either press the Tab key or click in the box below the **By Changing Cells:** label. As when entering the objective function cell reference, you can either

FIGURE 7.14
Anatomy of the
Microsoft Excel®
Solver Parameters
window for a linear
optimization model.

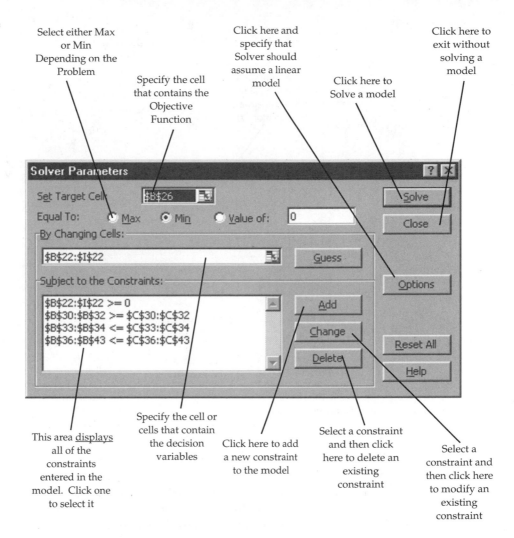

Select either Max
or Min
Depending on the
Problem

Specify the cell
that contains the
Objective
Function

Click here and
specify that
Solver should
assume a linear
model

Click here to
Solve a model

Click here to
exit without
solving a
model

This area displays
all of the
constraints
entered in the
model. Click one
to select it

Specify the cell or
cells that contain
the decision
variables

Click here to add
a new constraint
to the model

Select a constraint
and then click
here to delete an
existing
constraint

Select a
constraint and
then click here
to modify an
existing
constraint

type the cell references for the decision variables or you can click and drag on them in the actual spreadsheet model. A contiguous range of cells should be entered by specifying the first cell and the last cell of the range separated by a colon, as illustrated in Figure 7.14. Additional non-contiguous decision variable ranges can be listed by typing a comma and entering the next range, and so on.

The constraints need to be listed in the **Subject to the Constraints:** sub-window of the **Solver Parameters** window. Click on the **Add** button and you will see the **Add Constraint** window, as illustrated in Figure 7.15. Although you can enter each individual constraint one at a time, that can be very tedious for larger models. Alternatively, you can enter a range of constraints all at once. The process is the same for either method and you can enter the appropriate cell references by clicking on the specific cells in the actual spreadsheet. If you cannot see a cell that you want, then move the dialog box and/or scroll the spreadsheet to another area.

In the box under the **Cell Reference:** label, you should list the cell or range of cells corresponding to the left-hand-side (LHS) of a constraint or set of constraints. If you choose to enter a range of cells, it should only include contiguous constraint rows that have the same constraint relation (i.e., "≥", "≤", or "="). Next, click on the <= box in the middle of the window and hold the mouse button down. Drag down

Anatomy of the
Microsoft Excel®
Solver **Add
Constraint** window
for a linear
optimization model.

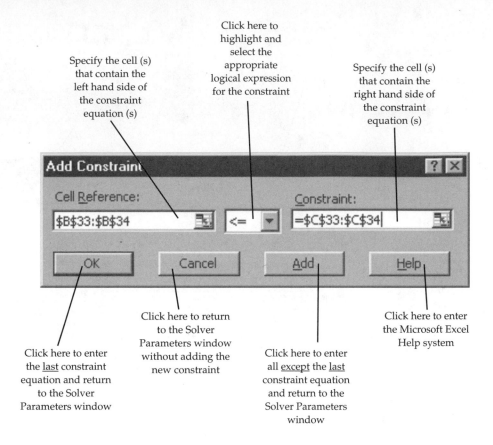

Specify the cell (s)
that contain the
left hand side of
the constraint
equation (s)

Click here to
highlight and
select the
appropriate
logical expression
for the constraint

Specify the cell (s)
that contain the
right hand side of
the constraint
equation (s)

Click here to enter
the last constraint
equation and return
to the Solver
Parameters window

Click here to return
to the Solver
Parameters window
without adding the
new constraint

Click here to enter
all except the last
constraint equation
and return to the
Solver Parameters
window

Click here to enter
the Microsoft Excel
Help system

and select one of the relations ($>=$ for "$\geq$", $<=$ for "$\leq$", or "$=$") depending on the specific constraint(s) that you are entering. When you have done this, the selected relationship will be displayed in the box and the cursor will be located in the box under the label **Constraint:**. Once there, you should list the cell or range of cells corresponding to the right-hand-side (RHS) of the constraint or set of constraints that you are entering. If you are entering a range of constraints, the number of elements contained in the left-side range must equal the number of elements in the right-side range. You can also enter a constant in the **Constraint:** box. This is especially useful when you are specifying that all the decision variables must be nonnegative.

When you have specified a constraint or set of constraints, you must add them to the model. This can be done in one of two ways. In the first way, click the **Add** button if you have additional constraints to define in the model. This will cause Microsoft Excel® to store the constraint(s) and present you with a blank entry screen for entering the next constraint(s). In the second way, click the **OK** button if you do not wish to add any more constraints at this time. This will store the current constraint(s) and return you to the **Solver Parameters** window. If you do not wish to store the constraint(s) that you have specified, simply click **Cancel** to return to the **Solver Parameters** window without adding the constraint.

Once you have added all of the constraints and have returned to the **Solver Parameters** window shown in Figure 7.14, you will see the constraints that you have entered in the box under the label **Subject to the Constraints:**. You can add additional constraints using the same procedure or you can click on one of the listed constraint equations to select it and press either the **Change . . .** or **Delete** buttons to modify or remove it from the list. Use the scroll bar at the side of the box if all of your constraints cannot be viewed in the display area at one time.

Finally, you need to click on the **Options . . .** button at the right side of the **Solver Parameters** window. Make sure that the box next to the label **Assume Linear Model** is checked. **This is most important!** If the box next to the label **Assume Linear Model** is not checked, then check it and click **OK**.

At this point there are three options open to you. If you click **Reset All**, the **Solver Parameters** window will **erase** all of the boxes in the window. Do **not** do this unless you want to start over with a different Solver model. You can also click the **Close** button. This will close the **Solver Parameters** window and return you to the original model spreadsheet. The work you have done will be saved and it can be opened again by selecting **Solver . . .** from the **Tools** menu. The current Solver model will be saved with your spreadsheet file, so that even if you quit the spreadsheet you can come back to the model at a later time and it will be just as you left it.

You can click the **Solve** button when you are ready to let the Solver compute the optimal solution of your model. When you do this, there will be a flurry of activity on the screen and you will not be able to use the screen for a very short while. Do not be alarmed, this is the way the Solver works on a problem.

Reading the Optimization Results

When the Solver has finished computing the optimal solution of the model, it will display the **Solver Results** window, shown in Figure 7.16. Note the message at the top of the window that indicates whether or not an optimal solution was found. Make sure that the radio button next to the label **Keep Solver Solution** is clicked. This ensures that the Solver will place the optimal values of the decision variables in the appropriate cells in the spreadsheet model. Click the **OK** button to return to the spreadsheet.

FIGURE 7.16
Anatomy of the Microsoft Excel® Solver **Solver Results** window for a linear optimization model.

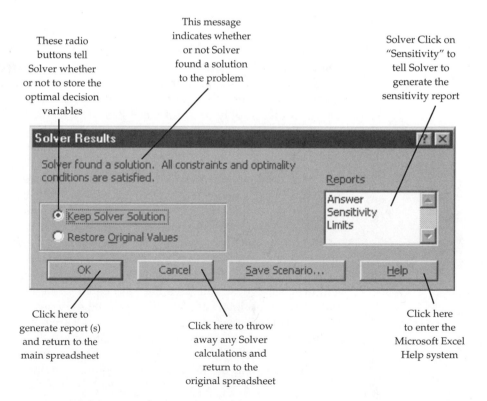

When the Solver is done, you will find yourself back in the spreadsheet model. You will notice that a few things have changed. Some or all of the decision variable cells and the objective function cell will have values in them. These values correspond to the optimal solution to the model. Note also that the LHS and the RHS of the constraints should have values corresponding to the LHS and the RHS of each constraint function evaluated using the optimal values of the decision variables.

You can run the Solver again by selecting **Solver . . .** and clicking **OK**. You should get the exact same results.

The following is a summary of the above remarks:

Reading the Optimization Results

Values of Decision Variables. The optimal value of each of the decision variables appears in the cells used to represent each of the decision variables.

Objective Function Value. The optimal objective function value appears in the cell that is used to represent the objective function.

Constraint Information. For each of the constraints, the value of the left-hand-side (LHS) and the right-hand-side (RHS) of the constraints (evaluated using the optimal values of the decision variables) appears in those cells that are used to represent the LHS and the RHS for each constraint.

To change the model by changing some of the data in the model, simply make the appropriate changes in the Data Section of your spreadsheet. However, the spreadsheet will not automatically re-solve the model for you unless you instruct it to do so. Therefore, after making any changes in the data of the model, you must re-instruct the computer to re-solve the model by selecting **Solver . . .** and clicking **OK** again.

Table 7.4 shows a spreadsheet representation of the NBS coal supply linear optimization model. In Table 7.4, the data for the model are contained in rows 1-14 of the table, and the decision variables are contained in row 18. The objective function cell is cell B21. The constraints of the NBS model are contained in rows 25-29 and rows 31-38. For each of these constraints, column B contains the left-hand-side (LHS) of the constraint and column C contains the right-hand-side (RHS) of the constraint. (For example, for the supply constraint, cell B25 contains the LHS, and cell C25 contains the RHS.) Table 7.4 shows the model after the optimal solution has been computed. The optimal value of the decision variables are shown in their respective cells in row 18. According to Table 7.4, then, the optimal solution is given by contracting for 55.0 mtons from Ashley, 600.0 mtons from Bedford, etc. Notice that these numbers correspond exactly to those given in Table 7.2. Also, according to Table 7.4, the optimal objective function value is $73,267.50 (in $1,000). Furthermore, the values of the LHS and RHS of each constraint are shown in columns B and C of the bottom section of Table 7.4. We can use these numbers to see which of the constraints are binding and which are non-binding. According to Table 7.4, we see that the supply constraint, the volatility constraint, the truck constraint, the Bedford capacity constraint, and the Gaston capacity constraint have the LHS equal to the RHS, and so are satisfied at equality at the optimal solution. Therefore, these constraints are the binding constraints. All of the other constraints in this model are non-binding constraints.

Table 7.5 shows a spreadsheet representation of the GTC production planning linear optimization model. In Table 7.5, the data for the model are contained in rows 2–7 of the table, and the decision variables are contained in row 10. The objective

TABLE 7.4

Spreadsheet solution of the NBS coking coal supply linear optimization model.

	A	B	C	D	E	F	G	H	I
1									
2	Resource	Ashley	Bedford	Consol	Dunby	Earlam	Florence	Gaston	Hopt
3	Capacity (mtons)	300	600	510	655	575	680	450	490
4	Union / Non-union	U	U	N	U	N	U	N	N
5	Truck / Rail	R	T	R	T	T	T	R	R
6	Volatility (%)	15	16	18	20	21	22	23	25
7	Price ($ / ton)	49.50	50.00	61.00	63.50	66.50	71.00	72.50	80.00
8									
9	Limits								
10	Demand	1,225							
11	Union	50%							
12	Volatility	19							
13	Rail Capacity (mtons)	650							
14	Truck Capacity (mtons)	720							
15									
16	Decision Variables								
17		Ashley	Bedford	Consol	Dunby	Earlam	Florence	Gaston	Hopt
18	Amount Purchased (mtons)	55.0	600.0	0.0	20.0	100.0	0.0	450.0	0.0
19									
20	Objective Function								
21	Total Purchase cost	$ 73,267.50							
22									
23	Resource Consumption								
24		Actual	Limit						
25	Supply	1,225	1,225						
26	Union	125	0						
27	Volatility	0.00	0.00						
28	Rail	505	650						
29	Truck	720	720						
30									
31	Ashley	55	300						
32	Bedford	600	600						
33	Consol	0	510						
34	Dunby	20	655						
35	Earlam	100	575						
36	Florence	0	680						
37	Gaston	450	450						
38	Hopt	0	490						

TABLE 7.5

Spreadsheet solution of the GTC production planning linear optimization model.

	A	B	C	D
1				
2	Resource	Wrenches	Pliers	Availability (1,000)
3	Steel	1.5	1.0	27
4	Molding	1.0	1.0	21
5	Assembly	0.3	0.5	9
6	Demand Limit	15.0	16.0	
7	Contribution to Earnings	$ 130.00	$100.00	
8				
9	Decision Variables	Wrenches	Pliers	
10	Amounts (1,000)	12	9	
11				
12	Objective Function			
13	Earnings ($1,000)	$ 2,460.00		
14	Contraints	Actual	Limit	
15	Steel	27	27	
16	Molding	21	21	
17	Assembly	8.1	9	
18	W-demand	12	15	
19	P-demand	9	16	

function cell is cell B13. The constraints of the GTC model are contained in rows 15–19. For each of these constraints, column B contains the (LHS) of the constraint and column C contains the (RHS) of the constraint. (For example, for the steel constraint, cell B15 contains the LHS, and cell C15 contains the RHS.) Table 7.5 shows the model after the optimal solution has been computed. The optimal value of the decision variables are shown in their respective cells in row 10. According to Table 7.5, then, the optimal solution is given by $W = 12.0$ and $P = 9.0$. Notice that these numbers correspond exactly to those determined when we solved the GTC problem graphically in Section 7.3. Also, according to Table 7.5, the optimal objective function value is $2,460. Furthermore, the values of the LHS and RHS of each constraint are shown in columns B and C of the bottom section of Table 7.5. We can use these numbers to see which of the constraints are binding and which are non-binding. According to Table 7.5, we see that the steel constraint and the molding machine capacity constraint have the LHS equal to the RHS, and so are satisfied at equality at the optimal solution. Therefore, these constraints are the binding constraints. All of the other constraints in this model are non-binding constraints.

Other Output Information. The output items just described are the obvious output information that you will want to know when modeling a problem using linear optimization. As it turns out, there are also two other categories of output information that are extremely valuable to know, called shadow prices and constraint range information, that are part of another type of output from the linear optimization model called the Sensitivity Report. The next section covers the general topics of sensitivity analysis and shadow prices in detail.

7.5 | SENSITIVITY ANALYSIS AND SHADOW PRICES ON CONSTRAINTS

Sensitivity analysis is concerned with the issue of how the optimal solution to a linear optimization model changes relative to changes in the data that underlies the problem at hand. In this section, we focus on the definition, interpretation, and use of one of the most important components of sensitivity analysis, namely shadow prices. Shadow prices have important implications for the way that linear optimization models are used to analyze complex management problems and are related to many comparative statics problems that arise in microeconomic analysis.

Shadow Prices on Constraints

Let us reconsider the Gemstone Tool Company (GTC) problem (Example 7.2). For the GTC problem, the relevant data for the linear optimization model was presented in Table 7.3. A mathematical description of the linear optimization model was developed in Section 7.1 and is restated here for convenience:

$$
\begin{aligned}
\text{maximize} \quad & 130W + 100P \\
\text{subject to:} \quad & \\
\text{Steel:} \quad & 1.5W + 1.0P \le 27 \\
\text{Molding:} \quad & 1.0W + 1.0P \le 21 \\
\text{Assembly:} \quad & 0.3W + 0.5P \le 9 \\
\text{W-demand:} \quad & W \le 15 \\
\text{P-demand:} \quad & P \le 16 \\
\text{Nonnegativity:} \quad & W, P \ge 0.
\end{aligned}
$$

The optimal solution of this linear optimization model was derived in Section 7.3 and is as follows:

$$W = 12, \quad P = 9,$$

(where the units are expressed in 1,000s of tools), and the objective value of this optimal solution (in $ per day) is:

$$\text{Contribution} = \$2,460.$$

Note that the current RHS of the steel constraint is 27. As we saw in the graphical solution method, the optimal solution of the model occurs where the steel constraint and the molding machine constraint are satisfied at equality. This solution is obtained as the solution to the system of two equations in the two unknowns W and P:

$$1.5W + 1.0P = 27$$
$$1.0W + 1.0P = 21.$$

Note that the first equation of this system is the equation for the steel constraint (at equality), and the second equation of this system is the equation for the molding machine constraint (at equality). The solution to this system is readily seen to be:

$$W = 12, \quad P = 9.$$

The objective function value of this optimal solution (in $ per day) is:

$$\text{Contribution} = 130 \times 12 + 100 \times 9 = \$2,460.$$

Now, suppose that we are given an extra 1,000 lb. of steel. Then the RHS of the steel constraint would change from 27 to $28 = 27 + 1$, and our new optimal solution would be the solution to the slightly modified system of equations:

$$1.5W + 1.0P = 28$$
$$1.0W + 1.0P = 21.$$

If we solve this new system of equations, the new values of W and P are:

$$W = 14, \quad P = 7,$$

whose new objective function value is:

$$\text{Contribution} = 130 \times 14 + 100 \times 7 = \$2,520.$$

Now notice that the objective function has increased by the quantity

$$\$60 = \$2,520 - \$2,460.$$

The added contribution from an extra 1,000 lb. of steel is thus $60. Therefore, GTC should be willing to pay up to $60/1,000 lb. for additional steel. The quantity 60 (in $/1,000 lb.) is called the **shadow price** of the steel constraint. More generally,

> The **shadow price** of a constraint is the amount of change in the optimal objective function value as the RHS of that constraint is increased by one unit, and all other problem data are kept fixed.

The shadow price also goes by a variety of other names. In some textbooks and trade articles, the shadow price is referred to as the dual price, the marginal price, or sometimes the marginal cost or the marginal value.

Let us now use the same methodology as above to compute the shadow price on the molding machine capacity constraint. Suppose that we are given an extra 1,000 hours of molding machine capacity. Then the RHS of the molding constraint would change from 21 to $22 = 21 + 1$, and our new optimal solution would be the solution to the slightly modified system of equations:

$$1.5W + 1.0P = 27$$
$$1.0W + 1.0P = 22.$$

Solving for W and P in this new system of equations, we obtain:

$$W = 10, \quad P = 12,$$

whose new objective function value is:

$$\text{Contribution} = 130 \times 10 + 100 \times 12 = \$2,500.$$

Notice that the objective function has increased by the quantity

$$\$40 = \$2,500 - \$2,460.$$

The added contribution from an extra 1,000 hours of molding machine capacity is thus \$40. Therefore, GTC should be willing to pay up to \$40/1,000 hours for additional molding machine capacity. The quantity 40 (in \$/1,000 hours) is the shadow price of the molding constraint.

We can also use our intuition to derive the shadow price of the assembly machine capacity constraint. Suppose that we are given an extra 1,000 hours of assembly machine capacity. Because the assembly machine capacity constraint is not a binding constraint, i.e., the optimal solution does not use all of the available assembly machine capacity, then adding additional capacity will not induce any change in the optimal solution or in the optimal objective function value. Therefore the shadow price on the assembly capacity constraint is zero, i.e., \$0/1,000 hours. Since GTC does not use all of its available assembly machine capacity, GTC would not be willing to pay extra for additional assembly machine capacity.

In fact, the argument we just used to show that the shadow price of the assembly capacity constraint is zero is quite general: If a constraint is not binding at the optimal solution, then the shadow price on the constraint will be zero.

We can argue in a similar manner to derive the shadow price of the wrenches demand constraint. Suppose that the demand for wrenches goes up by 1,000 tools per day, from 15,000 to 16,000 tools per day. Because the demand limit on wrenches is not a binding constraint, i.e., the optimal solution does not satisfy all of the demand for wrenches, then adding additional demand for wrenches will not induce any change in the optimal solution or in the optimal objective function value. Therefore, the shadow price of the wrench demand constraint is zero, i.e., \$0/1,000 tools per day. Since GTC does not satisfy all of the demand for wrenches, GTC would gain no additional contribution from an increase in the demand for wrenches. We can argue in a similar manner to derive that the shadow price of the pliers demand constraint is also zero, i.e., \$0/1,000 tools per day.

Table 7.6 summarizes the shadow price values that we have derived.

7.5.1 General Principles Governing Shadow Prices

Here we list some of the most important general principles governing shadow prices of a linear optimization model.

1. **One Shadow Price for each Constraint.** There is a shadow price corresponding to each regular constraint in a linear optimization model. In the GTC linear op-

TABLE 7.6

Shadow prices for the GTC problem.

Constraint	Shadow Price
Steel	\$60/1,000 lbs.
Molding	\$40/1,000 hours
Assembly	\$0/1,000 hours
W-demand	\$0/ 1,000 tools
P-demand	\$0/1,000 tools

timization model, there are five shadow prices, one for each of the five constraints in the problem.

2. **Unit of the Shadow Price.** The unit of the shadow price is the unit of the objective function divided by the unit of the constraint. For example, in the GTC linear optimization model, the unit of the objective function is in dollars ($) and the unit of the steel constraint is in 1,000 lb. Therefore, the unit of the shadow price of the steel constraint is $/1,000 lbs.

3. **Economic Information in the Shadow Price.** The shadow price for a given constraint is a mathematically derived quantity. It usually (but not always) has a very relevant managerial/economic interpretation, and usually contains extremely valuable economic information about the problem, which we would not otherwise be able to easily ascertain. For example, in the GTC linear optimization model, the shadow price on the steel constraint is the incremental value of steel to GTC, and the shadow price on the molding constraint is the incremental value of molding capacity to GTC.

4. **Relation of the Shadow Price to Microeconomic Theory.** In terms of microeconomic theory, the shadow price of a given constraint is the "marginal value" of the resource whose units are expressed in the constraint. For example, in the GTC linear optimization model, the shadow price of the steel constraint is the marginal value of steel to GTC.

We next list two additional properties of shadow prices that are of a more advanced nature and are intended only for readers who have a working knowledge of calculus.

- **Relation of the Shadow Price to Calculus.** The shadow price of a given constraint can be viewed as a derivative in the traditional sense of calculus. Let r denote the RHS value for a given constraint (in the GTC linear optimization model $r = 27$ for the steel constraint) and let $f(r)$ denote the optimal objective function value of the linear optimization model, as a function of the RHS value r. (In the GTC linear optimization model, $f(27) = 2,460$.) Then the shadow price of a given constraint is simply the derivative of the optimal objective value with respect to the RHS value of the constraint. That is, the shadow price is $f'(r)$. (In the GTC linear optimization model $f'(27) = 60$.) Written in a different way, the shadow price is:

$$\text{Shadow Price} = f'(r) = \frac{\Delta(\text{optimal objective function value})}{\Delta(\text{RHS value})}.$$

The shadow price of a given constraint is the change in the optimal objective function value per unit change in the RHS value of the constraint.

- **Relation of Shadow Prices to Lagrange Multipliers.** In many microeconomics courses, as well as elsewhere in most MBA curricula, the concept of Lagrange multipliers is encountered. Generally speaking, Lagrange multipliers are used in the solution of optimization problems where the variables must obey certain equations, and the Lagrange multipliers are used in the solution of the optimization problem involving these equations and the objective function. In this context, it is possible to interpret the shadow price of a given constraint as a generalization of a Lagrange multiplier for that constraint. If the constraint is a binding constraint, then the shadow price and the Lagrange multiplier are the same concept and take on the same value. However, the theory of Lagrange multipliers does not allow for inequality ("≤" or "≥") constraints, and so Lagrange multiplier theory cannot be applied directly to linear optimization models. (It should be pointed out that there is an extension of Lagrange multiplier theory called Kuhn-Tucker multiplier theory which does apply to linear optimization models.)

7.5.2 Obtaining Shadow Price Information from a Spreadsheet Model

In the case of the GTC linear optimization model, we have been able to derive the shadow price values for each of the five constraints in the problem "by hand," using a combination of simple arithmetic and management intuition. That is because the GTC problem is quite simple. For more typical linear optimization modeling problems, however, it is quite cumbersome to derive the values of the shadow prices by hand. Fortunately, the calculations needed to derive the shadow prices are easily done on the computer, and in fact, almost all commercial software programs for solving linear optimization models also compute all of the shadow price information automatically and easily. We next show how to obtain the shadow price information that is computed automatically in the spreadsheet linear optimization software Solver resident in Microsoft Excel®.

Step 1. Solve the linear optimization model by entering the **Solver** window under the **Tools** header at the top of the screen as usual.

Step 2. Click on **Solve** to solve the linear optimization model.

Step 3. After the model solves, the **Solver Results** window will appear. In a subwindow on the right called **Reports,** click on **Sensitivity** and hit **OK**. The Solver will produce a separate worksheet called **Sensitivity Report** for the linear optimization model. The Sensitivity Report contains all of the shadow prices for the model and is read as follows:

- The Sensitivity Report contains an upper and a lower table. The upper table in the report is entitled "Adjustable Cells" and the lower table is entitled "Constraints." The first three columns of the upper table show the optimal solution of the model. The last four columns of the upper table contain information that is rather technical and not very managerial in scope, and so is not covered in this text.

- The lower table lists a variety of information for each constraint. Under the column **Cell,** the table lists the cell where the left-hand-side (LHS) of each constraint appears in the spreadsheet. The second column shows the **Name** for each constraint. (The Solver picks a name by searching to the left and above for any appropriate cell with characters in it.) The third column is the **Final Value** column. This column presents the final value of the LHS of each constraint. The fourth column is the **Shadow Price** column, which lists the shadow price of each constraint in the model.

- The last two columns of the Constraints table contain other information regarding the "range" of the shadow price, which will be explained in the next subsection.

(Incidentally, under the **Reports** sub-window after the model solves, you can also ask for two other types of reports. One is called the **Answer** report, and the other is called the **Limits** report. We will not cover the information contained in these two other reports, because it is rather technical and not very managerial in scope.)

The Sensitivity Report for the Gemstone Tool Company linear optimization model is shown in Table 7.7. The shadow prices for the five constraints of the model are shown

TABLE 7.7

Spreadsheet sensitivity report for the Gemstone Tool Company linear optimization model.

	A	B	C	D	E	F	G
1	Adjustable Cells						
2	Cell	Name	Final Value	Reduced Cost	Objective Coefficient	Allowable Increase	Allowable Decrease
3	B10	Wrenches	12	0	130	20	30.00
4	C10	Pliers	9	0	100	30	13.33
5	Constraints						
6	Cell	Name	Final Value	Shadow Price	Constraint R.H. Side	Allowable Increase	Allowable Decrease
7	B15	Steel	27.0	60	27	1.5	2.25
8	B16	Molding	21.0	40	21	1.0	1.50
9	B17	Assembly	8.1	0	9	1E+30	0.90
10	B18	W-demand	12.0	0	15	1E+30	3.00
11	B19	P-demand	9.0	0	16	1E+30	7.00

in the fourth column of the lower part of Table 7.7. Notice that these shadow price values are the same as the shadow price values that were derived by hand earlier in this section.

7.5.3 Shadow Prices and Range Information

The shadow price of a given constraint is the incremental change in the optimal objective function value of a linear optimization model per unit increase in the RHS value of the constraint. For example, in the Gemstone Tool Company (GTC) problem, the shadow price of the steel constraint is $60/1,000 lbs. Therefore, GTC should be willing to pay up to $60/1,000 lbs. for additional steel. Put a slightly different way, the earnings of GTC would increase by $60 if GTC were to simply discover their steel on hand was increased from 27,000 lbs. per day to 28,000 lbs. Put still another way, the earnings of GTC would decrease by $60 if GTC were to discover that their steel on hand was decreased from 27,000 lbs. to 26,000 lbs.

One question that naturally arises when using this shadow price information is the extent to which the shadow price information is valid when the RHS value is changed in a more significant way. For instance, one might wonder if the earnings of GTC would still change at the rate of $60/1,000 lbs. if the availability of steel were to change from 27,000 lbs. up to 35,000 lbs. This is important to know especially if one is considering using the shadow price of $60/1,000 lbs. as a guide for negotiating the purchase price of additional steel. Steel is worth $60/1,000 lbs. "on the margin," but one might wonder to what extent this shadow price would be valid if GTC is considering a very large purchase of additional steel.

Fortunately, the computer-generated Sensitivity Report for a linear optimization model contains information on the range in which the shadow price information is valid. This is best illustrated by continuing the example of the GTC linear optimization model, whose Sensitivity Report is shown in Table 7.7. According to Table 7.7, the shadow price on the steel constraint is $60/1,000 lbs. This value is given in the fourth column of the lower part of the table. The sixth and the seventh columns of the lower part of the table contain the information on the range of RHS values for which the shadow price is valid. For example, according to the table, the "Allowable Increase" for the steel constraint is 1.5. This means that the shadow price of $60/1,000 lbs. is valid for increases in the RHS value of steel up to an increase of 1.5 thousand pounds, i.e., up to 1,500 lbs. of additional steel. If GTC were to consider additional purchases of steel, they should be willing to pay up to $60/1,000 lbs. for up to an additional 1,500 lbs. of steel. Beyond the value of 1,500 lbs. of additional steel, we do not automatically know what the incremental value of steel will be.

Again according to the table, the "Allowable Decrease" for the steel constraint is 2.25. This means that the shadow price of $60/1,000 lbs. is valid for decreases in the RHS value of steel up to a decrease of 2.25 thousand pounds, i.e., up to a decrease of 2,250 lbs. of steel. If GTC were to consider decreasing the amount of steel that they procure, their earnings would decrease by $60/1,000 lbs. as long as the decrease in steel did not extend beyond 2,250 lbs. of steel. Again, beyond the value of 2,250 lbs. less steel, we do not automatically know what the incremental affect on earnings would be.

Let us illustrate this range information again, using the molding constraint. According to Table 7.7, the shadow price on the molding constraint is $40/1,000 hours. This value is given in the fourth column of the lower part of the table. The sixth and the seventh columns of the lower part of the table contain the information on the range of RHS values for which this shadow price is valid. For example, according to the table, the "Allowable Increase" for the molding constraint is 1.0. This means that the shadow price of $40/1,000 hours is valid for increases in the RHS value of molding capacity up to an increase of 1.0 thousand hours, i.e., up to 1,000 hours of additional molding capacity. If GTC were to consider additional purchases of molding machine capacity, they should be willing to pay up to $40/1,000 hours for up to an additional 1,000 hours of molding capacity. Beyond the value of 1,000 hours of additional molding capacity, we do not automatically know what the incremental value of molding capacity will be.

Again according to Table 7.7, the "Allowable Decrease" for the molding constraint is 1.5. This means that the shadow price of $40/1,000 hours is valid for decreases in the RHS value of molding capacity up to a decrease of 1.5 thousand hours, i.e., up to a decrease of 1,500 hours of molding capacity. If GTC were to consider decreasing the amount of molding capacity that they have on hand, their earnings would decrease by $40/1,000 hours as long as the decrease in molding capacity did not extend beyond 1,500 hours of molding capacity. Beyond the value of 1,500 hours less molding capacity, we do not automatically know what the incremental affect on earnings would be.

7.5.4 Illustration of the Use of Shadow Price Information in the NBS Linear Optimization Model

Consider the New Bedford Steel coking coal supply problem (Example 7.1.) The management problem and its formulation as a linear optimization model has been presented in Section 7.1, and the computer solution to the problem has been shown in Table 7.4. The Sensitivity Report for this model is shown in Table 7.8.

We will start by analyzing the shadow price information for each of the constraints in the NBS linear optimization model, as follows:

Supply Constraint: According to the sensitivity report of the NBS linear optimization model presented in Table 7.8, the shadow price on the supply constraint is 61.50. Let us first derive the unit on this number. Because the unit of the objective function is $1,000, and the unit of the supply constraint is in 1,000 tons (mtons), the unit of the shadow price on the supply constraint is $1,000/1,000 tons, i.e., $/ton. Therefore, the shadow price on the supply constraint is $61.50/ton. This number represents the incremental change in the optimal objective function if the RHS of the supply constraint is changed by one unit, i.e., if the amount of coal that must be procured increases by one unit. Thus the shadow price of $61.50/ton is the marginal cost of coking coal to NBS.

According to the sensitivity report presented in Table 7.8, the allowable increase of the supply constraint is 5 and the allowable decrease is 25. This means that the shadow price of $61.50/ton is valid for RHS values in the range from a low value of $1,225 - 25 = 1,200$ mtons up to a high value of $1,225 + 5 = 1,230$ mtons. If the amount

TABLE 7.8

Spreadsheet sensitivity report for the New Bedford Steel linear optimization model.

	A	B	C	D	E	F	G
1	Adjustable Cells						
2	Cell	Name	Final Value	Reduced Cost	Objective Coefficient	Allowable Increase	Allowable Decrease
3	B18	Ashley	55	0.0	49.50	0.5	1.00
4	C18	Bedford	600	0.0	50.00	1.5	1E+30
5	D18	Consol	0	2.5	61.00	1E+30	2.50
6	E18	Dunby	20	0.0	63.50	0.125	0.05
7	F18	Earlam	100	0.0	66.50	0.05	0.125
8	G18	Florence	0	1.5	71.00	1E+30	1.50
9	H18	Gaston	450	0.0	72.50	1	1E+30
10	I18	Hopt	0	0.5	80.00	1E+30	0.50
11							
12	Constraints						
13	Cell	Name	Final Value	Shadow Price	Constraint R.H. Side	Allowable Increase	Allowable Decrease
14	B25	Supply	1,225	61.50	1,225	5	25
15	B26	Union	125	0.0	0	125	1E+30
16	B27	Volatility	0.0	3.00	0	20	100
17	B28	Rail	505	0.0	650	1E+30	145
18	B29	Truck	720	-1.00	720	20	3.33
19	B31	Ashley	55	0.0	300	1E+30	245
20	B32	Bedord	600	-1.50	600	4	25
21	B33	Consol	0	0.0	510	1E+30	510
22	B34	Dunby	20	0.0	655	1E+30	635
23	B35	Earlam	100	0.0	575	1E+30	475
24	B36	Florence	0	0.0	680	1E+30	680
25	B37	Gaston	450	-1.00	450	12.5	2.5
26	B38	Hopt	0	0.0	490	1E+30	490

of coal that must be procured were to increase from 1,225 mtons, then the additional cost to NBS would be \$61.50/ton for each additional mton, up to an additional 5 mtons. For increases above 5 mtons, we do not automatically know what the incremental cost to NBS would be. If the amount of coal that must be procured were to decrease below 1,225 mtons, then the savings in procurement costs to NBS would be \$61.50/ton for each mton, up to a decrease of 25 mtons. For decreases beyond 25 mtons, we do not automatically know what the incremental savings in procurement costs to NBS would be.

Truck Capacity Constraint: According to the sensitivity report of the NBS linear optimization model presented in Table 7.8, the shadow price on the truck capacity constraint is -1.00. Because the unit of the objective function is \$1,000, and the unit of the truck capacity constraint is in 1,000 tons per year (mtons per year), the unit of the shadow price on the truck constraint is \$1,000/1,000 tons per year, i.e., \$/ton per year. Therefore, the shadow price on the truck capacity constraint is -\$1.00/ton per year. This number represents the incremental change in the optimal objective function if the RHS of the truck capacity constraint is changed by one unit, i.e., if the capacity of coal that can be brought into NBS by truck increases by one unit per year. Thus, on the margin, an additional ton of capacity for coal by truck per year would decrease the objective function by \$1.00, because the shadow price has a minus sign. This makes sense, since additional capacity can only save NBS money, i.e., lower their procurement costs. The value of -\$1.00/ton per year is the marginal value of extra truck handling capacity.

According to the sensitivity report presented in Table 7.8, the allowable increase of the truck capacity constraint is 20 and the allowable decrease is 3.33. This means that the shadow price of −$1.00/ton per year is valid for RHS values in the range from a low value of $720 − 3.33 = 716.67$ mtons/year up to a high value of $720 + 20 = 740$ mtons/year. If the available trucking capacity were to increase from 720 mtons/year to some other value, then NBS's coal procurement costs would decrease by $1.00/mton for each additional mton of annual capacity, up to an additional 20 mtons of annual capacity. For capacity increases above 20 mtons of capacity, we do not automatically know what the incremental decrease in NBS's procurement costs would be. If the available trucking capacity were to decrease below 720 mtons/year, then the coal procurement costs to NBS would increase by $1.00/ton for each mton of reduced annual trucking capacity, up to a decrease of 3.33 mtons/year. For capacity decreases beyond 3.33 mtons/year, we do not automatically know what the incremental increase in procurement costs to NBS would be.

Rail Capacity Constraint: According to the sensitivity report of the NBS linear optimization model presented in Table 7.8, the shadow price on the rail capacity constraint is 0.0. Because the unit of the objective function is $1,000, and the unit of the rail capacity constraint is in 1,000 tons per year (mtons per year), the unit of the shadow price on the rail constraint is $1,000/1,000 tons per year, i.e., $/ton per year. Therefore, the shadow price on the rail capacity constraint is $0.0/ton per year. This number represents the incremental change in the optimal objective function if the RHS of the rail capacity constraint is changed by one unit per year, i.e., if the capacity of coal that can be brought into NBS by rail increases by one unit per year. This number is zero, of necessity, because NBS does not use all of the rail capacity that they have. Their rail capacity is 650 mtons per year, but they only use 505 mtons per year. Because the rail capacity constraint is not binding, the shadow price on the constraint is zero. The linear optimization model solution does not use all of the rail capacity. Therefore, an increase in the capacity would not affect the optimal solution or the optimal objective function value.

Ashley Capacity Constraint: According to the sensitivity report of the NBS linear optimization model presented in Table 7.8, the shadow price on the Ashley mine capacity constraint is 0.0. Because the unit of the objective function is $1,000, and the unit of the Ashley mine capacity constraint is in 1,000 tons per year (mtons per year), the unit of the shadow price on the capacity constraint is $1,000/1,000 tons per year, i.e., $/ton per year. Therefore, the shadow price on the Ashley mine capacity constraint is $0.0/ton per year. This number represents the incremental change in the optimal objective function if the RHS of the Ashley mine capacity constraint is changed by one unit per year, i.e., if the capacity of coal that can be brought to NBS from the Ashley mine increases by one unit per year. This number is zero, because the linear optimization model solution does not use all of the Ashley mining capacity. The Ashley mining capacity is 300 mtons per year, but they only use 55 mtons per year. Because the Ashley mine capacity constraint is not binding, the shadow price on the constraint is zero. The linear optimization model solution does not use all of the capacity of the Ashley mine. Therefore, an increase in the capacity would not affect the optimal solution or the optimal objective function value.

Bedford Capacity Constraint: According to the Sensitivity Report of the NBS linear optimization model presented in Table 7.8, the shadow price on the Bedford mine capacity constraint is −1.50, whose units are $/ton per year, i.e., −$1.50/ton per year. This number represents the incremental change in the optimal objective function if the RHS of the Bedford mine capacity constraint is changed by one unit, i.e., if the capacity of coal that can be brought to NBS from the Bedford mine increases by one unit per year. This number is negative because, as the linear optimization model solution indicates, the Bedford mine is a good value for NBS, and they would like to purchase as much coal from the Bedford mine as possible. Therefore, if the capacity of the Bedford mine were to increase, NBS would purchase more coal from Bedford (and less from elsewhere), and their supply costs would decrease by $1.50 per ton per year. Note that the value of $1.50 per ton per year is the value of increased capacity of the Bedford mine to NBS. Since the Bedford coal costs NBS $50/ton, NBS would therefore be willing to pay up to $51.50/ton (51.50 = 50.00 + 1.50) for the coal from the Bedford mine.

According to the sensitivity report presented in Table 7.8, the allowable increase of the Bedford mine capacity constraint is 4 and the allowable decrease is 25. This means that the shadow price of $-\$1.50$/ton per year is valid for RHS values in the range from a low value of $600 - 25 = 575$ mtons/year up to a high value of $600 + 4 = 604$ mtons/year. If Bedford's capacity were to increase from 600 mtons/year to some other value, then NBS's coal procurement costs would decrease by $1.50/ton per year for each additional mton of annual capacity, up to an additional 4 mtons of annual capacity. For capacity increases above 4 mtons of capacity, we do not automatically know what the incremental decrease in NBS's procurement costs would be. If Bedford's capacity were to decrease below 600 mtons/year, then the coal procurement costs to NBS would increase by $1.50/ton per year for each mton of reduced mine capacity, up to a decrease of 25 mtons/year. For capacity decreases beyond 25 mtons/year, we do not automatically know what the incremental increase in procurement costs to NBS would be.

Other Mine Capacity Constraints: An interpretation and analysis of the shadow prices on the other mine capacity constraints parallels that for Ashley and Bedford. The shadow prices of the capacity constraints for the Consol, Dunby, Earlam, Florence, and Hopt mines are all zero, because the linear optimization model solution does not use any of these mines at their capacities. The shadow price on the capacity constraints for the Gaston mine is $-\$1.00$/ton per year, and $1.00/ton per year represents the value of additional capacity at the Gaston mine to NBS.

Union Constraint: The union constraint states that the tonnage from union mines must exceed the tonnage from non-union mines. The shadow price on this constraint is zero, because the constraint is not binding at the optimal solution. The optimal solution calls for purchasing 675 mtons from union mines and 550 mtons from non-union mines. In order to understand the units on this shadow price, we need to examine the constraint carefully. The mathematical expression of the constraint is:

$$\text{Union: } A + B - C + D - E + F - G - H \geq 0.$$

As currently written, the constraint states that the quantity of coal (in mtons) from union mines minus the quantity of coal from non-union mines must be greater than or equal to zero. The RHS of the constraint is zero. If the RHS were to change from zero to 1, then the constraint would say that the quantity of coal (in mtons) from union mines minus the quantity of coal from non-union mines must be greater than or equal to 1 mton. The effect of such a change on the optimal objective function value would be zero, because the constraint is not binding at the optimal solution. Therefore, the shadow price on the constraint is zero.

Volatility Constraint: According to the sensitivity report of the NBS linear optimization model, the shadow price on the volatility constraint is 3.00. However, it is not easy to derive the units of this number; therefore it is also difficult to give a direct economic interpretation of this number. This is because the original volatility constraint, in its more "natural" form, was derived as:

$$\frac{15A + 16B + 18C + 20D + 21E + 22F + 23G + 25H}{A + B + C + D + E + F + G + H} \geq 19.$$

In order to make the constraint a linear constraint, we cleared the denominator and obtained the following equivalent constraint which is used in the NBS linear optimization model:

$$\text{Volatility:} \quad -4A - 3B - C + D + 2E + 3F + 4G + 6H \geq 0.$$

However, there are no natural units associated with this constraint, and there is no obvious interpretation of changing the RHS of this constraint from 0 to 1. Here is a case where the shadow price does not have a straightforward economic interpretation.

Let us now use all of the shadow price information discussed above to answer the following questions concerning the optimal solution to the NBS coking coal supply problem.

Question: What is the cost of coking coal on the margin, i.e., how much does an extra ton of coking coal cost NBS?

Answer: The shadow price of $61.50/ton is the marginal cost of coking coal to NBS.

Question: Should NBS consider expanding their trucking capacity? If so, how much should they be willing to spend?

Answer: Yes. The shadow price on the truck capacity constraint is $1.00/ton per year. NBS should be willing to spend up to $1.00/ton per year for additional truck capacity.

Question: Should NBS consider expanding their rail capacity? If so, how much should they be willing to spend?

Answer: No. NBS does not use all of its existing rail capacity, and so the value of additional rail capacity is zero.

Question: Should Stephen Coggins be willing to negotiate a higher price in order to get more coal from Bedford and/or Gaston? If so, how high should he be willing to go?

Answer: Yes. Stephen Coggins should be willing spend up to $1.50/ton extra, i.e., up to $51.50/ton, for additional coal from the Bedford mine. He should be willing to spend up to $1.00/ton, i.e., up to $73.50/ton, for additional coal from the Gaston mine.

Question: NBS currently has a management policy of procuring at least 50% of their coking coal from union mines. How much is this policy costing NBS? Should they consider amending this policy?

Answer: This policy is not currently imposing additional costs on NBS. This is because the union constraint is not a binding constraint.

7.6   GUIDELINES FOR CONSTRUCTING AND USING LINEAR OPTIMIZATION MODELS

In this section, we discuss several guidelines and rules for constructing and using linear optimization models.

General Rules of Thumb for Constructing a Linear Optimization Model

- **Identifying Decision Variables.** One guideline is to start by using decision variables that agree with intuition. Start by asking questions of the type: "What decision or decisions must I make in order to solve my problem?" Then try to translate those decisions into decision variables for the problem.

- **Identifying the Objective Function.** Typically, the objective function of a linear optimization model will take on one of the following two forms:

  (i)   maximize revenue minus cost,

  (ii)   minimize cost minus revenue.

  When formulating the objective function, one needs to make sure that all costs and revenue flows are accounted for once and only once. In addition, one needs to net out any sunk or fixed costs or otherwise unavoidable costs.

- **Identifying Constraints.** There is no overriding rule that governs how to identify the constraints for your problem. However, there are certain types of constraints that arise quite frequently in practice. These are resource-balance constraints, capacity constraints, quality constraints, and policy constraints. (However, this list is not exhaustive, and some problems might have constraints that fit none of these categories.) Nevertheless, each of these four types of constraints is discussed below.

  — **Resource-balance constraints.** An example of a resource-balance constraint is the steel constraint in the GTC problem, which is:

  $$\text{Steel:} \quad 1.5W + 1.0P \le 27.$$

  This constraint states that GTC cannot use more steel than it has available on a daily basis. The steel is a resource, and the constraint states that GTC cannot use up more of a resource than it has available. Another type of resource-balance constraint might state that one cannot use more of a resource than one produces.

  — **Capacity Constraints.** Capacity constraints usually state that one cannot operate a given activity beyond its capacity. For example, in the NBS coal supply model, there are the eight constraints:

  $$
  \begin{aligned}
  \text{Acap:} \quad & A \le 300 \\
  \text{Bcap:} \quad & B \le 600 \\
  \text{Ccap:} \quad & C \le 510 \\
  \text{Dcap:} \quad & D \le 655 \\
  \text{Ecap:} \quad & E \le 575 \\
  \text{Fcap:} \quad & F \le 680 \\
  \text{Gcap:} \quad & G \le 450 \\
  \text{Hcap:} \quad & H \le 490.
  \end{aligned}
  $$

Each constraint is a capacity constraint on the operations of the eight mining companies. For example, the Ccap constraint states that the annual coal production from the Consol mine cannot exceed the capacity of the mine, which is 510 mtons/year.

— **Quality Constraints.** A quality constraint usually governs a physical property of a mixture of items. For example, the volatility constraint in the NBS coal supply problem is a quality constraint. That constraint states that the average volatility of the coal supplied to NBS must be at least 19%. That constraint is formulated as:

$$\frac{15A + 16B + 18C + 20D + 21E + 22F + 23G + 25H}{A + B + C + D + E + F + G + H} \geq 19.$$

However, by clearing the denominator and moving all terms to the left-hand-side of the constraint, the volatility constraint is then stated as a linear constraint as follows:

$$\text{Volatility:} \quad -4A - 3B - C + D + 2E + 3F + 4G + 6H \geq 0.$$

— **Policy Constraints.** In many instances, constraints are the result of management policy. For example, in the NBS coal supply problem, management has a policy of procuring at least half of its coal from union mines. This is not a physical or even a legal restriction; rather, it is a policy restriction dictated by management, presumably designed around corporate goals.

- **No Unique Formulation.** There usually is not a unique "correct" formulation of a management problem as a linear optimization model. Unlike engineering or mathematical problems, management problems are usually not neatly defined. Therefore, there is usually more than one correct formulation of a management problem as a linear optimization model.

- **Equality versus Inequality Constraints.** Sometimes it may be unclear whether to use equality constraints ("=") or greater-than-or-equal-to ("≥") constraints for a particular part of the problem. Similarly, it may be unclear whether to use equality constraints ("=") or less-than-or-equal-to ("≤") constraints for a particular part of the problem. Intuition is usually the best guide in these circumstances.

Guidelines on Using a Linear Optimization Model

The following are common sense guidelines on the use of optimization models for solving problems that arise in management.

- **Think through the issues in your problem.** The use of a linear optimization model is never a substitute for thinking about the underlying problem. Sometimes, careful thought about the problem will reveal the optimal management strategy, and building and analyzing a linear optimization model is then unnecessary. Even when this is not the case, the linear optimization model is there to help you analyze the problem; the model itself is not a substitute for your own thinking and analysis.

- **Good data is essential.** A well constructed optimization model with poorly constructed data is as meaningless as no model at all. Poor data inevitably will produce solutions that are either just plain wrong or should not be acted upon. Judgment is needed as to where to focus your data acquisition activities and how much effort to put into refining the numbers.

- **Study the data in your problem.** Your judgment can only be enhanced with the help of a linear optimization model if you understand the data that is the input to the model. Only then will you be able to make sound management decisions based on the model.

- **Use the optimization model wisely.** Make plenty of "what if" runs. Perform plenty of sensitivity analysis runs on key data uncertainties, etc. Learn more about your problem by using the model to enhance your own insight and confidence regarding the problem.

7.7   LINEAR OPTIMIZATION UNDER UNCERTAINTY*

The development of the concepts of linear optimization models in Sections 7.1–7.6 of this chapter has presumed that all of the data for the linear optimization model are known with certainty. However, uncertainty and inexactness of data and outcomes pervade many aspects of most management problems. As it turns out, when the uncertainty in the problem is of a particular (and fairly general) form, it is relatively easy to incorporate the uncertainty into the linear optimization model of the problem. The following prototypical example will be used to develop and illustrate how this is done.

Example 7.3 – Steel Supply Planning at Gemstone Tool Company

Let us recall once again the Gemstone Tool Company (GTC) production planning problem, which was presented in Example 7.2. Recall for this problem that GTC would like to determine the number of wrenches (W) and pliers (P) to produce, in 1,000s, subject to constraints on the availability of steel, molding and assembly machine capacities, and market demand. The data for this problem has been presented in Table 7.3. The formulation of the problem as a linear optimization model was described in Section 7.1 and is re-stated here for convenience:

$$\text{maximize} \quad 130W + 100P$$

subject to:

Steel:	$1.5W + 1.0P \leq 27$
Molding:	$1.0W + 1.0P \leq 21$
Assembly:	$0.3W + 0.5P \leq 9$
W-demand:	$W \leq 15$
P-demand:	$P \leq 16$
Nonnegativity:	$W, P \geq 0.$

Recall that the solution of this linear optimization model is given by

$$W = 12, \quad P = 9,$$

with an optimized contribution to earnings of

$$\$2,460 = 130(12) + 100(9).$$

Planning under Uncertainty

For the current quarter, GTC had contracted with a steel supplier for the delivery of 27,000 lbs. of steel per day. This restriction was incorporated into the GTC linear optimization model as the steel availability constraint:

$$1.5W + 1.0P \leq 27.$$

Now suppose that GTC is planning for next quarter, and that they would like to determine how much steel to contract for with local suppliers for the next quarter. Suppose that steel contracts are typically arranged for daily deliveries over the entire quarter, and that the market price for such contracts is $58.00/1,000 lbs. of steel. Let us define the decision variable:

S = the amount of steel to contract for, for next quarter, in 1,000 lbs./day.

GTC would like to determine the optimal value of S. We suppose that the following aspects of the problem are known:

- The market price of steel is $58.00/1,000 lbs.
- The utilization of steel, assemby machine hours, and molding machine hours in wrenches and pliers is the same as given in the original problem.
- The molding machine capacity is the same as in the original problem, namely 21,000 hours/day.
- The demand for wrenches and pliers is the same as in the original problem, namely 15,000 wrenches per day and 16,000 pliers per day.
- The unit contribution to earnings of production of pliers is the same as in the original problem, namely $100/1,000 units.

However, we also suppose that the following aspects of the problem are uncertain:

- The assembly machine capacity for next quarter is uncertain. GTC has ordered new assembly machines to replace, as well as to augment, their existing assembly machines, but it is not known if these new machines will be delivered in time to be used next quarter. Let us suppose that the assembly machine capacity for next quarter will either be 8,000 hours/day (with probability 0.5) or 10,000 hours/day (with probability 0.5).
- The unit contribution to earnings of production of wrenches next quarter is uncertain due to fluctuations in the market for wrenches. Supppose that GTC estimates that the unit contribution to earnings of wrenches will be in the range between $90 and $160. For the sake of simplicity, let us suppose that this unit earnings contribution will be either $90 (with probability 0.5) or $160 (with probability 0.5).

The data for this problem is summarized in Table 7.9.

TABLE 7.9

Data for the Gemstone Tool Company steel supply planning problem.

	Wrenches	Pliers	Availability
Steel (lbs.)	1.5	1.0	S (to be determined)
Molding Machine (hours)	1.0	1.0	21,000 hours/day
Assembly Machine (hours)	0.3	0.5	either 8,000 hours/day or 10,000 hours/day
Demand Limit (tools/day)	15,000	16,000	
Contribution to Earnings ($/1,000 units)	either $160 or $90	$100	

GTC must soon decide how much steel per day to contract for, for next quarter. At the beginning of next quarter, the assembly machine capacity will become known. Also, at the beginning of next quarter, the unit earnings contribution of wrenches will become known. This sequence of events is shown in Table 7.10.

Stage-one and Stage-two

We will divide up the flow of time in our problem into two stages, which we refer to as "stage-one" and "stage-two," and where today (that is, the current quarter) is stage-one and next quarter is stage-two. In our steel supply planning problem, there is only one decision to make in stage-one, namely the amount of steel S to contract for, for next quarter. The decisions that must be made next quarter are the stage-two decisions. The stage-two decisions for our steel supply planning problem are the quantities of wrenches and pliers to produce next quarter. Note that these decisions do not have to be made until next quarter.

Note also that in this framework, there is uncertainty in stage-one about what the data for the problem will be in stage-two. That is, in stage-one, we do not yet know what the assembly machine capacity will be next quarter (either 8,000 hours/day or 10,000 hours per day), and we also do not know what the wrenches unit earnings contribution will be next quarter (either $160/1,000 units or $90/1,000 units). However, this uncertainty will be resolved prior to the start of stage-two.

Formulation of the Problem as a Linear Optimization Model

We begin the formulation of the steel supply planning problem by identifying the decision variables for stage-one. Recall that S is the amount of steel per day to contract for, for next quarter. The first-stage decision that GTC needs to make is the amount of steel per day to contract for, for next quarter, which is S.

The next step in the formulation of the model is to identify the decision variables for stage-two of the problem. In order to identify these decision variables, we first need to enumerate all of the possible "states of the world" that might transpire next quarter. Table 7.11 shows the four possible states of the world that might transpire next quarter with their associated probabilities. There are four possible states of the

TABLE 7.10

The sequence of events in the GTC steel supply planning problem.

Time	Event or Action
Today:	GTC must decide how much steel per day to contract for, for the next quarter.
Soon thereafter:	• GTC will discover the actual assembly machine availability for next quarter (either 8,000 or 10,000 hours/day).
	• GTC will discover the actual unit earnings contribution of wrenches for next quarter (either $160 or $90/1,000 units).
Next quarter:	GTC must decide the production quantities of wrenches and pliers.

TABLE 7.11

The four possible states of the world for next quarter.

State of the World	Assembly Machine Capacity	Unit Earnings Contribution of Wrenches	Probability
1	8,000 hours/day	$160/1,000 units	0.25
2	10,000 hours/day	$160/1,000 units	0.25
3	8,000 hours/day	$90/1,000 units	0.25
4	10,000 hours/day	$90/1,000 units	0.25

world for next quarter corresponding to the two possible assembly machine capacity values and the two possible unit earnings contributions of wrenches. For example, in Table 7.11, the first state of the world that might transpire is that the assembly machine capacity will be 8,000 hours/day and the unit earnings contribution of wrenches will be \$160/1,000 units. If we presume that the assembly machine capacity uncertainty and the wrenches earnings contribution uncertainty are independent, then the probability that the first state of the world will transpire is simply

$$0.25 = 0.50 \times 0.50$$

because there is a 50% probability that the assembly machine capacity will be 8,000 hours/day and a 50% probability that the unit earnings contribution of wrenches will be \$160. The probabilities of each of the four possible states of the world are shown in the fourth column of Table 7.11.

We then proceed by creating a decision variable for each of next quarter's decisions for each possible state of the world. We therefore define:

W_1 = the number of wrenches per day to produce next quarter, in 1,000s, if state-of-the-world 1 transpires,

P_1 = the number of pliers per day to produce next quarter, in 1,000s, if state-of-the-world 1 transpires,

W_2 = the number of wrenches per day to produce next quarter, in 1,000s, if state-of-the-world 2 transpires,

P_2 = the number of pliers per day to produce next quarter, in 1,000s, if state-of-the-world 2 transpires,

W_3 = the number of wrenches per day to produce next quarter, in 1,000s, if state-of-the-world 3 transpires,

P_3 = the number of pliers per day to produce next quarter, in 1,000s, if state-of-the-world 3 transpires,

W_4 = the number of wrenches per day to produce next quarter, in 1,000s, if state-of-the-world 4 transpires,

P_4 = the number of pliers per day to produce next quarter, in 1,000s, if state-of-the-world 4 transpires.

For example, the interpretation of P_2 is that P_2 is the quantity of pliers that GTC will produce next quarter if state-of-the-world 2 transpires, that is, if assembly machine capacity is 10,000 hours and the wrench unit earnings contribution is \$160.

We are now ready to construct the linear optimization model of the steel supply planning problem. The objective will be to maximize the expected contribution to earnings over all possible states of the world that might transpire next quarter. The expression for the objective function is:

$$\text{Objective} = 0.25 \cdot (160W_1 + 100P_1) + 0.25 \cdot (160W_2 + 100P_2)$$
$$+ 0.25 \cdot (90W_3 + 100P_3) + 0.25 \cdot (90W_4 + 100P_4) - 58.00S.$$

The constraints of the model will be the steel availability, assembly and molding machine capacity, and demand constraints, for each possible state of the world that might transpire next quarter. The resulting linear optimization model is as follows:

$$\text{maximize} \quad 0.25 \cdot (160W_1 + 100P_1) + 0.25 \cdot (160W_2 + 100P_2) +$$
$$0.25 \cdot (90W_3 + 100P_3) + 0.25 \cdot (90W_4 + 100P_4) - 58.00S$$

subject to

Steel1:	$1.5W_1 + 1.0P_1 - S \leq 0$
Molding1:	$1.0W_1 + 1.0P_1 \leq 21$
Assembly1:	$0.3W_1 + 0.5P_1 \leq 8$
W-demand1:	$W_1 \leq 15$
P-demand1:	$P_1 \leq 16$
Steel2:	$1.5W_2 + 1.0P_2 - S \leq 0$
Molding2:	$1.0W_2 + 1.0P_2 \leq 21$
Assembly2:	$0.3W_2 + 0.5P_2 \leq 10$
W-demand2:	$W_2 \leq 15$
P-demand2:	$P_2 \leq 16$
Steel3:	$1.5W_3 + 1.0P_3 - S \leq 0$
Molding3:	$1.0W_3 + 1.0P_3 \leq 21$
Assembly3:	$0.3W_3 + 0.5P_3 \leq 8$
W-demand3:	$W_3 \leq 15$
P-demand3:	$P_3 \leq 16$
Steel4:	$1.5W_4 + 1.0P_4 - S \leq 0$
Molding4:	$1.0W_4 + 1.0P_4 \leq 21$
Assembly4:	$0.3W_4 + 0.5P_4 \leq 10$
W-demand4:	$W_4 \leq 15$
P-demand4:	$P_4 \leq 16$
Nonnegativity:	$S, W_1, P_1, W_2, P_2, W_3, P_3, W_4, P_4 \geq 0.$

This linear optimization model is called a **two-stage linear optimization model under uncertainty** or more simply a **two-stage model.** This is because the model is constructed based on there being two time-stages (today and next quarter), and because there is uncertainty about the data for stage-two (the assembly machine capacity next quarter will be either 8,000 hours/day or 10,000 hours/day next quarter, and the wrenches unit earnings contribution will be either $160/1,000 units or $90/1,000 units next quarter).

Observations on the Two-Stage Model

Let us make several observations about the two-stage model that we have just constructed. First, notice in this linear optimization model that the objective function consists of the expected contribution to earnings from the daily production of wrenches and pliers in each state of the world, minus the cost of steel. Secondly, for each state of the world, we have our usual constraints on steel utilization, molding machine capacity and assembly machine capacity, and demand for wrenches and pliers. However, the model uses different values of assembly machine capacity (either 8,000 or 10,000 hours/day) corresponding to the different possible states of the world, consistent with the description of the four different states of the world in Table 7.11. Similarly, the model uses different unit earnings contributions of wrenches (either \$160 or \$90) corresponding to the different possible states of the world, also consistent with the description of the four states of the world in Table 7.11.

Notice as well that the model expresses the constraint that GTC cannot use more steel than it has contracted for delivery, in the four constraints:

$$1.5W_1 + 1.0P_1 - S \leq 0$$
$$1.5W_2 + 1.0P_2 - S \leq 0$$
$$1.5W_3 + 1.0P_3 - S \leq 0$$
$$1.5W_4 + 1.0P_4 - S \leq 0.$$

These four constraints state that regardless of which state of the world will transpire next quarter, GTC cannot utilize more steel next quarter than they have contracted for.

Interpreting the Solution of the Two-Stage Model

The optimal solution of the two-stage model is shown in Table 7.12. According to Table 7.12, the optimal value of S is $S = 27.25$. This means that GTC should contract today for the purchase of 27,250 lb./day of steel for next quarter. In order to interpret the optimal solution values of the decision variables W_1, P_1, W_2, P_2, W_3, P_3, W_4, and P_4, let us re-organize the optimal values of these eight decision variables into the format shown in Table 7.13.

We can interpret the optimal solution values in Table 7.12 and Table 7.13 as follows:

- Today, GTC should contract for 27,250 lb./day of steel for next quarter.

- Next quarter, if assembly hour availability is 8,000 hours/day and the contribution of wrenches is \$160, then GTC should produce 15,000 wrenches per day and 4,750 pliers per day.

- Next quarter, if assembly hour availability is 10,000 hours/day and the contribution of wrenches is \$160, then GTC should produce 15,000 wrenches per day and 4,750 pliers per day.

TABLE 7.12

The optimal solution of the linear optimization model of the GTC steel supply planning problem.

Decision Variable	Optimal Solution Value
S	27.25
W_1	15.00
P_1	4.75
W_2	15.00
P_2	4.75
W_3	12.50
P_3	8.50
W_4	5.00
P_4	16.00

TABLE 7.13

The optimal production plan for next quarter for the GTC steel supply planning problem.

State of the world Next Quarter	Production of Wrenches (units/day)		Production of Pliers (units/day)	
	Decision Variable	Value	Decision Variable	Value
1	W_1	15,000	P_1	4,750
2	W_2	15,000	P_2	4,750
3	W_3	12,500	P_3	8,500
4	W_4	5,000	P_4	16,000

- Next quarter, if assembly hour availability is 8,000 hours/day and the contribution of wrenches is $90, then GTC should produce 12,500 wrenches per day and 8,500 pliers per day.

- Next quarter, if assembly hour availability is 10,000 hours/day and the contribution of wrenches is $90, then GTC should produce 5,000 wrenches per day and 16,000 pliers per day.

Flexibility of the Two-Stage Linear Optimization Modeling Paradigm

The modeling framework for a two-stage linear optimization under uncertainty allows considerable flexibility in modeling uncertainty. Here we indicate how we can model a variety of different issues that might arise in this context:

Modeling different probabilities. We could have modeled different probabilities for different possible states of the world. For example, suppose that we presume that the following probabilities hold for the problem:

$$P(\text{assembly machine hours} = 8,000) = 0.8$$
$$P(\text{assembly machine hours} = 10,000) = 0.2$$

and

$$P(\text{wrench contribution} = \$160) = 0.7$$
$$P(\text{wrench contribution} = \$90) = 0.3.$$

Under these scenarios, the states of the world and their associated probabilities would be as shown in Table 7.14.

Modeling different numbers of states of the world. Suppose that there are seven different assembly machine capacity levels that might transpire next quarter, and that there are six different wrench unit earnings contributions levels that might transpire next quarter. Then we would have $42 = 7 \times 6$ possible states of the world, and would need $1 + 42 \times 2 = 85$ decision variables and $42 \times 5 = 210$ constraints in the model. Therefore, the number of distinct states of the world can increase the size of the model quite a lot.

Modeling different numbers of stages. We might want to model more than two stages: today, next quarter, the next quarter after that, etc. The same modeling principles illustrated here would then apply, but the resulting linear optimization model can become much more complicated, as well as much larger.

TABLE 7.14

The four possible states of the world for next quarter with different probabilities of transpiring.

State of the World	Assembly Machine Capacity	Unit Earnings Contribution of Wrenches	Probability
1	8,000 hours/day	$160/1,000 units	$0.56 = 0.8 \times 0.7$
2	10,000 hours/day	$160/1,000 units	$0.14 = 0.2 \times 0.7$
3	8,000 hours/day	$90/1,000 units	$0.24 = 0.8 \times 0.3$
4	10,000 hours/day	$90/1,000 units	$0.06 = 0.2 \times 0.3$

Summary of the Method for Constructing a Two-Stage Linear Optimization Model under Uncertainty

Although we have presented the two-stage linear optimization modeling technique in the context of a simple example, the methodology applies broadly for modeling linear optimization problems under uncertainty. Here we summarize the main steps in constructing a two-stage linear optimization model under uncertainty.

Procedure for Constructing a Two-Stage Linear Optimization Model under Uncertainty

1. Determine which decisions need to be made in stage-one (today), and which decisions need to be made in stage-two (next period).

2. Enumerate the possible states of the world that might transpire next period, what the data will be in each possible state of the world, and what is the probability of each state of the world occurring.

3. **Creating the decision variables:** Create one decision variable for each decision that must be made in stage-one. Create one decision variable for each decision that must be made in stage-two, for each possible state of the world.

4. **Constraints:** Create the necessary constraints for each possible state of the world.

5. **Objective function:** Account for the contribution of each of today's decisions in the objective function. Account for the expected value of the objective function contribution of each of next period's possible states of the world.

In order to use two-stage models effectively, we must have a reasonably accurate estimate of the probabilities of the future states of the world. Also, in order to keep the size of the model from becoming too large, it is important to limit the description of the different possible future states of the world to a reasonably low number.

There is great modeling power in two-stage linear optimizaiton under uncertainty. Indeed, to the extent that the most important decisions that managers need to make are concerned with optimally choosing actions today in the face of uncertainty about tomorrow, then the two-stage modeling framework is a core modeling tool.

7.8 | A BRIEF HISTORICAL SKETCH OF THE DEVELOPMENT OF LINEAR OPTIMIZATION

The following is a sketch of important events in the historical development of linear optimization. Although certain concepts related to linear optimization had been discovered by economists and mathematicians in the former U.S.S.R. (Soviet Union) as early as the 1930's, it was not until 1947 that the potential of linear optimization models was fully recognized. George B. Dantzig defined the linear optimization concept in the Spring of 1947 and invented the simplex algorithm in the Summer of 1947. In 1953, William Orchard-Hayes developed the first commercial software program for solving linear optimization problems using the simplex algorithm. By this time, economists and mathematicians were fully aware of the enormous potential for improved economic performance using linear optimization. In 1958, Professors Robert

Dorfman, Paul Samuelson, and Robert Solow published their landmark book *Linear Programming and Economic Analysis* (McGraw-Hill Book Company, 1958). (Two of these authors would later win the Nobel Memorial Prize in economic science.) In 1975, the Nobel Memorial Prize in economic science was awarded to Tjalling Koopmans and Leonid Kantorovich specifically for the application of linear optimization to economic science.

The next significant event in the development of linear optimization took place in 1984, when Dr. Narendra Karmarkar of AT&T Bell Laboratories developed a radically different and more efficient method for solving linear optimization problems using what is now called the "interior-point method." News of Dr. Karmarkar's algorithm was reported on the front page of the *New York Times,* as well as in the *Wall Street Journal, Time* magazine, and in other major periodicals around the world. Interior-point methods are now used to solve gigantic linear optimization problems (that is, problems with ten million decision variables or more). Today, managers and scientists routinely solve linear optimization models with thousands of constraints and decision variables on their personal computers. Larger computers are used to solve problems with one million decision variables or more.

7.9 | CASE MODULES

SHORT-RUN MANUFACTURING PROBLEMS AT DEC

Introduction

Digital Equipment Corporation (DEC) is the world's leading manufacturer of network computer systems and associated peripheral equipment and is the industry leader in systems integration with its networks, communications, services, and software products. Recent annual revenues were over $12 billion. Two-thirds of the revenue is derived from hardware sales and one-third is from software sales and services.

Successful introduction of new computer hardware products is important in the competitive computer industry. Rapid advances in chip technology have caused product life cycles to be short and steep, typically 2-3 years. Transitions from older products to new products must be carefully planned and executed. Both production shortfalls and obsolescence expense must be avoided.

The case before us examines one aspect of introducing and "ramping" a major new computer hardware product family. In the industry jargon, "ramping" refers to bringing a product into full production and sales.

Organization

The Manufacturing organization is comprised of several segments, see Figure 7.17. The External Procurement and Chip groups are responsible for supplying hardware components to internal (i.e., in-house) manufacturers of saleable (i.e., final) computer products. The Memory and Disk groups are responsible for supplying products that are either sold

FIGURE 7.17
The Manufacturing
organization at DEC.

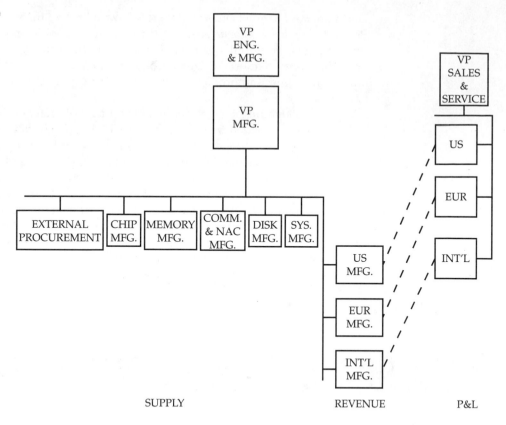

FIGURE 7.17
The Manufacturing organization at DEC.

separately as "add-ons" to customers' computer systems (such as extra hard disks or additional memory) or are used by the in-house computer System manufacturers. The computer System groups manufacture completely configured computer systems for sale to customers.

The Geographic Manufacturing groups are responsible for generating shipments to customers. They are the interface between Field groups and Manufacturing groups. It is their job to ensure that demand and supply are in balance and that orders are properly filled.

The Sales & Services organization (Field) generates sales and is responsible for the company P&L (profit and loss).

The Corporate Demand/Supply organization has an oversight role and ensures integration across the diverse Manufacturing and Field organizations.

Background

A new family of general purpose computer systems and workstations was announced in Q2-1988 (i.e., second quarter, 1988). (See Table 7.15 for a brief description.) This family represented a significant price/performance improvement over the existing products. Customer acceptance of the new product family was very strong.

Shipments of this new family of products had commenced in Q3-1988 and ramped slower than planned during the current quarter, Q4-1988. Two problems prevented supply from meeting overall demand. Chip supply from the in-house supplier had been limited as the chip manufacturing group worked to de-bug the new chip process technology. Similarly, the in-house disk drive manufacturing group was

TABLE 7.15

Product description of new family of products.

GP-1	High-end general purpose computer system. Large memory, disk storage, and expansion capability.
GP-2	Intermediate general purpose computer system. Moderate memory, disk storage, and expansion capability.
GP-3	Interim replacement for GP-2 using older disk storage devices.
WS-1	High-end workstation based on the GP-2 system.
WS-2	Entry-level workstation using older disk storage devices and enclosure. Limited memory and expansion capability.

TABLE 7.16

Revenue for each system.

System	List Price
GP-1	$60,000
GP-2	$40,000
GP-3	$30,000
WS-1	$30,000
WS-2	$15,000

- List price is an average across the 3 major Geographies. Effect of varying memory and new disk content on list price and mark-up is negligible.
- Allowances and discounts are roughly the same across the products and Geographies.
- Mark-up percentages are roughly the same across the products and Geographies.
- Most costs can be considered fixed over the one quarter time-frame.

TABLE 7.17

CPU chip set requirements.

System	# CPU Chip Set
GP-1	1
GP-2	1
GP-3	1
WS-1	1
WS-2	1

- Chip Manufacturing is a long lead time process. Chip supply is fixed at 7,000 sets for Q1-1989 with no possibility of an increase. This volume was based on prior market sizing estimates.

de-bugging the new state-of-the-art disk manufacturing process. While it wasn't unusual for problems to exist during the initial phases of a new product ramp, the anticipated continuation of these problems into Q1-1989 was becoming a serious concern.

The Revenue managers (whose job is to ensure that supply of products is delivered to meet demand) had responded to the shortages in a simple, straightforward way in Q3-1988. On the supply side, the majority of the scarce CPU chips were used to build the more valuable general purpose computer systems. (See Table 7.16 and Table 7.17 for product list price and chip set requirements.) On the demand side, customers were encouraged to order these more valuable systems through short-term marketing programs.

At least one of the new type of disk drives is required for the GP-2 and WS-1 system (see Table 7.18) and is a popular "add-on" in extra numbers on these two systems as well as the GP-1 system. (See Table 7.18. For example, the average demand for the new disk drive in the GP-2 system is 1.7 drives per computer system.) Due to the scarcity of these disk drives, the placement of disk drives were reduced as shown in the third column of Table 7.18 with a commitment to those customers who wanted additional add-ons to provide the additional drives when these restrictions were lifted.

Several new developments occurred in the middle of Q4-1988 that had a further impact on supply of systems in Q1-1989. The in-house disk supplier reduced com-

TABLE 7.18

Disk usage per system.

| System | Average Disks Per System | |
	Customer Preference	Constrained
GP-1	0.3	0
GP-2	1.7	1
GP-3	0	0
WS-1	1.4	1
WS-2	0	0

- GP-3 and WS-2 use other (non-constrained) disks. GP-1 use of the new disks is optional.
- Estimates are world-wide averages. Geographic estimates vary ±10%.
- Committed availability for Q1-1989 was recently reduced by 50% to 3,500 units. Further small reductions are possible and recovery to the previous level is also possible.
- The usage rate has been held at the constrained level since Q3-1988. Customer discontent has been increasing. Some key customers are insisting on greater than one disk per unit on their systems but the number of systems involved is unknown.
- Any spare drives will be shipped as add-ons to prior customers who were constrained at one drive per system.

mitted Q1-1989 availability by 50% to 3,500 units. The chip manufacturing group stated that CPU chip supply was capped at 7,000 sets. Industry-wide supply of 256K DRAMs had tightened. These were used on many system and memory products and were used extensively in the new family of computer systems. Supplies would fall about 10% short of the company's total need. Furthermore, there were unquantified potential shortages of communication modules and module handles, both of which were used in the new family of products. Finally, after two previous quarters of delayed delivery of the add-on disks (discussed herein), key customers were demanding shipment of their constrained computer system and disk orders.

It was clear to the Manufacturing staff that the problem had become much more complex. Emotions were running high. Revenue, profitability, and customer satisfaction were all at risk. They needed a rational analysis that would distill the multiple interrelated factors into something more manageable. A set of recommendations would have to be made to the manufacturing staff that was easily understood, supportable by all affected parties, and conducive to fast implementation. They needed to know which problems to focus on and what actions to take.

What recommendations would you make?

Key Issues and Uncertainties

One of the decisions that management must make concerns disk usage per system (see Table 7.18). Should they plan to satisfy customer preference for disks per system, or should they continue to manufacture products in the constrained mode of disks per system?

Another decision that management must make concerns configurations of DRAM usage in products. See Table 7.19. The first column shows the number of 256K DRAM boards required in each product. However, the GP-1 could be produced with two 1-meg DRAM boards instead of the four 256K DRAM boards. A decision needs to be made whether to produce the GP-1 with four 256K DRAM boards or with two 1-meg DRAM boards.

A third decision that must be made is where to start tackling the shortages of disks and of 256K DRAM boards. Manufacturing staff would like to concentrate their troubleshooting efforts on either decreasing the shortage of disks or decreasing the shortage of 256K DRAM boards. They would like a recommendation on which problem to concentrate their efforts.

TABLE 7.19

Memory usage of
DRAMs.

System	256K Boards Per System	1-Meg Boards Per System
GP-1	4	2
GP-2	2	—
GP-3	2	—
WS-1	2	—
WS-2	1	—

- Use of 1-meg DRAM boards on GP-1 has been technically qualified but not yet announced. An announcement could be made quickly.
- 1-meg DRAM boards will not be technically qualified on the other systems until Q2-1989.
- 256K DRAMs are used on roughly a dozen different steady-state memory and system products. A 10% shortfall in Q1-1989 on a base of several million DRAMs is expected. Assume enough sets of 256K DRAMs will be available to support 10–15,000 memory boards.
- 1-meg DRAMs are used on several new memory and system products and are in tight supply. Assume enough sets of 1-meg DRAMs will be available to support 4,000 1-meg boards.

TABLE 7.20

Demand mix.

System	Estimated Maximum Q1-1989 Customer Demand
GP-1	1,800
GP-3	300
GP FAMILY	3,800
WS FAMILY	3,200

- GP-1 demand capped due to market saturation in the prior two quarters.
- GP-3 is a temporary fill-in due to lack of GP-2 availability. Demand is limited.
- Total GP and WS family market size is based on previous market studies, though lack of supply in the prior two quarters could distort demand.

TABLE 7.21

Customer
satisfaction data.

System	Estimated Minimum Acceptable Supply
GP-2	500
WS-1	500
WS-2	400

- Supply had been skewed to the higher valued general purpose systems in the prior two quarters. Key customers are demanding that their workstation orders be filled as well.

Probably the most important uncertainties are the availability of the new disks and the availability of 256K DRAM boards. From the notes in Table 7.18, disk unit availability will be in the range of 3,000–7,000 units. From the notes in Table 7.19, 256K DRAM board availability will be in the range of 10,000–15,000 units.

Assignment:

(a) Formulate a linear optimization model that describes DEC's manufacturing problem.

(b) The spreadsheet DEC.XLS contains various data for this case. Using the data in this spreadsheet, construct a spreadsheet version of your linear optimization model and solve the model for the optimal solution.

(c) Solve other versions of the model for different assumptions on the data values and to help analyze some of the key issues in the case. What conclusions can you draw?

(d) Prepare a brief (two pages or less) but pointed memo of summary recommendations for action addressed to the manufacturing staff.

SYTECH INTERNATIONAL

Sytech International is a leading manufacturer of computers and peripheral equipment. Established in 1951, Sytech entered the market with an innovative operating system for its large mainframe computers. Recognizing that "user-friendly" software was the key to acceptance by the business community long before the term became popular, Sytech established a loyal following that allowed it to prosper. Sytech continued to demonstrate its awareness of business needs by being one of the first large computer manufacturers to market personal computers. Sytech is currently active in computer networking and office automation.

Sytech's corporate headquarters is located in Burlington, Massachusetts. Manufacturing plants are located in Burlington, Taiwan, and Ireland. These plants are operated as wholly owned subsidiaries of Sytech International. The foreign plants can typically manufacture products at a lower cost due to a combination of lower labor costs and/or more favorable corporate tax rates in Ireland and Taiwan. However, these governments also apply strict regulations regarding the various procedures for withdrawing capital from the subsidiaries in order to further promote investment and industrial development within their countries.

Although Sytech manufactures hundreds of products, management has found that for major manufacturing decisions, four product classifications are sufficient: large mainframe computers (MFRAMES), smaller minicomputers (MINIS), personal computers (PCS), and PRINTERS. The two major markets for Sytech products are North America (primarily the United States) and Europe (primarily Western Europe).

The Problem

Major sourcing decisions are made quarterly at Sytech. At the end of each quarter, management meets to review the production plans of the previous quarter and to generate new production plans for the upcoming quarter. The primary outcome of the meetings is a set of production targets for the three major manufacturing facilities. These preliminary production targets allow the plant managers to estimate the labor and component materials requirements at their plant for the next quarter. These estimates are ultimately used to adjust the labor force and to draw up long term supply contracts.

Although these quarterly meetings are from time to time political in nature, a large amount of hard quantitative analysis must always be completed in order to determine a set of good sourcing strategies. In what follows, we examine the data behind this analysis and the structure of the analysis itself. This data is contained in the spreadsheet SYTECH.XLS. Where possible, we will refer to the range of cells in this spreadsheet (e.g.[C22–F15]) corresponding to the data items as we describe their significance in the analysis.

The analysis begins in the marketing division in which demand forecasts are prepared for the upcoming quarter. These forecasts are shown in Table 7.22 [A4–C9]. As one would expect, the demand for PCs is significantly higher than the demand for Minis, which is in turn higher than the demand for mainframes. Furthermore, the

TABLE 7.22

Forecast demand.

Product	Market	
	North America	Europe
MainFrame	962	321
Mini	4,417	1,580
PC	48,210	15,400
Printer	15,540	6,850

projected demand in North America is more than twice that in Europe. Although there is some debate concerning the methods used by the marketing division to forecast demand, in the past its forecasts have been reasonably accurate.

From the marketing side of the organization, we move to manufacturing. Prior to the meeting, each plant manager is required to submit a report detailing the capacity limitations at his plant. The data summarizing these reports are shown in Table 7.23 [A13–C16]. Two capacity constraints are considered: space and labor. Space is required for product assembly and inventory storage. Labor is required for both primary manufacturing and assembly, but there are regulatory restrictions limiting the legal size of the labor force at each plant. The Burlington plant is by far the largest, being over twice the size of the Taiwan plant and nearly four times as large as the Ireland plant. However, the Burlington plant labor capacity is only 55% of the Taiwan plant labor capacity. The labor capacity at the Ireland plant is proportionally smaller than that in Burlington, making the capacity profile of the Ireland plant look much like a scaled down version of the profile of the Burlington plant.

To use the capacity data, we require utilization data. This information is shown in Table 7.24 [E4–G8]. The utilization information allows one to determine the amount of capacity (space or labor) required per unit of production. For example, to produce one MFRAME requires 17.48 square feet of space and 79 hours of labor, whereas the production of a PC requires only 3 square feet of space and 6.9 hours of labor.

The final data required to perform the analysis is supplied by the accounting department. This data is shown in Table 7.25 [A21–I25]. The numbers shown in Table 7.25 represent unit profit contributions. For example, a mainframe manufactured in Burlington and sold in the North American market will provide a contribution of $16,136.46 to total (after-tax) Sytech profit. The least profitable items are the PC's manufactured in Burlington for the European market. These contribute only

TABLE 7.23

Plant capacities.

Plant	Space (1,000 square feet)	Labor (1,000 hours)
Burlington	540.71	277.71
Taiwan	201.00	499.24
Ireland	146.90	80.17

TABLE 7.24

Resource utilization rates.

Product	Space/Unit	Labor Hours/Unit
MainFrame	17.48	79.0
Mini	17.48	31.5
PC	3.00	6.9
Printer	5.30	5.6

	MainFrame		Mini		PC		Printer	
Plant	North America	Europe	North America	Europe	North America	Europe	North America	Europe
Burlington	$16,136.46	$13,694.03	$8,914.47	$6,956.23	$1,457.18	$1,037.57	$1,663.51	$1,345.43
Taiwan	$17,358.14	$14,709.96	$9,951.04	$7,852.36	$1,395.35	$1,082.49	$1,554.55	$1,270.16
Ireland	$15,652.68	$13,216.34	$9,148.55	$7,272.89	$1,197.52	$1,092.61	$1,478.90	$1,312.44

TABLE 7.25

Unit profit contributions.

$1,037.57 per unit to Sytech profit. We will postpone our discussion of the relevant accounting methods employed at Sytech for arriving at the numbers in Table 7.25 in order to continue our examination of the analytical framework.

The Model

The information described above is assembled by the Management Science Group. There, it is analyzed and preliminary sourcing strategies are determined by using a linear optimization model of the Sytech manufacturing facilities. The linear optimization model formulation is shown in Figure 7.18.[1]

We use index i to denote the product categories. For example, we use the four symbols $L_1, L_2, L_3,$ and L_4 to refer to the labor utilization for MFRAMES, MINIS, PCS, and PRINTERS, respectively. Index j is used in a similar fashion to refer to the three plants. Hence, $SC_1, SC_2,$ and SC_3 refer to the total space available at Burlington, Taiwan, and Ireland, respectively. Finally, the index k corresponds to the two markets, so, for example, $D_{41},$ and D_{42} are used to denote the demand for PRINTERS ($i = 4$) in North America and Europe, respectively.

The decision variables, X_{ijk}, represent the quantity of product i manufactured at plant j and sold in market k. For example, X_{231} represents the number of minicomputers manufactured in Ireland for the North American market during the quarter. Thus, the values of the decision variables determine the sourcing decisions for the upcoming quarter.

FIGURE 7.18

The linear optimization model formulation.

Decision Variables:

X_{ijk}:   Quantity of product i manufactured at plant j and sold in market k, where:

$\quad i$:   Product: 1 = MainFrame, 2 = Mini, 3 = PC, 4 = Printer
$\quad j$:   Plant: 1 = Burlington, 2 = Taiwan, 3 = Ireland
$\quad k$:   Market: 1 = North America, 2 = Europe

Maximize
$$\sum_{i=1}^{4} \sum_{j=1}^{3} \sum_{k=1}^{2} C_{ijk}\, X_{ijk}$$

Subject to:

Space constraints:
$$\sum_{i=1}^{4} \sum_{k=1}^{2} S_i\, X_{ijk} \leq SC_j \quad \text{plants } j = 1, 2, 3$$

Labor constraints:
$$\sum_{i=1}^{4} \sum_{k=1}^{2} L_i\, X_{ijk} \leq LC_j \quad \text{plants } j = 1, 2, 3$$

Demand constraints:
$$\sum_{j=1}^{3} X_{ijk} \leq D_{ik} \quad \begin{array}{l}\text{products } i = 1, 2, 3, 4 \\ \text{markets } k = 1, 2\end{array}$$

$$X_{ijk} \geq 0$$

where

C_{ijk}:   Unit contribution for product i, manufactured at plant j, and sold in market k (shown in Table 7.25).
$\ S_i$:   Space utilization for product i (shown in Table 7.24).
$\ L_i$:   Labor utilization for product i (shown in Table 7.24).
SC_j: Total space available at plant j (shown in Table 7.23).
LC_j: Total labor available at plant j (shown in Table 7.23).
D_{ik}:   Demand for product i in market k (shown in Table 7.22).

---

[1]The spreadsheet SYTECH.XLS contains the linear optimization model in spreadsheet format suitable for solving using Microsoft Excel®. In the spreadsheet SYTECH.XLS, the decision variables are contained in cells [B61-I63], and the objective function is represented in cell [B71].

The objective is to maximize total Sytech profit for the upcoming quarter. The total profit is the sum of the profits at each of the wholly owned subsidiaries and the profit at Sytech itself. Though other objectives have been suggested, management feels that the profit maximizing strategy best serves the interest of the Sytech shareholders.

Total profit is calculated using the data shown in Table 7.25. These unit profit contributions are calculated as the sum of the unit contribution at the appropriate manufacturing plant and the contribution at Sytech International. Therefore, the objective function shown in Figure 7.18 represents the total profit at Sytech, and the optimal solution to the linear optimization model with respect to this objective function determines the sourcing decisions that will maximize total Sytech profits.

The model contains three sets of constraints: space constraints, labor constraints, and demand constraints. The space and labor constraints represent the physical capacities of the three manufacturing facilities. For example, the space constraint for the Ireland plant, (i.e., $j = 3$) is

$$17.48(X_{131} + X_{132}) + 17.48(X_{231} + X_{232}) + 3.00(X_{331} + X_{332})$$
$$+ 5.30(X_{431} + X_{432}) \le 146{,}900,$$

where the utilization coefficients are from Table 7.24, and the right-hand-side is from Table 7.23. The left side of the constraint represents the total amount of space required by the Irish plant to produce the products allocated to it (e.g. $X_{131}, X_{132}, \ldots, X_{432}$). The quantity $(X_{131} + X_{132})$ is the total number of mainframes produced in the Irish plant. Multiplying this by the utilization factor, 17.48, yields the total amount of space required to produce the mainframes. Summing over the four product categories gives the total space required in Ireland to meet the production targets in the upcoming quarter. The constraint forces this to be less than or equal to the amount of space available at the plant.

The labor utilization constraints have exactly the same form as the space utilization constraints. There is one labor constraint and one space constraint for each plant, resulting in a total of six resource constraints.

There is one demand constraint for each product in each market (a total of eight constraints). For example, the demand constraint for PCs in Europe is

$$X_{312} + X_{322} + X_{332} \le 15{,}400.$$

The left-hand side of the constraint represents the total number of PCs manufactured for Europe (obtained by summing over the three plants). This is then compared with the total forecast demand for PCs in Europe. With the demand constraints, a feasible sourcing strategy, as represented by the X_{ijk} variables, will satisfy the condition that total production of each product for each market does not exceed demand for each product in each market.

Prior to the quarterly planning meeting, the Management Science Group optimizes the linear optimization model under various scenarios. The results of the model are then analyzed by the group and a report is distributed to the plant managers and to the Manufacturing Strategy Committee, describing the conclusions and recommendations of the group. This report is then used to determine the manufacturing strategy for Sytech for the next quarter.

Review of the Data

Because the results of the Sytech model are relatively sensitive to the input data, the sources and derivations of these data command close scrutiny. As part of its report to the Manufacturing Strategy Committee, the Management Science Group has included the following analysis of the data used in the Sytech model.

Demand Forecasts

The marketing division has a good track record and its forecasts have been fairly accurate in the past. This is especially true of the aggregate forecasts used in the Sytech model.

The division has had difficulty forecasting demand for specific products (e.g. a specific mainframe model). They have also been unable to predict with accuracy the demand beyond a one year time horizon because of the dynamic nature of the computer industry. Nevertheless, their predictions of the demand for the four aggregate product groups over a one quarter time period have been fairly accurate, and there is no reason to believe that the forecasts used in the current model are any less accurate.

Capacity and Utilization Data

The physical capacity data shown in Table 7.23 are very accurate, since they are derived from fixed and easily measurable quantities. These capacity limitations will not change unless Sytech management decides to expand plant capacity at some later date. Whereas such expansion might or might not be economically justified, it is beyond the scope of the current study. Hence we assume fixed plant capacity in this analysis.

Computing the labor utilization data in Table 7.24 is straightforward. The managers know how many workers must work for how long on each product, and the wage and benefit rates are fixed by negotiated labor contracts.

The space utilization data, however, are less exact. Unlike labor, space used for producing a unit can be re-used for another unit when the first is completed. The space utilization is an average based on current production levels; the space devoted to manufacturing a particular unit divided by the number of units produced per quarter. Although this results in inexact data, the quality of the data is adequate for the planning purpose at hand, assuming that the level of production does not change drastically. In fact, these numbers have shown little quarter-to-quarter variation in the past.

Profit Contribution Data

The reliability of the unit contribution data shown in Table 7.25 is a more complex issue. It begs a larger question: How to determine the actual contribution of each product to corporate goals? This is never easy. Nevertheless, the method currently used to determine unit product contributions at Sytech is arguably better than any other given the limited information and the complexity of Sytech's corporate structure.

In order to understand the procedures used to derive these data, it is necessary to understand the global operation of Sytech, the tax laws in Ireland, Taiwan, and the United States, and the accounting procedures employed at Sytech. We briefly describe these elements in the following paragraphs.

The foreign manufacturing facilities are operated as wholly-owned subsidiaries of Sytech International. Sytech International operates with these subsidiaries by purchasing at an arms-length basis all of the products they manufacture. The price Sytech pays for the manufactured products is called the transfer price and is calculated as a fixed percentage of the final market price. This procedure for calculating the transfer price often leads to the apparent paradox of Sytech paying different prices for the same product depending on where the product is shipped. For example, if the transfer price is 40% of the market price, then Sytech would pay the Taiwan subsidiary 40% of the North American market value for PCs that were to be sold in the United States, and 40% of the European market value (which is usually slightly lower than the American market value) for those products shipped to Europe. Although this paradox can lead to complex accounting requirements, it is necessary because of the strict transfer pricing regulations imposed by both governments.

Governments closely regulate transfer pricing schemes because of the potential they offer for tax evasion. Consider the following example wherein computers are manufactured in Taiwan for sale in the U.S.: The U.S. corporate tax rate is 34%, and the Taiwan rate is 10%. Everything else being equal, Sytech International would choose to pay as high a transfer price as possible so that it could show a loss on the U.S. books and a gain on the Taiwan books. The total tax bill to Sytech International and the Taiwan subsidiary would decrease as the unit transfer price increased. To prevent this kind of tax evasion, most countries have specific regulations regarding transfer pricing methods. For example, section 482 of the U.S. Internal Revenue Code provides the Secretary of the Treasury with the following wide-reaching powers:

> In any case of two or more organizations, trades, or businesses (whether or not incorporated, whether or not organized in the United States, and whether or not affiliated) owned or controlled directly or indirectly by the same interests, the Secretary or his delegate may distribute, apportion, or allocate gross income, deductions, credits, or allowances between or among such organizations, trades, or businesses, if he determines that such distribution, apportionment, or allocation is necessary in order to prevent the evasion of taxes or clearly reflect the income of such organizations, trades, or businesses.

The tax effects of shifting the flow of funds can be understood by examining the various tax procedures. For the production facilities, taxes are based on gross profit, which is calculated as gross revenue from Sytech International (as calculated using the corresponding transfer prices) less labor, materials, overhead, shipping costs, and royalties to Sytech International. At Sytech International, taxes are based on gross revenues (that is, royalties plus market value of goods sold) less transfer payments, less overhead costs. The total tax bill is then determined as the sum of taxes paid by the three plants plus the taxes paid by Sytech International. The total net contribution is then determined as the sum of the profits of the four companies after tax plus the overhead. (Note: Overhead is deducted only for tax purposes. Since it does not represent a physical flow of funds, it must be added back in to the after-tax profit in order to determine the total profit contribution correctly.)

An Example of the Unit Profit Contribution Calculations

In order to understand the accounting procedures outlined above more clearly, we apply them to a small example. In our example, we wish to determine the unit contribution of a minicomputer (MINI) made in Taiwan for the European market. In other words, we wish to calculate the value of C_{222} in Figure 7.18. To perform this analysis, we shall trace the income effects of the production and sale of a unit of MINI (i.e. set $X_{222} = 1$). Table 7.26 [A27–E44] contains the accounting data required for this analysis, and Table 7.28 shows the itemized profit calculation procedure.

We start by analyzing the income statement for the Taiwan subsidiary. The revenues in Taiwan are derived solely from the transfer price paid by Sytech International, which is the product of the market value (sales price) and transfer price rate (see Table 7.26).

On the cost side, the Taiwan plant incurs the standard costs associated with the manufacturing industry. Labor costs are calculated by multiplying the number of hours required to manufacture one MINI (Table 7.24) by the labor burden rate per

TABLE 7.26

Manufacturing cost accounting information.

	Main Frame	Mini	PC	Printer
North American Sales Price	$40,270	$18,337	$3,376	$3,992
Europe Sales Price	$37,012	$15,776	$2,980	$3,635
Material Cost	$16,268	$5,163	$1,153	$1,545
Sytech Overhead Rate	14.10%	14.10%	14.10%	14.10%
Transfer Price Rates				
Burlington	50%	50%	40%	40%
Taiwan	50%	50%	40%	40%
Ireland	50%	50%	40%	40%
	Burlington	**Taiwan**	**Ireland**	
Manufacturing Data				
Labor Burden	$29.91	$9.17	$35.13	
Sytech Royalties	5%	5%	5%	
Income Tax Rates	34%	10%	11%	

	MainFrame		Mini		PC		Printer	
Plant	North America	Europe	North America	Europe	North America	Europe	North America	Europe
Burlington	$115	$321	$57	$277	$54	$265	$49	$148
Taiwan	498	465	238	231	231	227	221	220
Ireland	345	91	288	44	276	40	164	32

TABLE 7.27

Unit shipping costs.

hour in Taiwan (Table 7.26). The material costs are taken directly from Table 7.26, and the shipping costs are taken directly from Table 7.27. Finally, the Taiwan subsidiary must pay royalties to Sytech International for the use of its managerial expertise and manufacturing know-how. The royalty payments are calculated as a percentage of total revenues, so the cost to the Taiwan subsidiary is calculated as the product of revenues (that is, the transfer price) times the royalty rate shown in Table 7.26

The tax rate for Taiwan is shown in Table 7.26. The after-tax profit for the Taiwan subsidiary is calculated as revenues minus costs minus taxes.

Now, turning to the Sytech International books, the revenue to Sytech is derived from two sources: the market value for the MINI sold in Europe (shown in Table 7.26) and the royalty payments from Taiwan.

For the Sytech accounting, we distinguish between direct and indirect costs. Briefly, direct costs are those costs that increase proportionally to the volume of sales, and indirect costs are the fixed costs of doing business. The only direct cost is the transfer price paid to Taiwan. All of the indirect costs are put together on the books under the heading "overhead." The overhead charge is calculated as a fixed percentage of the market value (shown in Table 7.26).

We must distinguish between direct and indirect costs for tax purposes. The tax at Sytech International is based on the book profit, that is, the revenues less direct and indirect costs. However, for the purposes of our manufacturing model, we are primarily interested in the actual profit, that is, the profit that depends directly on the decisions we make with the model. Indirect costs impact the actual profit only through their impact on taxes. Therefore, after we calculate the taxes at Sytech International,

TABLE 7.28

Profit derivation for one MINI produced in Taiwan for the European market.

Income at Taiwan Subsidiary		
Revenues:		
Transfer Price:	7,888.00	15,776.00 × 50%: Market value times Transfer price rate [Table 7.26]
Costs:		
Labor:	288.86	31.5 × 9.17: Labor hours times labor rate [Table 7.24 and Table 7.26]
Material Costs:	5,163.00	Material Cost [Table 7.26]
Shipping cost:	231.00	Shipping Cost [Table 7.27]
Royalties to Sytech:	394.40	7,888 × 5%: Transfer price times Royalty rate
Profit before Taxes:	1,810.74	Revenue less costs
Taxes:	181.07	1,810.74 × 10%: Profit before taxes times tax rate [Table 7.26]
Profit after Taxes:	1,629.67	Profit before taxes less taxes
Income at Sytech		
Revenues:		
Market Value	15,776.00	Market Value [Table 7.26]
Royalties	394.40	7,888.00 × 5%: see above
Costs:		
Transfer price	7,888.00	15,776.00 × 50%: Market value times Transfer price rate [Table 7.26]
Overhead	2,224.42	15,776.00 × 14.1%: Market value times Sytech overhead rate [Table 7.26]
Profit before taxes:	6,057.98	Revenues less costs
Taxes:	2,059.71	6,057.98 × 34%: Profit before taxes times tax rate [Table 7.26]
Profit after taxes:	3,998.27	Profit before taxes less taxes
Overhead adjustment:	2,224.42	15,776.00 × 14.1%: Market value times Sytech overhead rate [Table 7.26]
Adjusted after tax profit:	6,222.69	After tax profit plus overhead adjust
Combined Income		
Profit at Taiwan Subsidiary:	1,629.67	
Profit at Sytech International:	6,222.69	
Total Profit	**7,852.36**	

we must adjust the after-tax profit by adding back in the overhead charge. The resulting adjusted after-tax profit is an accurate reflection of the actual profit contribution at Sytech International for MINIs produced in Taiwan for the European market.

The total profit contribution is then calculated as the sum of the contribution to the Taiwan plant profits and the contribution to the Sytech International profits.

The unit contribution and profit calculations described above are adequate representations of actual profits at Sytech. Thus, we use the contribution values calculated in this fashion in the objective function. This provides us with a good approximation of the effects of the sourcing decisions on the overall profitability of the firm. Having assessed the reliability and accuracy of the input data, we are prepared to run the preliminary model. The results of this initial model are presented in the next section.

The Base Case

At the beginning of the manufacturing planning session this quarter, the Sytech model was implemented with the data shown in Tables 7.22–7.27. This was called the "base case" since the input data were derived using the most likely demand forecasts and accounting data. There was, however, some concern that the labor burden at the Taiwan plant might be far too low, as there was considerable upward pressure on labor rates. Sytech management wanted to be prepared with alternative sourcing strategies if they were warranted by changes in these cost estimates.

Table 7.29 [A59–K66] shows the results of the base case optimization. The values of all of the decision variables are shown. For example, the number of printers made by the Burlington plant for the North American market is 15,540. Note that the total production shown in the totals row is less than or equal to the total demand in each market shown in Table 7.22 (and duplicated as the bottom line in Table 7.29).

The aggregate profit contribution is shown at the bottom of Table 7.29. This contribution is $194,244,024.67 for the base case. This value is the optimal objective value of the underlying linear optimization model.

Assignment:

The spreadsheet SYTECH.XLS contains the linear optimization model of Sytech's production planning problem. In each of the following questions, make appropriate changes in the spreadsheet and then re-optimize the model.

(a) Suppose that labor regulations have just changed in Ireland, decreasing the labor capacity at the Ireland plant to 78,000 man-hours.

   (1) Change the labor capacity at the Irish plant to 78 and re-optimize the model.

   (2) How does the solution change?

   (3) What is your intuition for why the solution changes in the way that it does?

(b) Suppose that labor regulations have just changed in Ireland, increasing the labor capacity at the Ireland plant to 95,000 man-hours.

   (1) Change the labor capacity at the Irish plant to 95 and re-optimize the model.

   (2) How does the solution change?

   (3) What is your intuition for why the solution changes in the way that it does?

(c) The InoTech Corporation has developed a new method for large integrated circuit assembly which would allow Sytech to reduce the labor requirement in Mini

| | MainFrame | | Mini | | PC | | Printer | | Slack or Surplus | |
	North America	Europe	North America	Europe	North America	Europe	North America	Europe	Space	Labor
Burlington	0	0	1,683	0	14,395	0	15,540	6,850	349,447	0
Taiwan	962	321	1,769	0	33,815	15,400	0	0	0	2,564
Ireland	0	0	965	1,580	0	0	0	0	102,412	0
Total	962	321	4,417	1,580	48,210	15,400	15,540	6,850		
Slack or Surplus	0	0	0	0	0	0	0	0		
Demand	962	321	4,417	1,580	48,210	15,400	15,540	6,850		

Total Profit Contribution is $194,244,024.67

TABLE 7.29

Production plan for the base case.

production from the current 31.5 hours per unit to 22.5 hours. This new technology would increase the space requirement per unit for production of both mainframes and minis from 17.48 to 19.0. To obtain the technology and set up the new process at any or all of Sytech's plants will require a capital investment of $12–14,000,000, depending on negotiations with InoTech. InoTech keeps the technology secure as a trade secret, but Sytech analysts believe that the technology will be public knowledge (and be much less expensive to acquire) within two years. Using the model to address this investment decision based on the base case production plan, answer the following:

(1) Should Sytech purchase and implement the InoTech innovation? What should Sytech be prepared to spend on this investment, i.e., how much is this investment worth to Sytech?

(2) What external factors would affect this investment decision that the model does not properly account for?

(d) Notice that the base case production plan calls for Minis to be produced at all three Sytech production facilities. As a possible cost-cutting option, Sytech is considering eliminating the production capability of Minis in Taiwan. This would result in an immediate estimated savings in fixed costs of $8.3 million (after taxes) per year associated with the management and maintenance of the Mini production operation in Taiwan. However, the current production plan of 1,769 Minis in Taiwan would have to be moved to other production facilities at some additional cost. Use the model to analyze the cost-effectiveness of this option. (Hint: You will need to augment the formulation with two additional constraints that force the production of Minis in Taiwan to be zero.)

FILATOI RIUNITI

The Italian textile industry

The northern regions of Italy are the heartlands of the Italian textile industry, providing textile products for many great Italian (and non-Italian) fashion houses. The industry's history reaches back to Roman times when Biella (a town in the northwestern Alps) was a center for wool production. Most of today's companies were founded at the turn of the century and have grown and thrived despite a series of twentieth century catastrophes, including the great Depression (which crushed the silk industry), World War II, and the flash floods of 1968 (which destroyed many of Biella's mills). The families that run the wool-producing companies, many of whose ancestors had worked the land for centuries, have always come back with great competitive spirit.

Sales in the entire Italian textile and apparel industry were about $50 billion in 1994 with exports of $23 billion, according to Italy's National Statistics Institute. The entire textile sector employs over 700,000 people. Italy's largest export markets in the textiles sector are Germany, France, Great Britain, the United States, and Japan. In 1994, over 1,200 companies exported textile products to the United States totaling about $625 million (over 6% of Italy's overall textile exports).

The major Italian textile companies are fighting hard to stay at the forefront of the world textile market, and the battles are numerous. Competition from east Asia, a tug-of-war with China over silk and cashmere exports, lack of sufficient qualified employees, and a fast-moving fashion industry (which requires the mills to create and deliver rapidly) are among the new challenges facing the industry. In the face of these challenges, many Italian textile firms are committed to making massive investments in state-of-the-art machinery and in research into new finishings.

Italian manufacturers are confident that Italian textile producers will always have an edge on the competition because of the high concentration of dyeing, finishing, and printing specialists in Italy. "Italy's textile sector is unique because there is this microcosm of small companies who are very creative and always up-to-date on the latest trends. They provide a constant stimulus and an endless source of ideas for manufacturers. In the end, this means continued creativity and flexibility of the industry," says industry spokesperson Enrico Cerruti. "The trump card for the Italian textile industry is its cultural tradition and human resources. . . . You can copy technology, you can copy design, but you can't duplicate the people here. It takes 100 years to build that and it's our greatest advantage."

How cotton yarn is produced

Prior to the Industrial Revolution textiles were spun by hand using a spinning wheel.

Today most commercial yarns are produced in textile mills, and although the tools and techniques used are different from hand spinning, most of the processes are still the same. Most yarns are spun from staple fibers made using one of three systems: the Cotton Process, the Woolen Process, or the Worsted Process. These processes vary only slightly from each other but they all include the three basic processes of preparation, spinning, and finishing.

The Cotton Process is used to spin cotton fibers between 3/4" and 2" in length. Synthetic fibers can also be blended with the cotton to form blended yarns. Likewise the Worsted and Woolen Processes are used to spin wool fibers and wool blends. The cotton process method employs the following steps:

1. **Preparation.**

   (a) **Opening & Loosening.** Upon arrival at the mill, the cotton bails are opened and loosened. This helps separate and clean the cotton before it is fed into carding machines. Impurities such as rocks, coins, and other solid objects (there are stories about bullets found in the raw cotton!) are removed.

   (b) **Carding.** Carding machines further loosen and separate the cotton fibers by passing the fibers between two rotating metal drums covered with wire needles. This aligns the cotton in a thin web of parallel fibers, which is formed into a rope-like strand called a sliver. The sliver is collected in a sliver can in preparation for roving. For high quality yarns the sliver is combed after carding to make the fibers more parallel and to remove smaller fibers.

   (c) **Drawing and Roving.** Slivers are then drawn out, blending the fibers and making them more parallel. No twist is added to the sliver during drawing, but several slivers can be blended together. Slivers can go through multiple drawings for further parallelization and blending. Drawn out slivers are then fed to the roving frame where they are drawn further while a slight twist is added. The roving strands are collected in cans and fed to the spinning machine.

FIGURE 7.19
The main steps of cotton yarn production.

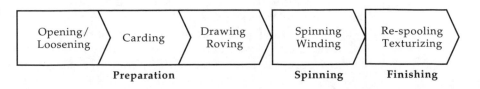

2. **Spinning and Winding.** The spinning machine draws out the roving strand, adds twist, and winds the yarn onto bobbins. The slivers, which are relatively short segments of cotton, are twisted against each other into a long, continuous strong yarn. Multiple bobbins of yarn are then wound onto larger spools called cheeses. Now the yarn is ready for texturing and dying and finally weaving into fabric.

3. **Re-spooling/texturizing.** Some finer qualities of thread require an additional step of spooling or passage in a gas-saturated room. This further step is necessary to chemically eradicate remaining impurities or to impart aesthetic and/or functional properties to the yarn.

Filatoi Riuniti

Filatoi Riuniti is a family-owned spinning mill located in Piemonte, a region in northwest Italy. Filatoi Riuniti produces cotton yarn, which is one the raw materials (together with wool) that is used to produce the fabrics that are then cut and sewn by Italian stylists into the worldwide famous Italian clothes.

Filatoi Riuniti was founded at the beginning of the 19th century by an Italian entrepreneur who built a spinning machine and began to produce cotton yarn on a low scale in the barn in his backyard. The company grew tremendously in the period 1880–1920. After World War I, Filatoi Riuniti benefited from the development of certain machine tool industries, and replaced and otherwise modernized most of their machine capacity. Unfortunately, after World War II, Italy had to rebuild its economy almost from scratch; Filatoi Riuniti struggled to remain solvent and it was many years before they had the capital needed to replenish and then expand their production facilities.

Filatoi Riuniti's current situation

For the past twenty years, Filatoi Riuniti had followed a strategy of rapid expansion to increase market share. As the Italian fashion industry grew in both stature and revenues, demand for Filatoi Riuniti's products increased, and management expected this pattern to continue. Filatoi Riuniti invested aggressively in new machine capacity to meet the demands of its current clients as well as to serve anticipated new customers. Filatoi Riuniti began to experience financial problems in the early 1990s and had to halt this expansion strategy due to an economic recession in Italy that was accompanied by a strengthening of the Italian lira:

> "Recession has hit the European textile industry from all sides . . . cotton yarn weavers are having an exceptionally hard time . . . . Some companies collapsed only to re-emerge shrunk to a third of their initial size" (Daily News Record, March 29, 1993).

> "The '80s . . . were very good in both sales and profitability, but there are market cycles and now we're facing a descending cycle. . . . The decrease in overall consumption of apparel, new competition, market problems in the U.S. and the strength of the lira against the deutsche mark and yen present uncertain signs for the future." (Daily News Record, December 5, 1993).

In the face of disappointing demand in the early 1990s, it might seem obvious that Filatoi Riuniti should have adjusted its production and its production capacity downward. Such down-sizing is not so easy to do in Italy's unionized industries. Italian trade unions achieved substantial gains in power and stature during the 1970s and 1980s. As a result, it was (and still is) very difficult for a company to lay off employees solely due to a fall in sales, unless the company could prove to the government that it was in severe financial distress. If the company could prove such financial distress, they could lay off employees (who would then be paid a minimal wage by the government). However, companies are very hesitant to take this course of action, because being labeled as "financially distressed" makes it almost impossible to buy from suppliers on account or to borrow money at low interest rates.

Filatoi Riuniti's management chose not to lay off any employees in the early 1990s. The resulting cash-flow problems severely limited the funds Filatoi Riuniti could use to increase their Spinning capacity (the second step). This was most unfortunate, since Filatoi Riuniti had previously expanded their Preparation machine capacity (first step) and Finishing capacity (third step), and their Spinning capacity needed to be expanded to fully balance their production facilities.

Outsourcing Spinning Production

With the recent upturn in the Italian economy, demand for Filatoi Riuniti's production is strong again, but Filatoi Riuniti's spinning machine capacity is insufficient to meet its production orders; and they decided six months ago to outsource part of the spinning production to six local family-owned spinning mills named Ambrosi, Bresciani, Castri, De Blasi, Estensi, and Giuliani (all six mills operate primarily for local markets such as Filatoi Riuniti). Filatoi Riuniti currently processes the raw material (combed cotton) and then sends part of the combed cotton to these six spinning mills for the spinning step. The semi-finished product is then returned to Filatoi Riuniti's production site where it is finished and stored until delivery to customers. The local mills charge higher prices for spinning finer yarns and for this reason Filatoi Riuniti has decided to spin as much as possible of the finer yarn sizes entirely in-house and to outsource only the spinning of low-end (coarser) yarns. Last month, for example, Filatoi Riuniti faced a total demand of 104,500 Kg of cotton and they outsourced 32,000 Kg of the spinning of the low-end sizes. Table 7.30 shows the production schedule and the prices charged by the six mills for February.

Milan Consulting Group Inc.

Last fall, Giorgio Armeni was named the new CEO of Filatoi Riuniti. Faced with a myriad of challenging issues at Filatoi Riuniti and sensing that Filatoi Riuniti's internal management team was not up to the task of radical internal re-engineering, he

TABLE 7.30

Outsourcing production schedule and prices charged to Filatoi Riuniti— February.

	Production Schedule for February (Kg)				Prices Charged to Filatoi Riuniti ($/Kg)			
	Size				Size			
Supplier	Extrafine	Fine	Medium	Coarse	Extrafine	Fine	Medium	Coarse
Ambrosi			3,000			13.00	10.65	9.60
Bresciani				12,000	17.40	14.10	11.20	9.45
Castri				10,000	17.40	14.22	11.00	9.50
De Blasi				1,000		14.30	11.25	9.60
Estensi					17.50	13.80	11.40	9.60
Filatoi R.	25,000	26,500	21,000					
Giuliani				6,000	19.75	13.90	10.75	9.40

	Demand to Meet					
Size	Extrafine	Fine	Medium	Coarse	Total	
(Kg/month)	25,000	26,500	24,000	29,000	104,500	

decided to hire Milan Consulting Group Inc. (MCG) to help address some of the company's ongoing problems. MCG's team was composed of Maurizio Donato, a junior partner, and Roberto Benello and Sofia Cominetti, two young associates in their first engagements. The three consultants spent four days at Filatoi Riuniti touring the production facilities, reviewing operations, interviewing managers, and studying mounds of data. After a weekend of hard thinking back in Milan, Maurizio Donato started the next Monday's project meeting with his two young associates with the words: "Our first priority is to find ways to reduce the costs that our client faces which are jeopardizing the future of the factory and the jobs of the almost 200 employees. Our goal is to come up with smart workable ideas, *e subito!*" He then outlined what he thought were four areas for obvious cost reduction:

(a) reducing machine down-time through improved inspection strategies,

(b) differential scheduling of machine maintenance,

(c) different management of overtime on production shifts, and

(d) improved outsourcing strategies from the six local spinning mills.

Roberto and Sofia immediately went to work on the analysis of these four proposals. They found that the total expected cost savings from the first three proposals would probably amount to roughly $200,000 per year. This was not a particularly large sum of money in comparison to Filatoi Riuniti's sales of $15 million (although it easily justified their consulting fees!). However, when they started to work on the fourth proposal, they immediately saw the potential for very large savings through more optimal outsourcing strategies with the six local spinning mills.

Optimizing the Outsourcing of Spinning Production

Filatoi Riuniti produces four different sizes of yarn (coarse, medium, fine, and extra fine) and there is an autonomous demand for each of the four sizes. Filatoi Riuniti can prepare enough raw cotton to meet their total demand, but they lack sufficient machine capacity to spin the four sizes of yarn, and as discussed above, they have been outsourcing part of the spinning production to six local mills: Ambrosi, Bresciani, Castri, De Blasi, Estensi and Giuliani. Table 7.30 shows February's spinning production schedule. Of the total demand of 104,500 Kg of yarn, 32,000 Kg were outsourced to the six local mills. All of the spinning of Coarse yarn was outsourced (29,000 Kg), and 13% of the spinning of Medium yarn was outsourced. The exhibit also shows the prices charged by the six mills to Filatoi Riuniti. The head of the purchasing department at Filatoi Riuniti said "We spin the finer sizes in-house and outsource the rest of the work. We outsource each yarn size to the lowest-price mill and then meet demand with the next-lowest-price mill." Roberto and Sofia thought that this outsourcing strategy could easily lead to sub-optimal outsourcing decisions, since outsourcing decisions were optimized only one at a time as opposed to optimizing all outsourcing simultaneously. In order to analyze the potential savings from optimizing the outsourcing of spinning production, they started to work with the client to identify the decision variables, the constraints, and the objective function to optimize.

Decision variables. Given the amount of each yarn size that Filatoi Riuniti needs to deliver to meet demand, the problem was how to allocate spinning production (both at Filatoi Riuniti and at the six local mills) in order to minimize costs. The decision variables of the optimization model are denoted X_{ij}, which represents the amount of yarn of size i that the company j would be assigned to produce. In this context,

$i = 1, 2, 3,$ and 4 means "extra fine," "fine," "medium," and "coarse," respectively. Similarly, $j = $ A, B, C, D, E, F, G mean Ambrosi, Bresciani, Castri, De Blasi, Estensi, Filatoi Riuniti, and Giuliani. See the blank table "Decision Variables" of the spreadsheet FILATOIR.XLS as a guide. Each X_{ij} must of course be nonnegative because none of the mills can produce negative amounts of spun yarn!

Variable Costs of Production. Roberto and Sofia knew the prices charged to Filatoi Riuniti by the six local mills (see Table 7.30). For internal purposes, they also needed to know Filatoi Riuniti's internal production costs in order to determine how much of each yarn size should optimally be produced internally versus externally. After a couple of days spent with the plant managers and the chief accountant, they came up with a fair estimate of the production cost for each of the four yarn sizes. See Table 7.31. The two blanks in the table indicate that Ambrosi and De Blasi cannot produce extra fine yarn.

Transportation costs. The yarn that is spun by the six local mills needs to be transported from Filatoi Riuniti to the mills for spinning and then be transported back to the production plant of Filatoi Riuniti in order to refine it and store it prior to delivery to customers. Sofia realized that they needed to obtain accurate data on transportation costs. One of the operations managers explained to her: "We have an agreement with a local truck company which takes care of all the transportation. The

Decision Variables X_{ij} Yarn produced by each factory (Kg/month) Size				Machine Hours Required for Production (Hours/Kg) Size				Production Capacity (Machine hours per
Supplier	Extrafine	Fine	Medium	Coarse	Supplier	Extrafine	Fine	Medium	Coarse	month)
Ambrosi					Ambrosi		0.400	0.375	0.250	2,500
Bresciani					Bresciani	0.700	0.500	0.350	0.250	3,000
Castri					Castri	0.675	0.450	0.400	0.250	2,500
De Blasi					De Blasi		0.450	0.350	0.200	2,600
Estensi					Estensi	0.650	0.450	0.400	0.250	2,500
Filatoi R.					**Filatoi R.**	**0.625**	**0.500**	**0.425**	**0.425**	**38,000**
Giuliani					Giuliani	0.700	0.450	0.350	0.400	2,500

Cost of Production ($/Kg) Size				Cost of Transportation ($/Kg) Size				Round trip distance
Supplier	Extrafine	Fine	Medium	Coarse	Supplier	Extrafine	Fine	Medium	Coarse	(km)
Ambrosi		13.00	10.65	9.60	Ambrosi	0.30	0.30	0.45	0.45	30
Bresciani	17.40	14.10	11.20	9.45	Bresciani	0.40	0.40	0.60	0.60	40
Castri	17.40	14.22	11.00	9.50	Castri	0.80	0.80	1.20	1.20	80
De Blasi		14.30	11.25	9.60	De Blasi	0.70	0.70	1.05	1.05	70
Estensi	17.50	13.80	11.40	9.60	Estensi	0.70	0.70	1.05	1.05	70
Filatoi R.	**18.25**	**13.90**	**11.40**	**8.90**	**Filatoi R.**	—	—	—	—	—
Giuliani	19.75	13.90	10.75	9.40	Giuliani	0.50	0.50	0.75	0.75	50
					($/Kg/Km)	0.010	0.010	0.015	0.015	

Demand to Meet (Kg/month)			
Extrafine	Fine	Medium	Coarse
25,000	26,000	28,000	28,000

TABLE 7.31

Production schedule, costs, and constraints—March.

contract with the truck company is very simple. They charge a fixed amount per kilometer per unit volume." Each product has a different density and therefore takes up a different volume per Kg. One Kg of finer product is more dense and so is less expensive to transport on a per Kg basis. Of course, each local mill is located at a different distance from Filatoi Riuniti. Armed with the contract with the truck company, a road map with the location of the six local mills, and product specification data, Sofia was able to estimate the transportation cost per Kg of each product for all the local mills. These numbers are shown in the table "Cost of Transportation" in Table 7.31. For example, it costs $0.01 per Kg per Km to transport fine yarn, and the round trip distance from Filatoi Riuniti to the Giuliani mill is $2 \times 25 = 50$ Km. Therefore, the table shows that it costs $(0.01 \times 50) = \$0.50$ to transport one Kg of fine yarn to Giuliani and back.

Resource consumption. Another important task was to understand the actual spinning machine production capacity of the six local mills and of Filatoi Riuniti itself. During the time spent with the plant manager, Roberto learned that production capacity is measured in machine hours per month and each product size requires a different amount of machine hours per Kg of product. He spent some more time with the plant engineer trying to estimate the six local mills' capacity in terms of machine hours per month and their production rate in terms of hours needed to produce one Kg of a given product size. Because each mill has different types of machines in different configurations, the number of machine hours required to produce one Kg of product differs among the mills. After a full day of work and very many telephone calls, fax, and email messages, Roberto and the plant engineer produced a table containing the production capacity and production rate per product for each of the six mills plus Filatoi Riuniti itself. These capacity and production rate numbers are shown in the two tables "Machine Hours Required for Production" and "Production Capacity" in Table 7.31. For example, at the Bresciani mill, it takes 0.70 hours to produce one Kg of extra fine yarn and there are at total of 3,000 machine hours per month available.

Product Demand. After talking to the marketing and sales manager at Filatoi Riuniti, Sofia estimated the demand for the four spun yarn sizes for March, which is shown in the table "Demand to Meet" in Table 7.31.

Armed with all of this data, Roberto and Sofia felt that they had enough information to solve for the outsourcing production strategy that would minimize the costs of producing spun yarn.

Assignment:

(a) Formulate Filatoi Riuniti's purchasing problem for the coming month (March):

   1. Write down the formula for the objective function of your model.

   2. Your model must have a capacity constraint for each local spinning mill. Write down the capacity constraints for the Ambrosi mill, for example.

   3. Filatoi Riuniti must meet demand for each of the four sizes of yarn. Your model must have a constraint for the demand for each of the four sizes of yarn. Write down the constraint for the demand for extra fine yarn, for example.

(b) Construct the spreadsheet for your optimization model. First, open the spreadsheet FILATOIR.XLS. Then complete your model and optimize it using the Solver. You will need to:

- create the objective function and the constraints in the appropriate place in your spreadsheet, and

- launch the Solver and optimize your model. Can you assume a linear model? What is the optimal supply strategy?

(c) Filatoi Riuniti should obviously consider increasing its spinning machine capacity. They could slightly expand the production capacity of the existing machines by renting an upgrade. This would increase their spinning production capacity by 600 hours/month. The monthly rental cost is $1,500/month. Would you recommend that they rent the upgrade? (Try to answer this question without re-optimizing your model.)

(d) Alternatively, Filatoi Riuniti could increase its spinning machine capacity by renting another spinning machine for the production of only medium size yarn, for a monthly rental cost of $3,000. The machine has a production capacity of 300 hours per month (the machine would run at the same rate of 0.425 hours/Kg). Suppose that the estimated production cost of running this machine is less than for Filatoi Riuniti's existing machines and is estimated to be $5.70/Kg (as opposed to $11.40/Kg for their existing machines according to Table 7.31). Would you recommend that Filatoi Riuniti rent the machine? (Try to answer this question without re-optimizing your model.)

(e) A new client is interested in purchasing up to 6,000 Kg/month of medium size yarn. What is the minimum price that Filatoi Riuniti should quote to this new client? Would it be a fixed price per Kg? Which additional question(s) might you ask this client? (In answering this question, assume that Filatoi Riuniti has not decided to expand its spinning machine capacity, and that Filatoi Riuniti does not want to change the prices that they currently charge their existing clients.)

(f) Your outsourcing production strategy optimization model is based in part on the prices charged by the local mills to Filatoi Riuniti and on an estimate of Filatoi Riuniti's internal production costs. The plant manager, the accounting department, and you estimate that Filatoi Riuniti's internal production costs could vary within a 5% range of the figures shown in Table 7.31. Would your recommendations change in the extreme cases? Why or why not?

(g) You estimate that the production capacity of one of your local mills, De Blasi, could vary within a 20% range of the figures shown in Table 7.31. Would your recommendations change in the extreme cases? Why or why not?

(h) Suppose that you present your proposed outsourcing plan to the owners of the Ambrosi mill. They complain to you that their mill cannot easily produce fine size yarn; in fact they presently can only produce medium and coarse size yarn, and they would incur substantial one-time set-up costs to ramp up for the production of fine size yarn. However, the optimal solution of the model indicates that it would be in Filatoi Riuniti's interests for the Ambrosi mill to produce fine size yarn. The owners want to maintain good business relations with Filatoi Riuniti, but they do not want to bear the full cost of ramping up for production of fine yarn. The contracts that Filatoi Riuniti currently has with its customers will not expire for at least another 12 months. Up to what amount would you be willing to share the one-time set-up costs for production of fine yarn with the owners of the Ambrosi mill?

(i) Suppose that you find out that one of the local mills, Giuliani, has the possibility of running an overtime shift (which would double their capacity) by paying its workers only 13% more the normal wage (it is a family-owned business). You know that the workers' salaries contribute to approximately 50% of the prices that the Giuliani mill charges Filatoi Riuniti for spinning yarn. The transportation cost component of the objective function would not change, of course. Modify the model in order to take into account this possibility and re-optimize. Does the optimal solution change? Why? [Helpful modeling hint: Think of the "overtime" part of this mill as a new mill with higher product costs.]

7.10 | EXERCISES

EXERICSE 7.1 A computer parts manufacturer produces two types of monitors—monochrome and color. There are two production lines, one for each type of monitor. The monochrome monitor line has a daily capacity of 700 units per day. The color monitor line has a daily capacity of 500 units per day. In department A, the tubes are produced for both monitor lines. In department A, the production of a monochrome tube requires one hour of labor, and a color monitor requires two hours of labor. Total daily labor hours in department A is 1,200 hours. In department B, the monitors are inspected. The monochrome monitor requires 3 hours of labor for inspection. The color monitor requires 2 hours of labor for inspection. A total of 2,400 hours of labor are available in department B. The monochrome monitor nets an earnings contribution of $40 per unit. The color monitor nets an earnings contribution of $30 per unit.

In order to maximize the net earnings of the company, we set up a linear optimization model with decision variables M for the daily production of monochrome monitors (in hundreds of monitors), and C for the daily production of color monitors (in hundreds of monitors). The linear optimization model is:

$$\text{maximize} \quad 40M + 30C$$

subject to:

M capacity:	$M \leq 7$
C capacity:	$C \leq 5$
A labor:	$M + 2C \leq 12$
B labor:	$3M + 2C \leq 24$
Nonnegativity:	$M, C \geq 0.$

(a) Solve the linear optimization model graphically. Show each constraint, the feasible region, and identify the optimal solution.

(b) Which two constraints are binding at the optimal solution? Solve these two constraints in the two unknowns to compute the optimal production plan exactly. What is M? What is C? What is the contribution to earnings?

(c) Consider the labor constraint for department A: $M + 2C \leq 12$. Suppose the number 12 was changed to 13, i.e., we had an additional 100 labor hours in department A. Re-solve the two equations in two unknowns to compute the new values of M and C, and the new optimal contribution to earnings.

(d) Compare the new contribution to earnings to the old contribution to earnings of part (b). What does the difference in the earnings indicate about the marginal value of labor in department A?

EXERCISE 7.2 The Magnetron Company manufactures and markets microwave ovens. Currently, the company produces two models: full-size and compact. Production is limited by the amount of labor available in the general assembly and electronic assembly departments, as well as by the demand for each model. Each full-size oven requires 2 hours of general assembly and 2 hours of electronic assembly, whereas each compact oven requires 1 hour of general assembly and 3 hours of electronic assembly. In the current production period, there are 500 hours of general assembly labor available and 800 hours of electronic assembly labor available.

In addition, the company estimates that it can sell at most 220 full-size ovens and 180 compact ovens in the current production period. The earnings contribution per oven is $120 for a full-size oven and $130 for a compact oven. The company would like to find an earnings-maximizing production plan for the current production period.

(a) Formulate the above problem as a linear optimization model.

(b) Solve the linear optimization model graphically. Plot the constraints, and identify each constraint and the feasible region. What is the optimal solution? Which constraints are binding at the optimal solution? What is the value of the objective function at the optimal solution?

(c) Consider the general assembly labor constraint. Suppose that the number 500 was changed to 510, i.e., the company has an additional 10 hours of general assembly labor. Re-solve the equations of the binding constraints to compute the new optimal solution. How does the new contribution to earnings differ from the contribution to earnings in part (b)? What is the marginal value of general assembly labor?

EXERCISE 7.3 A company manufacturing fine glass accessories produces color glass vases with a flower pattern. Each vase is produced from liquid glass by an artist glass-blower and then set in a storage room to cool to the room temperature. The vases are made in two sizes—large and small—but since the production processes are nearly identical, the two types of vases share the same resources.

Each vase, irrespective of its size, takes 20 minutes of the artist's work. The artist works 40 hours each week. A small and a large vase require 10 oz. and 20 oz. of colored glass, respectively. A total of 1,600 oz. of colored glass is available per week. In addition, a small vase occupies 2 units of storage space, whereas a large vase occupies 3 units of storage space. The total available storage space is 260 units. A small vase realizes an earnings contribution of $10.00 and a large vase realizes an earnings contribution of $12.00.

(a) Formulate the above problem as a linear optimization model with decision variables S and L, where S is the number of small vases produced and L is the number of large vases produced.

(b) Solve the linear optimization model graphically. Plot the constraints, identify each constraint, and identify the feasible region. What is the optimal solution? Which constraints are binding at the optimal solution? What is the value of the objective function at the optimal solution?

(c) Consider the storage capacity constraint. Suppose that the number 260 was changed to 270, i.e., the company has obtained an additional 10 units of storage space. Re-solve the equations of the binding constraints to compute the new optimal solution. How does the new contribution to earnings differ from the contribution to earnings in part (b)? What is the marginal value of the storage space?

EXERCISE 7.4 Craft Studio Furnishings (CSF) produces a unique line of cane furniture. The items currently on the market are table chairs, easy chairs, and love seats. The studio is considering introducing two new products: coffee tables and end tables, and is seeking to optimize their weekly production plan by means of a linear optimization model.

The production of any item consists of manufacturing a wooden frame, stretching the woven cane onto the frame, and finishing. Each procedure is performed by a different shop at the studio. Labor utilization by each product and hours of labor available in each shop are shown in Table 7.32. The contribution to earnings of each product is also shown.

In addition to the resource constraints mentioned above, CSF wishes to limit the production of the new products (coffee tables and end tables) to no more than 10 units each per week. The linear optimization model formulation is given below.

$$
\begin{aligned}
\text{maximize} \quad & 30TC + 44EC + 57LS + 55CT + 45ET \\
\text{subject to:} \quad & \\
\text{frame:} \quad & TC + EC + 1.3LS + 0.5CT + 0.5ET \le 40 \\
\text{stretching:} \quad & TC + 1.2EC + 1.5LS + 2CT + 1.5ET \le 80 \\
\text{finishing:} \quad & TC + 1.5EC + 1.7LS + CT + ET \le 60 \\
\text{coffee table limit:} \quad & CT \le 10 \\
\text{end table limit:} \quad & ET \le 10 \\
\text{nonnegativity:} \quad & TC, EC, LS, CT, ET \ge 0.
\end{aligned}
$$

The spreadsheet solution Sensitivity Report is presented in Table 7.33. Use the information in this report to answer the following questions:

(a) What is the optimal weekly production plan?

TABLE 7.32

Labor utilization and availability, and earnings contributions for Cane Studio Furnishings.

	Table Chair	Easy Chair	Love Seat	Coffee Table	End Table	Availability (hours)
Frame Manufacturing (hours)	1	1	1.3	0.5	0.5	40
Stretching (hours)	1	1.2	1.5	2	1.5	80
Finishing (hours)	1	1.5	1.7	1	1	60
Contribution to Earnings ($/unit)	30	44	57	55	45	

TABLE 7.33

Spreadsheet solution sensitivity report for the Cane Studio Furnishings linear optimization model.

	A	B	C	D	E	F	G
1	Adjustable Cells						
2	Cell	Name	Final Value	Reduced Cost	Objective Coefficient	Allowable Increase	Allowable Decrease
3	B12	Table Chair	0	-13.6	30	13.6	1E+30
4	C12	Easy Chair	4	0	44	6.294	0.154
5	D12	Love Seat	20	0	57	0.200	6.800
6	E12	Coffee Table	10	0	55	1E+30	32.8
7	F12	End Table	10	0	45	1E+30	22.8
8							
9	Constraints						
10	Cell	Name	Final Value	Shadow Price	Constraint R.H. Side	Allowable Increase	Allowable Decrease
11	G6	Frame	40	42.8	40	0.588	3.333
12	G7	Stretching	69.8	0	80	1E+30	10.2
13	G8	Finishing	60	0.800	60	5	0.769
14	G9	Coffee Table	10	32.8	10	2.222	10
15	G10	End Table	10	22.8	10	2.222	10

(b) What are the binding constraints? the non-binding constraints?

(c) Why is the shadow price of the stretching constraint zero?

(d) What is the economic interpretation of each of the shadow prices, for each of the constraints in the model?

EXERCISE 7.5 Best Wishes Company is a mail-order company that delivers gift baskets for businesses and individuals. They currently offer four different kinds of gourmet cheese gift baskets: "Four-Cheese," "Cheddars," "Party Box," and "Nachos Blend." Each of these different gift baskets comprises a different combination of cheeses, as indicated in Table 7.34. The far right column of the table shows the amount of each type of cheese that is available on a daily basis. The bottom row of the table contains the unit earnings contribution for each type of gift basket.

The company wishes to determine how many baskets of each type to produce in order to maximize the total earnings contribution. The linear optimization model for this problem is given below.

$$\text{maximize} \quad 6.99F + 7.99C + 5.99P + 8.99N$$

subject to:

$$\text{mild cheddar:} \quad 4F + 8C + 4P + 4N \leq 500$$
$$\text{sharp cheddar:} \quad 4F + 8C + 6N \leq 300$$
$$\text{swiss:} \quad 4F + 4P \leq 450$$
$$\text{monterey jack:} \quad 4F + 4P + 6N \leq 350$$
$$\text{nonnegativity:} \quad F, C, P, N \geq 0.$$

The spreadsheet solution sensitivity report for this linear optimization model is shown in Table 7.35. Using the information in this sensitivity report, answer the following questions:

(a) What is the optimal number of baskets of each type of gift basket to produce daily? What is the resulting contribution to earnings?

(b) What are the binding constraints? the non-binding constraints?

(c) Why is the shadow price of the Swiss constraint zero?

(d) What is the economic interpretation of each of the shadow prices, for each of the constraints in the model?

EXERCISE 7.6 A pottery manufacturer manufactures four different types of dining room service sets: English, Currier, Primrose, and Bluetail. Furthermore, Primrose can be made by two different methods.

Each dining room service set uses clay, enamel, dry room time, and kiln time, in the quantities shown in Table 7.36. The rightmost column in Table 7.36 shows the

TABLE 7.34

The four different gourmet cheese gift baskets offered by Best Wishes Company.

	"Four-Cheese" Basket	"Cheddars" Basket	"Party Box" Basket	"Nachos Blend" Basket	Daily Availability (oz.)
Mild Cheddar (oz.)	4	8	4	4	500
Sharp Cheddar (oz.)	4	8	0	6	300
Swiss (oz.)	4	0	4	0	450
Monterey Jack (oz.)	4	0	4	6	350
Contribution to Earnings ($/basket)	6.99	7.99	5.99	8.99	

TABLE 7.35

Spreadsheet solution sensitivity report for Best Wishes Company.

	A	B	C	D	E	F	G
1	Adjustable Cells						
2	Cell	Name	Final Value	Reduced Cost	Objective Coefficient	Allowable Increase	Allowable Decrease
3	B8	Four-Cheese	0	-0.001	6.99	0.001	1E+30
4	C8	Cheddars	23.4375	0	7.99	7.99	0.01
5	D8	Party Box	59.375	0	5.99	1.335	0.005
6	E8	Nachos Blend	18.75	0	8.99	5.9875	0.0025
7							
8	Constraints						
9	Cell	Name	Final Value	Shadow Price	Constraint R.H. Side	Allowable Increase	Allowable Decrease
10	G3	Mild Cheddar	500	0.748	500	150	250
11	G4	Sharp Cheddar	300	0.250	300	316.667	150
12	G5	Swiss	237.5	0	450	1E+30	212.5
13	G6	Monterey Jack	350	0.749	350	250	150

TABLE 7.36

Resource utilization and earnings contributions for the dining room service sets.

	English	Currier	Primrose Method 1	Primrose Method 2	Bluetail	Resource Availability
Clay (lbs.)	10	15	10	10	20	130
Enamel (lbs.)	1	2	2	1	1	13
Dry Room (hours)	3	1	6	6	3	45
Kiln (hours)	2	4	2	5	3	23
Contribution to Earnings ($/service)	51	102	66	66	89	

manufacturer's resource availability for the remainder of the week. Notice that Primrose can be made by two different methods. Both methods use the same amount of clay (10 lbs.) and dry room time (6 hours). But the second method uses one pound less of enamel and occupies three more hours in the kiln.

The manufacturer is currently committed to making the same amount of Primrose using methods 1 and 2. The formulation of the earnings maximization problem is given below. The decision variables E, C, P_1, P_2, B are the number of sets of type English, Currier, Primrose Method 1, Primrose Method 2, and Bluetail, respectively. We assume, for the purposes of this problem, that the number of sets of each type does not have to be a whole number.

$$\text{maximize} \quad 51E + 102C + 66P_1 + 66P_2 + 89B$$

subject to:

$$\text{Clay:} \quad 10E + 15C + 10P_1 + 10P_2 + 20B \leq 130$$
$$\text{Enamel:} \quad E + 2C + 2P_1 + P_2 + B \leq 13$$
$$\text{Dry room:} \quad 3E + C + 6P_1 + 6P_2 + 3B \leq 45$$
$$\text{Kiln:} \quad 2E + 4C + 2P_1 + 5P_2 + 3B \leq 23$$
$$\text{Primrose Equal:} \quad P_1 - P_2 = 0$$
$$E, C, P_1, P_2, B \geq 0.$$

The spreadsheet solution sensitivity report for this linear optimization model is shown in Table 7.37. Based on the information in Table 7.37, answer the following questions:

(a) What is the optimal manufacturing strategy, and what is the total contribution to earnings?

TABLE 7.37

Spreadsheet solution sensitivity report for the pottery manufacturing problem.

	A	B	C	D	E	F	G
1	Adjustable Cells						
2	Cell	Name	Final Value	Reduced Cost	Objective Coefficient	Allowable Increase	Allowable Decrease
3	C14	English	0.00	-3.57	51.00	3.57	1E+30
4	D14	Currier	2.00	0.00	102.00	16.67	12.50
5	E14	Primrose Method I	0.00	0.00	66.00	37.57	1E+30
6	F14	Primrose Method II	0.00	-37.57	66.00	37.57	1E+30
7	G14	Bluetail	5.00	0.00	89.00	47.00	12.50
8							
9	Constraints						
10	Cell	Name	Final Value	Shadow Price	Constraint R.H. Side	Allowable Increase	Allowable Decrease
11	C20	Clay (lbs.)	130.00	1.43	130.00	23.33	43.75
12	C21	Enamel (lbs.)	9.00	0.00	13.00	1E+30	4.00
13	C22	Dry Room (hours)	17.00	0.00	45.00	1E+30	28.00
14	C23	Kiln (hours)	23.00	20.14	23.00	5.60	3.50
15	C24	Primrose Equal	0.00	11.43	0.00	3.50	0.00

TABLE 7.38

The proportion of each metal in the alloys produced by Jordan Alloy Corporation.

Metal	W	X	Y	Z
Aluminum	0.30	0.40	0.10	0.15
Copper	0.30	0.10	0.25	0.40
Magnesium	0.40	0.50	0.65	0.45

(b) What is the economic interpretation of each of the shadow prices, for each of the constraints in the model?

(c) Suppose that the manufacturer can purchase an additional 20 lbs. of clay for $1.10/lb. Should the manufacturer make this purchase?

(d) Suppose that the number of hours available in the dry room decreases by 20 hours due to an unforeseen problem. What will be the new contribution to earnings?

(e) In the current model, the number of Primrose service sets produced using method 1 is required to be the same as the number of Primrose service sets produced by method 2. Consider a revision of the model in which this constraint is replaced by the constraint $P_1 - P_2 \geq 0$. In the reformulated model, would the number of Primrose service sets made by method 1 be positive?

EXERCISE 7.7 The Jordan Alloy Corporation produces alloys for aircraft construction. They manufacture four different alloys, denoted W, X, Y, and Z, from three basic metals, namely aluminum, copper, and magnesium. The contribution to earnings of these alloys are $35, $47, $60, and $140 per ton, respectively, for each of the four alloys W, X, Y, and Z. The monthly supplies of aluminum, copper, and magnesium are 600, 400, and 800 tons per month, respectively. The proportion of the metals in the alloys are shown in Table 7.38. For example, one ton of alloy W consists of 0.30 tons of aluminum, 0.30 tons of copper, and 0.40 tons of magnesium. The company believes that they can sell all of the alloys that they produce. The objective is to maximize the contribution to earnings.

(a) Construct a linear optimization model to determine how much of each alloy to produce in order to maximize the contribution to earnings.

Hint: You may want to start by defining the variables AW, AX, AY, and AZ to be the amount of each alloy that the company produces. Then the linear optimization model must capture the supply limitations, so that the constraint

$$0.30AW + 0.40AX + 0.10AY + 0.15AZ \leq 600$$

represents the supply limitation on aluminum.

(b) Solve the linear optimization model (on the computer). What actions would you recommend based on the optimal solution and the shadow price information?

EXERCISE 7.8 Nature's Best Frozen Foods company produces four different mixes of frozen ready-to-eat vegetables. The mixes consist of five different vegetables: carrots, mushrooms, green peppers, broccoli, and corn. The company manufactures four different mixes each sold in 10 oz. bags. The mixes are: "Stir Fry," "Barbecue," "Hearty Mushrooms," and "Veggie Crunch," and their contributions to earnings (per bag) are $0.22, $0.20, $0.18, and $0.18, respectively. The monthly supplies of carrots, mushrooms, green peppers, broccoli and corn are 150,000 oz., 80,000 oz., 135,000 oz., 140,000 oz., and 150,000 oz. per month, respectively. The compositions of the mixes are shown in Table 7.39. For example, one bag of "Stir Fry" mix contains 2.5 oz. of carrots, 3.0 oz. of mushrooms, 2.5 oz. of green peppers, 2.0 oz. of broccoli, and no corn. The company can sell all of the mixes that they produce.

(a) Construct a linear optimization model to determine the optimal product mix (i.e., how many bags of each mix to produce in order to maximize the contribution to earnings).

(b) Solve the linear optimization model (on the computer). What is the optimal product mix?

(c) What is the value of an extra ounce of green peppers?

EXERCISE 7.9 Johnson Electric produces small electric motors for four appliance manufacturers in each of three plants. The unit production costs vary from plant to plant, because of differences in production equipment and labor productivity. The unit production costs and monthly capacities are shown in Table 7.40.

The customer orders that must be produced next month are shown in Table 7.41. The unit transportation costs in dollars per unit are shown in Table 7.42. Johnson

TABLE 7.39

The composition of the products produced by Nature's Best Frozen Foods.

	"Stir Fry"	"Barbecue"	"Hearty Mushrooms"	"Veggie Crunch"
Carrots	2.5	2.0	0.0	2.5
Mushrooms	3.0	0.0	4.0	0.0
Green Peppers	2.5	2.0	3.0	2.5
Broccoli	2.0	3.0	3.0	2.5
Corn	0.0	3.0	0.0	2.5

TABLE 7.40

Plant production costs and capacities for Johnson Electric's three plants.

Plant	Electric Motor Production Cost ($/motor)	Monthly Capacity (Motors /month)
Arlington	$17	800
Binghamton	$20	600
Canton	$24	700

TABLE 7.41

Customer demand for Johnson Electric motors.

Customer	Demand (Motors/month)
Onyx, Inc.	300
Treble Company	500
Hilton Appliances	400
Dean Electric	600

TABLE 7.42

Transportation costs from plants to customers ($/motor) for Johnson Electric.

Plant	Customer			
	Onyx	Treble	Hilton	Dean
Arlington	$3.00	$2.00	$5.00	$7.00
Binghamton	$6.00	$4.00	$8.00	$3.00
Canton	$9.00	$1.00	$5.00	$4.00

Electric must decide how many motors to produce in each plant and how much of each customer's demand to supply from each plant, at least cost.

(a) Construct a linear optimization model to determine a production and distribution plan for Johnson Electric in order to minimize the total cost to Johnson Electric.

Hint: Notice that Johnson Electric must decide how many electric motors to produce at each plant and how many electric motors to ship from each plant to each customer. Let XAO, for example, be the decision variable defined to be the quantity of motors produced at the Arlington plant and shipped to Onyx, Inc. Let XAT, XAH, and XAD be defined likewise for the other three customers and let XBO, XBT, XBH, XBD, XCO, XCT, XCH, and XCD also be defined in a similar manner. Then the constraints in the problem should include plant capacity constraints such as:

$$XAO + XAT + XAH + XAD \leq 800,$$

and customer demand constraints such as:

$$XAO + XBO + XCO \geq 300,$$

for example.

(b) Solve the linear optimization model on the computer. What managerial actions would you recommend based on the optimal solution and the shadow price information?

EXERCISE 7.10 A New Hampshire produce company supplies organically grown apples to four New England specialty stores. After the apples are collected at the company's orchard, they are transported to any of three preparation centers where they are prepared for retail (by undergoing extensive cleaning and then packaging), after which the prepared apples are shipped to the specialty stores. The cost of transporting organic fruit is rather high due to the fragility of the product.

The company has three preparation centers available for use. Table 7.43 shows the unit shipping and preparation costs (in $/lb.) from the company's orchard to the preparation centers, as well as the preparation centers' monthly capacities. Demand at the specialty stores is shown in Table 7.44. The unit costs of transporting the apples from the preparation centers to the specialty stores is shown in Table 7.45.

The produce company must decide the amount of apples to prepare at each of the three preparation centers and how much of each specialty store's demand to supply from each preparation center, at least cost.

TABLE 7.43

Unit costs and monthly capacities at the three preparation centers.

Preparation Center	Unit Transportation and Preparation Cost ($/lb)	Monthly Capacity (lbs.)
1	$0.30	200
2	$0.60	450
3	$0.90	760

TABLE 7.44

Monthly demand for apples at four specialty stores.

Store	Monthly Demand (lbs.)
Organic Orchard	300
Fresh & Local	500
Healthy Pantry	400
Season's Harvest	200

TABLE 7.45

Unit transportation costs for transporting prepared apples from the preparation centers to the specialty stores, in $/lb.

Preparation Center	Organic Orchard	Fresh & Local	Healthy Pantry	Season's Harvest
1	$0.40	$0.60	$0.30	$0.70
2	$0.60	$0.60	$0.30	$0.70
3	$0.10	$0.70	$0.60	$0.90

(a) Construct a linear optimization model to determine the amount of apples to be prepared at each of the three preparation centers, and how much of each specialty store's demand to supply from each preparation center, in order to minimize the total cost of the operation.

Hint: Notice that the produce company must decide both the amount of apples to prepare at each preparation center and how many apples to ship from each preparation center to each store. Let $X1O$, for example, be the decision variable defined to be the quantity of apples prepared at preparation center 1 and shipped to the Organic Orchard store. Let $X1F$, $X1H$, and $X1S$ be defined likewise for the other three specialty stores, and define the appropriate decision variables for the other two preparation centers in a similar manner. Then the constraints in the problem should include preparation center capacity constraints, such as:

$$X1O + X1F + X1H + X1S \leq 200,$$

and store demand constraints, such as:

$$X1O + X2O + X3O \geq 300,$$

for example.

(b) Solve the linear optimization model on the computer. What managerial actions would you recommend based on the optimal solution?

EXERCISE 7.11 Dairy products are rich in many vitamins. However, when exposed to light even for brief periods of time, these vitamins tend to decompose, thus diminishing the nutritional value of dairy products. To avoid this undesirable effect, dairy products should be stored in specially designed packaging.

WonderPlastics is a company specializing in producing plastic products designed to meet special customer requirements. In particular, they supply five local dairy farms with plastic packaging suitable for storing dairy products. The plastic packaging is produced at WonderPlastics' two plants located in Amherst and Providence. The unit production costs and weekly capacities of the plants are summarized in Table 7.46, and customer demands are shown in Table 7.47. The cost of supplying the customers is different for the two plants. The unit transportation costs (in $/unit) are shown in Table 7.48.

The management of WonderPlastics must decide how many units of plastic packaging to produce at each of the two plants and how much of each customer's demand to supply from each plant, so as to minimize the total production and transportation cost.

(a) Construct a linear optimization model to determine how many units of plastic packaging to produce at each of the two plants and how much of each customer's demand to supply from each plant in order to minimize the total cost.

(b) Solve the linear optimization model on the computer. What managerial actions would you recommend based on the optimal solution and shadow price information?

EXERCISE 7.12 An investor is considering allocating $10,000 among five investment alternatives. The five alternatives and their respective fund categories, risk levels, and average annual returns are shown in Table 7.49.

TABLE 7.46
Production costs and monthly capacity at WonderPlastics' two plants.

Plant	Unit Production Cost ($/unit)	Weekly Capacity (units)
Amherst	$2.00	200
Providence	$3.00	210

TABLE 7.47
Demand for plastic packaging for WonderPlastics.

Customer	Weekly Demand (units)
1	60
2	100
3	110
4	50
5	80

TABLE 7.48
Unit transportation costs from plants to customers for WonderPlastics, in $/unit.

Plant	Customer				
	1	2	3	4	5
Amherst	$5.00	$3.00	$2.00	$6.00	$6.00
Providence	$7.00	$3.00	$3.00	$6.00	$7.00

TABLE 7.49
Information on five investment alternatives.

Name of Fund	Category of Fund	Risk Level	Average Annual Return
Adams	Money Market Fund	1	4.50%
Barney	Money Market Fund	2	5.62%
Chilton	Bond Fund	2	6.80%
Dunster	Bond Fund	3	10.15%
Excelsior	Aggressive Growth Fund	5	20.60%

The risk level of each investment is rated on a scale of 1 to 5, where 1 is very conservative, and 5 is very risky. The investor would like to maximize the average annual return on his investment subject to the following restrictions:

1. The average risk level of the entire investment should not exceed 2.5.

2. At least 30% of the investment should be placed in money market funds.

3. At most $2,000 should be invested in the aggressive growth fund.

Construct and solve a linear optimization model to determine the optimal allocation of the investor's money.

EXERCISE 7.13 A manufacturing company is anticipating an increase in demand for its products. However, management is concerned about the adequacy of their employees to meet the increased demand. This inadequacy, combined with high workforce turnover (5% of employees leave the company at the end of each month and must be replaced), will threaten the company's ability to meet the increased demand. Rather than simply hiring new workers, management is contemplating enrolling some or all of their employees in a month-long intensive training program. After the successful completion of the training program, an employee would receive an increase in salary; furthermore, the employee would sign a contract not to leave the company for at least 6 months.

The management believes that successful completion of the program would increase an employee's productivity by 20%. However, only 90% of the employees are estimated to be able to complete the training program successfully. (We assume that if the employee enrolls in the training program but does not successfully complete the program, then he or she will return to the workforce at the pre-training skill level, and that he or she can enroll in the program again at any time).

The monthly demand for **untrained** employees for the next six months is shown in Table 7.50. Note that if there are trained employees available, their higher productivity would allow management to satisfy demand with fewer employees. For example, the demand in month 1 can be satisfied with 100 untrained employees, or with 82 untrained and 15 trained employees (since $100 = 82 + (1.20) \times 15$).

An employee cannot be engaged in production and be enrolled in the training program during the same month. At the beginning of January, there are 145 (untrained) employees on the workforce. Monthly payroll costs to the company are $3,000 per untrained employee (engaged in either production or in the training program) and $3,300 per trained employee.

The company would like to design a training schedule for its employees that would minimize their total six-month payroll cost and allow them to satisfy the workforce demand throughout the six months from January through June. Construct and then solve a linear optimization model to design such a schedule. What is the optimal training schedule?

TABLE 7.50

The demand for (untrained) employees at a manufacturing company.

Month	Number of (untrained) employees required
January	100
February	100
March	115
April	125
May	140
June	150

Hint: The decisions that have to be made in this problem are how many untrained employees to allow to enroll in the training program each month. There will be similar conditions that have to be satisfied every month, and so as an illustration, let us consider the month of April. Let us re-name the months January through June as months 1-6. Then April is month 4, for example. The decision variables are as follows:

T_i = the number of trained employees available in month i, for $i = 1, \ldots, 6$.

UP_i = the number of untrained employees engaged in production in month i, for $i = 1, \ldots, 6$.

UT_i = the number of untrained employees enrolled in the training program in month i, for $i = 1, \ldots, 6$.

Then for $i = 4$, assuming that the 5% turnover rate among untrained employees who are currently engaged in production prevails, we would have the following constraints:

$UP_4 + 1.2T_4 \geq 125$ (the demand for employees engaged in production has to be satisfied)

$T_4 = T_3 + 0.9UT_3$ (the trained employees in month 4 consist of those in month 3 plus those who successfully complete their training in month 3)

$UT_4 + UP_4 = 0.95UP_3 + 0.1UT_3$ (the untrained employees in month 4 consist of those who remain from month 3 (less the 5% who leave the company every month) plus those who did not successfully complete the training program in month 3).

EXERCISE 7.14 A department store experiences a significant increase in the number of customers at the end of each year. To accommodate the customers, the store has to make sure there are enough sales representatives available. Starting in July of each year, the store starts hiring new sales representatives that have to be trained by the sales representatives already working in the store. The training takes one month, and one sales representative can train up to 25 new trainees every month. Experience has shown that one in every twenty trainees does not successfully complete the training. The estimated monthly demands for sales representatives for the second half of the year is shown in Table 7.51. As of July, 150 sales representatives are available for sales or training, and the personnel records indicate that 3% of representatives leave the store at the end of each month. Each trainee costs $1,900 per month, while each sales representative working or training costs $3,500 per month. It is the store's policy not to fire sales representatives in the second half of the year.

Construct and solve a linear optimization model to determine a hiring and training schedule for the months of July through December that meets the demand requirements at the least cost. What is the optimal hiring plan? What is the optimal training plan? What is the cost of the optimal plan?

TABLE 7.51

Estimated demand for sales representatives at a department store.

Month	Number of Sales Representatives Required
July	120
August	135
September	150
October	150
November	170
December	200

Hint: To see how to formulate this problem, let us denote the six months shown above as months 7, 8, 9, 10, 11, and 12. Thus, for example, August is month 8. The decisions we must make each month are:

(a) how many trainees to hire, and

(b) how to divide up the sales representatives into the tasks of sales and training.

We will have very similar conditions that must be satisfied every month. To illustrate how to formulate the problem, let us look in detail at month 9 (September). Let us define the following decision variables:

H_M = the number of trainees to hire in month M, for $M = 7, 8, \ldots, 12$.

R_M = the number of sales representatives on hand in month M, for $M = 7, 8, \ldots, 12$.

S_M = the number of sales representatives engaged in sales in month M, for $M = 7, 8, \ldots, 12$.

T_M = the number of sales representatives engaged in training in month M, for $M = 7, 8, \ldots, 12$.

Then for the month of September (month 9), assuming that average labor turnover rates prevail, we would have the following constraints:

$T_9 \geq (1/25)H_9$ (we need at least one trainer for every 25 trainees hired)

$R_9 = 0.97R_8 + 0.95H_8$ (the sales representatives in September consist of those who remain on from August plus those who successfully complete the training program in August)

$R_9 = S_9 + T_9$ (the number of sales representatives is the total of those representatives engaged in sales plus those representatives engaged in teaching)

$S_9 \geq 150$ (we need 150 sales representatives in September).

EXERCISE 7.15 (Investment Management under taxation) Last year, Ellen Grunbaum purchased s_i shares of stock i at price q_i, $i = 1, \ldots, n$. The current price per share of stock i is p_i, $i = 1, \ldots, n$. Ellen Grunbaum expects that the price per share of stock i one year from now will be r_i, $i = 1, \ldots, n$. If she sells any shares, she must pay a transaction cost of 1% of the amount transacted. In addition, she must pay a capital-gains tax at the rate of 30% on any capital gains at the time of the sale. For example, suppose that Ellen Grunbaum sells 1,000 shares of a stock today at $50 per share, which she had originally purchased at $30 per share. She would receive $50,000. However, she would have to pay capital gains taxes of $0.30 \times (50,000 - 30,000) = \$6,000$, and she would have to pay $0.01 \times (50,000) = \$500$ in transaction costs. Therefore, by selling 1,000 shares of this stock, she would have a net cashflow of $50,000 - \$6,000 - \$500 = \$43,500$. Now suppose that Ellen would like to sell enough shares of the stock in her portfolio today to generate an amount of cash C today for use as a down payment on a home. Formulate the problem of selecting how many shares of which stocks she needs to sell in order to generate the cash amount C, net of capital gains and transaction costs, while maximizing the expected value of her portfolio for next year.

EXERCISE 7.16 Central Airlines would like to determine how to partition their new aircraft serving Boston-Chicago passengers into first-class passenger seats, business-class passenger seats, and economy-class passenger seats. The plane has room to construct 190 economy-class seats, if they do not partition any sections for first-class or business-class seats. A section can be partitioned off for first-class seats, but each of these seats takes the space of two economy-class seats. A business-class section can also be included, but each of these seats takes the space of 1.5 economy-class seats. A first-class ticket yields a revenue of $1,600, a business-class ticket yields a revenue of $1,100, and an economy-class ticket yields a revenue of $500. Historical demand data indicate that demand for seats obeys the distribution shown in Table 7.52. Thus, for example, there is a 40% probability on any given day that there will be a demand for 25 first-class seats, 60 business-class seats, and 210 economy-class seats.

The airline would like to determine how to partition the aircraft into first-class seats, business-class seats, and economy-class seats, so as to maximize their expected revenue. Assume that once the aircraft is partitioned, it is prohibitively expensive to reconfigure the partition in the near-term. Also, assume that Central Airlines does not engage in the over-booking of any of their flights. Construct and solve a two-stage linear optimization model that will determine the optimal configuration of the space in the aircraft into first-class seats, business-class seats, and economy-class seats. What is the optimal configuration of the aircraft?

TABLE 7.52

The distribution of demand for seats at Central Airlines.

Intensity of Passenger Demand	Probability	First-class Passenger Demand	Business-class Passenger Demand	Economy-class Passenger Demand
High Demand	0.40	25	60	210
Medium Demand	0.30	12	30	170
Low Demand	0.30	5	9	150

Nonlinear Optimization

CONTENTS

THE FUNDAMENTAL CHARACTERISTIC OF A LINEAR OPTIMIZATION MODEL IS THAT THE objective function, as well as all of the constraints, are linear functions of the decision variables. In a variety of important management problems, the objective function and/or the constraints are *nonlinear* functions of the decision variables. This necessitates the study of the generalization of the ideas of linear optimization to that of nonlinear optimization, which is the subject of this chapter. We begin by focusing on three typical applications of nonlinear optimization models in management, namely (i) portfolio management, (ii) optimizing production and pricing decisions, and (iii) the optimal location of facilities. We then develop insight into the important differences between linear optimization and nonlinear optimization by examining a simple nonlinear optimization model in two variables. We next discuss spreadsheet solution methods for finding an optimal solution to a nonlinear optimization model, followed by a discussion of shadow price information on constraints in nonlinear optimization models. We then take a closer look at portfolio optimization problems and close the chapter with a classification of nonlinear optimization problems from the point of view of their ease of solvability.

| 8.1 | # FORMULATING A MANAGEMENT PROBLEM AS A NONLINEAR OPTIMIZATION MODEL |

A nonlinear optimization model is just like a linear optimization model except that the constraints, as well as the objective function, are not presumed to be linear functions of the decision variables. Indeed, the objective function can be a linear function or a curved (that is, nonlinear) function of the decision variables. Similarly, each of the constraints is not presumed to be a linear function of the decision variables; each constraint can be any linear or curved function of the decision variables. Let us consider several examples.

Example 8.1 — Optimal Portfolio Management at Marathon Investments, Inc.

One of the most important and useful applications of nonlinear optimization models is in the construction of so-called optimal portfolios of assets. The managers of large investment portfolios face the task of how to compose a portfolio of investment assets that meets the needs of their investors most efficiently. Typically, there are two primary objectives that a manager would like to optimize in composing a portfolio of investments in risky assets:

- maximize the expected return of the portfolio, and

- minimize the risk associated with the portfolio.

In almost every situation encountered in practice, these two objectives conflict with each other. That is, in order to achieve a higher expected return on the portfolio, one needs to incur a greater risk. Conversely, in order to achieve a lower risk level, one needs to expect a lesser return on the portfolio.

Suppose that Pat Glover is a portfolio manager for Marathon Investments, Inc. Suppose that Marathon is assembling a portfolio of assets of stock in Advent Communications, General Space Systems (GSS), and Digital Devices. The financial analysts at Marathon have gathered data and estimated the expected returns on these stocks, as well as standard deviation and correlation information on these stocks. This data is summarized in Table 8.1.

Let us consider Table 8.1 in detail. The annual return on investing in Advent is an unknown quantity. In some years, it is high, and in other years it is low. However, from historical data and careful scrutiny of market conditions, analysts at Marathon are able to estimate the mean of its annual return, which is estimated to be 11.0%. In a similar fashion, analysts at Marathon have estimated the standard deviation of the annual return of investing in Advent, which is estimated to be 4.00%. They have estimated the correlation of the return on investing in Advent with investing in GSS to be 0.160. Recall that the correlation of two random variables is a measure of the ex-

TABLE 8.1

Annual expected return, standard deviation, and correlation of stock returns for Advent Communications, General Space Systems, and Digital Devices.

Asset Name	Annual Expected Return (%)	Standard Deviation of Return (%)	Correlation		
			Advent	GSS	Digital
Advent	11.0%	4.00%			
GSS	14.0%	4.69%	0.160		
Digital	7.0%	3.16%	−0.395	0.067	

tent to which these two random variables vary together. Therefore, a correlation of 0.160 means that these two assets tend to yield a return on investment whose directions are somewhat similar. Analysts at Marathon have estimated the correlation of the return on investing in Advent with investing in Digital to be -0.395. This means that these two assets tend to yield a return on investment whose directions are opposite. When one goes up, the other tends to go down.

Marathon would like to determine which fraction of its investment dollars to invest in each of the three firms listed in Table 8.1. Let us define the following decision variables:

A = fraction of Marathon's investment dollars invested in Advent,

G = fraction of Marathon's investment dollars invested in GSS,

D = fraction of Marathon's investment dollars invested in Digital.

Because these variables are fractional quantities, they must satisfy the constraint:

$$A + G + D = 1.$$

The annual return of each stock is a random variable. Let us denote by R_A, R_G, and R_D be the annual return of Advent, GSS, and Digital, respectively. Let R be the total return of a portfolio consisting of a fraction A invested in Advent, a fraction G invested in GSS, and a fraction D invested in Digital. Then R is described in the following manner:

$$R = A \cdot R_A + G \cdot R_G + D \cdot R_D.$$

Notice that since R_A, R_G, and R_D are each random variables, then R is also a random variable. The expected value of R is simply the expected annual rate of return on the portfolio, and using the formulas of Chapter 2, we have:

$$E(R) = 11.0A + 14.0G + 7.0D.$$

Keep in mind that we would like to maximize the expected rate of return.

We next present an expression for the standard deviation σ_R of the annual return of the portfolio, which is a measure of the risk of the portfolio. As it turns out, by using a simple extension of the formula for the variance of a weighted sum of random variables (see Chapter 2), we can derive the following expression for the variance σ_R^2:

$$\sigma_R^2 = A^2\sigma_A^2 + G^2\sigma_G^2 + D^2\sigma_D^2$$
$$+ 2 A G \sigma_A \sigma_G \text{CORR}(R_A,R_G) + 2 G D \sigma_G \sigma_D \text{CORR}(R_G,R_D)$$
$$+ 2 A D \sigma_A \sigma_D \text{CORR}(R_A,R_D).$$

Substituting the information presented in Table 8.1 in the above formula, we obtain:

$$\sigma_R^2 = 16.0A^2 + 22.0G^2 + 10.0D^2 + 6.0A G + 2.0G D - 10.0A D.$$

Therefore, the standard deviation of the portfolio is expressed as:

$$\sigma_R = \sqrt{16.0A^2 + 22.0G^2 + 10.0D^2 + 6.0A G + 2.0G D - 10.0A D}.$$

Suppose that we would like to have an expected rate of return on our portfolio of 11.0%. Given that goal, we would like to choose those values of A, G, and D that yield an expected rate of return of 11.0% and that minimize the risk of the portfolio as measured by the standard deviation of the portfolio. This is accomplished by formulating the following optimization problem:

$$\text{minimize} \quad \sqrt{16.0A^2 + 22.0G^2 + 10.0D^2 + 6.0AG + 2.0GD - 10.0AD}$$

subject to:

Fractions: $\quad A + G + D = 1.0$

Target return: $\quad 11.0A + 14.0G + 7.0D \geq 11.0$

Nonnegativity: $\quad A, G, D \geq 0.$

The objective function of this nonlinear optimization model is the standard deviation of the portfolio (which measures risk), which we would like to minimize. The first constraint is the constraint stating that the fractions of the money invested in each of the three assets must sum to one. The second constraint states that the expected rate of return of the portfolio must be at least 11.0%. The third set of constraints states that we cannot invest negative amounts in any of the assets. (In practice, we might allow the possibility of "shorting" a particular stock, for example the GSS stock. This would be accomplished by allowing G to be nonpositive or nonnegative.)

Notice that the above problem is a nonlinear optimization problem, because the objective function is a nonlinear function of the decision variables A, G, and D.

Just as in the case of linear optimization modeling, it is possible to format this problem into a spreadsheet and to have the software compute the optimal solution to this problem. That is, the computer will compute those values of the variables A, G, and D that will satisfy all of the constraints and nonnegativity conditions, and will yield the minimum value of the standard deviation in the process. If one solves the problem this way, the optimal fractional allocation of the investors' money that minimizes the standard deviation of the portfolio is given by the assignment shown in Table 8.2.

According to Table 8.2, the optimal asset allocation in order to achieve an expected annual return of 11.0% with minimum risk is to invest 37.69% of each investment dollar in Advent, 35.61% of each investment dollar in GSS, and 26.70% of each investment dollar in Digital. The standard deviation of the resulting portfolio will be:

$$\sigma_R = \sqrt{16.0A^2 + 22.0G^2 + 10.0D^2 + 6.0AG + 2.0GD - 10.0AD}$$

$$= \sqrt{\begin{array}{c} 16.0(0.3769)^2 + 22.0(0.3561)^2 + 10.0(0.2670)^2 \\ + 6.0(0.3769)(0.3561) + 2.0(0.3561)(0.2670) - 10.0(0.3769)(0.2670) \end{array}}$$

$$= 2.4008\%.$$

Now let us look at an alternate version of the portfolio optimization problem. Instead of minimizing the risk of the portfolio subject to meeting a given minimal expected annual rate of return, Marathon might want to design their portfolio in order maximize the expected return of the portfolio subject to a restriction that limits the

TABLE 8.2

The optimal fractional allocation of assets to achieve an expected annual return of 11.0% with minimum risk.

Asset Name	Decision Variable	Optimal Fractional Allocation
Advent	A	0.3769
GSS	G	0.3561
Digital	D	0.2670

TABLE 8.3

The optimal fractional allocation of assets to achieve a standard deviation of at most 3.1% with maximum expected return.

Asset Name	Decision Variable	Optimal Fractional Allocation
Advent	A	0.3782
GSS	G	0.5339
Digital	D	0.0879

standard deviation of the portfolio to be at most a pre-specified quantity. For example, they may want the standard deviation of the portfolio to be at most 3.1%. Then the resulting optimization problem would be:

maximize $11.0A + 14.0G + 7.0D$

subject to:

Fractions: $A + G + D = 1.0$

Target risk: $\sqrt{16.0A^2 + 22.0G^2 + 10.0D^2 + 6.0AG + 2.0GD - 10.0AD} \le 3.1$

Nonnegativity: $A, G, D \ge 0.$

Notice that in this problem the objective function is a linear function of the decision variables, but one of the constraints involves a nonlinear function of the decision variables.

It is also possible to format this problem into a spreadsheet and to have the spreadsheet software compute the optimal solution to this problem. That is, the computer will compute those values of the variables A, G, and D that will satisfy all of the constraints and nonnegativity conditions, and will yield the maximum value of the expected annual return of portfolio in the process. If one solves the problem this way, the optimal fractional allocation of the investors' money that maximizes the expected annual return of the portfolio is given by the assignment shown in Table 8.3.

According to Table 8.3, the optimal asset allocation in order to achieve a standard deviation of at most 3.1% with maximum expected return is to invest 37.82% of each investment dollar in Advent, 53.39% of each investment dollar in GSS, and 8.79% of each investment dollar in Digital. The expected annual return of the resulting portfolio will be:

$$E(R) = 11.0A + 14.0G + 7.0D$$
$$= 11.0(0.3782) + 14.0(0.5339) + 7.0(0.0879)$$
$$= 12.250\%.$$

Example 8.2 — Optimizing Production and Pricing Decisions

Recall the Gemstone Tool Company (GTC) production planning model, which is Example 7.2 of Chapter 7. In the GTC production planning problem, the company would like to choose the number of wrenches to produce per day (in 1,000s), denoted as W, and the number of pliers to produce per day (in 1,000s), denoted as P, in order to maximize the contribution to earnings.

The corresponding linear optimization model was developed as follows:

$$\begin{aligned}
\text{maximize} \quad & 130W + 100P \\
\text{subject to:} & \\
\text{Steel:} \quad & 1.5W + 1.0P \le 27 \\
\text{Molding:} \quad & 1.0W + 1.0P \le 21 \\
\text{Assembly:} \quad & 0.3W + 0.5P \le 9 \\
\text{W-demand:} \quad & W \le 15 \\
\text{P-demand:} \quad & P \le 16 \\
\text{Nonnegativity:} \quad & W, P \ge 0.
\end{aligned}$$

Recall that the steel, molding, and assembly constraints arise from availability and/or capacity restrictions on the daily amount of steel, molding machine hours, and assembly machine hours that are available at the plant. The W-demand and P-demand constraints reflect the fact that at current market prices for wrenches and pliers, GTC cannot sell more than 15,000 wrenches per day and also cannot sell more than 16,000 pliers per day.

As shown in Chapter 7, the optimal solution to this problem is

$$W = 12 \quad \text{and} \quad P = 9,$$

and the contribution to earnings of this optimal plan is $2,460 per day.

Now notice that this model assumes implicitly that Gemstone Tool Company is a "price-taker," that is, that GTC is too small a firm to influence market prices for wrenches and pliers. Put differently, the market has set the prices on wrenches on pliers, and at those prices, GTC can earn $130 per 1,000 wrenches sold and can earn $100 per 1,000 pliers sold. However, because the market for wrenches and pliers is limited, GTC cannot sell more than 15,000 wrenches per day, and they also cannot sell more than 16,000 pliers per day.

Suppose instead that GTC has a very large share of the market and so is a "price-setter" in the markets for wrenches and pliers. The demand for each of GTC's tools will be a function of the price that GTC sets for each tool. Let P_W denote the price of wrenches (in $/1,000 wrenches) and let P_P denote the price of pliers (in $/1,000 pliers) that GTC sets for these tools. Suppose that GTC has used linear regression (and possibly other forecasting tools) to estimate the effects of setting prices P_W and P_P on the demand for wrenches and pliers that GTC faces, yielding the following estimated demand equations for wrenches and pliers, respectively:

$$D_W = 565.0 - 0.50P_W$$
$$D_P = 325.0 - 0.25P_P,$$

where D_W and D_P denote the demand that GTC faces for wrenches and pliers, given that GTC has set prices P_W and P_P on wrenches and pliers. These equations relate the price that GTC sets for each tool to the demand for each tool faced by GTC. Thus, for example, if GTC sets the price of wrenches to be $P_W = \$1,100$ per 1,000 tools, then GTC will face a demand for wrenches (in 1,000s) of

$$D_W = 565.0 - 0.50P_W = 565.0 - 0.50 \cdot 1,100 = 15.0.$$

Note, by the way, that the demand for each tool is a decreasing function of the price of each tool. This reflects the economic reality that as the price of a good goes up, the demand for the good goes down. Suppose also that the variable cost of producing wrenches and tools is as shown in Table 8.4. Then, for example, if GTC sets the price of its wrenches to be $P_W = \$1,100$ per 1,000 wrenches, the contribution to earnings of each wrench will be

TABLE 8.4

Demand equations, variable production costs, and unit contribution to earnings of wrenches and pliers at GTC.

	Wrenches	*Pliers*
Demand Equation (1,000)	$D_W = 565.0 - 0.50P_W$	$D_P = 325.0 - 0.25P_P$
Variable Production Cost ($/1,000)	$1,000.0	$1,200.0
Contribution to Earnings per tool ($/1,000)	$P_W - 1,000.0$	$P_P - 1,200.0$

$$\$100 = P_W - 1,000.0 = 1,100.0 - 1,000.0.$$

We can incorporate the demand equations and the variable production costs into the GTC production planning model by introducing the price of wrenches and the price of pliers as two new decision variables, P_W and P_P. The objective function, which is the total contribution to earnings, is now expressed as:

$$(W)(P_W - 1,000.0) + (P)(P_P - 1,200.0).$$

This expression simply states that the total contribution to earnings is the quantity of wrenches produced (W) multiplied by the contribution to earnings of each wrench ($P_W - 1,000.0$) plus the quantity of pliers produced (P) multiplied by the contribution to earnings of each pliers ($P_P - 1,200.0$). The amended optimization model then is:

maximize $(W)(P_W - 1,000.0) + (P)(P_P - 1,200.0)$

subject to:

Steel: $1.5W + 1.0P \le 27$

Molding: $1.0W + 1.0P \le 21$

Assembly: $0.3W + 0.5P \le 9$

W-demand: $W \le 565 - 0.50P_W$

P-demand: $P \le 325 - 0.25P_P$

Nonnegativity: $W, W_P, P, P_P \ge 0.$

Notice in this model that the decision variables include the price of wrenches (P_W) and the price of pliers (P_P). Also, the demand equations for wrenches and pliers are now included in the model, but are included here as inequalities. The reason for this is that we want to include the restriction that production of wrenches (W) cannot exceed the demand for wrenches ($565 - 0.50P_W$), which results in the following inequality:

$$W \le 565 - 0.50P_W$$

with a similar construction for pliers. Next, notice that the model includes nonnegativity conditions on the price of wrenches and the price of pliers, that is, $P_W \ge 0$ and $P_P \ge 0$, since prices cannot be negative quantities. Also notice in this model that the constraints are linear functions of the decision variables W, W_P, P, and P_P. However, the objective function is a nonlinear function of the decision variables, since the objective function involves multiplying two decision variables times each other.

It is also possible to format this problem into a spreadsheet and to have the spreadsheet software compute the optimal solution to this problem. That is, the computer will compute those values of the variables W, W_P, P, and P_P that will satisfy all of the constraints and nonnegativity conditions and will yield the maximum value of the contribution to earnings. If one solves the problem this way, the optimal solution to the problem turns out to be:

$$W = 13.818, \quad P_W = \$1{,}102.36, \quad P = 6.273, \quad P_P = \$1{,}274.91,$$

and the contribution to earnings is equal to $1,884.36 per day. This solution states that GTC should set the price of wrenches to be $1,102.36 per 1,000 wrenches, and that they should produce 13,818 wrenches per day. GTC should set the price of pliers to be $1,274.91 per 1,000 pliers, and they should produce 6,273 pliers per day.

Example 8.3 — Optimizing the Location of a Facility

Suppose a firm would like to choose the site of a new distribution center that will simultaneously serve its four sales centers located in Amherst (A), Bowdoin (B), Colby (C), and Dartmouth (D). Figure 8.1 shows the relative location of each of these sales centers in the coordinate plane, where each unit is one mile. Table 8.5 shows the daily number of deliveries that must be made to each sales center from the new distribution center, as well as the (x, y)-coordinates of each of the sales centers based on Figure 8.1. Suppose that truck delivery costs are $1.00 per mile for trucks that travel between the distribution center and the sales centers. The firm would like to determine where to locate the new distribution center, so as to service the sales centers with the lowest transportation cost.

Let us construct a nonlinear optimization model for this problem. Let $P = (x, y)$ be the location of the distribution center in the coordinate plane. The distance from $P = (x, y)$ to Amherst (point $A = (8, 2)$) is given by the distance formula

$$\sqrt{(x - 8)^2 + (y - 2)^2},$$

and since Amherst must receive 9 truck deliveries per day, the travel cost associated with the Amherst sales center is given by the following expression:

$$2 \cdot 9 \cdot \sqrt{(x - 8)^2 + (y - 2)^2}.$$

FIGURE 8.1

The location of the four sales centers.

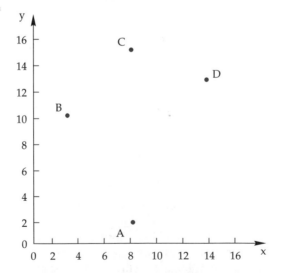

TABLE 8.5

Daily truck deliveries and coordinate positions of the four sales centers.

Sales Center	Code	Daily Number of Truck Deliveries	x-coordinate	y-coordinate
Amherst	A	9	8	2
Bowdoin	B	7	3	10
Colby	C	2	8	15
Dartmouth	D	5	14	13

The number "2" appears above because each truck must travel to the sales center from the distribution center and back again, for a total of 9 round trips, that is, 18 one-way trips. It is straightforward to derive the travel costs associated with the other three sales centers in a similar manner. Then the facility location problem of determining the location (x, y) of the distribution center is:

$$\text{minimize} \quad 2 \cdot 9\sqrt{(x-8)^2 + (y-2)^2} + 2 \cdot 7\sqrt{(x-3)^2 + (y-10)^2}$$
$$+ 2 \cdot 2\sqrt{(x-8)^2 + (y-15)^2} + 2 \cdot 5\sqrt{(x-14)^2 + (y-13)^2}.$$

Notice in this problem that the objective function is a nonlinear function of the decision variables x and y, and that there are no constraints.

Once again, it is possible to format this problem into a spreadsheet and to have the spreadsheet software compute the optimal solution to this problem. The computer will compute the coordinate values x and y of the location P of the distribution center that will yield the minimum value of the daily travel costs. If one solves the problem this way, the optimal solution to the problem turns out to be:

$$x = 6.95, \quad y = 7.47,$$

and the optimal daily travel cost is equal to $285.94. That is, the optimal location of the distribution center is at the point $P = (6.95, 7.47)$, and the optimized daily travel cost is equal to:

$$\$285.94 = 2 \cdot 9\sqrt{(6.95-8)^2 + (7.47-2)^2} + 2 \cdot 7\sqrt{(6.95-3)^2 + (7.47-10)^2}$$
$$+ 2 \cdot 2\sqrt{(6.95-8)^2 + (7.47-15)^2} + 2 \cdot 5\sqrt{(6.95-14)^2 + (7.47-13)^2}.$$

Now let us consider a richer version of this facility location problem. Suppose that zoning laws restrict the location of the distribution center to lie in the four-sided figure shown in Figure 8.2. Then, when the four sides of the figure are converted to linear constraints, the distribution center location problem can be written as:

$$\text{minimize:} \quad 2 \cdot 9\sqrt{(x-8)^2 + (y-2)^2} + 2 \cdot 7\sqrt{(x-3)^2 + (y-10)^2}$$
$$+ 2 \cdot 2\sqrt{(x-8)^2 + (y-15)^2} + 2 \cdot 5\sqrt{(x-14)^2 + (y-13)^2}$$

$$\text{subject to:} \quad x \geq 10$$
$$y \geq 5$$
$$y \leq 11$$
$$x + y \leq 24.$$

In this problem, the objective function is a nonlinear function of the decision variables x and y, and all of the constraints are linear functions of the decision variables x and y.

This nonlinear optimization problem can also be formatted into a spreadsheet and solved using spreadsheet software. The computer will compute the coordinate values x and y of the location P of the distribution center that will yield the minimum value of the daily travel costs subject to the constraints that the point P must lie in the four-sided region shown in Figure 8.2. If one solves the problem this way, the optimal solution to the problem turns out to be:

$$x = 10.0, \quad y = 7.40,$$

and the optimal daily travel cost is equal to $308.45. That is, the optimal location of the distribution center is at the point $P = (10.0, 7.40)$, and the optimized daily travel cost is equal to:

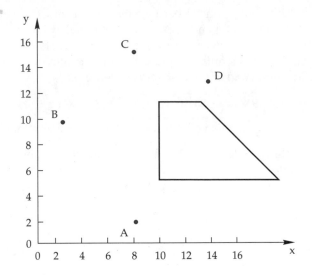

$$\$308.45 = 2 \cdot 9\sqrt{(10.0 - 8)^2 + (7.40 - 2)^2} + 2 \cdot 7\sqrt{(10.0 - 3)^2 + (7.40 - 10)^2}$$
$$+ 2 \cdot 2\sqrt{(10.0 - 8)^2 + (7.40 - 15)^2} + 2 \cdot 5\sqrt{(10.0 - 14)^2 + (7.40 - 13)^2}.$$

8.2 | GRAPHICAL ANALYSIS OF NONLINEAR OPTIMIZATION MODELS IN TWO VARIABLES

In this section we study the geometry of a nonlinear optimization model in order to understand which geometric ideas of linear optimization can be extended to nonlinear optimization, and which geometric ideas of linear optimization cannot be extended to nonlinear optimization.

Consider the following nonlinear optimization problem, which we will call problem P1:

$$\text{P1: minimize} \quad f(x, y) = \sqrt{(x - 14)^2 + (y - 14)^2}$$
$$\text{subject to:} \quad (x - 8)^2 + (y - 9)^2 \leq 49$$
$$x \geq 2$$
$$x \leq 13$$
$$x + y \leq 24.$$

Just as in the case of linear optimization, the **decision variables** in a nonlinear optimization problem are defined to be the unknown variables for which we would like to assign values. In problem P1, the decision variables are x and y. An assignment of the decision variables is a **feasible solution** of the problem if the assignment satisfies all of the constraints of the problem. In problem P1 above, the assignment $x = 7$ and $y = 10$ is a feasible solution: Straightforward computation shows that this assignment satisfies all of the constraints. The locus of all of the feasible solutions is called the **feasible region** of the problem. The **optimal solution** of a nonlinear optimization model is that feasible solution that optimizes the objective function value.

Now let us construct a graph of the feasible region of the problem P1. Just as in the case of linear optimization, we will do this by first plotting each of the constraints. The first constraint is

$$(x - 8)^2 + (y - 9)^2 \le 49.$$

Similar to the case of linear optimization, we first plot the constraint in equality form, that is, we first plot the points (x, y) that satisfy

$$(x - 8)^2 + (y - 9)^2 = 49.$$

Because this equation is precisely the equation for a circle in the plane whose center lies at the point (8, 9) and whose radius is 7 ($7 = \sqrt{49}$), the points that satisfy this equation form a circle. As one can easily test, the locus of points that lie inside the circle are precisely those points that satisfy the constraint inequality in the correct direction. Therefore, the locus of points that satisfy the first constraint will be the disk shown in Figure 8.3. All of the other constraints in this problem are linear constraints and can be plotted using the general method presented in Chapter 7. These other constraints are plotted in Figure 8.4, and the shaded region shown in Figure 8.4 thus represents the feasible region of problem P1.

FIGURE 8.3

The locus of points that satisfies $(x - 8)^2 + (y - 9)^2 \le 49.$

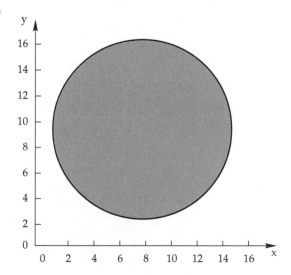

FIGURE 8.4

The feasible region of problem P1.

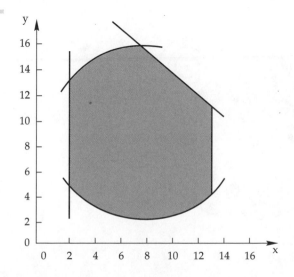

The next task is to plot the objective function isoquant lines. For the problem P1, the objective function is given by the formula:

$$f(x, y) = \sqrt{(x - 14)^2 + (y - 14)^2},$$

which is the distance from the point (x, y) to the point $(14, 14)$ in the coordinate plane. Therefore, the isoquant contours of this function will be an expanding ring of circles that are all centered at the point $(14, 14)$. This is shown graphically in Figure 8.5. In fact, Figure 8.5 indicates that the optimal solution of P1 is that point in the feasible region that is closest to the point $(14, 14)$. This point is $(x, y) = (12,12)$, which is where the isoquant of the objective function $f(x, y)$ just touches the constraint:

$$x + y \leq 24.$$

Now let us instead consider the following slightly altered nonlinear optimization model, called P2:

$$\begin{aligned}
\text{P2: minimize} \quad & f(x, y) = \sqrt{(x - 16)^2 + (y - 14)^2} \\
\text{subject to:} \quad & (x - 8)^2 + (y - 9)^2 \leq 49 \\
& x \geq 2 \\
& x \leq 13 \\
& x + y \leq 24.
\end{aligned}$$

This problem is almost identical to problem P1. The constraints of problem P2 are identical to the constraints of problem P1, and the objective function of problem P2 is of the same format as that of P1, except that the isoquant contours are centered instead at the point $(16, 14)$ in the coordinate plane. The graphical representation of the solution to problem P2 is shown in Figure 8.6. Notice that the optimal solution occurs where the isoquant of the objective function just touches the feasible region, which for this problem occurs at the point $(x, y) = (13, 11)$. This point is at the intersection of the following two constraints, which are both satisfied at equality at the solution:

$$x \leq 13$$

$$x + y \leq 24.$$

FIGURE 8.5

Graphical representation of the solution of problem P1.

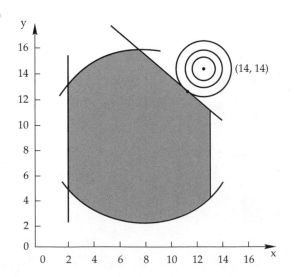

FIGURE 8.6

Graphical representation of the solution of problem P2.

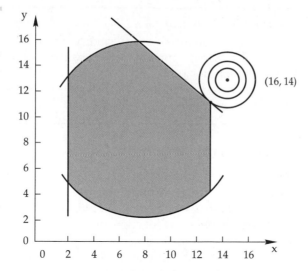

FIGURE 8.7

Graphical representation of the solution of problem P3.

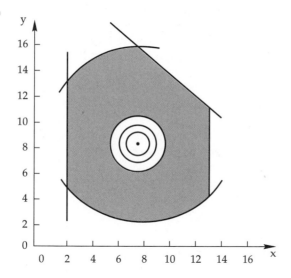

Finally, let us consider a third problem, which we will call problem P3:

$$\text{P3: minimize} \quad f(x, y) = \sqrt{(x - 8)^2 + (y - 8)^2}$$
$$\text{subject to:} \quad (x - 8)^2 + (y - 9)^2 \le 49$$
$$x \ge 2$$
$$x \le 13$$
$$x + y \le 24.$$

This problem is also almost identical to problems P1 and P2. The objective function is of the same format as that for P1 and P2, except that the isoquant contours are centered instead at the point (8, 8) in the coordinate plane. The graphical representation of the solution of problem P3 is shown in Figure 8.7. Notice now that the optimal solution to the problem occurs at the point (8, 8), and that this point satisfies all of the constraints of the problem at strict inequality.

We therefore have the following elementary observations regarding the solution of a nonlinear optimization model.

> *Two Insights from the Graphical Analysis of Nonlinear Optimization*
> - The optimal solution of nonlinear optimization model need not occur at a "corner point," nor even on the boundary of the feasible region of the problem.
> - When the optimal solution occurs on the boundary of the feasible region, the solution will be where the feasible region just touches the best isoquant of the objective function.

Local Versus Global Optimal Solutions

As stated earlier, the optimal solution to a nonlinear optimization model is that solution which is feasible (it satisfies all of the constraints) and optimizes the objective function value among all other feasible points. A **local optimal solution** is a feasible solution that optimizes the objective function among all feasible points near to itself. In the case of a nonlinear optimization model, it is possible for a solution to be a local optimal solution but not be the true optimal solution for the problem.

The problem of a local optimal solution is illustrated in Figure 8.8. In Figure 8.8, the feasible region is the "kidney-shaped" area in the figure, and the isoquants of the objective function are indicated by the contour lines with their respective objective values. Notice in Figure 8.8 that the point A is a local optimal solution, since all points near enough to A that are feasible have a larger objective function value. However, the actual optimal solution is at the point B, which has the best objective function value among all of the feasible points, that is, those points that lie in the feasible region. The optimal solution B is also called the **global optimal solution** to distinguish it from a local optimal solution.

Another illustration of a local optimal solution versus the global optimal solution is the following problem, which we call problem P4:

$$P4: \text{minimize} \quad f(x)$$
$$\text{subject to:} \quad x \le 7$$
$$x \ge 2,$$

where the function $f(x)$ is portrayed in Figure 8.9.

Problem P4 is simply an optimization problem in one variable, namely x. The feasible region of problem P4 is simply those values of x that lie between 2 and 7. It is plain to see from Figure 8.9 that the optimal solution to problem P4 is the point

FIGURE 8.8

Illustration of a local optimal solution that is not the global optimal solution.

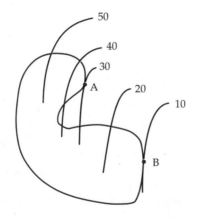

FIGURE 8.9
The objective function $f(x)$ of problem P4.

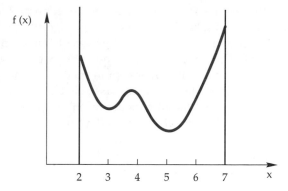

$x = 5$. However, the point $x = 3$ is a local optimal solution, because all of the feasible points near enough to $x = 3$ have a larger objective function value $f(x)$.

8.3 | COMPUTER SOLUTION OF NONLINEAR OPTIMIZATION PROBLEMS

In this section we discuss the relevant issues regarding the solvability of a nonlinear optimization model on the computer. We start with general principles of solvability of nonlinear optimization models. We then present detailed instructions on how to use the Solver Add-In function in Microsoft Excel® to solve a nonlinear optimization model formatted in a spreadsheet.

General Principles on the Solvability of Nonlinear Optimization Models

In general, a nonlinear optimization model is more difficult to solve than a linear optimization model. A linear optimization model is easy to solve by virtue of the fact that the optimal solution must correspond to a "corner point" of the feasible region, and that a corner point solution itself corresponds to the solution of a certain system of linear equations. However, as we have seen in Section 8.2, the solution of a nonlinear optimization model will not necessarily correspond to a corner point of the feasible region, and in fact, there are no identifiable systems of either linear or nonlinear equations whose solution will be the optimal solution of the model. For this reason, nonlinear optimization models are generally more difficult to solve than are linear optimization models.

There are a great many different types of algorithms (and corresponding software) that have been developed to solve nonlinear optimization models. Most algorithms and software for solving nonlinear optimization problems use rather sophisticated mathematical methods that ultimately rely on calculus and that work by computing derivatives, partial derivatives, and second partial derivatives. However, the information one derives from notions in calculus typically is "local" information. As a consequence, most algorithms and software for solving nonlinear optimization problems are only capable of computing a local optimal solution, rather than the global optimal solution. This is less than we would like to have in an algorithm and/or in a software package for solving nonlinear optimization problems. Research on better algorithms for solving nonlinear optimization problems is progressing quickly, and hopefully the capabilities for solving for global optimal solutions of nonlinear optimization problems will materialize in the next decade. But for now, it is important to note that most algorithms and software for solving nonlinear optimization problems are only capable of computing local optimal solutions. Even when the algorithm tells the user that it has "solved" the nonlinear optimization model, this usually means that the algorithm has found a local optimal solution. There is no inherent way of knowing if the algorithm has found the global optimal solution, except in special, although widely applicable, circumstances. (These circumstances are discussed in Section 8.6.)

Furthermore, the computational difficulty of solving a particular nonlinear optimization model depends very much on the underlying mathematical structure of the particular model. Some nonlinear optimization models are very easy to solve, while other nonlinear optimization models are very difficult to solve. The determination of the kinds of mathematical structures that are easy to solve and the ones that are hard to solve is a more advanced topic, which we cover in Section 8.6.

There are many software packages that are available for solving nonlinear optimization models. These packages vary quite a bit by their degree of functionality. Some software packages are only designed for very small problems, that is, problems with only a few decision variables and/or only a few constraints in the model. These less functional (and less expensive) packages might fail completely on certain problems, depending on the mathematical structure of the problem to be solved. In the better (and more expensive) software packages, the software will almost always compute a local optimal solution (but not necessarily the global optimal solution) even when the number of decision variables is very large and/or when there are a very large number of constraints in the model. The better software packages for solving nonlinear optimization problems are typically expensive to purchase and so are not automatically featured as part of any typical spreadsheet software. The Solver Add-In software resident in Microsoft Excel® is a medium-quality package and can be relied on for small problems but not for large problems.

Below is a summary of the key points just discussed:

Guideline 1: Unlike a linear optimization model, a general nonlinear optimization model can be very difficult to solve even with today's computers.

Guideline 2: Because algorithms for solving nonlinear optimization models rely on calculus, they are only capable of solving for a local optimal solution of the nonlinear optimization model, which is not necessarily a global optimal solution of the model.

Guideline 3: Some nonlinear optimization models are easy to solve, and others are difficult. The difficulty in solving a nonlinear optimization model depends very much on the model's own mathematical structure.

Guideline 4: Software for solving nonlinear optimization models varies with the degree of functionality and with the price of the software. The better software packages will solve nonlinear models with very many variables and/or constraints.

Using Spreadsheet Software to solve a Nonlinear Optimization Problem

In Chapter 7, we showed how to use the Microsoft Excel® Add-In function Solver to solve a linear optimization model. The Solver function can also be used to solve a nonlinear optimization problem. Below we indicate how to use the Solver to solve a nonlinear optimization model.

- **Basic construction of the model.** Format your nonlinear optimization model in a spreadsheet in the same way as you would a linear optimization model. This involves assigning decision variables, the objective function, and the constraint left-hand-sides (LHS) and right-hand-sides (RHS) with appropriate cells in the spreadsheet, exactly as in a linear optimization model. Enter the Solver in the usual way by selecting **Solver . . .** under the **Tools** header at the top of the spreadsheet. Just as in the case of a linear optimization model, one simply instructs the Solver which cells are the decision variables, which cell contains the objective function, and which cells contain the left-hand-side (LHS) and right-hand-side (RHS) of each of the constraints. This information is entered in the **Solver Parameters** window.

- **Make sure that "Assume Linear Model" is not checked.** Click on the **Options** button in the **Solver Parameters** window. This will bring up the **Solver Options** window. In the **Solver Options** window, make sure that the box next to the label **Assume Linear Model** is **not** checked. This is very important.

- **Changing the parameters in the "Solver Options" dialog box.** Unlike linear optimization models, the user might need to experiment with changing the parameters in the **Solver Options** dialog box when solving a nonlinear optimization model in order to achieve better solution quality. Each parameter option has a default setting that is appropriate for most problems. We now describe the meaning of some of the features in the **Solver Options** dialog box that are important for solving nonlinear optimization problems. (We do not discuss those options that are too technical or are not relevant for nonlinear optimization models.)

  — **Max Time.** This option allows the user to limit the time taken by the solution process. While the user can enter a value as high as 32,000 seconds or more, the default value of 100 seconds is adequate for most small problems. However, when solving larger nonlinear optimization problems, one needs to increase the limit beyond its default value.

  — **Iterations.** This option allows the user to limit the time taken by the solution process by limiting the number of interim calculations. The default value of 100 iterations is adequate for most small problems.

  — **Precision.** This option allows the user to control the precision of solutions and the accuracy of the numerical calculations. The level of precision determines whether the constraint left-hand-sides have the proper relation to the constraint right-hand-sides (either "$\leq$", "$=$", or "$\geq$") to within a certain precision. The "Precision" must be given as a fractional number between 0.0 and 1.0. A higher precision is indicated when the number entered has more decimal places, so that 0.00001 indicates a very high precision. When the precision is higher, the solution will more accurately satisfy the constraints in the problem. However, when the precision is higher, the Solver will need more time to find a solution.

  — **Tolerance.** This dialog box is not relevant for nonlinear optimization models, and so can be ignored.

  — **Convergence.** When the relative change in the target cell value is less than the number in the **Convergence** box for the last five iterations, the Solver stops. The "Convergence" must be given as a fractional number between 0.0 and 1.0. A higher Convergence value is indicated when the number entered has more decimal places, so that 0.00001 indicates a very high Convergence value. The higher the Convergence value, the more time Solver will need to take to compute a solution.

— **Assume Linear Model.** Remember to make sure that the box next to **Assume Linear Model** is not checked.

— **Show Iteration Results.** This option instructs the Solver to pause to show the results of each iteration.

— **Assume Non-Negative.** This option instructs the Solver to assume a lower limit of 0.0 for all adjustable cells (that is, decision variables) for which the user has not set a lower limit in the **Constraint** box in the **Add Constraint** dialog box.

- **Solving the model.** Once you have adjusted the various parameters in the **Solver Parameters** dialog box, you are ready to solve your problem. Click on **OK** in the **Solver Options** window and then click on **Solve** in the **Solver Parameters** window. The software will then proceed with the computations of a solution of your model. After a short amount of time, the **Solver Results** window will appear on the screen.

- **How to know if Solver has found a solution.** Look at the message in the **Solver Results** window. It should read "Solver found a solution. All constraints and optimality conditions are satisfied." If some other message appears in the **Solver Results** window, then Solver has not found a solution of the model. In this case, you might try to re-adjust some of the parameters and options in the **Solver Options** window and then try again to solve the model.

- **Reading the Optimization Results.** When the Solver has finished computing a solution of the model, it will display the **Solver Results** window. Note the message at the top of the window that indicates whether or not an optimal solution was found. Make sure that the radio button next to the label **Keep Solver Solution** is clicked. This ensures that the Solver will place the optimal values of the decision variables in the appropriate cells in the spreadsheet model. Click the **OK** button to return to the spreadsheet.

8.4   SHADOW PRICES INFORMATION IN NONLINEAR OPTIMIZATION MODELS

In Chapter 7, we introduced the concept of the shadow price of a constraint in the context of a linear optimization problem. Recall that the shadow price of a particular constraint is defined as follows:

> The **shadow price** of a constraint is the amount of change in the optimal objective function value as the right-hand-side (RHS) of that constraint is increased by one unit, and all other problem data are kept fixed.

As it turns out, the definition of the shadow price carries over exactly to the case of a nonlinear optimization model, that is, the same definition pertains. Furthermore, almost all commercial software programs for solving nonlinear optimization models also compute all of the shadow price information automatically as part of the solution methodology. Just as in the case for linear optimization models, the Solver Add-In function in Microsoft Excel® computes the shadow prices for nonlinear optimization models as part of the Sensitivity Report. We next indicate how to retrieve the shadow price information when using the Solver.

Obtaining Shadow Price Information from a Nonlinear Optimization Model formatted in a Spreadsheet

Step 1. Solve the nonlinear optimization model by entering the **Solver** window under the **Tools** header at the top of the screen as usual.

Step 2. Click on **Solve** to solve the nonlinear optimization model.

Step 3. After the model solves, the **Solver Results** window will appear. In a subwindow on the right called **Reports,** click on **Sensitivity** and hit **OK.** The Solver will produce a separate worksheet called **Sensitivity Report** for the nonlinear optimization model. The Sensitivity Report contains all of the shadow prices for the model and is read as follows:

- The Sensitivity Report contains an upper and a lower table. The upper table in the report is entitled **Adjustable Cells** and the lower table is entitled **Constraints.** The first three columns of the upper table show the optimal solution of the model. The fourth column of the upper table contains information that is rather technical and not very managerial in scope and so is not covered in this text.

- The lower table lists the relevant information for each constraint in the model. Under the column **Cell,** the table lists the cell where the left-hand-side (LHS) of each constraint appears in the spreadsheet. The second column shows the **Name** for each constraint. (The Solver picks a name by searching to the left and above for any appropriate cell with characters in it.) The third column is the **Final Value** column. This column presents the final value of the left-hand-side (LHS) of each constraint. The fourth column is entitled **Lagrange Multiplier.** This is the column which lists the shadow price of each constraint in the model. (For historical reasons, sometimes shadow prices are also called Lagrange multipliers. For our purposes, the two phrases "Lagrange multiplier" and "shadow price" are interchangeable and refer to the same quantity.)

To illustrate the definition as well as the practical use of shadow price information in nonlinear optimization, consider again the portfolio optimization problem introduced in Example 8.1. This problem is restated below for convenience:

$$\text{minimize} \quad \sqrt{16.0A^2 + 22.0G^2 + 10.0D^2 + 6.0AG + 2.0GD - 10.0AD}$$

subject to:

Fractions: $\quad A + G + D = 1.0$

Target return: $\quad 11.0A + 14.0G + 7.0D \geq 11.0$

Nonnegativity: $\quad A, G, D \geq 0.$

In this problem, the decision variables are A, G, and D, which denote the fraction of Marathon's investment dollars that Marathon Investments is planning to invest in Advent Communications, General Space Systems, and Digital Devices, respectively. The first constraint of the formulation states that the fractions of the investment dollars must sum to one. The second constraint states that the expected return of the portfolio must be at least 11.0%. The nonnegativity conditions reflect the restriction

TABLE 8.6

Spreadsheet representation of the Marathon Investments risk minimization model.

	A	B	C	D	E	F
1	Asset	Expected	Standard		Correlation	
2	Name	Return	Deviation	Advent	GSS	Digital
3	Advent	11.0	4.00			
4	GSS	14.0	4.69	0.160		
5	Digital	7.0	3.16	-0.395	0.067	
6						
7						
8	Decision Variables		Advent	GSS	Digital	
9			0.3769	0.3561	0.2670	
10						
11						
12	Standard Deviation		2.4008			
13						
14	Constraints					
15		LHS	RHS			
16	fractions	1.0000	1.0000			
17	target return	11.0000	11.0000			

TABLE 8.7

Spreadsheet sensitivity report for the Marathon Investments risk minimization model.

	A	B	C	D
1	Adjustable Cells			
2	Cell	Name	Final Value	Reduced Gradient
3	C9	Advent	0.3769	0
4	D9	GSS	0.3561	0
5	E9	Digital	0.2670	0
6				
7	Constraints			
8	Cell	Name	Final Value	Lagrange Multiplier
9	B16	fractions	1.0	-2.8937
10	B17	target return	11.0	0.4813

that Marathon cannot invest "negative" amounts in any of the three stocks, i.e., they are restricted from short-selling any stock.

Table 8.6 shows a spreadsheet representation of the above problem. As was stated in Example 8.1, this problem can easily be formatted into a spreadsheet and solved using the Solver Add-In function in Microsoft Excel®. Table 8.7 shows the Sensitivity Report for this model that is produced after the model has been solved. Recall from the previous discussion that the shadow prices for the two constraints of the model are shown in the "Lagrange Multiplier" column of the lower part of Table 8.7.

Let us now see how the shadow price information works in practice. Consider the "Target Return" constraint in this problem. According to Table 8.7, the shadow price on this constraint is 0.4813. This means that the optimal objective function value will increase at the rate of 0.4813 units per unit increase in the RHS of the Target Return constraint. We illustrate this mathematically as follows. The RHS of the Target Return constraint has the value 11.0%, and the optimal objective function value of the problem is 2.4008%. If the target return value of 11.0% were to change by an amount Δ, to $11.0 + \Delta$, then the optimal objective function value would increase by approximately 0.4813Δ. That is, the new optimal objective function value would be as follows:

$$\text{OPTIMAL OBJECTIVE VALUE} \approx 2.4008 + 0.4813\Delta.$$

This formula is an approximation, because all of the functions are in fact nonlinear. Also, this approximation is only valid for very small values of Δ.

Continuing the example, suppose that $\Delta = 0.1$. That is, we are interested in knowing the approximate change in the optimal objective function value as the RHS is increased from 11.0 to 11.1. Then according to the shadow price information, the new optimal objective function value will increase from 2.4008 according to the following rule:

$$\text{OPTIMAL OBJECTIVE VALUE} \approx 2.4008 + 0.4813\Delta$$
$$= 2.4008 + 0.4813 \times (0.1) = 2.4489.$$

Therefore, as the RHS changes by a small amount, the new optimal objective function value changes at the rate of 0.4813 times the change in the RHS. Note that unlike the sensitivity report for linear optimization problems, there is no range information in the sensitivity report for a nonlinear optimization problem.

8.5   A CLOSER LOOK AT PORTFOLIO OPTIMIZATION

Once again, let us recall the basic portfolio optimization problem of Marathon Investments, as developed in Example 8.1. The nonlinear optimization model is to determine the fraction of Marathon's investment dollars to invest in Advent Communications, General Space Systems, and Digital Devices in order to minimize the standard deviation of the portfolio while meeting the target expected annual return of 11.0%. This model has been constructed as follows:

$$\text{minimize} \quad \sqrt{16.0A^2 + 22.0G^2 + 10.0D^2 + 6.0AG + 2.0GD - 10.0AD}$$

subject to:

Fractions: $A + G + D = 1.0$

Target return: $11.0A + 14.0G + 7.0D \geq 11.0$

Nonnegativity: $A, G, D \geq 0.$

The computer solution to the model has been shown in the upper part of Table 8.7. This model is a prototypical basic portfolio optimization, in that it is the building-block on which more sophisticated portfolio models are built in practice.

Extensions of the Basic Portfolio Model

The basic portfolio model can be extended in several ways in order to accommodate a wide variety of types of constraints. For example, if we wanted the portfolio to be considered as a high-technology portfolio, we might want a constraint that stated that at least 70% of the portfolio was invested in computer manufacturing firms. This would be represented by adding a constraint to the model of the form:

$$A + D \geq 0.70.$$

In a similar way, other policy considerations, as well as government regulations that limit the range of investment possibilities, can typically be addressed through the addition of a variety of linear constraints to the model.

Note also that it is easy to see how this model can be extended to optimize a portfolio of hundreds of assets. The only difficulty would be to estimate the data for the model, i.e., the expected rate of return of each asset, as well as the standard deviation of each asset and the correlation table of each asset with each other asset. However, statistical packages combined with large data sets on stock market returns make this task fairly easy to accomplish.

The Efficient Frontier

To see the effect of modifying the required expected return, which we have previously set to be 11.0%, we can solve the preceding model for a variety of different values of the expected annual return. If we do this, we obtain the optimal solution information shown in Table 8.8.

For each value of the required expected return in Table 8.8, the optimal standard deviation is given in the second column. This standard deviation is the minimal standard deviation attainable for the required expected return. The fractional allocation columns in Table 8.8 contain the composition of the portfolio with minimum risk that produces the required expected return. For example, Pat Glover might decide that she would like Marathon's portfolio to have an expected rate of return of 12.0%, while minimizing the risk of the portfolio. Then she would instruct her staff to invest 37.77% of the investment dollars of the portfolio in Advent, 49.85% of the investment dollars in GSS, and 12.38% of the investment dollars in Digital. This combination will yield a 12.0% expected rate of return with a standard deviation of 2.9474%. Furthermore, no other portfolio with an expected return of 12.0% will have a lower standard deviation.

If we plot the numbers in the first and the second column of Table 8.8, we obtain what in financial economics is called the **efficient frontier** of the market for these three securities. This plot is shown in Figure 8.10. The efficient frontier is used by portfolio managers to determine the desired tradeoff between the expected rate of return and the acceptable level of risk of the portfolio, and the portfolio is then composed accordingly.

8.6   TAXONOMY OF THE SOLVABILITY OF NONLINEAR OPTIMIZATION PROBLEMS*

(This section contains somewhat more advanced material, and can be omitted without loss of continuity.)

As discussed in Section 8.3, software packages for nonlinear optimization problems typically are only able to compute a local optimal solution. Therefore, it is useful to understand and identify those problems for which a local optimal solution is also a global optimal solution. In order to do this, we need to develop some definitions related to the notions of a convex function and a concave function. This understanding will lead us to a classification of which nonlinear optimization problems are easy to solve and which problems are hard to solve.

TABLE 8.8
The effect of changing the required expected rate of return on the optimal standard deviation and on the optimal composition of the portfolio.

Required Expected Annual Return (%)	Optimal Standard Deviation (%)	Optimal Fractional Allocation		
		Advent	GSS	Digital
8.0%	1.8928%	0.3755	0.0872	0.5373
9.0%	1.8928%	0.3755	0.0872	0.5373
10.0%	2.0162%	0.3762	0.2136	0.4102
11.0%	2.4008%	0.3769	0.3561	0.2670
12.0%	2.9474%	0.3777	0.4985	0.1238
13.0%	3.5901%	0.3333	0.6667	0.0000
14.0%	4.6904%	0.0000	1.0000	0.0000

FIGURE 8.10

The efficient frontier.

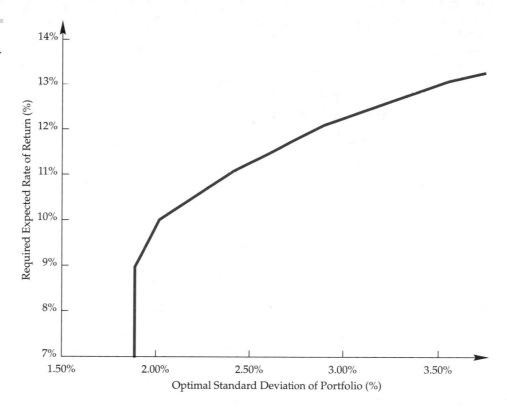

FIGURE 8.11

A convex function.

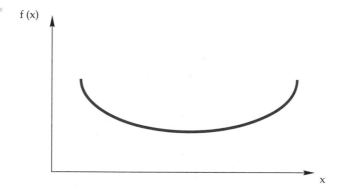

Convex optimization problems

The function $f(x)$ is called a **convex function** if $f(x)$ is shaped as in Figure 8.11, exhibiting **increasing** marginal values. The function $f(x)$ is called a **concave function** if it is shaped as in Figure 8.12, exhibiting **decreasing** marginal values.

By looking at the shape of a convex function, we see that a local minimum of a convex function will also be a global minimum of the function. In a similar manner, it is also true that a local maximum of a concave function is also a global maximum of the function.

Now suppose that $f(x, y)$ is a function of two decision variables. Then the function $f(x, y)$ is called a convex function if the line segment joining any two points on the graph of $f(x, y)$ lies above the graph of $f(x, y)$. Figure 8.13 portrays the typical shape of a convex function in two decision variables.

Similarly, a function $f(x, y)$ of two variables is called a concave function if the line segment joining any two points on the graph of $f(x, y)$ lies below the graph of

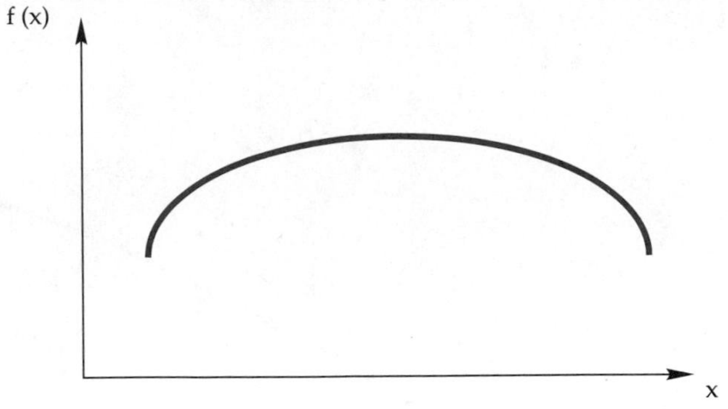

FIGURE 8.12
A concave function.

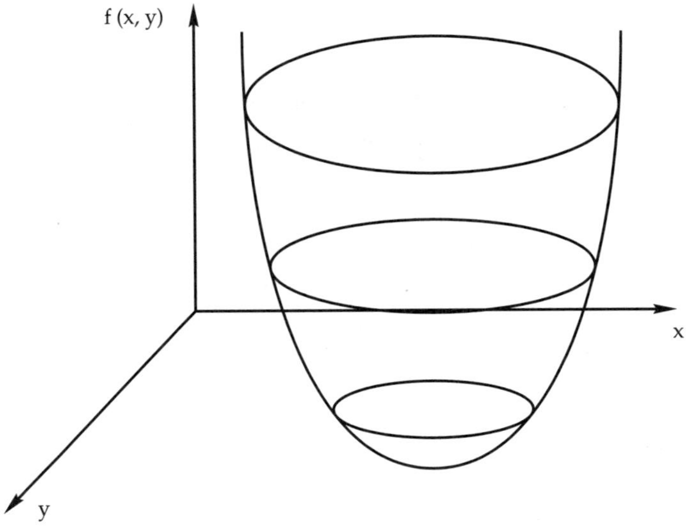

FIGURE 8.13
A convex function
of two variables, x
and y.

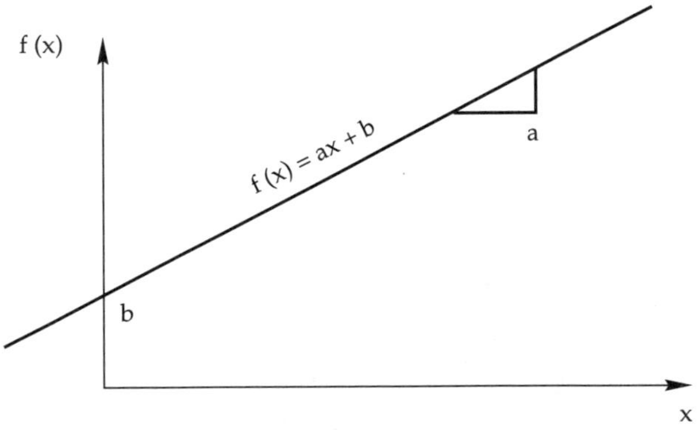

FIGURE 8.14
A linear function is
both convex and
concave.

$f(x, y)$. In more than two decision variables, the definitions of a convex function and a concave function generalize, but are more sophisticated.

What about linear functions? As it turns out, every linear function is both a convex function and a concave function. An example of a linear function is shown in Figure 8.14.

We now define a very important class of nonlinear optimization problems.

> A nonlinear optimization model is called **a convex minimization problem** if:
>
> (a) the objective function is a convex function that is to be minimized.
>
> (b) each of the equality constraint functions is a linear function.
>
> (c) each of the less-than-or-equal-to ("$\leq$") constraint functions is a convex function.
>
> (d) each of the greater-than-or-equal-to ("$\geq$") constraint functions is a concave function.

The important fact about a convex minimization problem is:

> If a nonlinear optimization model is a convex minimization problem, then a local optimal solution will also be a global optimal solution. Therefore, such problems will be relatively easy to solve on a computer.

The reason why it is relatively easy to solve a convex minimization problem is as follows. As stated earlier, algorithms for nonlinear optimization problems can easily and efficiently compute a local optimal solution. However, for a convex minimization problem, a local optimal solution is also the global optimal solution. Therefore, these algorithms will efficiently find the global optimal solution.

One can analyze maximization problems in a very similar way.

> A nonlinear optimization model is called **a concave maximization** problem if:
>
> (a) the objective function is a concave function that is to be maximized.
>
> (b) each of the equality constraint functions is a linear function.
>
> (c) each of the less-than-or-equal-to ("$\leq$") constraint functions is a convex function.
>
> (d) each of the greater-than-or-equal-to ("$\geq$") constraint functions is a concave function.

Similar to the case for convex minimization problems, the following is true:

> If a nonlinear optimization model is a concave maximization problem, then a local optimal solution will also be a global optimal solution. Therefore, such problems will be relatively easy to solve on a computer.

Table 8.9 below summarizes the discussion regarding the solvability of nonlinear optimization problems.

Let us now look at three special cases:

Case 1: The objective is to minimize a convex function, and all constraints are linear constraints. In this case, because all linear functions are both convex and concave, then the problem satisfies all four criteria to be a convex minimization problem and so is relatively easy to solve.

TABLE 8.9

Taxonomy of the solvability of nonlinear optimization problems.

Type of Problem	Level of Difficulty to Solve on a Computer
Linear Optimization Problem	Very Easy
Convex Minimization Problem	Relatively Easy
Concave Maximization Problem	Relatively Easy
General Nonlinear Problem	Difficult

Case 2: The objective is to maximize a concave function, and all constraints are linear constraints. In this case, because all linear functions are both convex and concave, then the problem satisfies all four criteria to be a concave maximization problem and so is relatively easy to solve.

Case 3: The problem is a linear optimization model, i.e., the objective function is a linear function, and all constraints are linear constraints. In this case, if the objective is minimization, the problem is a convex minimization problem, because all functions involved are both convex and concave functions. If, instead, the objective is maximization, the problem is a concave maximization problem, because all functions involved are both convex and concave functions. Either way, the problem is easy to solve.

Finally, it turns out that all three of the examples of this chapter (namely, Example 8.1, Example 8.2, and Example 8.3) are either convex minimization problems or concave maximization problems, and so all three examples are easy to solve on a computer.

8.7   CASE MODULES

ENDURANCE INVESTORS

Endurance Private Client Fund (EPCF)

Endurance Investors is a private asset management firm started five years ago by nine founding partners: four graduates of MIT's Sloan School of Management and five graduates of Harvard Business School. Endurance's early clients were predominantly institutional investors such as universities, employee pension funds, and endowments of charitable organizations. As the firm grew, the partners developed different funds to meet the demands of an expanding client base. Two years ago, Endurance added three different types of fixed-income securities funds. Last quarter, in order to meet the needs of a small but growing list of wealthy private clients, Endurance introduced a blue-chip fund called the Endurance Private Client Fund (EPCF).

The strategy for the Endurance Private Client Fund (EPCF) is to give private investors a pure play in a portfolio of the largest leading American companies with a manageable level of risk. EPCF is a portfolio consisting of stock investments in five specially selected blue chip companies (Boeing, Exxon, General Motors, McDonald's, and Procter & Gamble) plus a market index fund, the Standard & Poor's 500 Index fund. The fraction of the portfolio invested in each of these six assets was selected last quarter based on a portfolio optimization model that maximizes the annual expected return of the portfolio for a given allowable level of investment risk.

Asset Portfolios, Expected Return, and Standard Deviation

Given n potential assets (which in the case of EPCF are the $n = 6$ assets of stock in Boeing, Exxon, General Motors, McDonald's, Procter & Gamble, and the Standard & Poor's 500 Index fund), an asset **portfolio** is created by assigning a fractional amount of each investment dollar to invest in each of the n assets. For the Endurance Private Client Fund (EPCF), for example, a portfolio might consist of investing the fractional amounts in each of the six assets according to Table 8.10 below. For the portfolio described in Table 8.10, 10% of every investment dollar is invested in Boeing, 20% of every investment dollar is invested in Exxon, etc. Notice that the portfolio fractions, which are also referred to as the **portfolio weights,** sum to one.

Let us denote the portfolio weight for asset i by the variable X_i for $i = 1, \ldots, n$. Then these weights must satisfy:

$$\sum_{i=1}^{n} X_i = 1.0,$$

that is, the portfolio fractions sum to one. Also, in most typical applications, the portfolio fractions must be nonnegative, that is,

$$X_1 \geq 0, X_2 \geq 0, \ldots, X_n \geq 0.$$

In a typical portfolio setting, the portfolio manager aims to maximize the annual return of the portfolio, while keeping the risk to a minimum. The "return" of the portfolio is the expected annual return of the portfolio. In order to measure the expected return of the portfolio, we need to have data on the expected annual rate of return on each asset in the portfolio. Table 8.11 shows Endurance's newly revised estimates of the annual expected return (in % per year) and the standard deviation of the annual return (in %

TABLE 8.10

Example of a portfolio composition of the assets of the Endurance Private Client Fund.

Asset	Boeing	Exxon	General Motors	McDonald's	Procter & Gamble	S&P500
Asset Ticker	BA	XON	GM	MCD	PG	SP
Fraction of Portfolio	0.10	0.20	0.25	0.05	0.15	0.25

TABLE 8.11

Newly revised estimates of annual expected return and standard deviation of assets.

Asset	Ticker	Expected Return (% per year)	Standard Deviation of Return (% per year)
Boeing	BA	12.69604	19.05455
Exxon	XON	9.92170	12.03149
General Motors	GM	11.80725	24.79470
McDonald's	MCD	13.54907	21.69084
Procter &Gamble	PG	13.45906	21.80891
S&P 500	SP	13.04295	11.71033

per year) of the six assets for the coming year. The numbers in Table 8.11 have been developed by using a combination of relevant market data bases, basic statistical analysis, professional judgment, and market intuition by the partners at Endurance. Consider the data for Boeing in Table 8.11. Let B denote the annual rate of return on stock invested in Boeing in the coming year. Then B is a random variable, and the expected value of B is 12.69604% per year. The standard deviation of B is 19.05455% per year.

Suppose that the EPCF portfolio is comprised of the fractional weights shown in Table 8.10. Then the expected annual return of the portfolio can be computed as follows:

$$(0.10)(12.69604) + (0.20)(9.92170) + (0.25)(11.80725)$$
$$+ (0.05)(13.54907) + (0.15)(13.45906) + (0.25)(13.04295) = 12.1628\%.$$

This computation is valid because of the rule: "The expected value of the weighted sum of random variables is the weighted sum of the expected values of the random variables." More generally, if the expected annual return on asset i is μ_i and the portfolio weight on asset i is X_i for $i = 1, \ldots, n$, then the formula for the expected annual return μ of the portfolio is given by:

$$\mu = \sum_{i=1}^{n} \mu_i X_i.$$

As stated earlier, a portfolio manager aims to maximize the expected annual return of the portfolio, while keeping the risk to a minimum. The "risk" of the portfolio is usually measured as the standard deviation of the portfolio. In order to compute the standard deviation of the portfolio, we need to have data on the standard deviation of the annual return of each asset in the portfolio, as well as data on the correlation between the rates of return of the different assets comprising the portfolio. For the Endurance Private Client Fund, the newly revised estimates of the standard deviations of the annual returns of each asset are shown in the fourth column of Table 8.11. For example, the standard deviation of the annual return on stock invested in Boeing is 19.05455%. Table 8.12 contains the newly revised estimates of the correlations between the rates of return of the different assets. Like the numbers in Table 8.11, the numbers in Table 8.12 have also been developed by using a combination of relevant market data bases, basic statistical analysis, professional judgment, and market intuition by the partners at Endurance.

To illustrate the meaning of Table 8.12, let B denote the annual rate of return on stock invested in Boeing in the coming year and let G denote the annual rate of return on stock invested in General Motors in the coming year. Then B and G are both random variables. The quantity CORR(B, G) is the correlation of the two random variables B and G. According to Table 8.12, Endurance's newly revised estimate of CORR(B, G) is CORR(B, G) = 0.21902.

In general, if the correlation matrix of the rate of return of asset i and asset j is given by CORR(i, j) for $i = 1, \ldots, n$ and $j = 1, \ldots, n$, and if the standard deviation

TABLE 8.12

Newly revised estimates of the correlations between annual returns of assets.

	BA	XON	GM	MCD	PG	SP
BA	1.00000	0.20559	0.21902	0.43523	0.25849	0.49609
XON	0.20559	1.00000	0.11522	0.30249	0.21095	0.56073
GM	0.21902	0.11522	1.00000	0.32526	−0.17682	0.36528
MCD	0.43523	0.30249	0.32526	1.00000	0.14953	0.59082
PG	0.25849	0.21095	−0.17682	0.14953	1.00000	0.55053
SP	0.49609	0.56073	0.36528	0.59082	0.55053	1.00000

of the rate of return of asset i is given by σ_i for $i = 1, \ldots, n$, and if the portfolio weights are given by X_i for $i = 1, \ldots, n$, then the formula for the variance of the portfolio σ^2 is given by:

$$\sigma^2 = \sum_{i=1}^{n}\sum_{j=1}^{n}\sigma_i\sigma_j\mathrm{CORR}(i, j) \cdot X_i \cdot X_j.$$

Therefore, the standard deviation σ of the portfolio is:

$$\sigma = \sqrt{\sum_{i=1}^{n}\sum_{j=1}^{n}\sigma_i\sigma_j\mathrm{CORR}(i, j) \cdot X_i \cdot X_j}.$$

To illustrate the preceding formulas for the variance and the standard deviation of a portfolio of assets, suppose that the EPCF portfolio is comprised of the fractional weights shown in Table 8.10. Then the variance of the portfolio is computed by summing up all of the numbers in the "correlation table" (Table 8.12) for each of the pairs of assets multiplied by their standard deviations and by their corresponding portfolio weights. For the portfolio weights given in Table 8.10, the variance of the portfolio is given by summing up the 36 terms (one term for each entry of the correlation table of Table 8.12) as follows:

$$\begin{aligned}\sigma^2 = \ &(1.00)(19.05455)(19.05455)(0.10)(0.10)\\ &+(0.20559)(12.03149)(19.05455)(0.10)(0.20)\\ &+\cdots\\ &+(0.55053)(21.80891)(11.71033)(0.25)(0.15)\\ &+(1.00)(11.71033)(11.71033)(0.25)(0.25)\\ =\ &127.963\%^2.\end{aligned}$$

Therefore the standard deviation of the portfolio is:

$$\sigma = \sqrt{127.963} = 11.312\%.$$

The Portfolio Optimization Model for the Endurance Private Client Fund

The portfolio optimization model for the Endurance Private Client Fund (EPCF) was created last quarter by Brian Jackson (who had joined Endurance after working for several years for another asset management firm) in order to compute the optimal portfolio weights for the newly created EPCF portfolio. Brian's model is shown below:

$$\text{maximize} \quad \mu = \sum_{i=1}^{n}\mu_i \cdot X_i.$$

subject to:

$$\text{Fractions:} \quad \sum_{i=1}^{n}X_i = 1$$

$$\text{Stand. dev.:} \quad \sqrt{\sum_{i=1}^{n}\sum_{j=1}^{n}\sigma_i\sigma_j\mathrm{CORR}(i, j) \cdot X_i \cdot X_j} \leq 13.0$$

Max single: $X_i \leq 0.30$ for i = BA, XON, GM, MCD, PG, SP
Nonnegativity: $X_i \geq 0$ for i = BA, XON, GM, MCD, PG, SP.

The objective function is to maximize the expected return of the portfolio. The first constraint states that the fractions of the EPCF investment dollar invested in each of the six assets must sum to one. The second constraint states that the maximum allowable standard deviation of the portfolio must be less than or equal to the pre-specified target allowable standard deviation. This pre-specified standard deviation was set to TARGET = 13.0% last quarter. The fourth set of constraints disallows investing negative amounts in any of the portfolio assets (that is, no short selling is allowed).

The third set of constraints are called the "max single" constraints. These constraints were added to ensure that no more than 30% of the portfolio's funds was invested in any one of the six assets. Brian added these constraints in order to force the diversification of the portfolio. In their collective experience with portfolio management, Brian and the other fund managers have seen benefits from a marketing perspective in offering investors the maximum level of diversity in trying to achieve the mutual fund's objectives.

Guided by the output of the portfolio optimization model, the EPCF fund managers had chosen the portfolio weights for the EPCF portfolio at the start of last quarter. These initial portfolio weights are shown below in the third row of Table 8.13. As a result of changes in stock prices during the quarter, the fractions of the portfolio invested in each of the six assets changed during the quarter. At the end of the quarter, these portfolio fractions are now those shown in the fourth row of Table 8.13.

Brian Jackson's Problem

It is now the start of the new quarter, and Brian Jackson is working on the problem of revising the optimal portfolio weights for the EPCF portfolio based on the revised data estimates on asset performance. Brian has just put together the newly revised data on asset performance: the updated estimates of the expected rates of returns and the updated estimates of the standard deviation of the rates of return for the six assets (Table 8.11), and the updated estimates of the correlations between the rates of the return of the assets (Table 8.12). Brian has placed all of these new data tables in his spreadsheet portfolio optimization model, which is the worksheet ENDURANCE.XLS. However, as Brian has been working on this problem, he has realized that the model is incomplete in two ways that are explained as follows.

The first way that the portfolio model is incomplete has to do with the real costs of transactions related to changing the composition of the portfolio. Even with economies of scale and the use of discount brokers, the cost of buying and selling stocks for the EPCF portfolio is not trivial and is 0.5% of the dollar value of all stock transactions.

To see how transaction costs might affect the value of the EPCF portfolio, suppose for the sake of argument that the Endurance Private Client Fund has exactly $K = \$1,000,000$ in total assets invested only in Boeing and Exxon, as follows: 30% of the EPCF portfolio currently comprises stock in Boeing, and 70% of the EPCF portfolio currently comprises stock in Exxon. Suppose that Endurance is considering changing these values next quarter to new fractions X_1 and X_2 invested in Boeing and Exxon. Then the total amount of the transaction would be:

$$K \cdot (\, |X_1 - 0.30| + |X_2 - 0.70| \,)$$

TABLE 8.13

Asset fractions of the EPCF portfolio.

Asset	Boeing	Exxon	General Motors	McDonald's	Procter & Gamble	S&P500
Asset Ticker	BA	XON	GM	MCD	PG	SP
Initial Fraction of Portfolio	0.19	0.18	0.23	0.07	0.13	0.20
Ending Fraction of Portfolio	0.21	0.16	0.21	0.09	0.09	0.24

(where $|x|$ is the absolute value of the quantity x). The transaction costs associated with this transaction would then be

$$0.005 \cdot K \cdot (|X_1 - 0.30| + |X_2 - 0.70|).$$

Without accounting for transaction costs, the expected return of the new portfolio would be:

$$\mu = 12.69604 \cdot X_1 + 9.92170 \cdot X_2,$$

expressed as a percentage, where the expected return numbers are as shown in Table 8.11. In order to account for transaction costs, we need to subtract 0.5% of the total transactions from the above expression. Therefore the expected return of the portfolio (expressed as a percentage), after accounting for transaction costs, is:

$$\mu = 12.69604 \cdot X_1 + 9.92170 \cdot X_2 - 0.5 \cdot (|X_1 - 0.30| + |X_2 - 0.70|).$$

(The reason why we use "0.5" rather than "0.005" in the above expression is because the units of the expected return are expressed as a percentage.)

The second way that the portfolio model is incomplete has to do with limitations on the extent to which the portfolio weights might be allowed to change. For the coming quarter, Brian Jackson obviously wants the optimization model to determine new portfolio weights so as to optimize the expected return of the portfolio, given the new data in Table 8.11 and Table 8.12. However, Brian would rather not change these portfolio weights too dramatically from their current values in the last row of Table 8.13. The reason for this is that he is concerned that a large change in the composition of the EPCF portfolio might be viewed by some of the private clients as an indication that the fund managers do not have a sound investment strategy for the fund. In order to guard against this possibility, Brian has decided to include constraints in the model that will limit the absolute change in any of the portfolio weights to $\pm 15\%$ from their current value. For example, the current portfolio weight of Boeing stock is 21% of the portfolio, according to Table 8.13. For next quarter, Brian wants to limit the range of the portfolio weight in Boeing stock to be in the range from $(21 - 15)\%$ to $(21 + 15)\%$, that is, from 6% to 36% of the portfolio.

Assignment:
Part I

The data and the portfolio model for the Endurance Private Client Fund is contained in the spreadsheet ENDURANCE.XLS. This spreadsheet contains the new expected returns, standard deviations, and correlations for the coming quarter. However, other than the new data, the spreadsheet's optimization model itself is the old optimization model from the last quarter. Therefore, it does not contain any transaction costs, and it does not account for the new constraints that the maximum change in any asset's portfolio weight should be $\pm 15\%$ from its current value.

(a) (For this question, ignore the issue of transaction costs and the issue of the maximum change in the portfolio's weights.) One current policy at Endurance Investors is that the standard deviation of the Endurance Private Client Fund (EPCF) should be no greater than 13%. Another policy is that the percentage holding of any one asset in the fund should be no greater than 30% of the fund. Use the Solver X to maximize the expected annual return of the fund, subject to these two policy constraints.

(b) What are the optimal portfolio weights for next quarter? What is the expected annual return of the portfolio?

(c) Examine the shadow prices on all of the constraints. What do they tell you about the solution?

(d) Construct the **efficient frontier** of the portfolio. In order to do so, you will need to run the model for a variety of different values of the right-hand-side (RHS) of the standard deviation constraint. Plot the standard deviation as the independent variable (on the horizontal axis) and the maximized expected annual return as the dependent variable (on the vertical axis).

Part II

(e) Modify the model to incorporate the effects of transaction costs (at a cost of 0.5% of the transactions for both purchases and sales) and to incorporate the constraints that the maximum change in any asset's portfolio weight from the previous quarter should be ±15%.

(f) What are the optimal portfolio weights for next quarter? What is the expected annual return of the portfolio? How do these numbers differ from your answers in Question (b)?

(g) Examine the shadow prices on all of the constraints. What do they tell you about the solution? Again, how do the shadow prices differ from those in Question (c)?

(h) Create the **efficient frontier** of the portfolio. As before, run the model for a variety of different values of the right-hand-side (RHS) of the standard deviation constraint. Plot the standard deviation as the independent variable (on the horizontal axis) and the maximized expected annual return as the dependent variable (on the vertical axis).

(i) How is the efficient frontier different from your answer to Question (d)?

(k) Based on the model, what portfolio weights would you recommend for the Endurance Private Client Fund?

CAPACITY INVESTMENT, MARKETING, AND PRODUCTION AT ILG, INC.

Mr. Nelson Stein is the Chief Executive Officer of ILG, Inc., an engineering company that he founded almost a decade ago. ILG was an early player in the market for network routers and over the years ILG has acquired a well-deserved reputation for developing innovative networking products and bringing these products to the market very quickly and profitably. However, owing in part to its own success, the market for network routers and related technology is now quite competitive.

ILG has recently developed a new product, tentatively called the "Speed-demon" by the marketing department, that is able to speed up its network routers by a factor of ten or more. Nelson Stein felt that in order to be successful with Speed-demon, ILG would need to take care to coordinate capital planning, manufacturing, and marketing strategy for the new product. He therefore convened a meeting with Jonathan Barr, vice president of manufacturing at ILG; Jenny Thompson, vice president of marketing at ILG; Richard Bradley, chief financial officer at ILG; and Bill Zender, a member of Nelson Stein's staff who is also a recent business school graduate.

In the meeting, Nelson Stein first asked Jonathan Barr about cost estimates for building production capacity for Speed-demon. Jonathan Barr reported that since the technology required to produce Speed-demon is brand new, none of ILG's current production capacity could be used to produce the product. Using cost data from several of ILG's previous new capacity construction projects as the basis for a nonlinear regression model to forecast cost and capacity, Jonathan Barr's staff has estimated the cost of new capacity as follows: If x_1 is the amount of money (in dollars) invested in new capacity to produce Speed-demon in the first year, then the annual production capacity for the first year is estimated to be

$$c_1 = \frac{x_1}{200} + \sqrt{x_1}.$$

For example, if the company were to invest $x_1 = \$1,000,000$ in the first year on new capacity for Speed-demon, then the company would have the capacity to produce up to

$$\frac{1,000,000}{200} + \sqrt{1,000,000} = 6,000 \text{ units per year.}$$

Jonathan Barr expected that the cost of the required production technology will decrease over time, and thus it will be less expensive to expand capacity for Speed-demon in the following year. Jonathan Barr's staff has estimated that in year two, the same amount of investment would lead to 30% more capacity than in year 1. For example, if the company were to spend $x_2 = \$1,000,000$ at the beginning of the second year, then the production capacity added in the second year would be $7,800 = 1.30 \times 6,000$ units per year. Nelson Stein asked Jonathan how confident he felt about these cost/capacity estimates. Jonathan responded that he was confident overall, but that there was the most uncertainty about the 30% increase that he quoted for the second year. He explained that this number could vary between 20% and 35%.

Jenny Thompson then reported on the marketing analysis for Speed-demon. She estimated that there would be a demand for 4,000 units in the first year of production, even if ILG were not to expend any money on marketing promotions for the new product. She also added that her staff had estimated that every additional $400 spent on promotions for Speed-demon at the beginning of the first year would increase the demand by one unit. Regarding the second year of the product's life, she estimated that even if no money is spent on promotions at the beginning of the second year, the demand during the second year would be 75% of the demand during the first year. She also felt that a promotion strategy in the second year would be more cost-effective, as the new product would have already achieved some acceptance in the market. Her staff estimated that every $300 spent on promotions of the product at the beginning of the second year would lead to an incremental demand of one unit. Once again, Nelson Stein asked Jenny Thompson how confident she was in her staff's analysis. Jenny Thompson responded that she was most uncertain about the 75% number. This was her staff's best estimate, but she felt that the number could be as low as 60% or as high as 90%.

Richard Bradley then presented his estimates of profit margins. The finance group estimated that variable profit (that is, revenue minus variable production costs) for the first year would be $800 per unit sold. This number did not account for capacity investment costs or the cost of marketing promotions. The variable profit for the second year would be $850 per unit sold (again not including any additional investment cost in capacity or in marketing promotions). Due to the rapid changes in the market, everyone at the meeting understood that units produced during the first year would not have any sale value in the second year of the product life-cycle.

Nelson Stein decided that given the overall strategy of ILG, he was prepared to commit up to $2 million in capital to finance capacity construction/expansion and product promotion for Speed-demon. He also added that profits from units sold during the first year, as well as unspent funds from the first year, could be used to finance capacity expansion and product promotion for the second year. As he left the meeting, Nelson Stein instructed Bill Zender to prepare a recommendation for a spending and production plan for capacity investment, promotions expenditures, and production of Speed-demon. Nelson Stein's parting words were "By the way, Bill, can you email your recommendation to me by tomorrow morning?"

Assignment:

(a) Suppose you are Bill Zender. Formulate the problem of coordinating ILG's capacity investment, marketing, and production strategy for Speed-demon over the next two years as a nonlinear optimization model. Construct your model in a spreadsheet and solve for the optimal solution.

(b) On two occasions in the meeting, Nelson Stein asked Jonathan Barr and Jenny Thompson how certain they were about their numbers. Bill Zender is certain that Nelson would like to know the effect on the overall Speed-demon strategy of changes in the 30% number that Jonathan Barr reported. Replace the 30% value in your model with values in the range from 20% to 35% and re-solve your model. How do changes in this number affect the overall Speed-demon strategy?

(c) Bill Zender is certain that Nelson would like to know the effect on the overall Speed-demon strategy of changes in the 75% number that Jenny Thompson reported. Replace the 75% value in your model with values in the range from 60% to 90% and re-solve your model. How do changes in this number affect the overall Speed-demon strategy?

(d) What is your recommendation for a spending and production plan for capacity investment, promotions expenditures, and production of Speed-demon?

8.8   EXERCISES

EXERCISE 8.1

(a) In what ways is a nonlinear optimization model similar to a linear optimization model?

(b) What are the chief differences between a nonlinear optimization model and a linear optimization model?

(c) How do these differences affect the ability to solve a nonlinear optimization model on a computer?

EXERCISE 8.2 Consider the following nonlinear optimization problem:

$$\text{minimize} \quad f(x) = 25 - 76x + 61x^2 - 17x^3 + 1.94x^4 - \frac{1}{13}x^5$$

subject to:

$$x \le 10$$
$$x \ge 0.$$

Plot the objective function over the range of feasible values of x, namely $x \ge 0$ and $x \le 10$. Which values of x are local minima of $f(x)$? Which values of x are global minima of $f(x)$? Which values of x are local maxima of $f(x)$? Which values of x are global maxima of $f(x)$?

EXERCISE 8.3 A small manufacturing company has purchased a new machine to manufacture its product. The company estimates that the revenues from using this machine for t years is given by the formula:

$$\text{Revenue} = 4.0(1.0 - 0.75^t),$$

where the units are in millions of dollars. For example, if the machine is used for $t = 4.0$ years, the revenue would be:

$$\text{Revenue} = 4.0(1.0 - 0.75^4) = \$2.73 \text{ million.}$$

If the company stops using the machine, they can sell the machine for its salvage value. The company estimates that if they sell the machine after t years of use, the machine's salvage value would be

$$\text{Salvage value} = \frac{1.0}{1.0 + t},$$

where again the units are in millions of dollars. For example, if the machine is sold after $t = 4.0$ years, the salvage value would be:

$$\text{Salvage value} = \frac{1.0}{1.0 + 4.0} = \$0.20 \text{ million.}$$

What is the optimal time for the company to sell the machine?

EXERCISE 8.4 Consider the following nonlinear optimization problem:

$$\text{minimize} \quad f(x) = 0.5 + 47x - 31x^2 + 7.5x^3 - 0.77x^4 + \frac{1}{35}x^5$$

subject to:
$$x \leq 10$$
$$x \geq 0.$$

Plot the objective function over the range of feasible values of x, namely $x \geq 0$ and $x \leq 10$. Which values of x are local maxima of $f(x)$? Which values of x are global maxima of $f(x)$? Which values of x are local minima of $f(x)$? Which values of x are global minima of $f(x)$?

EXERCISE 8.5 Consider again the Magnetron Company production planning problem described in Exercise 7.2 of Chapter 7. In Exercise 7.2, it was assumed that the prices of full-size and compact microwave ovens are set so that the resulting unit contributions to earnings are $120 and $130 per oven for full-size and compact microwave ovens, respectively. As it turns out, the unit earnings contribution of $120 per oven for full-size ovens derives from the fact that Magnetron has set the price of a full-size oven to be $270, and the variable production cost of a full-size oven is $150 (and so the unit contribution to earnings is $120 = $270 − $150). Also, the unit earnings contribution of $130 per oven for compact ovens derives from the fact that Magnetron has set the price of a compact oven to be $230, and the variable production cost of a compact oven is $100 (and so the unit contribution to earnings is $130 = $230 − $100). As a next step in the marketing/production planning process, the company would like to determine the optimal combination of prices and production levels to maximize the overall contribution to earnings.

The changes in the prices of ovens will result in changes in demand. Suppose that Magnetron has estimated that the demand for their ovens is related to the prices they set as follows:

$$D_F = 490 - P_F,$$
$$D_C = 640 - 2P_C,$$

where D_F and D_C are the demands for full-size and compact ovens, and P_F and P_C are the respective prices set by Magnetron for full-size and compact ovens.

(a) Modify your model of the Magnetron production planning problem by introducing two new decision variables, P_F and P_C, and making corresponding changes to the demand constraints. Your new model should be:

$$\text{maximize} \quad F(P_F - 150) + C(P_C - 100)$$

subject to:

General:	$2F + C \leq 500$	
Electronic:	$2F + 3C \leq 800$	
Full-size demand:	$F \leq 490 - P_F$	
Compact demand:	$C \leq 640 - 2P_C$	
Nonnegativity:	$F, C, P_F, P_C \geq 0.$	

Verify that when $P_F = 270$ and $P_C = 230$, the demands are as specified in the linear model.

(b) Solve the nonlinear optimization model of part (a) to determine the optimal pricing and production strategy. What is the optimal strategy? What is the optimized contribution to earnings? Is the optimized contribution to earnings greater or lesser than that in the linear model? What actions would you recommend to the management of Magnetron?

EXERCISE 8.6 Health & Comfort, Incorporated (H&C) specializes in the production of hypoallergenic pillow and mattress covers for asthma and allergy sufferers. The covers are made out of a unique protective fabric. The manufacturing process consists mainly of two operations: cutting and sewing, which are performed by two separate departments. Table 8.14 shows the resource utilization and weekly resource availability for this problem.

H&C is one of the largest producers of hypoallergenic bedding, and it controls a large share of the market. As a consequence, the production level of each product at H&C influences the market price of the product, which in turn influences their unit earnings contributions. Econometric research indicates that this dependence can be represented as

$$E_P = 506 - 0.75P$$

for pillow covers, and

$$E_M = 653.5 - M$$

TABLE 8.14

Resource utilization and weekly resource availability at H&C.

	Pillow Cover	Mattress Cover	Availability per Week
Fabric (square feet)	8.75	60.5	40,000
Cutting (hours)	0.1	0.2	150
Sewing (hours)	0.4	0.3	500

for mattress covers (here P and M are the production levels of pillow and mattress covers at H&C, and E_P and E_M are the corresponding unit contributions to earnings in dollars per unit). H&C is seeking to maximize its earnings by selecting appropriate production levels of its products.

(a) Formulate a nonlinear optimization model of production for H&C in terms of the variables P,M,E_P, and E_M. (Note: Your model should have linear constraints and a nonlinear objective function.)

(b) Solve the model on the computer. What are the optimal production levels?

EXERCISE 8.7 An investor is considering allocating fractions of her investment dollars in common stock in four different companies for the next year: IBM, AT&T, General Motors (GM), and General Electric (GE). Based on statistical analysis of the market data, she has estimated the expected annual returns, as well as standard deviations and correlations of these annual returns. The results of her analysis are summarized in Table 8.15.

Answer the following questions by considering appropriate nonlinear portfolio optimization models.

(a) Suppose that the target expected return of the portfolio is 20%. What is the minimum standard deviation of the investor's portfolio? What is the optimal asset allocation?

(b) Suppose that the target standard deviation of the portfolio is 13%. What is the maximum expected return on the investor's portfolio? What is the optimal asset allocation?

(c) Using one of the models in (a) or (b), compute and plot the efficient frontier of this four-stock portfolio.

EXERCISE 8.8 A portfolio manager is designing a portfolio of stocks in three companies: Exxon (XON), Microsoft (MSFT), Oracle Systems (ORCL), plus the S&P500 index. Table 8.16 summarizes the manager's estimates of the expected annual returns, standard deviations, and correlations of the annual returns of the three companies' stocks plus the S&P500 index.

TABLE 8.15

Annual expected returns, standard deviations, and correlations for stocks of four companies.

Company	Expected Annual Return (%)	Standard Deviation of Annual Return (%)	Correlation IBM	AT&T	GM	GE
IBM	17.85	30.53				
AT&T	12.70	19.47	−0.035			
GM	19.33	27.07	0.182	0.104		
GE	22.99	15.00	0.124	0.305	0.396	

TABLE 8.16

Annual expected returns, standard deviations, and correlations for stocks in three companies plus the S&P500 index.

Company	Expected Annual Return (%)	Standard Deviation of Annual Return (%)	Correlation XON	MSFT	ORCL	S&P500
XON	14.67	12.17				
MSFT	33.20	24.47	0.158			
ORCL	59.36	37.72	0.078	0.241		
S&P500	11.91	8.66	0.579	0.302	0.282	

Answer the following questions by considering appropriate nonlinear portfolio optimization models.

(a) Suppose that the target expected annual return of the portfolio is 30%. What is the minimum standard deviation of the manager's portfolio? What is the optimal asset allocation?

(b) Suppose that the target standard deviation of the portfolio is 10%. What is the maximum expected return of the manager's portfolio? What is the optimal asset allocation?

(c) Using one of the models in (a) or (b), compute and plot the efficient frontier of this portfolio.

EXERCISE 8.9 John Brooks, managing director of the CYCOM Corporation, is trying to determine how to allocate CYCOM's research and development budget for the coming year. Six different projects are under consideration. John believes that the success of each and every project depends in part on the number of engineers assigned to the project. Let $x_1, \ldots, x_6$ denote the number of engineers assigned to projects $1, \ldots, 6$. According to internal corporate estimates, the probability that each project will be successful is given according to the function in the third column of Table 8.17. For example, according to Table 8.17, the probability that project 3 will be successful is

$$p_3 = \frac{x_3}{x_3 + 2.5}.$$

If John were to assign $x_3 = 5$ engineers to project 3, then the probability of success of the project would be:

$$p_3 = \frac{5}{5 + 2.5} = 0.667.$$

Table 8.17 also shows the start-up cost of each project and the estimated profit of each project if it is successful.

Cycom can assign up to 25 engineers to these six projects. The cost of an engineer is $150,000 (per year). An engineer can be assigned to more than one project. For example, $x_2 = 3.4$ means that 3.4 engineers are assigned to project 2, which means that 3 engineers are assigned to this project full-time and one engineer is assigned to this project only 40% of the time.

TABLE 8.17

The start-up cost of each project, the probability of success of each project, and the estimated profit of each project.

Project Number	Start-up Cost (in $1,000)	Probability of Success	Profit if successful (in $1,000)
1	$325	$\dfrac{x_1}{x_1 + 1.1}$	$1,750
2	$200	$\dfrac{x_2}{x_2 + 0.5}$	$700
3	$490	$\dfrac{x_3}{x_3 + 2.5}$	$1,300
4	$125	$\dfrac{x_4}{x_4 + 1.6}$	$800
5	$710	$\dfrac{x_5}{x_5 + 2.2}$	$1,450
6	$240	$\dfrac{x_6}{x_6 + 2.4}$	$1,300

If a project is unsuccessful, it incurs its full start-up cost, shown in the second column of Table 8.17. If the project is successful, it realizes the profit value shown in the fourth column of Table 8.17. This value includes the start-up cost of the project (but does not include the cost of engineers). Thus, for example, if project 1 is unsuccessful, it incurs a cost of $325,000. If project 1 is successful, it realizes a profit of $1,750,000.

(a) Construct and solve a nonlinear optimization model to determine the number of engineers to assign to each project that will maximize the expected contribution to profit of the six projects minus the cost of assigning engineers to the projects. What is the optimal solution?

(b) Construct and solve an optimization model that minimizes the standard deviation of the contribution to profit subject to the constraint that the expected contribution to profit (minus the cost of engineers) is at least $1.1 million. What is the optimal solution?

EXERCISE 8.10 Gerhard Kohl is the marketing manager of a large automobile dealership in the Cleveland metropolitan area. Gerhard would like to decide how to allocate his advertising budget of $1,500,000 for the coming month among the following four advertising options: late night television advertising (Option 1), prime time television advertising (Option 2), radio advertising (Option 3), and newspaper advertising (Option 4). Gerhard's market analysts have arrived at the following formulas to estimate the demand $d_1, \ldots, d_4$ for automobiles generated by each of the four options (in units per month) as a function of the advertising expenditures $x_1, \ldots, x_4$ of each option (in dollars), as follows:

$$d_1 = \frac{x_1}{500} + 3.0(x_1)^{0.5},$$

$$d_2 = \frac{x_2}{400} + 0.5(x_2)^{0.6},$$

$$d_3 = \frac{x_3}{600} + 0.2(x_3)^{0.7},$$

$$d_4 = \frac{x_4}{500} + 0.1(x_4)^{0.8}.$$

For example, if Gerhard were to spend $x_1 = $300,000 on late night television advertising, the demand generated by this advertising is estimated to be:

$$d_1 = \frac{300,000}{500} + 3.0(300,000)^{0.5} = 2,243 \text{ automobiles.}$$

Gerhard would like to determine how much money to allocate to each of the four options in order to maximize the total demand generated. Due to prior contractual commitments, he must spend at least $700,000 on television advertising (the first two options). Furthermore, it is the policy of the dealership to spend at least 10% more on newspaper advertising (option 4) than on radio advertising (option 3). Construct and solve a nonlinear optimization model of Gerhard's problem. What is the optimal allocation of the advertising budget? What are the binding constraints?

EXERCISE 8.11 Recall Example 8.3, which is concerned with the optimal location of a firm's new distribution center relative to four sales centers located in Amherst (A), Bowdoin (B), Colby (C), and Dartmouth (D). Figure 8.1 shows the location of the four sales centers, and the (x, y)-coordinates of each of the four sales centers is shown in Table 8.5. Now suppose that instead of locating the new distribution center to minimize the total travel costs, we instead are interested in minimizing the maximum travel distance to any one of the four sales centers. Then the resulting nonlinear optimization model is:

$$\text{minimize} \quad \max \left\{ \begin{array}{ll} \sqrt{(x-8)^2 + (y-2)^2}, & \sqrt{(x-3)^2 + (y-10)^2}, \\ \sqrt{(x-8)^2 + (y-15)^2}, & \sqrt{(x-14)^2 + (y-13)^2} \end{array} \right\}$$

(a) Solve this nonlinear optimization model on the computer. What is the optimal location of the distribution center?

(b) Now suppose that the location of the distribution center is constrained to lie in the four-sided region shown in Figure 8.2. Include the four constraints describing this region in your model and re-solve your model for the optimal location of the distribution center. Where should the distribution center be located?

Discrete Optimization

CONTENTS

IN MANY MANAGERIAL APPLICATIONS OF OPTIMIZATION MODELS, RANGING FROM personnel scheduling to capital budgeting, the decision variables are required to be assigned values that are whole numbers. An optimization model whose decision variables are required to be whole numbers is called a **discrete optimization model.** Discrete optimization is a very powerful modeling framework that provides great flexibility for expressing managerial problems as optimization models. However, discrete optimization problems vary in the degree of difficulty required in order to be solved on the computer, depending on certain characteristics of the particular problem at hand. In this chapter, we present the fundamental notions relevant for the managerial use of discrete optimization models. We begin by presenting several examples of discrete optimization that arise in practice. We then develop insight into the important differences between linear optimization and discrete optimization by examining a simple discrete optimization model in two variables. We finally discuss spreadsheet solution methods for finding an optimal solution to a discrete optimization model.

FORMULATING A MANAGEMENT PROBLEM AS A DISCRETE OPTIMIZATION MODEL

In this section, we introduce the fundamentals of discrete optimization by considering three examples.

Example 9.1 – An Airplane Manufacturing Problem

The CRISP Corporation manufacturers four types of small airplanes: model AR1 (a one-seat plane), model AR2 (a two-seat plane), model AR4 (a four-seat plane), and model AR6 (a six-seat plane). The AR1 and AR2 are typically purchased by private pilots, whereas the AR4 and AR6 are typically purchased by corporations to augment their corporate fleets. In order to enhance safety, the Federal Aviation Administration (F.A.A.) regulates many aspects of small airplane manufacturing. Typical F.A.A. manufacturing regulations and inspections are based on a monthly schedule, and as a result small airplane manufacturing is scheduled in monthly units. Table 9.1 shows the important manufacturing information for the airplanes at CRISP. The first row of Table 9.1 shows the maximum number of airplanes of each type that the F.A.A. has certified capacity for CRISP (in number of airplanes per month). The second row shows the time required to build each type of airplane (in days). The third row shows the number of production managers needed per airplane, and the last row shows the contribution to earnings from the production of each airplane.

The total number of production managers available next month is 60. CRISP's airplane manufacturing facility can simultaneously work on up to 9 airplanes at any given time. Therefore, the total number of manufacturing days available in the next month is 270 days (270 = 9 × 30 days per month).

Jonathan Kuring, head of manufacturing operations at CRISP, would like to determine the number of airplanes of each type to produce in the next month in order to maximize the contribution to earnings. Let us now formulate this problem as an optimization model. We will start by defining the following decision variables:

$$A_1 = \text{number of AR1 airplanes to produce next month,}$$
$$A_2 = \text{number of AR2 airplanes to produce next month,}$$
$$A_4 = \text{number of AR4 airplanes to produce next month,}$$
$$A_6 = \text{number of AR6 airplanes to produce next month.}$$

Notice that each of these decision variables must be a nonnegative whole number, that is, a number of the form 0, 1, 2, 3, ... This is because CRISP cannot manufacture a fractional quantity of an airplane in a month. There would be nothing wrong, for example, with assigning $A_1 = 7$, but it would be wrong to assign

TABLE 9.1

Production capacity, time to build, production managers needed, and contribution to earnings for the airplanes of CRISP Corporation.

	AR1	AR2	AR4	AR6
F.A.A. Maximum Production (airplanes per month)	8	17	11	15
Time to build (days)	4	7	9	11
Production managers needed per airplane	1	1	2	2
Contribution to earnings per airplane ($1,000)	62	84	103	125

$A_1 = 7.45$. Let us introduce a bit of notation: A nonnegative whole number is called an **integer.** The model of CRISP's production planning problem must therefore include the following restriction on the decision variables:

$$A_1, A_2, A_4, A_6 \text{ are integers.}$$

Then CRISP's production planning problem is easily seen to be:

maximize $62A_1 + 84A_2 + 103A_4 + 125A_6$

subject to:

Time to build:	$4A_1 + 7A_2 + 9A_4 + 11A_6 \leq 270$
Managers:	$A_1 + A_2 + 2A_4 + 2A_6 \leq 60$
AR1 capacity:	$A_1 \leq 8$
AR2 capacity:	$A_2 \leq 17$
AR4 capacity:	$A_4 \leq 11$
AR6 capacity:	$A_6 \leq 15$
Nonnegativity:	$A_1, A_2, A_4, A_6 \geq 0$
Integer requirement:	A_1, A_2, A_4, A_6 are integers.

Notice that this problem is quite similar to a linear optimization model, except for the requirement specified in the bottom row, which states that the decision variables must be integers.

Just as in the case of linear optimization modeling, it is possible to format this problem into a spreadsheet and to have the software compute the optimal solution to this problem. That is, the computer will compute those values of the variables A_1, A_2, A_4, and A_6 that will satisfy all of the constraints, the nonnegativity conditions, and the integer requirement, and will yield the maximum contribution to earnings in the process. If one solves the problem this way, the optimal production plan for CRISP is given by the assignment shown in Table 9.2.

Notice in Table 9.2 that the assigned values of the decision variables are indeed all integers. According to Table 9.2, the optimal production plan (that maximizes the contribution to earnings) is to produce 8 AR1 airplanes, 17 AR2 airplanes, 1 AR4 airplane, and 10 AR6 airplanes next month. The optimized contribution to earnings of this plan is:

$$\$3,277,000 = (62 \cdot 8 + 84 \cdot 17 + 103 \cdot 1 + 125 \cdot 10) \times 1,000.$$

The optimization problem for the CRISP production planning model is an example of an **integer optimization model,** which is defined as follows.

> An optimization model is called an **integer optimization model** if all of the decision variables are required to be integers (that is, nonnegative whole numbers), and all of the constraints and the objective function are linear functions.

TABLE 9.2

The optimal production plan for CRISP for next month.

Airplane Type	Decision Variable	Optimal Number to Produce Next Month
AR1	A_1	8
AR2	A_2	17
AR4	A_4	1
AR6	A_6	10

	Project 1	Project 2	Project 3	Project 4
Investment ($ million)	8	6	5	4
Anticipated Earnings ($ million)	12	8	7	6

An integer optimization model is also called by a variety of other names, including **integer program, integer optimization problem,** or **integer model.**

Example 9.2 – A Capital Budgeting Problem

Kearns & Associates is a medium-sized construction management firm. Jacob White, vice-president for planning at Kearns & Associates, is considering four possible capital projects for the firm to invest in during the coming year. Table 9.3 shows the investment required in each of the four projects as well as the anticipated earnings from each of the four projects over the next three years (net of the investment cost of each of the four projects).

Jacob has a budget of $15 million to spend on capital projects for the next year, and he would like to choose those projects that maximize the total anticipated earnings, subject to his capital budget constraint.

Let us now formulate this problem as an optimization model. Since Jacob must decide which of the four projects to choose for investment, we would like to have a decision variable for each of the four projects, and we would like that decision variable to represent either a "yes" or a "no" decision regarding the project. We will do this as follows. Let x_1 denote the decision variable that represents whether or not Project 1 is chosen and let us define x_1 as follows:

$$x_1 = \begin{cases} 1 & \text{if Project 1 is chosen,} \\ 0 & \text{if Project 1 is not chosen.} \end{cases}$$

That is, $x_1 = 1$ represents that Project 1 has been chosen, and $x_1 = 0$ represents that Project 1 has not been chosen. Let us now introduce a bit more notation. We will call a decision variable x a **binary** decision variable if x is required to be assigned only the values 0 or 1. Then the decision variable x_1 is a binary decision variable. Let us also define x_2, x_3, and x_4 similarly as follows:

$$x_2 = \begin{cases} 1 & \text{if Project 2 is chosen,} \\ 0 & \text{if Project 2 is not chosen.} \end{cases}$$

$$x_3 = \begin{cases} 1 & \text{if Project 3 is chosen,} \\ 0 & \text{if Project 3 is not chosen.} \end{cases}$$

$$x_4 = \begin{cases} 1 & \text{if Project 4 is chosen,} \\ 0 & \text{if Project 4 is not chosen.} \end{cases}$$

Then x_1, x_2, x_3, and x_4 are all binary decision variables. Jacob White's capital budgeting problem can now be formulated as the following optimization model:

$$\text{maximize} \quad 12x_1 + 8x_2 + 7x_3 + 6x_4$$

subject to:

$$\text{budget:} \quad 8x_1 + 6x_2 + 5x_3 + 4x_4 \leq 15$$

$$\text{binary:} \quad x_1, x_2, x_3, x_4 \text{ are binary.}$$

Notice that this problem is quite similar to a linear optimization model, except for the requirement specified in the bottom row, which states that the decision variables are required to be binary variables.

Just as in the case of linear optimization modeling, it is possible to format this problem into a spreadsheet and to have the software compute the optimal solution to this problem. That is, the computer will compute those values of the variables x_1, x_2, x_3, and x_4 that will satisfy all of the constraints and the binary variable requirements, and will yield the maximum anticipated earnings in the process. If one solves the problem this way, the optimal capital project selection at Kearns & Associates is given by the assignment shown in Table 9.4.

Notice in Table 9.4 that the assigned values of the decision variables are indeed all binary, that is, zeros and ones. According to Table 9.4, the optimal project choice (that maximizes the anticipated earnings) is to choose Project 2, Project 3, and Project 4. The optimized earnings of this choice is:

$$\$21 \text{ million} = 12 \cdot 0 + 8 \cdot 1 + 7 \cdot 1 + 6 \cdot 1.$$

The optimization model of the Kearns & Associates capital budgeting problem is an example of a **binary optimization model,** which is defined as follows.

An optimization model is called a **binary optimization model** if all of the decision variables are required to be binary (that is, zero or one), and all of the constraints and the objective function are linear functions.

A binary optimization model is also called a **0-1 integer optimization model.**

The use of binary decision variables can greatly expand the capability to model specific types of restrictions that can be used in an optimization model. For example, suppose that the capital budgeting problem that Jacob faces contains the following additional restrictions:

(a) The firm can only invest in at most two projects. This restriction can be formulated as the following optimization model constraint:

$$x_1 + x_2 + x_3 + x_4 \leq 2.$$

(b) If Project 4 is chosen, then Project 3 must also be chosen. This restriction can be formulated as the following constraint in the model:

$$x_3 - x_4 \geq 0.$$

TABLE 9.4

The optimal selection of capital projects at Kearns & Associates.

Decision Variable		Optimal Value
Project 1	x_1	0
Project 2	x_2	1
Project 3	x_3	1
Project 4	x_4	1

Note that if $x_4 = 1$, then this constraint forces $x_3 \geq 1$, and hence $x_3 = 1$.

(c) The firm cannot simultaneously invest in Project 1 and Project 3 due to legal restrictions. This restriction is modeled simply as:

$$x_1 + x_3 \leq 1.$$

Note that if $x_1 = 1$, then $x_3 \leq 0$ and so $x_3 = 0$.

If we add these constraints to the capital budgeting model, the new binary optimization model becomes:

$$
\begin{array}{rl}
\text{maximize} & 12x_1 + 8x_2 + 7x_3 + 6x_4 \\
\text{subject to:} & \\
\text{budget:} & 8x_1 + 6x_2 + 5x_3 + 4x_4 \leq 15 \\
\text{maximum of two:} & x_1 + x_2 + x_3 + x_4 \leq 2 \\
\text{projects 3 and 4:} & x_3 - x_4 \geq 0 \\
\text{projects 1 and 3:} & x_1 + x_3 \leq 1 \\
\text{binary:} & x_1, x_2, x_3, x_4 \text{ are binary.}
\end{array}
$$

Once again, it is possible to format this problem into a spreadsheet and to have the software compute the optimal solution to this problem. That is, the computer will compute those values of the variables x_1, x_2, x_3, and x_4 that will satisfy all of the constraints and the binary variable requirements and will yield the maximum anticipated earnings in the process. If one solves the problem this way, the optimal capital project selection at Kearns & Associates is given by the assignment shown in Table 9.5.

Notice in Table 9.5 that the assigned values of the decision variables are indeed all binary, and also that the assigned values of the decision variables satisfy all of the constraints in the revised model. According to Table 9.5, the optimal production plan (that maximizes the anticipated earnings) is to choose Project 1 and Project 2. The optimized earnings of this choice is:

$$\$20 \text{ million} = 12 \cdot 1 + 8 \cdot 1 + 7 \cdot 0 + 6 \cdot 0.$$

Example 9.3 — A Strategic Relocation Problem

TRD Corporation is a large computer manufacturer. TRD currently operates three service centers for their European customers, in London, Madrid, and Paris. Customers throughout Europe that have service contracts with TRD call their local office to request service when they encounter a problem with their mainframe computer. An engineer is then dispatched to the customer site from the service center. Often the engineer needs to order new parts that are then shipped from the service center to the

TABLE 9.5

The optimal solution of the Kearns & Associates capital budgeting model with the addition of extra constraints.

	Decision Variable	Optimal Value
Project 1	x_1	1
Project 2	x_2	1
Project 3	x_3	0
Project 4	x_4	0

customer site. Johan Ziegler, vice president of operations at TRD, has received complaints from several major customers about the timeliness of the service operation at TRD, with many customers having to wait more than two days for parts to reach the customer from the service center. At the same time, the shipping costs as well as the costs of maintaining the service centers have increased substantially.

Johan is considering relocating some of the service centers, and possibly decreasing their number from three to two in order to decrease operating costs. In addition to London, Madrid, and Paris, Johan is considering Hamburg and Rome as possible locations for service centers. Johan Ziegler's staff has assembled the cost information shown in Table 9.6, which contains the staff's best estimates of the annual operating costs for each of the five possible service center locations.

The major customers of TRD are located in five countries: England, Germany, Switzerland, Italy, and France. Table 9.7 shows the percentage of major customers in each of these five countries.

Table 9.8 shows the average shipping time (in days) from each of the potential service center locations to each of the five customer country locations.

Johan would like to determine the number and location of customer service centers. A reasonable objective would seem to be to minimize the total operating cost of the service centers, while maintaining some pre-specified service requirement. In particular, Johan has decided to require that the average shipping time to each of the five countries from the customer service centers should not exceed 1.5 days. Moreover, Johan would like to ensure that the average shipping time across all five countries should be at most 1.1 days.

Let us now construct an optimization model that will represent Johan Ziegler's problem. Let the index $j = 1, \ldots, 5$ denote the five potential service center locations, with $j = 1$ corresponding to London, $j = 2$ corresponding to Madrid, $j = 3$ corresponding to Paris, $j = 4$ corresponding to Hamburg, and $j = 5$ corresponding to

TABLE 9.6

Annual operating costs of five possible service center locations in $ million.

	Service Center Location				
	London	Madrid	Paris	Hamburg	Rome
Operating Cost ($ million)	20	15	22	21	16

TABLE 9.7

Percentage of TRD's major customers in each of five countries.

Country	Percentage of customers
England	25%
Germany	30%
Switzerland	15%
Italy	10%
France	20%

TABLE 9.8

Average shipping time, in days, from each of the possible service center locations to each of these five countries.

Country	Service Center Location				
	London	Madrid	Paris	Hamburg	Rome
England	0.5	2.5	1.5	2.0	3.0
Germany	2.0	3.0	1.0	0.5	2.0
Switzerland	3.0	2.0	2.0	1.5	1.0
Italy	3.0	1.0	2.0	2.0	0.5
France	1.5	2.0	0.5	1.0	2.0

Rome. Also, let the index $i = 1, \ldots, 5$ denote the five customer location countries, with $i = 1$ corresponding to England, $i = 2$ corresponding to Germany, $i = 3$ corresponding to Switzerland, $i = 4$ corresponding to Italy, and $i = 5$ corresponding to France. For $j = 1, \ldots, 5$ we define the following binary decision variables:

$$y_j = \begin{cases} 1 & \text{if location } j \text{ is selected,} \\ 0 & \text{if location } j \text{ is not selected.} \end{cases}$$

In addition, for $i = 1, \ldots, 5$ and $j = 1, \ldots, 5$, let us define the following decision variables:

$x_{ij} =$ the fraction of service requests from country i that will be serviced by location j.

Note that the decision variables x_{ij} are ordinary optimization decision variables, that is, they are not integer variables nor are they binary variables. The objective function is to minimize the annual operating cost of the service centers, which is:

$$\text{COST} = 20y_1 + 15y_2 + 22y_3 + 21y_4 + 16y_5.$$

The following constraint expresses the requirement for England that the sum (over all service centers) of fractions of requests for service from England to the service centers must sum to one:

$$\text{fractions1:} \quad x_{11} + x_{12} + x_{13} + x_{14} + x_{15} = 1.$$

Similarly, for each of the other countries, we will have a similar constraint:

$$\text{fractions2:} \quad x_{21} + x_{22} + x_{23} + x_{24} + x_{25} = 1,$$
$$\text{fractions3:} \quad x_{31} + x_{32} + x_{33} + x_{34} + x_{35} = 1,$$
$$\text{fractions4:} \quad x_{41} + x_{42} + x_{43} + x_{44} + x_{45} = 1,$$
$$\text{fractions5:} \quad x_{51} + x_{52} + x_{53} + x_{54} + x_{55} = 1.$$

We also need to ensure that the average shipping time for each country is at most 1.5 days. Let us consider England, for example. Let us denote the average shipping time from the service centers to England by the decision variable w_1. From Table 9.8, we have the following expression for w_1:

$$\text{shipping time1:} \quad w_1 = 0.5x_{11} + 2.5x_{12} + 1.5x_{13} + 2.0x_{14} + 3.0x_{15}.$$

More generally, if we denote the average shipping time to country i by the decision variable w_i, for $i = 1, \ldots, 5$, then we can use Table 9.8 to derive the following expressions for w_2, w_3, w_4, and w_5:

$$\text{shipping time2:} \quad w_2 = 2.0x_{21} + 3.0x_{22} + 1.0x_{23} + 0.5x_{24} + 2.0x_{25},$$
$$\text{shipping time3:} \quad w_3 = 3.0x_{31} + 2.0x_{32} + 2.0x_{33} + 1.5x_{34} + 1.0x_{35},$$
$$\text{shipping time4:} \quad w_4 = 3.0x_{41} + 1.0x_{42} + 2.0x_{43} + 2.0x_{44} + 0.5x_{45},$$
$$\text{shipping time5:} \quad w_5 = 1.5x_{51} + 2.0x_{52} + 0.5x_{53} + 1.0x_{54} + 2.0x_{55}.$$

Since Johan would like the average shipping time to each country to be at most 1.5 days, we include the following constraints:

$$\text{time bounds:} \quad w_1 \leq 1.5, \quad w_2 \leq 1.5, \quad w_3 \leq 1.5, \quad w_4 \leq 1.5, \quad w_5 \leq 1.5.$$

Furthermore, we also would like to ensure that the average shipping time across all countries is at most 1.1 days. Using the data from Table 9.7, we have the following constraint:

total shipping time: $0.25w_1 + 0.30w_2 + 0.15w_3 + 0.10w_4 + 0.20w_5 \leq 1.1.$

Another important requirement is to ensure that no customer is serviced from a service center that has not been chosen. Stated in terms of the decision variables, this requirement means that if $y_j = 0$, then $x_{ij} = 0$ for all country locations $i = 1, \ldots, 5$. For example, if the Madrid service center has not been chosen ($y_2 = 0$), then we must require that $x_{12} = 0$, $x_{22} = 0$, $x_{32} = 0$, $x_{42} = 0$, and $x_{52} = 0$. We can model this requirement by adding the following constraints:

logical: $x_{ij} \leq y_j$, for all $i = 1, \ldots, 5$ and $j = 1, \ldots, 5$.

Note that these constraints will ensure that if $y_j = 0$, then $x_{ij} = 0$. To see why this is true, notice that the variables x_{ij} are nonnegative, and also that $x_{ij} \leq 0$ if $y_j = 0$. Since also $x_{ij} \geq 0$, then $x_{ij} = 0$ whenever $y_j = 0$.

Finally, we need to model the requirement that the total number of service centers should be either 2 or 3. We model this requirement with the constraints:

number2: $y_1 + y_2 + y_3 + y_4 + y_5 \geq 2,$

and

number3: $y_1 + y_2 + y_3 + y_4 + y_5 \leq 3.$

Here is the complete optimization model:

$$
\begin{aligned}
\text{minimize} \quad & 20y_1 + 15y_2 + 22y_3 + 21y_4 + 16y_5 \\
\text{subject to:} \\
\text{fractions1:} \quad & x_{11} + x_{12} + x_{13} + x_{14} + x_{15} = 1 \\
\text{fractions2:} \quad & x_{21} + x_{22} + x_{23} + x_{24} + x_{25} = 1 \\
\text{fractions3:} \quad & x_{31} + x_{32} + x_{33} + x_{34} + x_{35} = 1 \\
\text{fractions4:} \quad & x_{41} + x_{42} + x_{43} + x_{44} + x_{45} = 1 \\
\text{fractions5:} \quad & x_{51} + x_{52} + x_{53} + x_{54} + x_{55} = 1 \\
\text{shipping time1:} \quad & w_1 = 0.5x_{11} + 2.5x_{12} + 1.5x_{13} + 2.0x_{14} + 3.0x_{15} \\
\text{shipping time2:} \quad & w_2 = 2.0x_{21} + 3.0x_{22} + 1.0x_{23} + 0.5x_{24} + 2.0x_{25} \\
\text{shipping time3:} \quad & w_3 = 3.0x_{31} + 2.0x_{32} + 2.0x_{33} + 1.5x_{34} + 1.0x_{35} \\
\text{shipping time4:} \quad & w_4 = 3.0x_{41} + 1.0x_{42} + 2.0x_{43} + 2.0x_{44} + 0.5x_{45} \\
\text{shipping time5:} \quad & w_5 = 1.5x_{51} + 2.0x_{52} + 0.5x_{53} + 1.0x_{54} + 2.0x_{55} \\
\text{time bounds:} \quad & w_1 \leq 1.5, \quad w_2 \leq 1.5, \quad w_3 \leq 1.5, \quad w_4 \leq 1.5, \quad w_5 \leq 1.5 \\
\text{total shipping time:} \quad & 0.25w_1 + 0.30w_2 + 0.15w_3 + 0.10w_4 + 0.20w_5 \leq 1.1 \\
\text{logical:} \quad & x_{ij} \leq y_j, \quad i = 1, \ldots, 5, \quad \text{and} \quad j = 1, \ldots, 5 \\
\text{number2:} \quad & y_1 + y_2 + y_3 + y_4 + y_5 \geq 2 \\
\text{number3:} \quad & y_1 + y_2 + y_3 + y_4 + y_5 \leq 3 \\
\text{nonnegativity:} \quad & x_{ij} \geq 0, \quad i = 1, \ldots, 5, \quad \text{and} \quad j = 1, \ldots, 5 \\
\text{integer:} \quad & y_j \text{ is binary, } j = 1, \ldots, 5.
\end{aligned}
$$

Note that this optimization model has 35 decision variables, namely 25 variables for the x_{ij}, 5 variables for the w_i, and 5 binary variables y_j.

Once again, it is possible to format this problem into a spreadsheet and to have the software compute the optimal solution to this problem. That is, the computer will compute those values of the variables y_j, x_{ij} and w_i that will satisfy all of the constraints and the binary variable requirements, and will yield the minimum operating cost. If one solves the problem this way, one obtains the optimal solution shown in Table 9.9, Table 9.10, and Table 9.11.

Let us now look at this solution in detail. Notice in Table 9.9 that the optimal choice of service centers is to choose Paris and Rome, at a total cost of:

$$\$38 \text{ million} = 20 \cdot 0 + 15 \cdot 0 + 22 \cdot 1 + 21 \cdot 0 + 16 \cdot 1.$$

According to Table 9.10, the optimal allocation of the service centers for each customer is as follows:

- All of England's customers should be served by Paris.

- 91.7% of Germany's customers should be served by Paris with the remaining 8.3% served by Rome.

- All of Switzerland's customers should be served by Rome.

- 67% of Italy's customers should be served by Paris with the remaining 33% served by Rome.

- All of France's customers should be served by Paris.

The shipping times for each country are shown in Table 9.11.

An interesting question regarding this problem concerns the tradeoff between operating costs and shipping times: If TRD operates more service centers (and hence

TABLE 9.9

Optimal value of the binary decision variables y_j.

	Service Center Location				
	London	Madrid	Paris	Hamburg	Rome
Decision Variable	y_1	y_2	y_3	y_4	y_5
Optimal Value	0	0	1	0	1

TABLE 9.10

Optimal value of the decision variables x_{ij}.

	Service Center Location				
Country	London	Madrid	Paris	Hamburg	Rome
England	0.0	0.0	1.0	0.0	0.0
Germany	0.0	0.0	0.917	0.0	0.083
Switzerland	0.0	0.0	0.0	0.0	1.0
Italy	0.0	0.0	0.67	0.0	0.33
France	0.0	0.0	1.0	0.0	0.0

TABLE 9.11

Optimal value of the shipping time decision variables w_i.

Country	Decision Variable	Optimal Value
England	w_1	1.5
Germany	w_2	1.083
Switzerland	w_3	1.0
Italy	w_4	1.5
France	w_5	0.5

incurs more operating costs), they should be able to decrease the shipping times to their customers. This issue is explored in Exercise 9.1.

The optimization model for the strategic relocation problem faced by TRD is an example of a **mixed-integer optimization model,** which is defined as follows.

An optimization model is called a **mixed-integer optimization model** if some of the decision variables are required to be either integer or binary, and other decision variables are allowed to be ordinary decision variables, and all of the constraints and the objective function are linear functions.

A mixed-integer optimization model is also called a **mixed-integer program.**

Summary of types of discrete optimization problems

Let us now review the terms we have introduced in this section. We have introduced three types of discrete optimization models, as follows:

- An **integer optimization model** is an optimization model for which all of the decision variables are required to be integers (that is, nonnegative whole numbers), and all of the constraints and the objective function are linear functions.

- A **binary optimization model** is an optimization model for which all of the decision variables are required to be binary (that is, zero or one), and all of the constraints and the objective function are linear functions.

- A **mixed-integer optimization model** is an optimization model for which some of the decision variables are required to be either integer or binary, and other decision variables are allowed to be regular decision variables, and all of the constraints and the objective function are linear functions.

9.2   GRAPHICAL ANALYSIS OF DISCRETE OPTIMIZATION MODELS IN TWO VARIABLES

In this section, we study the geometry of a discrete optimization model. We will see that the geometry of discrete optimization is very different from that of linear optimization.

Consider the following generic integer optimization model, which we will call problem IM:

$$\begin{aligned} \text{maximize} \quad & 150X + 112Y \\ \text{subject to:} \quad & 7.5X + 6Y \leq 90 \\ & 8X + 12Y \leq 138 \\ & 55X + 33Y \leq 600 \\ & X, Y \text{ are integers.} \end{aligned}$$

In problem IM, the decision variables are X and Y, and notice from the last row of the model that these decision variables are required to be integers. In problem IM, the assignment $X = 6$ and $Y = 5$ is a feasible solution: Straightforward computation shows that this assignment satisfies all of the constraints, and of course this assignment has integer values for the decision variables. Just as in linear optimization, the locus of all of the feasible solutions is called the **feasible region** of the problem, and the **optimal solution** of an integer optimization model is that feasible solution that optimizes the objective function value.

Now let us construct a graph of the feasible region of the problem IM. Just as in the case of linear optimization, we will do this by first plotting each of the linear constraints. If we plot the three linear inequality constraints in this model, we obtain the region shown in Figure 9.1.

We next need to plot those points in the (X, Y)-plane that have integer values. This is shown in the pattern of points in Figure 9.2. All of the dots in this figure correspond to values of X and Y that are integers.

In order to complete the picture of the feasible region of problem IM, we need to overlay the linear inequality constraints on top of the integer points in the (X, Y)-plane. This is shown in Figure 9.3. In Figure 9.3, we see that the feasible region of an integer optimization is a discrete set of points.

The next task in solving the problem IM is to plot the objective function isoquant lines and to move up one of these lines until it just touches the feasible region. This

FIGURE 9.1

The linear constraints in the integer optimization model.

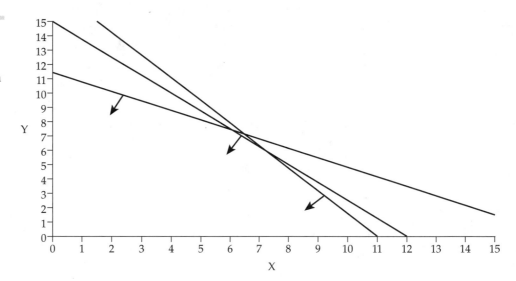

FIGURE 9.2

The integer points in the (X, Y)-plane.

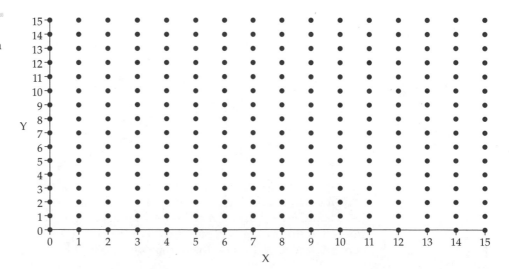

FIGURE 9.3
The feasible region of the integer optimization model.

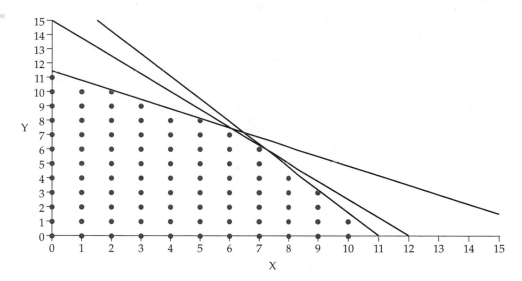

FIGURE 9.4
The feasible region and the optimal solution of the integer optimization model.

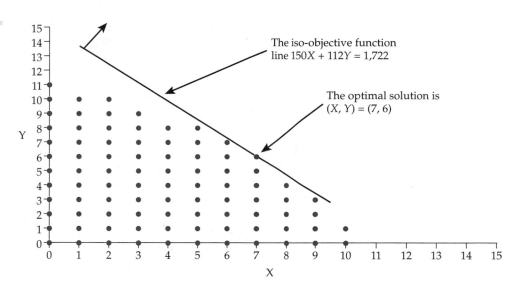

The iso-objective function line $150X + 112Y = 1{,}722$

The optimal solution is $(X, Y) = (7, 6)$

is shown in Figure 9.4. We see from Figure 9.4 that the optimal solution to problem IM is $(X, Y) = (7, 6)$, and the optimal objective function value is:

$$1{,}722 = 150 \cdot X + 112 \cdot Y = 150 \cdot 7 + 112 \cdot 6.$$

We therefore can make the following observations regarding the solution of an integer optimization model.

Observations on the Graphical Analysis of an Integer Optimization Model

- The feasible region is a collection of discrete points.

- Unlike a linear optimization model, the feasible region is not shaped at all like a polygon.

- There are no "corner points" of the feasible region.

- The "border" points of the feasible region do not necessarily correspond to where two constraints meet. This is very different from what we have observed in a linear optimization model.

9.3 COMPUTER SOLUTION OF DISCRETE OPTIMIZATION PROBLEMS

In this section, we discuss the relevant issues regarding the solvability of a discrete optimization model on the computer. We start with general principles of solvability of discrete optimization models. We then present detailed instructions on how to use the Solver Add-In function in Microsoft Excel® to solve a discrete optimization model formatted in a spreadsheet.

General Principles on the Solvability of a Discrete Optimization Model

In general, a discrete optimization model is much more difficult to solve than a linear optimization model. Recall that a linear optimization model is easy to solve by virtue of the fact that the optimal solution must correspond to a "corner point" of the feasible region, and that a corner point solution itself corresponds to the solution of a certain system of linear equations. However, as we have seen in Section 9.2, the solution of a discrete optimization model will not necessarily correspond to a corner point of the feasible region, and in fact, there are no identifiable systems of linear equations whose solution will be the optimal solution of the model. For this reason, discrete optimization models are generally much more difficult to solve than are linear optimization models.

Unlike the case for linear optimization, there is usually no one solution method that will work well on all discrete optimization models. The most commonly used method is called the "branch-and-bound" method for solving a discrete optimization model. This method works well for most small discrete optimization models, but can take a long time to solve certain large discrete optimization problems. In Section 9.4, we illustrate this method for those readers who are interested.

There are a variety of software packages that solve discrete optimization problems. Just as in the case of nonlinear optimization software, the better software packages for solving discrete optimization problems are typically expensive to purchase and so are not automatically featured as part of any typical spreadsheet software. The "Solver" Add-In software resident in Microsoft Excel® does have the capability to solve a discrete optimization problem. However, it is a medium-quality package and can only be relied on for small discrete optimization models, and not for large discrete optimization models.

Typically, but not always, a binary optimization model is a bit easier to solve than an integer optimization model, which in turn is usually a bit easier to solve than a mixed-integer optimization model.

Below is a summary of the key points discussed above:

Guideline 1: Unlike a linear optimization model, a discrete optimization model can be difficult to solve even with today's computers.

Guideline 2: Some discrete optimization models are easy to solve, and others are difficult. The difficulty in solving a discrete optimization model depends very much on the model's own mathematical structure.

Guideline 3: Software for solving discrete optimization models varies with the capability of the software to solve larger discrete optimization models (that is, those models with many decision variables and many constraints) and with the price of the software. The better software packages will solve discrete optimization models with very many decision variables and/or constraints.

Guideline 4: Roughly speaking, binary optimization models are typically easier to solve than are integer optimization models, which in turn are a bit easier to solve than mixed-integer optimization models.

Using Spreadsheet Software to solve a Nonlinear Optimization Problem

In Chapter 7, we showed how to use The Microsoft Excel® Add-In function "Solver" to solve a linear optimization model. The Solver function can also be used to solve a discrete optimization model. In this section, we indicate how to use the Solver to solve a discrete optimization model.

- **Basic construction of the model.** Format your discrete optimization model in a spreadsheet in the same way as you would a linear optimization model. This involves assigning decision variables, the objective function, and the constraint left-hand-sides (LHS) and right-hand-sides (RHS) with appropriate cells in the spreadsheet, exactly as in a linear optimization model. Enter the Solver in the usual way by selecting **Solver...** under the **Tools** header at the top of the spreadsheet. Just as in the case of a linear optimization model, one simply instructs the Solver which cells are the decision variables, which cell contains the objective function, and which cells contain the left-hand-side (LHS) and right-hand-side (RHS) of each of the constraints. This information is entered in the **Solver Parameters** window.

- **Integer and Binary Decision variables.** In a discrete optimization model, some or all of the decision variables might be required to be integer and/or binary variables. In order to add this requirement to your model, select the **Solver Parameter** dialog box and go to the **Subject to Constraints:** section and then click on the **Add** constraint button. Highlight those decision variable cells that are required to be integer or binary variables and place their cell references in the **Cell Reference** window of the **Add Constraint** dialog box. Next, click on the "≤" box in the middle of the window and hold the mouse button down. Drag down and select either "int" (for integer) or "bin" (for binary), depending on whether you are requiring the referenced cells to be integer variables or binary variables. Then click the **Add** button to complete the instruction. This procedure should be repeated for all groups of integer and binary constraints.

- **Make sure that "Assume Linear Model" is checked.** Click on the **Options** button in the **Solver Parameters** window. This will bring up the **Solver Options** window. In the **Solver Options** window, make sure that the box next to the label **Assume Linear Model** is checked. This is very important.

- **Changing the parameters in the "Solver Options" dialog box.** Unlike linear optimization models, the user might need to experiment with changing the parameters in the **Solver Options** dialog box when solving a discrete optimization model in order to achieve better solution quality. Each parameter option has a default setting that is appropriate for most problems. We now describe the meaning of some of the features in the **Solver Options** dialog box that are important for solving a discrete optimization problem. (We do not discuss those options that are too technical or are not relevant for discrete optimization models.)

— **Max Time.** This option allows the user to limit the time taken by the solution process. While the user can enter a value as high as 32,000 seconds or more, the default value of 100 seconds is adequate for most small problems. However, when solving larger discrete optimization problems, one needs to increase the limit beyond its default value.

— **Iterations.** This option allows the user to limit the time taken by the solution process by limiting the number of interim calculations. The default value of 100 iterations is adequate for most small problems.

— **Precision.** This option allows the user to control the precision of solutions and the accuracy of the numerical calculations. This option is not very important for discrete optimization problems.

— **Tolerance.** The tolerance is the percentage by which the target cell of a solution satisfying the integer or binary constraints can differ from the true optimal value and still be considered acceptable. A higher tolerance tends to speed up the solution process at the expense of a solution of lower quality. For example, if we set the tolerance to be 10%, we are only guaranteed to obtain a solution whose objective function value is within 10% of the optimal value. If, however, we decrease the tolerance to 1%, we will be guaranteed a solution that is within 1% of the optimal value. One might think then that it is best to set the tolerance to a very low level, perhaps even 0%, as this will force the computer to find the very best solution. However, because it is very difficult to solve many discrete optimization problems, setting the tolerance level too low will typically cause the computer to perform an excessive amount of computations in trying to find the best solution. The default value of the tolerance is 5%. At the end of this section, we illustrate the effect of changing the tolerance on the solution of the airplane manufacturing problem of Example 9.1.

— **Convergence.** The convergence parameter is only used for nonlinear optimization models, and so it is not important for discrete optimization models.

— **Assume Linear Model.** Remember to make sure that the box next to "Assume Linear Model" is checked.

— **Show Iteration Results.** This option instructs the Solver to pause to show the results of each iteration.

— **Assume Non-Negative.** This option instructs the Solver to assume a lower limit of 0.0 for all adjustable cells (that is, decision variables) for which the user has not set a lower limit in the Constraint box in the **Add Constraint** dialog box.

• **Solving the model.** Once you have adjusted the various parameters in the Solver Parameters dialog box, you are ready to solve your problem. Click on **OK** in the **Solver Options** window and then click on **Solve** in the **Solver Parameters** window. The software will then proceed with the computations of a solution of your model. After a short amount of time, the **Solver Results** window will appear on the screen.

• **How to know if Solver has found a solution.** Look at the message in the **Solver Results** window. It should read "Solver found a solution. All constraints and optimality conditions are satisfied." If some other message appears in the **Solver Results** window, then Solver has not found a solution of the model. In this case, you might try to re-adjust some of the parameters and options in the **Solver Options** window and then try again to solve the model.

- **Reading the Optimization Results.** When the Solver has finished computing a solution of the model, it will display the **Solver Results** window. Note the message at the top of the window that indicates whether or not an optimal solution was found. Make sure that the radio button next to the label **Keep Solver Solution** is clicked. This ensures that the Solver will place the optimal values of the decision variables in the appropriate cells in the spreadsheet model. Click the **OK** button to return to the spreadsheet.

Example 9.4 – The Effect of Changing the "Tolerance" Parameter on the Solution of the Airplane Manufacturing Problem in Example 9.1.

Recall the airplane manufacturing problem presented in Example 9.1 in Section 9.1:

$$\text{maximize} \quad 62A_1 + 84A_2 + 103A_4 + 125A_6$$

subject to:

Time to build:	$4A_1 + 7A_2 + 9A_4 + 11A_6 \leq 270$
Managers:	$A_1 + A_2 + 2A_4 + 2A_6 \leq 60$
AR1 capacity:	$A_1 \leq 8$
AR2 capacity:	$A_2 \leq 17$
AR4 capacity:	$A_4 \leq 11$
AR6 capacity:	$A_6 \leq 15$
Nonnegativity:	$A_1, A_2, A_4, A_6 \geq 0$
Integer requirement:	A_1, A_2, A_4, A_6 are integers.

Let us now study how the tolerance parameter affects the quality of the solution of this model that is computed by the Solver. Table 9.12 shows the solution to the problem, as reported by the Solver, for three different values of the "Tolerance" parameter, namely 5%, 1%, and 0%.

Notice in Table 9.12 that for lower values of the tolerance parameter, the objective value of the solution computed by the Solver improves. However, the Solver software must work harder and do many more computations in order to solve a discrete optimization with the tolerance parameter set to a lower value. For this reason, it is usually recommended to set the tolerance parameter to higher values, particularly for models with many integer or binary variables.

TABLE 9.12

The effect of the tolerance parameter on the solution computed by the Solver.

	Decision Variables				Contribution to Earnings
Tolerance	A_1	A_2	A_4	A_6	($1,000)
5%	8	17	11	1	3,182
1%	8	17	7	5	3,270
0%	8	17	1	10	3,277

| 9.4 | # THE BRANCH-AND-BOUND METHOD FOR SOLVING A DISCRETE OPTIMIZATION MODEL* |

In this section, we illustrate the primary method that is used to solve most discrete optimization problems, which is called the **branch-and-bound** method. This is the method that is used in the Solver in Microsoft Excel®.

We illustrate the branch-and-bound method by using this method to solve the capital budgeting problem in Example 9.2 in Section 9.1. Recall the capital budgeting model developed in Example 9.2:

$$\text{maximize} \quad 12x_1 + 8x_2 + 7x_3 + 6x_4$$

subject to:

$$\text{budget:} \quad 8x_1 + 6x_2 + 5x_3 + 4x_4 \le 15$$

$$\text{binary:} \quad x_1, x_2, x_3, x_4 \text{ are binary.}$$

The first step in the branch-and-bound method is to create a linear optimization model from the given problem that ignores the binary requirements. This linear optimization is as follows:

$$\text{maximize} \quad 12x_1 + 8x_2 + 7x_3 + 6x_4$$

subject to:

$$\text{budget:} \quad 8x_1 + 6x_2 + 5x_3 + 4x_4 \le 15$$

$$\text{bounds:} \quad x_1 \le 1, x_2 \le 1, x_3 \le 1, x_4 \le 1$$

$$\text{nonnegativity:} \quad x_1, x_2, x_3, x_4 \ge 0.$$

Notice that this linear optimization model is almost identical to the binary optimization model, except that the constraints

$$x_1, x_2, x_3, x_4 \text{ are binary}$$

are now replaced by the constraints

$$0 \le x_1 \le 1, \quad 0 \le x_2 \le 1, \quad 0 \le x_3 \le 1, \quad 0 \le x_4 \le 1.$$

This problem is called the **linear optimization relaxation** of the original problem. The solution of this problem is shown in Table 9.13.

Unfortunately, since x_3 is not binary in this solution, we do not have a binary solution yet. However, we know from the solution to the linear optimization relaxation that no binary solution can have an objective function value that is greater than $22.2 million. In fact, because all of the data for the problem are whole numbers themselves, no binary solution can have an objective function value that is greater than $22 million.

TABLE 9.13

The optimal solution of the linear optimization relaxation of the capital budgeting problem.

	Decision Variable	Optimal Value
Project 1	x_1	1
Project 2	x_2	0
Project 3	x_3	0.6
Project 4	x_4	1
Optimal Earnings Value ($ million)		22.2

The next step is to force x_3 to be binary. To achieve this, we **branch** on the variable x_3, creating two new linear optimization problems. In the first new linear optimization problem, we will add the constraint:

$$x_3 = 0,$$

and in the second new linear optimization problem, we will add the constraint:

$$x_3 = 1.$$

We then proceed to solve these two new linear optimization models. The solutions to these models are shown in Figure 9.5.

At this point, we know that the optimal binary solution has an objective function value that is no greater than $22 million, but we have not yet found a binary solution. Therefore, we will select one of the linear optimization models that we have just solved and we will branch on one of its variables. We will select the model that has the constraint "$x_3 = 1$," and we will branch on the variable x_4. After solving the two newly generated linear optimization models, we obtain the solutions shown in Figure 9.6.

Now notice that we still have not found a binary solution. Therefore, we select the linear model with the constraints "$x_3 = 1, x_4 = 1$," and we branch on the variable x_1. After creating and solving these two new linear optimization models, we obtain the solutions shown in Figure 9.7.

At this point, we have found the binary solution $x_1 = 0$, $x_2 = 1$, $x_3 = 1$, and $x_4 = 1$, with objective function value equal to $21 million. There is no need to continue branching from this point, as we have already found a binary solution. We also need not continue from the right-most branch in Figure 9.7, since that linear optimization model is infeasible.

FIGURE 9.5
The first branching in the branch-and-bound method.

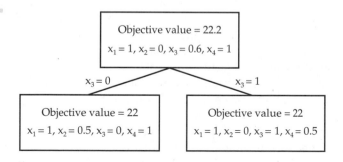

FIGURE 9.6
The second branching in the branch-and-bound method.

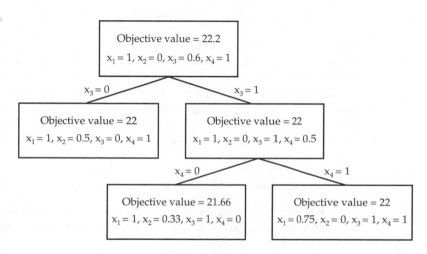

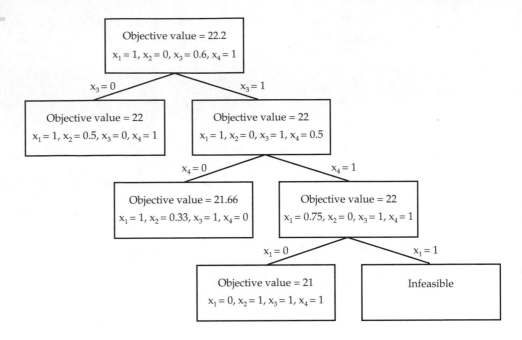

There are two more active linear optimization models. The linear optimization model with the constraints "$x_3 = 1, x_4 = 0$" has an optimal objective function value of $21.66 million. Once again, since all of the data for the problem are whole numbers, the best binary solution we can can hope for from this linear optimization model will have an objective value that is at most $21 million. Since we already have found a solution with value $21 million, we need not enumerate further from this point.

At this point the only remaining linear optimization to consider is the one whose constraints include "$x_3 = 0$." Its optimal objective value is $22 million. Since our best binary solution has an objective value of $21 million, it is possible that there might be a binary solution of this model with an objective function value of $22 million. We therefore must create two new linear optimization models from the model with the constraint "$x_3 = 0$": One of these models will have the additional constraint "$x_2 = 0$," and the other will have the additional constraint "$x_2 = 1$."

The linear optimization model with constraints "$x_3 = 0, x_2 = 0$" has an optimal objective function value of $18 million, and the linear optimization model with constraints "$x_3 = 0, x_2 = 1$" has an optimal objective function value of $21.5 million. Once again, since all of the data for the problem are whole numbers, the best binary solution we can can hope for from this linear optimization model will have an objective value that is at most $21 million. Since we already have found a binary solution with an objective function value of $21 million, we need not enumerate further from this point.

At this point there are no other active linear optimization models to solve, and so we have solved our binary optimization model at last. The optimal binary solution is $x_1 = 0$, $x_2 = 1, x_3 = 1$, and $x_4 = 1$ with an optimized objective function value of $21 million.

The steps of the branch-and-bound method are summarized as follows:

The Branch-and-Bound Method for Solving a Binary Optimization Model

1. Solve the linear optimization relaxation of the problem. If the solution is binary, it is the optimal solution of the binary optimization model. Otherwise,

create two new linear optimization models by branching on a fractional variable. Label these models as "active."

2. Any of the current linear optimization models is labeled "inactive" if any one of the following conditions are met:

    (a) The linear optimization model solution is binary.

    (b) The linear optimization model is infeasible.

    (c) The linear optimization model has a solution, but its optimal objective function value is no better than that of the best binary solution we have found so far.

3. Choose an active linear optimization model, and branch on one of its fractional variables.

4. Continue this process until there are no more active linear optimization models to consider.

The branch-and-bound method is a very effective method for solving large discrete optimization models. Occasionally, however, it might require the creation and the solution of many linear optimization models in the process. The Solver function in Microsoft Excel® uses an implementation of the branch-and-bound method to solve discrete optimization models. This implementation is capable of efficiently solving small and medium-sized discrete optimization models.

9.5   SUMMARY

Discrete optimization models can be used to extend the types of management problems that can be effectively analyzed with an optimization model. As a result, discrete optimization is a very powerful tool.

Discrete optimization problems are not easy to solve on the computer. Some discrete optimization models can take a large amount of computational effort to solve, even on today's computers. However, new methodological tools as well as faster computers now make it possible to solve ever-larger discrete optimization problems.

9.6   CASE MODULES

INTERNATIONAL INDUSTRIES, INC.

International Industries, Inc. is a $53 billion conglomerate that owns and runs a wide variety of businesses worldwide. The scope of these businesses (which are called "divisions" at International Industries) ranges from retail packaged foods to industrial machine tools to financial services. George Ye has been CEO of International Industries for the past six years. At a recent meeting of the Board of Directors, Mr. Ye had come under criticism for International Industries' poor performance in the last two years. In particular, the Board felt that Mr. Ye was not decisive enough in selling divisions that had been under performing, and that he was also not aggressively investing in new businesses (particularly in the computer and bio-technology sectors). To his credit, Mr. Ye had closed four divisions during his tenure as CEO (which were smart moves, even in hindsight), and he had invested more than $2 billion in a new worldwide-web-based internet division, and more than $1 billion in a new division involved in the development of industry-oriented financial software.

After the Board of Directors meeting, George Ye arranged a meeting with the Chief Financial Officer (CFO) of International Industries, Mr. Paul Glasser. George Ye asked Mr. Glasser to undertake a comprehensive re-evaluation of all of the divisions of International Industries. More specifically, he asked Mr. Glasser to recommend to him which divisions to sell, which divisions merited further investment of capital, and which should be maintained at status quo. Furthermore, he wanted this analysis completed within the next two months, in time for the next quarterly meeting of the Board of Directors.

Mr. Glasser retained the services of the consulting firm GCG, Inc. for assistance in this decidedly large and important undertaking. Mr. Glasser asked the directors of each of the fifty divisions of International Industries to submit a request for capital expenditures (with justification and back-up). For each division, Mr. Glasser wanted to decide whether International Industries should further invest in the division, maintain the division with no significant additional investment, or sell the division. Of course, it would also be nice to consider other investment options for each division, such as investing more or less than the requested amount, but with only two months to complete his analysis, Mr. Glasser honestly thought he would have to keep his decision framework purposely limited in scope.

For each of the fifty divisions and for each of the three decision choices (invest, maintain, or sell), Mr. Glasser asked the division vice president to report the investment amount required, the expected financial implications of the choice (measured in net present value (NPV)), and the cash flow implications of the choice for the coming year. With the help of the GCG consultants, each of the fifty divisions submitted the requested information. For example, consider the tool and die manufacturing division, which is division number 2. The summary information for division 2 is shown in Table 9.14. The plan to invest in this division consists of building a new factory in Mexico, buying new machinery, buying new computer systems, and expanding warehousing capacity. The plan to maintain this division merely requires upgrading obsolete equipment. The plan to sell this division involved funds expended for canceling leases and contracts and for severance packages for higher-level managers. The spreadsheet INT-INDUSTRIES-DATA.XLS contains all of the information collected by GCG for all 50 divisions.

TABLE 9.14

The investment required, net present value, and cash flow for next year for each of the three choices (invest, maintain, and sell) for the tool and die manufacturing division, which is division 2.

Choice	Investment Required (in $ million)	Net Present Value (in $ million)	Cash Flow for Next Year (in $ million)
Invest	300	−257	−200
Maintain	40	−16	35
Sell	400	1,100	1,600

Mr. Glasser needed to determine which decision (invest, maintain, or sell) to recommend for each division. His decision criterion was to maximize the net present value to International Industries, subject to cash flow considerations. The cash-flow considerations were that the total investment amount for next year could not exceed the total cash flow for next year.

Mr. Glasser also identified some choices that were interrelated, which he listed as follows in his discussions with GCG:

(a) For strategic reasons, if International Industries sells division 1, then they should invest in division 2 and vice versa. Similarly, if International Industries sells division 1, then they should sell division 3 and vice versa. Finally, if International Industries sells division 1, then they should sell division 4 and vice versa.

(b) If International Industries invests in division 6, then they should also invest in division 7 and vice versa.

(c) For diversification purposes, Mr. Glasser felt that at most one of the following choices could be made: sell division 3, sell division 4, sell division 5, maintain division 6, sell division 7, and sell division 9.

(d) Similarly, Mr. Glasser felt that at most one of the following choices should be made: invest in division 4, maintain division 6, sell division 2, sell division 6, sell division 8, sell division 12, and invest in division 14.

(e) Given the similarities of divisions 24 and 28, Mr. Glasser felt that if International Industries invests in division 24, then they should also invest in division 28.

(f) Similarly, if International Industries maintains division 30, then they should either maintain or invest in division 32.

Given that there are three choices for each of the fifty divisions, Paul Glasser realized that there were $3^{50} \approx 7.1 \times 10^{23}$ possible investment strategies to consider, which of course is an astronomical number. When he discussed this with the consultants at GCG, they pointed out to him that they thought they might be able to compute the optimal investment strategy by formulating and solving the decision problem as a discrete optimization problem. Mr. Glasser knew that even if he found the "optimal decision strategy" George Ye would most certainly ask him about the sensitivity of his decision to key financial assumptions. From previous experience, Paul Glasser also knew that George Ye would ask him not only for his "optimal" recommendation, but he would also ask Paul for his second-best and third-best alternative recommendations, etc.

Assignment:

(a) Suppose that you are an associate of the firm GCG. Using the data provided in the spreadsheet INT-INDUSTRIES-DATA.XLS, construct a discrete optimization model of the problem faced by International Industries. Solve the problem on the computer.

(b) What is the penalty for imposing restrictions (a)-(f) outlined above? That is, how much does the optimal NPV increase if these restrictions are removed?

(c) Propose a methodology to generate the second best and the third best solutions and find the second best and third best solution to your discrete optimization model.

SUPPLY CHAIN MANAGEMENT AT DELLMAR, INC.

It is early March, and Ron Mason has many reasons to feel good about his career. It has been only eight short years since Ron graduated from business school, and he has just been promoted to vice president of logistics at Dellmar, Inc. In fact, Ron is one of only five vice presidents at the company, which is quite an accomplishment.

Dellmar is a major manufacturer of commercial air-conditioning systems. Dellmar introduced its cost-efficient air-conditioning system "Cushion-Air-Pro" one year ago, and this system has been very successful in the marketplace. Customers have praised the system for its design, efficiency, reliability, and price. Orders for the Cushion-Air-Pro system have been growing rapidly.

However, the success of Cushion-Air-Pro has created serious logistics problems at Dellmar. Delays in stocking of Cushion-Air-Pro at Dellmar's national and regional distribution centers have resulted in long delays in satisfying customer orders. At the same time, there is widespread concern within Dellmar that inventory and transportation costs are excessive. In February, total inventory and transportation costs amounted to over $1.4 million. It was now up to Ron Mason to somehow figure out how to deliver Cushion-Air-Pro to customers on time, while simultaneously decreasing total inventory and transportation costs.

The Supply Chain for the Cushion-Air-Pro System

Dellmar manufactures the Cushion-Air-Pro system at its manufacturing plant in New Hampshire. The plant has the capacity to produce up to 50,000 Cushion-Air-Pro units per month. Given the success of the Cushion-Air-Pro system, Dellmar is considering increasing this capacity by an additional 10% at an additional cost of $55,000 per month in financing and operating costs.

Dellmar divides up its national sales into three regions: the East Coast, West Coast, and Midwest areas of the United States. Each region is served by a regional sales distribution center, whose locations are Wilmington, Delaware (serving the East Coast); Salinas, California (serving the West Coast); and St. Louis, Missouri (serving the Midwest). Dellmar operates two national distribution centers, one in Ohio (that serves the Midwest and the West Coast), and one in New Jersey (that serves the Midwest and the East Coast). Completed Cushion-Air-Pro units are shipped from the plant in New Hampshire to the two national distribution centers (in Ohio and New Jersey), where they are stored for shipment to the three regional sales distribution centers. In order to take advantage of economies of scale in shipping, shipments are scheduled for once a month. Dellmar keeps inventory both at the two national distribution centers as well as at the three regional sales distribution centers.

Transportation and Inventory Costs

The unit cost of shipping of a Cushion-Air-Pro system either from the plant to a national distribution center or from a national distribution center to any of the regional sales distribution centers is $10 per system. The fixed transportation costs of arranging for shipments are shown in Table 9.15.

The unit inventory cost per month at the national distribution centers in Ohio and New Jersey is $5 per unit per month, while it is $10 per unit per month at the regional sales distribution centers.

TABLE 9.15

Fixed transportation costs for the various routes at Dellmar.

Route		
From:	To:	Fixed Transportation Cost
New Hampshire	Ohio	$5,000
New Hampshire	New Jersey	$4,000
Ohio	West Coast	$4,000
Ohio	Midwest	$3,000
New Jersey	Midwest	$5,000
New Jersey	East Coast	$3,000

TABLE 9.16

Forecasted demand for Cushion-Air-Pro for April and May.

Sales Region	Month	Forecasted Demand (units)
West Coast	April	20,000
	May	20,000
Midwest	April	15,000
	May	25,000
East Coast	April	25,000
	May	30,000

TABLE 9.17

Estimated inventories of Cushion-Air-Pro at the end of March.

	Distribution Center	Units
National Distribution Centers:	Ohio	20,000
	New Jersey	10,000
Regional Sales Distribution Centers:	West Coast	2,000
	Midwest	1,000
	East Coast	2,000

The Demand for Cushion-Air-Pro Systems

Ron has asked the marketing department for a forecast of the demand for Cushion-Air-Pro systems for the next two months. The marketing department's forecast is shown in Table 9.16.

Inventories

Table 9.17 shows the estimated inventories of Cushion-Air-Pro units at each distribution center for the end of March, as prepared by Ron Mason's staff.

Ron Mason's Problem

Ron Mason would like to determine how many Cushion-Air-Pro units to manufacture each month, and how many units to ship to the distribution centers each month in order to minimize total transportation and inventory costs. Currently, there is no minimum inventory policy for inventories of Cushion-Air-Pro at any of the distribution centers. This helps to keep inventory costs down, but it does not allow for the flexibility to meet unanticipated surges in customer demand. Ron is thinking of increasing minimum inventories to 500 or possibly to 1,000 units in inventory per month at each distribution center (national as well as regional) as a hedge against such extra surges in demand for Cushion-Air-Pro. Last of all, Ron would like to make a recommendation on whether to increase production capacity at the New Hampshire plant.

Assignment:

(a) Construct a discrete optimization model of the problem of minimizing the total transportation and inventory costs over the months of April and May.

(b) In February, the total cost of transportation and inventory cost was $1.4 million, and the estimated cost for March is roughly the same amount. Using the model you have developed in question (a), what is the average monthly cost in April and May if the logistics operation at Dellmar is optimized? What should be Dellmar's production and shipping schedule? How much inventory should Dellmar keep at each distribution center?

(c) What is the effect on the total transportation and inventory cost if Dellmar decides to increase its production capacity by 10%?

(d) In order to decrease delays in filling customer orders, Ron is considering increasing the minimum inventory at each distribution center from 0 to 500 or possibly even 1,000 Cushion-Air-Pro units per month. Is it possible to institute such a policy given the current capacity of 50,000 units per month? Is it possible to institute this policy if plant capacity were to increase by 10%? What would be the effect of such a policy change on total transportation and inventory costs?

(e) What changes would you make in inventory policy, scheduling of shipments, and possible changes in plant capacity at Dellmar?

THE NATIONAL BASKETBALL DREAM TEAM

Rudy Dellamico has been the coach of the United States national men's basketball team for the last two years. The national men's basketball team is one of the 16 finalists for the world championship basketball tournament which is scheduled to take place in Barcelona next summer. Rudy is the chair of the player selection committee, which is responsible for selecting the 12 players that will comprise the "dream team" from among the best players in the National Basketball Association (NBA) and the National Collegiate Athletic Association (NCAA) men's basketball league. The committee has recently narrowed the field of possible dream team players to 20 players whose player statistics are shown in Table 9.18.

The players have been divided into four play positions:

- Players 1, 2, 3, 4, and 5 are designated as "playmakers," otherwise known as point-guards.

- Players 4, 5, 6, 7, 8, 9, 10, and 11 are designated as "shooting guards."

- Players 9, 10, 11, 12, 13, 14, 15, and 16 are "forwards."

- Players 16, 17, 18, 19, and 20 are "centers."

Notice that there are players that can play more than one position. For example, player 4 is both a playmaker and shooting guard. For balance purposes, the committee has decided that the team should consist of at least three playmakers, four shooting guards, four forwards, and three centers, which implies that some players who play multiple positions need to be selected.

Players 4, 8, 15, and 20 play in the NCAA, while all of the other players play in the NBA. The committee has decided that they would like at least two players from the NCAA to be included on the dream team.

After a lot of wrangling, the committee has decided that the average rebound ability among the 12 selected players should be at least 7 rebounds per game. Also, they have

TABLE 9.18

Player statistics for the national men's basketball dream team.

Player Number	Average Rebounds Per Game	Average Assists Per Game	Height (feet and inches)	Average Points Per Game	Defensive Ability (scale from 0 to 10)
1	1	7	5'11"	10	10
2	2	14	6'0"	14	9
3	3	12	6'4"	19	8
4	4	4	6'0"	18	6
5	5	9	6'3"	20	8
6	7	6	6'5"	21	10
7	7	8	6'8"	23	10
8	4	2	6'5"	13	5
9	8	2	6'10"	17	8
10	5	5	6'4"	25	8
11	10	6	6'10"	20	9
12	8	8	6'9"	30	10
13	10	2	7'3"	24	9
14	9	5	6'10"	15	7
15	6	3	6'10"	17	6
16	16	2	6'9"	3	6
17	11	1	7'4"	27	9
18	12	5	7'2"	26	10
19	11	1	7'3"	21	9
20	9	1	7'0"	14	8

decided that the average number of assists among the 12 selected players should be at least 6 assists per game. Furthermore, they have decided that the average points scored among the 12 selected players should be at least 18 points per game. Finally, the committee has decided that the average height of the players should be at least 6'7", and that the average defensive ability among the 12 selected players should be at least 8.5.

As if the selection problem were not already sufficiently complicated, alas there are compatibility problems among these highly-compensated athletic stars! Player 5 has declared that if player 9 is selected, then he will turn down any invitation to join the team. Also, players 2 and 19 can only be selected as a pair, since they have played on the same team for seven years and they feel that they are much more effective when they play together.

Finally, in order for the committee not to be accused of undue favoritism, at most three players from the same franchise team can be selected. Only one franchise team has more than three players among the list of 20 players: Players 1, 7, 12, and 16 all play for the same team, the Chicago Bulls.

Suppose that Rudy Dellamico would like to apply some real management science to the selection of the players for the dream team, and that his objective is to select the team with the highest average points scored per game subject to all of the requirements indicated above.

Assignment:

(a) The spreadsheet DREAM-TEAM.XLS contains all of the data shown in Table 9.18. Using this spreadsheet, construct and solve a discrete optimization model that can be used to select the national men's basketball dream team.

(b) How will the composition of the dream team be changed if the following constraints are changed as follows:

- the average number of rebounds among the 12 selected players needs to be at least 8 rebounds per game,

- the average number of assists per game among the 12 selected players must be at least 7 assists per game, and

- the average number of points per game among the 12 selected players must be at least 20 points per game.

(c) Rudy is thinking of also selecting two more players as alternates in case any of the 12 selected players is injured prior to the start of the world championship games in Barcelona. Propose a method for selecting the two alternates.

9.7 EXERCISES

EXERCISE 9.1 Recall the strategic relocation optimization model developed in Example 9.3 in Section 9.1. This exercise explores the issue of the tradeoff between operating costs and shipping times to customers in this problem.

(a) Construct and solve the mixed integer optimization model that was developed in Example 9.3. Verify that the optimal solution has a total annual operating cost of $38 million.

(b) Suppose that Johan would like to ensure that the average shipping time across all countries is 0.9 days on average instead of 1.1 days on average. Change your model and re-solve the model on the computer. What is the new optimal relocation strategy? What is the new annual operating cost?

(c) Decrease the upper limit on the average shipping time across all countries to 0.8 days, 0.7 days, and 0.6 days, and re-solve the model for each of these three values. What is the new optimal relocation strategy for each of these three values? What is the new annual operating cost for each of these three values?

(d) Recall from Example 9.3 that TRD currently operates three service centers in London, Madrid, and Paris. Now suppose that Johan would like to guarantee that the average shipping time across all countries is 1.0 days. However, suppose that there is an additional cost of $2 million per service center for closing any one of the current service centers, and that there is an additional cost of $3 million per service center to open a new service center. Modify your optimization model and solve for the new optimal solution to the problem in this case.

EXERCISE 9.2 Brian spends a large amount of time surfing the worldwide web. Table 9.19 shows the average number of hits and the average time to search for six different search engines that Brian has access to through his internet service. In order to most efficiently use his time, Brian has decided to use optimization in order to maximize the information he can find in the least amount of time.

TABLE 9.19

The average number of hits and the average time to search for six internet search engines.

Search Engine Company	Average Number of Hits	Average Time to Search (in seconds)
Company A	25	10
Company B	40	20
Company C	125	35
Company D	100	40
Company E	60	45
Company F	15	5

TABLE 9.20

Driving distances between the centers of six communities in minutes.

Town	Arlington	Belmont	Cambridge	Lexington	Concord	Winchester
Arlington	0	5	10	15	20	15
Belmont	5	0	8	10	15	12
Cambridge	10	8	0	15	20	10
Lexington	15	10	15	0	10	12
Concord	20	15	20	10	0	12
Winchester	15	12	10	12	12	0

TABLE 9.21

Estimated advertising revenue and television show categories for nine television shows.

Television Show	Advertising Revenue ($ million)	Public Interest	Contains Violence	Comedy	Drama
Cheers	6			yes	yes
Dynasty	10		yes		yes
L.A. Law	9	yes	yes		yes
Jake	4		yes		yes
Bob Newhart	5			yes	
News Special— the Middle East	2	yes	yes		
Focus on Science: The Fusion Issue	6	yes			yes
Beaches	7			yes	
Urban Action for Education	8	yes			

(a) Suppose that Brian has $T = 50$ seconds to find as many hits as possible. Construct and solve a discrete optimization model to choose which search engines Brian should use in order to maximize the average number of hits that he can obtain in this amount of time.

(b) Re-solve your model for $T = 100$ seconds, $T = 130$ seconds, and $T = 150$ seconds. How does the solution change?

EXERCISE 9.3 The Belmont Bank is considering placing ATM machines in the town centers of some of the following six communities: Arlington, Belmont, Cambridge, Lexington, Concord, and Winchester. The bank would like to purchase the minimum number of ATM machines needed to ensure that at least one ATM machine is within a ten-minute drive from the center of each of these six communities. The times required to drive between the communities are shown in Table 9.20.

(a) Construct a discrete optimization model of the problem faced by Belmont Bank.

(b) Solve your model on the computer. What is the optimal number of ATM machines that Belmont Bank needs to purchase? What is the optimal placement of these ATM machines?

EXERCISE 9.4 Sandy Arledge is the program scheduling manager for WCBN-TV. Sandy would like to plan the schedule of television shows for next Wednesday evening. Of the nine possible one-half hour television shows listed in Table 9.21, Sandy must schedule exactly five of these shows for the period from 8:00 p.m. to 10:30 p.m. next Wednesday evening. For each television show, its estimated advertising revenue (in $ million) is shown in the second column of Table 9.21. Furthermore, each show has been categorized into one or more of the categories of "Public Interest," "Contains Violence," "Comedy," and "Drama".

Sandy would like to determine a revenue-maximizing schedule of television shows for next Wednesday evening. However, she must be mindful of the following considerations:

- There must be at least as many shows scheduled that are categorized as public interest as there are shows scheduled that are categorized as containing violence.

- If Sandy schedules "Focus on Science—The Fusion Issue," then she must also schedule either Jake or L.A. Law (or both).

- Sandy cannot schedule both "Focus on Science" and "Urban Action for Education," as both of these shows are considered a bit on the dry side.

- If Sandy schedules two or more shows in the comedy category, then she must schedule at least one show in the drama category.

- If Sandy schedules more than three shows in the "contains violence" category, she will lose an estimated $4 million in advertising revenues from family-oriented sponsors.

(a) Construct a binary optimization model of Sandy's scheduling problem and solve the model on the computer.

(b) What is the optimal schedule of television shows for next Wednesday evening?

EXERCISE 9.5 The office manager of a large New York City-based accounting firm needs to replace the aging and out-of-style office furniture in their New York offices. The firm has decided to purchase new desk/chair/credenza furniture sets for all 2,000 offices in New York. The company has received bids from four different furniture companies who are willing to supply the furniture sets, as follows:

- Carolina Woodworks has bid to deliver up to 1,000 furniture sets at a cost of $2,500 per set and with a one-time delivery charge of $10,000.

- Nashawtuc Millworks has bid to supply up to 1,200 furniture sets at a cost of $2,450 per set and with a one-time delivery charge of $20,000.

- Adirondack Furnishing Designs has bid to deliver up to 800 furniture sets at a cost of $2,510 per set but with no delivery charge.

- Lancaster Artisan Company has bid to deliver 1,100 furniture sets at a cost of $2,470 per set and with a one-time delivery charge of $13,000.

(a) Construct a discrete optimization model to determine how many furniture sets to purchase from each of these four potential suppliers.

(b) Solve your model on the computer. What is the optimal purchasing strategy?

(c) Suppose that a fifth company, Delaware Mills, has submitted a bid to supply up to 1,000 furniture sets at a cost of $2,530 per set and a one-time delivery charge of $9,000. However, if the firm purchases between 1,000 and 1,500 furniture sets from Delaware Mills, then Delaware Mills will charge the firm only $2,430 for any and all additional furniture sets beyond the 1,000, and with an additional delivery charge of only $7,000. Incorporate this new bid into your model and re-solve for the optimal purchasing strategy.

EXERCISE 9.6 An airline operates a fleet of 15 jet aircraft, and each jet is equipped with one RR-3000 engine. The airline performs its own engine-related repairs and maintenance at its repair facility. The maintenance director is reviewing the spare parts ordering and stocking policy for the next three years. The RR-3000 engine is comprised of four main modules, simply called modules A, B, C, and D. Sometimes when aircraft are taken out of service for scheduled maintenance, the entire

TABLE 9.22

Forecasted module replacements and engine replacements for the next three years.

| | Engine Module | | | | Entire |
Year	A	B	C	D	Engine
1	5	4	4	2	1
2	2	1	1	7	0
3	3	4	3	0	2

TABLE 9.23

Forecast of prices of modules and entire engines for the next three years (in $ million).

| | Engine Module | | | | Entire |
Year	A	B	C	D	Engine
1	0.7	2.5	6.0	1.3	9.0
2	0.6	2.2	5.5	1.1	8.5
3	0.5	2.0	5.0	1.0	7.8

engine must be replaced because of extensive damage and wear. More often, however, only certain modules of the engine need to be replaced. Table 9.22 shows the forecasted replacements of individual engine modules and complete engines for the next three years.

The airline places orders for modules as well as entire engines at the beginning of the year with Jaguar Jet Engine Corporation, the manufacturer of the RR-3000 engine. Table 9.23 shows the projected prices of modules and entire engines that have been forecast for the next three years.

Note that entire engines cost less to purchase than the total cost of purchasing each of the four modules. Assume that the cost of "cannibalizing" an engine, that is, breaking an entire engine into four individual modules, is negligible compared to the cost of the four modules. The mix of modules and entire engines that the airline should order from Jaguar Jet Engine Corporation, therefore, should account for the economies of ordering entire engines. Assume that the airline does not have any inventory of modules or entire engines on hand, and that there are no inventory carrying costs. Construct and then solve a discrete optimization model to determine the order quantities of modules and entire engines for the next three years that minimizes the total costs of all purchases. What is the optimal purchasing schedule?

EXERCISE 9.7 The Ohio Truck Company produces two models of trucks at its factory in Columbus, Ohio: large trucks (the Warrior model) and small trucks (the Chomper model). The factory can produce only one type of truck every month, and so the production planning department needs to determine which model and how many of that model to produce each month. If the plant switches from producing one model one month to the other model the next month, they incur a switch-over cost of $15 million. Historically, the demand for both models has fluctuated significantly over the calendar year. It is now December, and the end-of-December inventory of trucks is expected to be 50,000 Warrior models and 50,000 Chomper models. Table 9.24 shows the forecasted demand for the Warrior and the Chomper models for the next twelve months.

The variable unit production cost for the first six months of next year is expected to be $7,000 for the Warrior model and $6,000 for the Chomper model. It is expected that these costs will increase by 10% after the first six months of next year due to anticipated higher labor costs under a new union contract. The factory can produce up to 100,000 Warrior models each month, or up to 110,000 Chomper models each

TABLE 9.24

Forecasted demand for the Warrior and Chomper models for the next twelve months.

Month	Forecast Demand	
	Warrior model (in 1,000s)	*Chomper model (in 1,000s)*
January	34	42
February	39	45
March	40	46
April	31	38
May	30	36
June	33	43
July	32	42
August	41	41
September	40	44
October	38	47
November	41	48
December	40	46

TABLE 9.25

The twenty courses that Linda is most interested in taking in her first year of business school.

Course Number	Course Title	Semester Offered	Course Prerequisites	Interest Level
1	Quantitative Methods	Fall		5
2	Microeconomics	Fall		5
3	Finance Theory	Fall and Spring		4
4	Strategy I	Fall		4
5	Strategy II	Spring	4	4
6	Accounting I	Fall		3
7	Accounting II	Spring	2, 6	3
8	Financial Engineering	Spring	1, 3	5
9	Statistics	Spring	1	4
10	Operations Management I	Fall		4
11	Operations Management II	Spring	1, 10	4
12	Marketing I	Fall		3
13	Marketing II	Spring	9, 12	3
14	Options and Futures	Spring	3	5
15	Information Technology I	Fall		4
16	Information Technology II	Spring	15	4
17	Entrepreneurship	Spring	4	4
18	New Product Development	Spring	10, 12, 17	3
19	Organizational Processes	Fall	4	3
20	Business Communications	Fall		5

month. The unit storage cost per month is $700 per truck for the Warrior and $600 per truck for the Chomper.

(a) Assume that it is now December and that the factory is producing Warriors this month. Construct a discrete optimization model to determine the production schedule of Warrior and Chomper model trucks for the coming year that will minimize the total cost of production, storage, and switch-over costs. Solve your model on the computer.

(b) What is the optimal production schedule for Warrior and Chomper model trucks?

EXERCISE 9.8 Linda Johansen, an incoming first-year MBA student, would like to determine her course schedule for her first two semesters of business school. Linda has created a list of twenty potential courses that most interest her, shown in Table 9.25. Linda has ranked her interest in each of these courses as a number between 3 and 5, as shown in the fifth column of Table 9.25.

Linda is allowed to take at most five courses in each semester. In determining her course schedule, Linda needs to consider the following:

- Linda can only take a course if she has completed or is concurrently taking all courses that are prerequisites for the course. The prerequisites for all twenty courses are shown in the fifth column of Table 9.25.

- In the Fall term, Linda must take at least three of the following five courses: Quantitative Methods (course 1), Microeconomics (course 2), Finance Theory (course 3), Accounting I (course 6), and Business Communications (course 20).

- If Linda takes Financial Engineering (course 8), she will not be allowed to take Options and Futures (course 14), because these two courses cover fairly similar material.

- Linda would like to take at least one course in Marketing (courses 12 and/or 13), and at least one course in Operations Management (courses 10 and/or 11).

Suppose that Linda's overall objective is to maximize her total interest level.

(a) Construct and solve a discrete optimization model that can be used to determine Linda's optimal course schedule. What is the optimal course schedule?

(b) Try to amend your model in order to generate a different solution with the same (optimal) objective value. What is the other optimal course schedule?

EXERCISE 9.9 Sarah Edwards manages a portfolio of technology and utility stocks in emerging markets that comprises various amounts of ten different stocks. Sarah routinely uses a nonlinear optimization model to optimize the portfolio. The portfolio weights for last month are shown in the second column of Table 9.26. The output of Sarah's nonlinear optimization model, which has determined the optimal portfolio weights for the current month, is shown in the third column of Table 9.26. For each of the ten companies in the portfolio, the fourth column of Table 9.26 indicates whether the company is a technology company or a utility company.

In order to trim the rather excessive transaction costs in emerging markets, Sarah would like to limit her portfolio to stocks in only six different companies, as opposed to the ten companies determined by the solution to her nonlinear optimization model. However, she would like her new portfolio of six stocks to be "close" to the portfolio determined by her nonlinear optimization model.

Let x_i be the decision variable that denotes the fraction of the new portfolio that will be comprised of stock in company i, for $i = 1, \ldots, 10$. The expression

$$|x_1 - 0.15| + |x_2 - 0.05| + \cdots + |x_{10} - 0.08|,$$

TABLE 9.26

Portfolio weights for the ten companies

Company Number	Last Month's Portfolio Weights	Portfolio Weights Determined by Sarah's Nonlinear Model for the Current Month	Stock Classification
1	0.12	0.15	Technology
2	0.08	0.05	Technology
3	0.07	0.08	Utility
4	0.14	0.11	Utility
5	0.17	0.14	Technology
6	0.06	0.09	Utility
7	0.09	0.08	Technology
8	0.04	0.08	Utility
9	0.18	0.14	Utility
10	0.05	0.08	Technology

which is the sum of absolute values of the differences between the final portfolio weights and the weights produced by the nonlinear optimization model, is a standard measure of how close the weights will be to those produced by the nonlinear optimization model.

Sarah would also like to take into account the following:

- Since transaction costs are proportional to the absolute value of the difference between the new portfolio weights and the portfolio weights from last month, it is desirable to impose the following constraint:

$$|x_1 - 0.12| + |x_2 - 0.08| + \cdots + |x_{10} - 0.05| \leq 0.60.$$

This constraint states that the sum of the absolute differences in portfolio weights between last month and the current month must not exceed 60%.

- Last month, the total portfolio weight in technology stocks was $0.12 + 0.08 + 0.17 + 0.09 + 0.05 = 0.51 = 51\%$. Furthermore, the total portfolio weight in technology stocks that is suggested by the solution of the nonlinear optimization model for the current month is $0.15 + 0.05 + 0.14 + 0.08 + 0.08 = 0.50 = 50\%$. Sarah would like to maintain the character of the portfolio as a balanced portfolio between technology and utility stocks. For this reason, she would like the total weight of the portfolio in technology stocks to be between 45% and 55%.

- All portfolio weights need to be nonnegative, that is, short positions are not allowed in the portfolio.

(a) Construct a discrete optimization model to determine the rebalanced weights of the portfolio that use only six stocks. Solve your model on the computer.

(b) What are the optimal portfolio weights suggested by your model?

Integration in the Art of Decision Modeling

CONTENTS

IN PREVIOUS CHAPTERS, WE HAVE CONCENTRATED ON SPECIFIC MANAGEMENT science models and tools (such as probability theory, statistical estimation, simulation, linear regression, linear optimization, etc.). In this chapter, we illustrate how management science models and tools are used in an integrative way in the management of a company. The purpose of this chapter is illustrative: to highlight how a company, or an entire industry, uses the various tools and models of management science in order to enhance its competitiveness.

We illustrate the integrative power of management science models and tools by focusing on three industrial sectors: the airline industry, the investment management industry, and the manufacturing sector.

We first present an overview of the uses of management science models and tools in the airline industry. We then expand this discussion into a detailed analysis of a certain set of models, collectively called revenue management models, that have revolutionized this industry over the last two decades. We next present a synopsis of how management science tools are used in the investment management industry. In both the airline industry and the investment management industry, a modeling-oriented philosophy in general, and management science models in particular, have completely changed the character of these industries in the last decade. Indeed, in both of these industries, management science modeling is no longer a luxury; it is indeed a necessity.

We conclude the chapter, and the book, with a snapshot of a year in the life of a typical manufacturing company. We show how a manufacturing company routinely uses many of the tools and models presented in this book as part of its suite of management practices. While the use of management science models in manufacturing is not currently as pervasive as in the airline and in the investment management industries, such uses represent the future of best-practices for tomorrow's successful companies.

<table>
<tr><td>10.1</td></tr>
</table>

MANAGEMENT SCIENCE MODELS IN THE AIRLINE INDUSTRY

The models and tools of management science, of the type that have been covered in this book, lie at the heart of the operations of virtually every successful passenger airline corporation. These models are used to determine the configuration of an airline's hub-and-spoke system, determine the airline's flight schedule, set fares and assign seat protection levels for fares, set overbooking levels for flights, assign crew to flights, assign aircraft to flights, schedule aircraft maintenance, control inventories of spare parts, determine detailed flight plans, re-route flights due to adverse weather, etc. In this section, we first present an overview of the types of management problems that are addressed using management science tools and models. We then look in detail at **revenue management models,** which have been used so successfully that they have actually revolutionized the operations and the economics of the entire airline industry.

Here are some of the more important uses of the models and tools of management science in the airline industry:

- **The Hub-and-spoke System Configuration.** A large airline operates with a hub-and-spoke system configuration. The cities served by the airline are the "spokes." However, certain of these cities are designated as "hubs" where very many flights are scheduled in such a way that passengers en route from one spoke to another will fly to a hub and then change planes to fly to their destination city. The critical decisions faced by the airline is where to locate their hubs to optimally take advantage of the geography of the markets that they serve and to retain customer satisfaction, while maintaining the economic advantages of the hub-and-spoke system overall. As the airline's route structure evolves over time, the airline must determine where to establish new hubs, where to close down existing hubs, and where to open and/or close spokes, etc. Typically, these decisions are made with the help of a binary optimization model to determine whether or not to place or remove a hub and/or spoke from the existing route system configuration. For these types of binary optimization models, the real challenge lies not in the construction of or in the solution of the model itself, but rather in developing the data that is used to describe the cost and revenue implications of various route system alternatives.

- **Demand Forecasting.** The forecasting of passenger demand for travel between pairs of cities lies at the core of many decisions about airline operations, from the determination of fares to the choice of the aircraft to fly between cities, to the physical configuration of the cabin into coach, business, and first-class seats. With today's network of computerized reservations systems, an airline typically has a vast array of data concerning historical demand on their flights. Most often, demand for reservations by flight and fare-class is modeled as a Normally distributed random variable, and so the challenge is to estimate the mean μ and the standard deviation σ of the distribution for every flight and fare class in the airline's reservations inventory. This is usually done with multiple linear regression models that account for past trends (over time) in conjunction with price levels of fares, economic trends, etc.

- **The Flight Schedule.** Once the airline has fixed its hub-and-spoke system and has reliable estimates of distributions of demand, the airline faces the task of constructing or modifying its flight schedule. Here the problem is to determine how many flights to schedule between spokes and hubs of the system. This problem is usually modeled as a very large mixed-integer optimization model, whose solution is used to develop the airline's overall flight schedule.

- **Fleet Assignment.** Once the flight schedule has been determined, the airline faces the task of assigning aircraft to each flight leg. The larger airlines operate as many as ten different types of aircraft, which vary by cabin capacity, configuration (the number of seats in coach, business, and first-class, etc.), fuel capacity (that determines how far the aircraft can fly), compatibility with airport maintenance facilities, compatibility with airport gate configurations, whether the aircraft is equipped for flight over water, etc. The problem faced by the airline is to determine which aircraft to assign to which flights in their schedule. The airline must bear in mind that once an aircraft is scheduled to arrive at a given city, the aircraft must then be reassigned to depart from that same city at a later time, after sufficient time to re-prepare the aircraft for flight (clean the cabin, unload and load baggage, re-board the aircraft, etc.). This problem is usually modeled as a very large binary optimization problem. The larger airlines estimate that their fleet assignment models contribute as much as $75 million per year to their earnings.

- **Crew Pairing.** Once the flight schedule has been determined and each flight has been assigned an aircraft, the airline must then assign a crew to the flight. Different crews are based in different cities, and there are complex government, management, and union regulations concerning how many hours a crew can work and rest in different periods of time. Furthermore, some crews are only trained for certain aircraft. And of course, all crews must return to their home city after several days of travel. The crew pairing problem is to determine which crews from which cities are assigned to which flights in a way that minimizes the overall cost to the airline. This problem is modeled as a binary optimization model. Crew pairing models have been used successfully by the larger airlines and their estimated cost savings is often on the order of $20 million per year.

- **Overbooking.** Approximately 50% of all airline reservations are either canceled or are no-shows. In the absence of intentionally overbooking of an airline's flights, upwards of 15% of all seats on a "full" flight would be empty and would be a lost revenue opportunity. For this reason, it is an economic imperative of any airline to intentionally overbook their flights. The obvious benefits (to the airline) of overbooking is the possibility of enhanced revenue due the possibility of fewer empty seats on a flight. This must be balanced against the risk of having a flight be overbooked at the time of departure, resulting in the cost of vouchers for paid passengers who are denied boarding, the cost of paying for fares for these passengers to fly on other airlines, and the loss of customer good-will. Most airlines use a relatively simple decision tree model to determine the optimal overbooking level for each flight in their flight schedule.

- **Revenue Management.** The term "revenue management" refers to the control and management of seat reservations inventory in a way that increases or maximizes the airline's profitability. In other words, revenue management has to do with selling the right seats to the right customers at the right prices (right for the airline, that is). This is such an important topic that we devote the entire rest of this section to revenue management modeling.

Background and Motivation for Revenue Management

Prior to the United States Airline Deregulation Act of 1978, airline fares and route structures within the United States were determined by the federal Civil Aeronautics Board (CAB). A carrier would be granted permission to fly a new route only if the CAB felt that it would not create "excessive competition or overcapacity" within that particular market, where a "market" is defined to be an origin-destination pair of cities, such as Chicago-Dallas or Atlanta-Philadelphia. Airfares were determined by a single formula loosely based on distance, but which also included a consideration for the overall cost structure of the industry.

In order to raise fares, carriers had to lobby together and convince the CAB that their costs had increased. After a lengthy review process, the CAB would decide whether or not fares should be raised. As such, the carriers within the airline industry had no incentive to compete with one another based on costs and thus chose to compete based on service. Piano bars and lounges were common on the upper decks of jumbo jets, and flights with only a few paying passengers onboard were not a major concern.

After 1979, however, the very nature of competition within the airline industry changed. Carriers were free to fly any route at any time and charge any price. Small upstart carriers, like Southwest Airlines and Nations Air, offered extraordinarily low fares. These upstarts threatened the major U.S. airlines, who suddenly found themselves having to compete on costs after years of consciously neglecting their overall cost structure. The major airlines recognized that they could not simply "match" the fares of these upstart airlines and hope to remain profitable in the long-run; thus, the science of **revenue management modeling** was born.

Revenue management models attempt to capture as much of the "economic rent" in a market as possible. The models aim to segment customers so that each customer pays exactly as much as the customer is willing to pay. As an example, consider a flight with 200 available seats that serves both business and leisure demand. Suppose that business passengers are willing to spend $1,200 for a ticket, whereas the price-sensitive leisure passengers are only willing to spend up to $400 for a ticket. Suppose that there are 100 business customers and 100 leisure customers for this flight.

If one were to charge a single high fare of $1,200, then the flight would receive revenues of $120,000 (= 100 × $1,200), but it would fly with 100 empty seats and forego potential revenue from leisure demand. Alternatively, one could charge a single low fare of $400. This would result in a full flight, but the revenues received would be only $80,000 (= 200 × $400). This scheme does not take advantage of the incremental revenue from business passengers, who are willing to pay as much as $1,200 for a ticket.

Ideally, one would like to have a third alternative of offering two fares: $1,200 for business passengers and $400 for leisure passengers. Observe that if this scheme were available, then the flight would receive revenues of $160,000 (= 100 × $1,200 + 100 × $400). Of course, it is not legal to discriminate among customers, charging different prices to different customers for the same product. (Moreover, if one were to ask customers to reveal the purpose of their travel, all customers would declare themselves to be leisure customers, regardless of their true status!)

One solution to this problem is to offer different "products" that legally distinguish between business and leisure passengers. For example, one could offer a $400 fare for tickets that are purchased fourteen days in advance, that require a Saturday night stay, and that is not refundable if unused. One could also offer a $1,200 fare for tickets that can be purchased any time prior to departure, that has no restrictions on Saturday night stays, and that is fully refundable if unused. The restrictions on the $400 fare make this product unattractive to business customers, who typically do not have the flexibility to schedule flights two weeks ahead of departure, and who prefer not to spend Saturday night away from home. In this way the airlines attempt to extract the highest possible revenue from every passenger and so optimize the revenue of the flight.

The previous example is a simplification of the problem, as business demand and leisure demand are both uncertain quantities. (For example, demand by business customers is typically modeled as a Normally distributed random variable.) Because of the fourteen-day advance purchase restriction on leisure fares, all demand for leisure fares will occur at least fourteen days before the flight departs. Suppose, for simplicity, that all demand for business fares will occur only within fourteen days of departure. Then, as potential leisure customers call in and purchase tickets, the question arises as to how many seats to set aside and *protect* for potential business customers. Continuing the example, suppose that in fact 170 leisure customers call in to request a booking. It might seem unwise to offer all of them a booking, as this would leave only 30 seats for potential business customers, who will be purchasing tickets only within fourteen days of departure. For this reason, airlines determine a number of seats to protect for business passengers, who may not purchase tickets until the day of departure. For this example, the airline might set a protection level of $L = 115$ seats. This means that $L = 115$ seats would be reserved for potential business demand and only $85 (= 200 - 115)$ seats would be available for leisure customers.

Of course, in setting the protection level to $L = 115$, one hopes that business demand will be at least 115 customers. This assumption might be wrong in two ways. First, business demand might be lower than 115 seats, and so turning away leisure demand would result in empty seats (and lost revenue). Second, business demand may be higher than 115 seats, in which case it would have been better to protect even more seats for the more lucrative business demand. It should be intuitive that there is some optimal value of the protection level L that optimally trades off these two possibilities and hence optimizes expected revenues to the airline. This is the essence of revenue management.

Revenue management is practiced by all of the major U.S. carriers to varying degrees of sophistication and by many other airlines worldwide (government control of fares limits its effectiveness in some regulated environments). Robert L. Crandall, former CEO of AMR and American Airlines, has stated:[1]

> I believe that revenue management is the single most important technical development in transportation management since we entered the era of airline deregulation in 1979 . . . . The development of revenue management models was a key to American Airlines' survival in the post-deregulation environment. Without revenue management we were often faced with two unsatisfactory responses in a price competitive marketplace. We could match deeply discounted fares and risk diluting our entire inventory, or we could

[1]"Yield Management at American Airlines," by Barry Smith, John Leimkuhler, and Ross Darrow, *Interfaces*, Volume 22, Number 1, January-February 1992.

not match and certainly lose market share. Revenue management gave us a third alternative—match deeply discounted fares on a portion of our inventory and close deeply discounted inventory when it is profitable to save space for later-booking higher value customers. By adjusting the number of reservations which are available at these discounts, we can adjust our minimum available fare to account for differences in demand. This creates a pricing structure which responds to demand on a flight-by-flight basis. As a result, we can more effectively match our demand to supply . . . . The development of the American Airlines' revenue-management system has been long and sometimes difficult, but this investment has paid off. We estimate that revenue management has generated $1.4 billion in incremental revenue in the last three years alone. This is not a one-time benefit. We expect revenue management to generate at least $500 million annually for the foreseeable future. As we continue to invest in the enhancement of DINAMO [the name of American Airlines' revenue management modeling system], we expect to capture an even larger revenue premium.

Revenue management models are applicable in a wide variety of industries that have advance reservations systems, a range of product prices segmented by service levels, a perishable inventory, and where customer cancellations and no-shows are part of doing business. Industries with these characteristics include the cruise line industry, the hotel industry (generating over $100 million annually for Marriott International, according to William Marriott Jr., Chairman and CEO of Marriott International), the automobile rental industry, and the passenger rail industry, among others. Most recently, revenue management models have begun to be used to set prices and protection levels for prime-time network commercial advertising in the network broadcast industry.

When an airline's route structure and fare structure are very simple, then it is straightforward to construct a revenue management model to determine optimal seat protection levels, using the fundamentals of probability together with decision tree models. This is shown in the Atlantic Air case at the end of this chapter. However, when an airline has a complex hub-and-spoke route system, one needs a more sophisticated system of models in order to captures the intricacies of the airline's more complicated operations. One such modeling system is developed in the illustrative example below.

Revenue Management at East-West Airlines

Suppose that East-West Airlines is a small airline that offers passenger air transportation between two major east coast cities, namely Boston and New York; two major west coast cities, namely San Francisco and Los Angeles; and one major midwest city, namely Chicago. East-West operates a hub in Chicago, at which passengers can change planes to their final destination. East-West Airlines owns and operates two identical Boeing 757 aircraft, each with a capacity of 200 seats. The daily schedule of these aircraft is shown in Table 10.1.

East-West offers both discounted (Q-Class) and unrestricted (Y-Class) fares. Discounted tickets must be purchased fourteen days in advance of flight departure. A Q-class ticket is non-refundable, non-changeable, and travelers must stay over a Saturday night at their destination. Unrestricted fare tickets can be purchased any time up until the departure time of the flight. A Y-Class ticket is fully refundable and can be changed simply by calling East-West's 24-hour Reservations Center.

TABLE 10.1

The daily flight schedule for East-West Airlines.

Aircraft Number	Departs: City	Time	Arrives: City	Time
1	BOSTON	8:00AM EST	CHICAGO	10:15AM CST
1	CHICAGO	10:45AM CST	SAN FRANCISCO	12:15PM PST
1	SAN FRANCISCO	5:30PM PST	CHICAGO	10:45PM CST
1	CHICAGO	11:59PM CST	BOSTON	4:30AM EST
2	NEW YORK	7:45AM EST	CHICAGO	10:15AM CST
2	CHICAGO	10:45AM CST	LOS ANGELES	12:15PM PST
2	LOS ANGELES	5:30PM PST	CHICAGO	10:45PM CST
2	CHICAGO	11:59PM CST	NEW YORK	4:45AM EST

TABLE 10.2

Prices of Q-Class and Y-Class fares for the westbound itineraries of East-West Airlines.

Itinerary From:	To:	Q-Class Fare Price	Y-Class Fare Price
BOSTON	CHICAGO	$200	$230
BOSTON	SAN FRANCISCO	$320	$420
BOSTON	LOS ANGELES	$400	$490
NEW YORK	CHICAGO	$250	$290
NEW YORK	SAN FRANCISCO	$410	$550
NEW YORK	LOS ANGELES	$450	$550
CHICAGO	SAN FRANCISCO	$200	$230
CHICAGO	LOS ANGELES	$250	$300

TABLE 10.3

The mean and standard deviation of the demand for travel on Mondays on westbound flights at East-West Airlines.

Itinerary From:	To:	Q-Class demand (Number of Passengers) μ	σ	Y-Class demand (Number of Passengers) μ	σ
BOSTON	CHICAGO	25.0	5.3	20.0	5.2
BOSTON	SAN FRANCISCO	55.0	5.1	40.0	6.0
BOSTON	LOS ANGELES	65.0	9.3	25.0	4.8
NEW YORK	CHICAGO	24.0	4.4	16.0	3.0
NEW YORK	SAN FRANCISCO	65.0	8.4	50.0	6.9
NEW YORK	LOS ANGELES	40.0	5.1	35.0	6.3
CHICAGO	SAN FRANCISCO	21.0	6.2	20.0	3.7
CHICAGO	LOS ANGELES	25.0	5.2	14.0	2.4

For the purpose of this illustrative example, we will focus exclusively on the westbound operations of East-West Airlines. Table 10.2 shows the westbound itineraries that East-West Airlines offers and their current prices for both Q-Class and Y-Class fares.

Modeling Demand with the use of Statistical Estimation

One of the many data-intensive challenges at any airline is the accurate forecasting of demand for the flights in the airline's flight schedule. Demand typically fluctuates by time of day and day of the week, as well as seasonally. Based on historical data and appealing to the Central Limit Theorem, demand for a given flight is usually modeled as a Normally distributed random variable with mean μ and standard deviation σ, where μ and σ are determined using statistical estimation. Table 10.3 shows East-West Airlines' estimates of the mean μ and standard deviation σ of demand for each of their eight westbound flights for a typical Monday. Such estimates are usually developed by computing the observed sample mean $\bar{x}$ and the observed sample standard deviation *s* based on recent historical data (typically the previous six months of flight bookings data) for the given flights, and then making adjustments based on judgments about any changes in the markets for different flights.

Optimizing the allocation of seats among itineraries and fare classes

Using the expected value information in Table 10.3, we can then compute the expected demand for seats on Mondays for each of the four westbound flight legs of East-West Airlines. This information is shown in Table 10.4. For example, the expected demand for seats on the flight leg from Chicago to San Francisco in Q-class is $55.0 + 65.0 + 21.0 = 141.0$. Notice in the last column of Table 10.4 that the total expected demand for seats exceeds the capacity of the aircraft (which is 200 seats) for every westbound flight leg. Therefore, it is imperative that East-West Airlines limit the number of seats that can be reserved for certain flights and certain fare classes, so as to optimize their revenues. We next indicate how to construct a linear optimization model that will optimally determine the number of seats that should be reserved for each flight and each fare class.

We start by defining the following sixteen decision variables:

BCQ, BCY = Number of passenger reservations on the flight from Boston to Chicago that should be accepted in classes Q and Y, respectively.

BSQ, BSY = Number of passenger reservations on the flight from Boston to San Francisco that should be accepted in classes Q and Y, respectively.

BLQ, BLY = Number of passenger reservations on the flight from Boston to Los Angeles that should be accepted in classes Q and Y, respectively.

NCQ, NCY = Number of passenger reservations on the flight from New York to Chicago that should be accepted in classes Q and Y, respectively.

NSQ, NSY = Number of passenger reservations on the flight from New York to San Francisco that should be accepted in classes Q and Y, respectively.

NLQ, NLY = Number of passenger reservations on the flight from New York to Los Angeles that should be accepted in classes Q and Y, respectively.

CSQ, CSY = Number of passenger reservations on the flight from Chicago to San Francisco that should be accepted in classes Q and Y, respectively.

CLQ, CLY = Number of passenger reservations on the flight from Chicago to Los Angeles that should be accepted in classes Q and Y, respectively.

The objective function of the linear optimization model is to maximize revenue. Using the price information in Table 10.2, we can express the revenue as follows:

$$\text{Revenue norm} = 200BCQ + 230BCY + \cdots + 250CLQ + 300CLY.$$

TABLE 10.4

The expected demand for seats on Mondays for each of the four westbound flight legs of East-West Airlines.

Flight Leg		Q-Class Demand (Number of Passengers)	Y-Class Demand (Number of Passengers)	Total (Number of Passengers)
From:	To:			
BOSTON	CHICAGO	145.0	85.0	230.0
NEW YORK	CHICAGO	129.0	101.0	230.0
CHICAGO	SAN FRANCISCO	141.0	110.0	251.0
CHICAGO	LOS ANGELES	130.0	74.0	204.0

The capacity of every flight leg is 200 seats, and so we must include the following capacity constraints for each flight leg:

BC Capacity:	$BCQ + BSQ + BLQ + BCY + BSY + BLY \leq 200,$
NC Capacity:	$NCQ + NSQ + NLQ + NCY + NSY + NLY \leq 200,$
CS Capacity:	$CSQ + BSQ + NSQ + CSY + BSY + NSY \leq 200,$
CL Capacity:	$CLQ + BLQ + NLQ + CLY + BLY + NLY \leq 200.$

Let us also include the constraint that the number of passenger reservations for each flight and each fare class must not exceed expected demand:

BCQ Demand:	$BCQ \leq 25$
BCY Demand:	$BCY \leq 20$
BSQ Demand:	$BSQ \leq 55$
BSY Demand:	$BSY \leq 40$
$\vdots$	$\vdots \quad \vdots$
CLQ Demand:	$CLQ \leq 25$
CLY Demand:	$CLY \leq 14.$

And of course, we must include the nonnegativity conditions:

Nonnegativity: $BCQ \geq 0, BCY \geq 0, \ldots, CLQ \geq 0, CLY \geq 0.$

The entire linear optimization model is therefore:

maximize	$200BCQ + 230BCY + \cdots + 250CLQ + 300CLY$
subject to:	
BC Capacity:	$BCQ + BSQ + BLQ + BCY + BSY + BLY \leq 200$
NC Capacity:	$NCQ + NSQ + NLQ + NCY + NSY + NLY \leq 200$
CS Capacity:	$CSQ + BSQ + NSQ + CSY + BSY + NSY \leq 200$
CL Capacity:	$CLQ + BLQ + NLQ + CLY + BLY + NLY \leq 200$
BCQ Demand:	$BCQ \leq 25$
BCY Demand:	$BCY \leq 20$
BSQ Demand:	$BSQ \leq 55$
BSY Demand:	$BSY \leq 40$
$\vdots$	$\vdots \quad \vdots$
CLQ Demand:	$CLQ \leq 25$
CLY Demand:	$CLY \leq 14$
Nonnegativity:	$BCQ, BCY, \ldots, CLQ, CLY \geq 0.$

This linear optimization model is designed to select how to allocate seats on each flight leg, while taking into account that passengers on certain flights occupy seats on one or more different flight legs. For example, a passenger on the flight from Boston to San Francisco will occupy a seat on the flight from Boston to Chicago and will occupy another seat on the flight from Chicago to San Francisco.

Notice that this linear optimization model comprises 16 decision variables and 20 constraints. The optimal solution of the linear optimization model is shown in Table 10.5 with an optimized total revenue over all flights of $182,280. It is evident

TABLE 10.5

The optimal solution of the linear optimization model to determine the number of reservations to accept for every flight and every fare class for westbound flights at East-West Airlines.

Itinerary		Q-Class Reservations Limit		Y-Class Reservations Limit	
From:	To:	Variable	Optimal Value	Variable	Optimal Value
BOSTON	CHICAGO	BCQ	25	BCY	20
BOSTON	SAN FRANCISCO	BSQ	25	BSY	40
BOSTON	LOS ANGELES	BLQ	65	BLY	25
NEW YORK	CHICAGO	NCQ	19	NCY	16
NEW YORK	SAN FRANCISCO	NSQ	44	NSY	50
NEW YORK	LOS ANGELES	NLQ	36	NLY	35
CHICAGO	SAN FRANCISCO	CSQ	21	CSY	20
CHICAGO	LOS ANGELES	CLQ	25	CLY	14

TABLE 10.6

The allocation of demand for seats on Mondays for each of the four westbound flight legs of East-West Airlines.

Flight Leg				
From:	To:	Q-Class	Y-Class	Total
BOSTON	CHICAGO	115	85	200
NEW YORK	CHICAGO	99	101	200
CHICAGO	SAN FRANCISCO	90	110	200
CHICAGO	LOS ANGELES	126	74	200

from the solution shown in Table 10.5 that all of the demand for Y-class fares is satisfied, and that the remaining seat capacity on each flight leg is then distributed optimally among Q-class fare demand.

Table 10.5 can be used to determine exactly how the seats of each westbound flight leg should be allocated. This is shown in Table 10.6. For example, the number of seats allocated for Q-class passengers on the flight leg from Chicago to Los Angeles is computed from Table 10.5 as

$$BLQ + NLQ + CLQ = 65 + 36 + 25 = 126.$$

This number is shown in the bottom row of the third column in Table 10.6.

Shadow prices, simulation modeling, and bid-price control policies for accepting fare reservation requests

One difficulty in using the above linear optimization model is that the model uses only the expected demand for each flight and each fare class. In reality, the actual demand is a random variable whose value is unknown, but whose distribution has been estimated, as shown in Table 10.3. For this reason, many airlines use the output of the linear optimization model in conjunction with simulation modeling to optimize the policies for accepting fare reservation requests. We now indicate how this is done.

Recall that the linear optimization model contains capacity constraints for each flight leg, namely:

BC Capacity:	$BCQ + BSQ + BLQ + BCY + BSY + BLY \leq 200,$
NC Capacity:	$NCQ + NSQ + NLQ + NCY + NSY + NLY \leq 200,$
CS Capacity:	$CSQ + BSQ + NSQ + CSY + BSY + NSY \leq 200,$
CL Capacity:	$CLQ + BLQ + NLQ + CLY + BLY + NLY \leq 200.$

TABLE 10.7

The shadow prices of the capacity constraints for the four westbound flight legs of East-West Airlines.

Flight Leg		
From:	To:	Shadow Price
BOSTON	CHICAGO	$150/seat
NEW YORK	CHICAGO	$240/seat
CHICAGO	SAN FRANCISCO	$170/seat
CHICAGO	LOS ANGELES	$210/seat

TABLE 10.8

Bid-Prices of all flights and fare classes for westbound flights at East-West Airlines.

Itinerary		Opportunity Cost ($/seat)	Q-Class		Y-Class	
From:	To:		Revenue ($)	Bid-Price ($)	Revenue ($)	Bid-Price ($)
BOSTON	CHICAGO	150	200	50	230	80
BOSTON	SAN FRANCISCO	320	320	0	420	100
BOSTON	LOS ANGELES	360	400	40	490	130
NEW YORK	CHICAGO	240	250	10	290	50
NEW YORK	SAN FRANCISCO	410	410	0	550	140
NEW YORK	LOS ANGELES	450	450	0	550	100
CHICAGO	SAN FRANCISCO	170	200	30	230	60
CHICAGO	LOS ANGELES	210	250	40	300	90

The shadow price for each of these constraints is computed along with the computation of the optimal solution of the linear optimization model. These shadow prices are shown in Table 10.7.

Now suppose that East-West Airlines' reservations center receives a request for a Q-class fare on their Monday flight from Boston to Los Angeles. If the airline were to accept the request, this action would effectively reduce the remaining capacity by one seat on both the Boston-to-Chicago flight leg as well as on the Chicago-to-Los Angeles flight leg. The opportunity cost of accepting such a request is therefore equal to the sum of the two shadow prices on each of these flight legs, that is:

$$\text{opportunity cost} = \$150 + \$210 = \$360.$$

The difference between the revenue of accepting the request and the opportunity cost is therefore $40 = $400 − $360. This difference is called the **bid-price** for the fare. Using the fares for all flights shown in Table 10.2 and the shadow price information shown in Table 10.7, we can easily compute the bid-price for each flight and fare combination. These bid-prices are shown in Table 10.8.

Intuitively, the fare with the highest bid-price is the most profitable for the airline. For this example, the Y-class fare from New York to San Francisco has the highest bid-price, which is $140. Under the bid-price control policy, all requests for Y-class fares from New York to San Francisco would be accepted. The next most profitable fare is the Y-class fare from Boston to Los Angeles, whose bid-price is $130. Requests for this fare would also always be accepted, because this flight does not use any shared resources with the flight from New York to San Francisco. The next highest bid-prices are the Y-class fare from Boston to San Francisco and the Y-class fare from New York to Los Angeles. Under the bid-price control policy, we would accept requests for Y-class fares from Boston to San Francisco only up to a certain threshold. The intuition for not accepting every request is because we would like to protect some seats for the most profitable routes, namely New York to San Francisco and

Boston to Los Angeles. Similarly, we would accept requests for Y-class fares from New York to Los Angeles only up to a certain threshold. In other words, we accept requests for a certain flight up to a certain threshold.

The practical problem with implementing the above bid-price control policy is to optimally determine the threshold levels for accepting reservation requests according to the priorities determined by the bid-price computation. This is where simulation modeling is used to great advantage. Most airlines construct a simulation model, based on the estimated demand distributions for flights and fares, that is run many times to test the revenue implications of different thresholds on reservation acceptance limits. By making many runs of the simulation model, airlines attempt to maximize the expected revenue of their entire flight schedule. The details of these models goes beyond the scope of this book. However, such models are of the utmost value to an airline: Revenue management models enhance revenues by upwards of $500 million per year for some large airlines.

When the flight schedule of the airline is simple, then in fact the threshold levels for accepting flight reservations can be determined by solving a simple equation. This is illustrated at the end of the chapter in the Atlantic Air case.

Section Summary

Management science tools and models are of critical importance in the management of today's large airlines which operate a complex route system and offer an array of fares on their flights. Revenue management models have revolutionized the operations and the economics of the airline industry. These models use or otherwise incorporate statistical estimation, linear regression, optimization modeling, and simulation modeling. Furthermore, revenue management models are now starting to have a fundamental impact on other industries that are characterized by advanced reservations systems, a range of product prices segmented by service levels, a perishable inventory, and where customer cancellations and no-shows are part of doing business. Industries with these characteristics include the passenger cruise line industry, the hotel industry, the automobile rental industry, the passenger rail industry, and the network broadcast industry, among others.

10.2 | MANAGEMENT SCIENCE MODELS IN THE INVESTMENT MANAGEMENT INDUSTRY

The investment management industry is concerned with the management of investments for clients ranging from giant institutional investors (such as employee pension funds, university endowments, etc.) to individuals who are saving money in their very first jobs. This industry has grown by leaps and bounds in the past two decades due to a variety of factors, including the deregulation of many financial markets, the economic growth of the world's largest industrialized nations, and the use of management science models and tools.

Management science models and tools are used in the investment management industry to analyze huge amounts of financial data, predict the future value of large pools of assets, optimally determine investment quantities that are efficient in terms of risk and return, and to automatically trade in a large number of assets in a large number of markets. One of the major motivations for using management science models in investment management is that such models have the ability to work with thousands of securities simultaneously, and the models are designed to rigorously control both risk and trading costs. This is in contrast with the traditional approach of "active" management that depends on a small group of professionals to research investment alternatives. Whereas these professional investment managers (presumably) bring a certain amount of expert judgment to bear on investment decisions, their more subjective approach cannot exclude institutional biases that are sometimes harmful to investment performance. In fact, the quantitative analysis division of today's typical investment firm manages much larger amounts of money than the more traditional "active" division of the firm.

Here are some of the more important uses of management science models and tools in the investment management industry:

- **Analysis of Financial Data.** The computerization and automation of financial markets has spawned gigantic amounts of financial data. It is now possible to conveniently amalgamate data on minute-to-minute price changes of thousands of financial instruments (stocks, bonds, Treasury bills, etc.) over large periods of time. This data is used to analyze trends in individual companies, in industrial sectors, and in financial markets as a whole. The data is also used to track and test for correlation among different financial assets and between asset returns and macroeconomic indicators (such as the inflation rate, various measures of the money supply, etc.). The management science tools that are used in such data analysis primarily are statistical estimation, including estimating means and standard deviations, and in computing confidence intervals for these financial estimates.

- **Forecasting Future Performance of Assets.** The ultimate purpose of most financial data analysis is to assist in estimating the probability distributions of the future performance of financial assets. Prices and/or rates-of-return of assets are usually modeled as Normally distributed random variables, and so the probability distributions are characterized by the mean μ and standard deviation σ of the distribution. There are a wide variety of management science tools and models that are used in forecasting the means and standard deviations of future asset performance. The most often-used model is multiple linear regression. The use of multiple linear regression was illustrated in the case "Sloan Investors, Part I" in Chapter 6. The independent variables in these models usually include firm-specific variables such as price-to-earnings ratios, industry-wide and economy-wide variables such as industry sales and economic growth variables, as well as other independent variables that might capture the idiosyncrasies of a particular company. The output of these models is a prediction of the expected price of the asset at some future date. This number is then typically adjusted up or down using the expert judgment of the investment analyst. The net result of such forecasting activities are predictions of the distributions of asset performance, which are then used to construct portfolios of assets.

- **Construction and Management of Efficient Portfolios.** As has been discussed extensively in Chapter 8, the determination of investment levels in different assets in a diversified portfolio, so as to efficiently trade off risk and return, is modeled as a nonlinear optimization problem. Such optimization models lie at the core of today's successful investment management firms. The "Endurance Investors" case in Chapter 8 describes a prototypical portfolio management optimization model. The case "Sloan Investor, Part II," at the end of this chapter, illustrates how regression models and optimization models are used in an integrated fashion to develop efficient portfolios of assets. More complex models are used to capture some of the subtleties of portfolio management, such as controlling trading costs and managing trades in the portfolio over time.

- **Determining Trading Strategies that Minimize Trading Costs.** One of the challenges in managing a portfolio of assets lies in keeping the portfolio efficient (that is, ensuring that risk is minimized and/or that return is maximized) while also not incurring excessive trading costs as the portfolio is constantly being rebalanced. In order to keep the portfolio from becoming unwieldy, most investment managers prefer that their portfolios contain only a relatively small number of assets. Furthermore, there is always the issue of the timing of trades. ("Should we make the trade today, or wait until tomorrow?") Many financial investment firms use a more complicated version of the basic portfolio optimization model that incorporates these considerations into their model. Such models use a combination of integer optimization (discussed in Chapter 9 and further illustrated in Exercise 9.9 at the end of Chapter 9), optimization under uncertainty (discussed in Section 7.7 of Chapter 7), and other modeling tools that go beyond the scope of this book.

- **Evaluation of Financial Assets such as Options and other Derivative Securities.** A derivative security is a financial asset whose price depends, at least in part, on the price and performance of one or more other securities. For example, a put option on the price of a company is a derivative security, as the price of the put option depends on the price of the stock in the company. The evaluation of the value of derivative securities such as put options is usually done with the help of simulation modeling tools and decision trees. This was illustrated in the case "To Hedge or Not to Hedge?" at the end of Chapter 5, where simulation modeling was used to evaluate the value of various currency put options.

The preceding is just a partial description of the various ways that management science tools and models are used throughout the investment management industry. The investment management industry is undergoing a steady revolution in its operations and practices as management science models become more extensively used.

10.3   A YEAR IN THE LIFE OF A MANUFACTURING COMPANY

Management science models are extremely useful in the management of manufacturing companies. While their use is not quite as pervasive as in the financial investment management industry and the airline industry, more and more manufacturing companies are finding it necessary to approach more of their central management problems with a modeling-oriented philosophy. In this section, and in the accompanying four cases at the end of the chapter, we illustrate the use of management science models at the Lexington Laser Corporation (LLC), which is a medium-sized manufacturing company that produces telecommunication equipment. (The name of the actual company is different; it has been disguised for use in this book.)

The Lexington Laser Corporation

Background

The commercialization of fiber optic technology over the past two decades has dramatically transformed the field of communications. The benefits of optical fibers—the tremendous information-carrying capability, distortion-free secure transmission, and minimal size and weight—have resulted in the rapid worldwide implementation of fiber optics. The technology came of age in the early 1980's, when the avail-

FIGURE 10.1
Penetration of fiber optics into a variety of communication applications.

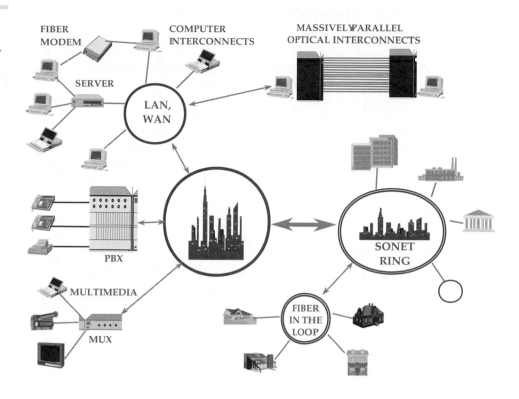

FIGURE 10.2
The process of fiber optic transmission.

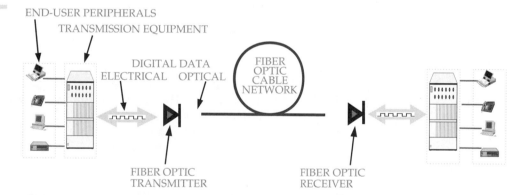

ability of laser diode sources and single-mode optical fiber ushered in the era of fiber optic communication. Figure 10.1 illustrates the penetration of fiber optics into a variety of communication applications.

The key components of a fiber optic communication link are the transmitter and the receiver. As illustrated in Figure 10.2, the fiber optic transmitter translates an electrical data stream of "0"s and "1"s (originating from the end-user peripherals) into an optical data stream of pulses of light. The optical signal travels across the optical fiber, and is then translated back into the original electrical signal by the fiber optic receiver. These transmitters and receivers are collectively known as optoelectronic components, because they are responsible for the translation of the communication signals between the optical and electrical domains.

The Lexington Laser Corporation

Aggressive commercialization of fiber optic systems has spurred the rapid evolution and deployment of broadband optical networks that serve an ever-advancing communications infrastructure. These advances have, in turn, created an enormous demand for fiber optic components.

Lexington Laser Corporation (LLC) was an early player in the component market, and its product line has grown (primarily through acquisitions) as the industry has evolved. LLC now serves short- and long-haul telecommunications, as well as data communications. Historically, LLC's strength has been its ability to develop and commercialize products with very different design and manufacturing profiles. The low-volume high-end components are usually hand-assembled, whereas commodity products are more often produced by highly automated robots in the same factory.

Long-Haul Telecommunications

The long-haul components were LLC's first product line, evolving over the 1980's. Until recently, the fiber optic portion of telecommunications was limited to relatively long-distance links. The key requirements for these optoelectronic components, which form the backbones of long-haul telecommunication links, are performance and reliability, with economic pressures playing a secondary role. Even today, these $500–$5,000 components are necessarily associated with expensive, sophisticated, labor-intensive manufacturing processes. These components typically operate at data rates of 2.5 gigabytes/second and above and can simultaneously carry upwards of 32,000 voice channels.

Short-Haul Telecommunications

Eighteen months ago, LLC acquired Bedford Laser, a manufacturer of components for the short-haul segment. Although the margins on these commodity products are lower than on the high-performance long-haul parts, LLC needed to deliver a broad suite of products to its customers. The recent availability of low-cost optoelectronics is paving the way for the extension of fiber optics ever closer to the consumer. Through communication network architectures that deploy these low-cost components between main switching centers and neighborhoods (and even individual homes), telephony service providers are (literally!) bringing the enormous advantages of fiber to our doorsteps.

The short-haul components' successful implementation hinges on the system provider's ability to economically deploy these devices in commodity-level quantities and at commodity prices (primarily in the range of $50–$200). These are relatively simple devices that typically are comprised of a low-cost laser chip, plastic lenses, and a simple housing.

Data Communications

In order to capitalize on the increasing data-communications bandwidth requirements driven by the growth of the Internet, six months ago LLC acquired Boston Datacom Components. In response to the challenges faced by today's data communications networks—limited bandwidth, data-hungry computing devices and applications, faster servers, and more users—fiber optics is being embraced as the technology that can alleviate the networks' bottlenecks. The shifting economics of the network architectures operating in the 10–200 megabytes/second region is driving the metamorphosis of the preferred communications medium from copper cable to fiber optic cable. In addition to the optoelectronic chips, these components typically include electronics interface chips for electrical signal formatting and timing recovery.

LLC Case Modules

In the case modules at the end of this chapter, we present four different cases, each representing a management problem faced by Lexington Laser Corporation over a recent year. A synopsis of these cases is as follows:

- **A Strategic Alliance for the Lexington Laser Corporation**

  In this case, Nick Lewis, vice president of Sales & Marketing at LLC, needs to determine whether or not to forge a strategic supply arrangement between LLC and Aspen Networks, and how to structure such an arrangement.

- **Yield of a Multi-Step Manufacturing Process**

  In this case, Julie Weller, vice president of Manufacturing at LLC, would like to determine the relationship between the number of laser starts per week, and the percentage of weeks that LLC is able to meet demand from Aspen.

- **Prediction of Yields in Manufacturing**

  This case is concerned with understanding the factors that impact on the yield in one of LLC's manufacturing processes. Steve Lo, a Manufacturing Engineering Manager at LLC, would like to determine which factors are causing the low yields in the pigtail step of the manufacturing of one of LLC's laser lines.

- **Allocation of Production Personnel**

  The problem addressed in this case is the efficient allocation of workers across tasks. Julie Weller, vice president of Manufacturing at LLC, would like to determine the most cost-effective allocation of workers by pay grade to the three different product lines at LLC.

  Each of these cases is well-suited for analysis and solution by the methods and tools of management science presented in this book.

10.4   SUMMARY

In this chapter, we have attempted to illustrate how management science models and tools are used in an integrative way in the management of a company. We have chosen examples from the investment management industry and the airline industry, and we have highlighted cases from a typical manufacturing enterprise. When used wisely, management science models and tools have enormous power to enhance the competitiveness of almost any company or enterprise. Indeed, we believe that the use of management science tools and models represents the future of best-practices for tomorrow's successful companies.

CASE MODULES

SLOAN INVESTORS, PART II

Recall that in the case "Sloan Investors, Part I," presented at the end of Chapter 6, the goal was to develop a multiple linear regression model that can be used to predict the expected future stock price returns for GM and IBM for Jim Theiser's new venture. Please take a moment to review Part I of this case before you continue. In Part II, the goal will be to build upon the analysis in Part I and to incorporate the optimization of risk into a model of portfolio performance.

As we saw in Chapter 8, an investor should be concerned not only with the expected return of her portfolio, but also with the risk that is incurred to achieve that expected return. Accordingly, professional money managers often spend considerable effort minimizing the risk of their portfolios. As we saw in Chapter 8, the problem of selecting how much to invest in each stock in a portfolio, in order to minimize risk subject to meeting a target expected return for the portfolio, can be formulated and solved as a nonlinear optimization model. As the target expected return is allowed to increase, the risk of the portfolio also increases. If we plot the minimum possible level of risk for every possible expected return, the curve that would be created is known as the **efficient frontier** of the portfolio (see Figure 8.10 in Chapter 8).

Although the process of computing the efficient frontier appears to be relatively straightforward, there are some very real obstacles to using the efficient frontier in practice. In theory, the efficient frontier is computed based on knowledge of future expected returns and future standard deviations and covariances among stocks. Unfortunately, it is impossible to know what these future values will be. Instead, they have to be estimated, using some combination of analysis of historical data (typically using a regression model) and expert judgment. As described in Part I of the case, Jim Theiser has used linear regression to estimate expected returns. To estimate future risk, Jim has decided to use the 12-month trailing standard deviation of historical returns, as well as the trailing 12-month sample covariances among the stocks in the portfolio. The use of the 12-month trailing standard deviations and covariances assumes that past risk is a predictor of future risk. Of course, this might or might not turn out to be valid. If Jim's estimates of expected return and risk do not have any future predictive power, then the optimization model that is supposed to minimize the risk of the portfolio will turn out to be minimizing noise! Jim is well aware of this situation, but he currently believes that there is sufficient predictive power from past data on the risk of stocks to make the data for the optimization model sufficiently reliable for use in practice.

Assignment:

In the assignment for Sloan Investors, Part I, you have already estimated the expected stock returns for two of the stocks in Jim's portfolio (IBM and General Motors) for the period January, 1996 through June, 1996. The spreadsheet SLOAN-INVESTORSII.XLS contains the expected returns for all 30 stocks in the Dow 30 index as well as the historical covariance matrix for each month between January, 1996 through June, 1996.

(a) Using the data in the spreadsheet SLOAN-INVESTORSII.XLS, construct a nonlinear optimization model and use the model to compute the efficient frontier for each of the six months from January, 1996 through June, 1996. (You need not be concerned with transaction costs in the construction of your model. Also, you can assume that Jim Theiser would prefer that you have no cash holdings, so that 100% of the portfolio's assets are invested in stocks during the entire six-month period.)

(b) Perform a simple calculation of the cumulative predicted expected return and standard deviation of the return of the Dow 30 index for the entire six-month period using an equal weighting for each of the 30 stocks in the Dow 30.

(c) Using the efficient frontier data computed in part (a), compute the cumulative predicted expected return over the entire six-month period for a suitably optimized portfolio with comparable risk to the Dow 30.

(d) Write a 2–3 page memo to Jim Theiser, providing him with the results of your analysis, as well as your opinion of the quality of the model. Please comment on whether you think that using historical risk as a future predictor is meaningful in this context. Also, list as many areas as possible where the model could be improved.

REVENUE MANAGEMENT AT ATLANTIC AIR

Brief History of Atlantic Air

Atlantic Air is a small, upstart carrier formed out of the large pool of highly qualified airline personnel left unemployed in the wake of many recent airline bankruptcies. Owned and operated by its pilots, flight attendants and support staff, Atlantic Air currently leases one jet with a capacity of 50 seats. Atlantic Air was able to lease this jet from Canadair after a canceled order from an ailing carrier. Atlantic Air has been given sole route authority to fly a shuttle-type operation between Boston and Elizabeth Island, a vacation destination off of the coast of Cape Cod. In addition to the many fine beach resorts and quaint New England inns located on the island, there is also a new convention center which has attracted a considerable amount of interest from businesses along the Atlantic coast.

Fare Products Offered

Recognizing that there exists a market for both business and leisure travel to Elizabeth Island, Atlantic Air's Pricing Department wishes to offer two different fare products on all of their flights :

- **Discounted Fare (Q-Class):** These tickets must be purchased fourteen days in advance of flight departure. They are non-refundable, non-changeable, and travelers must stay over a Saturday night at their destination.

- **Unrestricted Fare (Y-Class):** These tickets can be purchased any time up until flight departure. They are fully refundable and can be changed simply by calling Atlantic Air's 24-hour Reservations Center.

Demand Forecasts

The Sales Department at Atlantic Air has set the current prices for fares to be $250 and $750 per one-way ticket for Q-Class and Y-Class passengers, respectively. Atlantic Air's Business Planning Department has estimated the demand per flight for each of the two fare classes offered based on these prices and on historical data, using linear regression models and other forecasting tools. For each fare class, passenger demand is modeled using the Normal distribution. Table 10.9 shows the

TABLE 10.9

Estimates of the mean and the standard deviation of demand per flight for Q-class and Y-class passengers.

	Q-Class Demand	Y-Class Demand
Mean	$\mu_Q = 29.17$	$\mu_Y = 27.86$
Standard Deviation	$\sigma_Q = 7.29$	$\sigma_Y = 5.57$

TABLE 10.10

An example of protection levels and booking limits for an aircraft with 150 seats.

	Q-Class	Y-Class
Protection Level		20
Booking Limit	130	150

estimates of the mean and standard deviation of the demand (per flight) for Q-Class and Y-Class passengers.

The ratio of the standard deviation to the mean of the distribution of demand is known as the "K-factor" of demand in the jargon of the airline industry. For Q-Class passengers, the K-factor is $0.25 = 7.29/29.17$, and for Y-Class passengers the K-factor is $0.20 = 5.57/27.86$. The larger K-factor for Q-Class passenger demand reflects the relatively greater uncertainty associated with the more price-sensitive leisure travelers.

The Seat Allocation Decision

Since low-fare passengers are required to purchase their tickets fourteen days in advance of flight departure, it is necessary to "protect" or set aside a certain number of seats for the high-fare passengers, who tend to book their tickets only a few days (or hours) before departure. Thus, the number seats made available to low-fare (Q-Class) passengers is limited to the capacity of the aircraft minus the number of seats protected for the high-fare (Y-Class) passengers.

Airlines refer to this number of seats as the "booking limit" of a particular fare class. The booking limit for high-fare (Y-Class) passengers is simply the capacity of the aircraft, as you would never reject a request made by a Y-Class passenger in hopes of later selling that seat to a low-fare (Q-Class) passenger. For example, if we wish to protect 20 seats for Y-Class passengers on an aircraft with 150 seats, the booking limits for the two fare classes are as shown in Table 10.10.

The specific number of seats protected for Y-Class passengers is, in some sense, a gamble. For example, if we set the protection level too high, any seats not sold to Y-Class passengers by the time of departure will go empty (since Q-Class passengers cannot purchase tickets past the fourteen-day restriction). Each empty seat that was protected for a Y-Class passenger that could have been sold to a Q-Class passenger represents a lost revenue opportunity (equal to the Q-Class fare) for Atlantic Air.

On the other hand, if we set the protection level too low, we may wind up selling too many seats to Q-Class passengers, such that some Y-Class passengers wishing to purchase tickets are turned away due to lack of seat availability. A seat sold to a Q-Class passenger that could otherwise have been sold to a Y-Class passenger also represents a lost revenue opportunity, equal to the difference between the two fares. Revenue management models attempt to maximize expected revenue for a given flight by setting protection levels so as to precisely balance the upside and downside risks described above.

The Model

The decision to accept or reject a low-fare request can be formulated as the decision tree problem shown in Figure 10.3.

If an airline accepts a low-fare request, the revenues it earns is the price of the low fare. If the airline rejects a low-fare request, two outcomes are possible. First, it might be able to sell that seat to a high-fare customer, in which case the revenues it earns is the price of the high fare. Second, it might not be able to sell that seat to a high-fare customer, and so rejecting the low-fare request would result in an additional empty seat and no additional revenue.

The decision depends on x, the probability of being able to sell a high-fare ticket when a low-fare request is rejected. The decision tree suggests that a low-fare request is to be rejected if

$$(x)(\$\text{high-fare}) \geq (\$\text{low-fare}).$$

A useful approach for solving this problem is the following "marginal cost" analysis. Suppose that L is the number of seats already protected for high-fare passengers. Let us consider the question of whether it is better to protect an additional seat. The decision of whether or not an additional seat, which we will call seat $L + 1$, should be protected needs to be made when there is a low-fare request that would require seat $L + 1$. The decision tree associated with this problem is shown in Figure 10.4.

In Figure 10.4, p denotes the probability that the airline can sell at least $L + 1$ seats to high-fare customers. That is, p is the probability that high-fare demand will be at least $L + 1$:

$$p = P(\text{High-fare demand} \geq L + 1).$$

FIGURE 10.3
Decision tree that determines whether to accept or reject a low-fare request.

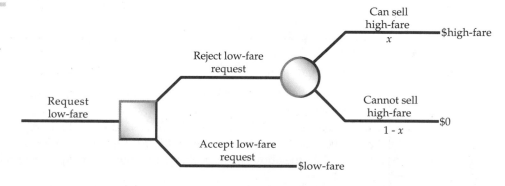

FIGURE 10.4
Decision tree that determines whether to accept or reject the low-fare request for seat $L + 1$.

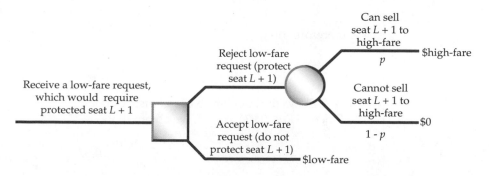

Let N_Y be the random variable representing high-fare demand; let P_Q denote the low fare and P_Y denote the high-fare. The decision tree suggests that seat $L + 1$ should be protected if

$$p \times (\$\text{high-fare}) \geq (\$\text{low-fare}),$$

which is equivalent to saying that seat $L + 1$ should be protected if

$$P(N_Y \geq L + 1) \geq \frac{P_Q}{P_Y}.$$

Conversely, given that L seats have been protected, an additional seat does not need to be protected if

$$P(N_Y \geq L + 1) < \frac{P_Q}{P_Y}.$$

This analysis suggests that the optimal protection level is that number L^* such that

$$P(N_Y \geq L^* + 1) = \frac{P_Q}{P_Y}.$$

However, because

$$P(N_Y \geq L^* + 1) = 1 - P(N_Y \leq L^*),$$

the above condition is the same as

$$P(N_Y \leq L^*) = 1 - \frac{P_Q}{P_Y} = \frac{P_Y - P_Q}{P_Y}.$$

Therefore, the optimal protection level L^* will satisfy the equation:

$$P(N_Y \leq L^*) = \frac{P_Y - P_Q}{P_Y}.$$

A simple example

Let us see how this equation works on a simple example. Suppose that N_Y, which is the demand for Y-class passengers on a given flight, obeys a Normal distribution with mean $\mu_Y = 55.0$ and standard deviation $\sigma_Y = 12.0$. Suppose further that fares are \$200 and \$800 per one-way ticket for Q-Class and Y-Class passengers, respectively. Then the above formula states that the optimal protection level L^* will satisfy:

$$P(N_Y \leq L^*) = \frac{P_Y - P_Q}{P_Y} = \frac{800 - 200}{800} = 0.75.$$

We therefore solve:

$$0.75 = P(N_Y \leq L^*) = P\left(\frac{N_Y - \mu_Y}{\sigma_Y} \leq \frac{L^* - \mu_Y}{\sigma_Y}\right) = P\left(Z \leq \frac{L^* - 55.0}{12.0}\right),$$

where Z obeys the standard Normal distribution.
Since $P(Z \leq 0.67) = 0.75$, we obtain that

$$\frac{L^* - 55.0}{12.0} = 0.67$$

and so

$$L^* = 55.0 + 12.0 \times 0.67 = 63.04 \approx 63.$$

The optimal number of seats to protect for Y-class passengers is thus computed to be $L^* = 63$ seats.

Note that the optimal protection level L^* depends only on the ratio of the low fare to the high fare and on the probability distribution of demand for the high-fare passengers. In the above model, the optimal protection level L^* does not depend directly on either the demand distribution for low-fare passengers or on the capacity of the aircraft.

The Spreadsheet Model

The spreadsheet AIRATL.XLS contains the simple model of seat protection developed above for the analysis of Atlantic Air. The data for the case is contained in the spreadsheet in cells B5:G9. The user-defined inputs for the spreadsheet are:

- the protection level L (in cell E14), and

- the capacity of the aircraft (in cell G6).

The spreadsheet computes the following output:

- the expected revenue for the protection level L (in cell E17)

- the optimal protection level L^* (in cell H14), and

- the expected revenue for the optimal protection level L^* (in cell H17).

Assignment:

(a) **Computing the Optimal Protection Level.** Without resorting to the spreadsheet, and instead using only the equation developed in the case, compute the optimal protection level L^* for Y-class fares for Atlantic Air.

(b) **Analysis of a New Lease Option.** Atlantic Air currently operates two round-trip flights per day (for a total of 4 flight legs) and operates 365 days per year, using a Canadair jet that they lease directly from Canadair. Canadair has recently had a canceled order for one of their larger jets (with a capacity of 75 seats), and would be interested in leasing this larger jet to Atlantic Air, allowing Atlantic Air to trade in their lease on their 50-seat jet. For an additional $1.5 million per year above their current lease price, Atlantic Air can trade in their 50-seat aircraft for a lease on a new 75-seat Canadair jet. The new jet has slightly higher operating costs ($2,000 more per flight leg, due to extra fuel burn) but does not require any changes in crew or maintenance equipment. Use the spreadsheet model AIRATL.XLS to analyze whether or not Atlantic Air should accept Canadair's offer. (Note: Do not worry about interest rates, inflation, taxes or depreciation. Simple cash flow calculations will suffice.)

(c) **Negotiated Group Discounted Fares.** Suppose that the Cambridge Consulting Group (CCG) is planning a strategy retreat for their partners on Elizabeth Island, and is hoping to negotiate a group discount on fares for the retreat. If there are 16 partners planning to attend the retreat, what is the minimum economically rational fare that Atlantic Air can charge CCG?

A STRATEGIC ALLIANCE FOR THE LEXINGTON LASER CORPORATION

The Opportunity

As he was driving home Friday evening, Nick Lewis, Vice President of Sales & Marketing at LLC, kept thinking about the interesting opportunity he had stumbled upon during last week's west-coast business development trip. It seems that Aspen Networks, an emerging company in the network business, has a requirement for a custom laser transmitter for one of their new transmission systems. Although there are industry-standard transmitters available from several established manufacturers, employing the industry-standard transmitter in next-generation transmission systems would require the system manufacturer to add functional building blocks external to the transmitter.

While this is precisely the approach that Aspen's competitors are pursuing, Aspen would like to incorporate additional functionality inside the laser module itself, in order to reduce the size (and the cost) of the transmission system. Because Aspen's strength is in communications systems—and not in optoelectronic components—they indicated that they are interested in forging a strategic supply arrangement with LLC (or perhaps some other optoelectronic component manufacturer) for the supply of custom laser transmitters. Aspen is confident that they can carve out a leadership position in the market with their new system—which could translate into $10 million in laser transmitter orders for LLC over three years. Nick was definitely excited about this potential opportunity for LLC.

After reviewing the technical specifications for the custom part with Peter Williams (VP of Engineering), it appeared that with minimal engineering investment LLC could adapt one of their existing designs to obtain the requisite functionality. Nick then started working with the manufacturing folks: Julie Weller (VP of Manufacturing) and Steve Lo (Manufacturing Engineering Manager). Together, they studied the new design, identified the new manufacturing challenges, and thought through the various options to manufacture the custom components.

Figure 10.5 illustrates the manufacturing process for the custom lasers. Julie and Steve felt that although there was sufficient excess capacity at LLC to produce the required laser chips, the rest of the process would require establishing a small dedicated manufacturing line at a cost of $800,000. It would take four months to build this facility—just three months before LLC would expect the first orders from Aspen.

Nick then tried to look more carefully at the numbers. The Aspen management team was optimistic that they could capture enough business to provide LLC with orders for 10,000 lasers over three years. Indeed, at a price of $1,000 per laser and 20% after-tax profit margins, this opportunity seemed profitable. However, as Nick studied the network market a bit closer, he learned that while Aspen had some leading-

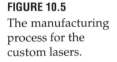

FIGURE 10.5
The manufacturing process for the custom lasers.

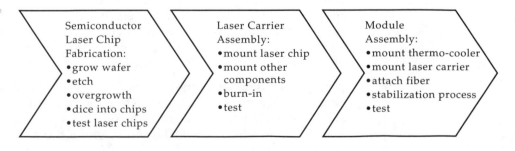

edge technologies and a novel approach, Aspen also had two established competitors, each promoting their own solution. After talking with several of Aspen's target customers, it became clear to Nick that while cost and performance—Aspen's key advantages over the competition—were important, there were many other considerations that customers focus on, such as comfort level with the particular technology, ease of deployment and maintenance, and reliability.

Nick also thought that given the rapid pace of technological innovation and commercialization in the communications industry, this custom laser would most probably have a relatively brief lifecycle of three years, and that much of the dedicated manufacturing facility would not have an alternate use beyond the third year. With input from Aspen and their customers, Nick estimated the best-case and worst-case revenues (corresponding to the range of Aspen's acceptance in the market) and post-tax profit projections as follows (see Figure 10.6):

- Best-case total revenue of $10 million over three years yielding after-tax profits of $2 million.

- Worst-case total revenue of $2,500,000 over three years yielding after-tax profits of $500,000.

- The probability of "Best-case" is subjectively estimated to be 70%.

At a meeting with the Aspen team, Nick explained his company's reluctance to invest in a custom manufacturing facility with an uncertain future. Hank Philips (purchasing manager of Aspen) then explained that Aspen has also been talking with another laser manufacturer to explore contract manufacturing of custom lasers. Although LLC was Aspen's first choice, the other manufacturer had already committed the resources for a dedicated line, and Aspen had even placed preliminary orders.

Nick then brought up the possibility for LLC to wait six months prior to committing to the dedicated line, in order to see how Aspen's new system fares in the marketplace. Hank explained that while they would be willing to work with LLC for the following two years, the laser orders they would place with LLC for years two and three would then be smaller by approximately 30%. Figure 10.7 shows Nick's estimate of the revenue stream from the supply alliance with Aspen, if LLC were to decide to wait six months to gauge Aspen's success in the marketplace before committing.

While the revenue opportunity was lower in the more conservative approach, waiting the six months prior to building the line would allow LLC to know exactly whether Aspen would be successful ("best-case") or not ("worst-case") in the mar-

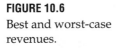

FIGURE 10.6

Best and worst-case revenues.

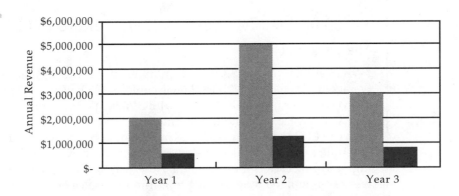

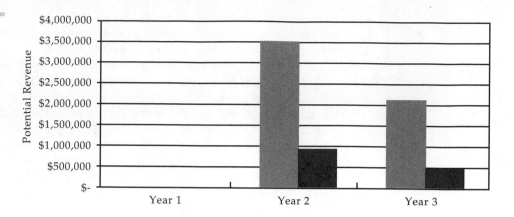

FIGURE 10.7

Best and worst-case revenues under the strategy of waiting six months before committing to build the manufacturing line.

ketplace. In the event Aspen was not successful, LLC would be spared the investment in a manufacturing facility that would not pay for itself.

Finally, Nick called his friend Frank Sullivan, who runs a market research firm focusing on fiber optic communications and networking. Frank was well-versed in the dynamics of Aspen's market, and he seemed to have a good sense of their target customers. He felt that by putting three analysts on the problem for two months, his company could give Nick an excellent assessment of Aspen's prospect in this market. The study would cost LLC $250,000. Of course, Nick was not as excited as Frank was about commissioning a market research study—Nick's previous experience indicated that such predictions are wrong 30% of the time.

As Nick drove home, he mulled over the options. His mind was racing: Build the facility or not? Hold off for six months to see whether Aspen is successful? Commission the market study? Knowing that Monday morning he would need to make a recommendation to the senior management team, he was anxious to apply the tools he had learned at business school. He thought wistfully to the times when only a grade was at stake. . . .

Assignment:

(a) Construct a decision tree of LLC's strategic supply arrangement decision problem.

(b) What practical aspects of the problem are not captured in your decision tree?

(c) Solve the tree. Propose and justify a recommended strategy for action.

YIELD OF A MULTI-STEP MANUFACTURING PROCESS

The Yield Problem

"What? Again? Julie—this is the third time this year we're missing a shipment to Aspen—what's going on?" Nick Lewis could not believe it. At the weekly meeting of the Manufacturing and Sales groups, Julie Weller (VP of Manufacturing) explained that they will have to miss another shipment to Aspen Networks. As the primary interface between LLC and Aspen, Nick was not happy about delivering this bad news—again.

Julie explained: "Nick, we've gone over this before. Your forecast keeps changing, and our cycle time—which, by the way, we've successfully reduced to three weeks—is still too long to react to last-minute sales orders. After all, our manufacturing process yields vary. The best we can do is estimate how many lasers we need to start each week, based on how many we need to yield. When you throw demand variability into the mix, it's not surprising we miss an occasional shipment. Look at the numbers—Aspen needs 500 lasers per week on average; I'm starting 800 every week, and yielding nearly 600—and we usually meet their demand."

Julie had a good point. The manufacturing operation had done a lot to reduce cycle time and was operating efficiently. The real culprits were the fluctuations in customer demand and in process yields. They both realized, however, that rapidly filling orders was critical to LLC's long-term success. After all, LLC is a second-source supplier to systems manufacturers who also have internal components divisions sourcing the same lasers. LLC's success was largely based on its ability to source components with shorter delivery times than those of their customers' internal organizations.

Nick thought out loud: "Julie, we know Aspen needs roughly 500 lasers per week and sometimes 10–20% more—why don't we just start enough lasers to yield enough for them, with an extra margin of safety?" Julie reluctantly acknowledged that this might be their only option for the near-term. However, she did point out: "If we don't pick the right quantities, our inventories will go through the roof. Furthermore, creating excess capacity is expensive, in terms of both capital equipment and staffing. This is clearly a trade-off between carrying excess inventory and customer satisfaction."

"Aha, now we're getting somewhere. Julie—let's take the guess-work out of this process. Why don't we simulate the production process and the customer demand, and quantify this trade-off between customer satisfaction and production starts? Why don't we take a week to collect the data on our manufacturing processes and demand fluctuations, and reconvene to make the decision."

The Data

The manufacturing process for the Aspen lasers consists of three steps: submount assembly, module assembly, and final test. Parts that successfully pass through one step go on to the next step. Those parts that fail are scrapped.

The weekly demand from Aspen for lasers has been 500 lasers on average, but it fluctuates. It is approximately Normally distributed, with a standard deviation of 50 lasers per week.

The data collected on yields of the manufacturing process steps is as follows:

- The submount assembly yield is approximately Normally distributed, with $\mu = 80\%$ and $\sigma = 5\%$.

- The module assembly yield is approximately binomially distributed, with the P(pass) = 95%.

- The final test yield appears to be evenly distributed between 90% and 100%.

Assignment:

(a) Construct a simulation model to estimate the distribution of the output of the manufacturing process and the distribution of the difference between supply and demand.

(b) What is the distribution of the output given the current policy of 800 starts per week?

(c) What is the distribution of the weekly demand?

(d) What is the distribution of the weekly surplus/deficit in supply/demand? How often will LLC miss a shipment according to this model?

(e) How many starts per week are required in order to guarantee that demand will be met 95% of the time? 99% of the time? 99.5% of the time?

PREDICTION OF YIELDS IN MANUFACTURING

The Yield Problem

As he drove home Thursday evening, Steve Lo's thoughts were on the yield problem that has plagued the long-haul product line. Although the yields across most of the manufacturing steps have held steady for the past year, the yield at one of the critical module assembly steps has fluctuated significantly over the past year. At this step—called the "pigtail" step (due to the coiled fiber's similarity to a pig's tail)—the optical fiber assembly is aligned to the laser chip and is welded into place with an accurately-placed high-power laser beam. Because this is one of the last operations in the manufacturing process, most of the product cost is already incurred. When a defective part is scrapped at this step, the effect on the bottom-line manufacturing cost is therefore painfully large.

For the past several weeks, the problem has gotten increasingly worse: Some fibers were breaking during the welding step, or the module failed the subsequent temperature cycling (implemented as a stability screen to verify the pigtail process). Steve was convinced that this was not random: These types of components have been in production for over three years with consistently high yields at the pigtail step. The pigtail yield degradation was clearly extraordinary, and it needed to be fixed. To complicate matters, there was tension and finger-pointing between the production operators, supervisors, and the manufacturing engineers. Everyone had a different theory as to what was going on: The engineers suspected that the operators were taking shortcuts under pressure, while the operators felt that poorly-serviced equipment was responsible. Steve had encountered situations like this before, and he knew that to resolve it, it was critical to quickly move beyond the squabbles and have everyone work together to fix it. "Easier said than done . . . ." he thought as he drove home.

Friday morning, Steve called a meeting of the entire team. "Folks, let's brainstorm all the possible factors that might be responsible for the low pigtail yield. Then let's collect all of the data we might need and make our assessment based on the facts. We should not rule anything out, nor should we have a preconceived notion of what factors actually matter." After much discussion, the team identified five factors that might have a significant impact on the pigtail yield. These factors represented the various judgements (and suspicions) of the parties:

1. **Operator Experience:** Some members of the team thought that the more-experienced operators may be more adept at carrying out the manually-intensive and complex alignment and weld operation. Although some of the operators had as much as four years of experience, some had 18 months experience or less.

2. **Recent Exposure to Pigtail:** There was concern in the team that because the operators were cross-trained and worked on multiple processes, a relevant factor might be the recent exposure to the pigtail operation.

3. **Time of Day:** One production supervisor hypothesized that although the rest of the factory was running at two or three shifts per day, the pigtail room was running only one shift per day. She had observed in the past that in the mornings, operators are distracted with set-up and planning activities, which perhaps disrupts their concentration on the first few production lots of the day.

4. **Room Temperature:** One engineer noted that the laser welders' performance is particularly sensitive to fluctuations in room temperature. He observed that the room temperature impacts the stability in some important laser welder parameters, such as weld time and total energy delivered to each weld. It was conceivable that sufficiently severe temperature fluctuations could alter the weld characteristics enough to alter the weld quality, and subsequently the yield. Fortunately, the room temperature is monitored and automatically logged throughout the day.

5. **Welder Maintenance:** One operator felt strongly that the maintenance schedule for the laser welder might be inadequate. The laser welders are "tuned up" annually as part of their maintenance schedule: Once a year each laser welder is disassembled, the cooling system is cleaned, the laser cavity is realigned, and the weld pulse timing is adjusted. The operator mentioned that on several occasions, the laser welders—which are monitored through statistical process control (SPC) on a daily basis—were found to be malfunctioning 2-3 months prior to their next scheduled maintenance.

Steve Lo asked his staff to gather relevant data on these five factors for the past year. Table 10.11 shows the results of this data collection effort, which took just over two full days to put together. The table shows yields of 55 randomly selected lots in the past year (in the last column). The second column of the table shows the number of years of pigtailing experience of the operator for each lot (in years). The third column of the table shows the percentage of time that the operator of the lot has spent in pigtail operations over the last year. The fourth column of the table shows the number of hours since the beginning of the shift that the lot was introduced into the laser weld process. The fifth column shows the average daily temperature in the welding room for each lot. And the sixth column shows the number of months that the laser welder has been in operation since its last tune-up. The data from Table 10.11 is also presented in the spreadsheet LLC-PIGTAIL.XLS.

Assignment:

(a) Perform a regression analysis of the data. Which factors appear to be relevant to the prediction of the pigtail yield? How relevant?

(b) What non-quantitative factors need to be considered in the prediction of pigtail yields?

(c) What next steps in the decision process would you recommend?

ALLOCATION OF PRODUCTION PERSONNEL

The Opportunity

It was 6 P.M. on a Friday, and Julie Weller was taking her daily walk-through of the manufacturing floor. The third shift was just coming on, and there was lots of activity. As she made her way past the workbenches and the Final Test area, she thought about the progress LLC's Manufacturing Department had made over the past 18 months. They had done a fairly good job with the integration of the two companies that LLC acquired—there were no lay-offs, and the operators from all three lines increasingly felt they were part of one team. The move to the larger facility—one that housed all three assembly lines—had gone smoothly. Operational metrics—yields,

TABLE 10.11

Data for five potential factors and yields for 55 randomly selected lots.

Lot Number	Operator Experience (Years)	Recent Exposure to Pigtail (% in last year)	Time of Day (hours)	Average Room Temperature (Fahrenheit)	Welder Maintenance (months ago)	Yield (%)
1	3.0	38	3	71	0	71
2	3.0	10	1	62	11	38
3	3.0	60	1	66	8	60
4	3.1	90	3	72	9	90
5	2.8	88	3	64	4	82
6	2.9	96	2	73	4	90
7	2.7	1	1	70	1	33
8	2.8	41	2	73	1	62
9	2.8	86	3	69	5	77
10	2.7	14	3	68	1	68
11	2.3	25	3	66	3	69
12	3.0	5	2	69	0	53
13	2.6	3	2	67	9	45
14	2.4	16	3	63	8	47
15	3.4	22	1	72	2	61
16	3.1	2	3	69	6	43
17	1.9	29	3	64	10	39
18	2.8	34	2	66	4	54
19	2.9	55	1	64	9	58
20	3.6	36	2	62	5	56
21	2.8	37	1	67	10	46
22	3.0	36	1	66	1	58
23	2.7	91	3	65	7	88
24	3.0	47	2	72	2	62
25	2.2	43	1	71	0	71
26	3.3	30	3	68	8	60
27	2.5	98	3	63	3	98
28	2.9	81	1	66	3	97
29	2.8	99	3	69	4	95
30	3.4	26	3	70	10	35
31	2.4	95	1	73	10	43
32	2.7	5	1	65	9	50
33	3.2	71	2	72	1	78
34	3.0	82	3	70	10	79
35	2.3	97	1	64	8	56
36	2.9	47	2	68	4	69
37	2.5	30	2	70	1	65
38	1.7	75	2	64	5	92
39	2.4	35	3	66	0	61
40	2.8	78	2	63	7	92
41	2.7	7	2	64	10	28
42	2.6	20	2	63	8	53
43	2.5	6	1	65	8	44
44	2.7	36	1	73	7	65
45	3.3	49	3	72	9	63
46	3.0	51	3	72	4	64
47	2.6	37	1	63	8	67
48	3.1	99	2	62	7	97
49	2.9	4	2	73	4	38
50	2.1	23	1	64	9	45
51	2.7	0	3	68	1	30
52	2.4	93	2	73	3	92
53	2.8	10	2	74	0	33
54	2.0	26	2	71	3	42
55	1.9	78	3	62	10	48

cycle times, delivery schedules—were maintained throughout the transition. Although Julie was proud of her team's progress, she was confident that the operational efficiency could be improved further.

Background

When Julie Weller joined LLC, the company only produced high-end components in its product line. Much of the assembly was handled by highly-skilled operators, many of whom had been with LLC for 7–10 years. On the contrary, their two recent acquisitions had been in less complex products, with more dependence on automated assembly techniques and equipment, and less dependence on skilled workers. As a result, LLC's three production lines had different types of workers, with different levels of skills, productivity, and wage scales. Table 10.12 summarizes this information.

Table 10.13 shows the hourly allocation of the workers across pay grades and product lines given that each operator works an average of 40 hours per week.

Given the fluctuation in demand, Julie had felt strongly that operators across all three product lines be cross-trained on each line's processes. That way, if demand for one product line falls, those operators would be able to help out on another line. After several months, all operators had been cross-trained on all of the processes across the three production lines.

Despite the cross-training, Steve Lo (Manufacturing Engineering Manager) noticed that there were still productivity differences between the workers, largely related to the experience and skill of the operators at the different pay grades. After reviewing the production records over the past several months, Steve put together the productivity table shown in Table 10.14.

TABLE 10.12
Staffing Allocation by product line and pay grade.

Pay Grade	Wage ($/hour)	Long-Haul Telecom (number of operators)	Short-Haul Telecom (number of operators)	Datacom (number of operators)
1	15.00	4	—	—
2	14.50	9	—	—
3	13.00	15	5	—
4	12.00	—	4	50
5	10.50	—	2	100
6	9.75	—	—	40

TABLE 10.13
Allocation of hours by product line and pay grade, per week.

Pay Grade	Wage ($/hour)	Long-Haul Telecom (hours)	Short-Haul Telecom (hours)	Datacom (hours)
1	15.00	160	—	—
2	14.50	360	—	—
3	13.00	600	200	—
4	12.00	—	160	2,000
5	10.50	—	80	4,000
6	9.75	—	—	1,600

TABLE 10.14
Productivity (parts/operator/hour).

Pay Grade	Long-Haul Telecom	Short-Haul Telecom	Datacom
1	2.00	1.20	2.00
2	1.80	1.08	1.80
3	1.62	2.50	1.62
4	1.80	2.16	1.45
5	1.62	1.93	1.31
6	1.30	1.74	1.20

TABLE 10.15

Weekly production
plan for next quarter
(parts/week).

Long-Haul Telecom	Short-Haul Telecom	Datacom
1,940	1,000	10,060

Table 10.15 shows the weekly production plan for next quarter that is used for planning purposes.

While Julie was confident that she could meet this production plan with her current staffing and allocation, she suspected that she could more efficiently utilize the workers. With the current allocation, there was no room for error—the workers were allocated 100% of their time. There was thus neither time for other projects, nor spare capacity (which often came in handy during end-of-quarter production rushes).

Assignment:

(a) Identify the most efficient allocation of the existing staff required to meet the production plan. While it is true that the total wages paid is constant, minimize the direct labor cost required to meet this production plan. This assumes that the excess operator time can be used for other projects. How much money does this reallocation save relative to the existing staffing allocation?

(b) As with any reorganization initiative, hard decisions must eventually be made regarding which employees to retain, which employees to lay off, and where to bring in new staff. Identify the most efficient allocation required to meet the production plan, without the constraint of keeping the existing staff. (You can assume that: (i) additional workers at any pay grade are available locally, and (ii) new workers in each pay grade will have similar productivity as the existing workers in that pay grade.) How much money does this reallocation save relative to the existing staffing allocation?

(c) Give an intuitive explanation for the differences between your answers to (a) and (b).

(d) What practical issues are missing from your model that might have an impact on staffing levels?

Appendix

TABLE A.1

Cumulative distribution function of the standard Normal distribution. If Z is a standard Normal random variable, then $F(1.34) = P(Z \le 1.34) = 0.9099$

z	0.00	0.01	0.02	0.03	0.04	0.05	0.06	0.07	0.08	0.09
−3.0	0.0013	0.0013	0.0013	0.0012	0.0012	0.0011	0.0011	0.0011	0.0010	0.0010
−2.9	0.0019	0.0018	0.0018	0.0017	0.0016	0.0016	0.0015	0.0015	0.0014	0.0014
−2.8	0.0026	0.0025	0.0024	0.0023	0.0023	0.0022	0.0021	0.0021	0.0020	0.0019
−2.7	0.0035	0.0034	0.0033	0.0032	0.0031	0.0030	0.0029	0.0028	0.0027	0.0026
−2.6	0.0047	0.0045	0.0044	0.0043	0.0041	0.0040	0.0039	0.0038	0.0037	0.0036
−2.5	0.0062	0.0060	0.0059	0.0057	0.0055	0.0054	0.0052	0.0051	0.0049	0.0048
−2.4	0.0082	0.0080	0.0078	0.0075	0.0073	0.0071	0.0069	0.0068	0.0066	0.0064
−2.3	0.0107	0.0104	0.0102	0.0099	0.0096	0.0094	0.0091	0.0089	0.0087	0.0084
−2.2	0.0139	0.0136	0.0132	0.0129	0.0125	0.0122	0.0119	0.0116	0.0113	0.0110
−2.1	0.0179	0.0174	0.0170	0.0166	0.0162	0.0158	0.0154	0.0150	0.0146	0.0143
−2.0	0.0228	0.0222	0.0217	0.0212	0.0207	0.0202	0.0197	0.0192	0.0188	0.0183
−1.9	0.0287	0.0281	0.0274	0.0268	0.0262	0.0256	0.0250	0.0244	0.0239	0.0233
−1.8	0.0359	0.0351	0.0344	0.0336	0.0329	0.0322	0.0314	0.0307	0.0301	0.0294
−1.7	0.0446	0.0436	0.0427	0.0418	0.0409	0.0401	0.0392	0.0384	0.0375	0.0367
−1.6	0.0548	0.0537	0.0526	0.0516	0.0505	0.0495	0.0485	0.0475	0.0465	0.0455
−1.5	0.0668	0.0655	0.0643	0.0630	0.0618	0.0606	0.0594	0.0582	0.0571	0.0559
−1.4	0.0808	0.0793	0.0778	0.0764	0.0749	0.0735	0.0721	0.0708	0.0694	0.0681
−1.3	0.0968	0.0951	0.0934	0.0918	0.0901	0.0885	0.0869	0.0853	0.0838	0.0823
−1.2	0.1151	0.1131	0.1112	0.1093	0.1075	0.1056	0.1038	0.1020	0.1003	0.0985
−1.1	0.1357	0.1335	0.1314	0.1292	0.1271	0.1251	0.1230	0.1210	0.1190	0.1170
−1.0	0.1587	0.1562	0.1539	0.1515	0.1492	0.1469	0.1446	0.1423	0.1401	0.1379
−0.9	0.1841	0.1814	0.1788	0.1762	0.1736	0.1711	0.1685	0.1660	0.1635	0.1611
−0.8	0.2119	0.2090	0.2061	0.2033	0.2005	0.1977	0.1949	0.1922	0.1894	0.1867
−0.7	0.2420	0.2389	0.2358	0.2327	0.2296	0.2266	0.2236	0.2206	0.2177	0.2148
−0.6	0.2743	0.2709	0.2676	0.2643	0.2611	0.2578	0.2546	0.2514	0.2483	0.2451
−0.5	0.3085	0.3050	0.3015	0.2981	0.2946	0.2912	0.2877	0.2843	0.2810	0.2776
−0.4	0.3446	0.3409	0.3372	0.3336	0.3300	0.3264	0.3228	0.3192	0.3156	0.3121
−0.3	0.3821	0.3783	0.3745	0.3707	0.3669	0.3632	0.3594	0.3557	0.3520	0.3483
−0.2	0.4207	0.4168	0.4129	0.4090	0.4052	0.4013	0.3974	0.3936	0.3897	0.3859
−0.1	0.4602	0.4562	0.4522	0.4483	0.4443	0.4404	0.4364	0.4325	0.4286	0.4247
−0.0	0.5000	0.4960	0.4920	0.4880	0.4840	0.4801	0.4761	0.4721	0.4681	0.4641
0.0	0.5000	0.5040	0.5080	0.5120	0.5160	0.5199	0.5239	0.5279	0.5319	0.5359
0.1	0.5398	0.5438	0.5478	0.5517	0.5557	0.5596	0.5636	0.5675	0.5714	0.5753
0.2	0.5793	0.5832	0.5871	0.5910	0.5948	0.5987	0.6026	0.6064	0.6103	0.6141
0.3	0.6179	0.6217	0.6255	0.6293	0.6331	0.6368	0.6406	0.6443	0.6480	0.6517
0.4	0.6554	0.6591	0.6628	0.6664	0.6700	0.6736	0.6772	0.6808	0.6844	0.6879
0.5	0.6915	0.6950	0.6985	0.7019	0.7054	0.7088	0.7123	0.7157	0.7190	0.7224
0.6	0.7257	0.7291	0.7324	0.7357	0.7389	0.7422	0.7454	0.7486	0.7517	0.7549
0.7	0.7580	0.7611	0.7642	0.7673	0.7704	0.7734	0.7764	0.7794	0.7823	0.7852
0.8	0.7881	0.7910	0.7939	0.7967	0.7995	0.8023	0.8051	0.8078	0.8106	0.8133
0.9	0.8159	0.8186	0.8212	0.8238	0.8264	0.8289	0.8315	0.8340	0.8365	0.8389
1.0	0.8413	0.8438	0.8461	0.8485	0.8508	0.8531	0.8554	0.8577	0.8599	0.8621
1.1	0.8643	0.8665	0.8686	0.8708	0.8729	0.8749	0.8770	0.8790	0.8810	0.8830
1.2	0.8849	0.8869	0.8888	0.8907	0.8925	0.8944	0.8962	0.8980	0.8997	0.9015
1.3	0.9032	0.9049	0.9066	0.9082	0.9099	0.9115	0.9131	0.9147	0.9162	0.9177
1.4	0.9192	0.9207	0.9222	0.9236	0.9251	0.9265	0.9279	0.9292	0.9306	0.9319
1.5	0.9332	0.9345	0.9357	0.9370	0.9382	0.9394	0.9406	0.9418	0.9429	0.9441
1.6	0.9452	0.9463	0.9474	0.9484	0.9495	0.9505	0.9515	0.9525	0.9535	0.9545
1.7	0.9554	0.9564	0.9573	0.9582	0.9591	0.9599	0.9608	0.9616	0.9625	0.9633
1.8	0.9641	0.9649	0.9656	0.9664	0.9671	0.9678	0.9686	0.9693	0.9699	0.9706
1.9	0.9713	0.9719	0.9726	0.9732	0.9738	0.9744	0.9750	0.9756	0.9761	0.9767
2.0	0.9772	0.9778	0.9783	0.9788	0.9793	0.9798	0.9803	0.9808	0.9812	0.9817
2.1	0.9821	0.9826	0.9830	0.9834	0.9838	0.9842	0.9846	0.9850	0.9854	0.9857
2.2	0.9861	0.9864	0.9868	0.9871	0.9875	0.9878	0.9881	0.9884	0.9887	0.9890
2.3	0.9893	0.9896	0.9898	0.9901	0.9904	0.9906	0.9909	0.9911	0.9913	0.9916
2.4	0.9918	0.9920	0.9922	0.9925	0.9927	0.9929	0.9931	0.9932	0.9934	0.9936
2.5	0.9938	0.9940	0.9941	0.9943	0.9945	0.9946	0.9948	0.9949	0.9951	0.9952
2.6	0.9953	0.9955	0.9956	0.9957	0.9959	0.9960	0.9961	0.9962	0.9963	0.9964
2.7	0.9965	0.9966	0.9967	0.9968	0.9969	0.9970	0.9971	0.9972	0.9973	0.9974
2.8	0.9974	0.9975	0.9976	0.9977	0.9977	0.9978	0.9979	0.9979	0.9980	0.9981
2.9	0.9981	0.9982	0.9982	0.9983	0.9984	0.9984	0.9985	0.9985	0.9986	0.9986
3.0	0.9987	0.9987	0.9987	0.9988	0.9988	0.9989	0.9989	0.9989	0.9990	0.9990

TABLE A.2

The value of c for a t-distribution with k degrees of freedom. For $k = 15$ degrees of freedom and $\beta = 95\%$, $c = 2.131$, that is, $P(-2.131 \leq T \leq 2.131) = 0.95$. When k is 30 or more, we use the Normal distribution.

Degrees of Freedom (k)	β = 90%	β = 95%	β = 98%	β = 99%
1	6.314	12.706	31.821	63.656
2	2.920	4.303	6.965	9.925
3	2.353	3.182	4.541	5.841
4	2.132	2.776	3.747	4.604
5	2.105	2.571	3.365	4.032
6	1.943	2.447	3.143	3.707
7	1.895	2.365	2.998	3.499
8	1.860	2.306	2.896	3.355
9	1.833	2.262	2.821	3.250
10	1.812	2.228	2.764	3.169
11	1.769	2.201	2.718	3.106
12	1.782	2.179	2.681	3.055
13	1.771	2.160	2.650	3.012
14	1.761	2.145	2.624	2.977
15	1.753	2.131	2.602	2.947
16	1.746	2.120	2.583	2.921
17	1.740	2.110	2.567	2.898
18	1.734	2.101	2.552	2.878
19	1.729	2.093	2.539	2.861
20	1.725	2.086	2.528	2.845
21	1.721	2.080	2.518	2.831
22	1.717	2.074	2.508	2.819
23	1.714	2.069	2.500	2.807
24	1.711	2.064	2.492	2.797
25	1.708	2.060	2.485	2.787
26	1.706	2.056	2.479	2.779
27	1.703	2.052	2.473	2.771
28	1.701	2.048	2.467	2.763
29	1.699	2.045	2.462	2.756

References

There is a very large number of reference texts on the various topics of management science. The objective of this section is to present a guide to some of the more pointed references on specific topic areas.

CHAPTER 1: DECISION ANALYSIS

The following are further references on decision analysis:

C. A. Holloway, *Decision Making under Uncertainty: Models and Choices*, Prentice Hall, 1979.

H. Raiffa, *Decision Analysis: Introductory Lectures on Choices under Uncertainty*, Addison-Wesley, 1970.

The Kendall Crab and Lobster, Inc. case was motivated by certain aspects of the Harvard Business School case Freemark Abbey Winery (9-181-027).

CHAPTER 2: FUNDAMENTALS OF DISCRETE PROBABILITY

There is a very large collection of books on probability theory. The following book presents probability theory in a managerial context.

J. McClave, P. Benson, and T. Sincich, *A First Course in Business Statistics*, Prentice Hall, 1998.

The following references present a more mathematical treatment of probability theory:

E. Parzen, *Modern Probability Theory and its Applications*, Wiley, 1960.

S. M. Ross, *Introduction to Probability Models*, Academic Press, 1997.

The Graphic Corporation case was motivated by certain aspects of the case Monitor Systems, Inc. in *Quantitative Methods in Management: Text and Cases*, by Paul A. Vatter, Stephen P. Bradley, Sherwood C. Frey, Jr., and Barbara B. Jackson, Richard D. Irwin, Inc., 1978.

CHAPTER 3: CONTINUOUS PROBABILITY DISTRIBUTIONS AND THEIR APPLICATIONS

In addition to the references in the previous chapter, a more advanced treatment of probability theory and its application is contained in the classical references:

W. Feller, *An Introduction to Probability Theory and its Applications*, Volume I, Wiley, 3rd edition, 1968.

W. Feller, *An Introduction to Probability Theory and its Applications*, Volume II, Wiley, 1971.

CHAPTER 4: STATISTICAL SAMPLING

The following references present introductory treatments of statistical methods at a level comparable to this text:

M. Hamburg, *Statistical Analysis for Decision Making*, Dryden Press, 1994.

R. A. Johnson and D. W. Wichern, *Business Statistics: Decision Making with Data*, Wiley, 1997.

Interesting business applications of sampling are contained in:

D. P. Foster, R. A. Stine, R. Waterman, *Basic Business Statistics: a Casebook*, Springer, 1998.

For a mathematical introduction to statistical sampling, see:

B. W. Lindgren, *Statistical Theory*, Macmillan, 3rd edition, 1976.

The Scallop Sampling case was motivated by Arnold Barnett's "Misapplications Reviews" column in *Interfaces*, March-April, 1995.

CHAPTER 5: SIMULATION MODELING: CONCEPTS AND PRACTICE

More detailed treatments of simulation modeling at a level comparable to this text are presented in:

J. R. Evans and D.L. Olson, *Introduction to Simulation and Risk Analysis*, Prentice Hall, 1998.

W. L. Winston, *Simulation Modeling Using RISK*, Duxbury, 1996.

For an advanced treatment of simulation methods, see:

G. S. Fishman, *Monte Carlo: Concepts, Algorithms and Applications*, Springer, 1996.

The Ontario gateway case was motivated by certain aspects of the Harvard Business School case Marsh & McLennan (9-171-303).

CHAPTER 6: REGRESSION MODELS: CONCEPTS AND PRACTICE

For a thorough and modern treatment of multiple linear regression, we refer the reader to:

T. Ryan, *Modern Regression Methods*, Wiley, 1997.

Interesting business applications of multiple linear regression are contained in:

D. P. Foster, R. A. Stine, R. Waterman, *Business Analysis Using Regression: a Casebook*, Springer, 1998.

CHAPTER 7: LINEAR OPTIMIZATION

For an introduction to optimization at a level comparable to this text, see:

W. L. Winston, S. C. Albright and M. Broadie, *Practical Management Science: Spreadsheet Modeling and Applications*, Duxbury, 1997.

For an introduction to optimization at a more mathematical level than this text, see:

S. P. Bradley, A. C. Hax and T. L. Magnanti, *Applied Mathematical Programming*, Addison-Wesley, 1977.

F. S. Hillier and G. J. Lieberman, *Introduction to Operations Research*, McGraw-Hill, 1995.

For a more advanced introduction to linear optimization, see:

G. B. Dantzig and M. N. Thapa, *Linear Programming*, Springer, 1997.

CHAPTER 8: NONLINEAR OPTIMIZATION

The references of the previous chapter also contain material on nonlinear optimization. A treatment of nonlinear optimization at a more algorithmic level is contained in:

W. L. Winston, *Operations Research: Applications and Algorithms*, Duxbury, 1987.

A more advanced reference for nonlinear optimization is:

D. Luenberger, *Linear and Nonlinear Programming*, Addison-Wesley, 1984.

CHAPTER 9: DISCRETE OPTIMIZATION

In addition to the references in Chapter 7, a modern treatment of discrete optimization can be found in:

L. A. Wolsey, *Integer Programming*, Wiley, 1998.

CHAPTER 10: INTEGRATION IN THE ART OF DECISION MODELING

A more extensive treatment of revenue management in the airline industry can be found in:

B. Smith, J. Leimkuhler and R. Darrow, "Yield Management at American Airlines," *Interfaces*, Vol. 22, Number 1, January-February 1992.

For an introduction to the finance industry, see:

R. A. Brealey, S. C. Myers, *Principles of Corporate Finance*, 5th edition, McGraw-Hill, 1996.

For an introduction to investment management, see:

Z. Bodie, A. Kane and A. J. Marcus, *Investments*, 4th edition, Irwin/McGraw-Hill, 1998.

For an introduction to models in manufacturing, see:

W. J. Hopp, M. L. Spearman, *Factory Physics: Foundations of Manufacturing Management*, Irwin, 1995.

Index